GEOGRAPHIC REGIONS

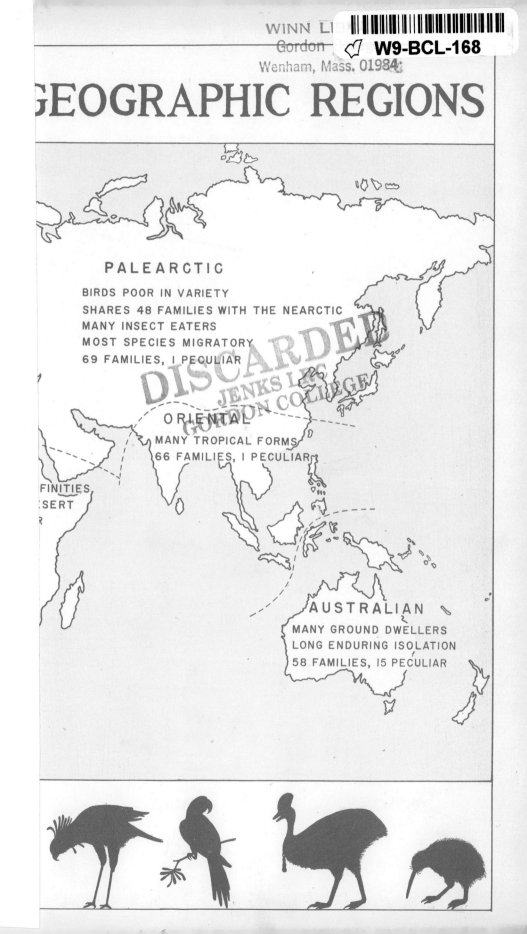

PALEARCTIC

BIRDS POOR IN VARIETY
SHARES 48 FAMILIES WITH THE NEARCTIC
MANY INSECT EATERS
MOST SPECIES MIGRATORY
69 FAMILIES, I PECULIAR

ORIENTAL

MANY TROPICAL FORMS
66 FAMILIES, I PECULIAR

FINITIES
SERT

AUSTRALIAN

MANY GROUND DWELLERS
LONG ENDURING ISOLATION
58 FAMILIES, 15 PECULIAR

ILLUSTRATED BY

NORMAN TOLSON

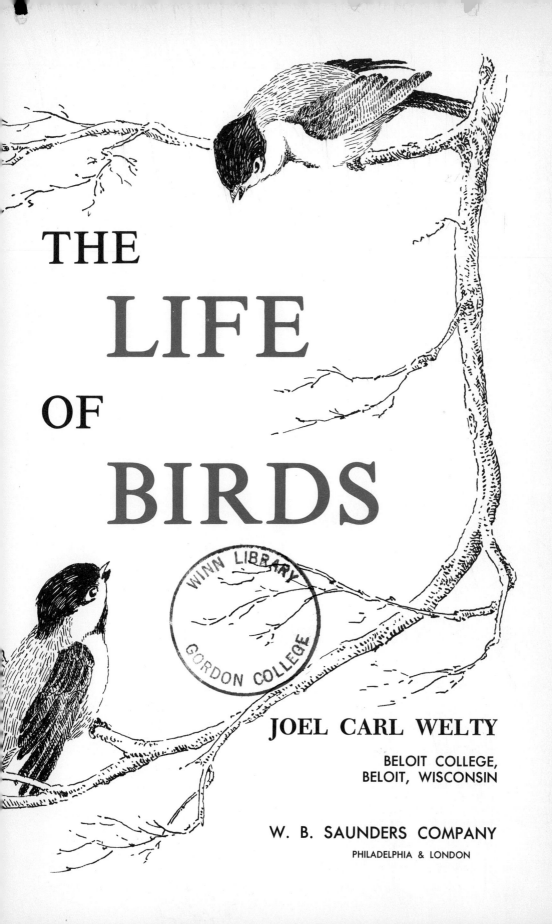

THE
LIFE
OF
BIRDS

JOEL CARL WELTY

BELOIT COLLEGE,
BELOIT, WISCONSIN

W. B. SAUNDERS COMPANY
PHILADELPHIA & LONDON

Reprinted July, 1964

The Life of Birds

For Susan

Preface

THE CHIEF AIM of this book is to present, simply and straightforwardly, the basic facts of bird biology. A second aim is to arouse in the reader a lasting enthusiasm for birds and for the wonderful things they do. If the first goal is attained, reaching the second should be insured by the facts themselves. They make a fascinating story when they are considered in relation to the live, throbbing bird and its problems of existence.

The book is directed toward the general student, and not toward the specialist. Most of the chapters can be read and understood by an interested reader without special preparation. For the more technical discussions of anatomy, physiology, and evolution, a good course in biology, either at the high school or college level, should provide enough background for an understanding of both the vocabulary and the concepts. Throughout the book, technical terms have been kept at a minimum.

The material used has been chosen for its applicability to the general principles of avian biology. These principles are, whenever possible, illustrated by vivid and pertinent examples. Important ornithological problems, solved and unsolved, are pointed out, as well as some of the ingenious experimental methods that have been employed to study them.

Notes from over 8000 separate books and articles have provided this material. Of these, about 900 seemed important enough to merit specific mention in the text and bibliography. All have been rigorously sifted for relevance and authenticity, but, even so, it is too much to hope that the book is completely free of errors, and any correction that a reader can provide will be welcomed.

One of the great difficulties in writing a general text on birds stems from a peculiar unevenness in the quality of ornithological writings. They run the gamut from ecstatic, subjective, undependable pieces about "our little feathered friends" to erudite and accurate, but sometimes stuffy, treatises on such themes as the metabolic uptake of radioactive isotopes. Sometimes the line between is hard to draw. For instance, scientific ornithologists frown on anthropomorphisms, for birds are not men, and definitely do not act like them. Avoiding anthropomorphic terms entirely, however, may result in clumsy or tedious pedantry. No sensible man ascribes vitalistic or animistic properties to a paved highway when he speaks of "treacherous" driving conditions, yet that one anthropomorphic word sums up information that would otherwise require several sentences to explain. Even the most confirmed mechanist speaks of "voluntary" muscles in animals supposedly bereft of any taint of free will. Accordingly, anthropomorphisms have been used here deliberately when their use promotes brevity, simplicity, or clarity. But choices of this kind make the compilation of a general text book such as this a somewhat hazardous business.

Ornithologists have suffered the disdain of other zoologists because of the occasional lapses from scientific objectivity of overenthusiastic amateur colleagues. Admitted with full standing to the great annual gatherings of American scientists are societies devoted to the study of fishes, reptiles, mammals, insects, and even microscopic protozoa, but not birds. Societies for bird study are relegated to a lower caste. Bird researchers have for years been treated as second-rate scientists, not worthy of the rank in academic peck order that is accorded even to a specialist in tapeworms.

It is, however, a paradoxical fact that many of the most fundamental principles and theories in modern biology have been discovered by ornithologists through researches on birds. The science of endocrinology was born in 1849 when Berthold transplanted the testis of one bird to another. Probably more has been discovered about the endocrine determination of sex through studies on birds than through studies on any other animals. Without the study of developing chick embryos, the science of embryology would be severely handicapped. In animal geography, Alfred Russel Wallace's great contributions were heavily influenced by his studies on the distribution of birds. It was through observations of the ground finches of the Galapagos Islands that Charles Darwin crystallized his grand concept of the origin of species through natural selection. Today, it is probable that more is known about the origin of species among birds than among any other vertebrates living in nature. Much of our knowledge of photoperiodism in animals stems from birds.

Not surprisingly, bird students have for years led all zoologists in the study of flight and migration. Research on the problems of orientation and homing, or how animals find their way, has been concentrated largely on birds. Moreover, in the field of behavior, the concepts of the particulate nature of instinctive action, releasers, displacement activities, imprinting, and territorial defense were all discovered by ornithologists. Taxonomically, birds are better known than any other class of animals. Through the banding or ringing of wild birds, more has been learned about the vital statistics of wild avian populations than has been learned about the populations of any other animal living under natural conditions.

This is by no means a complete list of the contributions to biological knowledge made by ornithologists, but it shows that their contributions have been very substantial. Moreover, the impressive list is growing. Birds are at last being accepted as scientifically respectable animals. Just as there have been periods of rapid radiation in the evolution of birds, so today there is a surge of experiment and rapid discovery in the science of ornithology. In the past 25 years the number of American graduate students taking their doctorates in ornithology has increased many times. This is in part due to a general increase of interest in birds, and in part to the development and availability of such new instruments and techniques as color-banding, mist-netting, tape recording, sound spectrography, color and high speed stroboscopic photography, aerial surveys, radar, telemetry, electrophoresis, chromatography, and radioactive tracers. I have tried to reflect some of the interest and excitement of these new discoveries in the pages that follow.

There are many intriguing and important problems in ornithology yet to be solved. Much remains to be learned about migration. Are some night migrants really guided by the stars? Will new techniques in physical chemistry and in genetics reveal unsuspected relationships in the classification of birds? What path does a breath of air take in passing through a bird's lungs? What is the function of the differently colored oil droplets in the retinas of birds' eyes? What are the chief causes of the ups and downs of population of grouse and other birds? The next few years offer the opportunity for students to learn the answers to these questions as well as to make important and stirring discoveries in other fields of bird study.

One of the joys in writing a book such as this comes from the cordial and generous help of many persons. My deep appreciation goes to the staff of the W. B. Saunders Company for their friendly and encouraging editorial aid. Working with them has been a pleasure as well as a valuable education.

It has been my exceptional good fortune to have the entire manuscript of *The Life of Birds* read and criticized by Margaret Morse Nice and Alexander F. Skutch. Their many suggestions were invaluable, and won my heartfelt gratitude. For other expert criticisms and suggestions on various chapters of the manuscript, I am much indebted to Albert Wolfson, William Behle, Eugene Odum, and Constance Nice.

My thanks go to Mary Claire Prendergast and Mary Elizabeth Storer for expert help in translating French ornithological works, to Hattie M. Chamberlin and Janet Nicoll for welcome assistance in reading proof, and to Catherine Crocker, Viola Welty, Gertrude Sweet, Dorothy Fuller, and Bartholomew Kunny for help in locating source material.

I am grateful to the publishers of *Scientific American* for permission to incorporate in Chapters 1 and 20 materials which previously appeared as articles in that excellent journal; to Norma Millay Ellis for generous permission to quote the poem by Edna St. Vincent Millay from *A Few Figs from Thistles* (Harper and Brothers, 1922); to Joel Peters for his

verses; to Robert Cushman Murphy for his permission to allow liberal quotation from his *Oceanic Birds of South America* (American Museum of Natural History, 1936); to all those whom I have quoted less extensively; and to Joseph Hickey and Eugene Odum for permission to use unpublished data on bird song and metabolism.

More than any other single reference, I have depended on Erwin Stresemann's classic volume, *Aves,* in Kükenthal and Krumbach's *Handbuch der Zoologie* (De Gruyter, Berlin, 1927–1934). I am happy to express my deep indebtedness to the author.

Even a brief scanning of the illustrations of this book will show how unusually fortunate I have been in obtaining the assistance of experts. My special gratitude goes to Ronald Austing, of Harrison, Ohio, and to Eric Hosking, of London, for their very helpful cooperation in providing the majority of the striking and instructive photographs that embellish this text. Sincere thanks go also to the following persons and institutions who provided excellent photographs: Salim Ali, D. L. Breeze, Christopher Doncaster, William Elder, John Emlen, M. D. England, Richard Fischer, Herbert Friedmann, Harry Hann, Henry C. Johnson, Howard J. Lee, Paul Lemmons, Hans Löhrl, Brooke Meanley, Nicholas Pastore, A. W. Schorger, Alexander F. Skutch, Robert Stabler, P. O. Swanberg, Lok Wan Tho, Benjamin Willier, and Ralph Yeatter; American Cyanamid Company, American Museum of Natural History, Australian News and Information Bureau, British Royal Radar Establishment, Expéditions Polaires Francaises, and Los Angeles County Museum.

For permission to reproduce an illustration from Heilmann's *The Origin of Birds* for Figure 23.4, I am indebted to Appleton-Century-Crofts. The illustration heading Chapter 23 is redrawn from the same source, while that heading Chapter 17 is after a photograph by Arthur A. Allen, and that for Chapter 9 is from a photograph by Eric Hosking. Figure 3.15 has been redrawn from *A Laboratory and Field Manual of Ornithology* by Olin Sewall Pettingill, Jr. To all these I extend thanks.

My chief regret in concluding preparation for the book's publication is that the artist, Norman Tolson, did not live to see in print the results of his dedicated and meticulous labor. I am extremely grateful to Magdalena Tolson for her help and advice in following through his fine work.

A college teacher enjoys a satisfying life, rich in tangible and intangible benefits. Among the tangible benefits is one not found in many other professions— sabbatical leave. To President Miller Upton and the Trustees of Beloit College I wish to express my gratitude for the sabbatical leave which made possible the writing of over half the manuscript for this book.

My final and deepest appreciation goes to my wife Susan for her patient help in typing the entire manuscript, reading proof, constructing the bibliography, and undertaking other tedious, eye-straining jobs. Throughout the book's long incubation period she has been a constant source of encouragement. We both hope for a healthy, lively hatchling that will provide instruction and pleasure to every student and every reader.

JOEL CARL WELTY

Beloit, Wisconsin

Contents

ONE

Birds As Flying Machines

There be . . . things which are too wonderful for me . . .
The way of an eagle in the air . . .
Proverbs 30:18, 19

The great struggle in most animals' lives is to avoid change. Physiological constancy is the first biological commandment. All animals must strive eternally to avoid enemies, to keep warm, well fed, internally moist, and supplied with oxygen, minerals, vitamins, and other substances, often within precise limits. Too great a change, especially in the internal economy of an animal, means death. If, for example, the concentration of salt in the blood of a man or a bird is increased or decreased by only one-half of one per cent, the animal dies. A Chickadee clinging to a piece of suet on a bitter winter day is doing its unconscious best to maintain the internal status quo—to maintain what the physiologists call homeostasis.

The spectacular fact that birds can fly across oceans, deserts, forests, and mountains tends to obscure the more significant fact that this ability to fly gives them exceptional opportunities for preserving their internal stability or homeostasis. Through flight, birds can search out the external conditions and substances they need to keep their internal fires burning clean and steady. A bird's wide search for specific foods and habitats makes sense only when considered in the light of this persistent, urgent need for constancy.

The power of flight has opened up to birds an enormous gaseous ocean, the atmosphere, and a means of quick, direct access to almost any spot on earth. They can eat in almost any "restaurant"; they can build their homes anywhere among

1

an almost infinite choice of sites, frequently beyond the reach of predators. Perhaps as a result of their supreme mobility, birds are, numerically at least, the most successful vertebrates on earth. There are roughly 28,500 species and subspecies of birds, as compared with 15,000 of mammals and 20,000 of fishes.

POSITION IN THE ANIMAL KINGDOM

Birds make up the Class *Aves* of the Subphylum *Vertebrata*, Phylum *Chordata*. They have descended from bipedal, lizardlike reptiles that lived in the Jurassic Period some 150 million years ago. Birds still show many reptilian affinities, such as their habit of laying eggs, the possession of scales on their beaks and legs, and the arrangement of many internal structures. This resemblance is so close that birds and reptiles are for convenience grouped together as the *Sauropsida*.

The three highest classes of vertebrates —reptiles, birds, and mammals— have adapted their reproduction to terrestrial life, largely through the evolution of an egg whose embryo is enveloped in a protective membrane called the amnion. Hence these three classes are grouped under the term *Amniota*, or amniotes. Among all animals, only birds and mammals have evolved the high, constant temperature ("warm-bloodedness" or homothermism) which makes energetic activity possible in all habitats and at all seasons. This, more than any other advance, is what makes these two classes the dominant vertebrates.

THE BIRD AS A FLYING MACHINE

At first glance, birds appear to be quite variable. They differ considerably in size, body proportions, color, song, and ability to fly. But a deeper look shows that in basic architecture they are far more uniform than, say, mammals. The largest living bird, the Ostrich, *Struthio camelus*, weighs about 144 kilograms (317 pounds) and is approximately 64,000 times heavier than the small Scintillant Hummingbird, *Selasphorus scintilla*, which weighs 2.25 grams (0.08 ounce). However, the largest mammal, a 136,200 kilogram (299,880 pound) Blue Whale, *Balaenoptera musculus*, weighs 59,000,000 times as much as the Pigmy Shrew, *Microsorex hoyi*, at 2.3 grams (0.08 ounce). Mammals, therefore, vary in mass nearly a thousand times as much as birds.

In body architecture, the comparative uniformity of birds is even more striking. Mammals may be as fat as a walrus or slim as a weasel, furry as a musk ox or hairless as a desert rat, long as a whale or short as a mole. They may be built to swim, fly, crawl, burrow, run, or climb. But the design of nearly every species of bird is dictated by one pre-eminent activity—flying. Their structure, inside and out, constitutes a solution to the problems imposed by flight. Their uniformity has been thrust upon them by the drastic demands that determine the design of any flying machine. Stringent natural selection has operated to convert a cold-blooded, groveling reptile into a light, warm-blooded, air-borne bird. Birds simply dare not deviate widely from sound aerodynamic design. Nature liquidates deviationists much more drastically and consistently than does any authoritarian dictator.

Birds were able to become flying machines largely through the evolutionary gifts of feathers, powerful wings, hollow bones, warm blood, a remarkable respiratory system, and a large, strong heart. These adaptations all boil down to the two prime requirements for any flying machine: high power and low weight. As early as 1679, the Italian physiologist Borelli in his *De Motu Animalium* (in Hall, 1951) showed an awareness of this power-weight relationship in birds:

"Such excessive power of the pectoral muscles seems to arise, firstly, from their large size . . . forming a dense and compact fleshy structure.

"Secondly . . . the body of a Bird is disproportionately lighter than that of man or of any quadruped . . . since the bones of Birds are porous, hollowed out to extreme thinness like the roots of the feathers, and the shoulder-bones, ribs, and wing-bones are of little substance; the breast and abdomen contain large cavities filled with air; while the feathers and the down are of exceeding lightness."

WEIGHT-REDUCING ADAPTATIONS

To lighten their airships, birds have thrown overboard everything possible that is not concerned with flight. Perhaps the most effective weight reduction has been accomplished in their bones. The skeleton of a pigeon accounts for 4.4 per cent of its total body weight, whereas that of a comparable mammal such as a white rat amounts to 5.6 per cent. This is in spite of the fact that the bird must have larger and stronger pectoral and pelvic girdles and appendages than a mammal, so that the full burden of locomotion may be supported either by the wings alone or by the legs alone—a problem not encountered by the typical quadruped animal.

The skeleton of a frigate bird with a seven-foot wingspread is reported by Murphy (1936) to weigh 114 grams (4 ounces), which is less than the weight of its feathers! Its plumage and breast muscles together make up at least 47 per cent of the total body weight. Although the bird skeleton is very light, it is also very strong and elastic—necessary characteristics in an air-frame subject to the great and sudden stresses of aerial acrobatics. This combination of lightness and strength depends mainly on the evolution of hollow, thin bones plus a considerable fusion of bones that are ordinarily separate in other vertebrates. The sacral vertebrae and the bones of the hip girdle, for example, are molded together into a thin, tube-like structure, strong but phenomenally light. The hollow finger bones are fused together; and some of them, in large soaring birds, show internal truss-like reinforcements much like the struts inside airplane wings. Similar struts are commonly seen in the hollow larger bones of the wings and legs. The paper-thin bones of a bird's skull show this type of reinforced construction to a remarkable degree. Coues, the early American ornithologist, called the beautifully adapted avian skull a "poem in bone."

Birds have reduced the long bony tail of their reptilian ancestors, and of *Archaeopteryx*, the first known bird, to a stunted vestige, the pygostyle. Rump muscles control the steering done by the tail feathers.

Figure 1.1. One of the chief adaptations which permit a bird to fly is its light skeleton. The dried bones of these two animals were weighed and compared. The entire skeleton of the rat weighed 5.61 per cent of its total live body weight; that of the pigeon weighed 4.43 per cent. The rat's skull weighed 1.25 per cent of its body weight; that of the pigeon weighed 0.21 per cent.

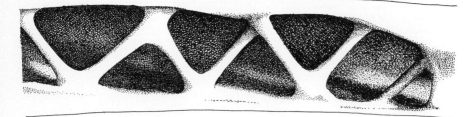

Figure 1.2. The metacarpal bone of a vulture's wing in long section. The internal bone struts are very like those in a Warren truss used in aircraft and bridge design. After D'Arcy Thompson.

Further skeletal reduction is found in the bird's hand (wing) where the finger bones are reduced both in size and number; two of them are completely missing and two of the other three fused together. Similar fusion and deletion occur in the leg bones.

Ribs are elegantly long, flat, thin, and jointed. They allow extensive movement for breathing and flying, yet are light and strong. Each rib overlaps its neighbor and thus reinforces its own strength with that of the adjoining rib. This arrangement provides the kind of resilient strength found in a woven splint basket. The sternum or breast bone is greatly modified in all flying birds by the addition of a thin, flat keel for the attachment of the large wing muscles.

Feathers, the bird's most distinctive and remarkable acquisition, are magnificently adapted for fanning the air, for insulation against the weather, for streamlining, and for reduction of weight. It has been claimed that for their weight they are stronger than any man-made substitute. Their flexibility allows the broad trailing edge of each large wing feather to bend upward with each downstroke of the wing. This produces the equivalent of pitch in a propeller blade, so that each wingbeat provides both lift and forward propulsion. The heat insulating value of feathers is so extraordinarily effective that it permits birds to live in parts of the Antarctic too cold for any other animal.

With the exception of the uropygial oil gland, no glands are found in the bird's skin. Nor are there bony plates like those worn by their saurian ancestors. Teeth have been eliminated in modern birds; consequently their jaw bones and jaw muscles need not be heavy.

In addition to light bones and light feathers, birds possess a weight-reducing system of air sacs that branch throughout the body, often even penetrating the hollow bones. The body of a feathered duck has a specific gravity of 0.6; that of a plucked duck, 0.9. Man and most other vertebrates have a specific gravity of about 1.0.

Further reduction in weight occurs in the urogenital system. Birds possess neither a urinary bladder nor a urethra to hold and discharge urine. Instead of watery urine, the kidneys excrete nitrogenous wastes, concentrated in the form of uric acid. This acid passes directly into the cloaca whose walls effect further concentration by absorbing still more water. The wastes, mixed with those of the intestine, become a concentrated whitish guano which is frequently voided. Nearly all species of birds possess only one ovary and oviduct (the left). They lay their eggs in the nest soon after the eggs are formed; development of the young does not occur in the body of the mother as in most mammals and in some reptiles. Furthermore, the sharply accented breeding season burdens the bird with heavy sex organs for only part of the year. Both ovaries and testes atrophy during the non-breeding season when they would be excess baggage. The sex organs of male and female Starlings, *Sturnus vulgaris*, were found by Bissonette to weigh 1500 times as much during the breeding season as they did during the rest of the year.

Even in the foods they select to fuel their engines, birds conserve weight. Just as an airplane cannot be powered by a wood-burning steam engine, so the metabolism of most flying birds is not powered by bulky, low calorie foods such as leaves and grass. Birds eat seeds, fruits, worms, insects, rodents, and the like—foods rich in calories. They burn "high test gasoline."

POWER-PROMOTING ADAPTATIONS

A basic law of chemistry holds that the speed of any chemical reaction roughly doubles with each rise in temperature of 10 degrees centigrade. In competitive Nature, the race often goes to the metabolically swift. Of all the million or so animals on earth, birds and mammals alone are warm-blooded or homothermal, and birds have evolved much the highest operating temperatures. Man with his conservative 37° C. (98.6° F.) is a metabolic slowpoke compared with some sparrows (42° C., 107° F.) or some thrushes (43.5° C., 110.5° F.). Birds burn their candles at both ends and live intense lives. Summer or winter, day or night, a bird's metabolic "engine" is always warm and ready for action.

Behind this high temperature in birds lie some interesting anatomical and physiological refinements. Flight itself would be utterly impossible in cool and frigid climates without homothermism. And homothermism, in turn, would be quite impossible without a warm coat of feathers. It seems probable that feathers evolved originally as an adaptation for heat conservation rather than for flight.

Besides eating an energy-rich diet, birds possess digestive equipment that processes their food rapidly, efficiently, and in large amounts. Fruit fed to young Cedar Waxwings, *Bombycilla cedrorum*,

passes through their digestive tracts in as little as 16 minutes (Nice, 1941). Other perching birds may take from one-half to two hours to pass food through their bodies. A young growing stork will gain one kilogram in weight for every three kilograms of fish and frogs eaten. Comparable figures for most mammals are one kilogram of growth for ten kilograms of food eaten. An examination of the excreta of birds shows that they utilize a very high percentage of the food they eat.

The breast muscles of a bird drive its propeller-like wings. In a strong flier, such as a pigeon, these muscles may account for as much as one-half the total body weight. On the other hand, some species —for example, vultures—fly largely on updrafts of air, as a glider does. In such birds the breast muscles are greatly reduced, and there are well developed wing tendons and ligaments which enable the bird to hold its wings in the soaring position with little or no effort.

A bird may have strong breast muscles and still be incapable of sustained flight because of an inadequate blood supply to these muscles. This condition is shown in the color of the muscles. The "white meat" of the breast muscles of a chicken or turkey indicates that they have so few blood vessels that they cannot fly far. On the other hand, the dark meat of their legs, in addition to the microscopic structure of the muscles, indicates a good blood supply, and an ability to run a considerable distance without tiring. If a Ruffed Grouse, *Bonasa umbellus*, is flushed four times in rapid succession, its breast muscles will become so fatigued that it can be picked up by the hand, unable to fly even a few feet. The blood supply is inadequate to bring fuel and oxygen and to carry away waste products fast enough to keep the muscles functioning. Xenophon's *Anabasis*, written about 400 B.C., relates the capture of bustards by exploiting this weakness:

"But as for the bustards, anyone can catch them by starting them up quickly; for they fly only a short distance like the partridge and soon tire. And their flesh was very sweet."

Birds, like mammals, have four-chambered hearts, which make possible a double circulation; that is, the blood makes a side trip through the lungs for gaseous purification before it is circulated through the body again. The bird's heart is large, powerful, and rapid in its beat. The following table, largely after Quiring (1950), gives the heart sizes and resting pulse rates for various species of animals, both cold- and warm-blooded.

ANIMAL	HEART AS PER CENT BODY WT.	HEART BEATS PER MINUTE
Boa constrictor, *Boa imperator*	0.31	20
Bull frog, *Rana catesbiana*	0.32	22
Man, *Homo sapiens*	0.42	78
Dog, *Canis familiaris*	1.05	140
Vulture, *Cathartes aura*	2.07	301
Crow, *Corvus brachyrhynchos*	0.95	342
Sparrow, *Passer domesticus*	1.68	460
Hummingbird, *Archilochus colubris*	2.37	615

In both birds and mammals the heart rate and the size of the heart in proportion to total body size increase as the animals get smaller. But the increase is significantly greater in birds than in mammals. Any man with a weak heart knows that climbing stairs puts a heavy strain on his pumping system. Birds do a lot of "climbing" and their circulatory systems are built for it.

The blood of birds is not significantly richer in hemoglobin than that of mammals. The pigeon and the mallard have about 15 gm. of hemoglobin per 100 cc. of blood, the same as man. However, the blood sugar concentration in birds averages about twice that found in mammals. And the blood pressure, as one would expect, is also somewhat higher: in man it averages 120 mm. of mercury; in the dog, 110 mm.; the rat, 106 mm.; the pigeon, 135 mm.; the duck, 162 mm.; and the chicken, 180 mm.

In addition to lungs, birds possess an accessory system of usually five pairs of air sacs connected with the lungs, which ramify throughout the body. Branches of these sacs often enter the larger bones of the body to occupy their hollow interiors, some of the sacs even penetrating into the small toe bones. The air sac system supplements the lungs as a supercharger, increasing the utilization of oxygen; and it also serves as a cooling system for the bird's speedy, hot metabolism which accompanies energetic muscle activity. It has been estimated that a flying pigeon uses one-fourth of its air intake for breathing and three-fourths for cooling.

The lungs of man constitute about 5 per cent of his body volume; the respiratory system of a duck, in contrast, makes up 20 per cent of the body volume (2 per cent lungs and 18 per cent air sacs). The anatomic connections of the lungs and air sacs in birds seem to provide a one-way traffic of air through most of the system, though this fact has never been experimentally established. Certainly, in man and all other mammals, the mixing of stale with fresh air at each inhalation by the sac-like, dead-end lungs, is inefficient. It seems odd that in the interest of efficient respiration, evolutionary selection has never produced a stale air outlet to animals' lungs, so that their linings could be constantly bathed by fresh air. In birds, the air sac system apparently approaches this ideal more closely than in any other vertebrate.

The active muscular exertion of breathing in birds is in exhalation, not in inhalation as in man and other mammals. Wing strokes cause rib compression which promotes easy breathing. Instead of "running out of breath" birds "fly into breath."

BALANCE, STREAMLINING, AND NERVOUS ADAPTATIONS

Any flying machine must be well balanced, with its center of gravity between and somewhat lower than the wings. In order to "trim ship" the weight of a bird's head has been drastically reduced through the elimination of teeth and heavy jaws and jaw muscles. A pigeon's skull weighs

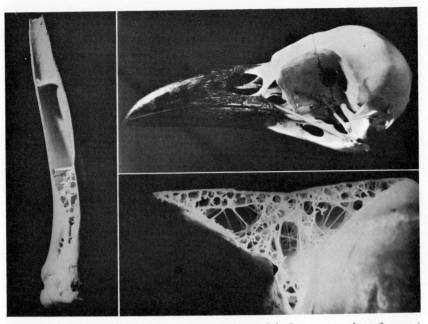

Figure 1.3. Why birds' skeletons are light in weight. At left, the upper arm bone (humerus) of a Golden Eagle, cut open to show its hollow interior. At upper right, the skull of a Common Crow which has been cross-sectioned between the eye sockets, and (below) the section magnified about three times. The network of bony braces provides rigidity with extreme lightness.

about one-sixth as much, proportionately, as that of a rat; its skull accounts for only one-fifth of one per cent of its total body weight. In a bird, the function of teeth has been largely taken over by the muscular gizzard (often with ingested grit substituting for teeth), located near the bird's center of gravity. This shifting of weight has eliminated the need of a long, counterbalancing tail such as birds' ancestors possessed.

Because birds must sometimes support their entire weight with their legs, and at other times with their wings, both the pelvic and pectoral girdles are strikingly adapted. The rigidly fused pelvic girdle is greatly elongated, so that when a bird alights on its legs, there is a firm support of the entire torso and its contents. There is a redistribution of the abdominal organs: the large gizzard and bulky air sacs have caused a downward and lateral displacement of the liver to the right, matching in position the ovary and oviduct to the left. This lateral broadening of the body, plus the requirements of egg laying, have resulted in a wide separation of the legs.

Rapidly flying birds normally have thoroughly streamlined bodies. The larger vane or contour feathers are responsible for the difference in appearance between the awkward angularity of a plucked bird and the streamlined sleekness of the feathered living bird. A bird has no external projecting ear lobes. It commonly retracts its "landing gear" legs within the belly-feathers while it is in flight. The smoothly streamlined Peregrine Falcon, *Falco peregrinus*, is reported to dive on its prey at speeds up to 288 kilometers (180 miles) per hour. Some rapid fliers have baffles in their nostrils to protect their lungs and air sacs from excessive air pressures. Even in the water, streamlined birds are among the swiftest of animals. An antarctic Gentoo Penguin, *Pygoscelis papua*, was once timed as swimming under water at about 36 kilometers (22.5 miles) per hour (Murphy, 1936).

Skillful flight demands sharp eyesight and quick muscle coordination. The eyes of a bird are relatively large, usually so large that the eye sockets meet in the center of the skull. In keeping with the need to reduce head weight, the eyes have relatively poor mobility as a result of reduced eyeball muscles. This is compensated for, however, by greatly increased neck flexibility.

Weight reduction, however, has not been promoted at the expense of the nervous system. The brain of a small perching bird weighs about ten times that of a lizard of the same body weight. It is about equal in size to that of a comparable rodent, but it is significantly smaller than the brain of an equal sized carnivore or primate. The relatively large forebrain and cerebellum of a bird are richly supplied with association centers, especially those concerned with muscle coordination. The optic lobes are relatively large. Nerve impulses are rapid. The sense of smell is apparently almost nonexistent; the olfactory lobes of the brain are reduced almost to vestiges.

The bird's success in adaptation to flight is best summed up by comparing its efficiency with that of a man-made airplane. The Golden Plover, *Pluvialis dominica*, a strong flier, fattens itself on Labrador bayberries in the autumn and then strikes off across the open Atlantic on a nonstop flight of some 3800 kilometers (2400 miles) to South America. It arrives there weighing about 56 grams (2 ounces) less than it did on its departure. This is the equivalent of flying a small airplane 256 kilometers (160 miles) on a gallon of gasoline rather than the usual 32 kilometers (20 miles), and the bird accomplishes this fuel economy in spite of the considerable handicaps of greater relative heat loss and greater friction inherent in its smaller body. Man still has far to go to equal such efficiency in flight.

SUGGESTED READINGS

There are a number of excellent general works on the biology of birds. Among the older books which still contain much useful information are Newton's encyclopedic *A Dictionary of Birds*, Pycraft's *A History of Birds*, Beebe's *The Bird*, Thomson's *The Biology of Birds*, and Allen's *Birds and their Attributes*. Among more recent general texts are those by Van Tyne and Berger, *Fundamentals of Ornithology*, Wallace, *An Introduction to Ornithology*, and Wing, *Natural History of Birds*. For very brief treatments of avian biology see Hann, *The Biology of Birds*, Hess, *The Bird*, and Heinroth, *The Birds*. The three most complete and authoritative works on birds are Grassé's Volume 15 (*Oiseaux*) in *Traité de Zoologie*, Stresemann's Volume 7 (*Aves*) in Kükenthal and Krumbach's *Handbuch der Zoologie*, and Marshall's *Biology and Comparative Physiology of Birds*.

TWO

The Kinds of Birds

Hast thou named all the birds without a gun?
Ralph Waldo Emerson, *Forbearance*

Any curious person observing the world of birds is struck by the varying degrees of resemblance and difference among them. His intellectual desire to "pigeonhole" diverse objects into systematic order leads him to place birds of the same general appearance together, and to give them a collective name: robins, ducks, eagles. Even savages feel this urge to classify. A tribe of natives in the mountains of New Guinea had 137 specific names for birds classified by scientists today as 138 species. Only one species was confused with another (Mayr, Lindsley, and Usinger, 1953).

Closer scrutiny of birds soon shows that there are larger and smaller differences. There are, for example, perching birds, with pointed beaks and separate toes, such as the robin and blackbird, and larger water birds with webbed feet and flat, rounded bills, such as ducks, geese, and swans. But while ducks, geese, and swans have similar feet and bills, they vary in length of neck. There are, in short, hierarchies of resemblances and differences: larger, deep-seated ones that determine the larger, more inclusive groups of birds, and smaller, more superficial ones that determine the smaller groups and eventually the individual "kinds" or species.

9

Two hundred years ago, when the Swedish naturalist Carolus Linnaeus set out to distinguish and name all the species of plants and animals, it seemed no great problem. There were not many species within his geographical horizons, and those he studied had sharply defined characteristics. He named a total of 564 birds and 4235 animals of different kinds.

Linnaeus realized that common or colloquial names were unreliable for purposes of permanent classification. Even today the name "robin" means one bird to an Englishman and a quite different bird to an American. The American Robin is much more closely related to the European Blackbird than it is to the European Robin, or, for that matter, to the American blackbirds. Common names often cause confusion when people talk and write about animals, particularly when such names are used in speaking to an international audience. Many birds, moreover, are too rarely seen to have common names.

To avoid these difficulties, Linnaeus gave each bird two Latin names, a generic name and a specific name. The European Robin, for example, he named *Erithacus rubecula*, which means "a kind of bird inclined to redness"; the European Blackbird he named *Turdus merula*, which means "thrush blackbird." The American Robin belongs to the same genus as the Blackbird, but is a different species, so he named it *Turdus migratorius*, which of course means "thrush which migrates." Originally these Latin names were meant to be descriptive, but in the course of time, relationships unknown in Linnaeus' day have been discovered, so that some names have become meaningless or mis-

leading if considered literally, though they remain convenient designations.

Using two Latin names as he did, Linnaeus established the principle of binomial nomenclature, which is still the basic system for naming all plants and animals. The science of classifying organisms is called taxonomy or systematic biology, and scientists, usually museum workers, who specialize in classifying and naming birds are called bird taxonomists or systematic ornithologists.

Linnaeus also provided Latin names for the larger, more inclusive categories of birds and other animals: Kingdom, Phylum, Class, Order, and Family. To illustrate: the American Robin and the European Blackbird resemble each other more closely than either resembles a Bluebird, so they are placed in the Genus *Turdus*. All three birds, however, resemble each other more closely than any one of them resembles a swallow, so the former are placed in the Family *Turdidae* (thrush family) and the latter in the Family *Hirundinidae* (swallow family). The thrushes and swallows still have enough basic features in common to be grouped into the Order *Passeriformes* (perching birds) as distinct, say, from the Order *Falconiformes* (hawks, eagles, falcons). And because all the 27 Orders of living birds possess the irreducible minimum of characteristics that define a bird, such as warm-bloodedness, feathers, and wings, they are placed in the Class *Aves*, the most inclusive bird category. Birds and other animals are thus arranged in a series of classifying hierarchies of decreasing inclusiveness from class to species.

Here are examples of the use of scientific terminology for four different kinds of animals, the last two both birds:

Kingdom:	Animalia	Animalia	Animalia	Animalia
Phylum:	Arthropoda	Chordata	Chordata	Chordata
Class:	Insecta	Mammalia	Aves	Aves
Order:	Hymenoptéra	Carnivora	Falconiformes	Passeriformes
Family:	Apidae	Felidae	Accipitridae	Turdidae
Genus:°	*Apis*	*Felis*	*Haliaeetus*	*Turdus*
Species:°	*mellifera*	*domestica*	*leucocephalus*	*migratorius*
Common name:	Honeybee	Domestic Cat	Bald Eagle	American Robin

° The genus and species are combined to form the scientific name.

Note that in the scientific name the Genus (plural Genera) is always capitalized; the species (plural also species) is not capitalized. According to the rules of international scientific nomenclature, the same generic name may not be used twice in the animal kingdom, but the specific name may be used frequently. In addition to the major classifications just listed, there are often intermediate classifications of Suborders and Superorders, Subfamilies, and so on. All backboned animals, for example, belong to the Subphylum *Vertebrata*.

Species containing populations of slightly different forms are commonly broken down into subspecies, sometimes called races. In this case they are given a trinomial scientific name. The Robin that breeds in northern North America is called *Turdus migratorius migratorius*, and the slightly different form that breeds in the southern United States, *Turdus migratorius achrusterus*. To the non-scientist the minor distinctions that separate these two races or subspecies are negligible, and he calls both groups Robins.

Just how many different kinds of birds are there? It depends on whom you ask. One authority will say that there are about 25,000 species in the world; another, 8600 species. Taxonomists can be grouped into "species" too: the "splitters" who delight in classifying birds according to minute differences, and the "lumpers" who differentiate species on the basis of larger differences. This discrepancy in techniques points up a central problem. No one has much trouble in distinguishing an eagle from a robin. But disagreements arise among observers when species and subspecies are to be differentiated.

On the Aleutian Islands off Alaska there lives a large, dark-colored Song Sparrow that is about twice as large as the light-colored, desert-dwelling Song Sparrow of southern Baja California. Had Linnaeus held these two birds in his hands he would undoubtedly have called them distinct species. Today we know that in North America there are 31 closely intergrading types of Song Sparrows, most of them living up and down the Pacific coast. These birds live as geographic populations, each population only slightly different from its neighbors. While the birds living at the north and south extremes of Song Sparrow range are distinctly different in size and coloration, it is quite apparent, as one travels from Alaska to Baja California, that the successive populations in between change gradually from large to small, from dark to light. Consequently the 31 population types are not classed as species but as subspecies of one Song Sparrow: the Aleutian giant is called *Melospiza melodia maxima* and the small California race, *Melospiza melodia rivularis*. The same sort of subspecific geographic populations occur among Bluejays, Red-tailed Hawks, Horned Larks, and many other birds.

So the answer to the question of how many kinds of birds there are depends on the answer to another question: What is a species? Linnaeus thought that all species were created in their different patterns, fixed and unchanging. Since Darwin's epochal publications a century ago, the species concept has itself evolved; it has undergone two fundamental changes. First, we now understand that through evolution one species arises from another pre-existing species. Therefore, birds related through evolutionary descent should show "family resemblances," and they do. Second, a species is no longer defined as a certain idealized type of bird with precisely defined shape, size, and color. Instead, today a species is defined as a living population in nature made up of birds (or other organisms) that have about the same structure, size, color, behavior and habitat, and breed with each other rather than with members of other similar groups. Subspecies are geographic races, or fractional populations, of species. Yet even this definition leaves room for argument. The most important single criterion of a species relates to inter-breeding. If two birds mate and have offspring which are fertile when they in turn intermate, the original pair are *likely* to belong to the same species. But this is not an infallible rule, for sometimes distant relatives may have fertile offspring, and close relatives may not.

CRITERIA OF RELATIONSHIPS

The problem of separating one species from another is especially difficult when the taxonomist is unable to observe the living populations in nature. Often he must work with only a few birds, perhaps museum specimens, or even fossils. In such cases, he can use only physical characteristics in attempting to describe and delimit a species. Linnaeus and other early taxonomists depended almost entirely on the external and internal structure (morphology) of an animal to determine its species. But morphology alone is often unreliable as a criterion of relationship. Herons, cranes, bustards, and Secretary Birds all have long legs, but are not at all closely related. An example of the hazards attendant on using morphological evidence is suggested by one of Delacour's (1946) observations regarding the Eurasian parrotbills. The species *Paradoxornis unicolor* has four toes and *Paradoxornis paradoxus* has only three. Yet the two species are otherwise so similar that they would be classed as two races of a single species. The taxonomist must always be alert to distinguish those similarities between animals that are the result of parallel evolution or convergent adaptation, and those that are due to a common heredity.

Morphological characters still have their use, however, in indicating relationships. The bones of a bird's skeleton—especially the structure of the palate, the number and shape of cervical vertebrae, and the structure of the sternum or of the leg bones—are very useful in determining some of the larger taxonomic categories. Muscles of the pelvic region have been used in classifying ospreys and vultures, and leg muscles have been used to separate genera of finches. The structure of tongue muscles has aided in classifying

parrots, and those of the voice box or syrinx, in classifying perching birds. Even the twistings of the intestines and the arrangement of the large arteries have taxonomic significance. Statistical studies of wing length, body length, and tail length have been helpful in identifying subspecies of birds. The distribution of feathers over the body and their sequence in molting have been used to differentiate many species. The speckled breasts of young Robins and Bluebirds help to reveal their membership in the thrush family.

Recently a type of micro-morphology has been employed, particularly in Japan by Yamashina, to help determine hereditary relationships. His microscopical studies of the chromosomes of birds, especially of ducks, pheasants, and pigeons, have confirmed some taxonomic determinations and cast doubt on others. The morphology and number of chromosomes of a bird do not necessarily reflect all the hereditary changes that distinguish it from other birds. Gene mutations, for example, are completely invisible, even to the eye of the electron microscope. Nevertheless, changes in chromosome morphology represent changes in heredity. Accordingly, a precise study of bird chromosomes does represent a direct attack on the hereditary stuff responsible for genetic differences. As such, it offers much promise in the difficult field of determining systematic relations between birds.

The tissue and fluids of every animal body are made up of protein compounds, which, for a given animal, are remarkably specific and stable. In recent years new techniques have become available for the analysis of these tell-tale proteins. The great advantage of using these methods is that most of them are quickly and easily employed, and that they can provide precise, quantitative, and completely objective data. Among these techniques, mainly from the field of physical chemistry, are the following:

1. Tests of blood serum and cellular antigen-antibody reactions of various kinds.

2. Photoelectric determinations of pre-cipitin turbidity.

3. Electrophoretic and chromatographic analyses of blood-, tissue-, and egg-proteins.

4. Osmotic pressure and filtration-rate measurements of various body fluids.

5. The determination of the sedimentation velocity of body and egg protein molecules with the ultra-centrifuge.

6. Study by electron microscopy of cells and cell inclusions.

7. Study of x-ray diffraction patterns of body extracts and secretions.

8. The physico-chemical analysis of the structure and weight of the hemoglobin molecule.

9. The chemical analysis of nucleoproteins.

10. Infra-red spectrometry of various body fluids.

There are, no doubt, other useful techniques now available or shortly to be developed that will still further refine this physico-chemical inquiry into animal relationships. The material basis of any species' heredity is determined by the molecular structure and location on the chromosomes of its genes. Lacking practical tools that will reveal and analyze the genes directly, probably our best hope for identifying the taxonomic relationships of any individual species is the development of delicate and precise tests that will identify the hereditary "finger prints" of the animal—its species-specific proteins.

In addition to these morphological and physico-chemical data, various physiological features offer suggestive clues to the relationships of birds. As with morphological features, the problem is to determine which physiological characteristics are stable and enduring, and which are plastic and quickly modified by evolutionary selection. Among physiological features that may be of taxonomic use are

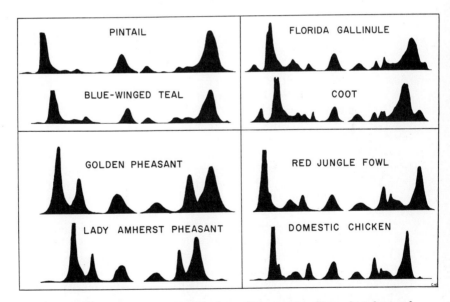

Figure 2.1. Electrophoresis patterns of fresh egg-white proteins of four selected pairs of related birds. For each pair, the patterns show clearly the chemical affinities of their egg proteins. These affinities corroborate morphological evidences of kinship between the birds. Vertical coordinates represent the concentrations of certain protein molecules of the egg white; horizontal coordinates show the distances the molecules moved while subjected to an electrical field. The two central peaks in each pattern are experimental artifacts and may be ignored in comparing curves. After McCabe and Deutsch.

body temperature, heart rate, blood pressure, oxygen dissociation, environmental resistance (to cold, starvation, lack of oxygen and water, and the like), digestion of food, basal metabolism, chronology of phases of the reproductive cycle, photoperiodic responses, fat deposition, hybrid sterility, endocrine and drug reactions, disease resistance, brain waves, and rate of development of embryos and nestlings.

Closely related to physiological characteristics are behavior patterns that throw light on hereditary relationships. Habitat preferences are quite varied in birds and often show distinct hereditary patterns. Obviously, water birds do not live in a desert. But even among closely related birds, different species and even subspecies have different habitat preferences. Within the single species of Song Sparrow, *Melospiza melodia*, one subspecies prefers salt marsh as a habitat; another, brushy meadow; still another, desert. Nesting sites can reveal taxonomic differences. Warblers of the genus *Vermivora* typically nest on or very near the ground, while those of the genus *Dendroica* nest in trees or shrubs. Many other behavior characteristics are equally diagnostic. Sometimes it is the differences that are significant, sometimes the similarities. Different species of bower-birds with almost indistinguishable plumage may construct different types of bowers. Males belonging to one group build a maypole-shaped bower; males belonging to another group, a trough-shaped one. Incidentally, the maypole builders have plain white eggs, the trough- or avenue-builders, heavily speckled ones.

The Tree Swallow, *Iridoprocne bicolor*, has two populations with quite different cold-weather food habits, according to Griscom (1945). The more northerly population survives freezing weather by eating bayberries. The southerly population may perish in sudden cold spells because it is completely dependent, as are most swallows, on insect food.

Certain deep-rooted behavior patterns indicate relationships between cormo-rants, boobies, albatrosses, and penguins (Murphy, 1936). All of these birds show an "ecstatic attitude" in which they posture with their neck and wings at right angles to the body; they sway while gaggling; they invert the neck and head over the back; they all use pebbles and feathers in courtship ceremonies; and none are able to recognize their normal food when it is out of water. Other behavior patterns of some use to the taxonomist include feeding, care of the young, nest sanitation habits, migration, flight patterns, song, and many modes of gregarious or social behavior.

There still remain a few other clues useful to the taxonomist in ferreting out bird relationships. Since modern bird species have evolved from previously existing species, recently derived species should not be very remote geographically or in the fossil record from their ancestors. Making due allowance for barriers and highways (difficult and easy routes of dispersal), the geographic distribution of birds over the earth provides valuable evidence of relationships. As would be expected, species that resemble each other most closely are generally closest together in space. Evidence from paleontology is greatly restricted by the small number of fossils found. The thin, delicate bones of birds do not well survive the processes of fossilization. The age of the strata in which the fossils are found is of great significance in determining systematic relationships. In North America nearly 500 kinds of fossil birds have been discovered and described, about half of them of species which still exist.

A surprising source of evidence for the classification of birds comes from their external parasites. Parasites are normally well adapted to their hosts. As birds evolved, their parasites evolved along with them, to such an extent that related species of birds today show related species of parasites. This relationship is known as Fahrenholz' Rule. As an illustration of its application, Rothschild and Clay (1952) make the point that although taxonomists have placed the African Ostrich and the South American Rheas in separate orders, largely on morphological grounds, they nevertheless both possess feather lice of closely related species belonging to the same genus, a genus which occurs on no other birds.

Finally, statistics are used, especially in the difficult realm of distinguishing subspecies. Just how different must the members of one population be from those of another of the same species to deserve subspecific rank? For practical purposes the "seventy-five per cent rule" is commonly applied. For example, if 75 per cent of the individuals of one geographic race differ recognizably from all the individuals of another race of the same species, they may be called a subspecies.

Although birds are the best known and most completely described class of animals, there still are many uncertain systematic relationships to be worked out. A subjective element remains in the determination of any taxonomic group: fallible human judgment is still a necessary tool for the taxonomist. There will probably continue to be controversies over classification in the ornithological journals for years to come. Probably the chief reason for this is the great structural and functional uniformity thrust on birds as they evolved into flying machines. This uniformity greatly restricts the diversity, so useful to taxonomists, found in other vertebrate classes.

To return to the question of how many different kinds of birds there are in the world, Mayr (1942) has shown that the present trend is to lump species together rather than to split them into smaller species. Groups of birds formerly described as species are now called subspecies or races of a single polytypic species. In 1910 the last complete list of the birds of the world recorded 19,000 species. Between 1910 and 1942, 8000 additional types were discovered, described, and named, but the total of all species by then had been reduced to about 8500. In 1946 Mayr estimated that there were then known 8616 species and 28,500 subspecies of living birds in the world. These belong to 166 families and 27 orders. New species are being discovered and classified at a steadily decreasing rate—at the present, about 6 species per year (Mayr and Zimmer, 1943). By contrast, between 6000 and 7000 new species of insects are described yearly. It is unlikely that more than one per cent of the birds on earth remain unclassified.

A SURVEY OF BIRDS OF THE WORLD

The list of birds of the world that follows is neither complete nor final, but it gives every order of known birds, living or fossil. It also gives every family of living North American birds (marked with an asterisk [*]) occurring north of the United States-Mexico boundary, as well as some of the numerically and biologically important families, living and fossil, of other continents. The list is roughly arranged in a sequence from the most primitive to the most highly evolved types. The family tree of bird relationships is of course branching, and cannot be represented by a linear sequence. A highly speculative diagram showing suggested bird relationships is shown in Figure 2.2. The arrangement of orders and families is after Wetmore (1951) and the number of species given for each family is taken from Mayr (1946). The names of orders are printed in large and small capitals and have the long suffix "iformes." Family names end in "idae."

CLASS AVES

Birds: Possess feathers; fore-limbs modified into wings; hind-limbs adapted to walking, swimming, or perching; mandibles with no teeth (in living species); light skeleton with much fusion; four-chambered heart; extensive airsacs throughout body; warm-blooded; no urinary bladder; oviparous; 8600 living species.

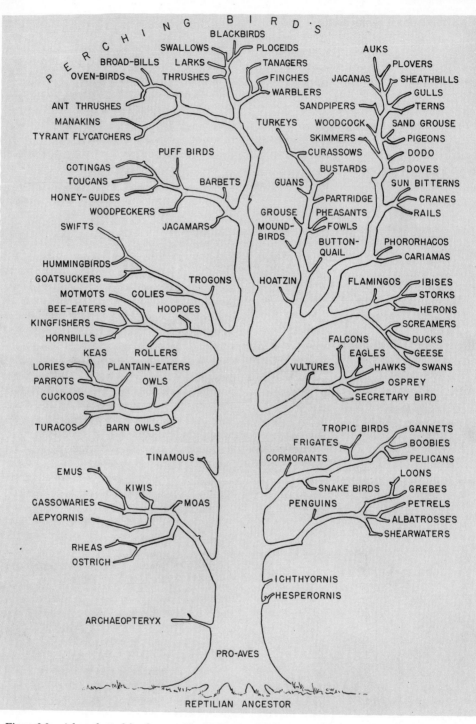

Figure 2.2.   A hypothetical family tree of birds showing possible relationships. Some of the kinships indicated here will no doubt be more accurately determined as more precise methods of taxonomic research are developed.

Subclass Archaeornithes

Ancestral birds: Fossil; lizard-like, with true teeth; three clawed-fingers, and a long bony tail of more than 13 vertebrae.

ARCHAEOPTERYGIFORMES. The oldest known birds; three fossils discovered in Jurassic stone quarries in Bavaria; pigeon-sized.

Archaeopterygidae: *Archaeopteryx;* 1 species.

Subclass Neornithes

True birds: Finger bones fused; tail vertebrae 13 or less; sternum flat or keeled.

SUPERORDER ODONTOGNATHAE. New World fossil birds.

HESPERORNITHIFORMES. Hesperornithidae:* *Hesperornis*—9 species; flightless, loon-like diving bird, with toothed jaws, from Upper Cretaceous of Kansas and Montana.

SUPERORDER ICHTHYORNITHES. New World fossil birds.

ICHTHYORNITHIFORMES. Ichthyornithidae:* 9 species; a crow-sized flying bird with a well-developed keel; Upper Cretaceous, Kansas and Texas.

SUPERORDER IMPENNES. Web-footed marine swimmers. Wing modified into a thin, powerful paddle; large keel; scale-like feathers.

SPHENISCIFORMES. Spheniscidae: Penguins; 17 species; Antarctica and cold waters as far north as the Galapagos Islands.

SUPERORDER NEOGNATHAE. Typical birds.

CAENAGNATHIFORMES. Fossil; possibly not a bird.

Caenagnathidae: *Caenagnathus;* 1 species; Upper Cretaceous of Alberta, Canada.

STRUTHIONIFORMES. Flightless walking birds. Flat sternum; heavy legs with 2 short toes; few feathers on head, neck or legs; small brain. Largest living birds,

Figure 2.3.   Adelie Penguin. Family Spheniscidae.

many over 2.2 meters tall; weighing 135 kilograms; precocial young.

Struthionidae: Ostriches; 1 species; Africa, Arabia.

RHEIFORMES. Flightless walking birds. Flat sternum; heavy legs with 3 toes; 1.2 meters tall; precocial young.

Rheidae: Rheas; 2 species; South America.

CASUARIIFORMES. Flightless walking birds. Flat sternum; stout legs with 3 toes; feathers with large aftershafts; 1.5 meters tall; precocial young.

Figure 2.4.   Ostrich. Family Struthionidae.

Casuariidae: Cassowaries; 6 species; Australia, New Guinea.

Dromiceidae: Emus; 2 species; Australia.

AEPYORNITHIFORMES. Fossil. Flightless terrestrial birds with flat sternum, rudimentary wings, 4 toes; varied in size between turkey and ostrich; laid largest known egg: 33 cm. by 24 cm.

Aepyornithidae: Elephant Birds; 12 species; Madagascar.

DINORNITHIFORMES. Fossil. Flightless terrestrial birds. Wings rudimentary or absent; flat sternum; 3 or 4 toes. Largest known birds; some were over 3 meters high. Became extinct about 300 years ago.

Dinornithidae: Moas; 8 species; New Zealand.

Anomalopterygidae: *Anomalopteryx* and relatives; 20 species; New Zealand.

APTERYGIFORMES. Flightless, terrestrial hen-sized birds. 4 toes, long bill with nostrils at tip; degenerate wings; feathers hair-like; nocturnal.

Apterygidae: Kiwis; 3 species; New Zealand.

TINAMIFORMES. Functional wings; keeled sternum; poor fliers; precocial young.

Tinamidae: Tinamous; 32 species; Central and South America.

GAVIIFORMES. Short legs located far back on heavy body; webbed feet; good divers; precocial young.

Gaviidae:° Loons; 4 species; Northern North America and Eurasia.

Figure 2.5.   Common Loon. Family Gaviidae.

PODICIPEDIFORMES. Short legs located posteriorly on body; lobate toes; rudimentary tail; good divers; precocial young.

Podicipedidae:° Grebes; 20 species; world wide.

PROCELLARIIFORMES. Marine birds with tubular nostrils; horny, hooked beak; oily plumage; long narrow wings; feet webbed, with rudimentary hind toe. Excellent fliers.

Diomedeidae:° Albatrosses; 14 species; mainly on southern oceans. Wandering Albatross, *Diomedea exulans*, has largest wingspread of all living birds: 3.5 meters maximum.

Procellariidae:° Shearwaters, fulmars, 56 species; world wide.

Hydrobatidae:° Storm Petrels; 18 species of small sea birds; world wide.

Pelecanoididae:° Diving Petrels; 5 species of small sea birds; south temperate and south polar seas.

PELECANIFORMES. Four toes united in one web; long beak; nostrils rudimentary or absent; possess a throat pouch (except Tropic Birds).

Phaëthontidae:° Tropic Birds; 3 species; tropical seas.

Pelecanidae:° Pelicans; 6 species; tropical and warm temperate seas.

Sulidae:° Boobies, Gannets; 9 species; world wide, excepting polar seas.

Phalacrocoracidae:° Cormorants; 30 species; world wide in fresh and salt waters; used by Japanese to catch fish.

Anhingidae:° Snake Birds; 1 species; tropical and subtropical fresh waters.

Fregatidae:° Frigate or Man-o'-war Birds; 5 species; tropical and subtropical seas.

CICONIIFORMES. Long necked and long legged waders; toes not webbed (except flamingos); often nest in colonies along shores or in marshes; one family with precocial young.

Ardeidae:° Herons, egrets, bitterns; 59 species; world wide.

Figure 2.6. Roseate Spoonbill. Family Threskiornithidae.

Figure 2.7. European Black Vulture. Family Accipitridae.

Ciconiidae:* Storks, jabirus, wood ibises; 16 species; world wide.

Threskiornithidae:* Ibises, spoonbills; 28 species; world wide.

Phoenicopteridae:* Flamingos; 6 species; tropical and temperate regions; precocial young.

ANSERIFORMES. Broadened bills containing many tactile nerve endings and with filtering ridges or "teeth" at margins; short legs with webbed feet (except screamers); body well supplied with down and oily feathers; precocial young.

Anhimidae: Screamers; 3 species; South America.

Anatidae:* Ducks, geese, swans; 145 species; world wide.

FALCONIFORMES. Diurnal birds of prey; strong bill, hooked at tip and sharp on edges; feet with sharp curved talons; keen vision; strong fliers as a rule.

Cathartidae:* New World Vultures; 6 species; Western Hemisphere.

Sagittariidae: Secretary Bird; 1 species; Africa.

Accipitridae:* Eagles, hawks, kites, Old World vultures, harriers; 205 species; world wide.

Pandionidae:* Osprey; 1 species; world wide.

Falconidae:* Caracaras, falcons; 58 species; world wide.

GALLIFORMES. Vegetarian, hen-like birds with short, stout beak, short rounded wings, and well developed tails; heavy feet adapted to scratching ground and running; often gregarious; commonly show distinct sex-dimorphism; nest on ground; precocial young; important game and domestic birds.

Megapodiidae: Megapodes or mound birds; 10 species; Australia and surrounding islands.

Cracidae:* Curassows, guans, chachalacas; 38 species; Central and South America.

Tetraonidae:* Grouse, ptarmigan; 18 species; Northern Hemisphere.

Figure 2.8. Prairie Chicken. Family Tetraonidae.

Phasianidae:° Quails, partridge, pheasants, jungle fowl, peafowl; 165 species; mainly Old World.

Numididae: Guinea fowl; 7 species; Africa, Madagascar.

Meleagrididae:° Turkeys; 2 species; Mexico and United States.

Opisthocomidae: Hoatzin; 1 species; young have two clawed-fingers; semi-precocial young; South America.

GRUIFORMES. Some birds long legged and long necked with strong flight (cranes); others smaller with shorter legs and necks, weak flight (rails and coots); rounded wings; prairie and marsh dwellers; precocial young.

Turnicidae: Bustard quails; 15 species; Africa, Eurasia, Indomalaya, New Guinea and Australia.

Gruidae:° Cranes; 14 species; world wide except South America.

Aramidae:° Limpkins; 1 species; South America and southern United States.

Rallidae:° Rails, coots, gallinules; 132 species; world wide.

Phororhacidae: *Phororhacos;* 8 species; fossil; large, flightless birds with enormous skulls 65 cm. long; Miocene deposits of Patagonia.

Otididae: Bustards; 23 species; Old World.

DIATRYMIFORMES. Fossil; large, stockily built, flightless birds, 2 meters high, with vestigial wings, and large, heavy skull; Eocene period.

Diatrymidae: *Diatryma;* 7 species; United States and France.

CHARADRIIFORMES. A large assemblage of 16 living families of shore birds, gulls, terns, auks, and others; toes usually webbed; compact plumage; strong fliers; often colonial; precocial young in most species.

Jacanidae:° Jaçanas; 7 species; long-toed lily-pad walkers; pantropical; precocial young.

Rostratulidae: Painted snipe; 2 species; South America, southern Africa, southern Asia, and Australia; precocial young.

Hematopodidae:° Oystercatcher; 6 species; laterally-flattened beaks; world wide; precocial young.

Charadriidae:° Plovers, turnstones, surfbirds; 63 species; world wide; precocial young.

Scolopacidae:° Snipe, woodcock, sandpipers; 77 species; world wide; precocial young.

Recurvirostridae:° Avocets, stilts; 7 species; world wide; precocial young.

Phalaropodidae:° Phalaropes; 3 species; Northern Hemisphere; precocial young.

Burhinidae: Thick-knees; 9 species; world wide except North America; semi-precocial young.

Glareolidae: Pratincoles, coursers; 16 species; Old World.

Stercorariidae:° Skuas, jaegers; 4 species; world wide, especially polar seas; semi-precocial young.

Laridae:° Gulls, terns; 82 species; world wide; semi-precocial young.

Rynchopidae:° Skimmers; 3 species; North and South America, Africa, southern Asia.

Alcidae:° Auks, murres, puffins; 22 species; north temperate and arctic seas; semi-precocial young.

COLUMBIFORMES. Pigeons and doves; short slender bill with cere (soft skin) at base; short legs; crop produces "pigeon's milk" to feed young.

Figure 2.9.   Sora Rail. Family Rallidae.

Figure 2.10.   Herring Gull. Family Laridae.

Pteroclidae: Sand-grouse; 16 species; deserts of Eurasia and Africa.

Raphidae: Dodos (extinct since 1700) and Solitaires (extinct since 1800); 3 species; Islands of Mauritius, Reunion, and Rodriguez.

Columbidae:° Pigeons, doves; 289 species; world wide.

PSITTACIFORMES. Narrow, hooked beak; upper mandible hinged movably to skull; fleshy tongue; large, rounded heads; toes, 2 front and 2 rear, with grasping claws; brilliant plumage; vary in size from 7 cm. to 90 cm.

Psittacidae:° Lories, parrots, macaws; 315 species; pantropical and subtropical.

CUCULIFORMES. Toes, 2 front and 2 rear; outer hind toe reversible. Many Old World cuckoos are brood parasites.

Musophagidae: Plantain-eaters; 19 species; Africa.

Cuculidae:° Cuckoos, road-runners, anis; 127 species; world wide.

STRIGIFORMES. Nocturnal predators; large, rounded head with large, forward-directed eyes set in feathered disks; large external ear-openings with flaps; short, powerful, hooked beak; strong, sharp talons; soft, fluffy plumage allows silent flight.

Tytonidae:° Barn owls; 11 species; world wide.

Strigidae:° Owls; 123 species; world wide.

CAPRIMULGIFORMES. Small bill with wide mouth usually surrounded by insect-netting bristles; small legs and feet; twilight insect feeders; majority lay eggs directly on ground.

Steatornithidae: Oil Bird; 1 species; cave dwellers; South America.

Podargidae: Frogmouths; 12 species; India, Australia.

Nyctibiidae: Potoos; 5 species; Central America and tropical South America.

Caprimulgidae:° Goatsuckers; 67 species; world wide.

APODIFORMES. Small birds with short legs and small feet; bill either small and weak (swifts), or long and slender with tubular or brushy tongue (hummingbirds); wings pointed.

Apodidae:° Swifts; 76 species (4 in the U.S.); world wide.

Trochilidae:° Hummingbirds; 319 species; includes some of the smallest birds on earth (*Mellisuga helenae* 6.3 cm. long); Central and South America; 15 species in the United States.

Figure 2.11.   Parrot. Family Psittacidae.

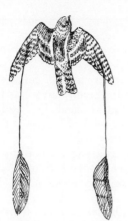

Figure 2.14.   Belted Kingfisher. Family Alcedinidae.

Figure 2.12.   Pennant-winged Nightjar. Family Caprimulgidae.

COLIIFORMES. Small birds; first and
fourth toes reversible; long tails.

Coliidae: Mouse-birds or colies; 6
species; Africa.

TROGONIFORMES. Short, stout bill; small
weak feet; usually iridescent green plumage with long tail; nest in cavities.

Trogonidae:° Trogons, Quetzal; 34
species; pantropical.

CORACIIFORMES. Strong, sharp bill;
third and fourth toes joined at base; nest
in cavities.

Alcedinidae:° Kingfishers; 87 species;
world wide.

Todidae: Todies; 5 species; West Indies.

Momotidae: Motmots; 8 species;
Central and South America.

Meropidae: Bee-eaters; 24 species;
Old World tropics and subtropics.

Coraciidae: Rollers; 16 species; Old
World.

Upupidae: Hoopoe; 1 species; Eurasia, Africa.

Figure 2.13.   Ruby-throated Hummingbird. Family
Trochilidae.

Bucerotidae: Hornbills; 45 species;
Old World tropics.

PICIFORMES. Toes, 2 front, 2 rear; nest
in cavities; no down on young or adults.

Galbulidae: Jacamars; 15 species;
Central and South America.

Bucconidae: Puffbirds; 30 species;
Central and South America.

Capitonidae: Barbets; 72 species;
pantropical.

Indicatoridae: Honey-guides; 13 species; often brood parasites; Africa,
India, Malaya.

Ramphastidae: Toucans; 37 species;
New World tropics.

Picidae:° Woodpeckers, piculets,
wrynecks; 224 species; strong,
gripping toes; long retractile
tongue with barbs; world wide except Madagascar and Australia.

PASSERIFORMES. Perching birds; toes, 3
front and 1 rear, adapted to perching; 12
tail feathers; 10 primary wing feathers.
This order contains over half of all known
birds. It embraces 69 living families, 53 of
which belong to the suborder Oscines
which have a well developed syrinx and
are known as Song-birds. Forty-nine of the
more important families are listed here.

Eurylaimidae: Broadbills; 14 species;
Indo-Malaya, Africa.

Dendrocolaptidae: Woodhewers or
woodcreepers; 63 species; Central
and South America.

Furnariidae: Ovenbirds; 209 species;
Central and South America.

Figure 2.15. Pileated Woodpecker. Family Picidae.

Formicariidae; Antbirds; 238 species; Central and South America.

Cotingidae:° Cotingas; 90 species; Central and South America.

Pipridae: Manakins; 59 species; Central and South America.

Tyrannidae:° Tyrant Flycatchers; 365 species; North and South America.

Pittidae: Pittas; 23 species; Old World tropics.

Menuridae: Lyrebirds; 2 species; Australia.

Alaudidae:° Larks; 74 species; Old World (1 species in America).

Hirundinidae:° Swallows; 75 species; world wide.

Campephagidae: Cuckoo-shrikes; 58 species; Old World.

Dicruridae: Drongos; 20 species; Old World tropics.

Oriolidae: Old World Orioles; 32 species; Old World.

Corvidae:° Crows, magpies, jays; 100 species; world wide.

Figure 2.17. Blue Jay. Family Corvidae.

Ptilonorhynchidae: Bower-birds; 17 species; Australia and New Guinea.

Paradisaeidae: Birds of Paradise; 43 species; New Guinea and Australia.

Paradoxornithidae: Parrotbills; 19 species; Eurasia.

Paridae:° Titmice; 65 species; Eurasia, Africa, North America.

Figure 2.16. Eastern Wood Pewee. Family Tyrannidae.

Figure 2.18. Black-capped Chickadee. Family Paridae.

Figure 2.19.   Wood Thrush. Family Turdidae.

Sittidae:° Nuthatches; 17 species; Northern Hemisphere, Australia, Madagascar.

Certhiidae:° Creepers; 17 species; Eurasia, Australia, North America.

Chamaeidae:° Wren-tits; 1 species; Oregon, California.

Timaliidae: Babblers; 261 species; Old World tropics.

Pycnonotidae: Bulbuls; 109 species; Old World tropics.

Cinclidae:° Dippers; 5 species; Northern Hemisphere and South America.

Troglodytidae:° Wrens; 63 species; New World, one species extending to Eurasia.

Mimidae:° Thrashers, mockingbirds; 30 species; New World.

Turdidae:° Thrushes; 304 species; world wide.

Sylviidae:° Old World warblers; 366 species; mainly Old World, Northern Hemisphere.

Regulidae:° Kinglets, goldcrests; 20 species; Northern Hemisphere.

Muscicapidae: Old World flycatchers; 328 species; Old World.

Prunellidae: Accentors, hedge sparrows; 12 species; Eurasia.

Motacillidae:° Pipits, wagtails; 48 species; world wide.

Bombycillidae:° Waxwings; 3 species; Northern Hemisphere.

Ptilogonatidae:° Silky flycatchers; 4 species; tropical America.

Laniidae:° Shrikes; 72 species; world wide except South America.

Sturnidae:° Starlings; 103 species; Old World (1 species introduced into North America).

Meliphagidae: Honey-eaters; 160 species; Australian region.

Nectariniidae: Sunbirds; 106 species; Africa, Asia, Australia.

Dicaeidae: Flower-peckers; 54 species; West Africa, Indo-Malaya, Australia.

Zosteropidae: White-eyes; 80 species; Africa, Asia, Australia.

Vireonidae:° Vireos; 41 species; New World.

Coerebidae:° Honeycreepers; 36 species; tropical America.

Drepanididae: Hawaiian honeycreepers; 22 species; Hawaiian Islands.

Parulidae:° Wood Warblers; 109 species; New World.

Ploceidae:° Weaver-finches; 263 species; Africa, South Asia, Australia (House Sparrow in North America).

Icteridae:° Blackbirds, troupials; 88 species; New World.

Thraupidae:° Tanagers; 197 species; New World.

Fringillidae:° Grosbeaks, finches, buntings, sparrows; 426 species; world wide except Australia.

Figure 2.20.   Rose-breasted Grosbeak. Family Fringillidae.

SUGGESTED READINGS

The authentic, well written, and beautifully illustrated book by Gilliard, *Living Birds of the World,* provides a stimulating introduction to bird classification. The twenty volumes by Bent on *Life Histories of North American Birds* are a rich mine of information on life history details, as also are the delightfully written volumes by Skutch, *Life Histories of Central American Birds*. The illustrated, five-volume *Handbook of British Birds*, by Witherby *et al.*, gives similar details for British and many European birds. In Van Tyne and Berger's *Fundamentals of Ornithology* will be found a brief, but excellent, illustrated summary of the families of living birds. For an introduction to sea birds, the volumes by Alexander, *Birds of the Ocean*, and Murphy, *Oceanic Birds of South America*, are recommended. For more technical, taxonomic reference, the following volumes should be consulted: American Ornithologists' Union *Check-list of North American Birds;* Ridgeway and Friedmann's *Birds of Middle and North America;* Peters' *Check-list of Birds of the World;* and Storer's chapter on the classification of birds in Marshall's *Biology and Comparative Physiology of Birds*. In German, the standard references are Niethammer's *Handbuch der Deutschen Vogelkunde*, and Heinroth and Heinroth's *Die Vögel Mitteleuropas*.

THREE

Skin, Scales, Feathers, and Colors

She plumes her feathers, and lets grow her wings
That in the various bustle of resort
Were all-too ruffled, and sometimes impair'd.
John Milton (1608–1674), *Comus*

Through the outside surface of every animal goes all traffic in materials and energy needed to sustain life. Birds, as creatures of land and air, and sometimes of water, have special needs. As a consequence, natural selection has provided them with a complex, highly adapted exterior.

THE SKIN OF BIRDS

Like all other vertebrates, birds possess a two-layered skin: epidermis on the outside and dermis underneath. Compared with other vertebrates, birds have a thin skin, extremely thin in owls and goatsuckers. As in man, the outer epidermis is composed of layers of flattened epithelial cells. These are capable of producing large amounts of keratin or horn, the substance of which hair and fingernails in man, and claws and scales in birds, are made. The inner layer, or dermis, a "housekeeping" layer, which supports and nourishes the epidermis, is a tougher, thicker, fibrous

26

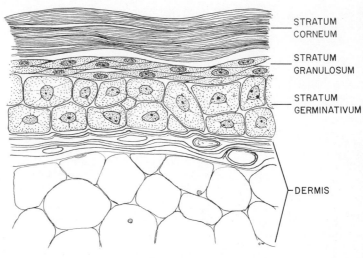

STRATUM CORNEUM

STRATUM GRANULOSUM

STRATUM GERMINATIVUM

DERMIS

Figure 3.1. A diagrammatic cross section of a bird's skin showing the typical layers. Magnification about 200×.

layer of connective tissue. It is penetrated by muscles, nerves, and blood vessels that supply the overlying epidermis and help to regulate heat loss. Its innermost layer is often rich in stored fat, valuable for shock absorption, heat insulation, and food storage. Dermal fat storage is particularly great in aquatic birds such as penguins, loons, ducks, albatrosses, petrels, and auks, and, during migration, in many passerine birds. Some species such as emus, boobies, pelicans, and nightjars possess subcutaneous air pockets that the bird may inflate at will. Smooth muscles located in the dermis are attached to the feather sockets. Their action permits the fluffing of feathers to increase the thickness of the insulating layer of trapped air, or the spreading of feathers for purposes of display or flight, or the pressing of feathers against the body for more rapid heat loss in hot weather.

Unlike mammals, birds possess no sweat glands. Sweat would merely plaster the feathers against the skin and hinder their normal functions. The only prominent skin gland is the uropygial or preen gland. As long ago as 1248 A.D., the Emperor Frederick II of Hohenstaufen (Wood and Fyfe, 1943) described this gland and its functions in his ornithological landmark, *The Art of Falconry.* Frederick described the organ as a double gland on the bird's

rump, supplied with a brush-like external opening. The gland secretes an oil which the bird squeezes out with its mandibles and places on its feathers and claws to keep them waterproof and in good condition. This accurate description of Frederick's was all the more remarkable in the light of recent ornithological controversies in which the gland has been erroneously held to be a scent gland, a poison gland, or used only to lubricate and polish the beak, or even to have some obscure electrical properties.

Actually, the preen gland may be two-lobed or single. It may or may not have a reservoir; and externally it may have a tuft of feathers at its opening, or a nipple. The gland is lacking in the adults of several species, including some parrots, bustards, doves, cassowaries, and the ostrich.

Studies by Elder (1954) have shown quite clearly that, at least in many waterfowl, the uropygial gland secretes a fluid containing fatty acid, fat, and wax, and that the act of preening automatically stimulates the flow of this secretion. He found further that birds whose glands had been experimentally removed suffered decided deterioration of their feathers, beaks, and leg scales (Fig. 3.2). There is good evidence that feathers supplied with the uropygial secretion have a significant amount of vitamin D, which may serve as

Figure 3.2. A normal Redhead Duck (left), contrasted with one whose oil gland had been removed. The role of the uropygial gland in feather-care is obvious. Photo from W. H. Elder and G. K. Brakhage.

a valuable supplement to the diet if swallowed during the preening exercise. Interestingly enough, young ducklings from which the preen gland had been removed displayed normal preening behavior but definitely shunned the water. Even 700 years ago Frederick II discovered that as a rule aquatic birds had larger oil glands than others. Recent experiments by Fabricius (1959) indicate that, at least in the Tufted Duck, *Aythya fuligula*, the uropygial gland is not an absolute requirement for waterproof plumage. Young ducklings whose oil glands had been removed had plumage as water-repellent as normal ducklings. The maintenance, by preening, of large amounts of finely distributed air among the ramifications of the feathers seemed to be responsible for their water repellency.

That the uropygial gland is of importance in waterproofing feathers is further seen in the Ascension Man-o'-War Bird, *Fregata magnificens*. This marine bird has a small pea-sized preen gland, and in consequence has feathers that become waterlogged when the bird alights on water or is caught in a rain storm (Murphy, 1936).

Many species of birds have patches of bare skin, especially on the head and neck: cassowaries, vultures, pelicans, hornbills, Galliformes, and others. These patches may be pigmented as in the turkey, or simply colored red by a rich supply of blood vessels. Many of them are in the form of fleshy lobes and contain a spongy connective tissue which, when inflated with blood, may become erect and turgid.

Among such structures are the combs of roosters, the fleshy eyebrows of some grouse, and the wattles of turkeys, pheasants, or cassowaries.

BEAKS, SCALES, AND CLAWS

The skin of a bird can produce a variety of structures depending on its location on the body. In one place it may remain skin, as in the naked head and neck of a vulture. In other places its epidermal cells may produce dense and compact scales, beaks, and claws, or light and complex feathers.

In some birds, including certain grouse and owls, the legs may be feathered as far as the toes, but in most birds the legs and feet are covered only with scales. As a rule, the epidermal cells of the skin build up the scales on their inner side as fast as they are worn away on the outside. Scales may be small and granular or large and plate-like. They provide a wonderfully tough, flexible, and easily cleaned covering for a bird's feet.

Claws are specialized scales protecting the toe-tips. They are well adapted for digging, scratching, fighting, and cleaning feathers. Each claw possesses a central basal mass of multiplying epidermal cells that become gradually keratinized and pushed forward, resulting in the horny finished claw. Many claws are curved because their upper surface grows more rapidly than their lower. As with other scales, claws are renewed from their bases about as rapidly as normal wear erodes their outsides. But in grouse the claws may be molted and renewed periodically as are the feathers.

Surprisingly, a few birds still possess claws on their wings, somewhat corresponding to nails on human fingertips. They are commonly found on the thumb in Falconiformes and Anseriformes, and on the second finger in the Ostrich, Rhea, and Hoatzin. At times claws are found also on the third finger of the Ostrich. The finger claws are well developed and quite functional in the young Hoatzin, which uses them to clamber about branches before it is able to fly.

As a consequence of their varied food habits, birds have evolved a great variety of beaks. All of them, however, arise in fundamentally the same way. They are essentially a compact layer of epidermal cells molded around the bony core of each mandible. The epidermis of the skin covering the upper and lower mandibles is stratified into three layers. Outwardly, as in the human skin, there is a horny stratum corneum which contributes directly to the formation of the beak. Inwardly, next to the dermis, is the stratum germinativum, where the epidermal cells actively multiply. Between these two layers is the stratum granulosum composed of two or three layers of cells in which keratohyalin granules are formed. These in turn are the forerunners of the keratin which is concentrated in the stratum corneum to make the beak, or rhamphotheca, proper.

The beak of a bird is normally hard and thick, especially at the tip, where wear is greatest. Frequently the edges, or tomia, are sharp, and useful for cutting food. In ducks the beak is hard only at its tip, and its sides are relatively soft and blunt. Its lateral margins are richly supplied with sensitive tactile nerve endings (Herbst corpuscles), useful in detecting seeds and insects in muddy water. Anyone who has ever held a handful of grain under water to feed a hungry duck can appreciate from the rapid disappearance of the grain the marvelous sensory discrimination of these pressure-sensitive corpuscles in the bird's beak. In a few species, such as the Woodcock, *Philohela minor*, the tactile corpuscles occur at the tip of the long sensitive beak, and aid the bird in detecting worms deep in soft soil.

In many species the tough horny material at the base of the upper mandible gives way to bare, thick skin adjoining the forehead. This region, called the cere, is also supplied with touch corpuscles. Frequently the cere is brightly colored, as in parrots and birds of prey.

Nostrils are usually situated in the upper mandible near its base or in the cere; but in the nocturnal kiwis, which find their food largely by scent, the nostrils are located at the tip of the beak. In petrels and albatrosses (Procellariiformes) the nostrils do not open directly outward but are carried forward in a covered tube, while in gannets they are entirely covered over.

Figure 3.3. The horny scales, talons, and beaks of birds are derived from the epidermis of the skin. Left: Scales and talons of the Bald Eagle. Right: Side and top views of the beak of the Pink-footed Shearwater.

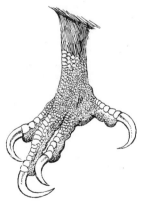
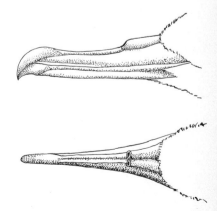

The Black Skimmer, *Rhynchops nigra*, is a shore bird that spends hours at a time flying just above the surface of the water with its upper mandible in the air, its lower mandible cutting the water. One-sided wear on the lower mandible would soon reduce it to a stump but for the remarkable fact that the lower mandible, adapted to the excessive friction, grows more rapidly than the upper. A Black Skimmer reared in captivity, lacking this water friction, will grow a lower mandible over twice as long as its upper mandible.

Ordinarily, each mandible of a bird is covered with a single horny sheath which is renewed from beneath as it is worn down on the outside. But on the vividly colored triangular beak of the Atlantic Common Puffin, *Fratercula arctica*, grow nine separate superficial scales: six on the upper mandible and three on the lower; and also one above and below each eye. These are apparently courtship ornaments, for they are all shed at the close of the reproductive period in August. This periodic molting of beak scales seems to be a primitive characteristic, reminiscent of the shedding of reptilian scales.

From the standpoint of evolutionary selection, beaks seem to be unusually plastic, and as a consequence are of little use taxonomically. For example, the stork, ibis, spoonbill, and flamingo have bills of widely different shapes, yet they are all members of the Order Ciconiiformes. Apparently the competition for food among these near relatives has promoted evolutionary divergence in their eating utensils.

FEATHERS

TYPES OF FEATHERS

No bird is without feathers, nor is there any other kind of animal that possesses feathers. The horny protein substance, keratin, seems to form the scales on the legs of a bird exactly as the scales of a reptile are formed, and in its earliest stages the development of a feather closely resembles that of a reptilian scale. Feathers probably evolved from reptilian scales into a primitive, heat conserving, fluffy insulation, and later into highly complex epidermal structures.

Though modern birds possess both feathers and scales, no intermediate stage between the two has ever been discovered. A feather may represent either an individual scale that has become enlarged and fringed, or else a coalescence of numerous hair-like filaments into a single unit. Possibly some day a Jurassic fossil animal will be found that reveals the intermediate stage between a scale and a feather.

There are five commonly recognized types of feathers: vaned or contour, down, semi-plume, filoplume, and powder down. The vaned feathers which chiefly cover a bird's body and give it its streamlined form are the contour feathers; those which extend beyond the body and serve for flight are called the flight feathers. Although they exist in great variety (a single feather will often suffice to identify a bird), in basic design they are all quite similar. Once formed, any feather is a dead horny structure without living cells. It receives nothing from the body but physical support.

The typical vaned feather is made up of a central shaft and a vane. The bare proximal (body) end of the shaft is called the calamus or quill. At its base, inserted in the skin, is a tiny opening, the inferior umbilicus, through which the growing feather received nourishment. This part of the shaft is circular in cross section. The portion of the shaft between the two webs of the vane is called the rachis. At the point where the calamus ends and the rachis and vane begin is another tiny opening on the under side, the superior umbilicus. At this point in many vaned feathers arises a secondary feather called the afterfeather or aftershaft. It is usually small and downy, but sometimes, as in the emu and cassowary, it is as large as the main feather. It is thought that this doubling of the distal (outward) parts of feathers was a device in primitive birds to provide a

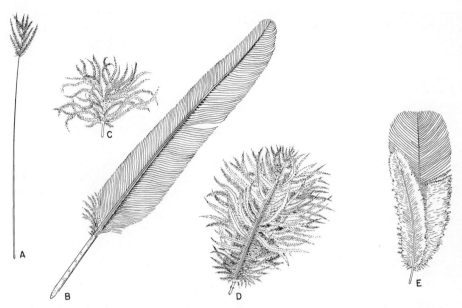

Figure 3.4.   Types of feathers. *A*, Filoplume, 3 ×; *B*, Vane or Contour, 1 ×; *C*, Down, 1 ×; *D*, Semi-plume, ½ ×; *E*, Pheasant Vane feather with Aftershaft, 1 ×.

thicker layer of insulation against heat loss.

From the superior umbilicus to its tip, the rachis is grooved on its inner surface and flattened on its sides. It divides the vane of the feather into two webs. These webs exhibit the most highly evolved and precisely adapted epidermal structures known. The flexible flatness of the vane, so valuable in flight, is achieved by means of numerous barbs or rami, small toothpick-like rods or filaments arranged in a closely parallel fashion on both sides of the rachis, running outwardly and diagonally toward the feather tip. They are fastened at their bases to the flat sides of the rachis, and their free ends mark the outer margins of the vane. There are usually several hundred barbs in each web. Those near the tip of the feather are likely to be stiff and flat, while those near the base are often loose and fluffy. Barbs are normally longest near the center of the vane and shortest at its ends.

The parallel barbs are held together in the flat webs by means of many tiny barbules or radii. These are, again, parallel filaments set in the two sides of each barb

much as the barbs are set in the two sides of the rachis. A single barb of a crane feather has about 600 barbules on each side, which means well over a million barbules for the entire feather. Here, however, the similarity of barbs and barbules ends, for there are two distinctly different types of barbules. Those branching out of the side of the barb toward the feather tip, the distal barbules, bear on their under sides many microscopic hooklets (hamuli), while the proximal barbules, on the side of the barb toward the feather base, present rounded ridges or flanges on their upper edges. The hook-bearing distal barbules on one barb overlap at right angles the smooth proximal barbules of an adjoining barb and cling to them with extraordinary tenacity to hold the barbs of a vane parallel and together against the pressure of moving air when the bird is flying. If two adjoining barbs are accidentally separated by some blow (i.e., the web becomes split), the bird needs merely to draw the feather between its mandibles to lock the barbule hooks and flanges together again and restore the entire web. Rachis, barbs, and barbules are all hard horny structures

Figure 3.5. A vaned (or contour) feather at increasing magnifications. A, 1×; B, 2.5×; C, 12.5×; D, 75×; E, 160×. In D and E are shown the tiny hooks which hold the overlapping barbules together to keep the vane a flat surface.

on the outside, but more or less hollow and filled with air inside.

Down feathers, like the basal portions of many vaned feathers, are downy because their barbules lack hooks. They are generally short fluffy feathers hidden under the contour feathers. They are abundant especially in ducks and in the downy young of many game birds and waterfowl.

Down feathers usually have no rachis. Their chief function is heat conservation.

Semiplume feathers are intermediate between vaned and down feathers in general structure. They have a rachis with barbs arranged in two rows as in a vaned feather, but the barbs lack hooks and flanges and therefore are loose and fluffy as in a down feather. Typically they occur

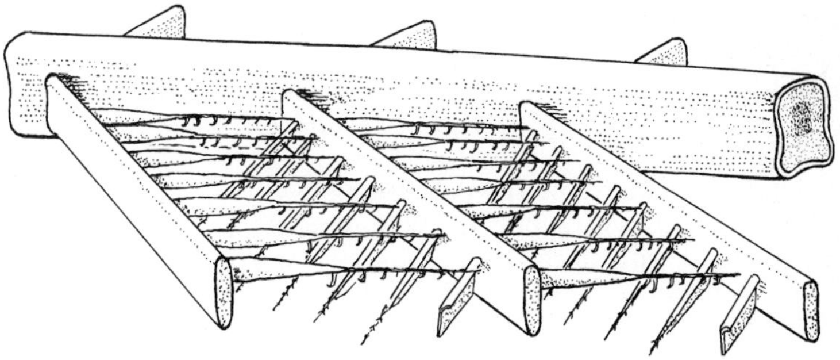

Figure 3.6. A diagram of parts of three barbs of a vaned feather, showing the hooking mechanism of the overlapping barbules. After T. I. Storer.

under a covering of contour feathers, generally along the sides of the abdomen but also at times along the neck and mid-back, and adjoining the large wing and tail feathers.

Filoplume feathers are the sparsely scattered "hairs" of a plucked fowl. They seem to be degenerate feathers that grow in circles of from one to ten around the bases of contour or down feathers. They are usually one-half to three-fourths the length of the covering contour feathers and have the shape of a slender whip. A weak tuft of barbs with hookless barbules may appear at the tip. The tactile "rictal" bristles surrounding the mouths of certain birds, such as flycatchers and goatsuckers, and used as insect nets, may be modified filoplumes. Aside from such a use, they have no known function. In cormorants and bulbuls they are especially abundant and visible in the neck and upper back regions. Ostriches and cassowaries do not have them at all.

Powder down feathers are unique in that they grow continuously and are never molted. They commonly grow in dense yellowish patches, especially on the breast, belly, or flanks of herons, bitterns, and tinamous. In other species, such as hawks and parrots, they are more diffusely scattered throughout the plumage. The barbs at their tips constantly disintegrate into a fine, talc-like, water resistant powder whose particles measure about a micron ($\frac{1}{1000}$ mm.) in thickness. Birds that lack preen glands often have abundant powder down feathers. The powder, scattered by preening or by fluffing the feathers, gives a metallic luster to the plumage of some

birds, and in general helps waterproof and preserve the feathers.

THE FUNCTIONS OF FEATHERS

Feathers are adapted to a variety of functions, the chief of which are heat conservation and flight. Small bodies cool much more rapidly than large ones. Yet the highly effective layer of insulating feathers clothing a tiny Black-capped Chickadee, *Parus atricapillus*, keeps it alive and warm through a long sub-zero winter night. Many birds carry more feathers in winter than in summer (Wetmore, 1936). A Carolina Chickadee, *Parus carolinensis*, taken on February 19, had 1704 contour feathers, while one taken on June 4 had only 1140. An American Goldfinch, *Spinus tristis*, had 2107 feathers on February 26, and another individual only 1901 on April 1.

In the Domestic Chicken, *Gallus gallus*, there is a genetic mutation known as "frizzled" in which all the feathers have weak stringy barbs that offer little insulation. In consequence, heat loss is rapid. Such a chicken will increase its metabolic rate about four per cent for every fall in outside temperature of one degree, whereas under similar conditions the metabolic rate of a normal bird will not vary (Srb and Owen, 1952). At high temperatures frizzled birds survive better than normal birds, which must pant in order to keep cool, since feathers preclude the development of sweat glands.

The flat, vaned contour feather is primarily an adaptation to flight, although it also sheds rain and has other protective functions. The distal tip of a large wing feather, or primary, has a streamlined cross section much like that of an airplane propeller. The way the trailing web of a primary bends upward during the downstroke of the wing provides both lift and a forward push to the body. An interesting adaptation in owls' wing-feathers ensures the silent flight so valuable to a nocturnal predator. On the leading edges of exposed primaries are located comb-like projections, while the trailing edges of the feathers are fringed somewhat like a shawl, and often the upper surface of each vane is downy. All these adaptations help to muffle the normal sounds of a blade-like object cutting the air. Further adaptation of feathers to flight will be considered in Chapter 21.

Oily feathers give buoyancy to a water bird by adding greatly to its volume while only slightly increasing its weight. The specific gravity of a feathered duck was determined by Heinroth (1938) to be 0.6, while that of the same bird plucked was 0.9. That is, a plucked duck weighs half again as much per unit volume as a feathered duck.

In several quite unrelated species, projecting primary wing feathers or tail feathers, usually with very narrow vanes, vibrate in flight so as to make sounds which may be used, for example, in courtship ceremonies. A Siberian snipe has several outer tail feathers narrowed so that they are little more than shafts. The passage of air through these feathers when they are widely spread during the spring courtship flight causes them to vibrate and

Figure 3.7. The feathers of the duck on the right have been treated with a wetting agent, or detergent, which destroyed their water-repellent quality and hence the duck's buoyancy. Photo from the American Cyanamid Company.

produce a "tremulous bleating" sound (Heinroth, 1938).

In both form and color, feathers have become modified into ornaments, recognition marks, concealing cloaks, and other useful aids to daily living.

Complex structures that they are, feathers need considerably more care than skin or hair. Preening with oil from the uropygial gland, or with powder down particles, or even with nothing at all, occupies a good share of the waking hours of most birds. Birds of the deserts and steppes where water is scarce take frequent dust baths, while those in more humid regions may take either dust or water baths. Preening commonly takes place after these baths and helps restore oil or powder down to keep the feathers in good condition. Bathing and preening, plus scratching with the claws, help allay itching, remove parasites, and clean the feathers. Preening is such a basic activity that it has achieved sufficient behavior momentum to become ritualized in courtship ceremonies.

The Growth of Feathers

Feathers grow from the base and not from the tip as do most plants. That is, the region of actively growing cells is always at the base of the feather next to the body.

The first evidence of a feather in the skin appears as a localized increase in epidermal and dermal cells to form a small papilla. This tiny pimple appears in an embryo chick of about six days incubation. The papilla continues to grow into a cone leaning toward the rear. At the same time its base sinks deeply into the bird's skin, creating a circular moat about the papilla. This moat with the surrounding epidermal cells becomes the feather follicle.

The cells of the papilla next begin to differentiate into several layers. On the outside is a single layer of very thin horny cells that become the epitrichium, a protective sheath. Next, inward, is the malpighian layer of epidermal cells which will grow into the structure of the feather proper. Enclosed within the malpighian layer is the core of the papilla, made up of dermal cells. This finger of dermal cells, with its rich supply of blood vessels, constitutes an internal pulp which provides nourishment for the growing feather, but contributes no cells to its structure.

As the malpighian layer develops, it differentiates into three layers: (1) a thin outer layer which forms a protective keratin sheath about the developing feather, (2) a thicker middle layer which is composed of large, rapidly growing epidermal cells which grow into the main structure of the feather, and (3) an internal, thin layer of cells which surround and protect the delicate dermal pulp. These last cells are represented in the completed feather only as a series of hollow pithy caps inside the transparent quill.

The first sign of differentiation into a vaned feather appears deep in the follicle in the collar of rapidly growing cells in the middle malpighian layer (Fig. 3.10). These cells begin to grow into a cylinder of parallel longitudinal ridges, something like pickets in a cylindrical fence. These pickets will become the barbs of the mature

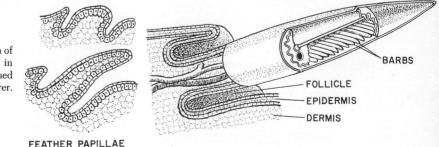

Figure 3.8. A diagram of three successive stages in the development of a vaned feather. After T. I. Storer.

FEATHER PAPILLAE

BARBS
FOLLICLE
EPIDERMIS
DERMIS

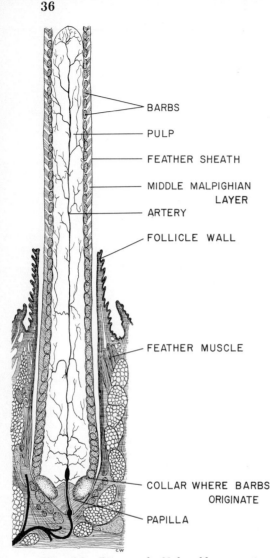

BARBS

PULP

FEATHER SHEATH

MIDDLE MALPIGHIAN
LAYER

ARTERY

FOLLICLE WALL

FEATHER MUSCLE

COLLAR WHERE BARBS
ORIGINATE

PAPILLA

Figure 3.9. Diagram of a 21-day-old regenerating breast feather of a White Leghorn rooster. After Lillie.

feather. As growth continues, two movements are discernible: the barbs grow in length, and the embryonic malpighian cells from which they originate migrate bilaterally from the ventral to the dorsal side of the collar, where the bases of the barbs unite to form an outward-growing projection, the rachis (Lillie and Juhn, 1938). Every barb originates at this ventral part of the collar. Tension between the surrounding sheath (layer 1 above), and the more rapidly growing middle mal-

pighian layer (layer 2), effects a secondary splitting of the barbs into the barbules. If the bases of the barbs do not migrate together to form a rachis, the feather will turn into a down feather with but a single circle of barbs on top of the quill. Possibly a secretion from the thyroid gland controls the formation of barbules, since its deficiency inhibits their appearance.

With continued growth of the vaned feather, the barbs become arranged on the two sides of the rachis, curving diagonally within the cylindrical sheath (layer 1). The first barbs to grow become the apical barbs of the completed feather; the last, the basal. Ultimately the feather stops growing. The rachis, barbs, and barbules become horny; the nourishing pulp is resorbed; the inferior umbilicus pinches shut; and the protective sheath splits open and is preened off, releasing the mature feather and permitting it to assume the characteristic flat form that makes the feather vane. The feather, now dead, has no more living traffic with the body. A small remnant of the malpighian and pulp cells remains as an embryonic germ at the base of the follicle after the feather has matured. Ordinarily each vaned feather is movable by means of several muscles attached to its follicle wall.

A typical feather germ grows a feather until it reaches a definite size, then it stops and the cells become dormant until that feather is molted. But in cocks of the Japanese Phoenix Fowl, a race of *Gallus gallus*, the central tail feathers may grow continuously up to six years without molting, and may reach a length of six meters. Usually, however, feather growth is strongly cyclic, and new feathers grow only at certain seasons. If a feather is accidentally removed, even in midwinter, the embryonic germ cells in the follicle will promptly grow a new one to replace it. To test the vigor of this regenerative capacity, Pearl and Boring (Stresemann, 1927) pulled out successive feathers from the same follicle on a Domestic Hen. They found that the follicle would regenerate no more than three times in a given inter-

Figure 3.10. Diagrams showing successive stages in the growth of a vaned feather from the collar of malpighian cells in a feather follicle. Barbs, which first appear in the ventral (V) part of the collar, migrate dorsally (D), and then outward. They are numbered in the order of their appearance. After Lillie and Juhn.

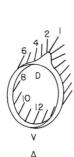

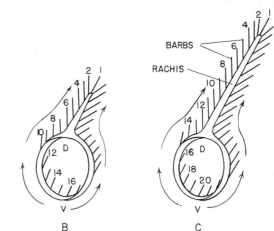

A   B   C

molt period. Then the follicle became inactive until the next normal molt period, at which it resumed activity.

Feathers grow at different rates, depending on the species of bird involved, its age, its diet and health, the part of the body concerned, the time of year, and even the time of day, nighttime growth being the slowest. As Frederick II observed, birds of prey, not subject to as many dangers as "inoffensive" species, can afford to grow their feathers more slowly. However,

"In land birds that nest on the ground and to whose young the parents bring no food (because they are able to get it themselves immediately after birth) the growth of feathers is most rapid and soonest completed. . . . Nature has with foresight provided that birds born in nests built on the ground are as early as possible provided with protective plumae and other feathers, because they are exposed to dangers. . . ." (Wood and Fyfe, 1943).

Young ground-nesting galliform birds develop their flight feathers most rapidly: some quail are able to fly when only a week old, and mound birds, Megapodiidae, a few hours after hatching. The primaries of the Yellow-shafted Flicker, *Colaptes auratus*, grow 5 to 7 mm. per day. A House Sparrow, *Passer domesticus*, replaced a complete primary in 12 days with an average growth of 4 mm. per day; while a Slate-colored Junco, *Junco hyemalis*, which had a tail feather pulled out in midwinter, grew a new one at the rate of 1.1 mm. per day. In general, the feathers

of large birds grow in absolute length more rapidly but in relative length less rapidly than the feathers of small birds. For example, the 285 mm. wing primary of the Hooded Crow, *Corvus cornix*, grows only $\frac{1}{32}$ of its length in 24 hours, while the 57 mm. primary of the Lesser Whitethroat, *Sylvia curruca*, grows $\frac{1}{17}$ of its length in the same time (Stresemann, 1927–1934).

FEATHER DISTRIBUTION

On primitive birds, feathers were probably rather evenly distributed over the body in a fine checkerboard pattern. Some traces of such an arrangement are still seen in present day species. The bodies of penguins, ostriches, and their relatives (ratites) are completely covered by feathers. But on most modern birds, feathers are distributed in scattered patches called pterylae or feather tracts, while the naked intervening regions are called apteria. Among birds with dense plumage such as ducks, the apteria are reduced in size and often covered with down.

Though species vary, most birds show the following pterylae (Fig. 3.11):

1. Capital tract, which covers the crown of the head.

2. Spinal tract, a quite variable pteryla which runs down the back from the head to the tail.

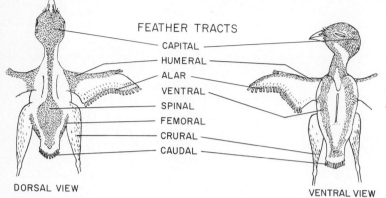

FEATHER TRACTS

CAPITAL
HUMERAL
ALAR
VENTRAL
SPINAL
FEMORAL
CRURAL
CAUDAL

DORSAL VIEW

VENTRAL VIEW

Figure 3.11. Feather tracts of a typical passerine bird.

3. Caudal tract, the pteryla of the tail feathers and the smaller contours which cover them (coverts).

4. Ventral tract, which runs from the throat to the breast, where it divides into two bands (with a naked apterium between them) which continue down the belly to the cloaca, where the bands unite. Very variable.

5. Humeral tract, which includes feathers of the upper arm and scapular region.

6. Alar tract, which includes the flight feathers and their coverts on the upper arm, forearm, and hand.

7. Femoral tract, which extends diagonally across the thigh.

8. Crural tract, which crosses the remainder of the leg.

The alar and caudal tracts carry the vaned feathers responsible for flight. The large feathers of the wings are called the remiges (Latin, *remex*, an oarsman). The largest and most distal remiges are crowded together on the hand, and are called the primaries. Their number varies from 9 to 12. The secondary remiges are the large quill feathers of the forearm or ulna. They vary in number from 6 in hummingbirds to as many as 37 in albatrosses. The tertiaries are the few remiges attached to the upper arm or humerus. In addition to these three groups of remiges are groups of smaller contours called coverts or tectrices (Latin, *tegere*, to cover), which act as rows of shingles to cover the quill bases of the larger remiges and to make aerodynamically smooth the upper and lower surfaces of the arm and hand. Attached to the bird's thumb are three or four short vaned feathers that make a separate little wing, the alula or spurious wing. The alula is especially

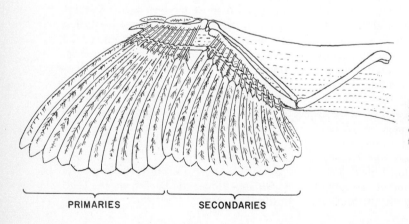

PRIMARIES   SECONDARIES

Figure 3.12. Primary flight feathers are borne on the hand of a bird's wing; secondaries, on the forearm.

prominent in wings which are short and rounded, such as those of gallinaceous birds. It increases the aerodynamic efficiency of the wing at the slow flight speeds common in ground dwellers.

On the rump are inserted the large tail feathers or rectrices (Latin, *rectrix*, a ruler or leader). These are usually straight, bilaterally paired feathers that range in number from 8 in anis to 24 in pheasants, but most commonly are 10 or 12. They are mainly concerned with steering and maintaining equilibrium in flight. In species that live near the ground they are usually quite short, but in expert flyers that maneuver with great skill they are relatively long.

The Number of Feathers

Birds vary in the number of feathers they carry, according to species, size, sex, age, metabolism, health, season, and geographic distribution. One might expect that adult birds of a given species taken at a given time of year would have a rather stable number of feathers. This was shown not to be the case in Wetmore's (1936) study of the number of vaned feathers in birds. For example, two female Song Sparrows, *Melospiza melodia*, on March 5 had 2208 and 2093 feathers respectively; two female Fox Sparrows, *Passerella iliaca*, on March 26, had 2648 and 2482. As mentioned earlier, birds carry more feathers in winter than in summer: two White-throated Sparrows, *Zonotrichia albicollis*, on February 22 had (male) 2556 and (female) 2710 feathers respectively, while two females taken October 4 and 8 had 1545 and 1508 feathers respectively.

Body size is the factor responsible for the greatest variation in feather number. A Ruby-throated Hummingbird, *Archilochus colubris*, had 940 feathers (June) and a Whistling Swan, *Cygnus columbianus*, had 25,216 (November). Actually, the hummingbird possesses more feathers per gram of body weight than the swan, which is to be expected since small bodies have relatively more heat-losing surface per unit of weight than large bodies. Perhaps the densest concentration of feathers is to be found in penguins. On the back of a young Gentoo Penguin, *Pygoscelis papua*, were counted 46 incipient or arrested feathers per square centimeter.

Further evidence of the importance of feathers to a bird is seen in their weight. Although they are "light as a feather," the total bird is also light, so that, relatively, feathers make up a major part of a bird's substance. A Bald Eagle, *Haliaeetus leucocephalus*, that weighed 4082 grams was found by Brodkorb (1955) to possess 7182 vaned feathers that weighed 586 grams, which was 14 per cent of the bird's total weight. The down feathers weighed an additional 91 grams. The vaned feathers alone weighed more than twice as much as the bird's skeleton, which weighed 272 grams.

The Molting of Feathers

In time, as feathers become worn they loosen in their follicles and drop out, and the feather germ in the base of the follicle promptly replaces the lost feather. Occasionally it is the growing of the new feather that pushes out the old one. In penguins, emus, and cassowaries the tip of the new feather penetrates the inferior umbilicus of the old, and the two generations of feathers become joined so that the birds wear some of their shabby old feathers on top of their new ones. Penguins particularly shed their old feathers nearly simultaneously so that they come off in sheets somewhat as a snake sheds its skin. When the new feathers are well along, the birds remove the older ones from their tips with bills and feet. Thus, in its cold habitat, the penguin is never without at least one coat of feathers.

In a typical molt a bird loses a few feathers at a time, usually the corresponding feathers on opposite sides of the body. At this time, normally at the close of the breeding season, some birds present a worn, ragged appearance, and they seek some sheltered retreat where they remain quietly until they can grow new feathers. The feathers do not fall out at random, but usually in a regular sequence, and of course they are replaced in the same sequence. There is much variation in molt pattern. Often, however, the large wing and tail feathers molt first, followed by a progressive molt of body feathers from rump to head. Within a single pteryla the internal rows of feathers molt first and the outside rows last. In most passerines and in many other groups there is a very precise order of molting the remiges. In the hand, for example, the first feather to molt is at the wrist, the last at the wing-tip; in the arm, the first feathers to fall out are at the two ends, the last in the center (Fig. 3.13). Tail feathers commonly molt centrifugally, that is, from the center outwards, the outer feathers falling when the innermost are completely replaced. In some species the order is reversed and the feathers are said to molt centripetally. In the Blue-footed Booby, *Sula nebouxii*, it appears that every other tail feather falls during a molt; each new feather then grows in beside an old one. Small owls are apt to lose all their tail feathers simultaneously, larger owls centripetally (Mayr and Mayr, 1954).

Many water birds (ducks, geese, swans, grebes, loons, and others) lose all their wing primaries at once, so that the birds are flightless for several weeks after the breeding season. Such a hazardous method of molting would never do for land birds, but water birds can tolerate it because, although flightless, they can find food and escape enemies by swimming on and under the water. This illustrates the widespread principle that functional and structural adaptations fit hand-in-glove with living conditions.

Male ducks normally have a colorful breeding plumage, but immediately after the post-breeding molt they take on a dull, inconspicuous coat, the "eclipse plumage," which they carry during the period of wing molt. This helps to conceal them from predators while they concentrate on growing new wing feathers. In late summer the drakes rather prematurely assume the bright colors of courtship plumage again, which they carry through the winter and to the end of the next breeding season. This early adoption of breeding plumage very likely promotes the wintertime pairing or "engagement" of ducks long before the spring breeding season. It also aids the male in distracting predators from the less conspicuous female while she is tending the growing young. In female ducks there is a major molt at the end of the nesting season and a partial molt of body and tail feathers late in the winter.

Other species also show useful adaptations in the timing of their molts. The Slender-billed Shearwater or Mutton Bird, *Puffinus tenuirostris*, molts its head and body feathers at its Tasmanian breeding

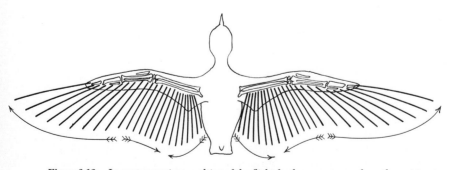

Figure 3.13.   In most passerines, molting of the flight feathers progresses from the wrist outward to the wing-tip, while the secondaries drop off first at the two ends of the forearm, and last in the center.

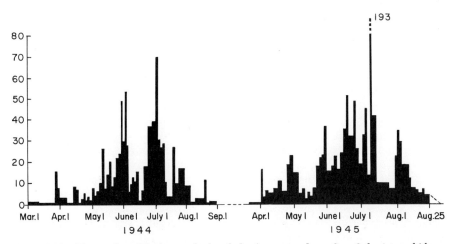

Figure 3.14.   The number of feathers molted each day (as averaged over 2- or 3-day intervals) by a female Golden Eagle during its second and third years of life. Some feathers were replaced annually; others, after two years. After Jollie.

grounds, but not its wing or tail feathers until it reaches the far-distant arctic waters where it spends its summer (Marshall and Serventy, 1956). In a twelve-year study of the Yellow-eyed Penguin, *Megadyptes antipodes*, of New Zealand, Richdale (1949) reports that the non-breeding adults molt earlier than the parent birds. This same delay in molt, which permits better care of the young by their parents, is found in numerous species. Among African hornbills (Bucerotidae), the female loses nearly all her feathers, practically to the point of nakedness, and then quickly renews them while incubating and brooding, imprisoned in her walled-in nest cavity, where she is fed by her mate. The male, however, and the non-breeding females, retain enough feathers to be able to fly. Likewise in the European Sparrow Hawk, *Accipiter nisus*, and Osprey, *Pandion haliaëtus*, the female molts her feathers during the quiet incubation and brooding periods, while the male who remains active, bringing food to the nest, postpones his molt until the young are flown (Heinroth, 1938). Similarly, in the Fulmar, *Fulmarus glacialis*, of Great Britain, the non-breeders molt in June and July, the breeders in August (Wynne-Edwards, 1939). Obviously, natural selection has had an influence in scheduling the time of molt.

Molts may require a brief period or may be prolonged over several months. Penguins, in their wholesale molt of feathers, require from about two to six weeks. After its chicks are raised, the well fed Yellow-eyed Penguin, *Megadyptes antipodes*, molts its feathers in 24 days, during which time the bird stays on land and does not eat. Some indication of the enormous energy required to grow a new coat of feathers is seen in the weight loss of these birds. The average adult male weighs 7.9 kg. at the onset of its molt, and 4.4 kg. at its end; the female, 7.6 kg. at the beginning, and 4.1 kg. at the end (Richdale, 1941). The Adelie Penguin, *Pygoscelis adeliae*, fattens up just before its post-breeding molt and then refrains from eating for from 9 to 17 days while it sheds its old coat and loses about 40 per cent of its weight. During this period the bird may stand on a cake of ice in one spot so long that it produces a melted depression embroidered with a ring of its castoff feathers (Cendron, 1953). The Purple Finch, *Carpodacus purpureus*, was found by Magee (1936) to complete its molt in the wild in about ten weeks. Observations on captive Golden

Eagles, *Aquila chrysaëtos*, by Jollie (1947), show that a complete molt requires two seasons. In the first season, extending from March 1st to August 30th, a one year old female eagle molted about 1850 feathers. The next year between mid-March and early September she molted a total of about 2600 feathers. Although the feathers were being shed, and new ones grown, continuously, there were decided peaks and troughs in molting activity (Fig. 3.14). Some of the feathers were molted each year, and others but once in two years. Most species of birds renew their wing feathers only once a year even though other feathers may be renewed twice. Cranes retain their wing feathers two years.

Such variability in molting patterns raises the question: What stimuli initiate the molting process? More research needs to be done on this question, but at present it is clear that both innate and environmental stimuli are involved. Different species of birds living under approximately identical conditions may exhibit quite different molting patterns and frequencies. Tropical ducks typically molt only once a year, whereas those of the temperate zone molt twice. Hybrids between ducks molting once and those molting twice a year have two molts a year (Stresemann, 1940). This fact alone clearly demonstrates a hereditary influence on molting.

In many species of birds, molting is intimately connected with the breeding cycle. Experimental manipulation of the reproductive cycle by castration, by injection of sex hormones, or by changing the daily exposure to light (or photoperiod) is commonly accompanied by plumage changes. There is evidence that in the Rock Ptarmigan, *Lagopus mutus*, temperature is the critical influence in setting the time of molt (Salomonsen, 1939). As mentioned earlier, whether a bird breeds or not often determines the time of its molt, breeding birds postponing their molt until the end of the reproductive season.

An African weaver finch, *Pyromelana*

franciscana, transplanted to Iowa, maintained its normal African molting schedule despite the changed environment and seasons. This innate triggering of two molts a year was attributed to the cyclic activity of its pituitary gland (Witschi, 1935). There is evidence that excess thyroid activity accelerates molting (as well as promotes barbule formation), whereas a deficiency of thyroid inhibits molting. But in recent studies on the Domestic Hen, using radioactive iodine as a tracer, molting seemed to be controlled by the decrease in ovarian activity and not by increased thyroid activity (Tanabe, Himeno and Nozaki, 1957).

The variable molting seasons in different species of Mexican hummingbirds seem to be related to local weather conditions which, in turn, regulate conditions of food supply and nesting materials. If, in dry weather, food is short and moss too brittle to be woven into nests, reproduction is prevented and molting occurs. Otherwise, the females molt after the end of the breeding season (Wagner, 1957). Molting of wing feathers in birds of various species may be brought on in winter by feeding them a diet rich in insects.

Just as plumage is in part under control of the breeding cycle, the breeding cycle may, in turn, be influenced by the plumage. In many species the bright colors and displays of the males in the springtime stimulate the activity of the sex organs in the female.

The various plumages in the life cycle of a bird follow one another in rather definite sequence: natal down, juvenal plumage, first winter plumage, first nuptial (breeding) plumage, second winter plumage, second nuptial plumage, and so on. Molts are named according to the plumage lost at the time: e.g., postjuvenal molt, postnuptial molt, and so on.

A bird's first coat of feathers is its natal down, which, as the name tells, is the plumage of down feathers the bird has at hatching or develops very shortly after. It usually lasts but a short time, several weeks in some cases, but may be worn as

NATAL   JUVENAL   FIRST WINTER

FIRST NUPTIAL   SECOND WINTER   SECOND NUPTIAL

Figure 3.15. Successive plumages in the first two years of a Rose-breasted Grosbeak. After Pettingill and Breckenridge.

long as a year in the King Penguin, *Aptenodytes patagonicus*, in which case, however, there are two generations of down, one succeeding the other. In the familiar downy duckling or baby chick this plumage is well developed. Often the natal down may be strikingly pigmented, which is not the case in the down of adult birds. In many of the perching birds, such as sparrows, warblers, and crows, the natal down feathers are but sparsely present and then only on isolated parts of the body, while in other species such as woodpeckers, jays, and swifts, down is completely lacking and the birds are born naked. The natal down is completely lost by the postnatal molt.

The juvenal plumage, which next appears, is composed largely of contour feathers which generally push out on their tips the natal down feathers. These contour feathers are often colored differently from those of the adult. The speckled breast feathers of the juvenile Robin, *Turdus migratorius*, are a familiar example. With the possession of contour and flight feathers, most juvenile birds are able to fly for the first time. As a rule, juvenal plumage replaces nestling down very rapidly—usually in less than three weeks in passerines.

The first winter plumage appears late in the summer of a bird's first year and, in form and coloration, may be typical of the bird's lifetime adult plumage, as in the chickadees. Or, as in the case of species in which the sexes vary in coloration, the first winter plumage of both males and females may resemble that of the adult female rather than that of the male.

The first nuptial plumage is the bird's first breeding cloak, and it normally appears late in the winter or early in the spring before the breeding season begins. If the bird is sexually mature, the color and pattern of the feathers may be that of typical adult birds. Since adult coloration is frequently controlled in part by sex hormones, a year-old bird that is not sexually mature may show diluted or incompletely developed coloration. Young Herring Gulls, *Larus argentatus*, which normally do not develop adult coloration until they are three or four years old, can be stimulated to grow plumage of adult pattern by injections of male hormones.

For those species that have two molts a year, the plumage, from the first nuptial plumage on, alternates annually between winter plumage and nuptial plumage. These plumages appear at the end of the breeding season (usually after a complete molt) and at the onset of the breeding period (following a partial molt). In many species the nuptial plumage is more vividly colored than the winter plumage. The male Scarlet Tanager, *Piranga olivacea*, possesses its dazzling scarlet and black plumage only for the breeding season; its winter plumage is dull green, yellow, and brownish.

In the many species that have only one molt a year, the feather change occurs normally just after the close of the breeding season, but in swallows and some accipitriform birds it occurs later on in the winter. In short, molting is such a variable process that few general rules about it can be laid down.

COLOR IN BIRDS

Birds are more vividly colored than any other class of vertebrates. Since they are able to fly from their enemies and to perch and nest in relatively inaccessible sites, they are somewhat removed from the selective pressures that impel earthbound animals to don inconspicuous coats. Further, their high metabolism produces waste products that may be discarded in the form of feather pigments.

Color in birds is produced in two ways: by pigments or by the physical structure of the feathers. Pigments are of two main sorts, melanins and lipochromes. Melanins produce the black, dull yellow, and brown colors. They occur in the form of sharply outlined, microscopic particles. They are nonsoluble in organic solvents, therefore they are not well known chemically. However, they appear to be the result of oxidation of a colorless chromogen, tyrosine, by an enzyme, tyrosinase. Lipochromes, on the other hand, produce the yellow, orange, and red colors (rarely the violet, blue, and green), and are generally diffused in fat droplets. They are alcohol-soluble carotenoids.

Melanin granules average about one micron in diameter and occur in two forms. The eumelanins, which under the microscope appear as rod-like particles, produce the blacks and grays of a bird's feathers. The phaeomelanins are in the form of oval granules and they produce the browns, red-browns, and yellow-browns. Melanin granules are formed in the cytoplasm of ameba-like chromatophore cells residing in the inner layer of malpighian cells of the feather germ. Long processes from each chromatophore reach out to distribute the pigment granules into the developing barbs and barbules. Although both types of melanin granules may be found in a single feather, with the eumelanins characteristically at the tip and the phaeomelanins at the base, a given chromatophore will form only one type of pigment (Stresemann, 1927–34).

The fat-soluble lipochromes exist in great variety but are generally of two main sorts: the carotenoids (related to vitamin A), which produce red, yellow, orange, and violet colors, and the porphyrin or pyrrol pigments (related to the hematin of the blood), which produce red, green, and brown colors. Porphyrins are often light-sensitive and will fade rapidly on exposure to sunlight. It is likely that some lipochromes are taken directly into the body and used unaltered as a pigment. Lipochromes are not produced by special chromatophore cells as are the melanins. One carotenoid pigment, ptilopin, from the fruit pigeon, will change through a sequence of colors when treated with alkali, from blue to violet, red, and orange (Stresemann, 1927–34).

A widely distributed carotenoid is zooerythrin, the red pigment in many birds such as the Cardinal, *Richmondena cardinalis*. Zooxanthin is the lipochrome that produces the bright yellow colors in canaries, orioles, and many other species, as well as the yellow beaks and feet of many water birds. Still other less common lipochromes have been identified in cotingas, plantain-eaters, turacos, and parrots, which produce reds, violets, greens, and other colors. The chemistry of many of these colors is still obscure.

Certain colors are produced by the

structure of the feather; they are due to the refraction and reflection of light. White daylight is broken up into different wave-lengths by the fine structure of a feather much as it is by the thin walls of a soap bubble. Blue is usually such a structural color; blue pigments are unknown in birds. Blue generally appears to be due to a particular arrangement of cells in the feather barb. There is some disagreement as to the effective structure in the barb responsible for the blue color. Bancroft (1923), Stresemann, and Heinroth (Fig. 3.16) hold that light refracted and reflected among fine tubes in thickwalled air chambers overlying pigmented cells emerges to the viewer as blue light. Gower (1936) maintains that in Blue Jays, *Cyanocitta cristata*, no hollow chambers are involved, but that very fine solid particles in a transparent dorsal layer of barb cells scatter the light so that it emerges blue. In both explanations the underlying heavily pigmented cells absorb other wave-lengths of light, allowing only the blue to be perceived. Further study of the phenomenon is needed. The fact that the blue color is caused by the feather's fine structure rather than by pigment is easily proved by crushing a blue feather with pressure; the blue color disappears, just as it does when a soap bubble collapses.

The shimmering play of colors known as iridescence is also due to structure and not to pigments. It is commonly seen in peacocks, hummingbirds, pigeons, and other birds. Iridescent feathers possess heavily pigmented distal barbules which are broadly flattened and twisted 90 degrees so that their flat surface is uppermost. This surface is covered with extremely thin laminated layers of horn, which, like thin soap bubbles, are thought to produce interference colors which change with the angle of incident light. The iridescent barbules of the Peacock, *Pavo cristatus*, are covered with three thin layers, each about 0.4 micron thick. Recent work by Schmidt (1952) indicates that iridescence may arise at the surface of the melanin granules and not in the horny lamellae. The dull velvet appearance of some ornamental feathers is physically the reverse of iridescence. The barbules possess many vertically directed bristles which absorb rather than reflect the light.

A given feather, even a single barbule, may contain different pigments. The various factors responsible for color at times cooperate to produce combination colors. For example, red and yellow pigments commonly produce orange; green is often the result of a yellow sheath of keratin on top of structural blue. Color intensity is usually a matter of pigment concentration. Eumelanin granules densely packed produce a black feather, and thinly scattered, a blackish-brown feather. A complete lack of pigment results in a white feather.

A feather once formed has no living traffic with the body and hence can receive no new pigments; nevertheless, its color may change. This is because of abrasion from physical wear and the bleaching

Figure 3.16. Blue colors depend on the structure of feathers, and not on pigments. *A*, The cross-section of a barb of a Blue Jay feather in which a layer of transparent cells containing fine, suspended particles is thought to produce the blue reflected light. After Gower. *B*, A barb of a tanager in cross-section. Very fine tubes surrounding air chambers are apparently the source of the blue color. After Stresemann.

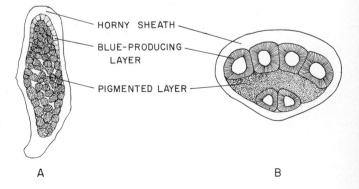

HORNY SHEATH

BLUE-PRODUCING LAYER

PIGMENTED LAYER

A   B

effects of sunlight. If the tips of feathers are colored differently from their remaining portions, their wearing away will expose different colors to the viewer (Fig. 3.17). Thus, the nuptial black bib of the House Sparrow, *Passer domesticus,* is the result of wintertime erosion of the lighter-colored tips of the breast feathers. Similar color changes occur in the European Brambling, *Fringilla montifringilla,* the Snow Bunting, *Plectrophenax nivalis,* and the Wandering Albatross, *Diomedea exulans.* Pigmented feathers are always more resistant to wear than unpigmented ones. With this fact in mind it is not surprising that the wing-tip primaries of many otherwise white birds are heavily pigmented: for example, storks, gulls, flamingos, herons, and pelicans.

Bleaching of the dark feathers of the South Polar Skua, *Catharacta skua,* occurs rapidly under the actinic rays of 24-hour sunlight in a dustless polar atmosphere. Red porphyrin colors are particularly sensitive to light. The pink breast feathers of certain gulls fade very rapidly when exposed to light, and the pale red down feathers of bustards turn into gray-white in a few minutes when exposed directly to sunlight. Sometimes color changes occur that cannot be explained as a result of either wear or bleaching. Feathers of some bee-eaters (Meropidae) gradually change from green to blue. It may be that in such cases preening accumulates enough oil in the feathers to account for the change.

Diet undeniably affects feather color in numerous species. Flamingos, *Phoenicopterus ruber,* ordinarily lose their red color

in captivity and do not regain it in subsequent molts. But the red can be restored by feeding them certain small crustaceans or even pure dyes. Bullfinches, *Pyrrhula pyrrhula,* become very dark colored if fed a diet of hemp seed. Captive Red Crossbills, *Loxia curvirostra,* that have faded to yellow will grow normal red feathers at their next molt if fed a diet containing rodoxanthin from the yew. Canaries will, in successive molts, gradually change from yellow to intense orange if fed red peppers (Beebe, 1906). Natives in various parts of the world change the colors of parrots by chemical treatment. For example, the green Amazon Parrot, *Chrysotis festiva,* will grow yellow instead of green head feathers if the sprouting feathers are rubbed with the skin secretions of the toad *Bufo tinctorius* (Wallace, 1889). It seems quite possible that variations in the coloration of different geographic races of birds may in part be due to varying amounts of certain foods, or even trace elements, available to them, but the problem needs further study.

Some zoologists believe that humidity is important in determining pigment intensity. It seems a fairly general rule that birds such as pipits, larks, and shrikes are darker when living in moist than when living in dry regions.

Age brings changes in coloration to birds as to other animals, including man. The larger gulls and albatrosses require several years before they assume adult plumage. Full coloration in the Bald Eagle, *Haliaeetus leucocephalus,* does not appear until the fourth or fifth year; and

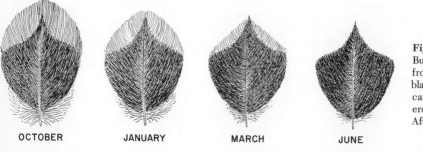

OCTOBER   JANUARY   MARCH   JUNE

Figure 3.17. The Snow Bunting changes its color from brown in October to black and white in June because of the wintertime erosion of feather tips. After Chapman.

in the California Condor, *Gymnogyps californianus*, until the fifth or sixth year. The eyes of accipitrine hawks change from yellow to orange with age; and the leg color of the Coot, *Fulica americana*, changes in successive years from blue-green to yellow-green to clear yellow, and finally to red-orange in mature adults.

Hormones also play a role in feather color, perhaps in conjunction with the sympathetic nervous system and its ganglia at the bases of feather papillae. Melanophore cells growing in tissue cultures are directly sensitive to sex hormones and anti-thyroid hormones (Mayaud, 1950). Sex dimorphism in the colors of Mallard Ducks, *Anas platyrhynchos*, is apparently due to the female sex hormone. Injection of this hormone into a male changes its plumage to the female type. The same situation prevails in the emphatically dimorphic parakeet *Eclectus*, in which the male is a vivid green and the female a brilliant red. Castrated males do not lose their colors, but castrated females take on typical male coloring. The female hormone inhibits male coloration.

Among species that alternate between colorful breeding plumage and drab resting plumage each year, it might be thought that some sort of a fixed hereditary schedule dictates the alternation between bright and dull feathers. That this is not necessarily the case was demonstrated by Beebe (1914) with captive Scarlet Tanagers, *Piranga olivacea*, and Bobolinks, *Dolichonyx oryzivorus*. Birds in breeding plumage that were given increased food and reduced hours of daylight put on weight, skipped the usual fall molt, and retained their bright feathers until the next spring. Then, with a return to normal conditions, the birds molted directly from one breeding plumage into another. That is, the drab winter plumage had been completely eliminated. Probably the unusual environmental conditions set up internal chemical chain reactions that resulted in the unorthodox plumage succession.

Length of day is known to exert a pro-found effect on the endocrine activity of birds, and this, in turn, on their plumage. Willow Ptarmigan, *Lagopus lagopus*, kept in outdoor cages in Norway were subjected by Höst (1942) to artificially controlled illumination so that their day-length could be arbitrarily shortened or lengthened. Birds subjected to long days in November and December took on breeding activities, molted their white feathers, and adopted brown summer plumage. Contrariwise, birds subjected to short days in summer molted and changed to white winter plumage. In fact, Höst could control the color of plumage at any time of year, regardless of the temperature, by manipulating light dosage. This subject of day-length influence or photoperiodism will be discussed further in Chapter 8.

Heredity, of course, plays a dominant role in controlling feather color. Just as there are no blue roses, there are no parrot-colored gulls. The hereditary genes in the feather germ which determine color are usually very stable. If, for example, melanoblast cells (the forerunners of pigment cells or melanophores) of a barred Plymouth Rock embryo donor are grafted into the base of the wing-bud of a White Leghorn 72-hour embryo host, the resulting wing of the chicken will have barred feathers characteristic of the Plymouth Rock (Willier, 1952). Pigments may even be exchanged between birds of different orders. For example, a White Leghorn chicken developed a black wing whose pigment came from the melanoblasts of a Common Crow, *Corvus brachyrhynchos*; and a White Wyandotte developed a grayish wing whose color came from a Robin, *Turdus migratorius* (Rawles, 1960). Skin from White Leghorn chicks was transplanted to the backs of chicks of five different breeds of various colors, and the grafts produced pure white feathers in every case (Danforth and Foster, 1929). The faithfulness with which the genes expressed themselves is all the more remarkable because the structure and shape of the feathers developed from the graft

Figure 3.18. A young White Leghorn rooster whose barred wing and breast feathers are the result of a graft, during its embryonic life, of pigment cells from a Barred Plymouth Rock embryo donor. After Willier and Rawles.

(i.e., whether cock-like or hen-like) were always like those of the host regardless of their origin.

Within hereditary limits there may be pronounced variation in feather color. Sometimes within a given species or race different color phases appear. Where two alternate forms of coloration appear within a single species, dimorphism or dichromatism is said to occur. In the Screech Owl, *Otus asio,* there are often, in a single brood, brown and gray birds; or in Barn Owls, *Tyto alba,* whitish and yellowish birds. There are light and dark phases in many species of hawks. Similar dimorphism is shown in the Kermdac Petrel, *Pterodroma neglecta* (black and brown phases), and in the Slender-billed Shearwater, *Puffinus tenuirostris* (dark gray and light gray). In the European Black-eared Wheatear, *Oenanthe hispanica,* males may be either white-throated or black-throated. Birds that show more than two color phases are said to show polymorphism or polychromatism. There are two species of African shrikes of the genus *Chlorophoneus* which

exhibit such diverse color phases (yellow, red, buff, or black) that each has unwittingly been classified into four species. The male Ruff, *Philomachus pugnax,* varies extremely in the color of its ruff and upper parts; they may be solid, spotted or speckled, sandy, buff, chestnut, glossy purple, rufous, or white.

Finally, genetic mutations may occur that affect not only feather color, as in melanism or albinism, but feather structure ("frizzle" in chickens), and may even cause the complete loss of feathers, as in a mutant form of pigeon. In the Domestic Hen alone dozens of mutations affecting feathers and their colors have been discovered.

THE USES OF COLOR

Colors in birds are mainly important for their effects on the behavior of other animals, including other birds. Nevertheless, colors have some intrinsic values to the bird. As mentioned, pigmented feathers are stronger and wear better than unpigmented feathers. Pigments absorb radiant heat, which at times is useful to the bird. Pigmented feathers stop the harmful ultraviolet rays of the sun, preventing sunburn of the bird's delicate skin. The Fairy Tern, *Gygis alba*, has thin, translucent white feathers, but a black skin, whereas its close relative the Noddy Tern, *Anoüs stolidus*, has dark, opaque feathers, but a light colored skin. Apparently the melanin is necessary, whether in skin or feathers, to shield the bird from the harmful actinic rays of the sun (Murphy, 1936).

Primarily, colors are useful to birds for concealment, for recognition, for courtship and other social functions, and therefore are important in their social life. Because of their wide-ranging and rapid flight, birds have special difficulty in matching their habitats, yet a surprising number of them do just that. The Snowy Owl, *Nyctea scandiaca*, and Greenland Gyrfalcon, *Falco rusticolus*, wear white plumage that resembles their arctic sur-

roundings. The Willow Ptarmigan mentioned earlier even changes its coat from a winter white to a summer brown to match the change in seasons. Many of the ground-dwelling birds such as the Galliformes have an inconspicuous brown color, while birds of the treetops like vireos and warblers often resemble the green sun-flecked foliage.

Sometimes the resemblance of a bird to its normal background is remarkably close. Larks of the family Alaudidae typically live on steppes where cover is thin and where they are quite exposed to predators. Field studies of larks by Meinertzhagen in Syria and Niethammer in Africa (Mayr, 1942) have shown a striking correlation between soil color and plumage color. Blackish subspecies of larks lived on black volcanic soil, reddish subspecies on red soil, and pale sand-colored subspecies on pale sandy soil. Not only did the color of the birds match the soil, but also their color pattern. "The birds will

Figure 3.19.   A female Woodcock on its nest, illustrating concealing coloration. Photo by G. R. Austing.

have a smooth, even coloration, if they live on a fine-grained, dusty, or sandy soil. If, on the other hand, they live on a pebble desert, they will have a coarse, disruptive pattern of coloration." Most remarkable of all, when Meinertzhagen attempted to chase reddish larks living on reddish soils to light lime soils only a few yards away, he was unsuccessful. Nor could he force the whitish larks living on light soil to descend on the non-matching red soils. The birds always alighted on soil matching their plumage, as though they were "conscious of the color of the soil that corresponds to their own coloration." A similar experience with a nightjar, *Caprimulgus aegyptius*, is related by Buxton (1923). Some twenty of these rather large birds habitually rested on the bare ground in a small one-acre field near Baghdad. In

spite of repeated visits to the place, he "never succeeded in detecting a Nightjar before it flew."

In India the Yellow-wattled Lapwing, *Lobipluvia malabarica*, lays its eggs directly on bare ground. On a narrow strip along the Malabar coast where the soil is red laterite with scattered particles of black ironstone, the bird lays reddish eggs with dark brown specks, very closely matching the ground (Cott, 1940). Elsewhere the species lays dark, earth-colored eggs that match ordinary soil.

Not only do birds at times match the general background, but in a few instances they match specific objects in it. Cott tells of Saville-Kent's experience with the Australian frog-mouth *Podargus*, which, when disturbed by a predator,

"... will at once straighten up stiffly and, with its mot-

Figure 3.20. Concealing behavior in the Screech Owl. The bird enhances its cryptic coloration by sleeking its feathers against the body, erecting its "horns," nearly closing its eyes, and by perching snugly against an upright branch. Photo by G. R. Austing.

tled feathers closely pressed to its body, assume so perfectly a resemblance to a portion of the branch upon which it is seated that, even at a short distance, it is almost impossible to recognize it. Under these conditions, in fact, it so readily escapes detection that several instances have been related to the writer in which people have actually placed their hand on the bird, when seated on a rail or log fence, before being conscious of its presence."

Bitterns, which commonly live among reeds, have streaked breasts which resemble the surrounding vegetation. When threatened by an enemy, a bittern will characteristically stretch its head and neck with the bill pointing skyward and the striped breast presented toward the intruder. W. H. Hudson tells of encountering the Little Bittern, *Ardetta involucris*, perched on a reed in an Argentine swamp. Hudson walked in a circle around the bittern, and the bird, while maintaining its mimetic pose, shifted its hold on the rush so as always to present its concealingly colored breast toward him. Even when Hudson several times pushed the bird's head down to its shoulders, it did not fly, but as soon as the hand was removed would resume its rigid vertical stance! Finally, when the bird was forced from its perch, it flew away.

Other cryptic postures are taken by the precocial young of many ground-nesting species. The young of various grouse, gulls, curlews, and other species will, when alarmed, squat low with head and neck stretched out flat on the ground and hold this pose as long as danger threatens. The survival advantage of such a pose is that, in addition to providing immobility, it tends to eliminate tell-tale shadows. Shadow elimination is partly attained in the great majority of adult birds and terrestrial vertebrates by "countershading." This refers to the development of darkest color on the back (where natural illumination is brightest) and lightest color on the belly of the animal (where illumination is weakest). The net effect of the contrary gradients of animal color and lighting is to reduce the three-dimensional roundness of the animal (as ordinarily indicated by shadows) and convert it into an inconspicuous, flat, even toned object. Experimental evidence of the effectiveness of countershading was obtained by de Ruiter (Tinbergen, 1957) at Oxford. He killed countershaded caterpillars and mounted them on twigs in a naturally planted aviary, half of them dark side up and half light side up. The European Jays, *Garrulus glandarius*, in the aviary "ate many more of the inverted (light side up) caterpillars than the others."

A further device used by some birds to escape detection is described by Cott as disruptive coloration. Both young and old Ringed Plovers, *Charadrius hiaticula*, possess, as their name suggests, a bold contrasting pattern of rings on the head, neck, and back, which optically break up the body into two pieces; they create a hiatus

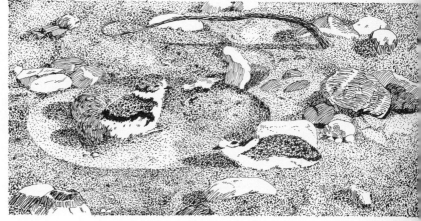

Figure 3.21. Concealment by disruptive pattern in the Ringed Plover. The bold markings tend to destroy the outline of the chicks as seen by a predator. The bird at the right shows the characteristic squatting posture of young galliform chicks when alarmed—an instinctive response which aids concealment by eliminating shadow. After Cott.

between head and body. This disruption of the visible form of the bird helps prevent its recognition *as a bird* by a potential predator. Disruptive marks like this are found in the downy chicks of snipe, woodcock, ducks, quail, and other species.

Some biologists have expressed doubts regarding the effectiveness of these various types of concealing coloration. They make the point that what seems concealing to man's eyes may not be so to the eyes of a bird's natural predator. The difficulties of arranging a natural experiment to test this point are considerable. However, experiments with wild birds preying on grasshoppers exposed against contrasting versus matching soil backgrounds were conducted by Isely (1938). They showed a 66 per cent survival of 114 protectively colored grasshoppers as against a 16 per cent survival of the same number of non-protectively colored grasshoppers. Similar results were obtained by Sumner (1934) after exposing minnows of background-contrasting and background-matching color to penguins. In nature, so pronounced a difference in survival would very quickly produce evolutionary consequences in population color. There is little reason to believe that the eyes of a bird feeding on insects or minnows would perform differently from the eyes of a hawk preying on another bird.

There are times in a bird's life when conspicuous or advertising coloration is of value. Conspicuousness may be gained by bright colors, sharp contrasts, bold patterns, or by behavior that exposes certain patterns or colors. Distinctive coloration can serve as a quick recognition mark for distinguishing friend from foe, or it may hold a flock of birds together. As in human affairs, conformity has its advantages. Birds that, through accident or mutation, have become altered in appearance, may not be accepted by others of their species. The male of a successfully mated pair of Ringed Plovers, *Charadrius hiaticula*, returned the next season with one foot missing. His wife abandoned him and mated with a new, unblemished male a half

kilometer away (Laven, 1938). Albino Chimney Swifts, *Chaetura pelagica*, have been repeatedly attacked by other Chimney Swifts; and an albino Robin, *Turdus migratorius*, was attacked by a normal Robin until it died of its injuries. Apparently a bird must wear the right clothes to attain social status within the species.

Patterns thought to serve as recognition marks are, for example, the white rump patch of the Yellow-shafted Flicker, *Colaptes auratus*, and the white outer tail feathers of the Junco, *Junco hyemalis*. These patterns are conspicuous in flight and may serve to keep the birds of a flock together. Many downy young shorebirds, although concealingly colored on head and back, possess snowy white wing feathers. When alarmed or lost, the young run about stretching their conspicuous wings high in the air.

Recognition marks also have sexual significance. The male and female Flicker are colored alike except for a pair of black mustache marks on the male's cheeks. In an experiment by Noble (1936), the female of an apparently successfully mated pair was caught and supplied with an artificial mustache. The male immediately attacked his mate as an intruding male rival! When the mustache of the female was removed, she was again accepted by her mate. In a reverse experiment performed by Vogt (Peterson, 1948) a stuffed female Yellowthroat, *Geothlypis trichas*, was placed in the territory of a singing male, which courted and copulated with her two or three times. Vogt then pasted a black mask over the female's face to make her resemble a male. The male returned "and was about to resume relations" when he noticed the mask, "bounced two full feet in the air and dashed away as if completely mortified." In the Magellanic Blue-eyed Shag, *Phalacrocorax atriceps*, of Tierra del Fuego, Murphy (1936) describes a white wing patch that appears immediately before mating, and, at the end of the breeding season, a short-lived white patch in the middle of the back that serves the birds "as an effective signal that

Figure 3.22. The Slate-colored Junco, whose white outer tail feathers, conspicuous in flight, may serve as recognition marks to birds of the same species. Photo by G. R. Austing.

the wearers of the patch have passed the point of being receptive toward amatory advances."

To a more limited extent, color may be used for threat or warning, that is, as an energy conserving device to avoid actual combat. Many birds spread their feathers and display their most striking colors when intimidating a competitor or intruder. The broadly spread feathers of a nuthatch before rivals at a feeding tray, or of one turkey cock before another, are common examples. Cott (1940) gives a striking example of an intimidation display in the Blue-fronted Amazon Parrot, *Amazona aestiva:*

"When alarmed or in danger this beautiful species throws its body forward into a horizontal position, partially spreads the wings in a horizontal plane, and widely fans out the tail, at the same time elevating its cobalt blue frontal fringe and green throat ruffle. This attitude effects the display of brilliant red areas on flight and tail feathers, which are normally concealed by a cryptic garment of green."

In addition to this optical onslaught the bird vibrates its feathers, causing a rustling sound, and, at the climax of its display, gives a staccato warning note "somewhat resembling the radio time signal!"

Finally, coloration is used by many birds in courtship ceremonies to attract mates, to stimulate them into sex-readiness, and to synchronize the male and female reproductive time schedules. Lack's (1943) remarks concerning the red breast of the European Robin, *Erithacus rubecula,* as a warning flag, apply also to courtship colors. "When a bird possesses a bright patch of color, one may guess that it plays a part in its life sufficiently important to outweigh the disadvantages of conspicuousness to its enemies."

Persuasive evidence that the bird is aware of its fine feathers is the fact that the colorful male almost invariably presents his showiest plumage directly before the female's eyes. Birds of paradise will assume quite grotesque poses to display their most colorful feathers, sometimes even hanging upside down from a branch. If a bird lacks gaudy feathers it may possess compensating colorful structures, such as combs, wattles, neck pouches, or even colored legs and feet, for courtship advertising service. The Blue-footed Booby, *Sula nebouxii,* will compete for the attentions of his intended by goose-stepping in front of her "raising his bright blue feet as high as possible and thrusting out his chest" (Murphy, 1936). Among phalaropes the female is more brightly colored than the male, and she does the active displaying in courtship. Not only is the male the drab, passive partner in courtship, but he stays home and incu-bates the eggs and raises the young single-handedly.

SUGGESTED READINGS

Old, but still valuable for general information on feathers and coloration, are Newton's *A Dictionary of Birds,* and Pycraft's *A History of Birds.* The paperback by the Heinroths, *The Birds,* has a brief but excellent section on molts of feathers. An excellent survey of feathers, molts and coloration is found in Van Tyne and Berger's *Fundamentals of Ornithology,* while a thorough and more technical account of feathers and pigmentation, emphasizing their embryonic development, is given in Rawles' chapter in Marshall's *Biology and Comparative Physiology of Birds.*

FOUR

Bones and Muscles

The caudal muscles, by means of which the male
Menura moves and manages his superb tail feathers,
must be of extraordinary complexity and flexibility, for
he is equally able to move each one of his sixteen
"display" plumes separately in any direction; to move the
whole sixteen in unison; to spread all or some of them in
a fan; to erect and depress them separately or in unison;
to fold some while the others remain erect; and to fold
all with a single movement.
Ambrose Pratt, *The Lore of the Lyrebird*

A good way to understand the distinctive modifications of a bird's body is to imagine the difficulties a bird would face in flying and perching if it were built on the plan of the lizard-like reptiles from which it descended. A lizard with feathers instead of scales still could not fly. For flight, extensive remodeling of the body architecture would be necessary. The long, bony tail of the reptile, which could contribute little to flight, would have to go. And with the tail gone, how could the creature maintain its balance while walking on its hind legs? Clearly, a shortening of the body axis would be necessary in order to concentrate the bird's weight over the legs and under the wings. To fly, the front legs must have powerful muscles, and these, in turn, demand a strong, well placed anchorage on the ventral side of the body—in other words, a well-developed sternum. The angels one sees in church windows are biological impossibilities; they lack the sternum and breast

55

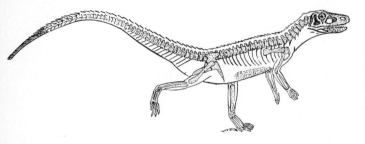

Figure 4.1. A restored skeleton of *Ornithosuchus*, a Mesozoic, bipedal, Pseudosuchian reptile thought to have been an ancestor of modern birds. Note the elongated body and the relatively simple hip and shoulder girdles. After Heilmann.

muscles needed to flap their impressive wings. These modifications birds have developed.

Then, too, unlike all other vertebrates, a bird must support its weight in two different ways: part of the time by its legs, part of the time by its wings. These alternating requirements have resulted in a skeleton more highly differentiated than that of any other vertebrate. The chief innovations that have met these demands are the two thin but extensive saucer-like plates, the synsacrum above and the sternum below. The muscles around these two hip and shoulder "girders" serve to propel the bird and to maintain its balance whether it is on its wings or on its legs. Since these are understandably the strongest and heaviest muscles of the body, it is essential, in a flying machine, that they be located near the center of gravity. As a consequence, the trunk axis of a bird is shorter than that of any vertebrate of corresponding size excepting the frog. The rigid synsacrum also permits a great reduction in the muscles of the back which, in four-legged vertebrates, or tetrapods, are used to bend the flexible back and to support it and the contents of the abdomen slung below.

As pointed out earlier, the avian skeleton achieves strength-with-lightness by being built with the greatest possible economy of materials. Some bones common to most of the higher vertebrates are completely eliminated; others are fused together. The bones that remain are usually highly mineralized and very strong. Many are "pneumatized" or filled with air spaces instead of bone marrow (Fig. 1.3). Early in a bird's life the larger bones are

filled with marrow, but this is often resorbed (within five weeks in a hen's humerus) and its place taken by outreaching extensions of the air sacs connected with the lungs. In some birds, hornbills for example, the air sacs penetrate even into the bones of the toes. Darwin owned a pipe whose stem was contrived from the hollow wing bone of an albatross.

Although pneumatization of bones is a great advantage to flying birds, not all birds show it. As a rule, small birds are less well pneumatized than large birds. Hollow bones are essentially lacking in gulls as well as in the flightless kiwi. In strong

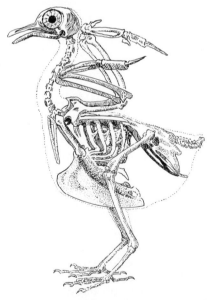

Figure 4.2. The skeleton of a pigeon, as contrasted with that of a reptile, is shorter and much more compact. The expanded pectoral and pelvic girdles are so located that either the wings or the legs may support the bird's body near its center of gravity. After Heilmann.

divers such as penguins, grebes, and loons, pneumaticity is very poorly developed, and in diving ducks it is less than in non-divers. The pneumatization of the skull of the House Sparrow, *Passer domesticus,* begins about 23 days after hatching and is completed when the bird is about 220 days old (Nero, 1951).

THE AXIAL SKELETON

To avoid disaster, a rapidly flying animal must see well, must possess superior motor coordination, and must make quick decisions. This means that birds, as compared with reptiles, must have large eyes and a large brain. The enlargement of these structures has had a profound influence on the form and size of the skull. The eyes of most birds are so large that they almost touch in the middle of the skull at the interorbital septum. In some instances they occupy so much space that they prevent the formation of part of this septum, so that there is a window between the two eye sockets (see Fig. 1.3). A ring of small, shingle-like bony plates, the sclerotic ring, encircles the eyeball in front—a protective device also found in the eyes of some reptiles. The larger the eyes, the more the brain is forced upward and backward into the bulging cranium. The enlargement of the eyes has been made at the expense of the sense of smell. The reduction in olfactory organs, and the substitution of a light, horny beak for a heavy jaw with teeth, have resulted in a great reduction in the size of the forepart of the skull.

Pneumatization of the skull occurs in most birds, although the kiwi shows no air spaces at all and the grebes only a few. There are usually two systems of air spaces in the skull: one, in and adjoining the upper mandible, which connects with the nasal cavity; the other, in the roof and base of the cranium and in the interorbital septum, which originates in the tympanic cavity.

Since birds have so specialized their front limbs that they are no longer useful for manipulating food, nesting material, and the like, the head and beak have had to take over these functions. Whereas in man and other mammals the skull articulates with the spinal column on two ball and socket joints (condyles), in birds, as in reptiles, one suffices. This allows the head greater freedom in movement. In most birds the opening for the spinal cord, the foramen magnum, has shifted from the rear of the skull to its lower side, especially in birds with large eyes, such as owls and hawks. In more primitive, small-eyed birds, such as the ducks, the opening is still at the rear.

As in reptiles, the lower mandible of birds is composed of several bones, and hinges on two small, movable bones, the quadrates. This allows a double-jointed, wide-gaping type of articulation not found in mammals. In many birds, not only is the lower jaw hinged to the skull, but the upper jaw also, normally at the forehead. By means of separate bar-like bones (the quadratojugal and jugal) which can slide along each side of the palate and which articulate with the quadrates, the upper mandible can be raised and lowered. As jaw muscles rock the quadrate bones to and fro, these shove forward or retract the jugal bars and palate which, in turn, raise or lower the upper beak. This action is very clearly seen in parrots.

The possibility of moving each mandible independently gives birds a much more precise control of the food they manipulate with their beaks. It also makes possible a wider gape, as in insect-catching forms, which accounts for increased success when feeding on the wing. A similar mechanism allows the raising of only the tip of the upper mandible in the Woodcock, *Philohela minor,* and other long-billed shorebirds. This latter adaptation permits the Woodcock to seize an earthworm deep in the ground without expending the energy needed to open its entire beak and push aside the soil for the whole depth which the beak penetrates.

A remarkable adaptation, both in skeleton and muscles, is seen in woodpeckers, hummingbirds, sunbirds, and others which are able to extend their tongues to a greater length than other birds. This permits them to exploit new food niches by probing deep in wood crevices for insects or deep in flower corollas for nectar. Such extreme extension of the tongue is made possible by a lengthening of the hyoid bones that support it, and the development of corresponding sheaths and muscles to house and move these bones. The roots of the hyoid bone are so greatly lengthened in the Green Woodpecker, *Picus viridis*, that they encircle the outside of the skull and their ends come to rest in the nasal cavity (Fig. 4.3). Whereas a sparrow can scarcely extend its tongue the length of its stubby beak, the Green Woodpecker can extend its barbed tongue four times, and the Wryneck, *Jynx torquilla*, five times the length of its upper beak (Hess, 1951).

The vertebral column of birds is subdivided, as in reptiles and mammals, into five regions: the cervical (neck), thoracic (chest), lumbar (loins), sacral (hip), and

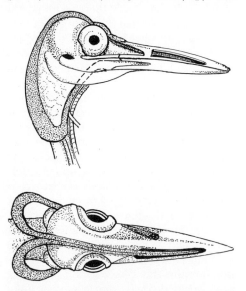

Figure 4.3. The highly protrusible tongue of the Green Woodpecker originates in the extremely long hyoid bones. These, sheathed by the muscles that move them, circle the back of the skull, cross its top, and end in the right nostril, which serves as a scabbard to hold them. After Leiber.

caudal (tail) regions. The number of vertebrae in the spinal column varies greatly, from 39 in a sparrow to 63 in a swan. The most characteristic feature of the avian backbone is its rigidity—a very necessary condition for effective flight as well as for an easy bipedal posture. The separate vertebrae are more or less fused together in all regions but the neck. Rails, however, are exceptional in that they possess very flexible spinal columns.

In the cervical region, as an adaptation to the increased use of the head as a manipulating tool, the vertebrae show extraordinary mobility. This is made possible by their peculiar "heterocoelous" articulating surfaces. These are saddle-shaped, with the anterior face of each vertebra convex up and down, and concave from side to side. The posterior face has corresponding curves to permit proper articulation. These complex vertebrae are supplied with bony processes above, below, and on the sides, for the attachment of ligaments and the complex muscles that move the neck. The ligaments that bind these vertebrae together are particularly stout on the upper side to counteract the weight of the long neck and head. An unusual modification of the neck vertebrae occurs in some herons and anhingas. A very long cervical vertebra in the mid-neck region has an articular surface so directed as to cause a sharp kink in the neck axis, which makes it look dislocated. This device seems to facilitate the lightning-like stabs these birds use in catching fish. The total number of cervical vertebrae varies from 11 in parakeets to 25 in swans, whereas the number in mammals, whether man or giraffe, is typically 7.

Thoracic vertebrae are those that bear the ribs. They vary in number from three to ten, and usually from three to five of them are fused together into a "dorsal bone." There are normally two or three free thoracic vertebrae just in front of the lumbar region to allow some movement between the dorsal bone and the following synsacrum. The thoracic vertebrae of penguins are not fused, a fact no doubt related to their fish-like swimming movements.

Ribs in birds have a double articulation with the thoracic vertebrae. They may reach only part way, or may extend all the way to the sternum on the lower side of the body. Those that reach all the way occur in two bony sections, an upper and a lower, that are joined almost at right angles to each other on the side of the chest cavity. On each upper rib section occurs a tab-like, backward directed projection, that strengthens the rib cavity by overlapping the adjoining rib to the rear. Interestingly enough, *Sphenodon* and some other reptiles possess such uncinate processes on their ribs. In powerful divers, such as guillemots and loons, there are extra-long uncinate processes that reach across two adjoining ribs, an adaptation that strengthens the rib cage against the pressures encountered in deep dives. As a further adaptation to diving, the entire rib cage in these birds is compressed and lengthened so that the body offers less resistance to passage through the water. The number of complete ribs in birds varies from three in some pigeons to nine in swans.

The next section of the spinal column, proceeding rearward, is the most extensively fused region of all. What in primitive ancestors were two or three sacral vertebrae have not only fused together in modern birds, but have also become fused with lumbar vertebrae in front and a few caudal vertebrae to the rear to make a paper-thin but rigid plate of bone, the synsacrum. The synsacrum embraces between 10 and 23 vertebrae in all. It has also expanded laterally to fuse intimately with the pelvic bones. With its ridges, braces, and projections, the synsacrum makes a wonderfully light and stiff framework for the support of the body by the legs.

The spinal column ends posteriorly in 12 or so caudal vertebrae (there were 22 in *Archaeopteryx*). About half of them, at the end of the tail, are welded together into a single broad bone, the pygostyle, which provides a support for the tail feathers. Movement in the entire backbone itself is possible in but three regions: the cervical vertebrae; between the dorsal bone and the synsacrum; and in some of the caudal vertebrae.

On the ventral side of the body where the ribs come together occurs the large, shield-shaped sternum. This bone, more highly developed in the bird than in any other vertebrate, protects the chest and part of the belly against physical blows, and, more important, provides a large, ideally placed surface for the attachment of the large wing muscles. In powerful fliers the sternum has a large, thin keel for the attachment of these muscles, and in flightless birds it may bear a very small keel or, as in ostriches (and man), none at all. Although the penguin is flightless it still has a distinct keel to which are attached the powerful muscles that move its flipper-like wings. The backbone, ribs, and sternum together form a flexible but strong box which houses the heart, lungs, and visceral organs of the bird.

THE APPENDICULAR SKELETON

The energetic thrust of each beating wing is translated to the body through a tripod of bones called the pectoral or shoulder girdle, embracing each side of the rib cage. These three bones are the scapula, coracoid, and furcula. This last bone is sometimes called the clavicle or "wishbone." Where the three bones come together there is an opening, the foramen triosseum, through which runs the tendon of the supracoracoideus muscle, referred to later. Where the scapula and coracoid unite, there is a hollow depression, the glenoid cavity, with which the chief bone of the wing, the humerus, makes a flexible ball and socket joint. A glance at a complete skeleton will show that the wings of the bird are attached above and slightly in front of the body's center of gravity—a necessary location for their function.

The scapula is a thin, blade-like bone bedded in muscles along the side of the spinal column. Interposed between the wing muscles and the ribs, it protects the latter. In strong fliers it is especially long. The stout coracoid bone braces the sternum against the powerful compression created when the chief breast muscles contract to cause the downbeat of the wing. Without this compression support of the coracoid, the muscular stresses of flapping flight would wreck the rib cage. The two halves of the shoulder girdle are united in front by the V-shaped furcula, which may or may not be attached to the sternum. Between the arms of the furcula pass the esophagus and windpipe on their way from the neck to the abdomen. In flightless birds the scapula and coracoid may be greatly reduced, or even absent as in the ostrich. In gliding birds such as the frigates, all three bones of the pectoral girdle may be rigidly fused together.

It is possible that the furcula of the goose has had more influence on human affairs than bones from any other animal, man excepted. In his book on bird folk-lore, Armstrong (1958) quotes a Bavarian physician, Dr. Hartlieb, writing in 1455 as follows:

"When the Goose has been eaten on St. Martin's Day or Night, the oldest and most sagacious keeps the breast bone and allowing it to dry until the morning examines it all round, in front, behind and in the middle. Thereby they divine whether the weather will be severe or mild, dry or wet, and are so confident in their prediction that they will wager their goods and chattels on its accuracy."

When Hartlieb asked an officer what sort of weather was impending, the latter drew a goose furcula from his doublet,

". . . and showed me that after Candlemas an exceeding severe frost should occur, and could not fail . . . [He] told me that the Teutonic knights in Prussia waged all their wars by the goose-bone, and as the goose-bone predicted so did they order their . . . campaigns."

To modify a walking leg into a wing requires extensive alterations. For lightness the bones are hollowed, reduced in number and size, and fused together. For compactness, while the wing is at rest, the arm folds closely against the body in a Z-shape. For the attachment of powerful muscles and large feathers, the bones are broadened and provided with prominent heads and crests. To convert the wing into a lifting plane, flat skin membranes—the pre- and post-patagia—are stretched between its front and rear edges and the body. Finally, the arm is equipped with rows of the largest feathers of the body, the primary wing feathers or the remiges. Activated by assorted muscles, the front leg is now ready to propel the bird through the air.

Among the details involved in the development of the wing are the shortening and broadening of the caudally-directed humerus which, with its large muscle-attachment surfaces, articulates in the glenoid fossa of the pectoral girdle. Near its proximal end, the humerus has a large hole through which its air chambers connect flexibly with the air sacs of the body. The broadened ulna of the forearm provides a base for the attachment of secondary flight feathers. Correlated with the reduced mobility of the hand, the number of wrist bones (carpals) is reduced to two, and the palm bones (metacarpals) to three, the second and third of which are fused together. Only three fingers appear in the hand of modern birds. The stubby thumb consists of a single small bone. It supports the three or four small feathers of the alula. The second finger is by far the largest: it consists of two broad segments on which are fastened the large primary flight feathers. The third finger is reduced to a single tiny bone. In the embryos of many species and the adults of a few (ostrich, hoatzin) there are claws on the ends of the fingers.

Adapted to running, perching, and occasionally to swimming, the pelvic girdle and the hind legs also show extensive remodeling of ancestral architecture. The bird's pelvis is greatly lengthened so that, welded to the synsacrum, it forms a thin but strong roof that covers about half of the body. The pelvis proper is made of three bones that come together at the leg socket or acetabulum. In the earliest archosaur reptiles from which birds descended, the pelvic bones radiated outward from the acetabulum somewhat as three spokes from a hub, the ilium upward and toward the midline of the back, the pubis downward and forward under the belly, and the ischium downward and toward the rear. In modern birds these bones have shown a more drastic modification than any others in the entire skeleton. The ilium has been greatly broadened and lengthened in an antero-posterior direction and firmly fused to the synsacrum. The ischium and pubis have each evolved into long, thin bars fused to the ilium anteriorly and directed sharply rearward, parallel to the backbone. In modern birds there are always openings left between the ilium and ischium and between the ischium and pubis, through which pass the chief nerves (and one muscle) that supply the legs. These bones do not unite or form symphyses at their distal ends, as they do in primitive reptiles, except in two birds: in the ostrich there is a pubic symphysis and in the rhea an ischial symphysis. The lack of such union leaves the under part of the pelvis open to accommodate the centrally placed abdomen. This openness also facilitates egg laying. Such a ventral location of the abdomen has necessitated spreading the legs apart and widening the pelvic girdle through which the legs support the body. The pelves of some parrots show a pronounced sexual dimorphism, that of the female being the wider. This is evidently an adaptation for egg laying. In running and climbing birds the pelvis tends to be wide, whereas in diving birds it tends to be narrow.

Since a bird's legs are still used largely for walking, leaping, and perching, they have not undergone as pronounced modification as its wings. The thighbone, or femur, is generally shortened and at times pneumatic. In most birds, especially those whose bodies are held horizontally, the short femur, buried in the flesh of the body, is directed somewhat forward so

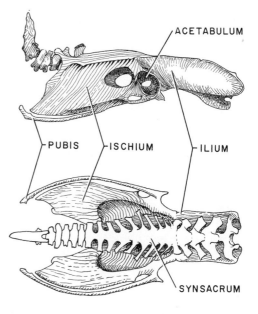

Figure 4.4. The pelvis of a Domestic Fowl as seen from the side and from below. The dome-like structure composed of the spinal column and the pelvic bones provides strength and rigidity with lightness.

that its distal end, from which the leg continues to the ground, will be near the bird's center of gravity. With their legs so wide apart, birds would still have trouble walking were it not for the rotation of the femur and knee joint that results in placing the foot under the bird's center of gravity. Usually at the knee joint there is, in loons, penguins, and other expert divers, a strong extension of the tibia, the cnemial crest. Leg muscles attached to this crest are provided with an oar-like leverage that greatly increases the thrust of their legs while swimming. This crest illustrates beautifully the way in which different bones may be adapted to the same end. In the giant fossil diver, *Hesperornis*, the cnemial crest consists of the large knee cap, or patella, fused to the end of the tibia. In the diving grebes it consists of contributions from both a conical patella and a prolonged tibia. But in loons, the cnemial crest is almost entirely an extension of the tibia, with but a tiny scale of a patella added to it. All three types of crests are very similar in appearance and serve exactly the same function, in spite of their different origins (see Fig. 21.14).

In the shank or "drumstick" the tibia is the main bone and the fibula is reduced to a splint. This change is related to a considerable loss in the ability to rotate the lower leg. Aside from the inward rotation already mentioned, birds have very little capacity to twist their legs or to step sideways. Their legs move in a rather limited fore-and-aft direction.

It is in the ankle joint that the avian leg shows its most striking changes. Whereas in mammals the ankle joint is usually composed of seven pebble-like tarsal bones, in birds some of these bones are fused to the end of the tibia, which thus becomes the tibiotarsus; and the remaining bones are joined to the three fused metatarsal bones, which all together as one bone are now called the tarso-metatarsus. Instead of a low, many-boned ankle joint, birds have acquired what is essentially an extra bone which greatly lengthens the leg: the tarso-metatarsus. This heel bone, now raised high above the ground, adds speed for running, reduces the risk of dislocation, and simplifies leg construction. In the embryo bird the separate tarsal bones are still distinguishable, but they soon lose their identity in fusion as the young bird matures. The fused metatarsal end of the tarso-metatarsus still shows its three-boned origin in many birds in the three ridges leading to three articular surfaces on which toes are placed. Grooves in and between these ridges serve as channels and pulleys for the tendons that operate the toes.

Modern birds may have two, three, or four toes, but never five. The first toe is generally directed backward and provides the considerable advantages of an opposable toe. The fourth toe in some owls, cuckoos, and plantain-eaters may at will be directed either forward or backward. Parrots and woodpeckers typically have their two outer toes directed backward and the two inner toes forward. In the ostrich, toes one and two disappear, and only toes three and four, greatly shortened, remain functional. This sort of toe reduction is characteristic of running birds. On the other hand, the toes may be greatly lengthened, as in jaçanas, for walking on floating vegetation.

In general, the bones of a bird, for all their mineral rigidity, have shown an evolutionary plasticity exceeded by no other system of the body. The problems of flight have placed unique and drastic demands on the bird's body, and its skeleton has responded with unique and drastic changes.

MUSCLES

As a result of adaptation to flight, the muscles of birds, like the bones, have become altered in both structure and distribution. The main changes have been in the locomotor muscles of the wings and legs. These massive muscles have been shifted ventrally, with a resultant improvement in aerodynamic balance. Anyone who has carved a fowl knows that the back is as spare in meat as the breast is abundant. The reduction of muscles on a bird's back has been made possible by the rigidity of the synsacrum and dorsal bone. These bones take the place of the fuselage of an airplane and eliminate the need of strong dorsal muscles (as, for example, the loin muscles in a mammal) to hold a flexible backbone against the stresses imposed by active flight or running.

Chief of the flight muscles is the large pectoralis which depresses the wing. It arises on the keel and furcula and is inserted on the under side of the humerus at some distance from the shoulder joint. On this muscle falls the main burden of supporting the bird in air. Acting as its antagonist is the supracoracoideus muscle that raises the wing. Rather than on the backbone where one might expect it, this muscle is also located ventrally, under the pectoralis muscle. It, too, arises on the keel; but whereas the pectoralis extends upward to attach directly on the humerus, the supracoracoideus ends dorsally in a tendon that passes through the foramen triosseum, where the three shoulder-girdle bones come together, and turns outward and downward to attach on the upper side of the humerus. By this arrangement, like a rope and pulley mechanism, the supracoracoideus exerts an upward force on the wing by a downward pull, and it keeps its main mass low in the body. These two paired muscles may together make up as much as one-fifth of a bird's weight. The supracoracoideus is especially well developed in diving birds that use their wings as paddles and brakes. In flightless birds both of these muscles are weak and poorly developed.

There are numerous other smaller muscles of the wing and shoulder girdle which pull the wing forward or backward, or which rotate the humerus so as to depress the leading edge of the wing (pronation) or to raise it (supination). Still others may flex or extend the wing, or stretch the skin flaps that occupy the angles of the wing.

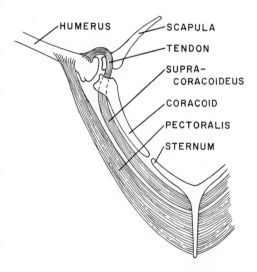

HUMERUS
SCAPULA
TENDON
SUPRA-
CORACOIDEUS
CORACOID
PECTORALIS
STERNUM

Figure 4.5. A cross section through a typical bird's breast muscles, showing how an ingenious rope and pulley mechanism permits the contracting supracoracoideus muscle to raise the wing, although the chief mass of this muscle lies low in the body. This arrangement promotes stable flight. After T. I. Storer.

Even the alula and individual feathers are subject to the control of an elaborate system of small muscles and tendons. All these muscles and their actions are important in making possible intricate control of bird flight.

As the keel is the chief anchorage for flight muscles, its size is a good index of a bird's capacity for flapping flight. Hummingbirds have relatively enormous keels, partly because small wings are less efficient than large, hence must be fanned more vigorously, and partly because hummingbirds apparently use both up and down strokes to apply power for flight. That is, the upstroke provides not merely passive recovery of the wing but also some forward, and at times backward, thrust. In the Ruby-throated Hummingbird, *Archilochus colubris*, the elevator breast muscles weigh nearly one-half as much as the depressors, whereas in the Robin, *Turdus migratorius*, they weigh but one-ninth as much (Savile, 1950).

Since the legs of birds still support the weight of the body from below as in reptiles, their muscles have not required as drastic remodeling as those of the wings. The major muscles of the legs provide forward and backward movement of the legs and very little lateral movement or rotation. Evidently, the ability of birds to escape their enemies by flight through the air has eliminated the necessity to develop the muscles and bone articulations that would make possible the zig-zag sort of running characteristic of rabbits. At any rate, most of the leg muscles are concerned with straightforward walking and running, with leaping into the air, with cushioning landings, and with grasping with the toes. In his detailed study of the Blue Coua, *Coua caerulea*, Berger (1953) listed 38 individual leg muscles. The main mass of these muscles is located in the thigh over the femur. A lesser amount is located in the shank or the tibiotarsus, and only six thread-thin miniature muscles are found in the tarso-metatarsus, just above the toes. The muscles in the upper parts of the leg flex and extend the lower

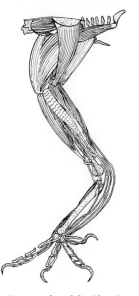

Figure 4.6. Leg muscles of the Blue Coua, showing how the heavier muscles of the leg, placed near the body, control the extremities by means of long, slender tendons. After Berger.

parts by means of strong, stringy tendons, sliding through sleeve-like sheaths and strategically placed (inside or outside of joints, for example) to provide the proper mechanical actions.

This concentration of the leg muscles on the upper leg has several advantages. First, it places most of their weight near the center of gravity, an important aid in flight. Second, it makes the outer ends of the legs light in weight, enabling them to be moved more quickly and with less exertion than would be the case were they, like human legs, more uniform in structure and thickness from top to bottom. Since the toes and the tarso-metatarsus are largely made of tough scales, tendons, and bones, they are, in spite of their exposed location and active use, much less subject to accidental damage and freezing than would be soft fleshy extremities. And of course the absence of major muscles at the distal end of the leg permits an economy in the distribution of blood vessels and nerves.

The muscles of the axial skeleton are primarily concentrated in the head, neck, and rump. Although birds have exchanged their teeth for muscular gizzards, they still possess complex muscles which move the beak. Investigations by Beecher (1951) of the jaw musculature of different blackbird species have shown a close correlation between muscle development and the type of diet eaten. Insect eaters such as members of the genus *Euphagus* have relatively weak muscles for closing the jaw. Seed eaters of the genus *Molothrus* have powerful jaw muscles. Meadowlarks of the genus *Sturnella* use the opening or gaping action of their bills in disturbing ground litter for food, and they have unusually strong gaping muscles.

Probably the most complex muscles in the bird are those which control the elaborately varied movements of its neck. Muscles of the neck are thin and stringy, interwoven and often subdivided and attached to one another. When a certain muscle has attached to its fascia sheath several other muscles leading in different directions, its motor action will be quite variable, depending on the contractions of its neighbors. A very transitory muscle appears on the upper neck and back of the head in the unhatched Domestic Chick. Not only is this muscle strategically located to provide exactly the force needed by the hatching chick to break out of its confining egg shell, but its size, according to careful studies by Fisher (1958), reaches its relative maximum on the 20th day of incubation, and the chick normally hatches on the 21st day. After the chick hatches, this muscle rapidly decreases in size (see Fig. 16.13).

Of considerable complexity are the rump and tail muscles of a bird. The pygostyle, which supports the tail feathers, is moved in various ways by these muscles. In addition, there are muscles that act directly on the feathers themselves: to fan them out, for example, when a bird alights.

Throughout the body there are dermal muscles that attach to all the contour feather follicles in a systematic fashion.

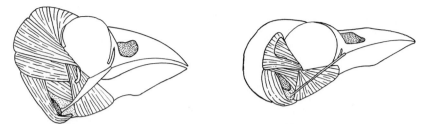

Figure 4.7.   Jaw muscles may be adapted to diet. The European Hawfinch (left) feeds on coarse seeds and even the pits of cherries, plums, and olives, cracking the latter by exerting with its mandibles a crushing force of 72 kg. (159 lbs). The Chaffinch (right) feeds on smaller seeds and insects, and has much weaker jaw muscles. After Mountfort.

These are smooth, or involuntary, muscles under the control of the sympathetic nervous system. Contour feathers are typically arranged in crossing rows in such a manner that any given feather is at the center of a hexagon marked out by its six nearest neighbors. The smooth muscles are so attached to the follicles of these feathers that, on proper stimulation, they can cause the feathers to be erected, depressed, or moved laterally. Other muscles in the skin, of the striated or voluntary type, can move entire patches of feathers, causing, for example, the erection or depression of the showy feathers of the pea-

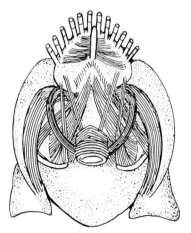

Figure 4.8.   Tail muscles of the Domestic Fowl. In some birds such as the Lyre Bird, these muscles are much more complex and permit a variety of movements, even of individual tail feathers. After du Toit.

cock. Still other skin muscles control the contents of the crop or the tension on inflated air sacs that play a part in the courting antics of some gallinaceous birds.

The skeletal muscles of the body may either be red in color or pale and whitish, as in the "dark" or "light" meat of a roasted turkey. These two kinds of muscles are distinctly different in structure and function. The white muscles are those which normally provide less sustained action than the red muscles. Many of the gallinaceous birds such as grouse, quail, pheasant, and chickens, have white breast muscles, and as a consequence are unable to undertake long flights. In spite of its powerful breast muscles, the Ruffed Grouse, *Bonasa umbellus*, makes an average flight of only 100 or 200 meters. If a given bird "is flushed three or four times in quick succession, it can be picked up by the hand, exhausted" (Edminster, 1947). The large pectoralis breast muscle is red in falcons, gulls, crows, sparrows, and other birds of strong flight.

Microscopically, the red muscles are built of finer fibers than the white, and their nuclei are located at the edges of the fibers, while the nuclei of white muscles are scattered through the fibers. In both muscles the nuclei are remarkably long. In human muscle fibers the nuclei are about four times as long as wide, whereas in bird muscles the ratio is 30:1 (Stresemann, 1927–1934). The color of the red fibers is due to the presence of the oxygen-carrying compounds, myoglobin and cyto-

Figure 4.9. The Squacco Heron of Europe, showing how muscles may control feathers, either sleeking them against the body or extending them in display. Photo by Hosking.

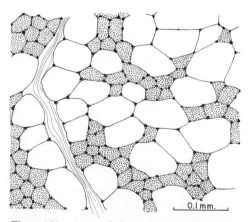

Figure 4.10. A magnified cross section of a pigeon's pectoralis breast muscle which contains both red and white fibers. The blood capillaries have been injected with India ink, and show as black dots. The narrow red muscle fibers (stippled) are more richly supplied with blood capillaries than the broad white fibers (clear). After George and Naik.

chrome, which are apparently absent or very rare in white muscles. Furthermore, red muscle cells have a higher content of mitochondria (microscopic respiratory bodies) than do white fibers and therefore are better able to carry on sustained oxidative processes (George and Naik, 1960a). In addition to these differences, red muscle fibers are provided with a richer supply of blood capillaries (Fig. 4.10) and a higher percentage of intracellular fat than white muscles. The amount of fat in the pectoralis breast muscle of the strongly flying King Crow, *Dicrurus macrocercus*, of India, was determined by George and Naik (1960b) to be 5.6 per cent, while that of the Domestic Chicken, *Gallus gallus*, was 0.98 per cent.

White muscles are reputed to contract more rapidly than red. In inactive caged birds the red muscles atrophy rapidly, but not the white muscles. These pronounced hereditary differences in the muscle structure of birds unquestionably play an important role in determining the nature of such life activities as flight, migration, dispersal, habitat preference, size of territory selected, and method of feeding.

SUGGESTED READINGS

Newton's *A Dictionary of Birds* has much useful material on the skeleton and muscles of birds. Another older reference still worth consulting is Shufeldt's monographic *Osteology of Birds*. Comprehensive treatments of both skeletal and muscular systems are found in Stresemann's volume *Aves*, in Kükenthal and Krumbach's *Handbuch der Zoologie*, and Portmann's chapter on the skeleton, and Oemichen's on the muscles, in Grassé's *Traité de Zoologie, Tome XV, Oiseaux.* Bones and muscles are treated largely from the standpoint of their taxonomic importance in Van Tyne and Berger's *Fundamentals of Ornithology.* Chapters with extensive, up-to-date information are those by Bellairs and Jenkin on the skeleton of birds, and Berger, on muscles, in Marshall's *Biology and Comparative Physiology of Birds.*

FIVE

Brain, Nerves, and Sense Organs

Embodied silence, velvet soft, the owl slips through the night.
With Wisdom's eyes, Athena's bird turns darkness into light.
Joel Peters, *The Bird of Wisdom*

Ever since the advent of bilateral symmetry, hundreds of millions of years ago, animals have been perfecting their organs of locomotion—fins, legs, paddles, wings—largely to escape their enemies or to overtake their prey. Any animal that goes places in a hurry has to know where it is going and has to direct its movements with considerably more alacrity and precision than does a jellyfish. Otherwise, disaster is certain. With the increasing velocity of their headlong flight across the landscape, animals have had to evolve more highly refined nervous mechanisms to handle their increasingly complex problems. An animal sees a moving shape in the distance. Is it friend or

foe—or possibly a breakfast? Shall I stand fast, attack, or flee? If I attack, shall it be with stealth or with a rush? These questions, of course, are stated in anthropocentric form, but the problems presented exist for all the higher vertebrates, though they may be solved (or not!) on a much lower intellectual plane than man would solve them.

The terrestrial vertebrates, to whom these problems of locomotion are especially acute, have solved them in a variety of ingenious ways. The rattlesnake, the eagle, the skunk, and the rhinoceros can afford to stand firm in the face of most enemies. The rabbit relies either on its concealing coloration and squats immovably, or seeks escape in zig-zag flight. Birds, in the main, have so perfected flight through the air as a means of locomotion that even the most fragile finch can wear a coat of gaudy colors and sing its penetrating song on a twig only two leaps away from its inveterate enemy, the house cat. But it must take care to perch two leaps away and not one! All these and other solutions to the problems posed by locomotion depend, of course, on a variety of nervous mechanisms. The organization and development of an animal's nervous system faithfully reflect the complexities and competence of its behavioral repertory. It is worth remembering in this connection that behavior itself is based on movement.

THE BRAIN AND SPINAL CORD

As the terrestrial vertebrates (reptiles, birds, and mammals) evolved, their brains, above all, had to keep pace with the increasingly complex problems of locomotion. Cold-blooded, sluggish reptiles have much smaller, simpler brains than do warm-blooded, *rapidly* moving birds and mammals. For example, a lizard weighing 24 gm. has a brain weighing 0.134 gm. (or 0.55 per cent of its body weight), and a Meadow Mouse, *Microtus drummondi*, weighing 23 gm., has a brain of 0.64 gm. (2.8 per cent), while a House Sparrow, *Passer domesticus*, weighing 23 gm., has a brain of 1.02 gm. (4.5 per cent) (Quiring, 1950).

Reptiles, birds, and mammals all have brains based on a common structural plan but varying considerably in internal neural pathways and in the relative proportions of parts. Both birds and mammals have evolved greatly enlarged cerebral hemispheres and cerebella. The olfactory lobes of birds are very small, suggesting their poor sense of smell. In the midbrain of both reptiles and birds the dorsally placed tectum has become prominent as a correlation center, especially for sight, while in mammals it is small and has lost most of its earlier coordinating functions.

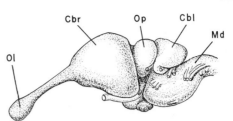

Figure 5.1. Brain of an alligator, side view. *Cbl*, Cerebellum; *Cbr*, cerebrum; *Md*, medulla; *Ol*, olfactory bulb; *Op*, optic lobe. After Romer.

In mammals the outer layer or cortex of the cerebral hemispheres becomes the chief coordinating center of body activities, whereas in reptiles the corpus striatum, which develops from the basal nuclei of the cerebral hemispheres, becomes an integrating center second only to the tectum in dominance. The cerebral cortex in birds is thin, not fissured, and relatively weakly developed compared to the cortex in mammals; but the bird's corpus striatum swells astonishingly in the floor of the cerebrum to become the dominant coordinating center of the brain. Here in the corpus striatum are located the bird's central controls for sensory perception and most of its instinctive behavior. Extirpation experiments have shown that different parts of the corpus striatum control eating, "talking," eye movements, locomotion, and those complex instincts related to reproduction, such as copulation, nest construction, incubation, and care of young. Although the cerebral cortex still functions in birds, it lacks the direct motor pathway to the spinal cord, the pyramidal

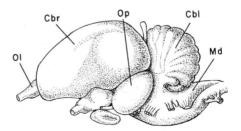

Figure 5.2. Brain of a goose, side view. Symbols as in Fig. 5.1. After Romer.

tract, which mammals have. As a consequence it is likely that direct conscious control of body motions is greatly reduced in birds as compared with mammals.

That the cerebral hemispheres of birds are not completely essential to the performance of complex behavior is proved by experiments in which they have been surgically removed. Pigeons whose cerebral cortex has been removed but whose striatum is intact, are able to mate and rear young. Removal of large sections of the corpus striatum results in serious disturbances in behavior (Prosser *et al.*, 1950). A falcon without hemispheres is able to capture a mouse, and a pigeon or Domestic Chick will pick up grain. But here the action stops, sterile and uncoordinated. The falcon blindly holds the mouse in its claws not knowing what to do next; the pigeon will not swallow the grain (Portmann, 1950). The essential difference between mammals and birds in brain coordination is that the brain of the mammal is dominated by the expanded top layer or cortex of the cerebral hemispheres, which has a high capacity for learning; whereas the bird is dominated by the expanded bottom layer or corpus striatum of the cerebral hemispheres, which seemingly lacks this capacity. Consequently, the behavior of a bird is largely mechanical, stereotyped, instinctive.

For all their size and importance, the corpora striata and cerebral hemispheres do not completely dominate body activities. Still lingering in the bird brain is a primitive compartmentalization or autonomy of regions that reminds one of brain mechanisms of fishes and amphibians. The psychic importance of the cerebrum, however, is indicated by Portmann's studies of the relative size of the cerebrum in relation to other parts of the central nervous system. Birds of superior intelligence, such as parrots and crows, have relatively larger cerebral hemispheres than the less intelligent fowls and pigeons.

The thalamus in birds, as in reptiles and mammals, is a visceral brain center. It shares control over visceral activities with the medulla and spinal cord, and acts as an intermediate transfer point between the spinal cord and corpus striatum for incoming sensory and outgoing motor messages. In birds the largest midbrain structures are the laterally bulging optic lobes. Their large size reflects the size and importance of the eyes in birds. It is chiefly because of the great size and the ventro-lateral location of the eyes and optic lobes that the brain in birds has been shifted upward and rearward in the skull. The optic lobes are intricately laced with nerve fibers and layered with gray neurons, to an extent which makes it seem likely that the lobes form a great visual association apparatus comparable to the visual centers of the human cerebral cortex. This interpretation would account for the fact that a pigeon deprived of its cerebral hemispheres can nevertheless fly and alight successfully on a perch. Birds are "eye-brained" animals to the same degree that many fishes are "nose-brained."

As one would expect of an animal showing superb muscular coordination in flight, birds have a large, well developed cerebellum. Its size is related to the large number of spino-cerebellar fibers from the spinal cord by which the muscle-sense, or proprioceptive, stimuli arrive from the body. As in other vertebrates, the cerebellum also receives impulses from the inner ear, which, along with the proprioceptive impulses, are assembled and reflexly used in coordinating body move-

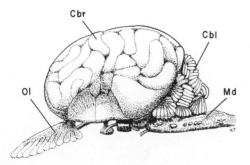

Figure 5.3.   Brain of a pig, side view. Symbols as in Fig. 5.1. After Petterson.

ments and in maintaining balance. Birds probably have a greater stake in precision of movement and equilibrium than any other animal, and accordingly the cerebellum is of crucial importance.

The medulla is the hindmost part of the brain. It lies under the cerebellum and gradually tapers into the spinal cord. It seems, as in man, to be a center for the reflex control of breathing. It also serves as a portal for the entrance of eight of the twelve cranial nerves. Only those cranial nerves having to do with smell and vision are located anterior to the medulla.

In other vertebrates the spinal cord is often shorter than the vertebral column, but in birds the two structures agree closely in length. As in all vertebrates, the spinal cord in birds gives off paired, spinal nerves, each with two roots, a dorsal sensory and a ventral motor root. As a rule, the sensory tracts within the spinal cord (bundles of nerves that carry sensory impulses to the brain) are smaller than the motor tracts. This condition results from a relative poverty of skin sense receptors, a condition promoted by the covering of feathers. Moreover, the fact that birds need not coordinate the movements of legs with wings as closely as quadrupeds must coordinate the movements of their four legs eliminates the need for considerable neural traffic between these two regions. There are cervical and lumbar enlargements in the spinal cord of birds, each associated with nearby nerve plexi supplying the wings and legs respectively. This is a typical vertebrate situation, but the lumbar enlargement is unusually and (so far) inexplicably large in birds. Some of its cells are richly stored with glycogen and lipids whose function is unknown.

Birds also possess an autonomic nervous system which, like man's, controls reflexes involving particularly the visceral organs and the circulatory system. The autonomic system is made up of efferent or outgoing nerve fibers that are grouped into two antagonistic systems. The sympathetic system, which arises in the thoracic and lumbar regions of the spinal cord, sends out impulses that serve to heighten the activity of the bird: they speed up the heart rate, constrict cutaneous blood vessels, and slow down the digestive activities; in short, they prepare the body for emergency action. Stimuli to the same visceral organs from the parasympathetic system, which arises in the brain and sacral spinal cord, produce exactly opposite results. They slow the heart beat, stimulate digestive processes, and in general place the viscera on a placid vegetative routine (Romer, 1949). Secretion of the hormone epinephrine into the blood stream produces effects on visceral organs that are indistinguishable from those caused by sympathetic nerve stimulation. It is thought that sympathetic nerve fibers secrete a substance very similar to or identical with epinephrine.

SENSE ORGANS
SENSE OF TOUCH

Birds are equipped with the varied sense organs that higher vertebrates typically possess, but with refinements and adaptations appropriate to their way of life. It is likely that a bird's skin possesses sense endings, much like those in man, which pick up stimuli interpreted by the brain as touch, pain, heat, and cold. Such endings are usually more abundant in skin that lacks feathers. The simplest receptors are nerves that zig-zag through the stratum germinativum of the skin and end in a disk-like network of fine nerve fibers. These nerve endings are probably the pain and temperature receptors.

More complex are the touch receptors which lie in the dermis of the skin and elsewhere. These are of two kinds: Grandry's corpuscles and Herbst's corpuscles. Grandry's corpuscles occur in the tongue and buccal cavities of ducks and owls. Each corpuscle resembles a sandwich composed of two bun-like sensory cells between which occurs a disk-like "filling" made of a flat terminal network of nerve fibrils. The function of these end-

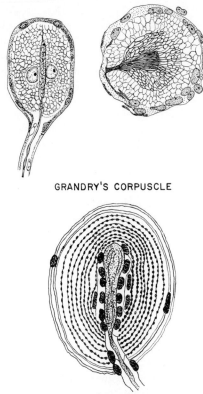

GRANDRY'S CORPUSCLE

HERBST'S CORPUSCLE

Figure 5.4. Touch, pressure, and vibration receptors from the bill of a duck. Grandry's corpuscle, in longitudinal and horizontal sections; Herbst's corpuscle, in longitudinal section. After Boeke and Clara, in Portmann.

It seems likely that, in addition to functioning as touch and pressure receptors, they also provide proprioceptive or muscle-sense impulses and are sensitive to low frequency vibrations. Bullfinches, *Pyrrhula pyrrhula*, whose ears had been removed, were trained by Schwartzkopff (1949) to respond to vibrations of from 100 to 3200 cycles per second. He found that an aggregation of hundreds of Herbst corpuscles between the tibia and fibula were the receptors. The individual Herbst corpuscle has a club-like core which is the swollen end of a sensory nerve. Arranged along two sides of this club are rows of large nuclei, and the whole core is encased in a capsule of concentric egg-shaped sheaths made of connective tissue (Fig. 5.4).

SENSE OF TASTE

The sense of taste seems to be poorly developed in birds. This is probably because birds as a group must snatch their food on the run and therefore have depended on their eyes for quick discrimination of good food from bad. Although the taste receptors of birds have apparently the same spindle-shaped construction as those of mammals, they never occur in "taste bud" aggregations visible to the naked eye. Compared with those of mammals, they are very few in number and occur at the sides and base of the tongue (never at the tip) and especially in the soft palate. Adult Domestic Pigeons, *Columba livia*, and Bullfinches, *Pyrrhula pyrrhula*, each have a maximum number of 50 to 60 taste buds. Experiments by Rensch (1925) showed that birds were sensitive to the four standard taste qualities of salt, sour, bitter, and sweet, and that their stimulus thresholds were about the same as in man. Some species of birds, such as parrots and other seed-eaters, are apparently insensitive to bitter tastes. Bread dipped in quinine powder and fed to parrots by Heinroth (1938) was accepted and eaten without protest. Simi-

ings is not certainly known, but is thought to be tactile. Herbst corpuscles are highly developed in birds and are very similar to the Pacinian (touch) corpuscles in mammals. They are found highly concentrated in the tongues of woodpeckers, in the palates and beaks of ducks and woodcock, and in the mouth flanges of helpless young "nidicole" or nest-dwelling birds. In the tip of the beak of a goose, 1800 Herbst corpuscles have been counted. They also occur in exposed patches of skin, in the feet, at the base of contour feathers, between muscles of the body, and in the connective tissues surrounding leg bones.

larly, seed-eaters and titmice ate grain dipped in picric acid. Ants, rich in formic acid, are eaten by many birds, including the Yellow-shafted Flicker, *Colaptes auratus.*

SENSE OF SMELL

As the small olfactory lobes of the brain indicate, the sense of smell is relatively unimportant to a bird. One need only imagine a winged bloodhound trying to follow a scent-trail in mid-air to realize in part why this is so. As Hesse has pointed out (Stresemann, 1927–1934), most volatile substances that stimulate the sense of smell produce heavy gases which quickly sink to the ground, where they can play almost no role in the orientation of a flying bird. It is significant in this connection that birds such as the kiwis, ducks, and snipe, which have relatively well developed olfactory lobes and nerves, are ground-dwelling species.

In the typical bird two nasal ducts, separated by a thin bony or cartilaginous partition, originate at the external nostrils, run across the palate of the upper beak and end in two large openings or choanae, which connect the tubes with the mouth cavity. Each of these tubes swells, in antero-posterior sequence, into three chambers. In each of these chambers the walls form either a fold or a spiral scroll or concha, which increases the surface over which inhaled air must pass. The first chamber or vestibule, adjoining the nostrils, is usually irregularly shaped, lined with epithelial cells, and has a rich blood supply. In the middle chamber the duct develops a prominent scroll of one to two-and-one-half turns—somewhat like a loosely rolled sheet of paper—and its surfaces are lined with a layer of ciliated epithelial cells. In ducks, the concha of the middle chamber may have up to five turns. The third chamber, which connects with the mouth cavity through the paired choanae, is usually the only one that has olfactory receptors in its lining epithelium.

Apparently the functions of the first two chambers are to moisten, warm, and clean the air a bird breathes. Because the choanae between the third chamber and the mouth are so large—much larger than the external nostrils in pelicans, for example—it seems probable that they carry odors from the mouth directly to the olfactory receptors. Thus, a bird is able to test food by smelling it while it is held in the mouth. Some falcons and owls that eat only fresh meat may pick up tainted meat, but will quickly throw it away after holding it in the beak a moment—presumably because the odors pass through the internal choanae to the olfactory epithelium (Stresemann, 1927–1934). The nocturnal kiwi has stunted eyes but a sharp sense of smell. Its nostrils are located at the tip of its long, probing bill, and the unusually well developed conchae of the second and third nasal chambers are both covered with an olfactory epithelium. Experimental studies indicate that the kiwi finds its underground prey (largely earthworms) by smelling them. Observations reported by Murphy (1936) on various species of albatrosses, skuas, and petrels in antarctic regions strongly suggest that these sea birds can detect meat, blood, and fat, particularly hot fat or oil spread on the surface of the sea, by their sense of smell.

Most studies, however, attribute a very poor sense of smell to birds. Ever since Darwin's and Audubon's famous (if inconclusive) experiments indicated that vultures were unable to find decaying meat by sense of smell alone, similar experiments have usually shown similar results. In a typical experiment, Vogt (1941) placed two slaughtered sheep 400 meters apart on a sterile desert near the coast of Peru. One carcass was left exposed and the other was loosely covered with a single layer of gunny sacks. Within one hour vultures and condors gathered about the exposed sheep, and they fed on it during the next few days. Although the blood seeped through the burlap of the covered carcass and it smelled strongly, the birds ignored it completely. Perhaps the best

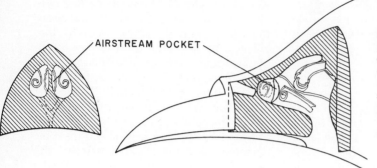

AIRSTREAM POCKET

Figure 5.5. Cross and longitudinal sections of the nasal chambers of a Fulmar, showing the location of the valve-like pockets which may serve sea birds as air-velocity sense organs to aid them in exploiting winds of varying speeds during dynamic gliding. After Mangold.

testimony to the olfactory obtuseness of vultures is found in McIlhenny's (1939) observations on Black Vultures, *Coragyps atratus,* attacking Common Skunks, *Mephitis mephitis.* In numerous instances the birds pressed a mass attack against an individual skunk, despite its discharge of musk, and then proceeded to pull the animal apart and to eat it!

The nasal equipment of birds possibly has other functions than smelling and air-conditioning. Experiments by Shelford and Martin (1946) suggest that chicks of the Ring-necked Pheasant, *Phasianus colchicus,* are able to discriminate differences in atmospheric humidity. Two of three chicks, placed individually in a circular chamber presenting a relative humidity gradient ranging from 40 per cent to 88 per cent, chose to remain in a region of approximately 72 per cent relative humidity, except for brief excursions to other parts of the chamber. Another possible function of the nasal cavity is suggested by the studies of the beaks of "dynamic gliders," such as the albatrosses, petrels, and fulmars, by Mangold and Fürst (Mangold, 1946). Dissections of the nasal chambers of these birds revealed a pair of small forward-opening pockets in the middle chamber which may act as organs for detecting variable pressures produced by differing external air-stream velocities. The nose of a bird is by no means a simple organ and further research into its structure and functions promises to be fruitful.

SENSE OF HEARING

Very probably, the ear arose in the earliest vertebrates not as an instrument for hearing but as an organ of equilibrium. As an organ of balance and motion-perception it reached such a high state of perfection even in the fishes that its basic structure has remained unchanged up the evolutionary ladder all the way to mammals. As an organ of hearing, however, it started out in the fishes as a simple, inefficient device which became progressively refined in the terrestrial reptiles, birds, and mammals.

As in mammals, the bird's ear is divided into three parts: the external, middle, and inner ears. The external ear ordinarily is merely a tube that carries sound waves from the surrounding air inward to the eardrum at its base. The middle ear in birds is essentially a cavity in which a rod-like bone, the columella, picks up sound vibrations of the eardrum and transmits them to a membranous oval window in the inner ear. The movements in the oval window, in turn, set up vibrations in the liquids of the inner ear. It is the inner ear which is the sensory receptor for both equilibrium and sound. Impulses of both kinds are carried from the ear to the brain by the eighth cranial, or auditory, nerve. The general construction of the inner ear in birds resembles closely that of crocodiles. It is a complex and delicate structure of bulbs and tubes (somehow reminding one of the contemporary vogue in abstract sculpture) and is called the membranous labyrinth. It is filled with a fluid about two or three times as viscous as water, the endolymph, and encased by the bony labyrinth of the intimately conforming bone of the surrounding skull. The membranous labyrinth does not adhere closely to the bony labyrinth, but is separated from it by a plasma-like fluid, the perilymph.

The central structures of the membranous labyrinth are two connected chambers, the utriculus above, and the sacculus below. Arching out from the utriculus are three semicircular canals, each arranged roughly at right angles to the other two: the anterior, the posterior, and the external or horizontal canals. At its lower end against the utriculus, each canal swells into a bulbous ampulla. Projecting downward from the sacculus like a curved finger is the endolymph-filled cochlear duct, the hearing organ.

In each membranous labyrinth there are six main sensory areas: one in the ampulla of each of the three semi-circular canals, and one each in the utriculus, the sacculus, and the cochlea. All sensory areas except that in the cochlea, the organ of Corti, have to do with perception of movement and position. In addition to these six sensory areas, there are two others of uncertain function, one in the utriculus and one at the tip end of the cochlea. The actual receptors inside the ampullae, utriculus, and sacculus are in the form of hair-like sensory cells on

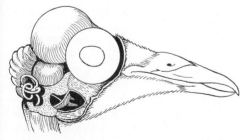

Figure 5.6. Dissected inner ear of the pigeon (below and left from the eye) showing the semicircular canals and, curving downward below them, the cochlea. After Krause, from Portmann.

whose tips is a gelatinous membrane. In the utriculus and sacculus this membrane becomes impregnated with calcium carbonate crystals, the so-called otoliths, which respond to gravitational pull and stimulate the nearest sensory cells to send impulses which the brain interprets as posture or position in space. In the ampullae, with which the semicircular canals connect, the sensory cells respond instead to linear and angular accelerations and send corresponding impressions to the brain. All these receptors collect stimuli from the inner ear, which together with others from the eyes and from proprioceptors in the body, are sent to the brain, where they are integrated to produce compensatory reflexes in the limbs and eyes, and in general maintain posture and balance.

Experiments on live pigeons reported by Coues (1903) revealed that sectioning of the horizontal canal caused the bird to move its head rapidly from side to side in a horizontal plane. The eyes oscillated in nystagmus and the bird showed a tendency to spin on a vertical axis. Cutting the anterior vertical canals caused the bird to move its head rapidly backward and forward and to turn forward somersaults, while cutting the posterior canals produced similar head motions and backward somersaults.

Bird songs and birds' imitations of sounds in the environment would make little sense unless birds themselves could hear. Hearing in birds depends on the cochlea of the inner ear, which appears to function in birds essentially the same way as it does in man. The organ of Corti, which is the auditory receptor in the cochlea, rests on a basilar membrane that, stretched from side to side, runs the length of the cochlear duct. On it rest the sensitive hair cells which are in contact with an over-arching tectorial membrane. When the endolymph vibrates in response to movements of the columella against the oval window, vibrations of different frequencies are thought to stimulate the hair cells at different levels along the basilar membrane. Impulses from these cells are then interpreted by the brain as sounds of different pitch. Although the cochlea of the average bird is approximately only one-tenth the length of the mammalian cochlea, it has about ten times as many hair cells per unit of length. This shorter, broader construction of the hearing mechanism of the avian ear suggests to Pumphrey (1961) that birds are less sensitive to a wide range of sound frequencies than mammals, but more sensitive to differences in intensities. Further, a bird is able to hear and respond to rapid fluctuations in song about ten times as rapidly as man can. This fact is proved by the ability of young birds to imitate other birds' songs that have intricacies which are inaudible to human ears but visible in sound spectrographs.

Several studies have been made of the range of hearing possessed by birds. A healthy, young human ear can detect sounds ranging from about 16 to 20,000 cycles per second. The range in birds, as determined either by conditioning or by delicate electro-physiological measurements of cochlear potentials, is shown by Schwartzkopff (1955) to extend from about 40 to 29,000 cycles per second for those birds studied. A few examples follow.

SPECIES	LOWER LIMIT (CYCLES PER SEC.)	UPPER LIMIT (CYCLES PER SEC.)
Mallard, *Anas platyrhynchos*	300	>8,000
Ring-necked Pheasant, *Phasianus colchicus*	250	10,500
Budgerigar, *Melopsittacus undulatus*	40	14,000
Long-eared Owl, *Asio otus*	100	18,000
Great Horned Owl, *Bubo virginianus*	300	>8,000
Starling, *Sturnus vulgaris*	700	15,000
Chaffinch, *Fringilla coelebs*	200	29,000
Serin, *Serinus canarius*	1,100	10,000
House Sparrow, *Passer domesticus*	675	11,500

In general, among related species the larger birds have deeper voices and a corresponding trend in hearing sensitivity. But Schwartzkopff points out that there are exceptions to this size-voice relation that have interesting references to behavior. For example, many owls have an unexpected sensitivity to high tones that correspond to the squeak of a mouse. Baby chicks are almost exclusively sensitive to the low clucks of the hen (400 cycles), while the hen shows an extraordinary sensitivity to the high cheeping of her chicks (above 3000 cycles).

Owls possess unique refinements in their hearing equipment which account for their amazing sensitivity to low intensity sounds. Externally many species have large, oblong ear-openings bordered in front with a fleshy, erectile flap or operculum, which is framed in small contour feathers. The whole arrangement resembles, and no doubt functions like, a cupped hand held in *front* of one's ear to reflect and concentrate sounds coming from the rear. A further refinement is seen in the striking asymmetry of the external ears. In many species (for example, of the genus *Asio*) the ear openings on the two sides of the head differ greatly in size and location. This asymmetry of sound-collecting structures seems to be helpful in pinpointing faint sounds in dim light, but in just what fashion is unknown. Coupled with these external adaptations, owls have very large eardrums, columellae, and cochleae. The wide head of the owl also helps it locate its prey, since the ear openings are far enough apart to create an appreciable time difference in the arrival of a sound they receive. Owls are said by Schwartzkopff to reach at least the human

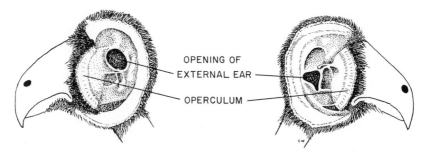

Figure 5.7. Left and right external ear openings of an owl (*Asio*), showing their marked asymmetry. After Pycraft.

difference threshold of 0.000,03 second. It is this slight time difference that tells us, for example, that a given sound is at our left instead of at our right. A bird is also able to detect the direction of a sound through the differences in intensity with which it strikes each ear. A sound coming from the left, for example, is louder in the left ear than in the right. By means of these two clues—difference in timing and difference in loudness—birds can locate sources of sounds with considerable precision. A Barn Owl, *Tyto alba*, using only its sense of hearing, can locate prey in total darkness with a deviation of only about one degree, both in the vertical and horizontal planes (Payne, 1961). Its ears are most sensitively directional with sounds above 9000 cycles per second.

As a final perfection, velvety feathers muffle the sounds of an owl's flight, so that in addition to hearing its prey very acutely, the owl makes no warning sound in swooping down for the kill.

SENSE OF SIGHT

A bird can gain more information about its surroundings through its eyes than through all its other sense organs together. An eye can detect the direction, distance, size, shape, brightness, color hue, color intensity, three-dimensional depth, and motion of an object. Combined with the other senses, sight can provide almost perfect information about one's environment. It is not surprising that natural selection

has improved on the first dim vertebrate eye, making continuous progress toward sharper acuity, color vision, three-dimensional perception, and other refinements in vision. The eye of the bird has reached a state of perfection found in no other animal.

The avian eye contains numerous legacies from its reptile ancestors, and today resembles in general the eye of living lizards. Variation in the eyes of birds is relatively slight, being no greater throughout the entire class Aves than it is within a single order or suborder of reptiles or amphibians (Walls, 1942).

Birds have enormously large eyes: hawks, eagles, and owls often have eyes actually larger than man's. Although the weight of the head in both Starlings, *Sturnus vulgaris*, and man is about one-tenth of the total body weight, the ratio of eye weight to head weight in man is less than 1 per cent; in Starlings it is about 15 per cent (Pumphrey, 1961). The value of the large size is, of course, that it provides larger and sharper images—most valuable qualities for rapidly moving animals. In shape the eyeball may be globose, or somewhat flattened in the optical axis, or, contrariwise, lengthened into a somewhat tubular form. As a rule, nocturnal birds such as owls have tubular eyes, and diurnal birds commonly have flattened or occasionally globose eyes. In most of its structures the bird's eye resembles the human eye. The eyeball is a three-layered organ with a tough scleroid coat on the outside. Toward the front this coat be-

Figure 5.8. and Figure 5.9.   A Saw-whet Owl striking and carrying off a mouse. Adaptations which enable most owls to be successful predators include a keen sense of hearing, eyes able to see in extremely dim light, and soft plumage which permits silent flight. Photos by G. R. Austing.

comes, with the overlying skin, the transparent cornea. Below the sclera comes the vascular and pigmented choroid coat, and on the inside of the eyeball, the sensitive retina which sends its impulses via the optic nerve to the brain. Just behind the cornea is the anterior chamber, filled with a clear fluid, the aqueous humor. It is followed, in the direction of the retina, by the pigmented iris, then by the crystalline lens, supported at its equator by the annular pad, or *ringwulst*, and the ciliary body. In the main body of the eyeball is

the gelatinous vitreous humor. The scleroid coat is reinforced by a circle of usually 11 to 16 small shingle-like bones, the sclerotic ring, surrounding the cornea.

The pigmented iris, containing circular and radial striated muscle fibers, controls the size of the pupil of the eye, much as a diaphragm controls the aperture of a camera lens. It shows extraordinary motility in birds, closing down the size of the pupil in bright light, and opening it in dim. The pupil is generally circular in shape but, when constricted, may be oval, slit-like as

Figure 5.9.

Figure 5.10. A Saw-whet Owl flying in the dark. Note the relatively large size of its eyes and their large pupils. Some owls are able to discern objects in dim light which is one-tenth to one-hundredth of that minimal for man. Photo by G. R. Austing.

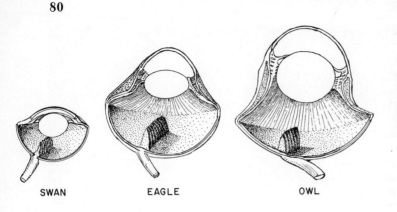

SWAN   EAGLE   OWL

Figure 5.11. Characteristic shapes of birds' eyes. Each figure represents the ventral half of the left eyeball. After Soemmering, from Walls.

in the Black Skimmer, *Rhynchops nigra,* or even square as in the King Penguin, *Aptenodytes patagonicus.* The lens is the highly refractive body in front of the vitreous chamber which, with some help from the cornea, brings rays of light to a focus on the retina. It is elastic, and when at rest its shape resembles a thick disk in diurnal birds and approaches a globe in nocturnal species.

In birds whose eyes have great power of accommodation (focusing) the lens is soft; contrariwise, it is very firm in eyes with low accommodation. The need for extensive and rapid changes in accommodation of a bird that catches insects on the wing, or of a bird that escapes its enemies by flying through trees and brush, is easily

seen. Reflecting this need, most birds have strong powers of near-and-far accommodation. Whereas a child has an accommodation of 13.5 diopters and a man aged 40 one of 6 diopters, a cormorant possesses the extreme accommodation of 40 to 50 diopters; chickens and doves, 8 to 12 diopters; and night birds such as owls, 2 to 4 diopters (Stresemann, 1927–1934). (A diopter is the reciprocal of the focal length of a lens in meters.) Owls, unable to focus their eyes on close objects, must back away from food offered them in order to fix it sharply in their eyes before they pounce. Penguins have practically no accommodation and are very near-sighted out of water (Heinroth, 1938).

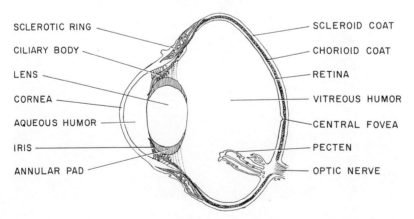

SCLEROTIC RING
CILIARY BODY
LENS
CORNEA
AQUEOUS HUMOR
IRIS
ANNULAR PAD

SCLEROID COAT
CHORIOID COAT
RETINA
VITREOUS HUMOR
CENTRAL FOVEA
PECTEN
OPTIC NERVE

Figure 5.12. A horizontal section of the eye of the European Buzzard, *Buteo buteo,* showing its major parts. After Portmann.

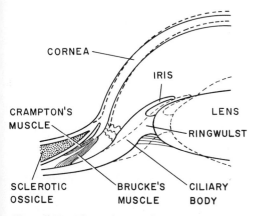

Figure 5.13. The mechanism of accommodation in a bird's eye. After Pumphrey, in Marshall.

The exact means by which the avian eye accommodates is not surely known, but there is general agreement that Brücke's muscles of the ciliary body act on the sclerotic ring and annular pad to bring pressure on the lens and thus change its shape. The action is thus different from that in the human eye, in which the ciliary muscles act to release a stretching tension on the lens, allowing the elasticity of the lens itself to determine its shape. In the case of some diving birds, such as cormorants, powerful iris muscles may squeeze the lens into a more rounded, shorter-focusing shape. On the other hand, one ring of ciliary muscles (Crampton's) in hawks and owls acts instead on the cornea to change its curvature and hence the focus of the eye. Still other

mechanisms may be employed in eye accommodation in birds. The third eyelid, or nictitans, in diving ducks, loons, and auks has in its center a clear lens-shaped window of high refractive index that serves the bird under water as a "contact lens" (Walls, 1942). An ingenious adaptation is seen in the machinery on the back of the eyeball which activates this third lid. The highly elastic nictitans is stretched across a bird's eye by means of a greatly lengthened tendon which circles the eyeball to the rear, passes through a sling in another muscle, the quadratus (which holds the tendon away from the optic nerve), and originates in the pyramidalis muscle which, with the quadratus, does the pulling. The inner surface of the nictitating membrane is covered with epithelial cells which possess brush-like processes, so that the cornea is *brushed* with tears at every flick of this thin, transparent lid. In addition the nictitans has on its margin a fold so slanted that it cleans the under surfaces of the eyelids on the reverse journey of each sweep, working much like a windshield wiper. The eyelids proper are generally moved by smooth muscles, hence slowly; and in most species the lids are used to close the eyes only in sleep, while the nictitans is reserved for blinking. Normally the eye is closed by raising the lower lid rather than lowering the upper lid as in man. However, in owls, parrots, toucans, wrens, and ostriches it is the upper lid that is the more movable. Owls use their upper lids to wink and

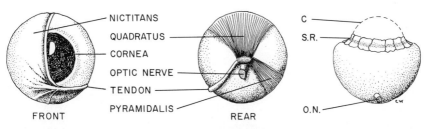

Figure 5.14. Left: Front and rear views of the eyeball of a Turkey, revealing the nictitating membrane mechanism. After Wolff, from Walls. Right: Eyeball of the Golden Eagle: *C*, cornea; *S.R.*, sclerotic ring; *O.N.*, optic nerve. After Walls.

their lower lids to close the eyes in sleep. In birds the lids expose only the cornea and none of the sclera; and since the lids follow the motions of the eyeball, they disguise the large size of the eyes.

Another feature of the bird's eye which links it to the reptiles and sets it apart from the mammals is the pecten, a pigmented, conical, highly vascularized body. It arises near the attachment of the optic nerve and juts out in the vitreous humor toward the lens. Whereas in reptiles the pecten is a simple, cone-like, vascular body, in birds it becomes an elaborate structure of thin folds richly supplied with small blood vessels (not capillaries). The folds either radiate out as spokes from a hub, or snake back and forth in accordion pleats. According to Walls (1942), over thirty theories have been proposed to explain the functions of the pecten, ranging from movement perception, light absorption, intra-ocular pressure regulation, and accommodation, to smoothing out blood pulsations in the eye and warming the eye in cold surroundings. The one function which most students consider established is the nourishment of the eye by diffusion through the vitreous body. If it has accessory functions, they must await experimental proof.

In its general pattern of construction the bird's retina is orthodox enough. From the outside (against the choroid coat) inward to the vitreous chamber it possesses the usual sequence of layers: pigment epithelium, sensory receptor layer (rods and cones), outer nuclear layer, inner nuclear layer, ganglion layer, and nerve fiber layer. The explanation of the perfection

of the avian retina lies in the abundance and distribution of these parts. Not only are the rods and cones more numerous and tightly packed than in other vertebrates, but the precisely layered conductive cells are also unusually abundant— so much so that the whole retina is from one-and-one-half to two times as thick as it is in most vertebrates (Walls, 1942). Just as the sharpness or resolving power of a photograph depends on the number and fineness of the silver grains that compose it, so the resolving power of a retina depends largely on the number and size of its sensory cells.

As in man, the point of sharpest vision, or highest resolution, is the fovea, where the overlying nervous and vascular tissues are thinned away and the visual cells are packed together in a funnel-shaped pit. Since it is normally the color-perceiving cones that are grouped in the fovea rather than the more sensitive rods, the fovea loses light sensitivity as it gains resolution. Anyone can test this by looking a little to one side of an extremely faint star and then looking directly at it (i.e., fixing it on the fovea) only to have it disappear. A further increase in the acuity of foveal vision is provided by the retinal cells themselves, which have a higher index of refraction than the adjacent vitreous body. Rays of light entering the eye and striking the slanting walls of the foveal pit will therefore be bent outward, thus magnifying any image that falls on the foveal cones about 13 per cent linearly, or 30 per cent in area (Walls, 1942). Surrounding the fovea is the so-called "central area" where resolution is higher than in

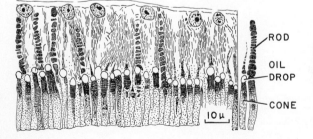

Figure 5.15. A cross-section of the rod and cone layer of the retina of the European Kestrel. In life, the oil droplets above the cones are colored yellow, orange, or red. After Rochon-Duvigneaud, from Grassé.

the remaining retina but lower than in the fovea.

Cones are more numerous than rods in the retinas of day birds, and rods more numerous than cones in night birds such as owls and goatsuckers. In the latter the rods are particularly long and thin. All birds have at least one central area, usually with a fovea, and many diurnal species, especially those that feed on the wing, have a second, temporally placed fovea, useful in binocular vision: e.g., hawks, terns, parrots, swallows, swifts, hummingbirds, and others. Terns and swallows of the genera *Sterna* and *Hirundo* have three foveae in each eye (Chievitz, *in* Stresemann, 1927–1934). Many birds have a horizontal streak or "central" area across the retina, usually with a fovea at each end. These are the hawks, eagles, swallows, ducks, terns, and many shore-birds. Such a device permits a sharp but economical scanning of the horizon without eye or neck movements. The Domestic Hen, as a price paid for its pampered existence, has no true fovea but only a shallow central area. Its visual acuity is correspondingly poor. The myopic South African Penguin, *Spheniscus demersus*, has only a horizontal central area and no fovea. In many diurnal birds of prey, the sensory cells are more numerous in the upper hemisphere of the eye (which perceives images from the ground) than in the lower hemisphere (which views the sky). As a consequence the Goshawk, *Accipiter gentilis*, for example, when it wishes to scan the sky more sharply, inverts its head either over its back or down near its belly (Stresemann, 1927–1934).

The "eagle-eyed" sharpness of birds' vision is borne out both by experimental studies on living birds and by microscopic examination of their eyes. Several species of thrushes, finches, and other passerines were trained by Donner (1951) to discriminate between a grating pattern and a solidly gray object of the same brightness to obtain food. By using coarser and finer gratings, he was able to determine the limits of a bird's visual acuity. For these

Figure 5.16. Many hawks and eagles have more sensory cells in the upper half of each retina than in the lower. Consequently, when they wish to scan the sky, they must invert their heads, as this Goshawk is doing, to obtain the sharpest vision. Photo by R. Stabler.

passerines he found that the finest detectable bars were subtended by visual angles of from 0.33 to 3.83 minutes of arc. This compared very favorably with man's minimum visual angle of about 0.64 minute, especially when one considers the small size of the eyes in these birds. A similar study of the gamecock's eyes, which have no fovea, revealed a minimum visual angle of 4.07 minutes.

Microscopically the bird's retina is shown to have even higher acuity. Outside the foveal region, the White Wagtail, *Motacilla alba*, has 120,000 visual cells per square millimeter of retinal surface, while man, even *in* the fovea, has only 200,000. As Walls remarks, the "grand champion of all foveae" is probably that of the European Buzzard, *Buteo buteo*, which boasts 1,000,000 cones per square millimeter of fovea, which must give it a visual acuity "at least eight times that of man." Even outside its fovea this buzzard probably has an acuity twice that of the human fovea.

To carry the mosaic perceptions of the retina to the brain where they are assembled into an image requires a great number of nerve fibers. The number of nerve fibers in a cross-section of the optic nerve has been determined by Bruesch and Arey (*in* Polyak, 1957) for various vertebrates. Here again, birds show their superiority over most other vertebrates. Man has somewhat over 1,000,000 nerve fibers coursing through each of his optic nerves. Other counts are: pigeon, 988,000; canary, 428,000; chicken, 414,000; duck, 408,000; pig, 681,000; cat, 119,000; dog, 154,000; alligator, 105,000; frog, 29,000; toad, 15,-500; *Necturus maculosus*, 362; goldfish, 53,000; bullhead, 26,000; sturgeon, 13,-500; brook lamprey, 5217; hagfish, 1579.

Not only do birds' eyes exhibit high visual acuity, but some of them show superb sensitivity under weak illumination. In experiments reported by Dice (1945), three species of owls (*Strix varia, Asio otus*, and *Tyto alba*) were able "to see and approach dead prey directly from a distance of six feet or more under an illumination calculated to be as low as 0.000,-000,73 foot candle." This almost incredibly low illumination is between one-hundredth and one-tenth the minimum light intensity that man requires. Experiments indicate that at least the eye of the Tawny Owl, *Strix aluco*, is incapable of responding to infrared radiation, so it is unlikely that owls "see" their prey by the heat they radiate.

Another adaptation which undoubtedly sharpens a bird's sight is the presence in many of its cones of colored oil droplets, one droplet to a cone. Diurnal birds typically possess red, orange, yellow, colorless, and, rarely, green oil droplets. Birds that are crepuscular or nocturnal have mostly colorless or pale yellow droplets. These colored droplets aid vision in at least two ways. First, they heighten the contrast of colored objects in the field of view. Most birds eat small objects such as

seeds, berries, and insects which are often colored unlike their immediate surroundings. If a red insect in green foliage is scanned by a bird having red oil droplets in its cone cells, the insect will "blink on and off," like a single blinking light bulb amid hundreds of steadily glowing bulbs, as its image sweeps across cones that do or do not possess red oil droplets. Secondly, the oil droplets may act as haze-piercing camera filters do, by holding back some of the glaring short wavelengths of light and allowing more of the longer waves to stimulate the retina. Since light is scattered by the molecules of water and gases in the atmosphere inversely as the fourth power of the wavelength, blue light is scattered the most and red the least; this is the Rayleigh Effect. By adopting a checkerboard sort of red filter, birds are probably able to see farther in hazy weather. It may not be merely a coincidence that early rising birds, such as most passerines and fowls, possess the greatest number of red oil droplets. The oil droplets probably have very little to do with color vision, but one cannot be sure. Much remains to be learned about them.

Diurnal birds are well supplied with retinal cones, and all diurnal birds that have been tested possess color vision. Chickens, pigeons, and thrushes are able to discriminate colors throughout the range of the visible spectrum. A pigeon can distinguish as many as 20 different hues while man can discriminate 160; but as Walls says, "the bird's real capacity in this regard is concealed, in any training technique, by its low intelligence." In some situations the pigeon was able to make finer color discriminations than a man. Rather surprisingly, even the Little Owl, *Athene noctua*, is able to distinguish red, yellow, green, and blue colors (Meijknecht, 1941).

The position of the eyes in a bird's head shows close correlation with its life habits. Inoffensive vegetarians, such as ducks, quail, and doves, have eyes laterally placed where they view possible enemies coming from any quarter. Hawks and other predators, intent on their next meal, have eyes directed more toward the front. Swifts and swallows, expert insect chasers, also have frontally directed eyes; they rely on their magnificent skill in flight to escape their enemies. Owls nearly match man with their frontal eyes, but unlike man's their eyes are almost immovably locked in their sockets. In compensation for this rigidity, they have flexible necks which allow them to twist their heads through at least 270 degrees. It seems likely that reflex compensatory movements, which in other animals are associated with the eyes, have spilled over into neck movements in some birds.

Birds sometimes reflect their special habits in their eye placement. The bittern, which feeds in shallow water, has eyes placed low in the head, so that they not only facilitate downward looking but also direct their sight at an intruder when the bird "freezes" with its head pointed skyward. The mud-probing Woodcock, *Philohela minor,* has its eyes shifted upward and backward to a position effective for preventing surprise attacks. Because of the location of its eyes, the Woodcock has more effective binocular vision of objects to the rear than of objects in front of it! Goatsuckers, cuckoos, and some crows may also converge their eyes toward the rear when disturbed by an object approaching from that direction.

The total field of view embraced by a bird's eyes depends on three things: the placement of the eyes, their mobility, and the angle of view that each eye subtends. Pigeons with their laterally disposed eyes (aided by plumage sleeked against the head to the rear) have a total field of view of about 340 degrees. In other words, they can see almost everything in the environment except the space occupied by their own bodies. Owls with their frontal eyes have a total field of 60 to 70 degrees. This optic parsimony is due to overlapping fields of the two eyes and also to the rigidly fixed and narrow fields of each individual eye.

When a hawk or a sparrow fixes an item of food before it with both eyes, the natural assumption is that the bird sees it in stereoscopic, three-dimensional vision as we do. There is no guarantee that this is a fact. There are, as Walls (1942) makes clear, numerous clues to distance perception that are available to any bird: size of retinal image—the larger the image, the closer the object; perspective, or the tapering shape of the object; overlap and shadow—near objects hide far objects; vertical nearness to the horizon; aerial perspective—hazy objects are more distant;

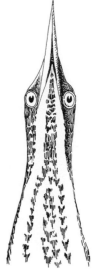

Figure 5.17. Left: Front and rear views of a Yellow-billed Cuckoo, a species able to converge its eyes on objects either in front of or behind its head. After Polyak. Right: a bittern's head viewed from below, showing its downward-facing eyes. After Berlioz, in Grassé.

and parallax, or change in the apparent angular movement of an object produced by lateral movement of the observer's eye.

One anatomical fact persuades some students that birds do not possess binocular stereoscopic vision. All of the nerve fibers of each eye, with very minor exceptions, pass directly across the optic chiasma to the opposite side of the brain. That is, the nerve fibers from one eye do not supply both sides of the brain, as in man, but only one. However, true binocular vision may not depend entirely on this interchange of fibers in the optic chiasma; the two sides of the brain may "compare notes" from the two eyes at higher internal levels and thus gain perceptions of depth or distance.

It is significant that those birds which most need and practice binocular vision (hawks, hummingbirds, swifts, swallows, and others) have a second, temporally-placed fovea in each eye. There is good reason to believe that, with the bird's eyes converged nasally, the two images of a single object focused on these foveae fuse in the brain and produce a true stereoscopic image. Even a bird like the pigeon with eyes directed sideward may have an overlap of the two individual eye-fields of from 6 to 25 degrees. The Kestrel, *Falco tinnunculus*, which has a 150 degree field of view for each eye, has a binocular overlap of 50 degrees. It is possible that some birds

—for example, penguins and hornbills— may have no binocular overlap whatever. However, most birds are capable of binocular fixation of an object before them and undoubtedly gain a good idea of its distance away by unconscious inference from any clues available to them. Their precisely oriented behavior admits no other interpretation.

Newly hatched chicks of the Domestic Fowl, *Gallus gallus*, were shown by Hess (1956) to possess innate stereoscopic depth perception. He fitted one-day-old chicks, which had had no previous visual experience, with prism goggles that displaced objects 7 degrees to the right. When these chicks were allowed to peck at a brass nail-head embedded in modelling clay, the marks of their pecks were scattered about the nail, but centered at a point 7 degrees to its right. Similarly scattered marks of the control chicks centered on the target. Tested again at three and four days of age, the control chicks showed increased accuracy: their pecks were less scattered about the nail. The pecks of the prism-wearing chicks were "clustered just as tightly as those of the controls," but were still displaced to the right as much as before. Similar experiments with prism goggles and food suspended in mid-air proved that newly hatched chicks rely on binocular vision for perceiving three-dimensional depth.

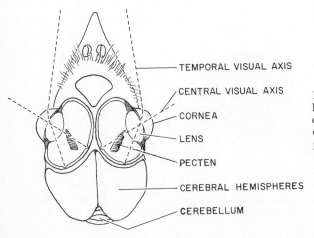

TEMPORAL VISUAL AXIS

CENTRAL VISUAL AXIS

CORNEA

LENS

PECTEN

CEREBRAL HEMISPHERES

CEREBELLUM

Figure 5.18. A horizontal section through the head of a Barn Swallow. With a slight convergence of the eyes toward the beak, a single object in front of the bird may be binocularly focused on the temporal foveae. After Polyak.

One further adaptation in the eye's structure that promotes binocular use is its twisted asymmetry. Both the cornea and lens of most birds' eyes are displaced toward the beak so that a ray of light passing through the pupil falls on the retina temporally rather than in its center. This modification reduces the amount of beakward rotation of each eye that is required to cause rays of light from a single object to focus simultaneously on the two temporal foveae. In other words, the eyes need not "toe in" so far to produce binocular fixation.

Even so, many birds very clearly use monocular vision in determining distances. This is the reason many shorebirds such as sandpipers bob their heads vertically. Raising and lowering the head quickly causes the object viewed to shift its relative position against the horizon, which enables the bird to judge its distance. Other birds practice optical fixation or "parallactic localization" of objects by similar means. Coots, *Fulica americana*, while swimming, and fowls, pigeons, and other ground-dwellers while walking, make rapid movements of the head forward and backward, apparently for object localization. In these birds the backward movement of the head normally compensates precisely for the forward movement of the body, so that, with regard to the immediate surroundings, the head occupies a series of fixed stations from which it may not only take unconscious triangulations of neighboring objects, but, while standing still, may detect more readily any moving object in the landscape. A steady eye can detect a moving fragment in the visible field much more easily than can a moving eye which causes the whole field to move also. This is no doubt the reason why a bird perching on a moving twig or telephone wire commonly holds its head in a precisely fixed spot even though its body may oscillate several centimeters with the branch. Above all, the eye of the bird must be sensitive to movement of any object in its surroundings, because moving objects mean either danger or food, and both are crucial in survival.

Even owls with their frontal eyes practice parallactic localization. Barn Owls, *Tyto alba*, and Tawny Owls, *Strix aluco*, frequently make oscillating horizontal movements of the head when intently observing an object. The Little Owl, *Athene noctua*, makes vertical movements, and still other owls reinforce their depth perception by rotating their heads in rapid vertical circles. These adaptations are quite logical when one considers the poor retinal acuity and limited accommodation found in owls.

Much experimental work remains to be done to solve some of the problems of acuity, sensitivity, color vision, and depth perception in birds. But from all the evidence at present available, one can at least be certain that birds are equipped with superb eyesight.

SUGGESTED READINGS

For a lucid and reliable treatment of the evolutionary relationships of the nervous system and sense organs of birds, see Romer's *The Vertebrate Body*. Excellent and comprehensive works, but in foreign tongues, are Stresemann's volume on *Aves* in Kükenthal and Krumbach's *Handbuch der Zoologie*, and Portmann's chapters on the nervous system and sense organs in Grassé, *Traité de Zoologie*. A brief but good discussion of sense organs is found in Wallace's *An Introduction to Ornithology*, and one in a more popular vein in Allen's *Birds and Their Attributes*. That sprightly classic on the eye, Wall's *The Vertebrate Eye*, is meaty, authentic, and has many references to birds. Polyak's *The Vertebrate Visual System* emphasizes anatomy and neurology but has much general information, some of it on birds. Much recent material on the nervous system and the sense organs will be found in the chapters by Portmann, Stingelin and Pumphrey in Marshall's *Biology and Comparative Physiology of Birds*.

SIX

Food and Digestion

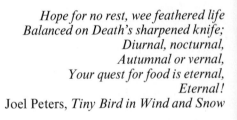

*Hope for no rest, wee feathered life
Balanced on Death's sharpened knife;
Diurnal, nocturnal,
Autumnal or vernal,
Your quest for food is eternal,
Eternal!*
Joel Peters, *Tiny Bird in Wind and Snow*

Two urges dominate nearly all the waking activities of a bird: hunger and love—self preservation and race preservation. These mainsprings of behavior are centered in the digestive and reproductive systems, although their workings are of course under nervous and endocrine control. As creatures with intense metabolism, birds require rapid, powerful, and efficient digestion of food. Although their digestive systems are basically similar in structure and function to those of reptiles and mam-

mals, they show numerous adaptations and refinements that support their special needs.

ANATOMY OF THE DIGESTIVE TRACT

While many birds possess a generalized type of digestive system capable of processing a mixed diet, most birds have digestive tracts adapted either to a plant or to an animal diet; this adaptation is evident throughout the entire alimentary canal. More detailed adaptations have also developed with specific feeding habits.

Starting where the food starts, with the beak, the correlation of food and food-handling machinery is obvious in many species. The main duties of the beak are to expose, seize, kill, and prepare food for swallowing. In birds of prey, the beak is a sharp-edged meat hook; in seed-eaters, a nibbling, crushing forceps; in shorebirds, a long, delicate probe; and in woodpeckers, a heavy, blunt pick. A multitude of adaptations to feeding habits have molded the bird's beak, showing that, adaptively, it is one of the more plastic parts of the alimentary system. In certain groups, such as birds of prey and gallinaceous birds, the beak shows great uniformity, while in others, such as the larks and ground finches (*Geospiza*), it does not. In only a few species does the beak vary between the sexes, but in the extinct Huias, *Heteralocha acutirostris*, of New Zealand, the bill was long and sickle-shaped in the female, short and conical in the male. The male used its stouter bill to dig holes in dead wood which the female then probed for wood-boring grubs.

The mouth or buccal cavity is generally roofed with a hard palate. Among seed-eaters the soft parts of the mouth are well supplied with relatively small mucous glands; but in aquatic species the glands are commonly scanty and may even be absent, as in the pelicans. For birds eating dry foods, the mucus moistens and lubricates the food to be swallowed. Salivary glands are usually present in the pharynx, and in seed-eaters are not only abundant but secrete a starch-digesting enzyme. In many swifts and swallows the dried saliva is used to cement their nests. The so-called Edible Swiftlet, *Collocalia*, of the East Indies, builds its nest entirely of dried saliva. Sometimes as many as three and a half million nests are shipped from Borneo to China in one year to be made into that well known delicacy, birds' nest soup. The glands of these swifts enlarge greatly during the nest-building season and atrophy

to the usual size immediately after. The same thing occurs, according to Stresemann (1927–1934), in the European House Martin, *Delichon urbica*, which builds its nest of mud mixed with saliva. Its salivary glands are two times as large during the nest-building period as later in the summer. The European Green Woodpecker, *Picus viridis*, has an unusually large salivary gland, seven centimeters long, which is in two sections, one of which secretes a watery solution, the other a sticky solution which coats the remarkably long, protrusible tongue with an insect-holding film. The large salivary glands of the Yellow-shafted Flicker, *Colaptes auratus*, are thought to function in neutralizing the formic acid of the numerous ants it eats.

Typically, the tongue of a bird is small, covered with a cornified epithelium, sharply pointed in front and supplied with papillae at the rear. In many species the tongue is very muscular and is used in manipulating food, but in fish-eaters, which swallow their prey entire, the tongue is greatly reduced. In the large pelican, for instance, it is a mere vestige about a centimeter long. Such fish-eaters as possess a respectable tongue use it primarily for closing the air passages in the mouth while holding prey under water. Because so many birds bolt their food quickly, their tongues and mouths are poorly supplied with taste endings. However, it is probable that all birds can taste foods, at least to a limited extent. Touch endings, on the contrary, are found widely distributed in the tongues and mouth parts of many birds. The tips of finches' and woodpeckers' tongues are thickly packed with tactile corpuscles. The beaks of parrots are also well supplied with them, a fact which becomes significant in the light of their "nose-rubbing" courtship ceremonies. In swallows the touch endings occur both inside and outside the beak tip, an appropriate distribution for catching insects on the wing.

The bills of ducks and geese are richly supplied, especially at the edges and tips, with tactile endings. According to Stresemann, these endings are grouped into peg-shaped sensory papillae, about 15 touch endings in a very restricted area. Each papilla contains Grandry corpuscles in its distal half and only Herbst corpuscles in the proximal half. Touch endings occur not only in the papillae, but are also scattered individually in the dermis of the beak, particularly along the edge of the palate, where as many as 27 per square millimeter have been counted in the Mallard, *Anas platyrhynchos*. This compares with 23 touch corpuscles per square millimeter in the most sensitive part of man's index finger. In the palatal epithelium of a duck's mouth there are about 18 Herbst and 14 Grandry corpuscles per square millimeter, or a total of about 6850 and 6300 respectively in the entire membrane (Stresemann, 1927–1934).

The esophagus, extending from the pharynx to the stomach, is usually provided with mucous glands and is somewhat muscular. Its size is related to the size of the food particles a species swallows. Insect-eaters, and species which break up their food before swallowing it, have narrow tubes, while species which swallow large items have a wide, distensible esophagus. Unlike mammals, birds seem to suffer no discomfort if food remains lodged in the esophagus. Many sea birds swallow fish so large that the birds go around for hours with the fish heads in their stomachs and the fish tails projecting from their mouths.

In many species the esophagus becomes enlarged into a storage chamber, the crop, where food remains until the stomach can accommodate it. The crop is usually located over the furcula and widens into a spindle-shaped or globular sac. In pigeons it becomes a large double sac which not only stores grain, but also secretes "pigeon's milk" for feeding the young squabs. In species that swallow insects alive and squirming, the esophagus and crop are frequently lined with a heavy epithelium which protects them against physical or chemical damage. Crops are generally prominent in grain-eaters, such

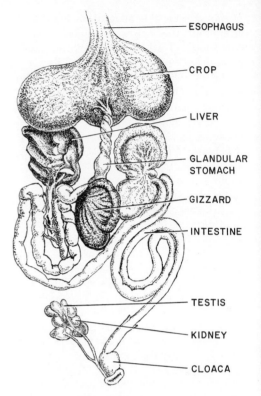

Figure 6.1. The digestive tract of a pigeon. After Schimkewitsch and Stresemann.

as game birds and pigeons. Their great virtue is that they permit their owners to gather and swallow food in a hurry, thus shortening their exposure to enemies while so occupied. Crops also permit hard seeds to be softened with mucus before further digestion in the stomach and intestines. No digestive glands are known to exist in the walls of the crop.

All birds possess two kinds of stomach: an anterior glandular stomach and a posterior muscular stomach or gizzard. The spindle-shaped glandular stomach is an innovation with birds, since only the muscular gizzard is found in reptiles. The inside of the glandular stomach is lined with columnar epithelial cells, the mucosa layer, richly supplied with tubular mucous glands. The layer next to this one, the submucosa, is the thickest layer of the stomach and is made up almost entirely of digestive glands. These are tubular glands, either simple or branched, and they secrete a peptic enzyme that attacks protein foods. The secretion is also highly acid and is able, in many flesh-eating species, to dissolve large bones.

Those species of birds which have efficient glandular stomachs, such as loons, pelicans, cormorants, gannets, owls, and accipiters, generally have weak, thin-walled muscular stomachs. It is mainly the herbivores that have powerful muscular stomachs: above all the seed-eaters, such as the pigeons, gallinaceous birds, and finches, although birds that eat molluscs and crustaceans in their shells may also have strong gizzards.

The gizzard is shaped something like a thick bi-convex lens, with striated muscles usually arranged in distinct bands. The mucous epithelium which lines the gizzard secretes a keratinous fluid that hardens into horny plates or ridges serving as millstones for the mechanical grinding of food. This work is furthered by the abrasive action of small bits of grit that many birds swallow, especially the grain-eaters. In time the grit eaten by a bird is worn away and must be replaced. There is evidence that if some grain-eaters are denied grit they will lose weight and eventually die. But experiments on Bobwhite Quail, *Colinus virginianus*, by Nestler (1946) showed that young and also adult breeding quail on a gritless diet survived as well as birds having grit. The gizzard of a domestic goose holds about 30 grams of grit; a duck, 10 grams; and a turkey, 45 grams. Gizzard stones associated with the fossil bones of Moas indicate that they carried as much as 2.3 kilograms of grit in their gizzards. Many petrels and penguins carry gizzard stones, but since they are fish-eaters and do not have very muscular gizzards, their function is problematical. Whalers claim that the penguins use the stones as ballast.

For many carnivorous species the gizzard is a trap that prevents sharp bones and indigestible fragments from proceeding down the alimentary canal. Such resistant items as teeth, feathers, fur, cellulose, or chitin may be rolled up into an elongated "pellet" and regurgitated by mouth. This is a normal occurrence in owls, accipiter hawks, gulls, goatsuckers, swifts, and grouse. The study of a bird's pellets tells much about its diet. The ability to regurgitate is sometimes put to other uses. Boobies and other sea birds often eat so many fish that they must disgorge some of them in order to take off in flight. And of course, many species regurgitate food that they have collected into the mouths of their young. Grebes are known to pluck their own feathers and eat enough of them to fill their stomachs. It is thought that these feathers either protect the stomach walls against sharp fish bones or plug the pyloric outlet of the stomach long enough for the fish bones to be dissolved before passing on into the intestine. The stomach exit in the Anhinga is covered with a grating of hair-like fibers whose function apparently is to prevent the passage of undissolved fish bones.

The two-lobed liver in birds is the largest gland in the body, and is larger than the liver in mammals of equal size. It seems to have the same functions as in mammals: primarily to store excess sugars, make bile, and excrete waste products from the blood. It is somewhat larger in fish- and insect-eaters than in meat- and grain-eaters. The pancreas likewise is relatively large in birds, and is larger in fish-, insect-, and grain-eaters than in meat-eating species. It secretes digestive enzymes that attack all three types of foods: fats, carbohydrates, and proteins.

The intestine is the chief organ of digestion and absorption of foods. In birds it is not sharply differentiated into regions as in mammals, but the tube is more or less looped or coiled between the muscular stomach and cloaca. As a rule, the intestine in meat- and fruit-eating birds is short, thin-walled, and broad; that of seed-eaters is long; that of fish-eaters relatively long, thin-walled, and of small diameter (Stresemann, 1927–1934). Among related species, larger birds have a relatively longer intestine than smaller species. This is true because, as solid objects become larger, their volume increases more rapidly than their superficial area.

If the linear dimensions of any object (whether cube, cylinder, sphere, or irregular form) are doubled, its surface area increases four times but its volume increases eight times. It is the mucous epithelium lining the inner surface of the intestine that absorbs the digested food needed for body growth and energy. If the intestine of a small bird is efficiently proportioned to its needs, a simple doubling of its length and diameter will not suffice for a bird twice its size, since the amount of absorbing epithelial surface does not increase as rapidly as the contents of the intestine. Hence, the originally efficient ratio of surface to volume is lost. This is the reason why the intestines of larger birds are proportionately narrower but longer than those of related smaller birds. In this way, more absorbing surface is provided. The absorbing surface is further greatly increased by the growth of hundreds of thousands of microscopic finger-like villi, which project inward toward the lumen from the mucous layer.

Similar adjustments in surface-volume ratios may be seen throughout the animal body. It is for this purpose of providing more surface on which digestive enzymes may act that beaks and gizzards break food into small particles. It is for similar reasons that capillaries, lung tubes, and even cells are very small. Inversely, this surface-volume relation helps us to understand why birds in cold climates are larger than their tropical relatives.

Toward the posterior end of the intestine, at the spot where, in mammals, the small intestine joins the large, there occur in many birds a pair of dead-end sacs or tubes, the caeca. In the more primitive species of birds the caeca are very large, particularly in the Galliformes. In grouse their combined lengths may equal that of the intestine, while in woodpeckers, parrots, swifts, passerines, and certain other groups, they are very small and may even be completely lacking, or converted into a patch of lymphatic tissue. The chief function of the caeca seems to be the absorption of water and digested proteins, and particularly the bacterial decomposition of crude fibrous foods. In many species the caecal wall is arranged in spiral ridges, which increase the area of its absorptive surface. The indigestible residue

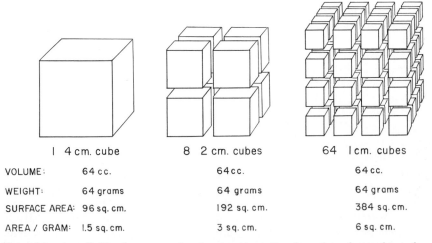

	1 4 cm. cube	8 2 cm. cubes	64 1 cm. cubes
VOLUME:	64 cc.	64 cc.	64 cc.
WEIGHT:	64 grams	64 grams	64 grams
SURFACE AREA:	96 sq. cm.	192 sq. cm.	384 sq. cm.
AREA / GRAM:	1.5 sq. cm.	3 sq. cm.	6 sq. cm.

Figure 6.2.   A small object has more surface in proportion to its volume than a larger object of similar shape. This simple geometric relationship is of great biological importance.

from the caeca is dark and moist, and is discharged independently of the whitish, drier intestinal feces. In the Domestic Hen there is one caecal discharge for about every ten intestinal defecations.

At the posterior end of the intestinal canal is the cloaca. It is divided by annular ridges into three regions. The anterior one, the coprodaeum, receives the excrement from the intestines; the middle urodaeum receives the discharges of the kidneys through the ureters, and of the genital organs through the vas deferens or oviduct; and the terminal proctodaeum stores the excrement. This last chamber is the largest of the three and it is supplied with powerful ejection muscles. On its dorsal wall is the bursa Fabricii, a lymphatic pocket prominent in young birds but generally atrophied in adults. It may have a thymus-like function in relation to sexual development, or it may be the site of white corpuscle manufacture. The cloaca is closed posteriorly by a horizontal opening, the muscular anus.

DIGESTION

Birds not only eat foods rich in energy and cell building materials, but they digest them more quickly and more completely than most animals do. As the food is taken into the mouth it is usually torn, cut, nibbled, or ground into small particles, moistened by the saliva and mucus, and swallowed. In some species, such as owls and many sea birds, the prey is swallowed entire, and the glandular stomach takes on the chemical job of dissolving its edible portions. In those species that possess a crop, the food remains there a variable time and becomes softened while waiting to enter the stomach. The crop is more an organ of storage than of digestion, but it is likely that a small amount of digestion of carbohydrates by saliva may take place there in birds, such as finches, which have large salivary glands.

It is primarily in the stomach that digestion begins. Here the gastric glands of the glandular stomach secrete a strong peptic enzyme and hydrochloric acid, which together attack proteins and break them down into peptones and proteoses. The stomach in which this digestion occurs has a high acidity: pH 2 to 3.5. In the Bearded Vulture or Lammergeier, *Gypaëtus barbatus*, of Mediterranean regions, an entire cow vertebra may be swallowed and digested in a day or two. Domestic Chickens with hyperacid gastric juice may develop stomach ulcers.

The grit in the gizzards of seed-eaters may not be indispensible but, at least in the Domestic Chicken, it increases the digestibility of whole grains and seeds by ten per cent. Rhythmic contractions of the muscular gizzard vary according to the quantity and hardness of the grain and grit inside. In the Domestic Hen, contractions vary between 1.5 and 3 per minute (Sturkie, 1954). The muscles of the gizzard are innervated with autonomic nerves, and, like the heart, will continue their contractions even when the stomach is removed from the body, because the gizzard has its own nerve net.

Considerable force is generated by the kneading walls of the gizzard. Experiments by Mangold (1929) and others revealed the following internal gizzard pressures, expressed in millimeters of mercury: buzzard (with weak carnivore gizzard), 8 to 26 mm.; hen, 100 to 150 mm.; duck, 180 mm.; goose, 265 to 280 mm.

Some early experiments by Réaumur in 1752 and Spallanzani in 1783 have been reported by Stresemann (1934). Réaumur found that a tube of sheet iron that could only be dented under a load of 36 kilograms (80 lbs.) was flattened and partly rolled up after being in the stomach of a Turkey, *Meleagris gallopavo*, for 24 hours. A Turkey will grind up in its gizzard 24 English walnuts in the shell in 4 hours. Even more striking are the results of Spallanzani's experiments. He found that a Turkey could grind to pieces 12 steel needles in 36 hours, and 16 surgical lancets in 16 hours!

As the food leaves the stomach and

Figure 6.3. A Turkey gizzard can exert powerful mechanical forces. Top row: At left, a thick-shelled pecan; and at right, a pecan broken after one hour in a Turkey's gizzard. Bottom row: At left, a hickory nut beginning to crack after 8 hours in the gizzard; and at right, a broken nut after 31 hours. Experimental pressures required to break similar hickory nuts varied from 56 to 152 kilograms (124 to 336 pounds). After Schorger.

passes into the intestine, it is mixed with digestive juices from the liver and pancreas, and possibly with juices from the walls of the intestine itself. Bile from the liver probably acts to neutralize the acid from the stomach and to emulsify fats in preparation for further digestion. The pancreatic juices probably digest all three classes of food, but precise work on their nature and action remains to be done. Once the food is digested, it is absorbed by the epithelial lining of the intestine, passed on into the blood stream, and distributed through the body. The crude fibers, digested with the help of bacteria in the caeca, are broken down in varying degrees, corn and wheat fibers being several times more digestible than oat or barley fibers. If the caeca of a hen are removed surgically, the percentage of corn fibers it can digest drops from about 17 per cent to zero; of oat fibers, from about 9 per cent to 1.3 per cent (Sturkie).

The high efficiency of avian digestion is shown in the relatively small amount of excrement they discharge. But this, too, is variable; birds such as grouse, which live part of the year on a low grade diet, discharge a greater amount of feces than meat-eaters. A better indication of the efficiency of digestion is the fact that growing young birds, such as storks, can gain one-sixth of a kilogram of weight each day from eating one-half kilogram of fishes and frogs (Heinroth, 1938). An extremely efficient conversion of food into body tissues is seen in the developing embryo. The weight at hatching of a Golden Eagle, *Aquila chrysaëtos*, was reported by Bent (1937) to be 73 per cent that of the egg.

The powerful action of a bird's digestive juices is seen in the speed with which foods are digested. Although a Domestic Hen requires 12 to 24 hours to digest a cropful of grain, a shrike can digest a mouse in three hours. Watery fruits pass through the alimentary canal very quickly: the seeds of berries eaten by young waxwings appear in their feces in as little as 16 minutes, and a thrush fed fruits of the elderberry will defecate the seeds 30 minutes later.

FOOD AND FEEDING HABITS

Birds show varying degrees of adaptation to the foods they eat. Some species, like the omnivorous crow, show no great specialization for any particular food; others, like the hummingbird, are highly adapted to their particular diet. The basic feeding adaptations of any species lie in such fundamentals as method and speed of locomotion; acuteness of sense organs; psychological bent; diurnal or nocturnal activity; character of beak and tongue; shape and strength of feet; type of plumage; physiological tolerance of such things as high and low temperatures, wet and dry habitats; and tolerance thresholds for certain food ingredients such as toxins, acids, salt, and roughage.

Birds are often said to be selective in their diets, but it must be remembered that they do not all enjoy the "a la carte" free choice that man does in a restaurant.

Natural selection through the years has greatly narrowed the menu for many birds so that they are compelled by their adaptations to dine "table d'hôte." Aesop's fable of the fox and the stork inviting each other in turn to dine out of unsuitable dinnerware illustrates the point.

One need only think of the absurdity of a woodcock attacking a rabbit, or a penguin hammering a dead limb for beetle grubs, to realize how limited many species are in their selection of food. It is undoubtedly true that most species have some freedom of choice in the food they eat, but it is also highly probable that what appears to be discriminating choice of preferred foods is actually a rigidly restricted diet imposed on the bird by structural or functional limitations or requirements. Specialization in one direction invariably closes doors toward adaptations in other directions. Even psychological limitations may in part prescribe a bird's diet. At the waterfront in Guayaquil, Ecuador, there was a slaughterhouse that dumped offal at the edge of the stream so that part of it fell in the water and part on land. The diners at this robust banquet were a marine and a terrestrial species which Murphy (1936) describes thus: "Here one can watch a completely amicable division of spoils between the Man-o'-war Birds [*Fregata magnificens*], and the Black Vultures [*Coragyps atratus*], for the latter ignore all the tidbits afloat as completely as the Man-o'-war Birds disregard whatever drops ashore." And yet, the Man-o'-war Birds pick sticks off the ground to build their nests!

Availability of food can play an important role in the diet of a species that enjoys some flexibility in food choice. In England, a normally insectivorous wren, *Troglodytes troglodytes*, which nested near a trout hatchery, fed its young largely or entirely on just-hatched young trout (Huxley, 1949). In southern Texas, six Peregrine Falcons, *Falco peregrinus*, preyed on a large colony of Mexican Free-tailed Bats, *Tardida mexicana*, although their diet is normally composed of pigeons,

ducks, passerines, and other birds (Stager, 1941). Analysis of regurgitated pellets and of food brought to nestlings of the Red-tailed Hawk, *Buteo jamaicensis*, in California showed an 18-fold increase in the consumption of young ground squirrels when they came out of their burrows in the spring. In areas where ground squirrels were reduced in numbers, reptiles were substituted in the diet, constituting 46 per cent of the bird's food (Fitch *et al.*, 1946). Great Blue Herons, *Ardea herodias*, sometimes dine on such exotic foods as young coots, young muskrats, domestic kittens, and pocket gophers (Wetmore, 1931). Occasionally the available food is quite unsatisfactory. The adult Ring-billed Gulls, *Larus delawarensis*, of one Atlantic coast colony ordinarily fed fish to their young, but when these failed they fed them berries and the young soon died (Lewis, 1941).

When a species becomes so adapted to its diet that it is restricted to a very few food items, or even a single one, it is said to be *stenophagous*. On the other hand, when it eats a wide variety of foods it is described as *euryphagous*. The Everglade Kite, *Rostrhamus sociabilis*, of Florida feeds exclusively on freshwater snails, which it extracts from their shells with its peculiarly hooked beak. The diet of the American Woodcock, *Philohela minor*, is said to be 86 per cent earthworms. An examination of 1500 crops of the Red Grouse, *Lagopus scoticus*, revealed that 77.5 per cent of its food was vegetable and 22.5 per cent animal; and that of the vegetable food, 94 per cent was composed of the leaves, fruits, and seeds of heather (Witherby *et al.*, 1941). The American Ruffed Grouse, *Bonasa umbellus*, on the contrary, eats some 374 kinds of plants and 131 kinds of small animals (Edminster, 1947).

As a stenophagous species increases the perfection of its feeding adaptations, it reduces, or may even eliminate, competition with other species for its special food. That is, it has the restaurant all to itself. But with this considerable advantage comes a price tag. If something should happen to reduce or eliminate the staple food of a stenophagous species, its survival is immediately and drastically threatened. Eelgrass is the staple food of the Brant, *Branta bernicla*, of the Atlantic coast of North America. Between 1931 and 1933 a great blight killed over 90 per cent of the coastal eelgrass, with the predictable result that about 80 per cent of the Brant wintering along that coast disappeared (Moffit and Cottam, 1941). A euryphagous species such as the Road Runner, *Geococcyx californianus*, of the southwest, would never be subjected to such a fate. It eats scorpions, tarantulas, snakes, centipedes, mice, rats, horned toads, small birds, eggs, numerous insects, fruits, and seeds (Bent, 1940).

Stenophagy and euryphagy are relative terms. A bird may be stenophagous at a certain stage in its life history or at a certain time of year, and euryphagous at other times. Among birds with stenophagous tendencies are hawks, eagles, doves, pelicans, geese, mergansers, penguins, hummingbirds, woodpeckers, parrots, swifts, kingfishers, and many passerine species. The more euryphagous species include many shore birds, gulls, some ducks, many gallinaceous birds, herons, crows, starlings, and several passerines (Mayaud, 1950).

Seasonal changes in diet have been observed, especially among non-migratory birds. From an analysis of the remains of 38,899 animals found in about 14,000 pellets of the Barn Owl, *Tyto alba*, taken between 1932 and 1943 in Denmark, it was apparent that there was a pronounced seasonal fluctuation in mice captured. In the summer, House Mice (*Mus*) accounted for 20 per cent of the catch and Field Mice (*Apodemus*) 16 per cent, while in winter the proportions were changed to 31 per cent and 7 per cent respectively (Lange, 1948). Near Davis, California, Barn Owls concentrated on House Mice (*Mus*) and Deer Mice (*Peromyscus*) in the spring, and Gophers (*Thomomys*) and Voles (*Microtus*) in the fall and early winter (Evans

and Emlen, 1947). An analysis of 4,000 stomachs showed that the Ruffed Grouse, *Bonasa umbellus*, in the northeastern states shifts between a diet that is predominantly buds and twigs in winter and spring to one of fruits and seeds in summer and fall (Edminster, 1947). A similar study of the stomach contents of the Rook, *Corvus frugilegus*, in Hungary showed that its food was three-fourths plant and one-fourth animal in winter, and almost exactly the reverse in summer.

Changes in diet may also be forced by periods of inclement weather. European White Storks, *Ciconia ciconia*, commonly shift their attention from fish and frogs to mice in periods of drought; and Hobbies, *Falco subbuteo*, will eat larger numbers of swifts in cold wet weather than in fair weather, the lack of flying insects in poor weather resulting in weakened swifts. It may well be that changes in diet, whether forced by a deficiency of the preferred food or stimulated by a special abundance of a new food (as in good lemming years or during times of grasshopper or mouse plagues), may result in permanent changes in food habits of a species. This would be especially likely to happen among young birds that learn some of their food habits from their parents. That permanent changes in diet do occur is evident in the diet of the native American Goldfinch, *Spinus tristis*, whose preferred foods are now the seeds of the Canada Thistle and Dandelion, both of which are introduced weeds that were not available to it before the settlement of North America by Europeans. It is certain that many species exhibit different diets in different geographic or ecological habitats. The Great Gray Shrike, *Lanius excubitor*, of Europe seems to feed largely on birds in Scandinavia; on insects, spiders, lizards, and shrews in Spain; and primarily on insects in desert regions. Of the six most important foods of the Ruffed Grouse in northern Ohio, only two are found in the list of the top six foods for that species in southern Ohio (Gilfillan and Bezdek, 1944).

It seems very likely that diet plays a

role in the evolution of birds. While it is obvious that specific adaptations may limit a bird in the food it may eat (a hummingbird's beak is unsuitable for gnawing acorns), it is probably no less true that the long-established diet of a species has a selective influence on the structure and function of a bird's feeding equipment. In this connection it is significant that closely related species living in the same habitat appear rarely to take the same foods in the same proportions.

The amount of food eaten by a bird depends on the species, health, age, and sex of the bird, on the season, time of day, food availability, and other factors. A study of food consumption by the birds and mammals of a 1000 hectare virgin forest in Czechoslovakia indicated that the total bird population consumed food equaling about 25 per cent of its weight daily; the mammals, 20 per cent (Turček, 1952). This fact accords well with the superior rate of metabolism in birds.

Periods of increased demands for energy or for body-building materials generally result in increased food intake. A female bird will increase its food consumption and also draw on fat reserves in the body during the egg-laying period. Experimental studies by Jordan (1953) on captive wild Mallards, *Anas platyrhynchos*, showed that in the early autumn the birds each consumed about 132 grams of grain daily, and in coldest winter about 150 grams. During fall and winter months the Mallard drakes ate about 15 per cent more food than the hens, but in the spring the hens consumed an average of 16.6 per cent more food than the drakes. Rapidly growing ducks between 8 and 9 weeks of age ate 44 per cent more food than adults —a statistic that parents with growing children will appreciate. In his experiments on a Masked Weaver, *Ploceus cucullatus*, weighing 40 grams, Schildmacher (1929) found that the bird ate 20 per cent of its body weight daily in an air temperature of 18° C., 25 per cent at 9° C., and 28 per cent at 7° C.

The surface-volume relationship referred to earlier imposes a heavy metabolic penalty on small warm-blooded animals. Small birds have relatively more heat-losing surface than large ones. A hummingbird is, in a sense, one fragment of an ostrich cut into 64,000 pieces, where every slice that is made creates more heat-radiating surface without adding a gram of heat-manufacturing tissue. Looking at it another way, an ostrich is nothing but a great heap of hummingbirds huddling together to keep warm. As a consequence, small species must eat relatively more food than large ones to make up their extra heat loss. Some examples of this relationship are seen in the figures in the adjoining table, taken from a survey by Nice (1938). The "weight of food" column gives the dry weight of the food eaten daily as a percentage of the bird's body weight.

The volume of food eaten per day will vary with the type of food. Watery ber-

Table 6.1. Bird Weights and Daily Food Consumption

SPECIES		WEIGHT OF BIRD (GRAMS)	WEIGHT OF FOOD (PER CENT)	AUTHORITY
Blue Tit	*Parus caeruleus*	11	30.0	Rörig
European Robin	*Erithacus rubecula*	16	14.7	Groebbels
Song Thrush	*Turdus ericetorum*	89	9.8	Groebbels
Mourning Dove	*Zenaidura macroura*	100	11.2	Nice
Blackbird	*Turdus merula*	118	7.3	Groebbels
Bobwhite	*Colinus virginianus*	170	8.8	Nice
Kestrel	*Falco tinnunculus*	200	7.7	Rörig
Buzzard	*Buteo buteo*	855–900	4.5	Rörig
Domestic Fowl	*Gallus gallus*	1800	3.4	Beck

ries will naturally be consumed in greater quantity than dried seeds or insects. A 57-gram Bohemian Waxwing, *Bombycilla garrulus*, was estimated to eat about 170 grams of the berries of *Cotoneaster horizontalis* in one day (Gibb, 1951). It is possible, too, that a bird may enjoy satisfying its appetite much as does man. The ancient Romans used to prolong the joys of dining by eating an emetic mushroom, *Russula emetica*, when they had stuffed to satiety, so that they would have room to continue their banquet. The Adelie Penguin, *Pygoscelis adeliae*, is reported by Murphy (1936) to stuff itself with opossum shrimps and cephalopods until its belly is distended, and then disgorge its food "so as to enjoy another Roman banquet without brooking the tedium of digestion."

As a general rule, birds eat most heavily early in the morning and again late in the afternoon, logical times in view of the long overnight fast. But here again there is great variation among different species. Birds that feed on small seeds and insects must eat fairly regularly throughout the day; but those that take in larger items, preying on animals or carrion, may feed very irregularly, sometimes going for days without eating. However, it is ordinarily only the larger species which are able to survive a fast of several days or weeks. Probably the world record for long fasting in birds is held by the male Emperor Penguin, *Aptenodytes forsteri*, which, in midwinter in the inhospitable antarctic, fasts about 60 days during the incubation of its single egg. The average fasting periods for seven marked male and female Adelie Penguins, *Pygoscelis adeliae*, were determined by Sladen (1953) to be at least 40 days for the incubating male and 21 days for the female. The Adelie Penguin also fasts an average of 12 days during its molting period, in which time the bird loses on the average 40 per cent of its weight (Cendron, 1953).

Experimental starvation studies by Jordan (1953) on wild Mallards, *Anas platyrhynchos*, showed that the birds could live without food under cool air temperatures (average, 14° C.) for slightly over three weeks. The hens showed much greater resistance to starvation than the drakes. Of the birds that died of starvation, the drakes lost 53 per cent of their original weight; the hens, 56 per cent. Surviving males lost an average 43 per cent of their original body weight, and the females, 44 per cent. These survivors were then fed unrestricted amounts of food for 28 days, at the end of which they were all in excellent health. Similar experiments by Gerstell (1942) indicated that Ring-necked Pheasants, *Phasianus colchicus*, can live without food for two weeks or more during severe winter weather; the wild Turkey, *Meleagris gallopavo*, one week; and the Hungarian Partridge, *Perdix perdix*, four or five days. The Weaver Finch, *Estrilda angolensis*, is said to die of starvation only four or five hours after its alimentary canal is completely empty. For House Sparrows, *Passer domesticus*, denied both food and water and kept in darkened cages, it was discovered by Kendeigh (1945) that survival time was closely related to environmental temperatures.. Birds survived the longest (67.5 hours) at 29° C. Below 21° birds died from their inability to maintain sufficient heat production, and above 35° they died from lack of sufficient water for cooling by evaporation.

Since small birds have such an intensified hunger problem, it is not surprising that a few species have evolved a special atavistic adaptation to solve it. Hummingbirds living at high altitudes in the Peruvian Andes stretch their slim fuel resources through the cold night by reverting to reptilian dormancy. Their body temperature drops from a daytime high of about 38° C. to a lethargic 14° C. at night (Pearson, 1953). Without this heat-conserving adaptation, such a small bird probably could not survive the night, except in a warm nest. Nestling European Swifts, *Apus apus*, are able to survive as much as ten days of fasting by reverting to cold-bloodedness. Although the adult

Swift is unable to assume dormancy, it is nevertheless able, through other physiological economies, to survive 4.5 days of fasting. Weight losses from fasting average 52.8 per cent in the nestlings and 38 per cent in the adults (Koskimies, 1950). These adaptations in both young and adult Swifts probably arose in response to the common hazard of cold, wet spells during which flying insects, their only food, are not available. The Poor-will, *Phalaenoptilus nuttallii*, of the southwestern states, can endure several months without food by a similar dormancy, its body temperature dropping to a low 6° C. Experiments by Marshall (1955) showed that dormancy was not caused directly by low environmental temperatures but by lack of food. The birds did not become torpid until they were denied food and had lost 20 per cent of their weight. Trilling Nighthawks, *Chordeiles acutipennis*, on the contrary, became torpid while very fat. Because they are able to migrate so easily, birds have not needed to adopt hibernation to the extent that mammals have.

Very little experimental work has been done on particular dietary needs of birds, but it is known, for example, that a seed-eating Bobwhite Quail, *Colinus virginianus*, must have a minimum of 11 to 12 per cent crude protein in its winter diet to maintain good health (Nestler, 1944). Experiments by Holm and Scott (1954) on wild ducks showed that an adult's diet containing 18.6 per cent protein food allowed satisfactory egg production and hatchability, but a 17 per cent protein diet did not. Young wild ducklings developed satisfactorily on a diet of 19 per cent total proteins or 8 per cent animal protein. In an experiment on 2,170 Bobwhite chicks, it was discovered that there was a direct relationship between survival time and the level of vitamin A in the diet (Harper *et al.*, 1952). Quail chicks fed a basal diet lacking vitamin A did not survive to an age of eight weeks.

Some years ago it was discovered that 70 per cent of the wild Turkeys, *Meleagris*

gallopavo, of Missouri lived on a single type of soil, Clarksville stony loam, derived from limestone. Habitats on other soils which appeared similar supported very meager populations or none at all (Allen, 1954). Subsequent nutrition experiments by Dale (1955) have shown that Ring-necked Pheasants, *Phasianus colchicus*, receiving limestone grit produced ten times as many eggs as those eating a similar diet but with granite grit. That the problem of supplementary items in the diet is not simple was revealed in an experiment on Bobwhites in which it was found that egg production, fertility, and hatchability "were affected by the calcium and phosphorus levels in the breeding diet of *their parents* a year before" (Allen, 1954). No doubt even minute amounts of trace elements in a bird's diet play a role in its health and survival. As more information from nutrition experiments becomes available, it will very likely show that bird distribution and possibly migration habits are linked with the soils and foods characteristic of a given species.

In addition to food, vitamins, and minerals, birds must have water. Most species have no difficulty securing water; they either drink it directly or obtain it through the watery foods they eat. Birds that live in deserts may get their water requirements from insects, succulent plants, or dew. As an adaptation to flight, birds have had to economize in the use of water. They have no sweat glands and they do not excrete watery urine. The walls of the cloaca absorb most of the water from the kidneys, and the walls of the intestines absorb much of it from the feces. The main water loss in a bird comes from respiration. A Domestic Pigeon, *Columba livia*, denied both food and water, will survive as long as 11 to 13 days at moderate temperatures, but one fed dried peas and given no water died after 4 to 5 days (Stresemann, 1927–1934). The increased metabolism involved in the digestion of food eaten requires increased respiration and hence increased water loss. A goose fed 50 grams of maize lost 42 grams of water daily through respiration, but one fed 100 grams of maize lost 68 grams of water. Birds denied food obtain water internally from the decomposition of body fats and proteins—the so-called "metabolic water."

Since sea water contains about 3 per cent salt and is three times as salty as a bird's body fluids, a severe salt-balance problem exists for pelagic sea birds. Are birds, like man, unable to drink sea water and remain alive? For years this problem has been debated by ornithologists, but only recently has the solution come to light. A bird's kidneys, which excrete only 0.3 per cent salt, are less efficient than man's in eliminating salt from the blood. A bird would need to excrete ten liters of urine in order to eliminate the salt taken in by drinking one liter of sea water. Obviously some other mechanism is called for. In sea birds the nasal glands on the surface of the cranium are salt-excreting glands. Experiments by Schmidt-Nielsen (1959) proved that gulls, petrels, and other sea birds excrete from these glands fluids which contain 5 per cent salt, a fantastically high concentration considering the osmotic problem involved. In petrels the fluid is forcibly ejected through the tubular nostrils (Fig. 6.4), but in other species it dribbles out of the internal or external nostrils. A gull given one-tenth its weight in sea water excreted 90 per cent of the contained salt within three hours, by means of the nasal glands. Mallard Ducks, *Anas platyrhynchos*, living in salt water habitats have much larger salt glands than those living on fresh water. Some sea birds are so specifically adapted to drinking salt water that they will die if denied access to it (Allen, 1925). The Adelie Penguin, *Pygoscelis adeliae*, on the other hand, can change abruptly from drinking sea water to drinking nothing but fresh water or eating snow (Murphy, 1936). Although salt, even in small quantities, may be lethal to some birds, it is necessary in the diet for various metabolic processes such as nerve-impulse transmission, blood clotting, and bone formation. Birds kept on a salt-free diet will eagerly eat pure salt when it is made available.

ADAPTATIONS FOR TAKING ANIMAL FOODS

There are probably almost as many

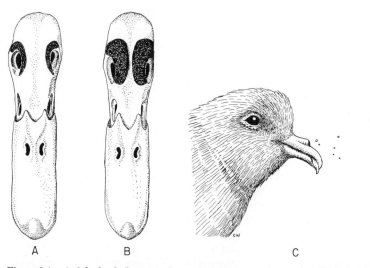

Figure 6.4. *A*, Salt glands (between the eyes) of a European race of Mallard Ducks living on fresh water are much smaller than those (*B*) of a semi-marine race living in Greenland. After Stresemann. *C*, A petrel forcibly ejecting salt droplets from its nostrils. After Schmidt-Nielsen.

Figure 6.5.   A Black Kite, Egyptian Vulture, and Griffon, ready to dine on a dead deer. The bare head and neck of the Griffon permit a more fastidious feeding on the deeper parts of the carcass. Photo by E. Hosking.

feeding adaptations, structural and functional, as there are species of birds. Only a few representative examples can be given here. Outstanding among the predominantly carnivorous birds are the diurnal predators (eagles, hawks, and falcons), and the nocturnal predators (owls). They all have strong hooked beaks and sharp powerful talons, the latter being used in grasping their prey. Where the feet have become weak, as in the vultures, the bird is compelled to feed on smaller, weaker prey, or on carrion. Owls differ from the diurnal predators in that they swallow their prey entire and digest the meat from the bones, fur, and feathers, then cast up this indigestible residue in several pellets. Owls have no crop. Eagles and hawks, on the contrary, tear their food apart, rejecting fur, feathers, and the larger indigestible parts before swallowing the nutritious parts. Because some of the food often remains, as a barrier, in the crop for a few hours, stomach pellets are not regurgitated as frequently as in owls.

Most commonly the prey of eagles and hawks is made up of smaller birds and rodents, but a few of the larger eagles concentrate on animals as large as themselves. The Harpy Eagle, *Harpyhaliaetus coronatus*, of South America feeds on sloths, peccaries, and monkeys; and the Crowned Eagle, *Stephanoaëtus coronatus*, of Africa specializes on monkeys, which it lures to their destruction with a soft whistle. A well fed, captive Long-eared Owl, *Asio otus*, will refuse to eat meat offered to it, but if it is presented live mice, it will continue to kill them (Räber, 1950). Apparently different behavior centers control killing and eating.

The rich food resources of the sea and fresh waters have been made available to fish-eating birds by a wide variety of adaptations. To hold the slippery fish, the upper mandible may be hooked at the tip as in pelicans, cormorants, frigate-birds, and albatrosses; or the edges of the mandibles may be serrated with "teeth" as in mergansers. Interesting parallel adapta-

Figure 6.6.   A Screech Owl eating a house mouse. Owls and parrots are exceptional in that their feet may be used to lift food to the beak. Note the large size of the eyes and their dark adapted pupils. Photos by G. R. Austing.

Figure 6.7.   The mouse is swallowed entire, and later the fur and bones are regurgitated in the form of cylindrical, felted pellets. Photos by G. R. Austing.

Figure 6.8. Pellets of the Saw-whet Owl are regurgitated once each day. By dissecting the pellets and studying the contained bones, beetle wing-covers, and other indigestible objects, a bird's diet can be reconstructed. Photo by G. R. Austing.

tions for the firm grasping of fish are seen in the spiny tubercles under the toes of both the fish-eating Osprey, *Pandion haliaetus,* and the fishing owls of the genus *Ketupa* which, significantly, lack the silent, downy feathers of their relatives that live on terrestrial prey. The Osprey has an enormous uropygial gland, which waterproofs its feathers.

Many fish-eating birds, such as the penguins, possess backward-slanting, horny projections on the tongue, palate, or other mouth parts that push and guide their slippery booty toward the esophagus. Some fish-eaters, like the herons and bitterns, have developed long wading legs, long mobile necks, and forceps-like beaks to seize fish and other aquatic prey. Their silent, immobile stance while awaiting a victim is a profitable behavior adaptation. Many aquatic species use their webbed feet and buoyant feathers to paddle about on the surface of the water to prospect for food. In their manner of foraging, the ducks fit into two categories: the surface-feeders which "tip up" to feed on small aquatic life, and the divers which plunge under the surface completely. These latter usually feed only a meter or two deep, but some Old Squaw Ducks, *Clangula hyemalis,* have been caught in fish nets set over 40 meters deep (Scott, 1938).

Among birds that dive for their food, there are those like the penguin or loon which dive from the surface, and those like the terns, gannets, pelicans, and kingfishers, which plunge in from some distance in the air. A pelican is so light and buoyant that it cannot get under water without a "running start." Many of the plunging divers are unable to maneuver in pursuit of their prey after they have submerged themselves. However, by virtue of their strong wings or powerful, posteriorly-placed legs, the penguins, loons, grebes, cormorants, mergansers, auks, and puffins have become agile underwater swimmers. These birds all seize fish between their mandibles, but the Anhinga uses its darting beak as a stiletto to impale its prey. Most good divers have heavy, vertically compressed bodies. Many fish-eaters, such as gulls, petrels, and albatrosses, seize their food from the surface of the water. An unusual type of surface feeding is found in the skimmers, *Rhynchops* sp., which fly just above the surface of quiet waters with their knife-like lower mandible cutting the water and apparently flipping small fish and crustaceans into the open mouth. The lower mandible, which grows more rapidly than the upper to compensate for the wear caused by water friction, is well supplied with touch corpuscles.

Many birds feed on molluscs. The oyster-catcher, *Haematopus* spp., has a stout, laterally-flattened bill which it inserts between the shells of a slightly gaping mussel and then twists so as to force the shells open. Many diving ducks pry small molluscs loose with the hardened nail at the end of their upper mandible and swallow them entire, digesting the shell and all. Many long-billed shorebirds probe the mud and sand for burrowing worms, small molluscs, and crustaceans. They frequently regulate their time of feeding not by the sun but by the tides. Gulls, crows, and even eagles are known to fly high over rocky ground with mussels, crabs, turtles, and nuts, and drop them to break them open and expose their

Figure 6.9. A Black Skimmer skimming. As an adaptation to the bird's remarkable mode of feeding, the lower beak grows about twice as rapidly as the upper. Photo by H. J. Lee, courtesy Newspaper National Snapshot Awards.

Figure 6.10. A European Nightjar yawning. The cavernous mouth, fringed with bristles, acts as an insect net for sweeping insects from the air while the bird is in flight. Photo by E. Hosking.

edible interiors. The Lammergeier, *Gypaëtus barbatus*, was given the name Ossifragus ("bonebreaker") in antiquity because of its habit of dropping bones to get at the marrow (Stresemann, 1927–1934). Similarly, eagles crack open tortoises by dropping them on rocks. Pliny says that the Greek poet Aeschylus met his death because an eagle, carrying a tortoise, mistook his bald head for a smooth rock. Aeschylus had remained out of doors all that day, fearful for his life, because an oracle had foretold that he would be killed by the fall of a house! (Thorndike, 1929.)

A horde of small birds depend on insects for their chief food. Some, like the flycatchers, perch on an exposed branch and sally out to snap up individual insects. Swifts, swallows, and some goatsuckers, with their rapid flight, weak feet, and wide, gaping mouths, feed constantly on the wing as animated insect nets. Many small species, such as titmice, nuthatches, and creepers, have strong feet for clinging to bark, and fine, pointed beaks for removing insects from the crevices. The woodpecker is adapted in several ways for digging out wood-boring insects and larvae. It has strong, grasping feet, stiff tail feathers to brace the body against the hammering head, a heavy skull, a strong, pick-like beak, and a tongue that is horny, barbed, richly equipped with tactile corpuscles, and astonishingly extensible. The European Green Woodpecker, *Picus viridis*, can stick out its tongue nearly 10 centimeters beyond the tip of its beak! After an insect gallery has been exposed by the beak, the long flexible tongue can explore its twistings, feel out, impale, and withdraw the larvae encountered. Sapsuckers, which specialize on sap and the insects attracted to it, have a tongue ending in thorny bristles. Industrious sapsuckers will dig about 30 holes a day, usually on the shady side of a tree, to start the sap flowing. At times they drink fermented sap and become too intoxicated to fly well. Lacking a long beak and tongue, the Galapagos Woodpecker-finch, *Camarhyn-*

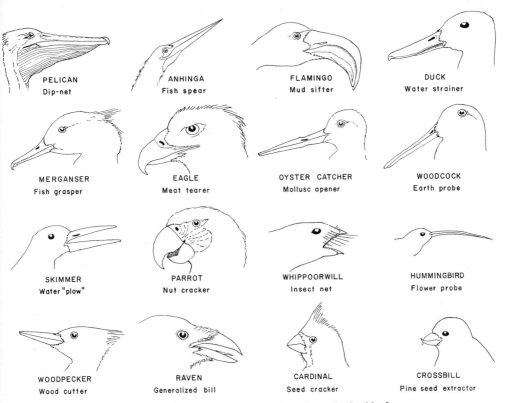

PELICAN
Dip-net

ANHINGA
Fish spear

FLAMINGO
Mud sifter

DUCK
Water strainer

MERGANSER
Fish grasper

EAGLE
Meat tearer

OYSTER CATCHER
Mollusc opener

WOODCOCK
Earth probe

SKIMMER
Water "plow"

PARROT
Nut cracker

WHIPPOORWILL
Insect net

HUMMINGBIRD
Flower probe

WOODPECKER
Wood cutter

RAVEN
Generalized bill

CARDINAL
Seed cracker

CROSSBILL
Pine seed extractor

Figure 6.11. Examples of bills adapted to different kinds of feeding.

chus pallidus, holds a cactus spine in its beak to pry insects out of cavities in dead wood. This finch is one of the very few tool-using animals of the world.

ADAPTATIONS FOR TAKING VEGETABLE FOODS

Birds eat all sorts of vegetable foods: roots, bulbs, stems, leaves, flowers, sap, nectar, fruits, seeds. A parrot in New Guinea, *Micropsitta bruijnii,* seems to specialize in eating fungi. Seeds are the preferred food of many vegetarian birds, both because they contain the most concentrated nourishment and because they are available at seasons when other foods are scarce.

Seed-eaters usually have short, heavy beaks operated by strong jaw muscles.

The beaks are commonly sharp at the edges and may have internal ridges against which seeds may be cracked or cut (Fig. 6.12). The tongue is likely to be muscular, scoop-shaped, and horny. Many species, like the doves, swallow the seeds entire; while others, like the finches and grosbeaks, shuck off the hard coat in the mouth. Still others, like the titmice, jays, and ravens, hold the seed with their feet and split it open with blows of the bill. Nuthatches, nutcrackers, and some woodpeckers place hard seeds in crevices of bark or rocks and attack them with their beaks. Crossbills, whose beak tips are laterally displaced and move past one another as the mouth is closed, use this remarkable adaptation to get behind conifer seeds in the cone and force them out.

Larger seeds are generally treated in the mouth or gizzard. Parrots, with their

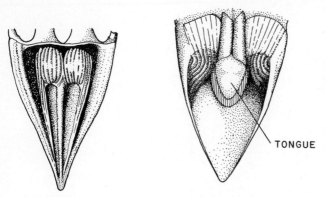

TONGUE

Figure 6.12. The upper jaw (left) and lower jaw (right) of the Hawfinch. The two ridged, horny mounds in each jaw serve as "anvils" for cracking nuts and fruit pits. Similar devices are found in the jaws of North American grosbeaks. A Hawfinch can crack olive pits which require a crushing force of 48 to 72 kilograms (106 to 159 pounds). After Mountfort.

powerful beaks, may crack nuts and seeds or may rasp them open by means of many abrasive ridges in the upper mandible opposed by a cross-wise ridge on the shorter lower mandible. Both mandibles are hinged to the skull and may be moved freely. The muscular tongue has a horny nail at its tip. Unlike most birds, parrots are able to hold food in one foot and lift it up toward the beak as they eat.

For eating extremely large fruits, the tropical fruit pigeons are described by Stresemann (1927–1934) as possessing three unusual adaptations in the beak, the stomach, and the intestines. The beaks of these birds spread open not only vertically but horizontally, as in snakes, to accommodate the enormous fruits they eat. One species, *Elaeocarpus graeffei*, swallows fruit pits as large as 30 by 50 millimeters! This is roughly the size of a small hen's-egg. The chief food of many fruit pigeons is the nutmeg, whose pulpy outside is rasped off by numerous horny, conical pegs lining the gizzard, as in *Ducula* spp., or by two opposed pairs of ribbed gizzard plates, as in *Ptilinopus* spp. These rasping surfaces are so hard that the pigeons need no grit in their stomachs. If a domestic pigeon eats a cherry it must regurgitate the seed because its intestines are not large enough to let it pass. But the intestines of fruit pigeons are exceptionally wide and short, so that they can easily pass, undamaged, nutmegs and other large seeds measuring 12.5 by 25 millimeters.

Smaller fruits and berries are eaten by many species, among them parrots, trogons, colies, toucans, manakins, waxwings, and flower-peckers. Only the pulp is normally digested and the seeds pass on through the alimentary canal. In many species, such as thrushes, starlings, and orioles, fruits are eaten only seasonally. Even some primarily carnivorous species, such as shorebirds and woodpeckers, occasionally eat fruits. When cold weather prevents their feeding on insects, Tree Swallows, *Iridoprocne bicolor*, may feed in great flocks on bayberries.

Buds and shoots of pine, willow, and heather are eaten by many grouse as a regular part of their diet, and by other species as emergency food when their usual source fails. Since such food is not rich in energy as compared with seeds, a great deal must be eaten to maintain normal levels of metabolism. As a consequence, grouse have exceptionally large caeca. The Capercaillie, *Tetrao urogallus*, which feeds mainly on conifer needles (an exceptionally low grade diet) is reported to excrete each day feces which, arranged in a single column, would extend about three meters (Stresemann, 1927–1934). Geese eat much aquatic vegetation and graze on grass; Brant occasionally eat marine algae as well as eel grass. The aberrant Hoatzin, *Opisthocomus hoazin*, is one of the few birds that eats leaves as a steady diet. This species eats hard leaves which it grinds, not with its small gizzard, but with its large, muscular crop which is lined with a tough, horny layer.

Some species, such as orioles and bullfinches, eat flowers and flower buds; but the flowers' main attraction for birds is their energy-rich nectar. Nectar-eaters, such as the honey-creepers, honey-eaters, sun-birds, and hummingbirds, generally have long beaks and long, extensible tongues which enable them to probe the depths of flower corollas for nectar. Often the narrow tongue has grooves on its surface so that, pressed against the palate, they may serve as tubes for sucking in the sweet juices. In honey-eaters and hummingbirds the hyoid bones of the tongue circle the skull as in woodpeckers, thus allowing much greater extensibility.

There is a mutual adaptation between the flowers of "ornithophilous" plants and the beaks of the birds that visit them. Not only do the bills of birds often fit the deep, tubular corollas of the flowers as a curved or straight blade fits its scabbard, but the flowers are typically red and without fragrance. Red colors are peculiarly attractive to hummingbirds and are ignored by at least the honey bee; and birds, with their inferior sense of smell, probably depend slightly if at all on floral fragrance, while many bees are strongly attracted by it. The nectar glands of these flowers flow with a bird-sized rather than an insect-sized abundance, and the nectar pots are so placed that few insects can reach them. Further, the reproductive organs of the flowers ripen at different times, the sticky pollen usually first, and are so placed that a bird visiting successive flowers will carry the pollen from one flower to another, thus promoting valuable cross-fertilization. While it is true that many nectar-eaters regularly eat insects as a protein supplement to their heavy carbohydrate diet, their chief interest in flowers is the nectar. Stresemann tells of one hummingbird kept alive nearly two months on sugar-water and flower nectar alone, and of another whose daily intake of nectar was twice the weight of its body.

Some plant species depend on birds to distribute their seeds. Many fruit-eating birds either regurgitate the seeds after digesting off the pulp, or pass them so rapidly through the alimentary canal that they not only emerge unharmed, but are often better prepared for germination by being softened and provided with dung to hasten their sprouting. Seeds that had passed through the digestive tract of a pheasant were found by Swank (1944) to germinate more quickly than those that had not. Some birds cache seeds in places where later on, if unretrieved, they may germinate. Others transport seeds, like those of the mistletoe, sticking to their beaks, or carried on muddy feet. In his well known experiment, Darwin (1859) once planted the seeds taken from a ball of mud obtained from the leg of a partridge. The mud had dried for three years, but 82 plants of at least five species germinated from the seeds.

ADAPTATIONS TO MIXED DIETS

Many species are able to eat a variety of both plant and animal foods, often depending on their availability. The ground scratchers, such as the Galliformes, commonly eat seeds, insects, roots, bulbs, or worms as they encounter them. Members of the crow family are well known for their catholic diet. Herring Gulls, *Larus argentatus*, which normally feed on fish, may in the summer move inland and feed largely on grain. An interesting consequence of this change in food is a temporary adaptation of the stomach: in the winter the stomach has a soft wall; in the summer the wall hardens (Thomson, 1923).

Ducks of the genus *Anas* may eat seeds, leaves, insects, worms, molluscs, and even small vertebrates. They possess a fringed and fluted beak marvellously adapted to sifting small food items from muddy water. Flamingos possess similarly fringed beaks which operate in an inverted position for sifting food from mud. Rather surprisingly, plankton-sifters among the sea birds are rare; but whale birds of the genus *Pachyptila* have laterally-placed, parallel plates arranged like teeth in a comb along the inner edge of each upper mandible. These undoubtedly sift food as baleen plates do in a whale (Murphy, 1936).

Peculiar Feeding Habits

In their constant struggle to keep alive, birds at times seek out and eat strange foods. In his monograph on the honey-guides, Friedmann (1955) tells of a Portuguese missionary in east Africa who wrote, in 1569, of these birds flying into his mission and eating the beeswax altar candles. It is well known that honeyguides lead men, ratels, and other animals to the nests of wild bees, where they feed on the honeycomb of the plundered nests. Although they eat bee larvae also, the birds may be kept alive on pure beeswax for as long as 32 days. Intestinal bacteria apparently help to break down the wax so that it may be digested and assimilated by the bird. Recent experiments have shown that the bacteria secrete a protein which inhibits the growth of tuberculosis germs, both in pure cultures and in guinea pigs.

Other relatively indigestible products sometimes eaten by birds are feathers and wool. As mentioned earlier, grebes often stuff their stomachs with their own feathers, probably for a mechanical effect. Crows and magpies have been observed plucking wool from the backs of sheep in snowy weather near Radolfzell, Germany —perhaps to add fat to their restricted menu (Mühl, 1954). Such a habit may have led to the striking predation of the Kea, *Nestor notabilis*, a New Zealand parrot which attacks sheep in times of winter famine. These birds use their powerful hooked beaks to tear through the wool and to feed on the flesh and fat underneath. In arctic regions where food is scarce, the Ivory Gull, *Pagophila eburnea*, feeds on the dung of polar bears, walrus, and seals. Puffins and petrels eat great amounts of whale dung (Mayaud, 1950). Post mortem studies of Flamingos, *Phoenicopterus ruber*, in southern France showed that their stomachs held great quantities of mud which contained only 6 to 8 per cent organic matter (Gallet, 1950).

Many accipiters and crows will turn to carrion when their favorite food is lacking. Larger albatrosses normally eat the poisonous, stinging Portuguese Man-of-war, *Physalia*, with impunity. Many species probably recognize, either innately or through sad experience, poisonous or stinging food items. Thomas Belt found a brightly colored poisonous frog in Nicaragua and tried without success to feed it to ducks and chickens. He finally enticed a young duck into taking it, but the duckling immediately cast it out and then "went about jerking its head as if trying to throw off some unpleasant taste." (Cott, 1940).

Feeding Associations

Birds sometimes associate with other birds or other animals in their endless search for food. Cormorants, Anhingas, and pelicans often join in bands to catch fish. In India, Heinroth observed one band of Anhingas several hundred meters long fishing cooperatively (Stresemann, 1927–1934). Brown Pelicans, *Pelecanus occidentalis*, at times form crude arcs and, beating their wings violently, swim toward shallow water where they scoop up the fish which they have driven before them. Lyre birds are often followed by smaller species which feed on the insects that they stir up. In similar manner, the Bee-eaters, *Merops nubicus*, ride on the backs of African bustards and ostriches to catch the insects they disturb; and egrets, kites, and herons follow elephants for the same reason. Tick-birds or ox-peckers eat the ticks on the buffalo and rhinoceros. Herodotus, who lived in the fifth century B.C., is credited with first telling the story of the Egyptian Plover, *Pluvianus aegyptius*, that entered the open mouths of live crocodiles to seek small particles of food there. Recently the story has been verified by several observers not only for plovers but for several other species as well. Food is where you find it. The titmice of English towns have recently learned how to peck open the caps of milk bottles left on house steps, and to drink the cream. The habit has spread to such an extent that in some localities it is unwise to leave milk bottles exposed, even in delivery trucks. It is well known that crows, gulls, and other birds follow the farmer to feed on the invertebrates and seeds that his plow turns up.

A very few species of birds have become parasitic on other birds for their food. Jaegers and frigate birds force weaker birds, such as terns, to disgorge the fish they have swallowed, which the parasites immediately seize in mid-air. The Laughing Gull, *Larus atricilla*, robs pelicans of fish they have caught, at times taking the food directly from the mouth of the larger bird.

There are some birds which prepare for future needs by storing excess food garnered in times of abundance. Titmice and nuthatches store insects and seeds in bark crevices during the spring and autumn for winter consumption. A three-year study of the Crested Tit, *Parus cristatus*, in Norway by Haftorn (1953), revealed that, of the food stored by the bird, 80 per cent was vegetable matter, mainly conifer seeds. Food was stored usually on the under sides of branches where it would be accessible in snowy weather, and three-fourths of all stored items were concealed in contact with lichens. Over one-half of the diet of the Crested Tit in a hard winter consisted of stored vegetable food. Haftorn thought that the birds remembered the type of locality rather than the exact spot where they had cached their food.

The Acorn Woodpecker, *Melanerpes formicivorus*, stores great numbers of acorns, each of which fits snugly in a hole that the bird has specially prepared in the bark of pine and oak trees; sometimes as many as 50,000 acorns are placed in one tree (Bent, 1939). Occasionally the food-storing instinct fails, and the bird stores pebbles instead of acorns. Jays of different species are known to hide food in crevices and holes in the ground. In an English oak grove, between 30 and 40 Jays, *Garrulus glandarius*, were observed by Chettleburgh (1952) to collect an estimated 200,-000 acorns in October and bury them about a kilometer away. In this case, the observer thought the birds remembered the localities of their caches.

The Nutcracker, *Nucifraga caryocatactes*, in Sweden lives on hazel nuts and spends its full time for three months in the autumn gathering and storing the nuts. In a series of observations by Swanberg (1951), the birds were observed to fill their throat pouches at the hazel thickets and fly as far as six kilometers to bury them in their spruce-forest territories, in small heaps covered with moss or lichens. The Nutcrackers live on the nuts over winter and feed their young on them the next spring. Apparently the birds remember where they have stored the nuts, for of 351 excavations, some of them through snow 45 centimeters deep, 86 per cent were successful.

SUGGESTED READINGS

The various volumes of Bent's *Life Histories of North American Birds* give extensive information on the feeding (and other) habits of most native species. In Marshall's *Biology and Comparative Physiology of Birds* are interesting and well documented chapters by Storer on feeding adaptations in birds, and by Farner on the digestive system and digestion. Van Tyne and Berger's *Fundamentals of Ornithology*, and Wallace's *An Introduction to Ornithology*, each contain good accounts of the feeding habits of birds.

SEVEN

Blood, Air, and Heat

*Darting, hovering helicopter
Fueling at a flower,
Tell me how your engine-heart
Generates such power!*
Joel Peters, *The Frustrated Engineer*

Weight for weight, birds eat more food, consume more oxygen, move more rapidly, and generate more heat than any other vertebrates. In no other vertebrate do the fires of metabolism burn more furiously than in a tiny humming-bird. Two organ systems that are basic to this intense metabolism are the circula-tory and the respiratory systems. Each of these systems shows striking adaptations for carrying out its strenuous functions.

THE CIRCULATORY SYSTEM

The chief functions of the circulatory system are to transport digested foods, oxygen, minerals, and hormones to the cells of the body, to remove carbon di-oxide and other metabolic wastes, to regu-late the water content of tissues and, in part, their hydrogen ion concentration (pH) and temperature. The circulatory system also plays a central role in the pre-vention and control of disease.

Structurally, the circulatory system of birds is much like that of reptiles and mammals. However, only mammals and birds are warm-blooded, and only they possess completely separate circulation paths for arterial and venous bloods. This is made possible by a four-chambered heart, the two right chambers of which pump used blood to the lungs for gaseous refreshment while the two left chambers circulate the fresh blood throughout the rest of the body. Reptiles and all other vertebrates are eternally doomed to cold-blooded sluggishness because their three- or two-chambered hearts can pump only mixed blood which is unable to support a high enough level of oxidation to maintain high body temperatures. Among the reptiles, the crocodilians possess four-chambered hearts, but their venous and arterial bloods nevertheless become mixed because of interconnections between the left and right aortae.

The heart in birds is larger and more powerful than that of reptiles or mammals of comparable size. The muscular walls of the left ventricle are more than three times as massive as those of the right ventricle. Small birds generally have relatively larger hearts than larger birds. This relationship undoubtedly stems from their need for higher metabolism. The figures in Table 7.1 from Portmann (1950), Quiring (1950), and Sturkie (1954) illustrate this inverse relationship.

Heart size seems also to be related to evolutionary position. The chart shows

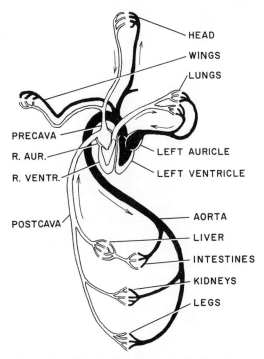

Figure 7.1. The circulatory system in birds, in simplified diagrammatic form. Black vessels contain "fresh" or oxygenated blood; white vessels contain "used" blood charged with carbon dioxide.

that the primitive Pheasant has a much smaller heart than the advanced Raven, although both birds have the same body weight. Within a given species, heart size usually increases both with altitude and with latitude. That is, it is larger in alpine races, in response to the need for more rapid circulation in the colder, thinner

Table 7.1.   Heart Weight in Relation to Body Weight

SPECIES	BODY WEIGHT (GM.)	HEART WEIGHT (GM./KG. BODY WT.)
Ostrich, *Struthio camelus*	123,000	0.98
Domestic Goose, *Anser anser*	4,405	8.00
Domestic Chicken, *Gallus gallus*	3,120	4.40
Domestic Duck, *Anas platyrhynchos*	1,685	7.44
Pheasant, *Phasianus* sp.	1,200	4.7
Raven, *Corvus corax*	1,200	10.0
Pigeon, *Columba livia*	297	13.80
Bluebird, *Sialia sialis*	29	17.00
Hummingbird, *Amazilia tzacatl*	4.8	23.71

air; and in polar races, in response to the need for greater heat production. In their study of heart-altitude correlation in 119 birds of 12 passerine species, Norris and Williamson (1955) found that the heart weights of species living between 2200 and 3400 meters elevation in California averaged roughly one-fourth heavier than heart weights of the same species living at altitudes below 260 meters.

As a rule, the heart beats more rapidly in birds than in mammals, but its rate depends upon several variables. There is an inverse relationship between body size and heart rate. A Turkey, *Meleagris gallopavo*, at rest, for example, has a heart which beats about 93 times per minute; a Robin, *Turdus migratorius*, 570 times per minute. Exercise, of course, raises the heart rate. A Black-capped Chickadee, *Parus atricapillus*, asleep has a rate of about 500 times per minute, but after strenuous exercise this rate is doubled (Odum, 1941). A drop in air temperature of about 8° C. caused an incubating Catbird, *Dumetella carolinensis*, to increase its heart rate 26 per cent. This increase probably reflects heightened metabolism to combat accelerated heat loss at the lower temperature. The temperature of the bird itself has the opposite effect on heart rate: the colder the bird, the slower the heart rate; the warmer, the faster. This is probably the chief reason why birds, which have higher temperatures, have faster heart rates than mammals of comparable size. As a general rule, the heart rate of any animal will double or treble for every 10° C. rise in body temperature (Prosser, 1950). At least in chickens, heart rate has little to do with blood pressure. The heart rate of a normal adult chicken may vary from 250 to 400 beats per minute "without causing appreciable changes in blood pressure" (Sturkie, 1954).

Experimental studies by Eliassen (1957) revealed that birds (e.g., guillemots, puffins, eiders) under simulated diving conditions slowed down their heart rates by more than 50 per cent, but with little effect on blood pressure.

As a rule, blood pressure is somewhat higher in birds than in mammals, and several times higher in birds than in reptiles, amphibians, fish, or invertebrates. Ordinarily blood pressure in male birds is higher than in females. Various determinations of arterial blood pressure in adult chickens show a variation of from 130 to 189 mm. of mercury for systolic and 85 to 160 mm. for diastolic pressure. Systolic pressures for small birds were determined by Woodbury and Hamilton (1937) as follows: Domestic Pigeon, *Columba livia*, 135 mm.; Starling, *Sturnus vulgaris*, 180 mm.; Robin, *Turdus migratorius*, 118 mm.; Canary, *Serinus canarius*, 130 and 220 mm. For comparison, among examples given by Prosser of mean arterial blood pressures, expressed in millimeters of mercury, are the following: Man, 100; horse, 175; dog, 110; bat, 50; crocodile, 40; frog, 26; salmon, 64; catfish, 35; shark, 22; lobster, 7; mussel, 0.8; earthworm, 5. Experimental lowering of the body temperature of a chicken decreases both its heart rate and its blood pressure.

Apparently, birds in their adaptation to respiratory and circulatory efficiency have pushed their blood pressures close to the margin of mechanical safety. A Cardinal, *Richmondena cardinalis*, exhausted from repeated territorial battles with another male Cardinal, died from the effects but showed no external damage. A postmortem examination revealed a 7 mm. wound in the heart ventricle, probably caused by the great pressure generated in the heat of battle (Dilger, 1955). Similarly, a Field Sparrow, *Spizella pusilla*, with a ruptured aorta, and a Baldpate, *Mareca americana*, with a ruptured right auricle, were presumably the victims of intense excitement (Walkinshaw, 1945; Hammond, 1948).

Probably as a result of selecting domestic Turkeys, *Meleagris gallopavo*, for rapid growth and heavy meat production, Turkey breeders have unwittingly selected strains with high blood pressures and weak arteries. A study by Ringer and

Rood (1959) revealed that males of the Broad Breasted Bronze variety of Turkey averaged a systolic blood pressure of 296 mm. of mercury at 22 weeks of age, and some individual birds had pressures as high as 400 mm. (Blood pressures over 150 mm. are considered abnormally high for man.) As a consequence, some Turkey flocks have suffered high mortalities from aortic rupture followed by internal hemorrhage.

Since the tranquilizing drug reserpine reduces nervous tension and lowers blood pressure in man, it has been used by turkey growers to reduce losses from aortic rupture. In one South Dakota flock of 3500 birds, there had been at least 57 deaths from aortic rupture by the time the birds were 13 weeks old. The flock was then divided into two groups of equal size: a control group, and an experimental group that was given 0.5 mg. of reserpine with each pound of food. In the next 11 days, 14 birds in the control group died, whereas not one of the reserpine-treated birds succumbed (Carlson, 1960).

Very little work has been done on the nervous control of heart rate and blood pressure in birds, but evidence suggests that it is similar to that in mammals. Peripheral stimulation of the vagus nerve, a cardioinhibitor, slows the avian heart to one-half or one-third its normal rate and reduces blood pressure from 150 to 100 mm. of mercury in the chicken. Contrariwise, stimulating vasomotor centers in the medulla may cause constriction in the smaller arteries, which will raise blood pressure as much as 48 per cent (Sturkie, 1954). Under normal pressure it takes the blood an average of six seconds to make a complete circuit of the body of an adult chicken.

In broad outline, the architecture of a bird's circulatory system is very similar to that of reptiles and mammals. Figure 7.1 shows the main paths of blood flow in a bird. The arterial trunks of birds resemble those of reptiles more than those of mammals. They are derived, as in all vertebrates, from the embryonic aortic arches. Of the six pairs of arches in the embryo, the first, second, and fifth shrink to insignificance or disappear completely; the third pair contributes to the carotid arteries which supply the head; the right arch of the fourth pair becomes the trunk of the aorta and the left half disappears (just the reverse of the situation in mammals); and the sixth pair become the pulmonary arteries. In accord with the heavy demands for blood by the breast and wing muscles, the brachial and pectoral arteries are relatively huge. Similar regional adaptations in arterial supply are found throughout the body. The venous system shows comparable adjustments to special avian needs. The two jugular veins draining the head are joined by a cross-vessel near the skull, so that if, for example, a twist of the neck should cramp shut the right vein, the blood could return to the heart via the left jugular. The paired kidneys are supplied with portal veins, a primitive feature not found in mammals. Blood from the posterior regions of the body flows through the iliac (portal) veins to the kidneys, where, by means of prominent valves at the juncture of the iliac and renal veins, the blood may either be deflected into the kidneys where nitrogenous wastes are removed, or pass directly on to the heart via the renal veins. The hepatic or liver portal system in birds functions as it does in other vertebrates to screen the blood coming from the intestines and to store or transform the food it carries.

Compared with reptiles and mammals, birds have a poorly developed lymphatic system. The dead-end lymph capillaries collect into larger vessels which parallel the larger blood vessels and eventually join the blood system at the thoracic duct. Lymph hearts are found in all bird embryos, usually near the sacral vertebrae; but they ordinarily disappear in adults, although they remain functional in a few species such as ostriches, cassowaries, gulls, storks, and some passerines (Stresemann, 1927–1934).

The spleen in birds is relatively small, has feeble muscles, and apparently is not the important blood storage organ which it is in mammals. In birds it varies seasonally in volume, being larger in summer than in winter. It is the site of white blood corpuscle formation and red corpuscle destruction.

As in other vertebrates, the blood of birds is made up of a fluid plasma and of formed elements. The plasma, which is 80 per cent water, is chemically very complex and in some regards remarkably stable in composition. It contains various salts in solution; digested foods such as glucose, fats, and amino acids; special blood proteins thought to be formed in the liver; waste products (mainly carbon dioxide and urea); gases, hormones, vitamins, and small amounts of other substances.

The constituents of the blood plasma of a normal, adult chicken are shown by Sturkie (1954) to vary chemically, according to age, sex, health, state of egg production, kind of food eaten, and recency of feeding. Laying hens, for example, have about two times as much blood calcium and three to five times as much blood lipids and fatty acids as non-laying hens. The increase in fats seems due to the secretion of estrogen from the ovary of the laying hen. Glucose level in the blood drops with age. Chickens 18 months old have only 80 per cent the blood glucose of those three months old. The average concentration of glucose in avian blood is about twice that of mammalian blood.

Total blood proteins in birds may vary from 2.30 grams to 6.10 grams per 100 cc. of blood serum. The plasma proteins in males are lower than those in females, a fact suggesting an influence of sex hormones. The chief functions of plasma proteins, as given by Sturkie, are to maintain the normal volume of the blood and water content in tissues by osmotic pressure, and to combat disease. The globulin protein is more concentrated in chicken blood than in mammalian blood. Since globulins manufacture antibodies, this may be the reason chickens are particularly good antibody producers. However,

on the debit side of the ledger is the fact that chickens, and probably other birds as well, suffer a remarkably high incidence of arteriosclerosis. In a study by Dauber (1945), 45 per cent of chickens over a year old showed visible damage to the aorta alone. Experimental administration of cholesterol and of estrogen increased incidence of atherosclerosis, or fatty plaque deposits, in arteries.

Making up the formed elements of the blood are the erythrocytes or red corpuscles, the leukocytes or white corpuscles, and the tiny, spindle-shaped thrombocytes concerned with blood coagulation. The same kinds of granular and non-granular leukocytes are found in birds and in mammals; however, their relative numbers are greater in birds. In human blood, for example, there is one leukocyte for every 700 erythrocytes, while in bird blood there is one leukocyte for every 100 to 200 erythrocytes. The chief function of the leukocytes is to protect the body against disease. For some unknown reason, the proportions between the two types of leukocytes fluctuate during each day. In the male Starling, *Sturnus vulgaris*, for example, the granular neutrophils make up 26 per cent of the leukocytes and the non-granular lymphocytes 59 per cent of the leukocytes in the morning, whereas in the afternoon the respective proportions are 43 and 38 per cent. In the female Starling the respective proportions in the morning are 9 and 79 per cent, and in the afternoon 22 and 59 per cent (Portmann, 1950).

Erythrocytes are nucleated as in reptiles, bi-convex, and oblong in outline. They vary in size from 9.5 to 20 micra in length and 5.5 to 10 micra in breadth. (The circular human red corpuscle is about 7.7 micra in diameter.) The largest avian corpuscles are found in the ostrich and its relatives, the smallest in the hummingbirds. As a rule, the more highly evolved birds have smaller red corpuscles, in greater numbers and supplied with richer hemoglobin, than do the primitive species. Good fliers have, in relation to their size, smaller erythrocytes than poor fliers. The smaller red corpuscles with their relatively greater surface for lively gas exchange illustrate once more the great biological significance of the surface-volume ratio (Stresemann, 1927–1934).

In birds the number of corpuscles per cubic millimeter of blood varies from 1.5 to 6.6 million, whereas in mammals the number varies from 2.0 to 19.4 million. There is a rough negative correlation between bird size and corpuscle number, as the examples, largely from Portmann, illustrate in Table 7.2.

The numbers of corpuscles (in millions per cubic millimeter) of a few representative lower vertebrates provide another explanation of their metabolic sluggishness (Prosser, 1950): lizard, 1.4; alligator, 0.85; frog, 0.5; *Necturus*, 0.05; carp, 1.6; catfish, 2.4; ray, 0.2; lamprey, 0.2.

Within a given species, the number of red corpuscles will vary according to sex, hormones, time of day, season of the year, and very probably the altitude at which the bird lives, and other factors. Male birds generally have a higher red corpuscle count than females. This suggests that sex hormones play a role in corpuscle frequency. Experimental studies by Domm and Taber (1946) showed that the red blood corpuscles in adult male chickens dropped from about 3.25 to 2.48 million per cubic millimeter after castration, whereas mature females of the same breed had about 2.6 million both before

and after castration. The obvious implication that male hormones, or androgens, were responsible for higher concentration in normal males was tested by injecting androgens into male and female castrates. In both types of birds the red counts rose to the approximate concentration of corpuscles in normal males. Further experiments showed that the thyroid hormone also influenced erythrocyte frequency, male chickens with thyroid glands removed having about three-fourths as many red corpuscles as the controls had. Females were unaffected. In general, Domm and Taber found that the Domestic Hen has more erythrocytes in the fall and winter than in the spring, and more at midnight than at noon.

Rather surprisingly, the hemoglobin content in the blood of birds is slightly less than that in mammalian blood. But, what is more important, the hemoglobin of birds is more efficient than mammalian hemoglobin in carrying oxygen to the tissues. The "life" of a red corpuscle in a chicken is thought to be about a month, but a human red corpuscle keeps working for about 120 days before it is destroyed.

Erythrocytes are formed mainly in the bone marrow of adult birds, although in passerines they are also formed in the spleen and liver (Portmann, 1950). Leukocytes are formed in large numbers early in the life of a bird by the liver, spleen, kidney, pancreas, and *bursa fabricius*. In the adult bird the spleen and caeca are the main organs producing them.

Table 7.2.   Body Weight and Erythrocyte Count

SPECIES:	BODY WEIGHT (GM.):	ERYTHROCYTES (MILLIONS PER CUBIC MM.):
Hummingbird, *Chrysolampis elatis*	2.4	6.59
Junco, *Junco hyemalis*	20	6.2
Blackbird, *Turdus merula*	85	6.4
Quail, *Coturnix coturnix*	100	5.0
Pheasant, *Phasianus colchicus*	1,170	4.8
Peacock, *Pavo cristatus*	4,500	2.7
Ostrich, *Struthio camelus*	120,000	1.9

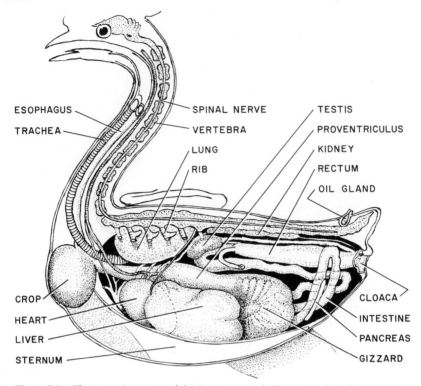

ESOPHAGUS
TRACHEA
SPINAL NERVE
VERTEBRA
LUNG
RIB
TESTIS
PROVENTRICULUS
KIDNEY
RECTUM
OIL GLAND
CROP
HEART
LIVER
STERNUM
CLOACA
INTESTINE
PANCREAS
GIZZARD

Figure 7.2. The internal anatomy of the Domestic Fowl. The air sacs have been removed. After T. I. Storer.

THE RESPIRATORY SYSTEM

As in all animals the chief function of the respiratory system in birds is to supply the living cells of the body with oxygen and to rid them of carbon dioxide. This exchange of gases requires that the lungs and accessory tubes and sacs suck in fresh air and push out used air, and that the blood carry the oxygen of the air from the lungs to the capillaries embracing the various body cells where, by osmosis, the oxygen is given up, and the carbon dioxide is absorbed for the return trip to the lungs. The hemoglobin of the red corpuscles is primarily responsible for the transport of oxygen, and the hemoglobin and blood plasma together are responsible for the transport of carbon dioxide.

In order to meet the rigorous demands for air consumption that intense living,

flight, and song impose on them, birds must have ample and efficient breathing machinery, as indeed they have. Not only is their respiratory system the most efficient known among all vertebrates, but it is unique in basic structure. Man and other mammals breathe by means of a cul-de-sac respiratory system in which inhaled fresh air is mixed with residual stale air remaining in the dead-end alveoli of the lungs, which can never be completely emptied. Birds, on the contrary, have a complex system of sacs and interconnecting tubes that make possible a more thorough bathing of the lung cells with fresh air.

The lungs are the center of the breathing system, and the place where gas exchange between the air and the blood occurs. Lungs are relatively smaller in birds than in mammals. The lungs of man occupy about five per cent of his body volume, but those of a duck take up only two per cent. However, the duck's lungs and air sacs together occupy about 20 per cent of the body volume.

As air is inhaled, it passes from the nasal chambers through the mouth and pharynx into the upper end of the windpipe or trachea via the slit-like glottis. At the top of the trachea is a cylindrical box, the larynx, whose skeletal support is provided by cartilaginous rings which generally become ossified in maturity. The larynx is a reptilian hang-over with no vocal cords, and is not as important to birds as it is to mammals. It leads directly to the trachea proper.

The trachea, which conducts air from the mouth cavity toward the lungs, forks into two short tubes, the bronchi, and these connect directly with the two lungs. The trachea is reinforced with a series of cartilaginous rings which in most species turn into bone in the adult. In mammals they remain cartilage throughout life. These rings are joined together by tough bands of fibrous connective tissue. In the female Emu, *Dromiceius novaehollandiae,* the central tracheal rings are not closed on the ventral side, and the open space is bridged with an elastic tissue that can be blown outward until a melon-sized balloon appears on the bird's neck, to the accompaniment of a loud booming noise. Normally the trachea does not follow the course of the neck vertebrae but is located to their right and parallel to the esophagus. Occasionally, in geese, cranes, shorebirds, and others, it is extraordinarily long and serves as a resonating tube to amplify the voice of the bird. This additional length may be provided by tracheal loops or coils located between the breast muscles and the skin, or at the base of the furcula, or in the thorax. In the Whooping Crane, *Grus americana,* the trachea is nearly as long as the bird itself, and about half its length is coiled in the keel of the sternum. If man had a trachea proportionately as long as that of the Whooping Crane, normal breathing would not suffice to keep him alive; the trachea

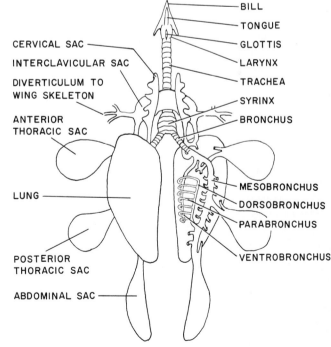

Figure 7.3. A simplified diagram of the respiratory system in birds. After Hazelhoff; Brandes and Hirsh.

BILL
TONGUE
CERVICAL SAC
GLOTTIS
INTERCLAVICULAR SAC
LARYNX
DIVERTICULUM TO
WING SKELETON
TRACHEA
SYRINX
ANTERIOR
THORACIC SAC
BRONCHUS

MESOBRONCHUS
LUNG
DORSOBRONCHUS
PARABRONCHUS

POSTERIOR
THORACIC SAC
VENTROBRONCHUS

ABDOMINAL SAC

would merely become filled with stale air shuttling back and forth. This emphasizes the fact that, in birds, the lung and air sac system allows for relatively deep breathing which ensures the presence of oxygen-rich air in the lungs, even though the air has traveled down a long trachea. It also reveals the principle that natural selection may lead to extravagant extremes in adapting to one need (courtship "song," in this case) at the expense of other vital needs (efficient breathing). A peculiar arrangement occurs in penguins in which a median partition divides the trachea into two tubes for nearly its entire length—possibly a device to withstand water pressure in deep dives.

At the point, generally above the sternum, where the trachea divides into the two bronchi, the syrinx or voice box appears. The syringes show great variety in structure, but generally there are three main types: the tracheal, bronchotracheal, and bronchial. A few species have no syrinx whatever (vultures, ostriches, and some storks). Male ducks and mergansers have a simple form of tracheal syrinx in which the last few rings enlarge and fuse together to form a chamber called the tympanum. It functions as a resonance box, devoid of muscles or vibrating membranes. In other birds the tympanum may have gaps in the tracheal rings across which a stretched membrane vibrates to produce sounds when rapidly expired air agitates it. In the Oil Bird, *Steatornis caripensis*, the syringes are purely bronchial enlargements.

The commonest type of syrinx is the bronchotracheal (Fig. 7.4). In this type the last three to six rings at the base of the trachea enlarge to form the tympanum, to which is added posteriorly two chambers made of the enlarged first three horseshoe-shaped rings of each bronchus. The whole forked box is supplied with muscles and vibrating membranes, and becomes the chief voice instrument of most birds. Inside the tympanum, where the trachea forks into the two bronchi, is a vertical, bony ridge, the pessulus, on which is a

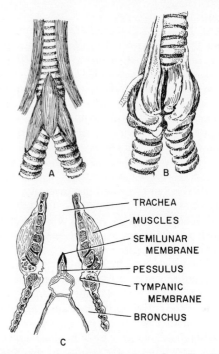

Figure 7.4. A, The syrinx of a tyrant flycatcher, *Colopteryx galeatus*, a bird with limited powers of song. After Müller, in Stresemann. *B*, Syrinx of the Babbling Thrush, *Melampitta gigantea*, showing the more complex musculature associated with greater musical virtuosity. After Mayr, in Stresemann. *C*, A longitudinal section of the syrinx of the male Blackbird, *Turdus merula*. After Haecker, in Stresemann.

vibrating, semilunar membrane which extends into the tympanic cavity. The mouth of each bronchus is somewhat constricted into a narrow slit by internal and external tympanic membranes. Not only these membranes, but others in the walls of the tracheal and bronchial tubes, may be acted upon by muscles that can stretch or relax them. Or the muscles may regulate the size of the air slits, or expand or contract or change the tensions on the half rings of the bronchi. There is great variety in the construction of syringes, but the complexity and perfection of a bird's song are closely related to the number of syrinx muscles that act on these various membranes and rings. Poor singers, like the manakins or falcons, may have but two or three pairs of syringeal muscles, but true song birds typically have seven pairs and may have as many as nine. In some species there are accessory structures, such as the long trachea of the Whooping Crane, or the simple enlargement of the trachea, the bulla, in ducks, which may act as resonance chambers to modify the sounds originating in the syrinx. In many species the male does the singing, even though the female possesses a well-formed syrinx. The chief reason why the sexes differ in song is not because of great structural differences in their syringes, but because song is primarily under the control of nerves and hormones. It is true, however, that in many female birds the syringeal muscles are more weakly developed than in the males.

The bright red lungs of birds are strikingly small, highly vascularized, and relatively inelastic. Above, they are firmly attached to the ribs and thoracic vertebrae. The lower sides are covered with connective tissue on which are inserted several small, weak muscles which originate on the ribs. In the higher reptiles and mammals the bronchi entering the lungs fork again and again into ever smaller tubes, much as the trunk and branches of a tree subdivide until they

end in twigs, the lung "twigs", being microscopic air sacs or alveoli. In birds, however, each bronchus passes through the ventral side of the lung and emerges at its posterior end to enter the large, thin-walled air sacs of the abdomen. Inside the lung, each bronchus, now called a mesobronchus, loses its reinforcing rings and gives off four to six secondary tubes called ventrobronchi, which in turn subdivide into the ultimate respiratory units, the parabronchi. The parabronchi are small parallel tubes, each several millimeters long and less than one-half a millimeter in diameter. There are about 1000 of them in each lung of a chicken. Their thin epithelial walls are punctured with the openings of hundreds of tiny, branching and anastomosing "air capillaries" (Fig. 7.5) which extend outward and are intimately surrounded by a profuse network of blood capillaries. It is between these air and blood capillaries that the gas exchange between the lungs and blood takes place.

Unlike the blind alveoli of mammalian lungs, the parabronchi are open at each end. Ventrally, they connect with the ventrobronchi, and dorsally, with the dorsobronchi. In each lung there are two rows of dorsobronchi, six to ten in each row, which join the parabronchi with the meso-

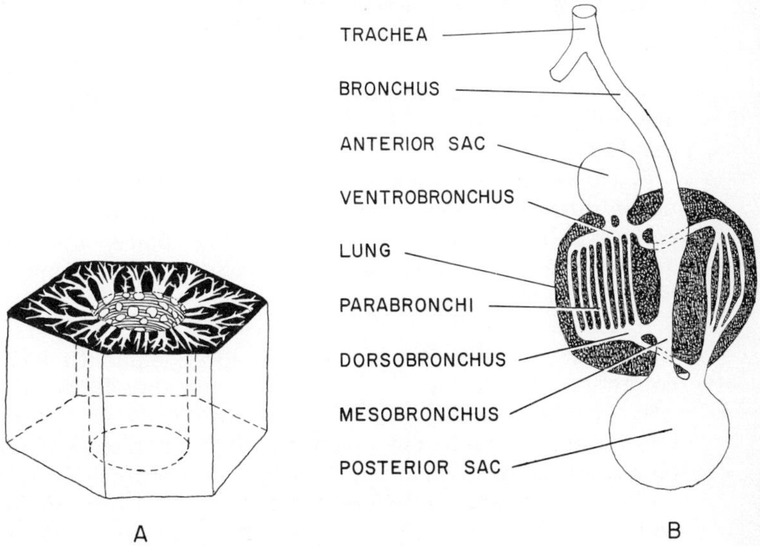

Figure 7.5. *A*, A diagram of a section of a parabronchus, showing the radiating air capillaries. After Hazelhoff. *B*, A diagrammatic scheme to show the chief paths of air circulation through a bird's lung. After Zeuthen, in Portmann.

TRACHEA

BRONCHUS

ANTERIOR SAC

VENTROBRONCHUS

LUNG

PARABRONCHI

DORSOBRONCHUS

MESOBRONCHUS

POSTERIOR SAC

A   B bronchus. Both anteriorly and posteriorly the mesobronchi and their branches connect with the nine air sacs of the body. These air sacs act as air reservoirs in the bronchial circuit rather than as air terminals. Thus, the lungs are provided with a system of interconnecting tubes and sacs which allows a relatively continuous flow of air across respiratory surfaces. Air is not drawn *into* the lungs so much as *through* them.

There has been much discussion and conjecture regarding the precise path that air takes in ventilating the lungs. Some students have postulated an antagonistic pumping action between the anterior and posterior air sacs which causes a two-way flushing of the lungs with air. Others have suggested a series of valves or sphincter muscles to control the direction of air flow. Although the problem is by no means settled, there seems to be general agreement on the following:

1. The air sacs are connected with the trachea and bronchi by means of large tubes, whereas the parabronchi are similarly connected with the mesobronchi by means of small tubes—seemingly a poor arrangement for efficient breathing.

2. Parabronchi have muscular walls which may constrict and thus limit the amount of air which passes through them.

3. The anterior air sacs have a higher carbon dioxide content than the posterior sacs.

4. The air sacs do not operate antagonistically. Air pressure studies indicate that they all fill and empty simultaneously.

5. No valves have been discovered that might direct the flow of air in certain pathways, but a deflecting "dam" which may have such a function occurs in each mesobronchus.

6. Circular smooth muscles occur in the walls of the parabronchi which may act to control the flow of air.

7. At each inhalation, the anterior air sacs receive preponderantly stale air; the posterior sacs, fresh air.

The best current explanation consistent with these facts holds that air enters the parabronchi by way of the dorsobronchi and leaves by way of the ventrobronchi— possibly during both inspiration and expiration. The fresher air in the posterior air sacs presumably is received directly from the trachea, bronchi, and mesobronchi. On its way out it passes partly through the ventrobronchi, parabronchi, and dorsobronchi, partly into the anterior air sacs, and partly directly to the exterior via the mesobronchus. There is also the possibility that air in the various air sacs may be recirculated through the lungs. The problem provides rich opportunities for further research.

There are in the typical bird's body four pairs of air sacs plus one unpaired sac, making a total of nine. Most of them are placed dorsally in the body, a fact which helps stabilize flying by lowering the body's center of gravity. The sacs are all thin-walled, with very little musculature and with a very poor supply of blood vessels, so they cannot be considered as primary respiratory organs. The unpaired air sac is the interclavicular, located anteriorly. It sends diverticula into the larger pneumatic bones such as the sternum, pectoral girdle bones, and humerus. Associated with the cervical vertebrae and sending lateral branches posteriorly are the paired cervical sacs. Also anteriorly placed are the prethoracic pair of sacs. Posterior in the body are the postthoracic and abdominal pairs of sacs, the latter supplying air to the pneumatic bones of the sacrum, pelvis, and legs. In general, large flying birds have well developed pneumatic bones, while small fliers have few or none. Birds with pneumatic wing bones are able to breathe through the broken and exposed humerus, even though the trachea may be closed, but apparently this does not hold true for the femur. In addition to the breathing tubes already mentioned, there are sets of recurrent bronchi or saccobronchi which branch out into the lungs and parabronchi from all air sacs except the cervical.

Undoubtedly, the air sacs play a dominant role in aerating the lungs; but they are not indispensable, at least in some species, because birds can still breathe, with reduced volume, after the sacs have all been destroyed (Sturkie, 1954). The sacs probably help cool the body during vigorous exercise through the internal evaporation of water. It may be that during energetic exercise rapid ventilation is more necessary for heat removal than for acquiring oxygen. It has been estimated by Zeuthen (1942) that a pigeon flying 70 kilometers an hour produces about 27 times as much heat as when at rest, and that this activity requires about three times as much air flow for heat removal as it does for lung respiration. Certainly, the air sacs are well placed among the body organs for the efficient removal of excess heat. It is also possible that the abdominal air sacs, which are in contact with the testes, serve as an analogue of the mammalian scrotum to lower their temperature and facilitate spermatogenesis (Cowles and Nordstrom, 1946).

For aquatic birds the air sacs provide valuable buoyancy. Swimming species have particularly large abdominal and postthoracic sacs whose volume can be controlled for diving or floating. In aquatic species that plunge from the air into the water for their food, the air sacs act as a buffer to protect the body against disabling shocks. It seems probable that the abdominal sacs aid the abdominal muscles in the acts of defecation and egg-laying. The air sacs even play an important role in the courtship of many species, analogous to sartorial finery in the human species. The male Frigate Bird, *Fregata aquila*, and the male Prairie Chicken, *Tympanuchus cupido*, inflate their showy neck bladders through diverticula of the cervical air sacs. The yellow external balloons of the Prairie Chicken also act as resonators for its booming courtship call. Among those species that have long-drawn-out songs, the air sacs may serve as air reservoirs.

Birds do not possess a heavy muscular diaphragm to provide the mechanical force needed for breathing. As a conse-quence, breathing depends on the movements of the body wall, especially the thoracic cage. With every inspiration the cage increases in vertical dimension, particularly toward the rear. As its volume is increased, air moves into the lungs, and particularly into the air sacs, to fill the partial vacuum thereby created.

It is likely that the rate of breathing is controlled in birds, as it is in mammals, by a respiratory center in the medulla of the brain. A special panting center is located in the mid-brain. Experimental studies indicate that the breathing center responds to changes in the temperature and pH of the blood, to carbon dioxide inhalation, and even to the position of the body (Sturkie, 1954). The panting center is stimulated by a rise in its own temperature. If the body temperature of a pigeon is raised from 41.7° to 43.6° C., its breathing rate will increase from 46 to 510 times per minute, and the volume of air breathed, from 185 to 610 cubic centimeters per minute (von Saalfeld, 1936). The evaporative cooling that this brings about takes place largely in the air sacs.

The rate at which a bird breathes varies with species, age, sex, size, activity, air temperature, time of day and other factors. As a rule, the smaller the bird the faster its breathing rate.

Because of their large air sacs, and because fresh air probably passes through the lungs during both inhalation and exhalation, birds have a larger capacity of air per breath, and therefore do not need to breathe as rapidly as mammals of comparable size to get the same supply of oxygen. Table 7.3, based on unpublished data from Eugene Odum, illustrates this relationship.

As in man, the breathing rate in birds speeds up with vigorous exercise. A House Sparrow, *Passer domesticus*, tested by Odum, had a basal or resting breathing rate of 50 cycles per minute, and this increased to 102 per minute while the bird was quietly held in the hand for ten minutes, and to 212 after the bird had been excitedly flying about a room. Miniature

Table 7.3.   Electronically Determined Basal Heart and Breathing Rates of
Small Birds and Mammals While at Rest and at
Thermoneutral Temperatures (from Odum)

BIRDS, SPECIES	BASAL HEART RATE (PER MINUTE)	BASAL BREATHING RATE (PER MINUTE)	RATIO OF HEART RATE TO BREATHING RATE
House Wren, *Troglodytes aëdon*	450	83	5.4 – 1
Black-capped Chickadee, *Parus atricapillus*	486	64	7.6 – 1
Song Sparrow, *Melospiza melodia*	450	63	7.1 – 1
Canary, *Serinus canarius*	514	57	9.0 – 1
Cardinal, *Richmondena cardinalis*	375	45	8.3 – 1
Average			7.5 – 1
MAMMALS, SPECIES			
Short-tailed Shrew, *Blarina brevicauda*	470	186	2.5 – 1
Deer Mouse, *Peromyscus leucopus*	395	135	2.9 – 1
Flying Squirrel, *Glaucomys volans*	250	91	2.8 – 1
Chipmunk, *Tamias striatus*	230	65	3.5 – 1
Average			2.9 – 1

telemetry devices have recently been developed that are small enough to be carried by birds while in otherwise normal flight. These devices are able to broadcast back to recording instruments such information as breathing rates, heart rates, and blood pressure variations in freely flying birds. Using this technique, Eliassen (1960) found that the heart rate of flying ducks increased only slightly over that while they were resting (from about 240 to about 300 beats per minute).

Several observers are of the opinion that wingbeats in flying birds are synchronized with breathing mechanics, a fact which, if true, would promote both the efficiency of respiration and of cooling the body. However, a flying crow may give a call which lasts through several wingbeats —a fact which proves that breathing and wing strokes are not necessarily synchronized in a flying bird.

Electronic studies of the respiratory rate of Black-capped Chickadees, *Parus atricapillus*, by Odum (1943) showed that their basal rate, while asleep at an air temperature of 11° C., was 65 per minute; and at 32° C., 95 per minute—an acceleration related to the need for removing heat. The few species which undergo temporary dormancy or hibernation slow down their breathing rates along with other metabolic activities. Torpid nestlings of the European Swift, *Apus apus*, breathe a minimum of eight cycles per minute during long fasts imposed by cold, wet weather (Koskimies, 1950). In House Wrens, *Troglodytes aëdon*, whose body temperatures were changed experimentally by Baldwin and Kendeigh (1932), birds whose breathing rate at normal body temperatures (38°–41.5° C.) was 92 to 112 per minute slowed down to a minimum of 28 per minute at 23° C. and rose to a rate of 340 per minute at the maximum tolerable body temperature of 47° C. (116° F.).

A bird that dives deeply in the water faces a special respiratory problem. To reduce buoyancy it must reduce the amount of air in its air sacs. Consequently, any air reserves it may have in them will be curtailed. In the duck, as in most mammals, the heart rate slows during a dive; and in penguins the oxygen consumption by tissues is reduced to 20 to 25 per cent of the normal resting rate (Prosser, 1950). It seems probable that in birds, as in diving mammals, muscle sugar or glycogen is broken down anaerobically to lactic acid in order to provide the needed energy. Such anaerobic glycolysis, while eliminating the immediate need for oxygen, would flood the blood with lactic acid, thus creating an "oxygen debt" which would be repaid when the bird returned to the surface. High tolerance of the breathing center to carbon dioxide, as has been demonstrated in seals and porpoises, also occurs in diving birds to enable them to prolong their time under water. The Mallard Duck, *Anas platyrhynchos*, has been experimentally held alive under water as long as 16 minutes, and even 27 minutes with its trachea closed. Voluntarily, birds stay under water for much shorter times, usually less than a minute; but the Common Loon, *Gavia immer*, has been known to stay under for 15 minutes. Great numbers of Old Squaw Ducks, *Clangula hyemalis*, have been caught and drowned in Lake Superior commercial fishing nets set 21 to 27 meters deep. (As many as 27,000 were so destroyed by one single fishing crew in the spring of 1946!) Undoubtedly these birds required a fairly long immersion to feed at such depths. Loons have been taken in fish nets set 55 meters (180 feet) deep (Schorger, 1947).

ENERGY METABOLISM

Metabolism is the sum total of chemical activities in a living organism which provide energy for heat, movement, irritability, growth, repair, and reproduction. This energy is all obtained from the oxidation of foods eaten by the animal: carbohydrates, fats, and proteins. A given quantity of food will provide a precisely specific amount of energy, whether burned in a bomb calorimeter in the laboratory or in the body of a live animal. The energy consumed by an animal may be measured directly, by the caloric value of the food consumed, or indirectly, by the amount of oxygen consumed to oxidize that food and release its energy. Not all the food eaten by an animal is converted into useful energy. Some is used for growth. Some foods are not completely digested, and the digestion of food itself creates heat which, except in cold weather, is of no use to the animal.

Basal metabolism is the resting metabolism of a fasting animal in an environment neither warm enough nor cold enough to create energy problems. It is possible that some small birds have two basal metabolic rates, one while they are resting and another, somewhat lower, while they are asleep. Blake (1956) suggests that the sleeping rate may represent partial torpidity as an energy saving device. Not only do smaller birds (and other animals) have relatively more surface than larger ones, but for their size they consume oxygen at a higher rate. Basal oxygen consumption in an animal varies in direct proportion to its surface area, or it varies as the 0.73 power of its body weight.

As unusually energetic animals, birds need amounts of energy greatly beyond those required for minimum resting existence. To start with, they have a higher basal metabolism than most mammals because, as a class, they are small animals. Moving in vertical as well as horizontal directions, and at great speed, they require more energy than most other animals, just as hill-climbing requires more energy than walking on a level surface. The tiny hummingbird probably demonstrates the highest metabolic rate and the greatest metabolic range of any vertebrate. Experiments by Pearson (1950) on captive Anna's Hummingbirds, *Calypte anna*, and Allen's Hummingbirds, *Selasphorus sasin*, which weighed between 3.75 and 4.32 grams, revealed that their daytime consumption of oxygen while resting ranged from 10.7 to 16.0 cc. per gram of body weight per hour. During periods of hovering flight their oxygen consumption rose to 85 cc./gm. per hour for Allen's Hummingbirds, and 68 cc./gm.

per hour for Anna's Hummingbirds. At night these birds became torpid, their body temperatures dropped to within a few degrees of the environmental temperature (24° C.), and their oxygen consumption dropped to below 3 cc./gm. per hour. It would seem unlikely that such small birds could live through the night should their metabolic fires continue to burn even at the relatively slow daytime resting rate, yet incubating females maintain their warm body temperatures both day and night.

Maintaining a higher body temperature than other animals results in a steeper temperature gradient between body and environment, hence a more rapid heat loss. Undaunted by these handicaps, birds have successfully penetrated the most frigid regions populated by any animal. The Emperor Penguin, *Aptenodytes forsteri*, breeds in antarctic temperatures as low as −62° C. (−80° F.)—"one of the most remarkable physiological feats known among warm-blooded animals" (Murphy, 1936). It is not surprising, in view of this fact, that the Emperor is the largest penguin, weighing, with its thick layers of fat, between 26 and 43 kilograms (57 to 94 pounds).

In order to achieve their high metabolic rates, birds have had to adapt themselves in various ways. As a rule, they eat foods rich in energy: seeds, fruits, nectar, insects, fish, rodents, and the like. The rich concentration of glucose in their blood

(about double that of human blood) promotes higher levels of metabolism. At those times of year when birds migrate, breed, and molt, their energy requirements are sharply increased. In unconscious anticipation of these extra demands, many species accumulate deposits of fat which tide them over periods of strenuous living. To conserve the heat they generate, they have reduced or eliminated heat-radiating projections such as external ears and fleshy tails and legs; they have covered the body with heat-conserving feathers and, in many aquatic species, with layers of insulating fat. No bats are found in polar regions, for the wings of bats and other flying mammals are living membranes with networks of blood vessels, while the main expanse of a bird's wings is made of lifeless feathers which conserve rather than dissipate heat. Exposed skin in many birds is reduced to a minimum. Many birds, when perching in cold weather, will stand on one foot with the other tucked into their belly feathers; and many also tuck their beaks among feathers of the body. The unfeathered legs of many birds dissipate large amounts of heat. The Domestic Fowl, while standing, loses 40 to 50 per cent more heat than while sitting; and by tucking its head under its wing, it reduces heat loss by 12 per cent (Deighton and Hutchinson, 1940). Although air sacs are probably most useful in cooling the body, paradoxically they may also conserve heat.

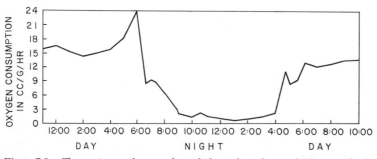

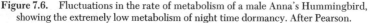

Figure 7.6.   Fluctuations in the rate of metabolism of a male Anna's Hummingbird, showing the extremely low metabolism of night time dormancy. After Pearson.

Since air is a poor conductor of heat, the more superficial air sacs, particularly if they contain relatively static air, may act to protect the body from heat loss in cold weather.

The main function of hemoglobin in the blood is to pick up oxygen in the lungs and give it to the oxygen-hungry cells throughout the body. In spite of the fact that avian hemoglobin has a somewhat weaker affinity for oxygen than mammalian hemoglobin, it nevertheless is more efficient in oxygen transport because it gives up oxygen more readily than does mammalian hemoglobin. A study of the difference in oxygen concentration in arterial and venous bloods of the duck and pigeon shows a utilization of 60 per cent, compared with 27 per cent in man (Prosser, 1950). Both the high temperatures and the high carbon dioxide concentrations in body tissues of birds promote a generous dissociation or unloading of oxygen by the red blood cells.

Birds consume energy at variable rates, depending on a variety of conditioning factors. As mentioned earlier, size is an important factor. The resting metabolism of a hummingbird, as measured by its oxygen consumption, is about 12 times that of a pigeon, 25 times that of a chicken, and 100 times that of an elephant. If an elephant's tissues generated heat as rapidly as a hummingbird's, the elephant, unable to lose heat rapidly enough, would cook to death. Apparently hummingbirds and shrews have reached the smallest size theoretically possible for warm-blooded animals. Animals significantly smaller would probably not be able to eat food fast enough to avoid starvation (Pearson, 1953). And, of course, warm-blooded birds and mammals metabolize energy at much faster rates than do cold-blooded animals. A resting canary consumes about 4 cc. of oxygen per gram of body weight per hour, but the cold-blooded Goldfish, *Carassius auratus*, consumes only 0.12 cc./gm. per hour; an earthworm, 0.06 cc./gm. per hour; and a sea anemone, 0.013 cc./gm. per hour. With their much

lower rates of metabolism, cold-blooded animals do not readily suffocate, which explains why miners keep canaries instead of goldfish in mines to detect foul air.

The degree to which activity accelerates metabolism is illustrated by the hummingbirds mentioned above. While flying, a hummingbird consumes about 30 times as much oxygen as when it is torpid and coasting through the night with only its "pilot light" burning. As a bird or a man grows older, its metabolic rate slows down. When one month old a Domestic Chicken consumes about twice the oxygen it does when 12 months old. Sex also influences metabolism. In chickens the metabolic rate of males is higher than that of females. When males are castrated their rate drops about 13 per cent (see p. 143). The thyroid gland has a profound effect on metabolism. Overactivity of the gland elevates, and underactivity depresses, metabolic rate (Sturkie, 1954). Removal of the thyroid glands causes heat production in a chicken to drop 14 per cent; and in a goose, 15 to 33 per cent. Diseases that affect the thyroid gland, or that cause fevers, likewise influence metabolic rate.

The molting and growth of feathers require added energy. The metabolic rate of the Chaffinch, *Fringilla coelebs*, rises about 25 per cent while it is regenerating its flight feathers; and that of the Domestic Fowl, *Gallus gallus*, rises about 45 per cent during the autumnal molt (Koch and de Bont, 1944).

METABOLISM AND TEMPERATURE

All animals are either cold-blooded or warm-blooded, poikilothermal or homothermal. Actually, a poikilothermal animal is one whose body temperature approximates that of its environmental medium, while a homothermal animal maintains a relatively warm body temperature independent of environmental temperatures. Only mammals and birds are homothermous. Homothermy confers rich benefits on its possessors, but at a heavy metabolic price. Warm-bloodedness makes possible an internal physiological stability, which in turn makes an animal independent of many environmental restrictions, particularly thermal limitations. Only two species of reptiles, for example, are found living inside the arctic circle; but hordes of homothermous birds live and breed there.

As pointed out in the first chapter, the race in competitive nature usually goes to the metabolically swift, and the constant high temperatures of homotherms make a high level of metabolism possible throughout the year. Homothermism also provides an enormous and obvious psychic advantage to birds and mammals, but one commonly overlooked. The rate and extent of animal learning depend heavily upon frequency and recency of experience. Even man forgets new mental acquisitions very quickly if they are not soon repeated. Warm-bloodedness makes possible a continuity of experience that powerfully supports the learning process. Most of the little that the slow, chilly brain of a reptile might learn is probably forgotten during the periods of nighttime or winter dormancy.

Birds have higher and more variable temperatures than mammals. Adult mammals range roughly between 36° and 39° C., while birds range from 37.7° to 43.5° C., the majority of them from 40° to 42° C. In extensive studies of bird temperatures, Baldwin and Kendeigh (1932) found the average resting temperature of 29 passerine species to be 40.4° C. Recent work by Udvardy (1953) found a mean resting temperature of 311 passerines to be 40.6° C. and of 90 Charadriiformes, 40.09° C. Primitive species tend to have lower temperatures than more advanced species; the kiwi, for example, has a body temperature of 37.8° C. As a general rule the body temperature of small birds fluctuates more than that of large birds; that of a House Wren, *Troglodytes aëdon*, may fluctuate 8° in 24 hours; that of a Robin, *Turdus migratorius*, about 6°. The domestic duck, on the other hand, varies its temperature only about one degree in the course of a day.

There is a fairly close but inverse relationship between the weight of a bird and its temperature. Body temperatures of various species plotted against the logarithm of their adult weights show a linear correlation—the smaller the bird, the higher the temperature. With every tenfold increase in body weight there is, roughly, a decrease of 1.5° C. in body temperature. The same correlation holds for large mammals; but, surprisingly, for mammals with weights of less than about five kilograms, body temperatures become lower with decreasing weight, rather than higher as in birds (Rodbard, 1950). This contrast is probably due to the fact that fur is a poorer insulator than feathers, so that a small mammal, with its relatively large surface, cannot maintain as high a body temperature as a small bird.

The daily cycle of activity and rest is understandably accompanied by a temperature cycle. Diurnal birds have their highest temperatures late in the afternoon and their lowest in the early morning. Nocturnal species, such as the owls and the Kiwi, have their maximum body temperatures at night, when they are most active. Torpidity in hummingbirds, swifts, and goatsuckers, already referred to, is a temporary poikilothermy which helps a small bird meet its most drastic metabolic crises. A torpid Poor Will, *Phalaenoptilus nuttallii*, whose body temperature was 5° C., had a metabolic rate only 3 per cent of that at normal body temperature (Bartholomew *et al.*, 1957). Dormancy and hibernation are much more generally resorted to by mammals than by birds, probably because mammals have poorer insulating coats and are less able to escape the rigors of winter by migration.

Seasonal variations likewise occur in avian temperatures. In the adult Domestic Hen, heat production is highest in February and lowest in July and August (Sturkie, 1954). To maintain a constant high body temperature in spite of environmental temperature changes, a bird requires not only foods rich in energy, and heat-producing tissues, but also a precise heat-regulatory mechanism. Either the produc-

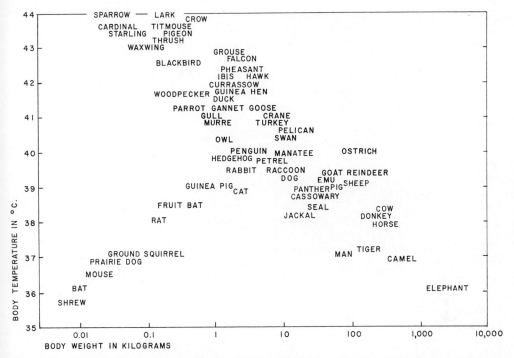

Figure 7.7. Weights of birds and mammals plotted against their body temperatures. Birds show a negative correlation between weight and temperature. Mammals show the same relation, but only down to forms about 5 kg. in weight; then, as mammals get smaller, their temperatures decrease, probably because fur does not insulate against heat loss as well as feathers do. After Rodbard.

tion of heat or its rate of loss may be controlled to maintain a steady temperature. Both the dilatation of blood vessels in the skin and the increase in the rate of breathing accelerate heat loss in warm weather. The water evaporated from the respiratory channels of a bird takes the place of that from the sweat glands of a mammal. The Budgerigar, *Melopsittacus undulatus*, whose normal respiration rate is about 72 to 120 per minute, increases its breathing rate to 185 to 300 per minute at an air temperature of 37° to 38° C. Mourning Doves, *Zenaidura macroura*, drink about four times as much water at 39° as at 23° C. A dove without water for 24 hours at 39° lost 15 per cent of its body weight (Bartholomew and Dawson, 1954). In extreme heat, pelicans, goatsuckers, and many other species resort to panting to increase the cooling ventilation of respiratory passages. In very cold weather most birds ruffle their feathers and thus create

a thicker, warmer layer of insulation. Young nestlings will huddle together in cold weather, and spread out to expose more heat-radiating surface in hot weather. In similar manner, parent birds will brood their young closely on cold days and shade their young with their outspread wings on hot days. Significantly, it is among the smallest species of birds in England, the Goldcrest, *Regulus regulus*, Wren, *Troglodytes troglodytes*, Long-tailed Tit, *Aegithalos caudatus*, and creepers, *Certhia* spp., that one occasionally finds sleeping aggregations in cold weather. As many as 50 Tits have been found huddled together in a ball-like mass on cold winter nights (Tucker, 1949). As another behavior pattern adapted to heat-retention, ptarmigan and other species burrow into loose snow to spend the night in bitter weather. Snow Buntings, *Plectrophenax nivalis*, may spend the night and even a major part of the day buried in the

Figure 7.8.   A feathery ball of about 15 Tree Creepers, huddled together to keep warm on a cold winter night in southern Germany. The tails of 8 are clearly visible. Photo by Hans Löhrl.

snow when the air temperature is between −30° and −37° C. Evolutionary selection has taken a hand in this heat-conservation problem by generally insuring that birds living in colder climates have larger bodies than their relatives living in warm climates. Thus, large arctic species have comparatively small surface areas, and consequently lose less heat per unit of weight than their smaller tropical relatives, who have comparatively large surface areas. This principle, known as Bergmann's Rule, has wide geographic and ecological implications.

When physical mechanisms for heat conservation do not suffice and the body temperature begins to fall, the bird's muscles begin to shiver; oxygen consumption increases; and extra heat is generated. A House Sparrow, *Passer domesticus,* for example, will maintain a body temperature of 41.5° C. at both 37° and 0° C., but at 0° will produce twice as much heat as at 37°. There is evidence that a temperature control center exists in the thalamus or hypothalamus of the bird's brain, and that it responds to temperature receptors in the skin, to internal temperatures in the body, and to hormones. The temperature center controls the reactions of the bird (feather erection, panting, shivering, and the like) either directly by autonomic nerve impulses or indirectly through endocrine secretions. A thermosensitive center in the hypothalamus of cold-blooded vertebrates controls blood pressure and is possibly the forerunner of the temperature regulating center in birds and mammals (Rodbard, 1953).

Chicks of megapodes ("incubator birds") are exceptionally precocial in that they apparently possess a well developed control of body temperature when they emerge from the shell. In other species this capacity to regulate body temperature develops more slowly. In her study of the development of thermal regulation in young birds, Mrs. Nice (personal letter) found that temperature regulation starts early but develops slowly in the downy, alert chicks of precocial species, whereas it starts later but develops more rapidly in altricial nestlings—those young which emerge from the shell blind, naked, and usually cold-blooded. The precocial chicks of the Bobwhite, *Colinus virginianus*, have some capacity to regulate body temperature even before hatching, and when one day old can maintain homothermy, but only within a narrow, rather elevated temperature range. Precocial young European Oystercatchers, *Haematopus ostralegus*, in an air temperature of· 14° C. maintained body temperatures of 31° C. at 3 hours of age, and of 33° at 5 hours of age, ten minutes after being brooded by adults. At 18, 23, and 30 hours of age, body temperatures were 37°, 39°, and 41°, all at 14° air temperature (Barth, 1949). As a general rule, altricial young acquire a relatively stable homothermism when between one and two weeks old (Fig. 17.20). The single downy young of Wilson's Petrel, *Oceanites oceanicus*, is brooded in an antarctic burrow by its parents only the first day or two after hatching. From then on it remains unattended all day long in an air temperature of 5° C. Its temperature control appears at the age of two days. This seems to be an evolutionary adaptation to the peculiar habits of the adults in an inhospitable environment. The young of the closely-brooded Adelie Penguin, *Pygoscelis adeliae*, in the same chilly habitat, do not establish homothermy until about the fifteenth day.

The establishment of temperature regulation is no doubt largely a hereditary matter, but it may be conditioned by environmental factors. Experiments by Ryser and Morrison (1954) on the precocial young of the Ring-necked Pheasant, *Phasianus colchicus*, revealed that re-

peated thirty minute exposures to moderate cold (20° C.) during the first two or three days resulted in a slight drop in body temperature (2° to 4° C.) and an impairment in the development of cold resistance. Altricial young of Snowy Owls, *Nyctea scandiaca*, however, steadily improved their cold resistance even though their body temperatures would drop to 25° C. during the frequent periods of adult absence from the nest.

Young chicks of the European Capercaillie, *Tetrao urogallus*, are precocial and hàtch out relatively homothermous, but with a weak temperature-regulating mechanism. The temperature of newly hatched dry chicks is 37.9° C. and it increases steadily until the chicks achieve normal adult temperature of 41.6° C. on the 18th day. However, chilly, wet weather causes heavy mortality among the chicks because they must spend so much time keeping warm under the hen that they starve to death, even though food be near and plentiful (Hoglund and Borg, 1955).

For every species of bird there is a range of environmental temperatures, known as the range of thermoneutrality, which has little or no effect on metabolism. But temperatures above and below this range will result in increased heat production by the body. The zone of thermoneutrality for the fowl ranges from 16.5° to 27.5° C. (Sturkie, 1954). If the air temperature drops below 16.5°, heat production in the bird increases to maintain its body temperature. If the air temperature drops still farther, the body temperature of the bird will eventually fall, because heat production cannot keep up with heat loss, and the bird will die. If the air temperature is raised much beyond the upper limit of thermoneutrality, heat loss mechanisms cannot keep pace with heat production, with the result that the bird's body temperature will rise, eventually causing death. Birds vary greatly in their survival time under low temperatures: chickens are superior to canaries, and pigeons are much superior to either. Of

25 fasting pigeons subjected to an air temperature of −40° C., the majority survived 72 hours, and four of them survived over 144 hours. But fasting pigeons plucked of their feathers survived less than half an hour (Streicher *et al.*, 1950).

It is in this zone of thermal neutrality that birds seem best able to withstand hunger. Conversely, well nourished birds can withstand extreme temperatures better than hungry birds. A sparrow with an empty stomach will die if its body temperature is allowed to descend to 32.8° C., but if it is well nourished, it will survive a drop to 21° without difficulty (Portmann, 1950). An individual bird may exhibit very different resistance to hunger at different seasons. A bird which survives an empty stomach only an average of 48 hours in summer, in an air temperature of 34°, may survive an average of 67 hours in winter in exactly the same temperature. Presumably, fat storage in the winter enables the bird to maintain the necessary metabolism longer than in summer. It is interesting that the normal body temperature of birds is much closer to the upper limit of thermoneutrality than to the lower. A small rise in body temperature is much more likely to be fatal than a comparable drop in temperature. Birds live close to their maximum metabolic limits. A fasting sparrow in summer, living under an air temperature of 34° C., can expect a maximum survival time of about 48 hours. A rise in air temperature to only 39° C. will cut down its survival time to an average of about 14 hours.

Because of physiological limitations such as these, birds are forced to seek out habitats suitable in climate, food availability, water, and other necessities. This may mean different habitats at different seasons of the year—in short, migration. The Yellowhammer, *Emberiza citrinella*, in north and central Europe can withstand a minimum winter temperature of −36° C. It has thick plumage and is sedentary. Its close relative, the Ortolan Bunting, *Emberiza hortulana*, has sparser plumage and can withstand a minimum of only −16° C. Although it breeds in the same regions as the Yellowhammer, it is compelled by its physiological limitations to migrate to Africa for the winter. Experiments by Kendeigh (1945) have shown that a House Sparrow, *Passer domesticus*, deprived of food will, under an air temperature of −22° C., survive only four hours; at −18°, less than 14.5 hours —the length of a temperate zone winter night; and at −14°, 19 hours. Hungry birds survived longest (67.5 hours) at 29° C. With a rise in air temperature from 29° to 46° C., the survival time decreased at the rate of four hours per degree. Such considerations alone clearly prescribe the northern geographic limits of a bird's winter residence. Without much doubt, the metabolic idiosyncracies of a species have a great deal to do with its geographic distribution and its migratory or sedentary tendencies.

SUGGESTED READINGS

A great deal of information on the physiology of birds is concentrated in Sturkie's *Avian Physiology*. Marshall's *Biology and Comparative Physiology of Birds* contains comprehensive chapters on the respiratory system by Salt and Zeuthen, and on metabolism by Farner, and a brief chapter on the circulatory system by Simons.

EIGHT

Excretion, Reproduction, and Photoperiodism

While the Cock, with lively din,
Scatters the rear of darknes thin,
And to the stack, or the Barn dore,
Stoutly struts his Dames before . . .
John Milton (1608–1674), *L'Allegro*

A seemingly illogical association occurs in vertebrates between the reproductive and excretory systems. In function they have nothing to do with each other, yet in origin and structure they are intimately related. Both systems arise from adjacent ridges of mesodermal cells in the roof of the embryonic body cavity. As an example of their close relationship, the primitive drainage tube of an embryo kidney is taken over by the reproductive system and becomes a sperm duct in the adult bird.

EXCRETION

As in other vertebrates, the kidneys of a bird maintain a homeostatic balance in the concentration of various salt ions in the blood. They also remove various waste products from the blood, particularly those that result from nitrogen metabolism. The kidneys are located behind the lungs in a depression against the sacral vertebrae and the pelvis. As a consequence of rapid metabolism in birds, their kidneys are roughly twice as large as those of

131

comparable mammals. Except in ostriches, there is no urinary bladder, and the urine drains directly by way of the ureters to the cloaca. This arrangement provides one of the weight-saving adaptations that aid flight.

In structure a bird's kidney is much like that of a reptile. It has the two layers— medulla and cortex—of the mammalian kidney, and externally it is usually divided into three lobes, which are again divided into many small lobules. In each lobule is a central vein around which radiate the functional units of the kidney, the nephrons or renal bodies. These are constructed, much like those of mammals, of a renal corpuscle where wastes, salts, glucose, and water filter out of the blood into a renal tubule. In the tubules the water, glucose, and salts are selectively absorbed back into the blood via a network of tubule-clinging capillaries; the wastes, in a concentrated form, pass on down the tubules to the ureter. The renal corpuscles of a bird are smaller and more numerous than those of a mammal. In one cubic millimeter of kidney tissue there are in a bird between 90 and 500 renal corpuscles, as against only 4 to 15 in a mammal (Benoit, 1950). The total number of renal corpuscles in both kidneys of a bird ranges from 30,000 in small passerines to over a million in ducks and geese. As described earlier, the kidneys of a bird receive both arteries and veins, the latter breaking up into a renal portal system. In this the bird kidneys resemble those of more primitive ancestors rather than those of mammals.

The urine in the renal tubules becomes progressively more concentrated through the absorption of water by the walls of the tubules, the walls of the cloaca, and possibly the walls of the rectum. By the time urine is discharged from the body it has combined with fecal material to form a white or cream-colored paste. The urine of birds differs from that of mammals in its high concentration of uric acid rather than urea, and in the preponderance of creatine over creatinine. About 60 per cent of the nitrogenous wastes excreted by the kidneys of birds are in the form of uric acid. The great advantage of excreting uric acid is that it is relatively insoluble in water, so that once it is formed (in the liver) and excreted (in the kidneys), water may be reabsorbed from it until the uric acid is nearly dry and can be discharged from the body with very little water loss. It is this water-saving type of excretion of nitrogenous wastes which makes it possible for desert birds, and also reptiles, to exist solely on the water they obtain from the insects they eat.

One might assume that the excretion of uric acid instead of watery urine was an invention of birds to reduce weight, but for the fact that reptiles show exactly the same trait. The evolutionary significance of uric acid excretion is made clear by Benoit, who points out that this complex type of excretion is restricted to those two classes of oviparous vertebrates which

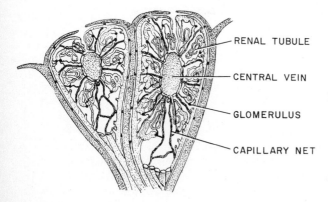

RENAL TUBULE

CENTRAL VEIN

GLOMERULUS

CAPILLARY NET

Figure 8.1. Two lobules of a bird's kidney, in section. After Spanner, from Benoit.

have adopted an exclusively terrestrial type of reproduction. Reptiles and birds lay eggs that develop in a gaseous rather than an aqueous medium. Only gaseous exchanges can occur between the developing, metabolizing embryo in the egg and the surrounding air. Nitrogenous wastes cannot be eliminated in a gaseous form; consequently they must accumulate inside the egg shell. In the soluble form of urea such wastes would quickly poison and kill the growing embryo, but in the nearly insoluble form of uric acid they can be stored harmlessly in a large transitory "bladder," the allantois, until the bird or reptile hatches. The allantois of the newly hatched bird contains a heavy load of uric acid crystals, which are then eliminated via the intestines. In the developing fish or amphibian egg this excretory problem does not exist, since the urea of nitrogen metabolism quickly diffuses outward into the surrounding water; in mammals the maternal placenta carries away the urea from the growing fetus. Natural selection, making an adult virtue of embryonic necessity, has preserved the uric-acid excreting machinery in birds and reptiles to promote their conquest of air and habitation of dry land.

REPRODUCTION

The Origin of Reproductive Organs

The reproductive organs, or gonads, of birds produce the male and female reproductive cells which unite to produce the next generation. The male gonad is the testis, which produces the male sex cells or spermatozoa; the female gonad is the ovary, which produces the female sex cells or ova. The two gonads also secrete hormones which regulate the development and functioning of many body structures.

Racial survival for any species depends heavily upon the efficiency of its reproductive system. Animals have evolved in two contrary directions to promote the survival of their kind. Most of the lower vertebrates and most invertebrates produce great numbers of eggs only to abandon them in water; they gamble, in a sense, on the probability that at least one or two eggs will survive the formidable hazards of an inhospitable environment. Reptiles, birds, and mammals, on the other hand, produce very few eggs, but either endow them with protective shells and a generous supply of food for an early and vigorous start in life, or carry and nourish them within the mother's body. Birds provide further care for their eggs by laying them in protective nests, incubating them, and caring for the young when they hatch. An oyster laying millions of eggs each year is probably no more successful in perpetuating its kind than a sea bird which lays only one egg a year.

Normally, the sex of a developing embryo is initially determined by the sex chromosomes it receives from its mother. Female birds produce two kinds of eggs which differ from each other in the kinds or numbers of sex chromosomes. In the fowl, for example, half of the eggs contain a male-determining sex chromosome and half do not. All sperm, however, are alike, and each contains a male sex chromosome. If an egg containing a sex chromosome is fertilized by a sperm with its sex chromosome, the egg with two male chromosomes will become a rooster. If the egg lacking a sex-chromosome is fertilized by a sperm, the result is a hen, because the one male-determining sex chromosome is overbalanced by the influence of female-determining genes that reside on other than the sex chromosomes.

Regardless of this genetic determination, all embryos start out in life with the essential primordia for forming all the organs of either sex. Which sex a given individual turns into depends, apparently, on enzymes produced by the sex chromosome genes (heredity determiners). These enzymes presumably control the growth and differentiation of cells whose hormones, in turn, control the differentiation of primordial sex cells into either male or female organs. Later on, the sex organs themselves secrete hormones which influence behavior and affect the development of secondary sex characters such as feather shape and color, combs, and spurs. The sex of a bird is normally, but by no means irrevocably, determined at fertilization. Spontaneous and experimental reversals of sex are well established facts.

In the dorsal wall of the visceral cavity, there occur in the early embryo, according to Domm (1955), sex cords which will develop into the sperm-forming tubules if the bird becomes a male, or into the ovary if it becomes a female. Likewise, each embryo starts out with two sets of tubes, the Wolffian and Müllerian ducts. If the animal becomes a male, each of the Wolffian ducts develops into a sperm duct, or vas deferens, and the Müllerian ducts atrophy. The reverse occurs in the developing female, except that only the left Müllerian duct becomes the oviduct, and only the left ovary develops. Both structures normally atrophy on the right side of the body in females. All evidence indicates that hormones control this early sex differentiation in bird embryos. Male hormones, in general, stimulate the development of male structures and the inhibition of female structures in embryos, regardless of the genetic sex. Likewise female hormones promote the development of female organs and inhibit that of male organs in either embryonic sex. As Domm makes clear, the hormones have no power of originating organs or their primordia; they can only "activate or inhibit primordia already laid down." In the embryos of chickens and passerines, sexual differentiation begins during the fifth day of development.

THE MALE REPRODUCTIVE SYSTEM

The essential sex organs in the male bird are the paired testes located just ventral to the anterior end of the kidneys. The testes are generally bean-shaped and their size varies according to season: at their maximum during the breeding season they may be 200 or 300 times larger than at other times of the year. During this seasonal maximum the two testes of a duck may equal one-tenth of its body weight (Benoit, 1950). The left testis is commonly larger than the right. Each testis is composed of numerous seminiferous tubules which give rise to enormous numbers of spermatozoa. As in other vertebrates, the sperm that arise from the tubule cells pass through three stages: (1) Small cells, called spermatogonia, which line the periphery of each tubule, multiply by mitotic cell division until millions are formed. (2) Some of the older spermatogonia move inward toward the central cavity of the tubule and begin a period of growth, increasing about twice in diameter. They are now called spermatocytes. (3) The spermatocytes become spermatozoa through a process of maturation which involves halving the number of chromosomes in each cell—reducing them from two of each kind to one. The spermatozoa, with vibrating tails and a reduced load of heredity determiners, find their way out of the testis and pass into a wavy, ciliated

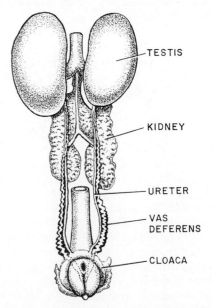

Figure 8.2. The reproductive and excretory organs of the male bird. After Jull; and Sturkie.

tube, the vas deferens, where they accumulate, ready to fertilize the female. During the breeding season the vas deferens also increases greatly in size, especially at its caudal end next to the cloaca, and acts as a sperm storage sac. In the Robin, *Turdus migratorius*, this seasonal increase in capacity may be 120-fold.

Fixed to the ventral wall of the cloaca in primitive birds such as the ostrich or ducks is an erectile, grooved penis which guides the sperm from the male into the cloaca of the female during copulation or "treading." In more advanced species, copulation simply involves the approximation of male and female cloacas, usually while the male stands on the female's back, although some swifts are reported to copulate in flight. A prodigious number of sperm are passed from the male to the female at each coition: 200 million in the pigeon, four billion in the Domestic Chicken (Stresemann, 1927–1934).

A physiological peculiarity of sperm cells is their inability to develop at high temperatures. Warm-blooded mammals have solved this problem by hanging the testes outside the body in a scrotal sac. Such an arrangement would be obviously unsuitable for birds, both because of heat loss in cold weather and because it would disrupt the aerodynamic efficiency of the bird's smooth streamlined shape. So birds keep their testes inside the body, but solve the problem of the heat vulnerability of sperm in three possible ways. First, during the breeding season the testes may migrate until they are in close contact with the cooling abdominal air sacs (Cowles and Nordstrom, 1946). Second, in many birds whose body temperatures are too high for the production of spermatozoa by day, the nocturnal drop in body temperature makes sperm production possible at night (Riley, 1937). Third, the caudal storage region of the vas deferens in some species swells into a cloacal protuberance whose temperature, for example, in several finches, may be 4° C. cooler than the internal body temperature (Wolfson, 1954).

After insemination of the female takes place, the spermatozoa swim up her oviduct and fertilize the egg at its upper end. In the Domestic Hen they may travel the length of the oviduct in as little as 26 minutes. The time lapse between copulation and the laying of the first fertile egg averages about 72 hours in the Domestic Hen, but may be as short as 19.5 hours. The highest percentage of fertile eggs is found in chickens two or three days after copulation, and good fertility occurs up to five or six days, but then drops rapidly. However, an occasional fertile egg may be had even 30 days after mating (Sturkie, 1954). Experiments on the hen of a Mallard, *Anas platyrhynchos*, by Elder and Weller (1954) showed a maximum duration of fertility of about two weeks after a separation from the male. During isolation from the drake, fertility of eggs laid the first week was 64 per cent; the second week, 37 per cent; and the third week, less than 3 per cent. There seems little if any relation between frequency of copulation and the number of eggs laid. In the Griffon Vulture, *Gyps fulvus*, pairs copulate at frequent intervals for an entire month and the female lays only one egg; whereas the hen Turkey, *Meleagris gallopavo*, will lay 12 to 15 eggs after a single copulation. Even when hen Turkeys are inseminated but once every 30 days, they still produce eggs that are 83 per cent fertile (Burrows and Marsden, 1938).

Occasionally eggs may develop and hatch without benefit of fertilization. In Turkeys such fatherless chicks are more likely to appear after the hens have been vaccinated for fowl-pox. Parthenogenesis, or the development of embryos in unfertilized eggs, is especially common in the Beltsville Small White strain of Turkeys. Eight years of selection for parthenogenesis by scientists at the United States Agricultural Research Center at Beltsville, Maryland, has increased the incidence of parthenogenetic eggs from 17 to 40 per cent, and also has increased the number of eggs reaching advanced stages of development. In 1960, 15 parthenogenetic young

Turkeys were hatched, all of them males, and all with the normal diploid complement of chromosomes. One of these birds provided semen to fertilize 14 female Turkeys, nearly half of whose eggs were fertile; of the fertile eggs, some 80 per cent hatched (Olsen, 1960).

Not only do the testes produce sperm that transmit the hereditary traits of the male to the next generation, but they act as endocrine glands that produce the male hormones or androgens. Between the tubules of each testis are interstitial cells, or cells of Leydig. These are considered the source of the male hormones which are so influential in determining the secondary sex characters. The Leydig cells are unusually rich in lipids and in mitochondria. With the seasonal enlargement of the testes comes a corresponding increase in the activity of interstitial cells and an increase in the secretion of androgens into the blood stream. It is this springtime increase in the concentration of male hormones in the body which excites courtship with its songs and bright colors in the male bird; as Tennyson puts it, "In the spring a livelier iris changes on the burnished dove."

THE FEMALE REPRODUCTIVE SYSTEM

Corresponding to the testis in the male is the ovary in the female, located high in the abdominal cavity. This organ, responsible for the manufacture of the eggs, or more properly the ova, is not paired; only the left ovary develops in most birds, and the right ovary and oviduct (Müllerian duct) dwindle to insignificance. If the functional left ovary of a bird is experimentally removed, the vestige of the right ovary will develop into a testis-like organ. The reduction in ovaries from two to one is in part an adaptation to reduce ballast in a flying machine, but also is an arrangement which protects the developing egg. If birds had paired ovaries and oviducts, a sudden jolt of the body, as in alighting, might crack mature eggs located side by

side in the parallel oviducts. Even so, in some birds of prey, especially in the genera *Accipiter, Circus,* and *Falco,* both left and right ovaries persist and function. However, even in these cases it is usually only the left oviduct which develops and carries the eggs. Abnormal ducks with two functional ovaries have been known to lay two eggs in one day.

Like the testes, the ovary enlarges greatly during the breeding season, then shrinks almost to invisibility for the rest of the year. At its maximum, it resembles a bunch of various-sized grapes. Each "grape" will become the yolk of a complete egg. In reality the yolk is the ovum, a single giant cell (about 30 mm. in diameter in the chicken) greatly enlarged with stored food, and surrounded with a nourishing sphere of connective, epithelial, and vascular cells, the follicle. All the ova develop from much smaller follicles in the cortex or outer layer of the ovary. The central part, or medulla, of the ovary is composed mainly of connective tissues and blood vessels. The follicles may number over 25,000 in the ovary of a Rook, *Corvus frugilegus,* and of these, only 5 or 6 follicles mature each year; the great majority never develop into mature ova. Those few destined to mature grow very slowly. In 9 months a Rook follicle increases in size from about 0.05 mm. to 3.5 mm. in diameter. But then it grows very rapidly and reaches the mature size of 14.6 mm. in only 4 days (Benoit, 1950). This rapid increase in size is accounted for largely by the laying down of concentric layers of fat and protein food. The egg yolk of the Domestic Hen is composed of 48.7 per cent water, 32.6 per cent fat, 16.6 per cent proteins, 1 per cent carbohydrates, and 1.1 per cent minerals (Romanoff and Romanoff, 1949).

The pattern of growth and maturation of the ovarian follicles is regulated by the follicle-stimulating hormone of the anterior pituitary gland. In males the pituitary provides a similar hormone which stimulates testes growth. A second pituitary secretion, the luteinizing hormone, stimulates the growth and activity of the interstitial cells in both the ovary and testes, and controls the discharge of the ovum from its follicle. Later in the reproductive cycle, the pituitary gland liberates a third hormone, prolactin, which depresses the production of both the follicle-stimulating and luteinizing hormones, and initiates broodiness (nesting and incubation) in a bird. When a follicle reaches maturity, the outer envelope of cells and blood vessels ruptures; the ovum (yolk) breaks out and is swept into the open end of the oviduct. This release of the ovum from the follicle and ovary is called ovulation, and it normally takes place within 15 to 75 minutes after the laying of the preceding egg by the chicken, or four to five hours after laying by the pigeon (Sturkie, 1954). From their microscopic origin to the large mature ova, the female reproductive cells pass through essentially the same cell division stages as the maturing sperm cells. At maturity both types of cells have the reduced or haploid number of chromosomes (single chromosomes), so that fertilization restores the diploid number (paired chromosomes) characteristic of the body cells of the bird.

As in the testes, there are certain cells in the ovary which secrete sex hormones. It is thought that scattered interstitial cells between the follicles, and probably the follicles themselves, are the sources of these hormones. Both male and female hormones are produced by the ovary.

In the mature female the oviduct is a long, winding tube through which the ovum progresses, and in which it acquires layers of albumen, shell membranes, shell, and pigment. The oviduct wall is built up of three layers: an outer connective tissue serosa, a thick layer of circular and longitudinal muscles to move the egg by peristalsis, and an inner glandular epithelial layer which secretes the various substances added to the ovum.

Longitudinally, the oviduct can be divided functionally into five regions. The first is the funnel-shaped infundibulum, whose contractile folds envelop the ovum as it breaks out of the ovarian follicle. Ovulation stimulates the activity of the oviduct. At the time the follicle ruptures and the ovum is released, the infundibulum will actively engulf any suitable object. Cork balls have been experimentally substituted for ova, with the result that the bird laid eggs with centers of cork instead of yolk. Between periods of ovulation the infundibulum is not receptive. The ovum remains in it only a short time —about 18 minutes in the chicken—and then is moved on into the second and largest section of the oviduct, the magnum. This portion, lined with glandular and ciliated cells, secretes layers of albumen (egg-white) around the ovum. The albumen-secreting glands of the magnum are activated by ovarian hormones, and cease their secretion once the ovary becomes inactive. The developing egg remains in the magnum about three hours in the Domestic Hen, and then passes by peristalsis to the third region, the narrow isthmus. Here the egg remains about an hour and a quarter while it receives the shell membranes.

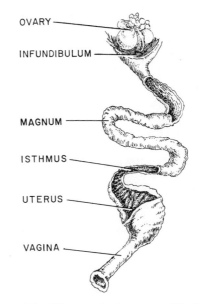

OVARY

INFUNDIBULUM

MAGNUM

ISTHMUS

UTERUS

VAGINA

Figure 8.3. The reproductive organs of the female bird. After Sturkie.

The egg spends most of its time—18 to 20 hours in the hen—in the fourth section of the oviduct, the large muscular uterus, or shell gland, where it acquires some watery albumen and its external limy shell. During the last few hours in the uterus the egg becomes pigmented. The uterine glands which color the egg secrete pigments that are related to blood and bile pigments. Perhaps this is an adaptive method of getting rid of wastes, for the colors of the eggs of some open-nesting birds are highly concealing. Whether an egg has diffuse coloring, speckles, streaks, or blotches seems to depend on its relative motion while the tiny pigment glands are applying colors (Thomson, 1923). The terminal section of the oviduct is the vagina, whose mucous glands and muscular walls aid in laying the egg. The total time the egg takes to pass through the oviduct varies according to species: it is about 24 hours in the Domestic Hen, and about 41 hours in the pigeon.

During the breeding season a bird's oviduct weighs from 10 to 50 times as much as during periods of sexual inactivity. Both the size and activity of the oviduct are closely dependent on ovarian hormones. If a laying hen has its ovary removed, the oviduct ceases its secretion and regresses to its inactive size. The injection of various sex hormones, male and female, will powerfully stimulate the growth of the oviduct in immature females of various species. Ovarian hormones injected into a Domestic Chick will cause its oviduct to increase in size forty-fold. Male hormones, likewise, will vigorously stimulate oviduct growth, and will also stimulate hens to assume male copulatory behavior. If male hormones (androgens) and female hormones (estrogens) are injected simultaneously into a female Starling, *Sturnus vulgaris*, they seem to cooperate in stimulating the oviduct (Benoit, 1950).

The laying of an egg seems to depend partly on unidentified hormones secreted by the ruptured follicles, and partly on autonomic innervation of the powerful muscles of the uterus and vagina. Hormones and drugs which cause muscle con-

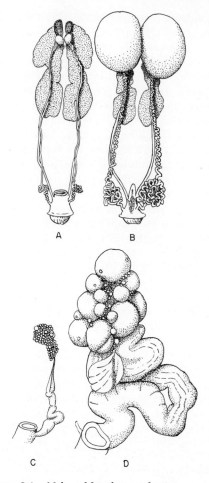

Figure 8.4. Male and female reproductive organs of the House Sparrow, before and after treatment with hormones. *A*, Male organs, quiescent phase. Weight of left testis, 0.5 mg. *B*, Male organs after 17 daily injections of 0.1 ml. (20 D.R.U.) of pregnant mare serum. Weight of left testis, 345 mg. *C*, Female's ovary and oviduct in quiescent phase. Weight of ovary, 10 mg. *D*, Female organs after 16 daily injections of 2 rat units (2 D.R.U.) of hypophyseal extract. Weight of ovary, about 500 mg. After Witschi. *A* and *B*, × 1½; *C* and *D*, × 2.

traction induce premature egg-laying. The intravenous injection of 0.1 to 0.2 cc. of obstetrical (posterior) pituitrin will stimulate a hen to lay an egg in three to four minutes (Sturkie, 1954). Some species of birds, such as warblers, tanagers, and finches, lay their eggs early in the morning, shortly after sunrise. Other species, such as manakins and anis, lay their eggs around noon. That some species possess a psychic control over egg-laying is demonstrated by brood parasites such as cowbirds and cuckoos. These birds can control to within a few seconds the time when they surreptitiously lay their eggs in the nests of their hosts. Most birds seem to be *determinate* layers, in that they lay a certain number of eggs and then stop, regardless of the fate of the eggs. Other birds, *indeterminate* layers, continue to lay eggs until a definite number has accumulated in the nest. In some way, at present unknown, the clutch of eggs then stimulates the anterior pituitary to secrete a prolactin-type hormone which induces regression of the ovary and initiates incubation behavior.

Considerable metabolic expenditure is involved in the laying of a clutch of eggs. The twelve eggs laid by the Spotted Crake, *Porzana porzana*, weigh one-fourth more than the bird itself. About 35 per cent of the egg mass represents yolk synthesized by the ovary, and 65 per cent represents albumen, membranes, and shell synthesized by the oviduct (Stresemann, 1927–1934). Since the eggs of a clutch are commonly laid at intervals of one or two days, rarely more, this means that these materials or their precursors must be made available quickly and copiously to the glands that produce the eggs.

The character of a bird's blood during the egg-laying period clearly reflects this seasonal devotion to egg manufacture. In a laying bird, fatty substances in the blood (phospholipids, fatty acids, and neutral fats, but not cholesterol) increase from three- to eighteen-fold over those in a non-laying or male bird. This great increase in blood lipids, which occurs shortly before and during laying, is stimulated by ovarian hormones. Estrin injected into immature hens (and also roosters) will double their concentration of blood lipids within twelve hours (Sturkie). Estrogens also stimulate the deposit of fat in body tissues of birds of either sex (Fig. 8.5).

Blood-sugar concentration in a laying hen is about twice that in a non-layer or a male. Although experimental studies of blood-sugar mechanisms have given conflicting results, it seems probable that hormones from the thyroid gland and the adrenal cortex are of chief importance in regulating carbohydrates in the blood.

Blood calcium, important for the formation of the eggshell, is essentially doubled in the laying hen or pigeon. Using radioactive calcium as a tracer, Comar and Driggers (1949) found that about 70 per cent of the calcium in an eggshell is obtained by eating, and about 30 per cent is from calcium stored in the body. The

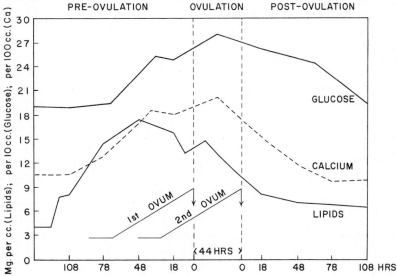

Figure 8.5. Changes in the chemical constituents of a pigeon's blood, associated with the ovulation of its two eggs. After Riddle; and Sturkie.

large bones of the body act as storage chambers for the extra calcium needed for the shell. As the ovarian follicles grow, they apparently secrete hormones which stimulate a heightened absorption by the intestine of calcium from the food eaten, and also promote a rapid and massive storage of calcium in the hollow bones of the body. Mature female pigeons, for example, have solid bones, while males have hollow bones. Injection of estrogen in various species has increased bone-calcium deposition. Evidence indicates that hormones of both the ovary and parathyroid glands cooperate to regulate the level of blood calcium. Neither one alone is effective, but together they regulate the calcium resources of the body for bone construction or destruction, and for eggshell secretion (Benoit, 1950). Apparently the female bird stores calcium in the bones only to withdraw it via the blood each time she needs to secrete an eggshell. The habit which many female birds have of eating the eggshells after their young have hatched may be an instinctive method of restoring depleted calcium reserves.

Not all birds attain sexual maturity with equal speed. As a rule, small species of birds become sexually mature sooner than large species. Some species lay eggs when very young: some tropical Ploceidae when only eight weeks old; the African finch, *Amadina erythrocephala*, when two months old; the Budgerigar, *Melopsittacus undulatus*, at three months; button quail, Turnicidae, before they are four months old (Steinbacher, 1936). Among larger birds that reach sexual maturity after some years, records of birds in the wild are understandably difficult to obtain. White Storks, *Ciconia ciconia*, are reported by Schüz (1936) to reach full sexual maturity ordinarily when four years old, but occasionally not until they are five. Studies of the Satin Bower-bird, *Ptilonorhynchus violaceus*, by Marshall (1954), suggest that the males become sexually mature when they are four or five years old—a remarkable age for a passerine bird. Three individual Mutton Birds

or Slender-billed Shearwaters, *Puffinus tenuirostris*, banded as nestlings, were observed by Serventy (1957) to nest for the first time when they were five, six, and seven years old.

An interesting characteristic of many species is that all the structures and functions of their reproductive apparatus do not come to full bloom at the same time. Herring Gulls, *Larus argentatus*, in immature plumage may pair, build nests, and copulate, but lay no eggs. Their reproductive instincts are apparently out of step with their gonads. Year-old White Storks, *Ciconia ciconia*, do not return to their European birth-nests but remain for the summer in their African winter quarters. Two-year-olds may return and claim nests, but do not breed. Three-year-olds often breed, but either raise fewer young than older birds or none at all (Schüz, 1936). Year-old female Starlings, *Sturnus vulgaris*, Bluebirds, *Sialia sialis*, and other passerines commonly begin laying later in the season and lay fewer eggs than older birds. In his study of gonad development in 485 specimens of the California Gull, *Larus californicus*, Johnston (1956) discovered that the testes of first-year birds showed no significant enlargement; those of second-year birds were about one-fourth adult size; and those of third-year birds about one-half adult size. First- and second-year birds did not breed, but among the three-year-olds a few females and about half of the males were thought to breed. A similar study of 215 male Red-winged Blackbirds, *Agelaius phoeniceus*, by the Wrights (1944) showed that the testes of year-old birds are smaller and develop maximum breeding size later in the season than those of older birds. The older birds maintain maximum testis size for a period of 50 to 75 days; the year-old birds, for a period of 30 to 55 days. Although the year-olds produce spermatozoa, they fail to breed, perhaps because breeding is psychologically dependent on ownership of territory, and available territory has already been preempted by older males.

In a 17-year study of the Yellow-eyed Penguin, *Megadyptes antipodes,* in New Zealand, Richdale (1954) discovered that fertility in females 2 years old was 18 per cent; 3 years old, 82 per cent; 4 years old, 95 per cent; 5 to 15 years old, 93.7 per cent; over 15 years, 91.7 per cent. Sexual maturity also seems to vary with sex in certain species. In Yellow-eyed Penguins, 3-year-old males seemed to be less fertile than 3-year-old females. Only 7 per cent of the 2-year-old males nested, whereas 48 per cent of the 2-year-old females nested. Among Starlings studied in Holland by Kluijver (1935), the majority of the females bred when a year old, but most males not until they were 2 years old.

Sexual maturity is also a matter of geographic distribution. The Black-headed Gull, *Larus ridibundus,* rarely breeds in the Baltic when a year old, but it commonly breeds in Holland, Switzerland, and Hungary at that age. Starlings seldom breed in Latvia at one year of age, but regularly do in Hungary (Steinbacher, 1936).

SECONDARY SEX CHARACTERS

One of the more exciting discoveries in ornithological history was made by Crew (1923), who found an Orpington chicken which changed its sex. This bird, a laying hen for three and one-half years, changed its external appearance, became a rooster, and sired two chicks. An autopsy of the bird revealed two functioning testes and a shriveled left ovary, probably destroyed by a tumor. Here was a natural, spontaneous reversal of sex which strikingly revealed the bisexual potentiality of birds. Since Crew's observations, much experimental work has been done on sex and sexual characteristics in birds. The majority of these experiments involve the manipulation of sex hormones through castration, grafting of sex organs, or the injection of hormones.

Birds, more than any other vertebrates, commonly show pronounced somatic differences between the male and the female. Although at hatching both sexes usually look the same, in many species they soon begin to differ in plumage, color, combs and spurs, size, song, and reproductive behavior. These differences are known as secondary sex characters (the primary characters being the gonads themselves), and they are largely due to the actions of sex hormones. The extravagant development of these "badges of sex" in many birds is very likely related to their

Figure 8.6. Experimental manipulation of secondary sex characters in the Domestic Fowl. Top row, left to right: normal male; castrated male; castrated male with grafted ovary. Bottom row: normal female; castrated female; castrated female with grafted testes. After Zawadowsky, from Benoit.

ROOSTER   CAPON   CAPON + OVARY

HEN   POULARD   POULARD + TESTES

heightened metabolism, the great velocity of their behavior reactions, and their fugitive mode of living. A male bird, showing off his fine feathers and splendid voice before his intended, has to make a persuasive impression in a hurry, before either one of them is frightened away by some predator. And competition with other males of the same species has undoubtedly played a role in intensifying these secondary sex characters. Darwin developed this theme into his principle of sexual selection.

If the two testes are removed from a young male chicken, it will grow into a capon instead of a cock or rooster. The bird will fail to develop a large comb and wattles, but it will retain its spurs. Instead of long glossy tail feathers it will develop dull, henny feathers; it will lose its proud posture and pugnacity and will no longer crow. In short, it loses most of the secondary characters which distinguish a cock from a hen. A castrated hen, or poulard, will develop a smaller comb; it will grow spurs where none existed before; at its next molt it will develop capon-like plumage. If now the capon has an ovary grafted into its belly, it will develop externally into a very close replica of a hen except that it will retain its spurs. If a testis is grafted into a poulard, the bird will take on the external appearance of a cock, spurs and all. Similar results are obtained when appropriate sex hormone injections are substituted for the grafts (Benoit, 1950). If androgens (testosterone and androsterone) are injected into one-

day-old chicks and the injections continued from five to ten consecutive days, the chicks will develop large combs and wattles, and some of them will begin crowing when only three days old (Kosin, 1942)! Recent experiments by Pincus and Hopkins (1958) have shown that merely dipping the pointed end of a fertile hen's egg into a solution of diethylstilbestrol in ethanol (10 mg./100 ml.) for ten seconds caused a feminization of male chicks, as revealed by their external genitalia. Sixteen weeks later, however, these "reversed" chicks developed normal testes. Masculinization of female chicks was not as easily accomplished by this method.

Such experiments as these show that there are two classes of secondary sex characters. In one group are those stimulated by sex hormones: combs, wattles, plumage, song, and sex instincts. The other group includes those characters which are inhibited by sex hormones, as the spur is by estrogens.

Other endocrine glands than the gonads also play important roles in the development and function of body structures; and some of them, such as the anterior pituitary or the thyroid, interact intimately with the gonads. Throughout the life of the bird there continues a complex interplay of endocrine secretions, many details of which are only now being discovered. In broad outline, the endocrine activities in a bird are similar to those in man and other mammals.

Not all secondary sex characters re-

Figure 8.7. Eighteen-day-old chicks of the Domestic Fowl. The one on the left was injected with the male hormone testosterone, which caused precocious development of male characteristics. After Selye, from Zuckerman.

spond with equal sensitivity to hormone dosage. That is, different parts of the body have different thresholds to hormone modification. The feathers on a bird's back, for example, have a lower threshold (i.e., they are more sensitive) to hormone modification than those of the throat. Work by Juhn *et al.* (1931) showed that there was a direct relationship between the speed of feather growth and the height of hormone threshold. It should be remembered that some somatic characters are irrevocably determined by heredity and cannot be modified by hormones. A crow will remain black no matter what hormones course through its blood. Albino crows are the result of genetic and not endocrine modification. A convincing experiment which illustrates the relative roles of genes and hormones in determining somatic characters was performed by Willier and Rawles (1940). They grafted a piece of head-skin ectoderm from the 72-hour embryo of a Barred Plymouth Rock chicken to the wing-bud base of a male White Leghorn embryo of the same age. The chicken which resulted had white feathers all over the body except for typical Barred Rock feathers on its wing (Fig. 3.18). The genes in the graft determined the pigment pattern of the feathers, but the wing-location and hormones of the host (White Leghorn) determined their size, shape, and male character.

Secondary sex characters are of course not limited to the outside of the body. Male and female birds show internal sex dimorphism in both structure and function. Some of these differences are unquestionably due to hormones; others are due to heredity. In chickens and pigeons, for example, the blood is richer in red corpuscles in males than in females, and this difference disappears in castrated males. The heart of a capon is only one-half as large as that of a cock. Castration of a cock will lower its respiration rate 30 per cent (Benoit, 1950).

Numerous instinctive behavior patterns are influenced through the effects of sex hormones on the nervous system. Experiments by Davis and Domm (1941) have revealed that much of the behavior related to reproduction is hormone-influenced: for example, the crowing of the rooster, its combativeness, and copulation pattern. These all disappear in castrates. If, however, a capon is injected with male hormones (androgens), it will begin to crow and embark on courtship conquests of hens. A poulard injected with female hormones (estrogens) will crouch and accept copulation from a cock; injected with androgens it will crow and show other forms of male behavior. Apparently some forms of behavior are common to both sexes and may be called forth in either by appropriate hormones. Interestingly, a capon will assume copulation behavior when injected either with androgens or estrogens, but only androgens will induce crowing.

Not only are psychic activities subject to endocrine control, but endocrine activity itself is subject to psychic control. Experiments by Matthews (1939) with a female pigeon demonstrated that it would lay eggs quite readily if it were placed in a cage with a male pigeon; somewhat less readily with a female pigeon; and not at all if isolated completely from other birds. However, when it was accompanied by a mirror in its cage it began to lay! Among birds which breed in large colonies, such as gulls and terns, there is often communal breeding in which wave-like spasms of copulation overrun the colony. This promotes synchronized breeding which is advantageous because it means that the chicks will all hatch at about the same time. This simplifies the problem of their defense against predators, because the parent birds can cooperate in the protection of the helpless young of the community, and predators are able to exploit them as a source of food only during a very limited time. Accordingly, the predator is unable to build up a heavy population dependent on the leisurely exploitation of a longer-enduring food source. In his studies of gull colonies, Darling (1938) concluded that synchronous breeding was more likely to occur in large than in small colonies. His observations showed that nesting occurred earlier, more eggs hatched, and more young were fledged in large colonies than in small. Predatory Hooded Crows, *Corvus cornix*, were more likely to rob colonies with widely-spaced nests than those with closely-spaced nests. Similar social suggestibility in breeding has been shown in the Tricolored Blackbird, *Agelaius tricolor*, and the House Sparrow, *Passer domesticus*, but not in the colonial-nesting Redwinged Blackbird, *Agelaius phoeniceus*.

Infectious breeding behavior is not necessarily dependent on sex-ripeness. Pellets of crystalline testosterone were implanted under the skin of wild male California Quail, *Lophortyx californicus*, during the non-breeding season, by Emlen and Lorenz (1942). The quail were marked for field identification and released. Although the birds did not show complete breeding behavior, they crowed, became pugnacious toward other males, and paired with females. Untreated, wild control males showed contagious behavior and also paired with females, even though this was not during their normal breeding season.

SEX RATIOS

Unequal sex ratios commonly occur among birds. In ducks, for example, studies of many species have shown a marked preponderance of adult males (sometimes as high as 3:1) over females. In the Australian Honey-eaters, (Meliphagidae), there are genera in which males seem to be ten times as numerous as females (Mayr, 1939). Some examples of sex ratio determinations from relatively large samples are given in Table 8.1. In most instances these birds were adults which had been trapped for banding studies.

The reasons for these unequal ratios are not easily determined. Without doubt there are various forces which operate to produce a selective bias in sex ratios. Since different observers often obtain different sex ratios for the same species of bird, it is clear that published sex ratios may be more apparent than real. Errors in determining the actual sex ratio of a species may be due to the method, the time, or the place of sampling the population. A sample of 8000 Mallards, *Anas platyrhynchos*, from hunters' bags in Illinois revealed a sex ratio of 57 per cent males to 43 per cent females, while 3700 Mallards caught in banding traps in Illinois at the same time showed 74 per cent males (Hawkins, 1940). Apparently, male ducks enter traps more readily than do females. Since similar sex ratios from banding traps are obtained before and after hunting seasons, it seems unlikely that there is a sex-differential in duck mortality from hunting.

Table 8.1.   Sex Ratios in Wild Birds

SPECIES	TOTAL NUMBER OF BIRDS	PER CENT MALES	PER CENT FEMALES	SOURCE
8 species of ducks	"thousands"	67	33	McIlhenny
10 species of ducks	40,904	60	40	Lincoln
15 species of ducks	10,180	54	46	Beer
Pintail Duck	5,707	73	27	McIlhenny
Mallard Duck	21,723	52	48	Homes
Blue-winged Teal	5,090	59	41	Bennett
Bobwhite Quail	45,452	53	47	Leopold
Crow	1,000	53	47	Imler and McMurry
House Sparrow	20,931	55	45	Piechocki
Evening Grosbeak	3,914	54	46	Magee
Redwinged Blackbird	6,480	84	16	McIlhenny
Boat-tailed Grackle	5,333	33	67	McIlhenny
Cowbird	4,281	74	26	McIlhenny

Differential sex migration may also introduce large errors in determining adult sex ratios of a species. Apparently male Mallards do not migrate south as extensively as do the females. In the autumn in Illinois the sex ratio was 74 per cent males to 26 per cent females, while in Louisiana in the winter it was 50 per cent to 50 per cent (Petrides, 1944). In Great Britain there is evidence that the older drakes, particularly among the diving ducks, do not migrate as far south in winter as do the females and young ducks, the drakes "far outnumbering the latter in the north of the winter-range, while in the south the reverse is the case" (Tucker, 1943). A further bias in sex ratios may result from the habit several species have of segregating by sex in flocks. The Redwinged Blackbird and other Icteridae show this trait in their winter quarters. Studies of California Quail by Emlen (1940) showed a progressive increase in the proportion of males to females through the winter and spring, indicating a heavier loss of females. In early fall the ratio of males to females was 51:49; in winter, 53:47; and in late spring, 56:44. In Nice's (1937) comprehensive study of the Song Sparrow, *Melospiza melodia*, she discovered that although the sex ratio was nearly balanced early in the spring, by the end of the nesting season there were between 8 and 10 per cent fewer females than males. The incubating females were probably subject to heavier losses than the males. Mayr suggests that in certain species the heavy casualties among males fighting for territory redress the balance in the spring.

Actual (rather than apparent) sex ratios for many adult birds may be largely determined by environmental forces which favor one sex above the other. Very probably the sexes are often differentially vulnerable to predation (including hunting by man), diseases, accidents, parasites, malnutrition, temperature extremes, and other hazards. Male ducks show evidence of being more susceptible than the females to lead poisoning (Wetmore, 1919). The females, on the other hand, are probably much more vulnerable to predators in the many species in which they alone incubate the eggs and care for the young.

The sex ratio of a species at hatching, which is often impossible to determine in a live bird, may already be different from the genetically determined sex ratio at fertilization. From the moment an ovum is fertilized it begins to face the hazards of existence. It may not even survive the trip through the oviduct, and many eggs do not survive the process of incubation. Further, certain genes may disturb the original sex ratio by differentially weakening or killing the embryos. This is particularly true of sex-linked lethal genes, which affect more females than males.

In addition to these and other sources of sex-ratio bias in birds, there is probably a fundamental bias introduced by evolutionary adaptation. It is possible that among species with differential sex vulnerability, or with special sex habits such as polygyny or polyandry, genetic selection has produced an unequal basic sex ratio in the fertilized eggs to meet the special needs of the adults (Mayr, 1939).

THE SEASONAL REPRODUCTIVE CYCLE

One striking characteristic of bird reproduction is its sharply periodic nature. When the proper season arrives, a bird seems to throw all its physiological resources into an intense and concentrated effort to produce the next generation. This effort usually comes at a time of year when environmental conditions are most benign for the raising of young. The survival value of telescoping the breeding season into a short period becomes apparent when one recalls the added burden a bird must carry when its gonads greatly enlarge to produce reproductive cells and hormones. One consequence of the soft life of domestication is the loss of much of this accentuation in breeding. Wild pigeons nest two or three times a year; the domestic pigeon, seven or eight times. The Domestic Chicken, genetically selected for continuous reproduction, can produce sperm or eggs throughout the year; but it is not noted for its prowess in flying. Modifiability of the annual reproductive rhythm has undoubtedly been exploited by natural selection to produce the various breeding timetables exhibited by different birds throughout the world.

With the beginning of the breeding season come not only changes in the size of the gonads but also drastic changes in the bird's physiology and behavior. Like so much other avian behavior, that related to reproduction is often inflexibly stereotyped. A typical sequence in the reproductive behavior of the male starts with selecting and defending the nest territory. This may be followed by courting and pairing with the female, and then, in many species, helping her to build the nest. The final stage may involve helping to care for the young. The automatic nature of these successive stages may be demonstrated experimentally. If, while a pair of Tricolored Blackbirds, *Agelaius tricolor*, are building their nest, some young from another pair are placed in the nest, the adults will not respond to the food calls of the young, and may even incorporate the

young into the structure of the nest (Emlen, 1941). Apparently the nest-building and egg-laying stage of the sex cycle inhibits the care-of-young stage. Later, when the nest is finished and the eggs laid, the adult blackbirds will accept and feed introduced nestlings. Similar chronological rigidity of instincts has been observed in many other species. After the young have become independent, the parent birds usually enter a period of sexual quiescence which may last until the beginning of the next breeding season unless, as in some species, they raise two or more broods each season.

In the northern hemisphere the breeding seasons of birds generally follow spring in its northward march across the land. The breeding cycle is often timed so that the young birds will hatch out when their standard food is abundantly available, and the weather mild. This means that species with long incubation periods must begin their breeding cycle earlier than rapid breeders. The Horned Owl, *Bubo virginianus*, for example, begins breeding in Florida about December 1; in Pennsylvania, mid-February; and in Labrador, late March. Some birds breed nor-

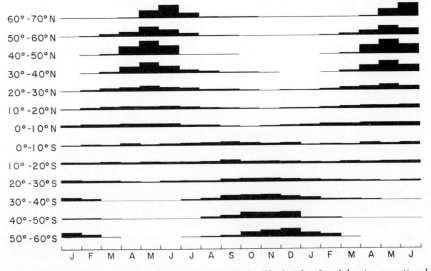

Figure 8.8.   The relation of breeding seasons to latitude. The height of each bar is proportional to the number of species normally producing eggs during that month of the year at that latitude. After Baker.

mally earlier or later than other species at the same latitude. At the latitude of Washington, D.C., the Bluebird, *Sialia sialis*, lays its eggs around April 1; the American Goldfinch, *Spinus tristis*, around July 1.

As one travels north from the equator, the summer season becomes progressively shorter. As a consequence, birds breeding in higher latitudes (and also at higher altitudes) may either shorten the time needed to raise a brood or reduce the number of broods per season. Even races within the same species show adaptations of this sort. In California there are two races of the White-crowned Sparrow. One, *Zonotrichia leucophrys nuttalli*, is a year-'round resident in the vicinity of Berkeley. It takes up territory, pairs, and raises three broods of young in 6.3 months. The other, *Zonotrichia leucophrys pugetensis*, winters in the same locality but migrates north to breed around Puget Sound, some 1200 kilometers away, where it raises three broods in only four months. Although these two races are exposed to the same environmental influences in winter, their gonads develop at strikingly different times and rates (Blanchard, 1941). The Prothonotary Warbler, *Protonotaria citrea*, normally produces two broods per year in Tennessee but only one in Michigan. The European Song Thrush, *Turdus ericetorum*, raises only one brood in south Finland, but raises three and possibly four in Italy, where the summer season is several times longer (Siivonen, 1939).

As a general rule, the breeding seasons of birds begin about 25 days later for each 10 degrees of latitude as one progresses northward from the Tropic of Cancer. However, many species are insensitive to the effects of latitude. When the conifer seeds on which it lives are abundant, the erratically wandering Red Crossbill, *Loxia curvirostra*, is able to breed in any month of the year, and its breeding season rarely comes in the same month for two consecutive years (Griscom, 1937). Since seasonal fluctuations in temperature dwindle to insignificance as one approaches the equa-

tor, it is understandable that wide-ranging species may lose their latitude-breeding correlation in the tropics. The Noddy Tern, *Anoüs stolidus*, has a definite cyclic breeding season in the Dry Tortugas off Florida (24° N. latitude), but breeds throughout the year on St. Paul Rocks (1° N. latitude) in the Atlantic (Murphy, 1936). More puzzling is the performance of the Pied Cormorant, *Phalacrocorax varius*, of southwest Australia, which breeds in the spring (November) on Albrohos Island, but in the autumn on the mainland only some 50 kilometers away (Serventy, 1938). Similarly, the Sooty Tern, *Sterna fuscata*, which shows great geographic irregularity in the timing of its breeding cycles, begins breeding in April on Manana Island, a small islet off Oahu, Hawaiian Islands, and in late October on neighboring Moko Manu, an islet merely 17 kilometers distant! Two explanations have been advanced to account for this peculiar situation. It may be that these two colonies represent northern and southern races of Sooty Terns, and that in migrating to the Hawaiian Islands to breed, they brought with them their ancestral northern- and southern-hemisphere breeding seasons. Or it may be that the recently established breeding colony of Sooty Terns on Manana Island has been forced into a new breeding rhythm, through some sort of mass suggestibility, by the established Noddy Terns which also breed there in April. However, on Ascension Island in the South Atlantic (8° S. latitude), the Sooty Terns breed not once each year but once every 9.7 months (Chapin and Wing, 1959). That is, the birds nest five times in every four years, quite out of synchrony with any possible natural season. The fact that a cycle of 9.7 calendar months corresponds closely with one of 10 lunar months, and also that this species is commonly active by night, suggests a possible breeding synchrony with phases of the moon. A similar correlation for nightjars has been suggested by Wynne-Edwards (1930).

Phenomena such as these immediately

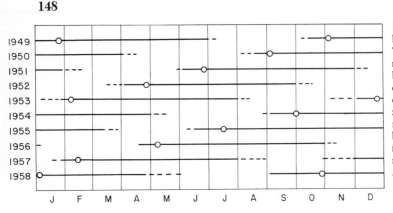

Figure 8.9. The non-annual breeding cycle of the Sooty Tern. This species, nesting near the equator, returns to breed on Ascension Island every 9.7 calendar months, or every tenth full moon. Horizontal lines show the approximate length of stay on the breeding grounds, and circles indicate the dates of the first reported eggs in each season. After Chapin and Wing.

raise the question: What stimulus sets off the breeding cycle in birds? Is it an innate physiological rhythm or is it some stimulus from the environment? The overwhelming majority of wild birds show a sharply accented breeding season once a year, followed by a period of sexual quiescence. In most species the breeding season occurs during the same months each year. Such facts as these strongly suggest an environmental stimulus. However, when wild species are transplanted from the southern hemisphere to the northern, with the subsequent seasonal displacement of six months, a few of them, such as the Emu, *Dromiceius novaehollandiae*, the Budgerigar, *Melopsittacus undulatus*, the Slender-billed Shearwater, *Puffinus tenuirostris*, and the Gouldian Finch, *Poëphila gouldiae*, tend to hold on to their southern-hemisphere breeding rhythm in spite of the changed seasons. European storks removed to Peru breed there at the same time of year that storks do in Europe. Most species, however, adapt quickly, and change their sex rhythm to match the change in seasons.

Many experiments and observations have been made to determine in what way environmental stimuli may influence the reproductive rhythm in birds. Since spring and early summer are the typical breeding seasons for most birds, the environmental changes which occur as winter gives way to spring have been widely investigated: changes in temperature, day-length, light intensity, rainfall, food, exercise. Some evidence has been secured that each of

these seasonal changes may play a part in triggering the annual cycle in birds, but only one—the springtime increase in day length—shows a predominant influence, at least among birds of temperate and boreal zones. Warmer temperatures seem to play a secondary role, and in equatorial regions rainfall is of great significance.

Numerous observations show that a warm early spring is accompanied by earlier nesting in many species. In southern Michigan in 1938, the last 20 days of April were unseasonably warm, and the Prothonotary Warblers, *Protonotaria citrea*, nested two weeks earlier than in cooler 1937 (Walkinshaw, 1939). Unusually warm spring weather in Holland not only allowed the Starlings and Titmice to nest earlier, but permitted two broods of young that season instead of the usual one. In Great Britain in 1953 the last three weeks of November and all of December were unusually warm. Many resident Blackbirds, *Turdus merula*, Song Thrushes, *Turdus ericetorum*, Robins, *Erithacus rubecula*, Starlings, *Sturnus vulgaris*, and House Sparrows, *Passer domesticus*, nested. Of 27 nests of the first three species, young were hatched in nine nests, and were fledged from four in December and January (Snow, 1955). Apparently, warm weather at either end of the reproductive season may stimulate breeding.

In tropical regions which have pronounced rainy seasons, the reproduction of most birds is closely tied to rainfall. The Galapagos finches (Geospizinae), made famous by Darwin, apparently breed from late December to April, during the Galapagos Islands wet season. In desert regions particularly, birds have become physiologically adapted to drought to such an extent that their sexual cycles are quickly responsive to rainfall or to its effects; the birds may begin nesting and egg-laying only a few days after the rains begin. However, should the rains fail, the gonads will remain quiescent and the birds will not breed, even for several seasons if the drought continues (Keast and Marshall, 1954). Nowhere is the stimulating effect of rain on reproduction more diagrammatically illustrated than in Eritrea. Unlike the rest of tropical Africa, eastern Eritrea has its rainy season between November and April. Correlated with this wet season is the breeding cycle of 73.5 per cent of the land birds, which nest between December and March, and a rear guard of 15 per cent which breed in April and May. However, in central and western Eritrea the rains come in summer, and only 9 per cent of the birds breed in the December-March period, and 28 per cent in April and May. Individual species have tailored their reproductive rhythms to fit the rains. *Euodice cantans* breeds in eastern Eritrea from February to April, and in western Eritrea from August to November (Smith, 1955).

The exact mechanism by which rain, or its effects, stimulates the breeding cycle is as yet unknown. In Argentina the Black Skimmer, *Rynchops nigra*, seems to have synchronized its sex cycle with the dry season. For protective isolation from its enemies it nests on the sandbars of large rivers when the water is at low ebb (Murphy, 1936). A striking synchrony in colonial breeding brought on by rain is illustrated in the Red-billed Quelea, *Quelea quelea*, of Africa. This destructive, sparrow-like pest which lives in enormous colonies of up to ten million birds "is precipitated into mass nesting by prolonged rainfall," with the result that their "eggs all hatch at about the same time and the shells tumbling from the nests resemble falling snowflakes" (Gilliard, 1958).

That rain itself may not be the immediate stimulus which synchronizes the sex cycle with cycles in humidity and drought is illustrated by the Stagemaker Bower-bird, *Scenopoeetes dentirostris*, of Australia, which begins its bower building, courtship, and song during the driest season of the year, at which time its gonads begin to mature. Its young subsequently appear at the beginning of the rainy season when food is abundant. Presumably some "anticipatory" stimulus initiates the breeding cycle. Very likely food acts as the ultimate breeding stimulus only in this distant and indirect fashion, although Davis (1940) suggests that a change in the diet of the Smooth-billed Ani, *Crotophaga ani*, from vegetable to animal matter, shortly after the rains begin, provides the immediate stimulus for the development of its gonads. The effects of rain, rather than rain itself, seem to bring on the breeding cycle of the Australian Zebra Finch, *Poëphila castanotis*. It breeds quite regularly in semi-arid regions which are well irrigated, whereas in a similar climate where irrigation is lacking, it apparently breeds only after rainfall (Frith and Tilt, 1959). As a compensatory adaptation to counter the effects of unproductive dry seasons, this species is able, in a humid season, to breed at the age of two months (Wagner, 1957).

As a result of his pioneer experiments with the Junco, *Junco hyemalis*, Rowan (1929, 1938) believed that birds subjected to artificially lengthened days were stimulated into sexual activity by increased exercise and wakefulness. However, later experiments by Riley (1940) and others, involving enforced exercise in rotating cages but in darkness, failed to confirm Rowan's work. Benoit and Ott (1944) produced sexual activation in a duck, artificially restrained from physical activity, merely by means of increased day-length. If exercise has any effect on gonad activation, it must be very minor.

PHOTOPERIODISM

For centuries the Japanese have practiced the art of *Yogai* which consists in forcing caged birds to sing in mid-winter by lengthening their days with candlelight for three or four hours each day after sunset in the fall. The Dutch similarly used to stimulate various finches to sing prematurely in October, then employed them to entice fall-migrating relatives into traps. Poultry raisers for years have stimulated winter laying in hens by illuminating coops for added hours at night. These alterations in the reproductive cycle caused by manipulating the length of day are all manifestations of photoperiodism—the natural response which many plants and animals make to day length.

Since the early photoperiodic experiments on birds by Rowan (1938) and Bissonette (1937), numerous experiments involving photoperiodism have shown clearly that the winter and springtime increase in day length stimulates the springtime growth and activity of gonads in birds; and that artificial increase in day length at other times of the year may stimulate precocious gametogenesis in birds. No other type of external stimulus —heat, exercise, wakefulness, diet, rain— has been demonstrated to induce precocious gametogenesis *in darkness* (Burger, 1949). In an experiment to test the relative values of light versus heat as stimuli to gonad development, Suomalainen (1937) divided 25 Great Tits, *Parus major*, into two groups in January in Finland. One group was kept indoors where it was warm, the other outdoors in the cold. One-half of each group was subjected to continuous electric light, day and night; the other half had natural lighting. Gonads developed only in those birds receiving artificial lighting, irrespective of temperature. Similar results have been obtained with other species.

In equatorial regions where day length is nearly constant throughout the year, photoperiodic responses in birds are attenuated. Since the sun swings overhead twice a year, there may be two breeding seasons a year in some species. Tropical species which breed once a year may synchronize their sex cycle with the northward movement of the sun, as in the Accipitriformes, or with the southward movement, as in the Charadriiformes and Gruiformes (Baker, 1938). In tropical regions with pronounced wet and dry seasons, rainfall as a stimulus may override the weak photoperiodic effect of slight changes in day-length. Some northern-hemisphere species spend their winters in the southern hemisphere far south of the equator. Since they arrive each spring at their northern breeding grounds ready to lay eggs, it may be the *shortening* of day length which trips their reproductive mechanism each year. It may also be true that an immediate external stimulus to initiate the breeding cycle is not needed in the southern hemisphere. It is quite possible that some endocrine cycle, locked in synchrony with the environmental conditions of the northern breeding season, possesses a momentum (or a recovery state) which initiates gonad development at the proper time in the southern hemisphere, regardless of environmental conditions as long as they are not inhibitory.

The way in which the breeding cycle begins and runs its course is described by Marshall (1954) and Eisner (1960) somewhat as follows. External stimuli, such as increased day length, rain, or the sights and sounds of courtship behavior, are registered in the bird's brain, which, through the hypothalamus, stimulates the anterior lobe of the pituitary gland into seasonal activity.

In the male, the pituitary releases into the blood a testis tubule-ripening hormone which promotes the formation of spermatozoa, and an interstitial cell-stimulating hormone which causes the interstitial (or Leydig) cells to produce male sex hormones, or androgens. These, carried by the blood, stimulate the development of secondary sex organs such as the sperm duct, have a regulatory effect on the pituitary, and, acting on the brain, probably stimulate instinctive courtship and mating behavior.

In the female, the anterior pituitary re-

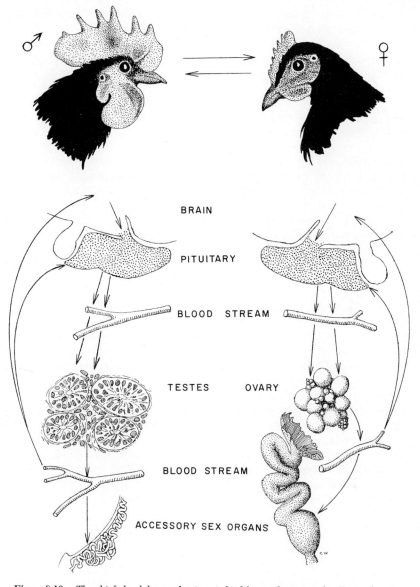

Figure 8.10. The chief glandular mechanisms in birds' reproductive cycles. For explanation, see text. Adapted from Marshall.

leases into the blood stream a follicle-ripening hormone that stimulates the growth of the egg follicles, and also a luteinizing hormone that is thought to stimulate interstitial cell development. As the ovary develops, it liberates into the blood the female sex hormone, estrogen. This causes the growth and activation of accessory sex organs, stimulates courtship and mating behavior, and probably inhibits the further production of the follicle-ripening hormone in the pituitary. The pituitary is thought to release prolactin, which may inhibit follicle and interstitial cell development in the ovary, and inaugurate broodiness (incubation and care-of-the-young behavior) in the hen.

Not all these endocrine reactions are

thoroughly established, and other pituitary and gonadal secretions probably play a part in the reproductive cycle.

A typical photoperiod experiment consists in subjecting a sexually quiescent male bird to an artificially lengthened day. Usually in three or four weeks the bird produces sperm, a sign of mature sexual activity. Even ducks on a starvation diet respond positively to added illumination in three weeks. According to Benoit (1950), an experimental day length of 15 hours (alternating with 9 hours of darkness) will stimulate testes maturation in a normal, quiescent duck in 12 to 15 days. In optimum situations, the testes will increase in volume 10 times in 10 days, 80 times in 20 days. This maturation of the testes includes complete maturity of sperm, interstitial cells, and sperm ducts. Female ducks seem somewhat less sensitive to artificial photoperiodic stimulation, and only rarely reach sufficient sexual maturity to lay eggs, although Bissonnette and Csech (1936) induced pheasants to lay fertile eggs in January in Connecticut. Similarly, "night lighting" has stimulated other species of birds to lay eggs out of season; rats, mice, and sheep to breed precociously; and brook trout to spawn in December instead of March. Photoperiodic control of reproduction is obviously a deep-seated mechanism in many vertebrates.

Continued experimentation in photoperiodism has revealed further details of its action. Young male ducks illuminated by lights of equal intensity but of different wave lengths, or colors, show a maximum response in testes development under red light, a very feeble response under blue, and none at all under infrared rays (Benoit, 1950). Further experimentation by Benoit has revealed the surprising fact that radiation of the retina of the eye is not essential to photoperiodic stimulation. If a duck with its eyes removed has a quartz rod inserted in one orbit, oriented so as to carry the light directly to the hypothalamus, or even the rhinencephalon, of the brain, the light will powerfully stimulate the pituitary, and through it, the gonads. In this case, too, the gonads are not affected by infrared rays, but are powerfully stimulated by red rays, and as much or more so by blue. Since the longer red rays penetrate the tissues of the head more effectively than blue rays, this fact may account for the difference in the stimulating effect of blue light through the retina and optic nerves as compared with its more direct effect through the quartz rod. But the photoperiodic effect of lengthening days normally seems to operate via the retina, optic nerve, and nerve centers of the brain to stimulate the anterior pituitary to release its gonadotropic hormones. Severing the stalk that con-

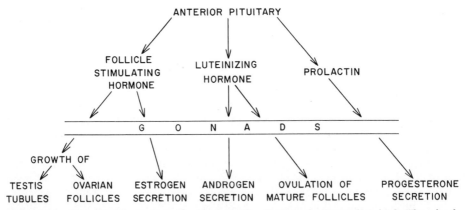

Figure 8.11.   The role of the pituitary gland in controlling the reproductive cycle in birds. The role of prolactin in stimulating progesterone secretion has not been firmly established. After Eisner.

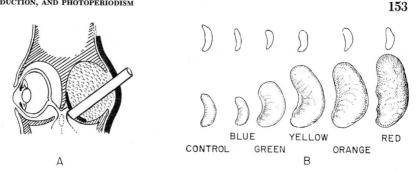

Figure 8.12. *A*, A horizontal section of the head of a Mallard Duck with its right eye removed, the socket filled with cotton, and a quartz rod inserted for conducting light directly to the brain. *B*, Different responses in the growth of testes in normal Pekin Ducks under different wave lengths of light of equal intensity and equal photoperiod. Top row shows sizes of testes at the beginning, and bottom row, at the end of each experiment. After Benoit.

nects the pituitary with the floor of the brain immediately stops all photoperiodic stimulation in spite of continued illumination.

While intensity of light has some stimulative effect on birds, it is no substitute for long days. Starlings, *Sturnus vulgaris*, subjected to a constant day length of 10.5 hours, produced no spermatozoa whether under 25 watt electric bulbs (which shed 5 footcandles at mid-cage), or under increasingly powerful lights up to 500 watts (190 footcandles) (Burger, 1939). On the other hand, a weak red light of only 1.7 footcandles intensity was sufficient to induce complete spermatogenesis when applied for long days (Bissonnette, 1932). Photoperiodic experiments on House Sparrows, *Passer domesticus*, by Bartholomew (1949) showed that in winter, 16-hour days of 10 footcandle intensity were as effective in stimulating spermatogenesis as 16-hour days with much higher intensities of illumination; but in the fall, 16-hour, 10 footcandle days were much less effective than 16-hour days with higher intensities. In this experiment, the minimum light intensity to cause full spermatogenic development was 0.7 footcandle. Slight testicular activity was obtained even with 0.04 footcandle illumination.

Experiments such as the foregoing suggest that the basic rhythm of the reproductive cycle is an inherent but modifiable rhythm of the anterior pituitary gland. That the sex rhythm may be inherent in the pituitary and not the gonads is suggested by the facts that castrated birds may still exhibit annual plumage changes (normally synchronized with the sex cycle), and that gonads in normal birds will respond to gonad-stimulating injections when they are normally quiescent.

Additional complexities of the photoperiodic mechanism have been revealed by experiments in which the dark period of each day is interrupted by one or more short periods of light. Bobwhite Quail, *Colinus virginianus*, were sexually unresponsive to an artificial day of 10 hours of light and 14 hours of darkness; but if one hour of the 10 hours of light was used to interrupt the dark period, the quail's gonads were stimulated to develop (Kirkpatrick and Leopold, 1952). It appears that the effects of light carry over beyond the end of the light period, and that interrupted dark periods may increase photoperiod stimulation by increasing the total carry-over time. It was further discovered that the rate of gonad development varied inversely with the length of the longest dark period each day.

The primacy of the pituitary gland in regulating the reproductive cycle is also shown by the so-called refractory period, during which light or other forms of gonad stimulation (via the pituitary) are

Figure 8.13.   In the winter a Starling's bill is black and its feather-tips white-spangled as shown here. In the spring, increasing day-length, acting through the endocrine glands, causes the bill to turn yellow. The white feather-tips are worn away and the bird's plumage becomes a solid, iridescent black. Photo by G. R. Austing.

ineffective. Adult Golden-crowned Sparrows, *Zonotrichia coronata*, and three subspecies of male White-crowned Sparrows, *Zonotrichia leucophrys*, fail to respond to long-day photoperiodic stimulation of the gonads between the end of the breeding season and about the first of November. Paradoxically, 15.5 to 21 hours of daylight applied to these birds before the end of their natural refractory period served only to prolong it 203 days in the White-crowned and 310 days in the Golden-crowned Sparrow (Miller, 1954). In many species, the normal termination of the refractory period may be marked by singing and by weak courtship behavior. Presumably, the refractory period represents a weakening or exhaustion of some critical component of the innate sexual rhythm. When this lack is repaired, the bird is again ready for another reproductive cycle. Should this recovery from exhaustion occur at the wrong time of year, the inhospitable conditions of the environment may act as a brake and hold

back the full velocity of reproductive activities until the following spring. Where inhibiting conditions do not occur, the species may resume breeding immediately after the end of the refractory period. This may account for the 9.7-month breeding cycle of the Sooty Tern, *Sterna fuscata*, on Ascension Island. A great body of evidence now indicates that environmental conditions such as temperature, rain, and, above all, length of day, may act as triggers to synchronize an inherent rhythm of activity of the pituitary with the rhythm of conditions essential for the successful production and raising of young.

Not only are these various physical stimuli from the environment essential to the triggering of the innate reproductive rhythm of the bird, but psychic stimuli frequently play an important role. The contagious effect of hormone-treated quail on the sex behavior of untreated controls was mentioned earlier. The fact that many species of birds will lay a new set of eggs when one is destroyed provides an illustration of psychological stimulation of the reproductive processes. The European Robin, *Erithacus rubecula*, is reported by Lack (1940) not to breed unless it is supplied with a psychological prop in the form of territory possession. A fascinating example of a psychological influence on sex rhythm is provided by the synchronous breeding of the White Ibis, *Threskiornis aethiopicus*. In west Java, this colonial species builds nests close together on large platforms, each of which holds 20 to 25 nests. The nests on one platform will have eggs or young all of the same stage, while those of another platform may be of a very different stage. For example, on August 22 one platform held only young that were six weeks old, while a neighboring platform held only eggs (Hoogerwerk, 1937). Psychologically synchronized breeding of this sort also occurs in gulls, terns, flamingos, and many other colonial species. In certain species, the larger the colony, the earlier and more successful the breeding. In many species of gulls, and no doubt other birds, a certain threshold of numbers appears to be necessary before the birds will breed at all (Darling, 1938); but in other colonial nesting species, such as penguins and petrels, sexually mature adults can breed even though isolated in single pairs. It may well be that the Heath-hen, *Tympanuchus cupido cupido*, was hurried into extinction when the last remnant on Martha's Vineyard fell below the numbers necessary for successful courtship and breeding.

SUGGESTED READINGS

General works with good bibliographies which provide extensive material on reproduction in birds are Sturkie's *Avian Physiology* and Jull's *Poultry Breeding*. In Grassé's *Traité de Zoologie* there are excellent chapters by Benoit on the urogenital system, endocrine glands, and photoperiodism. For the anatomy of the urogenital system see Bradley and Grahame's *The Structure of the Fowl*. In Wolfson's *Recent Studies in Avian Biology* is an excellent chapter by Domm on sex differentiation. The introductory chapters of Marshall's *Bower-Birds* contain information on reproductive physiology and the timing of the sex cycle. In Marshall's *Biology and Comparative Physiology of Birds* there are two excellent chapters by Marshall on the anatomy and function of the reproductive organs, and one by Witschi on sex differentiation and secondary sex characters.

NINE

Behavior

A well-laid scheme doth that small head contain,
At which thou work'st, brave bird, with might and
    main...
In truth, I rather take it thou hast got
By instinct wise much sense about thy lot...
            Jane Welsh Carlyle (1801–1866),
                To a Swallow Building Under Our Eaves

Birds are popularly considered to be not only intelligent animals, but animals possessing many of the more commendable human traits and emotions. A bird seems to be very clever to find its way in migration over great stretches of trackless forests and seas. It seems grateful when, in return for the privilege of nesting in man's back yard, it sings its cheerful songs. It appears foresighted when, to raise its young, it builds warm sheltering nests; and tenderly devoted when it incubates its eggs, broods, feeds, and defends its young, sometimes at the cost of its life. This pretty, anthropomorphic picture of birds has, through the centuries, become embedded in songs, proverbs, and folktales: Robin Redbreast covering the lost babes with leaves, the birds listening to St. Francis' sermon, Genghis Khan's pet falcon striking the poison cup from his hand, and Noah's dove returning with an olive branch.

Though this anthropomorphic appraisal is misleading, the fact remains that birds are remarkable for many achievements which man, with all his brain power, would find it hard to duplicate. Ages of natural selection have provided birds, far more than man, with instincts that are highly adapted to solving routine problems of daily living. As an example, the Nutcracker, *Nucifraga caryocatactes*, buries caches of hazelnuts in the autumn, and, months later, accurately locates them in deep snow and digs them up to keep itself alive when food is scarce. It also feeds its young on buried nuts the following spring before other sources of food become abundant (Swanberg, 1951). Although this behavior is probably largely instinctive, it insures the Nutcracker's survival as well as if the bird were intelligent and foresighted.

But when environmental changes occur, instinctive behavior cannot always adapt to the new circumstances. The automatic, spur-of-the-moment actions that usually characterize birds as a class then produce strange results. Several species of woodpeckers store acorns in small cavities, usually one acorn to a hole, and feed on them later in the year when those on the ground have become unavailable. Their instinct to store food normally serves, like the Nutcracker's, the same purpose as human foresight. But one Acorn Woodpecker, *Melanerpes formicivorus*, found a small knothole in the wall of a closed cabin and spent the entire fall dropping hundreds of acorns through it to the floor below. Similar stories are told of Red-headed Woodpeckers, *Melanerpes erythrocephalus*, fruitlessly "storing" acorns in holes running completely through telephone poles. This is instinct gone awry. Many people have observed birds for days on end vigorously attacking their reflections in windows or in automobile hubcaps. Penguins during the breeding season have been known to brood not only eggs but stones, dead and dried chicks, and even lumps of ice, while other species have been observed incubating light bulbs, golf balls, corncobs, and tobacco tins. The Pediunker Petrel, *Adamastor cinereus*, of Tristan da Cunha, and the Pinkfooted Shearwater, *Puffinus creatopus*, of Mocha Island off the coast

of Chile, are repo͟͟ like moths into a͟ smother the fire wit͟ ies (Murphy, 1936).

More revealing are͟ tions of the Carib͟ *Fregata magnificens*, an͟ Booby, *Sula nebouxii*, ͟ close together in mixe͟͟͟͟ as though nothing had ever o͟͟͟ed to mar the eternal friendship between the two." Once they are in the air, however, an extraordinary change in behavior occurs. A Booby laden with fish is bullied and terrorized by a Frigate-bird until it disgorges the fish, which is then seized by the pursuing Frigate-bird.

Whereas humans frequently respond to an integration of many stimuli spread over hours and days, a bird more often responds to the stimulus of the moment. Blue-footed Boobies attack and kill the downy young of Kelp Gulls, *Larus dominicanus*, which may wander into their nesting territories; and the Kelp Gull, with poetic reciprocity, eats the eggs and young of the Booby. A young Kelp Gull, attacked by a Booby, will give its distress call, which will draw the attention of adult Kelp Gulls. They fly toward it, screaming as though bent on a crusade of righteous retribution. However, if a gull on the way to succor the defenseless chick should see an exposed egg of a Booby, it will digress from its altruistic course, filch the egg, and calmly devour it to the accompaniment of strident dinner music from the beleaguered chick. This is not to say that birds are completely lacking in intelligence, but to point out that bird behavior cannot be accurately described in terms of human conduct.

For years, bird behavior has been a notoriously thorny subject, whose interpretation and logical treatment have been the despair of ornithologists. One can safely disregard the sentimental "bird lovers" who interpret all bird behavior in human terms. More serious students have generally allied themselves with one or the other of two antagonistic schools of be-

...r: mechanism and vitalism. Mecha-
...sts tend to follow the teachings of Loeb,
Pavlov, Watson, and others, and attempt
to describe an animal as a reflex machine
whose most complex and apparently purposive acts can be explained entirely in
terms of objective matter and energy.
Mechanism is an atomistic school of behavior, which considers an organism as a
"mosaic" made up of the sum of a great
many stimulus-response elements, a "re-
public of reflexes," as von Uexküll described a sea urchin. "The legs move the
animal," and not vice versa. Vitalists, on
the other hand, maintain that the animal
is an oligarchy which moves its own legs,
that the whole is greater than the sum of
its mechanistic parts. They postulate a
subjective vital force—entelechy, soul, or
instinct—which drives and directs the behavior of the animal, and which may
exhibit purposiveness. Philosophically,
mechanism denies foresight: the animal
does what it does because it cannot help
itself; it is a product of blind forces. Vitalism, on the other hand, has a place for
foresight: the animal has a goal in mind
and acts with purpose to achieve that
goal. Since both hypotheses straddle the
ancient philosophical dilemma of mind
and matter, neither can be satisfactorily
proved or disproved.

In the early days of ornithology, bird
behavior was assumed to be directed by
a vitalistic spirit or soul inside each bird.
Since a noumenal soul has no phenomenal
aspects susceptible of scientific study, very
little progress was made in the analysis of
bird behavior. Early in this century, however, mechanism enjoyed wide support by
students of animal behavior, and it provided a vigorous and fruitful impetus to
the objective study of bird life. In recent
years, a refined variety of vitalism has re-
gained respectability among zoologists.
Neither mechanism nor vitalism alone
seems adequate to account for all the facts
of animal behavior. As a consequence,
many modern students, while avoiding
strict teleology, make use of both concepts
in studying and interpreting animal be-

havior. They recognize the dangers of
excess in the direction either of extreme
subjectivity or of extreme objectivity, and
agree with Julian Huxley that one should
be "neither guilty of anthropomorphizing
a bird, nor of the equal intellectual mis-
demeanor of 'mechanomorphizing' it and
reducing it to the false oversimplification
of a mere system of reflexes." Or, as
D'Arcy Thompson (1942) puts it, "Still,
all the while like warp and woof, mechanism and teleology are interwoven together, and we must not cleave to the one
nor despise the other; for their union is
rooted in the very nature of totality." Fortunately, it is possible to study bird behavior inductively, without forcing one's
observations and discoveries to fit into any
preconceived philosophical scheme. This
is the approach followed by the great
majority of modern students.

THE GENERAL NATURE
OF BIRD BEHAVIOR

Behavior in birds, as in all animals, is
largely directed toward self- and racial-
survival. It is, in effect, an internally directed system of activities which strives
to maintain the physiological stability of
the body in the face of many environmental hazards, such as heat and cold, sun
and rain, food lack, competition, predators, and parasites. It is also a system that,
through reproductive behavior, tends to
guarantee the continuation of the species.
There are many paths to survival of which
cleverness is one, but it is not necessarily
the most successful one. As Heinroth
(1938) remarks, it is no disgrace for a partridge to be stupid, so long as it lays 16
eggs a year! There are, of course, many
structural adaptions which fit birds for
different niches in life: uropygial glands
and webbed feet to exploit aquatic habitats, sharp eyes and a hooked beak for a
life of predation, stilt legs for wading in
marshes. But they are of no value until
brought into action through various forms

of behavior. Birds show an extraordinarily rich variety of behavior patterns, the most characteristic of which is flight itself. Flight has proven to be an enormously successful evolutionary venture, but one that has cost birds dearly in mental development. In effect, flight has become a substitute for cleverness; birds solve many potential problems merely by flying away from them. Natural selection rarely evolves more or better adaptations than are needed to solve the most pressing problems of existence. Accordingly, like the poor little rich girl who never needed to lift a finger to help herself, birds, because of their rich endowment of wings, have never felt great need to develop clever brains. As a consequence, much of their behavior is, by mammalian standards, fragmentary, stereotyped, and at times amazingly stupid.

The way any animal behaves depends in large part on its behavior equipment: the sense organs or receptors, the correlating nervous system, and the effectors or muscles and glands. Since all of these structures are inherited, there exists a solid hereditary base for the behavior patterns exhibited by any given species. In birds and some other vertebrates, this hereditary component looms so large that Lorenz (1950) considers their behavior not as something which they "may do or not do, or do in different ways, according to the requirements of the occasion, but something which animals of a given species 'have got' exactly in the same manner as they 'have got' claws or teeth of a definite morphological character." Just as the cat with its retractile claws behaves quite differently in fighting and tree-climbing from the dog with its dull, non-retractile claws, or a sniffing dog with its keen sense of smell from a bird with its poor sense of smell, so, to a lesser degree, a hawk with its keen eyesight will differ in its behavior from an owl which possesses eyes of high sensitivity but poor acuity. And just as the inherited quality of its sense organs prescribes limits to an animal's behavior, so does the inherited quality of the correlating central nervous system and of the

Figure 9.1. Many passerine birds instinctively recognize and show antagonistic behavior toward owls and other predators. Here a Mockingbird is attacking a Great Horned Owl. Photo by G. R. Austing.

effectors. Some of the more subtle interrelations of these structural elements of behavior probably account for such patterns of behavior as the innate antagonism many passerine birds show toward owls, or toward the parasitic cuckoos (illustration at head of chapter). Much of the basic framework of a bird's behavior repertory is thus hereditary or innate, although abundant evidence has also shown that birds are capable of intelligent learning.

INNATE BEHAVIOR

No animal acts in a vacuum. Its behavior always takes place with reference to an environment, internal as well as external, from which the animal is constantly being bombarded with potential stimuli, and toward which it in turn gives off stimuli. The degree to which a given behavior pattern is modifiable by its give and take with the environment—that is, by experience—is broadly a measure of learning or intelligence. Behavior patterns highly resistant to such modification are said to be innate. While for purposes of general description it is useful to distinguish between innate and learned behavior, some students of behavior believe that no sharp line can be drawn between the two. Even so, it is difficult to imagine that there is any element of learning in the gaping responses of a newly hatched bird, or in the cessation of peeping of *unhatched* grouse chicks when their incubating mother gives a warning call as a hawk sails overhead.

There are different grades of inborn behavior. The simplest is the *reflex*, a quick automatic response of an organ to a simple stimulus, as in the blinking of an eye, or the familiar knee-jerk in the doctor's office. A *kinesis* is the non-directional active movement of the whole organism in response to a continuing stimulus, like the aimless scurrying of cockroaches when a light is turned on. A *taxis* represents oriented locomotion toward or away from the acting stimulus, as in the moth flying into the candle's flame.

An *instinct*, as the most complex form of innate behavior, is more difficult to define. Its nature has been the subject of perennial argument. Some ornithologists, such as Lack, think the term should be abandoned. Historically, the word has been freighted with a great variety of meanings, and this makes its modern use at times precarious. However, no generally accepted substitute term is available at the present time.

A usable definition of an instinct may be made, based largely on the work of Thorpe (1956) and Lorenz (1950), though it is a tentative definition and many exceptions can probably be found to its various aspects. An instinct is an inborn, particulate, stereotyped form of coordinated behavior, characteristic of a given animal species. A general internal "drive" or nervous tension sets instinctive behavior in action and possibly determines its direction. Such behavior is released completely, rather than guided, by environmental stimuli. An instinctive act weakens with repetition (i.e., its stimulus threshold rises), and gets stronger with disuse (its threshold lowers), until in certain situations the instinctive behavior may be performed without apparent stimulus. Inborn in the animal is a disposition to recognize and pay attention to certain stimuli or environmental conditions, and to ignore others. Normally, instinctive behavior is directed toward ends that promote survival. Implicit in many definitions of instinct is the idea that an animal does not realize the end of its actions but performs them blindly. This notion, of course, cannot be easily proved or disproved. If, however, one grants that an animal has memory, one can hardly deny that it knows the consequences of repetitions of instinctive acts.

Some skeptics deny the reality of instinct, but the hybrid behavior of certain hybrid birds gives convincing evidence of its existence. Some species of lovebirds of the genus *Agapornis* carry fibrous building materials to their nests in their beaks; others carry them tucked in their rump feathers. Dilger (1962) crossed a Fischer's Lovebird, *Agapornis personata fischeri*, which typically carries nest materials in its beak, with a Peach-faced Lovebird, *Agapornis roseicollis*, which carries materials stuffed in its feathers. When the hybrids began to build nests they "acted as though they were completely confused," unable to concentrate effectively on either inherited pattern of carrying materials. After three years the hybrids learned to carry materials successfully in their beaks, but they still made futile attempts occasionally to tuck fibers in their feathers.

In his pioneering study of pigeons, Whitman (1899) discovered that much of their behavior was *particulate*, in that a given action was automatic and relatively independent of the activities of the organism as a whole. It is difficult to believe that Whitman's interpretation of instinctive behavior was written so long ago and not today:

> "It is quite certain that pigeons are totally blind to the meanings we discover in incubation. They follow the impulse to sit without a thought of consequences; and no matter how many times the act has been performed, no idea of young pigeons ever enters into the act. They sit because they feel like it, begin when they feel impelled to, and stop when the feeling is satisfied. Their time is generally correct, but they measure it as blindly as a child measures its hours of sleep . . . The same holds true of the feeding instinct. The young are not fed from any desire to do them good, but solely for the relief of the parent."

The modern study of comparative animal behavior or ethology can be said to date from Whitman's work.

As an example of the particulate nature of instinctive behavior, Lorenz describes how a Muscovy Duck, *Cairina moschata*, will respond to the distress cry of a Mallard duckling, *Anas platyrhynchos*, by defending it, but will then respond to its coloration pattern by killing it as it would any strange, small, nest enemy. Similar particulate responses in Sooty Terns, *Sterna fuscata*, were observed by Watson (1908). An adult tern will vigorously drive a strange tern chick from its nesting area. Should the chick, however, avoid the jabs of the adult and touch its breast, a new instinctive response is immediately thrown into gear, and the adult accepts the chick as one of her own and "solicitously" broods it. If, on the other hand, the chick is driven away, sometimes dripping blood, and attacked by another adult tern, the chick's distress call will evoke another response in the first adult, which will then rush from its nest to rescue the strange chick and drive off its attacker! Obviously, this is not the kind of response a human mother would accord an infant in distress. It reveals the compartmentalized nature of instinctive behavior. The adult tern is a creature of the moment, responding in quick succession to strangeness, to breast contact, or to distress calls, all with sublime impartiality. It is when a bird's behavior "miscarries" in this fashion that its automatic and particulate nature is most evident.

Pondering such non-adaptive examples of instinctive behavior, Craig (1918) came to the conclusion that in much of its behavior an animal aims not at survival but at the *discharge* of these automatic actions which Craig called *consummatory* actions. The general preparatory restlessness or striving which leads toward the consummatory act he called *appetitive behavior*. Appetitive energy may be discharged through specific consummatory acts or may result in spontaneous behavior, such as aimless or exploratory wandering.

Elaborating this discharge principle, Lorenz (1950) proposed his widely accepted releaser hypothesis of instinctive behavior. He explains the rigidly stereotyped nature of instinct by assuming that within each animal there are a number of inborn movement forms which he calls *fixed action patterns*. Each of these hereditary patterns embraces motor, sensory, and integrating elements, all in one rather rigidly organized packet. The fixed action patterns of a given species are as specific and constant as its anatomical characteristics, and consequently just as useful for taxonomic purposes. Further, each pattern somehow generates its own nervous tension or *specific action potential* in the central nervous system. This tension builds up as long as the specific action pattern remains quiescent, but is consumed with its activation.

The discharge of a specific action pattern corresponds to Craig's consummatory act, and produces some sort of satisfaction to the animal. That is, the animal's unconscious goal in instinctive behavior is the discharge of fixed action patterns, and not survival. Every specific action pattern remains blocked until its correlated *innate releasing mechanism* receives a specific sign stimulus, called a *releaser* by Lorenz, which releases the block and allows the action to be discharged. A given releaser is related to a given innate releasing mechanism as a key to a lock.

In his remarkable studies of the Jackdaw, *Corvus monedula,* Lorenz (1952) discovered that any animal, man included, which carried a dangling or fluttering black object, would become the focus of a furious attack by these birds. One's im-

Figure 9.2. The head of a stuffed Cuckoo is enough to release attacking behavior in two Willow Warblers. Photo by E. Hosking.

mediate guess might be that these highly gregarious birds mistake the black object for a Jackdaw and rush to its aid, or at least attempt to drive off the dangerous predator. But the releasing stimulus in this case does not need to resemble a bird at all closely. Lorenz's first experience with the phenomenon came when he withdrew some black swimming trunks from his pocket. Immediately he was "surrounded by a dense cloud of raging, rattling jackdaws, which hailed agonizing pecks upon my offending hand." Even a Jackdaw carrying to its nest a black wing-feather of a raven is subject to attack by other Jackdaws. On the other hand, when Lorenz held unfeathered, baby Jackdaws in his hand, their parents were not in the least disturbed. But on the day their quill feathers burst open and turned the baby birds black, he was immediately and furiously attacked by the parents. "Dangling black" is the releaser of an innate predator-attacking mechanism in adult Jackdaws. The behavior is not released by the situation as a whole, nor by those elements in it that a human would consider significant, but instead by some characteristic part of it to which the innate releasing mechanism, through the sense organs, is "tuned." As a result of their classical experiments with cardboard silhouettes of various kinds of birds in flight, Lorenz and Tinbergen (Tinbergen, 1948) discovered that both outline and movement were significant visual characteristics in releasing fear reactions in such birds as Willow Ptarmigan, *Lagopus lagopus.* A generalized silhouette (Fig. 9.4) when moved in one direction released fright reactions, but moved in the opposite direction did not. Apparently, the silhouette when moving in one direction suggested a hawk; when moving in the other direction, a goose.

The food-begging response of a newly hatched Herring Gull, *Larus argentatus,* is released by the sight of its parent's red-spotted beak presenting food near by. In an attempt to analyze this stimulus situation, Tinbergen and Perdeck (1951) pre-

Figure 9.3. Two Stonechats attacking a stuffed Cuckoo. In the excitement of discharging a belligerent fixed action pattern, released by the sight of the Cuckoo, the male Stonechat has seized his protesting mate's foot. Photo by E. Hosking.

sented newly hatched chicks with artificial bills of various sizes, shapes, and colors. They discovered that to be an effective releaser the bill must have a definite shape and a red patch near its tip, which is characteristic of the species. Further, to be most effective, the bill should be held low, near the chick, pointing downward, in motion, and with something protruding from its outline (food). As a quantitative measure of the relative effectiveness of different kinds of bills and heads, presented under different conditions, the number of pecks made by the chicks toward the experimental models was recorded for comparable exposures. A moving head, for example, received 100 pecks, and a still head only 31; a near object, 81 pecks, a far object, 6 pecks. A bill with a red patch near its tip received four times as many pecks as one with none. A solid red bill released about twice as many pecking responses as a bill of any other solid color. The color or shape of the parent's head had no effect on the peck frequency of the young. A head colored

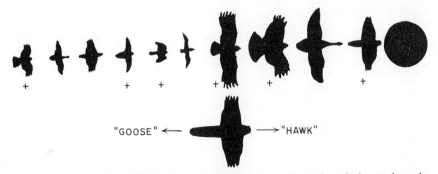

Figure 9.4. When cardboard models like the above were moved through the air above defenseless birds, the models marked "+" released fright or escape responses. The generalized bird shown below released fright responses only when moved toward the right. The releaser in every case was "short neck." After Lorenz and Tinbergen.

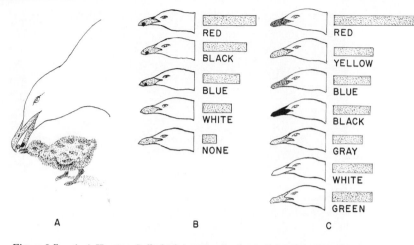

Figure 9.5. *A*, A Herring Gull chick begging for food. *B*, Models of Gull heads, with varied patches on the bills, used to release begging responses in newly hatched chicks. Bars indicate the relative frequencies of the chicks' responses. *C*, Bars indicate the releasing values of Gull models with bills of varying solid colors. All figures after Tinbergen.

black or green released as many responses as a normally white head. The inborn concern of the chick was for the bill and its general character (Fig. 9.5).

Quite unexpectedly, certain artificial stimuli were found to be more effective releasers than their natural counterparts: a normally shaped bill received 100 pecks, but an abnormally long and thin bill, 174 pecks. Likewise, a normal bill with its single red patch on the lower mandible received 100 pecks, but an abnormal bill with a bull's-eye pattern (circle and central dot) of the same size and color re-

Figure 9.6. An example of a super-normal releaser. An Oystercatcher will attempt to incubate a gigantic artificial egg in preference to its own (foreground) or that of a gull (left). After Tinbergen.

ceived 116. In fact, a long, thin, red rod, with three white rings near its end, elicited begging more readily than a real gull's head. Such unusually evocative stimuli were called super-normal releasers —the goal and envy of every advertising executive. Lorenz emphasizes the point that these releasers or "sign stimuli" generally exhibit *relational* properties, and are not simple, absolute qualities or quantities. Neither a limp black rag nor a man standing alone elicits the mobbing attack of Jackdaws, but the rag dangling from a man's hand, or from a dog's mouth, releases the typical anti-predator assault. Releaser experiments by Tinbergen and Kuenen (1939), using cardboard models on young thrushes, have shown that they will gape toward the nearer, the higher, and the smaller of two objects. All three of these pairs of relations are characteristic of the parent bird's head and body while feeding its young. Each of these relational stimuli alone has the power to release the begging response in the young, and all of them together combine, in what Tinbergen calls "heterogeneous summation," to release the same consummatory response under natural conditions.

Convincing support for the theory of hereditary fixed action patterns is provided by the experiments of von Holst and von Saint Paul (1962) on the Domestic Fowl, *Gallus gallus*. By inserting electrodes several millimeters deep into the brain of a rooster or a hen, they were able to stimulate the brain with weak (0.2 to 1.2 volts) alternating currents. Depending on the region stimulated, and the voltage used, they were able to elicit at will a great variety of complex behavior patterns that are normally associated with such everyday activities as feeding, preening, sleeping, courting and fighting. A rooster, for example, if unstimulated, will ignore a nearby stuffed weasel. But when the appropriate center of its brain is stimulated electrically, it will respond toward the weasel with the following stereotyped sequence of actions: "alertness, visual fixation, approach, attitude of rage, attack with spurs, and triumphant call." This complex train of actions, very different from a simple reflex, is brought on by a single, simple, electrical stimulus.

According to Tinbergen, there exists in each animal a hierarchy of functional integrating centers on different levels, one level superimposed on another. Each level is activated by nervous potential descending from the level above. Blocks between these levels, each with its innate releasing mechanism, prevent the discharge of motor impulses until an appropriate releaser opens them to allow their passage. If motivational impulses flowing downward from a higher center toward a lower remain blocked, they may be diverted into appetitive behavior or general motivational drive. Other influences which contribute drive to these centers are hormones, sensory stimuli, autonomic impulses from the viscera, and possibly self-generated stimuli from the centers themselves. The blocking or "damming up" of action potential results in lowering the threshold for the stimuli required to release a given action; in other words, it raises the pressure behind the block, sometimes to such a level (threshold zero)

that the action goes off without any external stimulus at all. Such action is called *vacuum activity* or overflow activity. In other instances, the nervous tension may "overflow" into other channels and activate the discharge of irrelevant or eccentric *displacement activities*, activities which make no sense according to human standards. Such displacement activities may also occur when an animal is somehow frustrated or prevented from performing the normal instinctive act, or when antagonistic drives are stimulated at the same time. A Song Sparrow, *Melospiza melodia*, confined in a cage, tugged strings and attacked straws when his rival alighted outside (Nice, 1943); and grackles, jays, and ravens have been observed attacking boughs and grass when their nests were threatened by man (Skutch, 1946). When thwarted in the performance of an instinctive act, Lapwings, *Vanellus vanellus*, make displacement feeding movements; crows and jays hammer on a branch; shorebirds assume the head-tucked-in-wing sleeping posture; many passerines strop their bills on a twig; and falcons will attack other birds previously unmolested (Armstrong, 1950). Displacement activity in other birds may take the form of bathing, preening, nest-building, copulation, grass-pulling, drinking, or singing. Among mammals, frustration results in a cat's washing itself, or an ape grooming its fur. Armstrong suggests that in man, "betel-chewing, gum-chewing, straw-sucking and smoking and like activities are so widespread . . . and seem so often to be in essence or origin a means of relieving tension that they may be regarded as modified forms of displacement feeding."

Under certain conditions, a bird will exhibit a low intensity or incipient instinctive response. Such activity is called by Lorenz an *intention movement*, which results from low internal tension or low specific action potential. He considers both intention movements and, particularly, displacement activities as "reliable indicators of the present 'mood' of an animal" or of "its present internal state of specific readiness for certain activities." As such, he believes that many of them have become visually prominent, ritualized, social releaser signals for other members of the same species. This would account, for example, for some of the grotesque displays that many birds use in courtship ceremonies.

One of the significant differences between an instinctive response and a reflex movement is the fact that the instinctive act, once begun, rolls on to completion even though the external stimulus which set it off ceases acting. For example, a goose rolling a displaced egg back into its nest by hooking it in with its lower mandible will carry the motion all the way to the nest even though the egg be snatched away in mid-journey. Probably the most famous example of such instinctive *performance momentum* was provided by Lack's (1943) experiments with a mounted Robin, *Erithacus rubecula*. He wired this stuffed bird on top of a two-meter stick and placed it in the territory of a female Robin which vigorously sang and attacked the dummy for 40 minutes. Lack then removed the mounted bird and went off to his breakfast, but chancing to look back he saw the hen Robin return repeatedly to the spot where the stuffed bird had been, and deliver violent pecks at the empty air! In various species, similar instinctive inertia may endure, after a fashion, for several days. As a probable example of this, Common Murres, *Uria aalge*, and many other birds which have lost pipped eggs or small young, will for two or three days return to the empty nest site and perform the food-offering ceremony (Johnson, 1941).

In much of their behavior animals exhibit a directiveness or an apparent purposiveness, since their various behavior patterns seem to promote biologically desirable ends. Thorpe (1956) is of the opinion that an animal's perception itself involves "an actively organizing, possibly a purposive, element" and that its general drive, which is most characteristically ex-

pressed in appetitive, exploratory behavior, has an element of "expectancy" which is dimly akin to purpose. Intelligence seems chiefly to be displayed in appetitive behavior, while consummatory acts generally follow rigid patterns.

It should be made clear that this theory of fixed action patterns and innate releasing mechanisms is but one of several attempts to explain some of the enormous complexities of inborn behavior in birds. It is the theory that is currently most attractive to students of bird behavior. It will undoubtedly be subject to alteration as more facts about bird behavior accumulate.

Other less widely held explanations of inborn behavior are based on Watsonian behaviorism, in which the animal is considered to be largely a mosaic made up of mechanistic reflexes; or on the Gestalt psychology of Köhler and others, in which the animal is considered to be an integrated, self-regulating entity that responds not to single, simple releasers in the environment, but to the whole complex environmental situation—the "Gestalt."

One of the key indications that a given behavior is inherited rather than acquired is provided by its frequency among related birds. If all the members of a given species or genus exhibit a given behavior, it is presumptive but not conclusive evidence that the trait is inborn. In his behavior studies of a half-dozen species of European titmice, Hinde (1952) found that they agreed remarkably in their acrobatic behavior patterns, and differed mainly in appearance, voice, and ecology. Similarly, the Horned Lark of North America and the Shore Lark of Great Britain, different races of the same species, *Eremophila alpestris*, both have the same peculiar habit of building a sort of flagstone terrace of pebbles or sheep-droppings outside their ground-level nests. These races have very likely been isolated from each other for thousands of years, yet the instinctive pattern continues. Tameness, shyness, and belligerence commonly "run in families" and very likely are based on hereditary behavior patterns. Phalaropes, puffbirds, kinglets, and titmice are relatively tame, confiding birds, while oystercatchers, Roseate Spoonbills, *Ajaia ajaja,* and Redshanks, *Tringa totanus,* are shy, wild species. Sometimes even within a single genus birds demonstrate strikingly different traits. The Ringed Penguin, *Pygoscelis antarctica,* is bold, pugnacious and quarrelsome, and when approached by man is likely to charge, whereas the Gentoo Penguin, *P. papua,* a "calm philosopher," turns tail, and the Adelie Penguin, *P. adeliae,* stands its ground (Murphy, 1936). There are, of course, differences in temperament between individuals of the same species. These, too, may be genetic or they may be acquired. When Common Terns, *Sterna hirundo,* are trapped and banded, some "tolerate it to an incredible degree, others react immediately and drastically" (Austin, 1947). Behavior in birds also varies with sex, age, period in the reproductive cycle, habitat, and other variables, so it is usually very difficult to determine the origins of any given behavior.

Among forms of behavior which show great stereotypy are those that have to do with care of the body surface: bathing, dusting, anting, and preening. Many land birds and all aquatic species bathe in water, while ground-dwelling game birds and dwellers on steppes and deserts bathe in dust. Some birds of prey, kinglets, and sparrows bathe in both water and dust. Passerines "bathe hurriedly with continuous movement, hawks and pigeons wallow motionlessly between bouts of violent splashing" (Goodwin, 1956). To bathe in water, most species immerse the head, suddenly raise it, and then begin beating the wings. The inborn nature of bathing movements is seen in the fact that four-week-old Goshawks, *Accipiter gentilis,* may go through bathing movements on the bare ground on seeing a brood-mate splashing in water (Bond, 1942). Preening seems invariably to follow bathing. While sun-bathing, most birds adopt a characteristic pose, leaning sideways and extending one wing and half of their tail feathers toward the sun. In a summary of observations of sun-bathing birds (mainly passerine), Gibb (1947) found that in 13 species, seven exposed their backs to the sun, four faced the sun, and two did both. Juvenile birds seemed to indulge in sun-bathing more than adults. Except in such birds as anhingas and cormorants, which need to dry out their wet feathers after diving, the reasons for sun-bathing remain obscure. Heat alone may be the stimulus to sun-bathe, according to Lanyon (1958), who observed hand-raised passerines "sun-bathing" in the dark while in the path of forced hot air from a space heater. The suggestion has been made that uropygial oil, irradiated by the sun, produces vitamin D, which the bird ingests while preening. The question needs more study.

A widespread but very puzzling instinctive activity of birds called *anting* has only recently attracted the study of ornithologists. It is a stereotyped behavior pattern in which the bird treats its feathers with ants or substitute materials. Anting occurs in either a passive or an active form. In passive anting, seen in crows, the bird spreads its wings, ruffles its plumage, and "sits down" on an active ant hill to let the angry ants crawl through its feathers. In active anting, practiced, for example, by orioles, jays, and starlings, the bird seizes one or more ants, and strokes or jabs them among its feathers. In active anting, the bird usually anoints ventral parts of the body, particularly under the wings and tail. Often, in its contortions to place ants among the under-tail and rump feathers, the bird steps on its own tail and tumbles over backward. Sometimes the bird will eat the ants after anting, and at other times will discard them. The ants used are often those that spray or exude pungent, aromatic, or repugnant fluids. While ants are the standard objects used, birds have been observed "anting" with substitutes such as beetles, bugs, wasps, orange peel, raw onion, hot chocolate, vinegar, hair tonic, cigarette butts, burning matches, and smoke. Whitaker (1957) has listed 148 species of birds which have been observed anting with at least 24 kinds of ants and over 40 substitute materials. When Whitaker exposed a hand-raised Orchard Oriole, *Icterus spurius,* to ants on 80 different days, the bird anted on 67 of them. Individual anting sessions commonly lasted 45 minutes.

Various explanations of anting have been proposed by different authors: the bird wipes off the ant's formic acid before eating it; the live ants eat or repel the bird's external parasites; ant fluids produce pleasurable effects, relieve itching, or act as a medicinal tonic on the skin; ant fluids provide physical protection for the feathers. But so far, no explanation of anting has been generally accepted.

In addition to these body-care instincts, birds show numerous other inborn behavior patterns related to feeding, fighting, courtship, nest-building, care of young, sleeping, social relations, and other activities. Many of these forms of instinctive behavior are considered in other chapters.

LEARNED BEHAVIOR AND INTELLIGENCE

Examples given thus far have perhaps made it appear that birds are capable of little, if any, intelligent behavior. While it is probably true that typically a bird's action is largely stereotyped and instinctive, it does not follow that it is non-adaptive or stupid. Instinctive behavior may be as adaptive as intelligent behavior. A great deal depends on the circumstances in which the behavior occurs. A species living for centuries on an isolated oceanic island with no enemies has no need to maintain instinctive wariness or predator-defense mechanisms. If its instinctive ways of feeding, bathing, courting, and breeding fit its requirements for survival, the species prospers. But once man introduces rats or cats on the island, the bird's "trusting disposition" is no longer adaptive, and the species may become extinct. This has happened all too frequently.

Actually, it is generally hazardous to label a given form of behavior as pure instinct, or another as completely learned. There are probably few specific action patterns so rigid that they cannot be modified by experience, nor any learned behavior completely free of some kernel of instinct.

Learning is the adaptive modification of behavior as the result of experience. By "adaptive modification" is usually meant a change that promotes individual and racial survival. The degree to which an individual animal can adaptively modify its behavior is ordinarily considered a measure of its intelligence.

Examples of learning in wild birds are difficult to establish with much certainty, so that most of the observations in this field are the results of experiments on confined birds. However, an unusual and widespread example of natural learning in birds appeared recently in the British Isles. Since 1921 there has been a growing practice among titmice and other birds (at least eleven species) of opening milk-bottle caps and drinking the cream (Fisher and Hinde, 1949). The birds attack the milk bottles usually a few minutes after they have been left at the door. Different methods may be used, even by the same bird, in getting at the milk. Cardboard and paper tops may be removed, or the paper torn off layer by layer. Metal foil tops are punctured and then torn off in thin strips. There are even reports that troops of tits follow milk carts down the street and open the bottle tops while the milkman is busy with his deliveries. Such pilfering of milk from man-made bottles can scarcely be inborn behavior, although the tearing of paper and of paper-like bark is a common trait of tits, which were the first birds reported to open milk bottles. Other species probably picked up the habit by associative learning, after watching the tits' success.

Similar adaptive modifications of behavior to artificial situations are seen in gulls and other birds which follow tractors during spring plowing to feed on the small

Figure 9.7. An example of learning in wild birds. In England, titmice and other birds have learned to open milk bottles and to drink the cream. Left: A Blue Tit removing the cardboard cap from a milk bottle. Right: A Great Tit puncturing a cap. Photos by D. L. Breeze.

animals turned up; in Pigeon Hawks, *Falco columbarius,* which follow slow trains in northern Mexico and prey on the small birds that are stirred up (Kenyon, 1942); or gulls that learned to appear and feed on the dead fish available after each mine-destroying explosion off the coast of Holland following World War II (Vleugel, 1951). Similarly, birds such as the House Sparrow, *Passer domesticus,* and Chimney Swift, *Chaetura pelagica,* which have adjusted their nesting habits to man-made structures, must have exercised some degree of learning.

One problem that complicates the study of learning concerns maturation. Does an older bird fly more expertly than a young one because of experience, or because its nerves, muscles, reflexes, and instincts have matured and are capable of more polished action? Is improvement in song based on practice, on maturation, or on both? Much reproductive behavior is clearly dependent on the maturity of the endocrine glands, particularly the pitu-

itary and sex glands. Without experimental controls, it is often impossible to discriminate maturation from learning. Consequently, caution is required when one interprets behavior that is apparently learned.

HABITUATION

Learning occurs at different levels of behavior. In his book on learning and instinct, Thorpe (1956) differentiates such types of learning as habituation, trial and error, insight, imprinting, and other forms. Much of the discussion that follows is based on Thorpe's contributions.

Perhaps the simplest form of learned behavior is *habituation,* or learning *not* to respond to meaningless stimuli. It is a common observation that birds nesting in the vicinity of busy highways and railroads soon learn not to be disturbed by the rush and noise of traffic. Pigeons, Killdeer, *Charadrius vociferus,* and Bob-

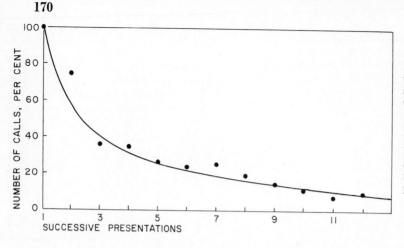

Figure 9.8. The habituation curve of Chaffinches showing their response to a live owl placed in their aviary. Each dot represents the average number of alarm notes per bird for that day, expressed as a percentage of the number given on the first presentation. After Hinde.

white, *Colinus virginianus,* have become habituated to the sound of near-by gunfire. A Robin, *Turdus migratorius,* built its nest and reared its young on the rocking arm of a Michigan oil-well pump. Very likely the bird started building its nest at one of the frequent intervals when the pump was inactive, but eventually it learned to stay on the nest when the pump arm rose and fell about a meter with every stroke. A quantitative study of habituation in the Chaffinch, *Fringilla coelebs,* was made by Hinde (1954) by counting the number of alarm notes or "chinks" the birds made on successive 20-minute, one-a-day presentations of a live Little Owl, *Athene noctua,* in their aviary. After five daily presentations, the alarm notes dropped to less than 30 per cent of the rate on the first day, and after 12 days to about 10 per cent. Birds are more likely to remain responsive to significant or meaningful stimuli because they are followed by reinforcement: i.e., either punishment or reward.

TRIAL AND ERROR

In *trial and error* learning, the animal selects one response from among several possible responses to solve a problem. Thorpe points out that this kind of learning is anticipatory in that the motor conditioning that accompanies the perform-

ance of the problem precedes the reinforcement of a successful trial. He considers appetitive motivation as "necessary before the process of trial and error learning can begin." Puzzle boxes and mazes are commonly used to study trial and error learning in birds. Various passerine species were taught by Sadovnikova (1923) to run the fairly complex Hampton Court maze in from 20 to 50 trials. Although runways of a maze represent a much less natural situation to a bird than to a rat, birds and rats have been taught to run mazes in approximately the same number of trials. Birds, however, appear to show more individual variation in performance. In nature, trial and error learning is probably involved when birds learn to discriminate palatable from unpalatable seeds or insects, or when they learn to choose the right kind of materials for building a nest. European Jays, *Garrulus glandarius,* use twigs to build their nests and know that they are inedible, so they do not seek twig caterpillars. However, if a jay through chance finds a twig caterpillar, it eats it and immediately seeks and pecks at all similar objects in the surroundings until, finding only twigs, it learns again to avoid them—and twig caterpillars—as a source of food (de Ruiter, 1952).

Play is undoubtedly an activity with an important component of trial and error learning. Young birds do not indulge in as much play as young mammals do, probably because so much of a bird's behavior repertory is instinctive. Nevertheless, the young of many birds do play and thereby learn more about their environment, and improve skills that will be of use in adult life. A young Prairie Falcon, *Falco mexicanus*, was watched by Munro (1934) as it played with a prey-sized piece of dried cow manure. The bird would repeatedly drop the manure in mid-air and immediately swoop down and retrieve it before it had fallen more than a few meters. Later the bird descended to the ground, tossed the piece of manure in front of it, fluttered after it and pounced on it several times in succession. Similar playing with twigs, leaves, feathers, pine cones, and other inanimate objects has been reported for various species from swallows to eagles. Birds also at times play with each other. Gyrfalcons, *Falco rusticolus*, have been observed in mock aerial combat. Common Eiders, *Somateria mollissima*, were watched by Roberts (1934) riding down a rapid tide current in a fjord, only to walk back across a narrow strip of land and ride down again and again, apparently for the pure joy of it. Jackdaws, *Corvus monedula*, and other Corvidae enjoy a "game" of soaring together in rising air currents, swooping to earth and then repeating the performance over and over. Such activities very likely furnish the satisfaction of discharging consummatory actions, and conceivably provide something akin to the "fun" children get from skipping rope or playing tag.

INSIGHT LEARNING

A much higher form of behavior called *insight learning* is defined by Thorpe as an organization of perception that permits the apprehension of relations. Thorpe adds that "insight learning involves the production of a new adaptive response as a result of insight or as the solution of a problem by the sudden adaptive reorganization of experience." In everyday terms,

one would say that the animal suddenly "sees through" or understands a problem, and without further ado is able to solve it. The use of tools in solving a problem, as in the case of apes using a stick to reach a banana, is generally considered a demonstration of insight. Tool-using is very rare among birds, but the fact that it exists at all is significant. The Indian Tailorbird, *Orthotomus sutorius*, perforates the edges of broad leaves with its beak, and then draws them together with strands of cottony fibers to form its cocoon-like nest. Colored fruit pulp and masticated charcoal are applied to the walls of its bower by the Satin Bower-bird, *Ptilonorhynchus violaceus*, by means of a "brush" or sponge-like wad of fibrous bark (Marshall, 1954). The most striking tool user among birds is the Galapagos Woodpecker-finch, *Camarhynchus pallidus*, which employs a cactus spine to probe holes and crevices too deep for its short bill. When an insect runs out, the bird drops its tool and eats the insect (Lack, 1947). It is not known whether this behavior is inborn, learned by imitation of other birds, or learned by each individual through insight into the problem. The fact that only this one species of bird is known to do the trick suggests that the bird must have at least some instinctive tendency to handle spines or similar objects. Various species of tits and other birds can be taught to obtain food tied to the end of a suspended thread by pulling up a loop of the thread and holding it with a foot while the bird reaches with its beak for the next pull. The bird's rapid and unfumbling solution of this problem convinces Thorpe that the act involves insight. Thorpe relates that European Goldfinches, *Carduelis carduelis*,

"are so adept at this trick that they have for centuries been kept in special cages so designed that the bird can subsist only by pulling up and holding tight two strings, that on the one side being attached to a little cart containing food and resting on an incline, and that on the other to a thimble containing water. This was so wide-spread in the sixteenth century that the Goldfinch was given the name 'draw-water' or its equivalent in two or three European languages."

A similar performance by wild birds is reported from many parts of Norway and Sweden by Homberg (1957). In the early spring Hooded Crows, *Corvus cornix*, pull up fishermen's lines set through holes in the ice to steal the fish or bait. A bird will seize the line with its beak, walk slowly backward with it away from the hole as far as it can, and then walk forward *on top of the line*, thus preventing its slipping back into the water. At the hole it will again grasp the line and repeat the process until the fish or bait is accessible.

Various other examples of possible insight learning in wild birds have been noted. In one instance reported by Lovell (1958), a Green Heron, *Butorides virescens*, repeatedly placed bits of bread in the water, and fed on the small fish which came to nibble on them. The heron did not eat the bread, and drove away other water birds which attempted to. It appeared to be intentionally using the bread as fish bait.

In an illuminating series of experiments with Canaries, *Serinus canarius*, Pastore (1954) taught birds to discriminate *uniqueness* in stimuli. Birds were first taught to seek food hidden under the one among nine covering objects which differed from all the others. For example, nine small depressions or wells were covered with eight aspirin tablets and one wood screw. Under the wood screw, the

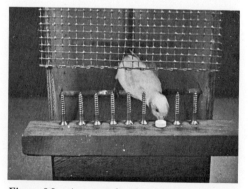

Figure 9.9. An example of insight learning. This Canary has been taught to discriminate the abstraction "uniqueness." It has learned to seek food hidden under the one different object (here an aspirin tablet) among nine. After Pastore.

unique or different object, a grain of food, was hidden. The bird was taught to push aside all objects until it uncovered the food, its reward. In the second trial there were eight screws and one aspirin tablet, the food this time being hidden under the unique object, the aspirin tablet. In successive trials the reward was placed in different wells, chosen at random, and under either a screw or an aspirin tablet, but always under the one unique object among the nine. After about 160 trials, the average Canary would succeed in learning to choose the unique object 15 times out of 20. In a second series of trials, the two sorts of stimulus objects were changed from aspirin tablets and screws to some other pair of objects: for example, chess pawns and bolts. In all, each Canary was trained to distinguish the unique object in a total of 21 different pairs of objects; and with each successive version of the problem, the birds improved their performance (Fig. 9.10). In short, they learned to respond to the abstract concept of "uniqueness," and not merely to the physical attributes of the stimuli.

After training his smartest Canary, a female named Phyllis, to feed from a food-bin on a post, Pastore elevated the bin beyond the reach of the bird, whose wing feathers had been clipped, and trained her to tug a toy truck on tracks by means of a string until it stopped so near the post that she could perch on the truck to reach the food. Next the string was threaded through a cardboard partition. On one side of the partition the bird could see the truck and post, but could not pull the string. On the other side she could pull the string, but could not see the truck and post. Pastore now began placing the truck at two different distances from the post so that from one position a single tug on the string sufficed to place the truck beside the post, and from the other position two tugs were required. In a series of trials in which the two distances were randomly interspersed, the bird learned after 2600 trials to match the distance of the truck from the post with the appropriate num-

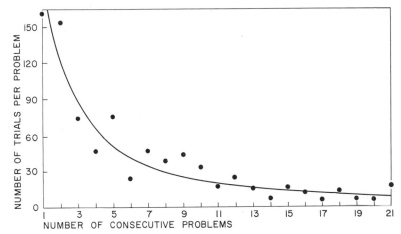

Figure 9.10. The learning curve of Canaries trained to distinguish "uniqueness." Each point represents the number of trials needed for a bird to select the unique object, in that particular problem, 15 times out of 20 (averaged for four birds). The curve reveals steady improvement on successive problems. After Pastore.

ber of tugs from behind the partition. After 6000 trials she learned to correlate four different amounts of tugging with four different distances. This remarkable performance showed clearly that the bird "discriminated among four different distances, retained a given discrimination while tugging behind the partition, discriminated among four different types of tugging responses and, finally, correlated the four types of tugging responses to the four distances." Obviously, the bird was able to make spatial discriminations, to remember, to form concepts, and to behave with insight.

Insight learning may also be involved in the ability some birds have to "count" objects. For example, a Raven, *Corvus corax,* was trained by Koehler (1951) and his students to open one of five boxes. The boxes had two, three, four, five, and six spots on their lids, and the key to the "correct" box was given by a neighboring key card which held the same number of spots. The size, shape, and distribution of spots on both key card and boxes were constantly changed to avoid secondary clues, so that the results indicated clearly that the bird was distinguishing numbers, and numbers alone. Of course, the numbers had no names and probably had no qualitative difference in the bird's mind, any more than one pencil tap in a series is different from any other. An African Gray Parrot,

Psittacus erithacus, was trained by Braun (1952) to pick up three pieces of food after hearing three auditory signals, and four

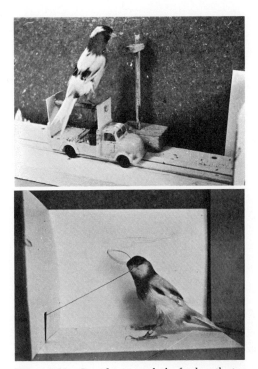

Figure 9.11. In order to reach the food on the top of the post, the Canary must perch on the toy truck which is pulled by a thread. The bird has learned to pull the thread, from behind a cardboard screen which hides the truck, the required number of tugs to position the truck beside the post. After Pastore.

pieces after hearing four signals. Such a problem, demanding a shift in sense modalities from hearing to vision, must have been considerably more difficult for the bird to master than a problem involving no such change. But the results substantiate all the more clearly the conceptual nature of the bird's behavior. It was dealing with the abstract concept "three," although it had no word for it. Parrots and other species have demonstrated an ability to distinguish between six and seven visual objects, and between six and seven auditory signals in sequence.

SUGGESTED READINGS

For Suggested Readings see the end of Chapter 10.

TEN

Social Behavior

. . . In the pond
The finely checkered duck before her train
Rows garrulous . . .
James Thomson (1700–1748), *The Seasons*

A remarkable form of learning has only recently received the attention of students of behavior, though it was innocently demonstrated long ago by the famous pet of Sarah Josepha Hale's nursery rhyme:

Mary had a little lamb,
Its fleece was white as snow;
And everywhere that Mary went
The lamb was sure to go.

This kind of learning is called *imprinting,* a name suggested by Lorenz (1935) as the result of his experiences with incubator-raised goslings. These young of the Gray Lag Goose, *Anser anser,* lacking a mother, reacted toward Lorenz by following him wherever he went, and eventually making him their substitute parent. Repeated experiments show that these young geese become attached to the first large moving object that they see and follow after they hatch. This is usually their mother, but in her absence it may be a human being or an inanimate object, and the attraction is so strong that they later completely ignore their real mother. In fact, if the attachment continues to adulthood, the bird may react sexually toward the object on which it is imprinted. Lorenz tells of a Budgerigar, *Melopsittacus undulatus,* that adopted a swinging ping-pong ball as its companion, and to which it addressed its typical caressing behavior. Other species have become imprinted on boxes, balloons, oil drums, dinner bells, wooden dummies, and other objects.

Imprinting has been demonstrated in a great variety of precocial species—ducks, geese, coots, Domestic Chickens, turkeys, pheasants, and quail—and even in such altricial species as owls, ravens, doves, and finches. Different species of birds show varying degrees of imprintability. The young of wild Mallards, *Anas platyrhynchos*, and Canada Geese, *Branta canadensis*, imprint very readily; those of the Ring-necked Pheasant, *Phasianus colchicus*, very poorly. Family groups or coveys of mixed species have been experimentally established through imprinting (Cushing and Ramsay, 1949). In order to hybridize two different species of wild pigeons, Craig (1908) found that he had to raise the young of one species under foster parents of the other. Then, when these young grew up, they mated by preference with birds of the same species as their foster parents.

Imprinting is usually an extremely rapid and abrupt form of learning, ordinarily confined to the first hours or days in the life of the individual. It is extraordinarily stable, responds to very generalized stimuli, and is characteristically found in precocial species such as ducks, geese, and gallinaceous birds. Although the fixation of an imprinted bird on its object is extremely rigid, and often long-lasting, it is not always irreversible. A male South American bittern or Tiger Heron, *Tigrosoma lineatum*, was hand-raised by Portielje (1921) of the Amsterdam Zoo, and became imprinted on him, addressing its social and courtship behavior toward him. Later, a female was obtained and placed with the male. He at first ignored her, but after being left alone with her for a time, he courted her, and together they raised several broods. However, the foster father had to take pains to keep his distance. Whenever he appeared, the male heron would vigorously drive the female from the nest, and "turning to his keeper, perform the ceremony of nest-relief, inviting Portielje to step into the nest and incubate!" (Lorenz, 1937.)

For some species the moving object that stimulates imprinting can be very generalized; for others it must be moderately specific in form. A young European Coot, *Fulica atra*, for example, may be equally imprinted on three widely different objects (a yellow football bladder, a black wooden "moorhen," and a 2 x .6 x .6 meter canvas box), by following each moving object once each day.

Reward, or reinforcement of learning, in the ordinary sense, is not required for the initial imprinting. In fact, Thorpe tells of Coots between 20 and 60 days old that persisted in following their "companion parent" as many as 100 runs with but one-minute intervals for rest, without the reaction weakening. And instead of a reward the birds were mildly punished at the end of each run by being caught and picked up with their legs dangling. Seemingly, the following behavior itself, and proximity to the object followed, are sufficient reward. If young ducklings, however, are not given the opportunity of following an object daily, their following behavior soon wanes, and may be lost (Mrs. Nice, personal letter). Following behavior normally ends with the end of the juvenile period.

Most experimental studies of imprinting have been concerned with young birds following visible moving objects, that is, visual imprinting. There is good evidence that auditory imprinting occurs in young birds, and possibly olfactory imprinting occurs in young mammals. In certain species of birds, if the baby does not hear its own parents, or other birds of the same species, sing while it is still young and imprintable, its song as an adult will not be typical of the species. Birds apparently differ markedly in the degree to which vision or hearing may be employed in imprinting. Attempts at auditory imprinting in young birds have been futile in the case of Mallards, but successful in Wood Ducks, *Aix sponsa*. On the other hand, Mallard young imprint vis-

Figure 10.1. The greater the effort a duckling makes to follow a moving decoy, the more firmly it becomes imprinted on the decoy. Here a duckling is scrambling over a ten centimeter barrier to keep pace with the decoy. After Hess.

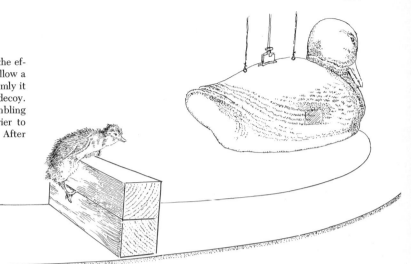

ually very easily, and Wood Ducks, very poorly. This difference, as Klopfer (1959) makes clear, derives from the facts that Mallards nest in the open, while Wood Ducks nest in tree cavities. Young Mallards can see their mother when she leaves the nest to lead them to water; young Wood Ducks can not.

In a series of experiments aimed at revealing some of the details of the imprinting mechanism, Hess (1959) allowed newly hatched Mallard ducklings, *Anas platyrhynchos*, to follow a mechanically operated decoy duck, painted to resemble a male, around a circular runway. Each duckling was given a 10-minute imprinting run of about 55 meters behind the male decoy, which uttered man-made sounds, "GOCK, gock, gock, gock," as it circled the runway. The duckling was then automatically returned to a box and placed in a brooder until it was tested for the strength of the imprinting effect. This was done by placing the now-imprinted duckling half-way between two model ducks, the male to which it had become imprinted and a similar decoy painted like a female. If the duckling followed the original male decoy the response was recorded as positive; any other response was considered negative. With this technique, Hess found that the greatest number of positive responses came from those duck-

lings imprinted between 13 and 16 hours after hatching. The imprinting effect dropped off very quickly with increased age. At 24 hours after hatching, 80 per cent of the ducklings not only failed to follow moving objects, but either avoided them or showed signs of fear. At 30 hours, all the ducklings behaved negatively. As a result of his experiments, Hess concluded that the critical period for imprinting begins as the young hatchlings are able to move about on their legs, and rapidly wanes with the onset of fear, since a fearful animal will "avoid rather than follow a potential imprinting object." The fact that young European Coots, *Fulica atra*, are wild and difficult to tame beyond eight hours after hatching indicates an extremely brief imprinting period.

Further experiments by Hess showed that the distance a duckling traveled was more significant than the duration of the imprinting period. A duckling following slowly after the decoy for 10 minutes was not as thoroughly imprinted as one following rapidly for 10 minutes. That is, the greater the distance traveled, up to about 15 meters, the stronger the imprinting. This suggested that imprinting depended somehow on the energy expended in following the decoy. To test this hypothesis, Hess placed in the runway hurdles ten centimeters high which had to be cleared

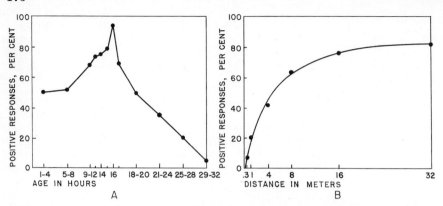

Figure 10.2. A, The age at which ducklings are most strongly imprinted by following a decoy. Each dot is the average test score of ducklings imprinted at that age. Mallard ducklings imprint best on a moving object at about 16 hours after hatching. B. The greater the distance traveled by a duckling during imprinting, the stronger the imprinting. After Hess.

by the ducklings, and discovered that those birds which made the greatest exertions to follow the decoy made the highest imprinting scores. Recent experiments with young mice have shown that physical stress (in this case, handling) early in life promotes superior avoidance learning later. Levine and Lewis (1959) have discovered that such handled mice show a greater depletion of adreno-ascorbic acid in the adrenal glands after subjection to cold than do non-handled mice. These findings raise the distinct possibility that chemophysiological mechanisms may be basic to imprinting.

The adaptive survival value of early and emphatic imprinting of the young on the mother is easy to understand in species like ducks and geese. In these birds, the mother gathers her brood of a dozen or so about her and leads them off to a pond the first day—leads them to food, safety, and education. Within the first 32 hours, as the imprinting machinery runs down, the young are progressively reinforced in their learning to recognize and depend on their mother by her coloration, her characteristic movements, quacking, and so on. By their second or third day of life, the imprinting mechanism is not only unnecessary, but could be a threat to survival should it persist, leading

the ducklings into hazardous adventures with enemies as well as with other "unsympathetic" ducks. Briefly, the adaptive significance of imprinting seems to be to gather the extremely impressionable and vulnerable young around a tutor who immediately begins to teach them the hard facts of survival in an unfriendly world.

In addition, imprinting enables the young quickly to learn the characteristics of their own species. This information, later on, is of great importance when the bird selects its mate. Experiments by Bambridge (1962) have shown that if male Domestic Chicks are exposed to a colored cellulose toilet float (4 x 11.5 cm.) during their critical imprinting period and the 7 days following (days 2 to 9 after hatching), and injected daily with testosterone propionate from the fifth day of life on in order to stimulate precocious sexual development, they will attempt to copulate with the float when 19 days old. Control chicks, given equal exposure to the float but *after* the critical imprinting period (days 10 to 17 after hatching), will ignore or avoid it.

It is obvious that imprinting has a hereditary basis. Ducklings that were highly imprintable were segregated by Hess and, when mature, bred separately from ducks which had a history of poor imprinting. The offspring of the more imprintable ducks were, as expected, more easily imprinted than those from the less imprintable parents. The test scores of the more imprintable ducklings were more than three times as good as those of the "poor imprinters." As to the basic nature of imprinting, Hess points out four distinct differences between imprinting and associative learning with food as a reward. In a visual discrimination problem in learning by association, practice trials spaced apart, with rest periods in between, produce the quickest learning. In imprinting, on the contrary, massed trials, requiring continuous effort, are more effective than spaced trials. Secondly, in associative learning, recency of experience is most effective, whereas in imprinting, primacy —the influence of the first imprinting object encountered—is most effective. Thirdly, punishment or painful stimulation increases the effectiveness of learning by imprinting, whereas it elicits avoidance of the painful stimulus in associative learning. Lastly, the tranquilizing drug meprobamate reduces imprintability in young chicks and ducklings nearly to zero, but has no deleterious effect on their ability to learn a color discrimination problem by association.

BIRD AGGREGATIONS

"Birds of a feather flock together," and sometimes flock with other kinds of birds as well. It is a rare bird that leads a solitary life outside the breeding season. Both diurnal and nocturnal birds of prey are usually examples of this minority group. On the other hand, birds rarely unite into permanent year-round flocks. The great majority of birds come together at different times of year, for different reasons, to form a great variety of homo- and heterospecific aggregations, large or small, and tightly or loosely organized. Certain solitary species which show pronounced intolerance of other individuals

during the breeding season may form flocks after their gonads decline in activity. Many other species, including most sea birds, come together in colonies for the breeding season.

Usually these colonies are formed of one species of bird, but sometimes they are of mixed groups. For example, mixed breeding colonies on Danish islands are reported by Salomonsen (1947) to contain a nucleus of Black-headed Gulls, *Larus ridibundus*, with about one-half as many Common Gulls, *Larus canus*, one-third as many Sandwich Terns, *Sterna sandvicensis*, plus a scattering of Kittiwakes, *Rissa tridactyla*, and Herring Gulls, *Larus argentatus*. This last species is not tolerated within the colony, and nests only on its margins, while the Sandwich Terns force their way into the center of the Black-headed Gulls, whom they drive outward and whose eggs they destroy.

Some species of birds that breed in isolated pairs migrate together in flocks— many ducks and geese, for example. Chimney Swifts, *Chaetura pelagica*, spend the night, during migration, clinging to the inside walls of large chimneys, often several thousands of birds in one chimney. Common Goldeneyes, *Bucephala clangula*, form compact, floating rafts of hundreds of birds to spend the winter night on a lake or river. Swallows, finches, crows, and many other species often spend the night roosting in enormous aggregations. During the irruptive invasion of Switzerland by Bramblings, *Fringilla montifringilla*, in the winter of 1950–1951, an estimated 72 million birds roosted in two small (6.8 hectare) pine woods every night (Mühlthalen, 1952). In cold weather, European tits, creepers, wrens, kinglets, and other small species sometimes gather in compact homospecific masses and spend the night sleeping in a feathery ball. As many as 50 Long-tailed Tits, *Aegithalos caudatus*, were observed in one such slumber party (Tucker, 1943). That low temperatures

Figure 10.3. A breeding colony of Gannets. Many species of birds often nest in large colonies, where mutual stimulation promotes reproductive success, and where collective defense against enemies aids survival. Photo by E. Hosking.

Figure 10.4. Starlings assembling before going to roost for the night. Photo by E. Hosking.

are not the only stimulus for such aggregations is suggested by the existence of other sleeping parties among tropical birds. Skutch (1944) observed 16 Prongbilled Barbets, *Semnornis frantzii*, pack into one small tree cavity to spend the night; and Pycraft (1910) writes of woodswallows (Artamidae) huddling together on tree branches, and colies (Coliidae) hanging upside down on branches in small, compact clusters during the night.

Roosts may also be heterospecific. In both winter and summer, mixed flocks of grackles, *Quiscalus* spp., Cowbirds, *Molothrus ater*, Robins, *Turdus migratorius*, Starlings, *Sturnus vulgaris*, and other species concentrate to spend the night. In one deciduous grove of about two hectares near Lexington, Kentucky, a winter roost of Starlings, Grackles, and Cowbirds was estimated to contain between onehalf and several million birds. Their numbers caused many branches to break and their guano accumulated 10 centimeters deep on the ground in some places (Loefer and Patten, 1941). In the Mississippi Valley, winter roosts of blackbirds commonly contain a million, and some have been estimated to contain as many as 15 million birds.

Not all mixed groups of birds are sleeping aggregations, nor are they all large. In both temperate and tropical regions there occur small mixed bands of birds which travel together while feeding. In an analysis of 169 such bird parties in Northern Rhodesia, Winterbottom (1949) found that each party contained an average of 7.8 species. In Europe, small mixed flocks of itinerant tits, nuthatches, treecreepers, and occasionally woodpeckers wander through the forests stirring up and eating whatever food they encounter.

Since these and other varieties of bird groups are so common, it is natural to speculate on what survival advantage there may be in bird societies. Without doubt, some birds congregate in breeding colonies simply because suitable nesting spots (e.g., isolated islands) are hard to find. Different species may be thrown together simply because they have similar ecological or other preferences. Some small bird groups may be no more than a family which remains together, as happens in Canada Geese, *Branta canadensis*. But in many flocks or colonies there are demonstrable advantages (and occasional disadvantages) in group living. In species such as the Cowbird which, raised as it is by foster parents, must be innately gregarious, flocking probably satisfies an instinctive urge. In many colonial species there is strength and security in sheer numbers. Large, closely packed colonies of gulls, for example, are less subject to predation by crows than small colonies. The more pairs of eyes that there are on the alert for predators, the more likely their detection. Further group benefits are possible in searching for food, in heat conservation, care of young, and particularly in education, both of adults and of young. Pycraft (1910) makes the point that gregarious species seem to be numerically stronger than related solitary species: e.g., Rooks and Jackdaws versus ravens; swifts versus goatsuckers; plovers versus rails.

COLLECTIVE BEHAVIOR

Even the most casual observation shows that much bird behavior is socially conditioned; that is, one bird's behavior depends in part on how other birds behave. In colonies of gulls and terns, one alarm cry may set off a contagious panic of cries and up-flights by thousands of birds. Perhaps by the same nervous mechanism that makes yawning infectious in man, great waves of instinctive behavior may suddenly sweep a gull colony, and just as suddenly fade away. As one would expect, there are species differences in these behavior epidemics. In a colony off the coast of Scotland that contained two species (Lesser Black-backed, *Larus fuscus*, and Herring Gulls, *Larus argentatus*) Richter (1939) noted that courtship display and copulation spread infectiously only among members of the same species, but that alarm, place-changing, preening, and sleeping spread from one species to the other. This mass conformity in instinctive behavior has been given the descriptive name *panurgism*. Infectious behavior of this sort is by no means restricted to colonial species. When one of Mrs. Nice's (1939) hand-raised Song Sparrows, *Melospiza melodia*, bathed, ate, preened, or flew to her desk, others were likely to do the same.

Often the concerted action of a group of birds is not merely the simultaneous release of a fixed action pattern, but a continuing performance that requires a constant adjustment of the individual's behavior to that of the group. The group flights of pigeons or shore birds with their split-second coordination and breath-taking precision furnish a common example. Adelie Penguins, *Pygoscelis adeliae*, are said by Murphy (1936) to drill in aggregations of thousands at the edge of the sea ice. During these drills, which may last for hours, "the penguins turn about and face in unison, and behave in many respects as though the horde were a single organism" or were responding to the orders of an individual prompter.

Sometimes, as in the case of these penguins, the concerted behavior seems to make little sense to humans, but in other instances the survival value is apparent. A straggling flock of Coots, *Fulica atra*, paddling on the water, will close ranks and jam together at the approach of an attacking Bald Eagle, *Haliaeetus leucocephalus*. The eagle is able to pick off only isolated stragglers, and the coots instinctively behave as though they knew this (Munro, 1938). In the same manner, Starlings close ranks in the air when attacked by a falcon. The group fishing formations of long lines of cormorants and pelicans probably have some of the efficiency of a long seine in catching fish. In the simultaneous diving of many water birds to feed on fish, the advantage may lie in the fact that in escaping one bird a fish plunges into the open beak of another. Murphy quotes Coker's description of diving Blue-footed Boobies or Piqueros, *Sula nebouxii*, thus: "We saw an actual cloud of thousands of piqueros flying over a school of anchobetas, when suddenly they began to fall, hundreds at a time until practically the whole cloud was precipitated into the sea . . ."

SOCIAL FACILITATION

When a hungry Domestic Hen, *Gallus gallus*, is allowed to feed at a pile of grain, it will eat until satisfied and then stop. If another hungry hen is then introduced, the satisfied hen will resume eating and consume an average 34 per cent more grain; or if three hungry hens enter the scene, she will stuff herself with an average 53 per cent more grain (Bayer, 1929). This is an example of *social facilitation*: the way in which the behavior of one animal may be enhanced by that of its associates. As an indication of the deep-rooted phyletic nature of social facilitation, fishes of various species will also eat more in a small group than they will when isolated from each other; and Goldfishes, *Carassius auratus*, will learn to run a simple maze more quickly in small groups than they will by themselves (Welty, 1934). Spontaneous gaping, which appears in young Starlings when they are only an hour or two old, disappears after four or five days in isolated birds, but it will persist up to 11 days in groups of young where mutual stimulation occurs (Holzapfel, 1939). Mutual stimulation varies at times according to the size of the group. In banding young Arctic Terns, *Sterna paradisaea*, Tiedemann (1943) found that in large, densely populated colonies they tended to run away from the human invaders, but in less dense colonies they "froze" in or near their nests, and were difficult to find. Williamson (1949) found that Arctic Skuas, *Stercorarius parasiticus*, living in a colony will often fly at and strike human intruders with their wings, but pairs living alone will not; likewise, Arctic Terns attack intruders more readily in large than in small colonies. The advantages of synchronized breeding in bird colonies have already been mentioned.

Social facilitation in such cases often seems to depend on a numerical threshold. According to Fisher (1952), Fulmars, *Fulmaris glacialis*, not only have less reproductive success in small colonies than in large, but are unlikely to breed at all if their colony contains less than 8 to 12 pairs.

At times it is difficult to distinguish between social facilitation and "instruction" of young birds. When young of Common Gulls, *Larus canus*, two or three weeks old are frightened, they take to the water. If the sea is quiet the adults leave them alone; but if it is rough, some dozen or so adults form a semicircle about them and, with splashing wings, shepherd the young back to the shore (Törne, 1939). Young Jackass Penguins, *Spheniscus demersus*, are coaxed or driven into the water the first time and given expert "demonstrations" of swimming maneuvers by their parents. Swallows often entice their hungry fledglings from the nest by flying slowly by with a tempting insect in their mouths.

Whether true imitation enters into these situations is a moot point. The results, however, suggest that something akin to imitation is involved. At a Louisiana hunting club, free-living decoys and tame crippled geese were called to their evening feeding with beating on a tin pan. Numbers of wild geese would accompany the tame ones on such occasions, even feeding from the caretaker's hand, but at other times they were unapproachable (Hanson and Smith, 1950). Facilitation of behavior can also work between species. In mixed colonies of Black-headed Gulls, *Larus ridibundus*, and Common Terns, *Sterna hirundo*, the young gulls, which swim a great deal, facilitate swimming in the young terns. Young terns swim much less in colonies that lack gulls (Frederikson, 1940).

It seems probable that social facilitation can work against the interests of a group of birds and become instead what might be called social impedance. Common Terns and Roseate Spoonbills, *Ajaia ajaja*,

will sometimes desert their nests in a body as the result of a minor disturbance. When the Audubon Society put up a big sign announcing that the Brown Pelicans, *Pelecanus occidentalis*, on Pelican Island, Florida, were protected, the wary birds immediately deserted the place (Griscom, 1945)! Rooks, *Corvus frugilegus*, habitually pilfer sticks from each others' nests, usually slyly and with restraint; but at times contagious waves of wholesale thievery spread through rookeries and cause serious nest destruction (Ogilvie, 1951). In a maze-learning problem with Budgerigars, *Melopsittacus undulatus*, Allee and Masure (1936) found that paired birds learned less readily than single birds. In the long run, social facilitation must produce more adaptive advantages than disadvantages for a species. Anything else would mean extinction.

Patterns of socialized behavior probably become established in the individual bird through initial instinctive reactions plus various types of learning which are mainly shaped and strengthened by experiences with parents and brood mates early in life. In his experiments with Domestic Chicks only two or three hours old, Collias (1952) found that pairs of them "were very slow to approach one another or failed to come together, even when only five or six inches apart, until after they had experienced some minutes of bodily contact, following which the members of each pair rapidly came together when separated by short distances." To a cold and hungry chick a broody hen represents a "complex of attractive stimuli including warmth, contact, clucking and movement; and repeated exposure to these stimuli, as well as the food guidance and protection that a hen gives her chicks, helps to strengthen the family bond" and the chick's social behavior patterns.

SOCIAL ORGANIZATION

Anyone who has raised Domestic Chickens has very likely wondered at the frequent bullying that goes on, and even more at the refusal of some of the worst-treated hens to fight back. Baby chicks live in pens together quite amicably, but after a few weeks begin to peck and jump at one another. With increased fighting, certain individuals come out on top, and other "hen-pecked" individuals consistently give way. By the time the chicks are about seven weeks old, the flock has become organized into a social hierarchy of dominance and submission called a *peck order*. In Curlews, *Numenius arquata*, this order is achieved only three weeks after hatching. The bird at the top, who wins the greatest number of contests, is called the Alpha bird or despot, and the one at the bottom of the social ladder, the Omega bird. Alpha has earned the right to peck all other birds in the flock; Beta may peck all but Alpha; Gamma may peck all but Alpha and Beta; and so on down to poor Omega, who is able to peck no one with impunity. Flocks of poultry are not always arranged in such a linear order, but may be organized in triangles (A pecks B pecks C pecks A) or polygons. Once a high-ranking hen achieves her social status she rarely has to fight to maintain it; the merest threatening gesture will cause a subordinate hen to make way for her highness. Both the threatening gesture and the reaction of submission seem to have become symbolic formalities in many species. A submissive Jackdaw, *Corvus monedula*, for example, bends his head low and turns the nape of his neck toward his superior when they meet. He knows his place!

Social hierarchies of this sort are commonly found where animals are thrown into close contact with one another, such as in artificial pens or in natural colonies. They occur in a great variety of birds, in mammals (including man), reptiles, and even fish. In many birds, social hierarchies occur during the breeding season only; but in Jackdaws, which live in permanent flocks, the peck order persists throughout the year. In some species, as in flocks of titmice, doves, or canaries, the peck order is rather loosely organized; but in chickens and Jackdaws it is rigorously constructed.

As to rigidity, there seem to be two sorts of peck orders. If, after one or a few belligerent encounters, one bird establishes its superiority over another, and the submissive bird accepts its status from then on, the dominant bird is said to possess a *peck right* over the subordinate bird. If, however, the two birds continue to jockey for dominance, the bird which wins the majority of encounters is said to have *peck dominance* over the other (Allee, 1936).

High status in the peck order carries such rewards as priority at the feeding trough, watering tank, and dust bath, the warmest spot on the roost, and fewest abrasions from combat. The advantages to the species of flock organization derive mainly from the fact that it prevents incessant fighting and allows time for more constructive pursuits. Two flocks of hens were compared by Guhl (1956) to see what effect social disorganization had on productivity. One flock was allowed to maintain a stable peck order; the other was disrupted by frequently shifting its members. The birds in the disorganized flock "fought more, ate less food, gained less weight and suffered more wounds."

Attainment of status in a flock does not always depend on strength or belligerence, although they are commonly important factors. In European Jays, *Garrulus glandarius*, the dominant or submissive status is assumed without physical combat and seems to depend on psychological factors. In some species, territory seems to be an important ingredient in attaining dominance. Seneca perceived this nearly twenty centuries ago when he remarked, "The cock is at his best on his own dung-hill." Strange Canaries, *Serinus canarius*, introduced into a cage of resident birds usually take subordinate positions (Shoemaker, 1939); and low-ranking pigeons allowed to remain in a given area will dominate a superior pigeon when it first enters the area (Noble, 1939). One of two male Song Sparrows, *Melospiza melodia*, which owned adjacent territories was captured, caged, and placed in the territory of its dominant neighbor. The stronger male attacked the cage furiously and attempted to get at the weaker bird. When a feather of the latter projected outside the cage, the dominant bird seized it and the bird in the cage died, apparently of fright. In some subtle way, the ownership of territory gives a bird moral support, possibly in the same way that a team of schoolboys finds it advantageous to play on their home grounds. This psychological support from territory applies to flocks as well as individuals. A winter flock of Black-capped Chickadees, *Parus atricapillus*, with a known peck order, was moved 2.5 kilometers from their own territory into that of another established flock by Odum (1941). The transplanted birds, strangers in the new territory, assumed subordinate positions in the combined flock while it lasted. In heterospecific winter flocks of European birds, there seems to be a kind of species hierarchy in which Nuthatches, *Sitta europaea*, dominate Great Tits, *Parus major*, and Great Tits lord it over Blue Tits, *Parus caeruleus*, who in turn bully Marsh Tits, *Parus palustris* (Armstrong, 1949).

Once a peck order is established in a flock, it can be maintained only if its members recognize and remember the various individuals in the flock. One Domestic Hen, for example, was able to distinguish 27 others in four different flocks. In order to check the clues a bird uses to recognize other individuals in a flock, Schjelderup-Ebbe (1935) altered the appearances of the heads of hens in a stable flock by placing bonnets over combs, or dyeing their combs or feathers. A transformed hen was treated as a stranger in the flock, and had to fight to reestablish her position in the peck order. In a series of experiments on the peck order in two large flocks of young hens, it was found that the surgical removal of combs and wattles consistently lowered a bird's rank in the social organization (Marks *et al.*, 1960). Apparently head furnishings on a bird can become symbols of status just as does gold braid on a military uniform.

A capacity for discriminating recognition of various objects in its surroundings is highly important to a bird, and is both an instinctive and learned ability. Many species of passerine birds recognize an owl instinctively (Hartley, 1950); and newly hatched ducklings seem instinctively to swim toward the ecological type of aquatic habitat characteristic for their species (Fabricius, 1951). But the recognition of individuals in a flock must obviously depend on experience. The male European Robin, *Erithacus rubecula*, is able to recognize his mate at least 27 meters away (Lack, 1943). Individual birds may be recognized not only by their appearance but also by their calls. Tinbergen (1939) noticed that Herring Gulls, *Larus argentatus*, reacted differently to the alarm calls of different members in a colony; when bird A called they merely became attentive, but when B called they flew off in alarm. Apparently bird A was psychologically related to the boy who called "Wolf, wolf!" when there was no wolf.

Because of the difficulties of long-continued observations in the field, the stability of peck order in wild birds has received little study. In a flock of Domestic Hens the despot may retain her dominant position for life; and in a flock of hand reared Herring Gulls, a straight-line dominance hierarchy was established when the young were 23 days old, and remained unchanged for 18 months (Goethe, 1953).

Sex plays a role in social hierarchy among many species. Roosters are normally dominant over hens. The male Chaffinch, *Fringilla coelebs*, is dominant over the female in winter, but during the nesting season the dominance is reversed. In a captive winter flock, females with under parts dyed red, in imitation of the male, dominated normal females (Marler, 1955).

The psychic subtleties of peck order are further revealed by realignments when birds of different status mate. In his semi-wild flock of Jackdaws, Lorenz (1952) noted that in the union of a high-ranking male and a low-ranking female, the wife took on the status of her husband.

"The extraordinary part of the business is not the promotion as such but the amazing speed with which the news spreads that such a little jackdaw lady, who hitherto had been maltreated by eighty per cent of the colony, is, from today, the 'wife of the president' and may no longer receive so much as a black look from any other jackdaw."

Social dominance is also related to breeding success. In a flock of Domestic Chickens with several roosters, the dominant rooster normally is most successful in mating with hens, and the Omega rooster the least. In one flock, Guhl (1956) found that the rooster lowest in the peck order was completely suppressed sexually and failed to mate with hens he knew even when the other roosters were removed from the flock; he was "psychologically castrated." Hens high in social rank, on the contrary, are less likely to submit to coition than those low in rank, and in adoption experiments are less willing to accept strange chicks than are low-ranking hens (Ramsay, 1953).

In order to determine whether a male hormone had any influence on social hierarchy, Allee and Collias (1938) injected doses of testosterone propionate in hens of low social standing. The injections slowed down egg laying and stimulated comb growth and crowing. The treated hens successfuly revolted against their superiors and achieved top status which, once won, was retained even though injections ceased and the other secondary effects of the treatment disappeared. Hens whose ovaries have been removed lose their aggressive behavior and decline in social status. The injection of male hormones into female Canaries, male and female doves, and even female swordfish, in every instance raised their social rank. However, neither castration nor injections of massive doses of testosterone affected the social position of Starlings, *Sturnus vulgaris*. Their aggressive, rank-determining behavior is apparently controlled by other means than sex hormones (Davis, 1957).

The aggressive pugnacity associated with hierarchy-building in many birds seems a distressingly wasteful way to achieve social stability. On close inspection, however, it is seen that violent physical conflict rarely enters into the process. Instead, most social species depend on ritualized behavior patterns, intention movements, and the like, which shed little if any blood. So ingrained have these actions become that Darling (1952) believes that they are in many instances essential to the survival of a species. In the Atlantic Murre, *Uria aalge*, for example, he points out that fighting "seems to intensify the urge to incubation rather than vanquish a neighbor as a competitor for space. The greater the amount of fighting, social preening, crowding, and calling, the greater the amount of apparent general satisfaction and welfare." And in some species such as the Prairie Chicken, *Tympanuchus cupido*, and Ruff, *Philomachus pugnax*, "formalized fighting has reached such a degree of organization that it is doubtful whether successful reproduction would be possible without it." In addition there is, very likely, still some truth in the old proverb, "Only the brave deserve the fair," or to put it in Darwinian terms, only the vigorous, highly endowed deserve offspring.

SUGGESTED READINGS

Thorpe's *Learning and Instinct in Animals* is a well documented, basic text. In *Mechanisms in Animal Behaviour* current authorities briefly discuss their specialties. For a brief, well organized resume of recent work in bird behavior, see Emlen's The Study of Behavior in Birds, in Wolfson, *Recent Studies in Avian Biology*. Tinbergen's *The Study of Instinct* gives a full and clear discussion of the releaser concept, and his *Social Behaviour in Ani-*

mals is a good, brief introduction to the subject. Lorenz's *King Solomon's Ring* has a choice collection of authentic anecdotes on bird behavior. Grassé has an excellent chapter on social organization in Grassé's *Traité de Zoologie*. For a life history study emphasizing behavior, see Lack's *The Life of the Robin*, Armstrong's *The Wren*, or Nice's *Studies in the Life History of the Song Sparrow II.*

ELEVEN

Songs, Calls, and Other Sounds

Hark! how the cheerefull birds do chaunt theyr laies . . .
The merry Larke hir mattins sings aloft;
The Thrush replyes; the Mavis descant playes;
The Ouzell shrills; the Ruddock warbles soft . . .
Edmund Spenser (1552–1599), *Epithalamion*

Nowhere else in the animal kingdom has sound production become as highly perfected or as widely used as it has among birds. Wherever man travels, whether on land or sea, mountain or plain, arctic tundra or tropical jungle, he is rarely beyond the reach of some bird's call. With an uncommonly lavish hand, natural selection has produced in birds an extraordinary variety of songs, calls, and other sounds. Some hint of this variety is seen in the "booming of the Emeu, the harsh cry of the Guillemot, . . . the plaintive wail of the Lapwing, the melodious whistle of the Wigeon, 'the Cock's shrill clarion,' the Cuckow's 'wandering voice,' the scream of the Eagle, the hoot of the Owl, the solemn chime of the Bellbird, the whip-cracking of the Manakin, the Chaffinch's joyous burst, the hoarse croak of the Raven, . . . the bleating of the Snipe, or the drumming of the Ruffed Grouse" (Newton, 1896).

A few species of birds have no voice— for example, storks, some pelicans, and some vultures. The vast majority of birds produce vocal sounds of one sort or another. More than one-half of all living birds are "songbirds," members of the order Passeriformes, suborder Oscines,

188

and they all possess specialized voice apparatus. Birds of other orders are less well endowed musically, and are generally restricted to calls instead of songs, although a few species like the Mourning Dove, *Zenaidura macroura*, Killdeer, *Charadrius vociferus*, and tinamous have simple and often beautiful songs. It is likely that the superior mobility of birds and their capacity for flight have made increased and complex sound production both useful and relatively safe.

It is difficult to make a sharp distinction between calls and songs, but for general purposes a call may be defined as "a brief sound with a relatively simple acoustic structure" (Thorpe, 1956), whereas a song, as a rule, is longer and consists of a series of notes, or a single note repeated, arranged more or less in a specific pattern.

Considerable variation in song is commonly shown both by birds of a given species and also by a single individual bird. Differences in song between birds of the same species are usually not great enough to obscure the basic species pattern. That is, despite their variations, the songs are still recognizable as the songs of a Robin or of a White-throated Sparrow; they are, in effect, "variations on a theme." Some species show much greater variation in song than others. Nearly 900 variations in the song of the Song Sparrow, *Melospiza melodia*, have been recorded by Saunders (1951), with as many as 20 different songs by an individual bird. On the other hand, the individual Field Sparrow, *Spizella pusilla*, usually sings but one song, which it repeats over and over. In general, it is the male of a species which does the singing, but in a few species such as the Cardinal, *Richmondena cardinalis*, and the Rose-breasted Grosbeak, *Pheucticus ludovicianus*, and many

Figure 11.1.   Among the true songbirds, or Oscines, few families excel the Fringillidae in beauty and variety of song. This charming portrait, by G. R. Austing, shows a male White-throated Sparrow, well known throughout North America for its plaintive "Poor Sam Peabody" song.

tropical wrens, the female sings nearly as well as the male.

THE FUNCTION OF VOICE

The importance of song to a bird can be partly judged by the amount of time the bird devotes to it. In an all-day study of an unmated Song Thrush, *Turdus ericetorum*, Rollin (1945) discovered that the bird on April 9th spent 10 out of the 24 hours singing, 9 hours roosting, and 5 hours eating and in other activities. One of Mrs. Nice's unmated Song Sparrows on May 11th spent 9 hours singing, 9 hours sleeping, and 6 hours eating and in other occupations. A Red-eyed Vireo, *Vireo olivaceus*, watched by de Kiriline (1954), sang 22,197 songs in the course of one day. It is inconceivable that an activity demanding such a large share of a bird's time and energy could survive the winnowing of natural selection unless it had definite survival values.

Since the first vocal land-dwellers, the frogs and toads, used voice almost exclusively to promote reproduction, it seems reasonable to assume that bird song originated in sex calls. However, one can with almost equally good logic assume that bird calls were first used to release nervous tension, as in the involuntary cry of a man or dog when in pain or when suddenly frightened. The first assumption, however, gains support from the fact that bird song usually reaches its highest complexity and greatest volume and vigor during the breeding season. Whatever their undiscoverable origins, today the songs and other utterances of birds clearly have a variety of functions. They may be grouped tentatively under three major headings: reproductive, social, and individual.

REPRODUCTIVE FUNCTIONS

To proclaim the sex of an individual.
To induce another individual to reveal its sex.

To indicate vigor and dominance in an individual.
To advertise for and to allure a mate.
To establish sovereignty over territory.
To stimulate and synchronize sex behavior.
To strengthen the pair bond.
To signal changes in domestic duties.
To identify the individual to his mate, parent, or offspring.

SOCIAL FUNCTIONS

To serve as a "password" for species identification.
To rally a flock for collective action.
To hold a flock together, as in dense foliage or at night.
To intimidate or drive away enemies or competitors.
To convey information, as about enemies and food.
To educate offspring and newcomers.

INDIVIDUAL FUNCTIONS

To discharge nervous energy or provide emotional release.
To perfect song through practice—and the possibility that some birds sing for the joy of it should not be arbitrarily ruled out!

Some of the functions listed are perhaps open to question, and undoubtedly there are other functions that have not been mentioned. The whole subject of sound production in birds is filled with subtle complexities and awaits more investigation. The recently developed electronic techniques which enable one to analyze bird sounds qualitatively and quantitatively should help to answer some of the interesting problems involved in bird song. Another promising technique involves a study of the behavior of deaf birds. Hüchtker and Schwartzkopf (1958) removed the cochleas of 16 Bullfinches, *Pyrrhula pyrrhula*, and kept them in flight cages with normal birds. For over a year these birds sang as well as normal birds. Deafness had no influence on their peck order, nor did it disrupt their normal reproductive functions, such as pair formation, nest building, copulation, or incubation. However, since the deaf parents could not hear the hunger calls of their nestlings, the young were fed so poorly that they soon died of starvation.

Good evidence that birds use calls as location notes to keep flocks or pairs together is found in two species of western towhees. The Brown Towhee, *Pipilo fuscus*, lives in grassy areas where vision is unimpeded, and the male sings only when unmated, presumably to attract a mate. The Rufous-sided Towhee, *Pipilo erythrophthalmus*, lives in shrubby habitats with obstructed vision, and the male sings throughout the nesting season (Quaintance, 1938). This same principle of using location notes is often illustrated by a single species. For example, the Pine Siskin, *Spinus pinus*, gives calls when foraging in dense foliage, but is silent in open fields. Well over two centuries ago the significance of location notes was grasped by that amazingly "modern" ornithologist, Baron von Pernau of Steinach, Austria, whose voluminous writings on bird behavior remained in obscurity until brought to light by Stresemann (1947). In his first book on birds, published in 1702, von Pernau writes,

"The Wood-Lark [*Lullula arborea*] eagerly follows the attraction call, in contrast to the Skylark [*Alauda arvensis*] that does not care about it; the reason for that difference probably is that God's inexpressible wisdom, which shines forth from the humblest things, did not implant in Skylarks that method of attracting each other, because they can see their companions on the flat field and can find them without such help, whereas the Wood-Larks, when flying among bushes and over completely wild ground, would often lose each other if they did not utter the attraction call constantly." (Stresemann's translation).

One would have to search long and hard to find in modern literature a better statement of the function of location notes.

The use of call notes for sexual and individual recognition is illustrated by the Emperor Penguin, *Aptenodytes forsteri*, of Antarctica. In this species, the trumpeting call of the male is rather musical and the final note long drawn out, whereas that of the female is a cackle with a short final note. Superimposed on these sexual differences in calls are individual differences, so that these similarly colored birds are able not only to recognize the sex of a stranger but to recognize their own mates and young. The young of the King Penguin, *Aptenodytes patagonica*, of South Georgia gather together in nurseries or "crèches" when five or six weeks old. Studies of banded birds by Stonehouse (1956) "showed that parents fed their own chicks exclusively, recognizing them primarily by sound and calling them out of the crèche with distinctive 'call signs,' to which their own chick responds."

In many species of birds the male sings vigorously until he finds a mate; then his songs either become much less frequent or cease altogether. Regarding the Song Sparrow, *Melospiza melodia*, Mrs. Nice remarks, "I often say to myself on nearing a territory where silence reigns over night, 'Such and such a male must either be dead or married,' and upon careful search I find either two birds or none." (Lack, 1943). The male Wood Warbler, *Phylloscopus sibilatrix*, before obtaining a mate sings at intervals of 25 seconds to 2 minutes, but afterward at intervals of 4 to 10 minutes (Mountfort, 1935). Without much doubt, song in such cases serves the function of attracting a mate. Some of the larger species of birds, such as certain hawks and crows, have no courtship calls; they depend on their large size and on courtship flights to impress the opposite sex. Owls, on the other hand, as nocturnal birds, have loud voices for amorous communication in the dark.

BIRD VOCABULARIES

For many years most naturalists have agreed that certain birds can communicate with their own kind by uttering different calls. For example, when a Com-

Figure 11.2. A male Great Horned Owl, showing the peculiar posture assumed while hooting. As nocturnal birds, owls have appropriately louder voices than the daytime predators, the hawks and eagles. Horned Owls hoot most frequently in mid-winter during the courtship season. Photo by G. R. Austing.

mon Crow, *Corvus brachyrhynchos*, discovers an owl perching in the woods, it gives what is called a rallying or assembly call, and other crows within hearing answer the call and fly to join the first crow in "mobbing" the owl. Sound tape recordings of the crow's assembly call were amplified and broadcast with loudspeakers by the Frings (1957) while they themselves remained hidden in woods where crows at the time were neither seen nor heard. Within a few minutes crows were attracted to the locality and came practically to the speaker. Crow alarm calls, on the contrary, quickly repelled the crows. In later experiments, the Frings exchanged sound tapes of crow calls with French ornithologists, and discovered the interesting fact that French crows ignored the alarm calls of American crows but that over one-half of the French crows responded to the broadcast of an American crow assembly call. Whereas all three species of French crows reacted to the raucous assembly calls of Jackdaws, *Corvus monedula*, or the hunger calls of nestling Rooks, *Corvus frugilegus*, American crows were unmoved by them. This ingenious type of research into the significance of bird vocabularies promises to throw considerable light on the evolution and phylogenetic relationships of bird songs and calls.

At times great roosts of Starlings, *Sturnus vulgaris*, and other birds in trees and buildings become nuisances. A loud broadcast of the distress call of a Starling was found by Frings and Jumber (1954) to be effective in disbanding flocks of Starlings, but it had no appreciable effect on Grackles, *Quiscalus quiscula*, or Robins, *Turdus migratorius*, in the flocks. In an attempt to drive away flocks of gulls from dumps and canneries, the alarm call of a Herring Gull, *Larus argentatus*, was broadcast. It dispelled not only this species but also two other species of gulls, the Great Black-backed Gull, *L. marinus*, and the Laughing Gull, *L. atricilla* (Frings et al., 1955). When the gulls became habituated to the alarm and it ceased to be effective, it was found that they could be attracted away from the areas to be cleared by broadcasting a food-finding call—a powerful attractant—from a neighboring locality.

In short, birds possess voice repertoires, or vocabularies, that enable them to "talk" to one another, but probably not with intention as humans do. Calls and songs seem always to be given instinctively and to be understood instinctively. This is indicated in the reaction of many gallinaceous young to their mother's calls. Gross describes how the just-hatched chicks of a Prairie Chicken, *Tympanuchus cupido*, come running to their mother if she gives her "brirrb brirrb" call, but immediately "freeze" into motionless lumps when she gives her shrill warning call (Bent, 1932). The young of the Hazel Grouse, *Tetrastes bonasia*, are reported by Pynnönen (1950) to react to four different kinds of parental warning notes which notify them of four different kinds of danger. Various ornithologists have attempted to "translate" the vocabularies of different species of birds. One of the pioneers in this field, Schjelderup-Ebbe (1923), distinguished ten different calls in the Domestic Chicken, *Gallus gallus*, each with its own significance. The Smooth-billed Ani, *Crotophaga ani*, was found by Davis (1940) to give 13 calls of considerable variety ("shouts, chucks, chuckles, whines, quacks, whews," and others) which were used as flock calls, alarm notes, territory defense calls, morning rising notes, pairing calls, and others. The male House Wren, *Troglodytes aëdon*, is reported by Kendeigh (1941) to have three different types of songs: territorial, mating, and nesting. A domestic Pigeon, *Columba*

livia, is said by Goodwin (1956) to possess four basic calls: an advertising coo, display coo, distress call, and excitement call. Eleven different notes have been identified in the House Sparrow, *Passer domesticus*, which are used as species identification notes, love call notes, a male social song, a scream, a flight signal, a danger signal, and so on (Daanje, 1941). It is interesting that in this species the infantile call note persists in the adult as a call for fledged young, as a female invitation to coition, and as a nest-relief call.

Warning calls sometimes indicate distinctions between types of danger. A Domestic Rooster, for example, has two danger calls: one, a "gogógogock," indicates danger approaching on the ground—as a man or a dog; the other, a long-drawn-out "raaaaay," warns of danger from the air —as a hawk (Heinroth, 1938). Similarly, a Field Sparrow, *Spizella pusilla*, gives a "chip-chip-chip" call when a man or a crow approaches; but for a flying hawk it utters a penetrating "zeeeee," which causes all small birds in the vicinity to seek cover (Walkinshaw, 1945). Many small birds throughout the world give essentially the same two warning calls. The European Chaffinch, *Fringilla coelebs*, for example, gives a short, low, "chink-chink-chink" when it sees a static, dangerous enemy, such as a hawk, perched in a tree. This call often attracts other "chinking" small birds which then proceed to mob

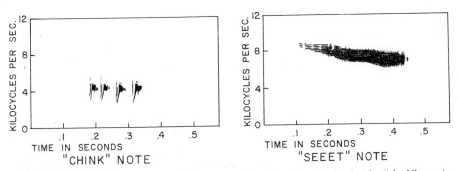

Figure 11.3. Sound spectrograms of the two warning calls of the Chaffinch. The "chink" note is easily located because of its low frequency (long wave length), short duration, and sharp beginning and end. The "seeet" note is difficult to locate because of its high frequency, long duration, and gradual beginning and end. After Thorpe.

the hawk. If, however, the hawk is flying, the Chaffinch gives a "seeet" call and, like the Field Sparrow, flies into the shrubbery along with other species of small birds which heed and repeat the warning call. Careful analyses by Thorpe (1956) using sound oscillograms or sound spectrograms revealed quite unexpected attributes in these two warning calls. Not only do they communicate to other birds the presence of two importantly different kinds of danger—one static and one in motion—but they reveal the location of the caller in the case of the "chink" call, and hide the location of the calling bird in the "seeet" call. Thorpe points out that the chief difference between these two calls is that the "chink" note is easy, the "seeet" call extremely difficult, to locate. The "chink" call is of such low frequency (Fig. 11.3) that the bird's two ears can detect phase differences in the approaching sound waves. Further, the abrupt, click-like nature of this call allows the two ears to detect differences in the time of its arrival, and hence the direction from which it comes. Contrariwise, the source of the high-pitched "seeet" calls is difficult to locate because their high frequencies probably prevent the detection of phase differences, and their slurred beginnings and endings mask differences in the time they reach the two ears. Thus, the "seeet" call warns of danger without revealing to the predator a clue as to the location of the calling bird.

Still more remarkable is the fact that, at least in Jackdaws, *Corvus monedula*, calls may be used to transmit acquired knowledge from one generation to the next— that is, to pass on tradition. The previously mentioned experiments of Lorenz (1952) with Jackdaws showed that any person who carried a black, fluttering object would provoke an angry, rattling attack by these social birds. Further, if one provokes this reaction two or three times in succession, he becomes in the Jackdaws' minds an enduring enemy, even when he is not carrying a black object. Therefore, they will attack him with their rattling calls whenever he appears. Most remarkable of all, the young will learn from their parents to do the same, even though the young would otherwise show no antagonism toward the person.

SOUND-MAKING APPARATUS

The voice-box of the bird is not the larynx, as in mammals, but the syrinx, a structure peculiar to birds, which is located at the lower end of the trachea where the two bronchi join. The location of the syrinx near the lungs rather than in the throat is one more instance of efficient weight distribution which improves the aerodynamic balance of the bird's body.

Constructed somewhat like a woodwind instrument, the box-like syrinx and its associated trachea set air columns in vibration when air from the lungs is forced through two pairs of elastic membranes stretched across the openings where the two bronchi enter the syrinx. Muscles situated within the membranes, and more particularly muscles outside the syrinx proper, control the tension of these membranes as well as of those stretched between the successive bony or cartilaginous rings of the syrinx walls. Changes in the tension of these membranes result in changes in the pitch of a bird's voice just as different tensions on a violin string will change its pitch. Different muscles, by pulling differently on the syringeal rings, can alter the timbre of the voice. Varying air pressure from the lungs is chiefly responsible for varying sound intensity or volume, although it also has some effect on pitch. As a rule, the greater the number of muscles activating a syrinx, the more varied the songs and calls it will produce; but this correlation is only roughly true. Crows have very intricate syringes with seven pairs of muscles, but are very poor songsters. Lyre birds (Menuridae), on the other hand, have very primitive syringes but are consummate mimics. Naturally, the contraction of syringeal muscles depends on their innervation, so

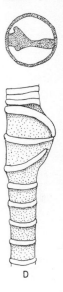

Figure 11.4. The syrinx of the Variegated Tinamou, seen from the right side, in four stages of contraction and extension. The circles above show corresponding cross sections that reveal the condition of the vocal membranes and the opening (shaded) between them. *A* produces high-pitched, and *D*, low-pitched tones. After Beebe.

A

B

C

D

that either hereditary or learned patterns of muscle-nerve coordination are basic to a bird's typical song.

Various resonating bodies act with the vibrating membranes of the syrinx to affect the quality of a bird's voice. Very probably the volume and carrying quality of a bird's voice depend more on resonance than on air pressure from the lungs. The trachea itself acts very much like a resonating organ pipe, and its effect depends on its length, diameter, and rigidity. As a rule, the longer and wider the trachea, the deeper a bird's voice; the shorter and narrower the trachea, the higher the voice. In the Plain Chachalaca, *Ortalis vetula*, the adult male has a trachea lengthened by a loop which is lacking in young males and females, and its voice is consequently an octave lower than theirs (Sutton, 1951). This length-pitch relationship was experimentally studied by Myers, who cut the trachea of a live hen in the middle and exposed the caudal portion through the skin of the neck. Before the operation the average pitch of the hen's voice was lower (375 cycles per second) than afterward (500 cycles per second) (Stresemann, 1927–1934). In hens, the sternotracheal muscles shorten the length of the trachea by one-third or one-fourth by compressing together the ten tracheal rings nearest the syrinx. When the trachea is so shortened, the pitch of the hen's voice rises. Several species of birds, such as the Whooping Crane, *Grus americana,* and Trumpeter Swan, *Olor buccinator,* possess enormously lengthened windpipes which provide a deep trombone-like quality to their calls. In these birds, part of the long trachea is coiled within the swollen keel of the sternum. The trachea of the Whooping Crane is 147 centimeters long, and 71 centimeters of its length are looped back and forth within the sternal keel. In the Australian Trumpeter Manucode, *Phonygammus keraudrenii* (a bird of paradise), the male carries its fantastically long windpipe coiled under the skin of its breast. An unusual modification of the trachea is found in penguins. Here the trachea is split into two asymmetrical halves by a sagittal septum. This arrangement permits a penguin to sound two notes at the same time. It is thought that the braying of the Gentoo Penguin, *Pygoscelis papua,* is produced both by expiration and inspiration of air. At least, when air is either blown out of or drawn into the trachea and syrinx of a dead penguin, sound is produced (Murphy, 1936).

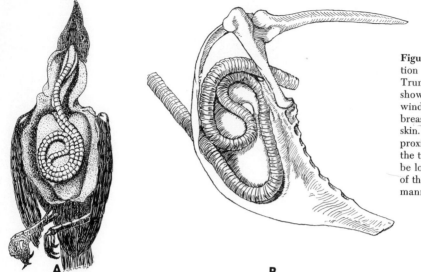

Figure 11.5. *A.* A dissection of the adult male Trumpeter Manucode showing the long, coiled windpipe between the breast muscles and the skin. After Rüppell. *B.* Approximately one-half of the trachea of a crane may be looped within the keel of the sternum. After Portmann.

For most species of birds, however, sound is produced only by the expiration of air.

Other forms of resonance chambers are provided by air sacs in various parts of the body. The paired cervical sacs of many Galliformes are inflated during the breeding season to add both resonance to courtship calls and visual appeal to the male's appearance. The ostrich, rhea, and some bitterns, grouse, bustards, pigeons, and other species can inflate the esophagus with swallowed air to increase the effectiveness of their calls. The Sage Grouse, *Centrocercus urophasianus*, may increase the volume of its esophagus 25 times by this means. The Emu, *Dromiceius novaehollandiae*, makes its booming call through the resonant help of a long inflated air sac in the neck, parallel to the trachea and connected with it through a narrow slit.

NON-VOCAL SOUNDS

Some of the sounds which birds make are not vocal at all, but are mechanically produced by the action of their feathers. The "drumming" of the Ruffed Grouse, *Bonasa umbellus*, is produced by the vigorous fanning of its wings while the bird is perched on a log. Among goatsuckers, owls, doves and larks are several species which make loud clapping noises in flight as their wings strike together. The Common Nighthawk, *Chordeiles minor*, is known in certain localities as the "bull bat" because of the whirring roar of its wing feathers when it pulls up sharply from its steep dives during courtship flights.

In many species certain feathers of the wings are specially modified for sound production. In the Woodcock, *Philohela minor*, the three outer wing feathers are remarkably narrowed and stiffened, so that, when they are spread apart during the springtime courtship flight, the air rushing between them causes them to vibrate with a high, whistling sound. This same type of feather adaptation is found in the wing feathers of certain ducks, bustards, doves, hummingbirds, cotingas, manakins, and others. Two different types of sound-making adaptations are found in the feathers of male manakins (Pipridae) of tropical America. *Manacus manacus* has its five outer wing primaries greatly narrowed and stiffened, and uses them in flight to make loud sounds. While perching, the bird can make snapping or explosive sounds by striking together the

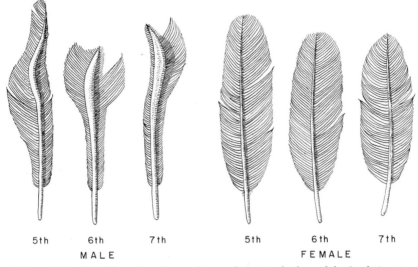

5th   6th   7th   5th   6th   7th

MALE   FEMALE

Figure 11.6. The fifth, sixth, and seventh secondary wing feathers of the South American manakin, *Machaeropteryx deliciosus*, showing the club-like thickened feather shafts of the male, which are thought to act somewhat like castanets in producing sounds. The seventh feather in each case is seen from below; the others from above. After Sclater.

thickened feather shafts of its secondary wing feathers. Quite remarkably modified are the swollen, club-shaped shafts of the fifth, sixth, and seventh secondaries of the wings of the male manakin *Machaeropterus deliciosus* (Fig. 11.6), which are thought to be somehow snapped together in the folded wing during courtship ceremonies. The wing bones that support these feathers are also abnormally thickened, very likely in correlation with their support and noisemaking activity (Newton, 1896).

Tail feathers also can be adapted to sound-making. The outer tail feathers of the European Snipe, *Capella gallinago*, are much stiffer than the central feathers, and their vanes are held together with more barbule hooklets than in normal tail feathers. In courtship flight, these stiffened feathers spread outward into the air stream and set up a rapid, humming vibration. This humming takes on a tremulous character, something like the bleating of a goat, because of air pulses created by the fluttering wings. Some species of snipe have extra tail feathers apparently adapted to the sole function of making courtship sounds. While the European Snipe has but 14 tail feathers, the Pintail Snipe, *Capella stenura*, has 26 feathers, the outer eight pairs of which are sharply narrowed and stiffened for the creation of sound (Fig. 11.7).

Besides using their feathers, birds may make non-vocal sounds with their beaks, either by hammering them on dead limbs or tin roofs as many woodpeckers do, or by clapping their mandibles together as storks and owls do. That a woodpecker's hammerings have courtship significance is seen in the male Great Spotted Woodpecker, *Dendrocopus major*, which drums on dead limbs between 500 and 600 times a day during courtship, but only 100 to 200 times a day, and sometimes not at all, after it secures a mate and begins nest building (Pynnönen, 1939). Several members of the grouse family make audible noises by stamping their feet on the ground during the courtship period. The vast majority of bird sounds, however, are produced by the syrinx, trachea, and associated vocal organs.

Figure 11.7. Upper, the Old World Common Snipe; and lower, the tail of the Pintail Snipe, showing the narrowed outer tail feathers which make bleating sounds during courtship flight. After Mayaud.

THE NATURE OF SONG

There is a rough correlation between the size of a bird and the pitch of its voice. Large birds, such as owls, cranes, and crows, have low-pitched voices while smaller birds, such as finches and warblers, have high-pitched voices. It seems reasonable to assume that birds' ears, either through physical structure or through nervous function, are best able to hear sounds of about the same frequencies as they themselves produce. An exception to this principle certainly occurs in some owls whose ears seem particularly sensitive to high-pitched squeaks, but this is an understandable adaptation to the voices of mice and other small rodents on which they prey. In careful studies of sound tracks of bird songs on films, Brand (1938) determined that the average frequency of the songs of 59 passerine species was

about 4280 cycles per second, which is a frequency slightly above the highest note of a piano, or an octave and a half above the top note reached by a coloratura soprano. Wood Warblers (Parulidae) averaged about 5350 c.p.s., thrushes (Turdidae) about 2890 c.p.s., Blackbirds, Meadowlarks, and Orioles (Icteridae) about 2890 c.p.s., and sparrows and finches (Fringillidae) about 4800 c.p.s. The highest frequency found was that of the Blackpoll Warbler, *Dendroica striata*, whose highest-pitched note reached 10,225 cycles per second.

Songs are commonly differentiated, largely on a basis of loudness, into two groups. *Primary songs* are loud songs generally concerned with the daily business of making a living and perpetuating the race. Primary songs are courtship songs, territory defense songs, special signal songs to other birds as when warning of enemies, and songs representing emotional outbursts. Ordinarily, primary song is periodic, at its height during territory selection and courtship, and reduced or suspended during the raising of the young. *Secondary songs* are weak, muted, "whisper songs" or "subsongs" which carry only a short distance and probably have little significance for other birds. They are characteristic of young males, some adult females, and of adult males outside the breeding season. Secondary song may be the means by which a bird "keeps its hand in" and practices singing while the external demands for loud song do not exist. The subsong of the young male Chaffinch, *Fringilla coelebs*, is thought by Thorpe (1956) to be the raw material out of which primary song is constructed, analogous to the various sounds a human baby makes before it learns to speak. Many of these sounds the infant, or young Chaffinch, ceases to produce when it does not hear them uttered by its parents or other adults.

A number of song birds practice synchronized singing, either singing simultaneously in duets, or singing alternately in an antiphonal fashion. Such singing is found among barbets, tyrant flycatchers and wrens of Central and South America, bush shrikes, and even penguins. While observing a pair of African bush shrikes, Allen (1925) heard one male "utter a series of ringing notes like measured beats of an anvil, while the mate replied with a series of double notes exactly timed to fill the interval between the anvil strokes. This pretty duet lasting several seconds was done with such precision as to give the impression of a single bird singing." One of the common wrens of Central America, *Thryophilus modestus,* is called "Chinchirigüi" after its loud antiphonal song. Skutch (1940) relates that "one member of the pair calls *chean-cheery,* while the mate answers *gwee;* they repeat these sharp whistles over and over again with great rapidity, and never a break in continuity, as though the sounds arose from a single throat. So perfectly are the voices synchronized that only when the two are on opposite sides of the hearer do they betray their secret."

THE ECOLOGY OF SONG

Like a man who claims he sings his best while taking a bath, most birds are definitely influenced in their song by environmental conditions. Males of many species demand a favorite exposed perch or "singing post" from which they woo their mate or proclaim their sovereignty over real estate. Common examples come quickly to mind: the male Cardinal, *Richmondena cardinalis,* or Brown Thrasher, *Toxostoma rufum,* singing from the tip-top branch of a tree; the Vesper Sparrow, *Pooecetes gramineus,* or Eastern Meadowlark, *Sturnella magna,* on a fence post; or the Field Sparrow, *Spizella pusilla,* atop a mullein stalk. Birds of the prairies, plains, or arctic barrens, lacking suitable song posts, sing on the wing: Bobolinks, *Dolichonyx oryzivorus,* Horned Larks, *Eremophila alpestris,* and Snow Buntings, *Plectrophenax nivalis.*

Birds living in dense vegetation, such as rain forests or thick reed beds, characteristically have loud and persistent voices as a means of keeping in touch with each other. The vegetation not only obstructs vision, but it absorbs sound. While making a sound film in marshes near Vienna, Goethe (1941) discovered that the reeds so deadened sounds that men only 20 to 30 meters apart were unable to hear each other's movements. This fact, he thought, was sufficient to explain the loud calls of most marsh birds.

The helpless open-nest-living young of many species remain comparatively silent until they are able to fly, but the young of hole-nesting species are well enough protected so that they can, and do, make noise with impunity. The young of colonial nesters are also inclined to be noisy, since the adults in the colony can usually repel invaders through the weight of their numbers.

Weather has a decided influence on bird song. Both cool weather and very hot weather depress the amount of singing in most species, as do rain and wind. A study of the European Blackbird, *Turdus merula,* at a winter roost, by Colquhoun (1939), showed a negative correlation between vocalization and wind. On a windless evening there were 68 calls in the period between 30 minutes after sunset and complete darkness; with an 8-kilometer-per-hour wind there were 22 calls, and with a 24-kilometer-per-hour wind, no calls. The calling of the Tawny Owl, *Strix aluco,* has also shown a negative correlation with wind velocity. An example of the effect of temperature on song is found in the tallies of calls per minute of Chuck-will's-widow, *Caprimulgus carolinensis,* by Harper (1938). At 16° C. (60° F.) this species gave 16 to 22 calls per minute, and at 24° C. (76° F.), 22 to 29 per minute. Latitude has profound effects on bird song. To determine its effects on the Yellowhammer, *Emberiza citrinella,* Rollin (1958) counted the number of songs delivered by an individual per day both in Britain and in arctic Norway. In Britain individuals sang 2,279 to 3,482 songs per day, while in northern Norway one sang only 488 songs. Whether these differences in the volume of song production were caused by day length, light intensity, temperature, or some other factor that varies with latitude remains to be determined.

CYCLES IN SONG

Most birds show a seasonal variation in song that is mainly correlated with breeding activities and hormone production. The richest, fullest song generally comes in the spring when birds are busy with territory establishment and courtship. Unmated males commonly sing much more abundantly than mated males. After a pair is mated and the duties of rearing a family begin, song generally wanes or may cease altogether. For obvious reasons, birds rarely sing on or near the nest. If a male loses his mate he may immediately resume singing to advertise for a new one. As a rule, birds are completely silent during the period of molt. With the incipient growth of gonads in the fall comes a return of singing in many species, but it is ordinarily a subsong, weak, intermittent and incomplete. With the arrival of cold winter weather, most species cease singing until the following spring. The annual singing schedules for numerous species of birds have been worked out by Saunders

(1947, 1948), and the relative times for the onset and cessation of song for different species show a striking regularity from year to year (Fig. 11.9). Not all temperate zone birds stop singing in the wintertime. The Cardinal, *Richmondena cardinalis*, Tufted Titmouse, *Parus bicolor*, and Winter Wren, *Troglodytes troglodytes*, sing sporadically through the winter, and the male European Robin, *Erithacus rubecula*, sings its best in late fall and winter while establishing winter territory.

For most species, hormones probably play a dominant role in determining the time of year a bird sings. The injection of male hormones into Chaffinches, *Fringilla coelebs*, will bring them into full song in mid-winter (Poulsen, 1951). Sometimes Canaries, *Serinus canarius*, that have been imported as singing males, weaken in song and after a month or so quit singing altogether. Suspecting that these were females which had been injected with male hormones, Herrick and Harris (1957) treated young female Canaries with testosterone phenyl acetate and discovered that after 9 days of treatment the birds began to chirp, and after 12 days of treatment they sang a sustained, vigorous song indistinguishable from that of males. The treatments were then suspended and after about a month the songs waned, and in 5 weeks ceased entirely. There is also some evidence that singing may be related to thyroid activity. Küchler (1935)

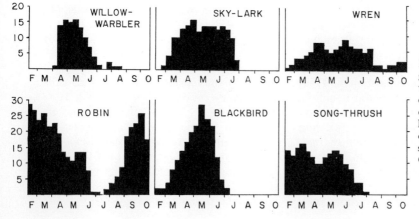

Figure 11.8. Histograms showing seasonal variation in the numbers of individuals of different European species heard singing during daily habitat census studies from February to October. After Cox.

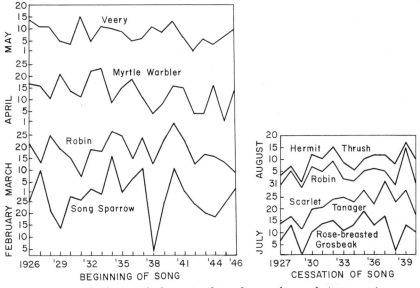

Figure 11.9. Graphs showing the beginning dates of seasonal song, during successive years, for four species of birds in southwestern Connecticut; and the dates of ending seasonal song for four species in Allegany State Park, N.Y. The downward trend of the curves in the spring and their upward trend in the autumn probably are due to the recent gradual warming trend in the climate of the northern hemisphere. After Saunders.

found that the European Robin and Yellowhammer have simultaneous peaks in both song and thyroid activity, and that these peaks occur in both spring and fall.

Most birds which are active by day begin their singing at dawn. At this time of day the most vigorous singing ordinarily occurs. It then gradually tapers off until it reaches low ebb early in the afternoon. Toward evening singing often increases again until gathering dusk stops it for the day. Early in the breeding season many species sing most of the day, but later they confine their singing largely to early morning and evening hours. There are many exceptions to this schedule: wrens and vireos are likely to sing with unabated vigor throughout the long spring day. The Vesper Sparrow, *Pooecetes gramineus,* and Wood Thrush, *Hylocichla mustelina,* although diurnal species, do some of their best singing an hour or more after sunset, and the Eastern Wood Pewee, *Contopus virens,* sings its best before sunrise. A few diurnal species occasionally sing late at night: the Domestic Rooster, *Gallus gal-*

lus, Black-billed Cuckoo, *Coccyzus erythrophthalmus,* Nightingale, *Luscinia megarhynchos,* Sedge Warbler, *Acrocephalus schoenobaenus,* Skylark, *Alauda arvensis,* and Mockingbird, *Mimus polyglottos.* Contrariwise, a few nocturnal species which normally sing at night may, like the Tawny Owl, *Strix aluco,* occasionally sing by day. Finally, there are a few species which are neither strictly diurnal nor nocturnal, but are crepuscular and sing mainly early in the morning or late in the evening: for example, the Woodcock, *Philohela minor,* and Common Nighthawk, *Chordeiles minor.*

Shakespeare's Romeo and Juliet were warned to end their dangerous tryst by their knowledge of bird song times:

Juliet: Wilt thou be gone? It is not yet near day:
        It was the nightingale, and not the lark,
        That pierced the fearful hollow of thine ear;
        Nightly she sings on yond pomegranate-tree:
        Believe me, love, it was the nightingale.

Romeo: It was the lark, the herald of the morn,
        No nightingale: look, love, what envious
          streaks
        Do lace the severing clouds in yonder east:
        Night's candles are burnt out . . .

Some birds, like the American Robin, *Turdus migratorius*, sing as soon as they awaken. The European Robin, however, begins singing about three minutes after awakening; the Blackbird, *Turdus merula*, five to six minutes; and the Chaffinch, 15 to 20 minutes after awakening (Scheer, 1951). As a rule the time of a species' awakening song is closely related to the time of sunrise so that a bird's first song of the day occurs earlier and earlier as spring progresses and the sun rises earlier each day. The Song Sparrow's first song is given each day at about the time of civil twilight, or approximately one-half hour before sunrise when the sun is six degrees below the horizon (Nice, 1938). In January and February the first song is given about five minutes after civil twilight, and in March to June, from three to six minutes before civil twilight. With the lengthening of spring days, many birds rise and sing earlier not only with regard

to the clock, but also more minutes before sunrise, so that by early summer in England, the Skylark begins singing at 2 A.M. The Chaffinch, which sings about 15 minutes after sunrise in February, sings 27 minutes before sunrise in June (Armstrong, 1949).

Such facts as these suggest that light intensity is the chief trigger which sets off awakening song in birds. Several studies have shown this to be true for a variety of species. Observations by Emlen (1937) of the rising time of a Mockingbird on 86 mornings between December 1 and April 1 showed that neither humidity nor temperature correlated with the time of awakening song. Only light intensity showed a consistent positive correlation with the time of the first song. On bright mornings the bird sang about 29 minutes before sunrise, and on cloudy mornings, 13 to 19 minutes.

Pioneer studies of the relationship be-

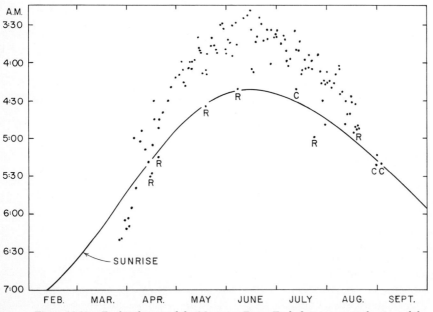

Figure 11.10. Daybreak song of the Mourning Dove. Each dot represents the time of the first song given each day at Madison, Wisconsin, 43° N. Latitude. Note how the reduced light of rainy (R) and cloudy (C) mornings delayed the first song on those days, and that the longer the day, the earlier the song with reference to the time of sunrise. After unpublished data of Aldo Leopold, courtesy of J. J. Hickey.

tween light intensity and morning song were made by Allard (1930) in the vicinity of Washington, D.C. He found that certain species like the Robin, *Turdus migratorius*, Cardinal, *Richmondena cardinalis*, and Song Sparrow, *Melospiza melodia*, sang their awakening songs in very dim light, whereas other species, such as the House Wren, *Troglodytes aëdon*, did not begin singing until the daylight was 150 to 200 times brighter. He also found that some of the earliest singers sang earlier than usual on mornings when there was a bright moon. It is well known that the Mockingbird, *Mimus polyglottos*, will sing throughout the night if there is a full moon.

Using a sensitive photometer, Aldo Leopold studied the relationship between morning song and light intensity by making hundreds of observations on 20 species of birds over a period of four years, in the vicinity of Madison, Wisconsin

(Leopold and Eynon, 1961). As a result of these painstaking observations, Leopold confirmed the fact that cloudiness delayed the time of the first morning songs of birds, and that a bright moon, at least for the Robin, caused earlier singing. One unexpected, and as yet unexplained, observation was that birds of six different species living in the city began their morning songs an average 10 minutes later than the same species living on a farm in the country. The intensities of incident sky light during the beginning of morning song by the Robin, Cardinal, and Song Sparrow were .023, .022, and .015 foot candle respectively, on clear mornings in April. The intensity of light at the beginning of civil twilight was determined as .04 foot candle. Leopold also found that the light intensity required to stimulate awakening song in the morning was significantly less for 9 passerine species than the light intensity coinciding with song cessation in

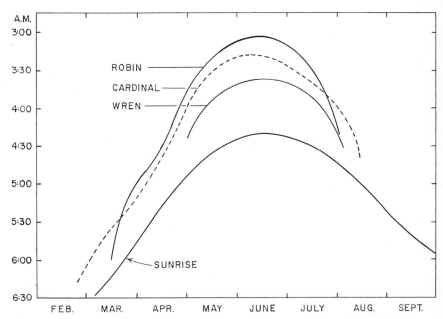

Figure 11.11. Smoothed curves showing the mean daily time of daybreak song for the American Robin, Cardinal, and House Wren, for different months of the year at 43° N. Latitude. After unpublished data of Aldo Leopold, courtesy of J. J. Hickey.

the evening. The Robin, for example, sings in the morning with a light intensity only one fifty-seventh of that in the evening when it ceases singing. This difference perhaps reflects an adaptation to the need of silent preparation for going to roost at the end of the day, and possibly also the need for seeking a second resting place should the first one chosen prove to be unsuitable.

There is an inverse relation between light and singing in nocturnal species. Field observations of the nocturnal Poorwill, *Phalaenoptilus nuttallii*, showed that the beginning of its activity at dusk and its cessation at dawn coincided with a light intensity of less than one foot-candle (Brauner, 1952). The Tawny Owl in Denmark begins its evening calling from about 9 minutes after sunset in August-September to 34 to 46 minutes after sunset in December-January; and its last call for the night occurs about 26 minutes before sunrise in August-September and about 56 to 66 minutes before sunrise in December-January. In this species wind and cold weather have a definite depressing effect upon its calls (Hansen, 1952).

A natural experiment that reveals dramatically the correlation between light and song occurs during a total eclipse of the sun. After the solar eclipse of June 30, 1954, in Sweden, appeals by press and radio for information on bird song brought in 107 reports (Ehrström, 1956). The diurnal songbirds stopped singing for about 15 minutes during the darkest period of the eclipse. The light intensity at which singing stopped was much higher than that at which it was resumed. Nocturnal species sang during totality and became quiet as light increased afterward. The Willow Warbler, *Phylloscopus trochilus*, which commonly sings at night, sang through the eclipse.

Since distance from the equator affects the length of daylight, there are latitudinal differences in the hours of waking song. The Robin, *Turdus migratorius*, not only begins its continuous morning song earlier in the higher latitudes (as early as 12:58

A.M. at 60 degrees N. latitude) but sings longer once it starts (89 minutes at 60 degrees N. lat.; 42 minutes at 38 degrees N. lat.) (Miller, 1958). Tinbergen (1939) found that Snow Buntings, *Plectrophenax nivalis*, arose earlier each day as spring progressed in Greenland until about May 1 when they began their activities at 1:00 A.M. Although the days continued lengthening until the summer solstice, the birds refused to rise any earlier. Even at that, they took only two or three hours of sleep each day.

The daily rhythm of activity and song may be inverted in certain species during the breeding and migration seasons. In the antarctic spring, for example, the Snow Petrel, *Pagodroma nivea*, is said to be active by day, but in the summer, only at night. During nocturnal migration flights, many diurnal species do not sing; but often they give short chirps or location notes, presumably to hold the flock together.

THE INHERITANCE AND LEARNING OF SONG

Do birds sing the songs they do because they learn them from their parents or because they inherit them? Baron von Pernau, writing early in the 18th century, had some shrewd ideas on the subject (Stresemann, 1947):

> "One has to consider that a young bird of any species, which neither hears an adult of its kind nor has another young around itself, never will attain its natural song completely, but will sing rather poorly. . . . There is nothing more agreeable than to hang a well-singing Tree Pipit [*Anthus trivialis*], which has a very long-drawn-out song, next to several young Chaffinches [*Fringilla coelebs*]. . . . If, by this method, one cause three or four finches annually to adopt a Tree Pipit's song . . . one can within some years, quite fill a forest with such-like song."

Modern experiments in bird song have confirmed part but not all of Baron von Pernau's conclusions.

Obviously, the physical structure of a bird's vocal machinery sets limits on the bird's capacity to modify its song, whether by learning or by genetic mutation or cross-breeding. One can no more extract a canary's warble from a goose than he can a flute's trill from a tuba. But within these rather broad limits, the question still remains: to what extent is a bird's song innate, and to what extent acquired? The fact that parrots (including Budgerigars), starlings, and other birds can be taught to repeat words and other sounds is well known. Is this an exceptional trait limited to a few species and to exceptional training conditions, or is it an ability common to many other species and occurring under natural conditions?

The simplest experimental approach to this problem is to raise young birds from incubation to vocal maturity in complete isolation from sounds of their own species. This has been done with a number of species and has shown that the song of some is almost entirely innate; in others, it is largely learned; in still others, it is partly innate and partly learned. Bobwhite Quail, *Colinus virginianus*, that are incubator-raised give the typical *bob white* call. Six European Blackbirds, *Turdus merula*, which were raised individually in sound-proof rooms, and four which were surgically deafened, developed songs that were characteristic of the species in all but the pitch and duration of certain notes (Messmer and Messmer, 1956). Other Blackbirds reared in acoustic isolation, by Thielke-Poltz and Thielke (1960), were experimentally exposed to various songs when 28 and 29 days of age, and reproduced these songs when 122 days old, one bird faithfully reproducing a stanza it had heard only 12 times. European White-throats, *Sylvia communis*, reared by Sauer (1954) in sound-proof isolation, developed completely typical call notes and songs, proving that in this species their utterances are completely innate and not learned. Experiments and observations by Poulsen (1951) convinced him that song was innate in the Reed Bunting, *Emberiza schoeniculus*, Wood Warbler, *Phyllosco-pus sibilatrix*, and Tree Pipit, *Anthus trivialis*, but learned in the Linnet, *Car-*

duelis cannabina, and Skylark, *Alauda arvensis*. In Song Sparrows, *Melospiza melodia*, a species which sings a great variety of songs, Nice (1943) found that the length, rate of delivery, and triple-phrased nature of the song were innate, but that the quality was acquired. Wild male Song Sparrows were never known to sing the songs of their fathers or grandfathers. A young Bullfinch, *Pyrrhula pyrrhula*, on the other hand, learns its song by imitating its father. One that had been raised by Canaries learned a typical Canary song. Four years later, descendants of this bird still sang faithful reproductions of Canary phrases (Nicolai, 1959).

Very convincing evidence that the song of the Chaffinch is partly innate and partly acquired is presented by Thorpe (1956), who made sound spectrograms of wild birds, birds reared in auditory isolation, and birds kept under still other experimental conditions. With electronic equipment he was able to secure graphic records of the frequency, amplitude, and time duration of even the most complex bird songs. A Chaffinch raised in complete auditory and visual isolation revealed the basic hereditary song pattern of the species. It had a song in three phrases, lasting about two seconds, and made up of a crescendo series of notes that ended in a single note of high pitch. All the refinements and flourishes that separate the typical song of a wild bird from this basic pattern must be learned, although the innate foundation is specific enough to prevent the Chaffinch from learning the distinctly different songs of other species. However, two young, unrelated Chaffinches reared in the same cage, but acoustically isolated from other birds, will acquire abnormal but essentially identical songs. Each bird is stimulated and guided by the other ("the blind leading the blind") in developing its song. Unable to follow the example of a wild bird's song, they turn out the best they can in duplicate copies. Spectrograms of the songs of such birds reared together show extraor-

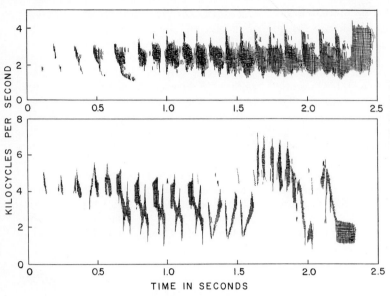

Figure 11.12. Sound spectrograms of Chaffinch songs. Above: the basic innate pattern of a hand-raised bird kept in auditory isolation. Below: the normal song of a wild bird. After Thorpe.

dinarily detailed resemblances between their song patterns, which, moreover, are distinctly different from the spectrograms of other pairs similarly raised in isolation (Fig. 11.13). When a Chaffinch is about eleven months old there is a critical period of about six weeks in which the bird learns its song pattern. Once the song is learned and sung vigorously for a few days, it becomes fixed for life, even though the bird may live among other Chaffinches singing quite different patterns.

The age at which a young bird first sings varies considerably according to species. Young Song Sparrows begin to sing as early as their 14th day after hatching (Nice, 1943), and the young of many other passerine species, before they are a month old. The recrudescence of adult song that occurs in many birds toward the end of the breeding season may well be a naturally selected device to impress upon the impressionable young the characteristic species song. There is some evidence that imprinting of song may occur under such conditions. Koehler (1951) tells of a six-weeks-old hand-raised Nightingale, *Luscinia megarhynchos,* which was exposed to the song of a Blackcap, *Sylvia atricapilla,* for ten days in July. The fol-

lowing January, when the Nightingale first began to sing, it sang the Blackcap song.

Mimicry in bird song is a well established fact. Mockingbirds, *Mimus polyglottos,* are well known to imitate the calls and songs of other species of birds. One Mockingbird, whose voice was recorded by Cornell University scientists, uttered songs of at least thirty other species of birds. Among some of the better mimics are the Catbird, *Dumetella carolinensis,* Brown Thrasher, *Toxostoma rufum,* Starling, *Sturnus vulgaris,* European Marsh Warbler, *Acrocephalus palustris,* European Red-backed Shrike, *Lanius collurio,* Black Thrush, *Turdus infuscatus,* birds of paradise of New Guinea and Australia, and lyrebirds and bower-birds of Australia. Some 50 different Australian species have been listed by Marshall (1950) as possessing the powers of mimicry. The lyrebird (Menuridae), a relative of the crow, is said to mimic not only other birds, such as owls and the Laughing Jackass or Kookaburra, *Dacelo novaguineae,* but the voices of people, the rustling of parrot wings, and even auto horns. Marshall (1954) also lists some of the sounds mimicked by the Australian Spotted Bower-bird, *Chlamydera macu-*

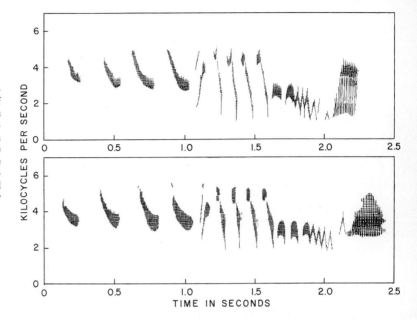

Figure 11.13. Sound spectrograms of the songs of two unrelated Chaffinches reared together but in auditory and visual isolation from all other birds. Note how nearly identical the songs are, and yet how different from a typical wild Chaffinch song. After Thorpe.

lata: the crying of cats, barking of dogs, sheep walking through dead branches, wood-chopping, twanging wire fences, and the calls of many birds. This bowerbird is said to mimic the call of a certain eagle so faithfully as to cause a hen and chickens to run for cover. Thorpe (1956) relates the story of a German woman who had a Bullfinch, *Pyrrhula pyrrhula,* trained to sing "God Save the King." A Canary, in an adjoining room, after a year learned the tune from the Bullfinch. At times, if the Bullfinch would pause over-long between the third and fourth phrases of the song, the Canary would pick up the tune and finish it!

It is difficult ordinarily to see what advantage a bird derives from a talent for mimicry. Mimicry appears to represent a type of displacement activity or an outlet for surplus drive. Evidence that such behavior may occasionally be useful, however, is presented by Gaukrodger (cited by Marshall, 1954) who related that if he approached the nest of a bower-bird, and the noisy mimicry of the female, at a distance from the nest, failed to attract his attention, the bird would "suddenly almost fall to the ground and with neck stretched out, feathers ruffled and wings spread, she would creep through the grass pretending helplessness."

It seems somewhat surprising that natural selection apparently has not exploited voice mimicry in birds for the same ends that Batesian mimicry achieves in the realm of animal coloration: that is, the singing of sham songs for ulterior gain. Perhaps a start in this direction is found in the hissing sounds made by many hole-nesting species, notably titmice and wrynecks. Some naturalists believe that these sounds warn away predators that mistake the sounds for the hissing of a snake. The African Crowned Eagle, *Stephanoaëtos coronatus,* may possibly employ voice-mimicry to capture the monkeys on which it feeds. The male is reported by Maclatchey (1937) to hide in foliage near a band of monkeys and whistle softly. This attracts the old males, which approach threateningly. The eagle then strikes at the nearest monkey and flies off with him. Maclatchey found that he could attract enraged monkeys to within a few meters by whistling in the same fashion. It is conceivable that a good mimic like the Mockingbird obtains a more exclusive sovereignty of its territory by warning away all species whose songs it imitates, but apparently this problem has not been studied. In his study of the Smooth-billed Ani, *Crotophaga ani*, in Cuba, Davis (1940) discovered that when a Mockingbird mimicked the anis' alarm note it caused them to give the fright reaction, even though there was no cause for fear.

SONG POPULATIONS

Some years ago there was a radio program in which the master of ceremonies attempted, often successfully, to locate within the United States the home localities of various participants by listening to their accents or geographic dialects. Birds may similarly show geographic population differences in song. An example of a local dialect is found in the "rain-call" of the Chaffinch. Local populations of Chaffinches only a few kilometers apart may have distinctly different rain-calls (Sick, 1939). Likewise, local populations of White-crowned Sparrows, *Zonotrichia leucophrys*, in California show different community song patterns (Petersen, 1941). When the songs of more than 200 species of African birds were studied by Benson (1948) he found that 33 of them showed geographic variations. Since about 1920, a new type of song has been spreading among the Blackcaps, *Sylvia atricapilla*, of southwestern Europe. This new variation is called the "Leier song," and it consists of a series of brief notes inserted within the regular song. It originated in the Alps and has now extended through southern Germany, southern France, Spain, and Mediterranean regions, spreading at the rate of about five kilometers per year (Morike, 1953). The method by which this new song is spreading through the Blackcap populations is very probably the same that caused Thorpe's Chaffinches to sing like their neighbors—by "learned

tradition." The fact that the Blackcaps are no longer learning the established, traditional song of the species may be explained by assuming some structural, physiological, or neurological "preadaptation" with which the new song (once a bird hears it) fits better than the old one. Certainly in the Chaffinch the great variety of songs spread through local populations all over Europe are no more inherited than the cockney accent of the "fair lady," Eliza Doolittle, in Shaw's *Pygmalion*. But once a dialect is established in a Chaffinch it is less malleable to corrective instruction than it was in Miss Doolittle's case.

These community patterns in bird song may have some significance in promoting group cohesion and stimulation, but they are probably of much more importance as agents of reproductive isolation which prevent the interbreeding of different populations of birds of the same species. Such reproductive isolation is of extreme importance to the evolution of any species.

SUGGESTED READINGS

For good discussions of the general principles of bird song, see Van Tyne and Berger, *Fundamentals of Ornithology*, or Wing, *Natural History of Birds*. An excellent discussion of the problem of innate versus acquired song is found in Thorpe, *Learning and Instinct in Animals*. For books on the identification of bird songs see Mathews, *Field Book of Wild Birds and Their Music*, and Saunders, *A Guide to Bird Song*. An English calendar for the song periods of many European birds is given in Witherby *et al.*, *The Handbook of British Birds*.

TWELVE

Territory

The gull claims only nest-room for her ground,
But if an interloper there be found,
All heaven echoes with protesting sound.
Joel Peters, *Every Man's House*

A common springtime sight on the grassy lawns of yards and parks is the clamorous fighting and chasing that goes on between two American Robins. This is the territorial fighting that occurs between two birds, usually males, when both lay claim to the same piece of land for a living site. The same sort of thing occurs in many other species of birds which are landed proprietors and commonly defend their property with all the vigor they can command. Various fishes, lizards, mice and other mammals—man, unfortunately, not excepted—engage in similar battles over land ownership.

Another frequently reported springtime activity of many birds is "reflection fighting" or the attack by a bird on its reflected image in a window or a mirror. Here the bird apparently mistakes its reflection for an intruder of the same species on its property. Every day between May 2 and July 11 a Brown Towhee, *Pipilo fuscus*, fought its reflection in a university laboratory window at Berkeley, California, sometimes visiting the window as often as 15 times a day and striking the window as often as 53 times a minute (Ritter and Benson, 1934). Several observers have experimented with mirrors to study the reactions of birds to their images. A mirror set up on an English lawn in early April was attacked for hours on end by male Pied Wagtails, *Motacilla alba*, male Blackbirds, *Turdus merula*, and male Great Tits, *Parus major*. The females, however, were indifferent to their images (Brown, 1937). Toward the end of April the birds' antagonism to their images decreased, and in May it disappeared altogether, illustrating the fact that territorial fighting is usually seasonal.

HISTORY OF THE TERRITORY CONCEPT

The concept of territory ownership in birds goes back in history at least as far as Aristotle (*ca.* 350 B.C.) who wrote "Each pair of eagles needs a large territory and on that account allows no other eagle to settle in the neighborhood" (Nice, 1953). In the next century, Zenodotus observed that "One bush does not shelter two Robins"; and much later, in 1622, Olina wrote of the European Robin, *Erithacus rubecula,* "It has a peculiarity that it cannot abide a companion in the place where it lives and will attack with all its strength any who dispute this claim" (Lack, 1943). Thoughtful observations by later naturalists began to reveal some of the complications of the territory concept. The remarkably perceptive Baron von Pernau wrote in 1707:

"On the other hand the Nightingale is forced, for the sake of her feeding requirements, to chase away her own equals, for if many would stay together, they could not possibly find enough worms and would inevitably starve. Nature therefore has given them the drive to flee from each other as much as possible. . . . The Chaffinch gives the most pleasure by the males, as soon as the sun in March gets stronger, selecting a special place, just as other birds do, often consisting of a few trees, and by afterwards not allowing another male to show up there. They sing very fervently all day long from the tops of such trees, to induce one of the passing females (that always arrive last in migration) to come down" (Stresemann, 1947).

Gilbert White of Selborne, writing in 1772, introduced a new notion into the slowly growing concept of territoriality:

"During the amorous season such a jealousy prevails amongst male birds that they can hardly bear to be together in the same hedge or field. . . . It is to this spirit of jealousy that I chiefly attribute the equal dispersion of birds in the spring over the face of the country" (Nice, 1941).

The first comprehensive modern definition of territory came from Bernard Altum in his book *Der Vogel und Sein Leben*, published in 1868. Although his ideas gained currency in Germany, they did not spread to other countries. The following excerpts from Altum are in Mayr's (1935) translation.

"It is impossible, among a great many species of birds, for numerous pairs to nest close together, but individual pairs must settle at precisely fixed distances from each other. The reason for this necessity is the amount and kind of food they have to gather . . . together with the methods by which they secure it. All the species of birds which have specialized diets and which . . . limit their wanderings to small areas, cannot and ought not settle close to other pairs because of the danger of starvation. They need a territory of a definite size, which varies according to the productivity of any given locality.

"It is, of course, natural that the most suitable localities will be most sought by the species preferring them. Large numbers will gather in such places, overcrowding them, while other available territories would be empty if pairs were not kept apart by force. This force is used by the male as soon as another gets too close during the breeding season. The interloper is immediately attacked in the most violent manner, and driven to a distance that is determined by the size of the required territory."

Altum goes on to show that song is used both as a proclamation to fix territorial boundaries and as an invitation to females to join the singing male.

A great impetus to the study of bird territory was given by the publication of Howard's (1920) book, *Territory in Bird Life*. Howard emphasized the instinctive intolerance of males for each other during the breeding season, the means by which males advertised their territories, the value of a territory for its exclusive food supply, and the possibility of extremely small, nest-centered territories in the case of birds nesting in colonies.

Numerous definitions of territory have appeared in recent years. They range from very brief statements such as Noble's (1939) "Territory is any defended area," to long discourses covering several paragraphs. Almost every definition, however, embraces the two ideas presented by Craig (1918): (1) an appetite for a place, and (2) an aversion to other members of the species except the mate. An excellent working definition of territory is offered by Mrs. Nice (1941):

"The theory of territory in bird life is briefly this: that pairs are spaced through the pugnacity of males towards others of their own species and sex; that song and display of plumage and other signals are a warning to other males and an invitation to a female; that males fight primarily for territory and not over mates; that the owner of a territory is nearly invincible in his territory; and finally that birds which fail to obtain territory form a reserve supply from which replacements come in case of death to owners of territory."

FUNCTIONS OF TERRITORY

As is already apparent, territory has no single, simple, over-all function. The uses of territory may differ for the individual bird, the mated pair or its family, a colony of birds, or a species. The significance of territory for a singing male is at times strikingly different from its significance for the female or for the nestlings; and territory has still different meanings for the species. Considered broadly, territory produces its effects, including numerous advantages and some disadvantages, through the isolation of birds, by spreading them apart, by providing geographic stability, and by giving its owners certain psychological advantages.

The first of these functions of territory —the isolation of birds from others of their kind—produces immediately apparent advantages. An isolated male in his territory is unmolested in his courtship of any female that may enter the territory. Once the breeding cycle begins, territory reduces interference with pairing, copulation, nest building, and the rearing of young. Ownership of a territory provides more or less of a monopoly of the food resources nearby (particularly important in adverse weather) and of nesting materials. Since isolation means fewer contacts with strangers, fighting is reduced and energy thus saved. Also, the hazards of promiscuity are reduced and family stability thereby promoted. This, of course, is extremely important in many species for the rearing of young. The monopolistic feature of territory probably arose out of the drastic nature of intraspecific competition. A Robin's worst enemy—his greatest competitor—is not a hawk or a cat. It is another Robin which seeks from the environment exactly those kinds of food, those nesting sites, and that kind of a mate, that all Robins seek.

Closely related to, yet different from, the advantages of isolation, are those arising from the dispersion of individuals. The mutual antagonism of male birds resembles the restless, mutual repulsion of the molecules of a gas under pressure, seeking always to fill all available space. Such a spreading out of birds of a given species regulates population density and prevents overpopulation. As von Pernau and Altum both pointed out, if birds of a given species gathered only where food is most abundant or most easily obtained, their concentrated appetites might shortly bring on famine, while in other neglected habitats food remained uneaten. Dispersion thus promotes the efficient exploitation of food, nest materials, nest sites, and other requirements. The possibility of overpopulation, should there be no territorial safeguards, was clearly demonstrated in a drastic field experiment conducted in a small piece of Maine forest by Hensley and Cope (1951). In a 16 hectare (40 acre) spruce-fir woods there were 154 territory-holding male birds of various species at the beginning of the experiment in early June, 1950. Through the use of firearms this population was reduced to 21 per cent of its original size by June 21, and held at about that level by the continuous shooting of new arrivals in the woods until July 11. By that time a total of 528 adult birds had been killed. (Students should realize that an experiment of this kind can be conducted only by special authorization of conservation authorities, and must be aimed at solving a definite scientific problem.) New males moved into the woods and established territories as quickly as territories were vacated by the removed birds. It seems obvious that there were surplus males available—males without territories and living in less desirable habitats—waiting to rush in and fill the vacuum the moment a given territory became unoccupied. Territorial spread thus works to create a stand-by population of birds ready to take over in times of emergency and to keep the optimum habitats producing birds.

Although concrete evidence is lacking, there is a strong possibility that the geographic dispersion of birds reduces the incidence of disease by reducing the opportunities for contagion. The earlier game management practice of winter-feeding of gallinaceous birds in concentrated spots has been modified for certain species to avoid the spread of disease, and the raising of Domestic Fowl in "broiler factories" on raised screens rather than on the ground is done to prevent epidemics of ground-transmitted disease. Certainly, the fact that birds are scattered over a large area rather than locally concentrated makes it more difficult for predators to find and kill them. Instead of sitting down to a meal of several birds in one spot, the predator has to travel and search for each individual it catches.

A function of territory commonly overlooked is evolutionary selection within the species, which may be promoted by geographic spread. Birds pushed by expansive territorial forces to the periphery of a species' range may be forced into nontypical habitats where they must eat somewhat different foods, use strange nest materials or nest sites, experience new ranges of climatic extremes, and so on. Some of these marginal birds may find that they already possess adaptations to one or more of the new conditions. In general they will, of course, lead the lean, arduous life of pioneers, but like their human counterparts, some small groups of them may occasionally "strike it rich" in the form of evolutionary adaptive divergence encouraged by ecological or geographic isola-

tion. It may well be that ecological divergence, brought on by territorial pressure, has resulted, for example, in altitudinal races of related species such as the European Ptarmigan, *Lagopus mutus*, of the alpine zones, and the Red Grouse, *Lagopus scoticus*, of the lower moors and bogs (Huxley, 1942). If the general principle is true that the less well-adapted an animal is to its environment the more drastic the winnowing of natural selection, then certainly the peripheral birds of a given population, exposed to a somewhat unfriendly environment, will be subject to a more intense selection pressure than the better adapted, more comfortably located central birds. Further, small fragments of a peripheral population have excellent chances of being reproductively isolated from the main population of their species —another important species-making factor. In these ways, territory can be a powerful adjunct to natural selection.

Another important aspect of territorialism is that it gives an individual the advantage of perfect familiarity with one small area. After a bird settles down on its territory and explores its surroundings, it soon learns where to go for food, the best escape routes when predators attack, where to find nest materials, and similar facts necessary to survival. Moreover it comes to know its neighbors "personally," and establishes a practical and more or less pacific *modus vivendi* with them based on their relative aggressiveness. In that way, a bird in familiar environs can become a creature of habit and thereby save itself the wear and tear of much trial and error learning. The community stability enjoyed by a territory-owning bird is roughly comparable to the law and order of a settled human community (also based in large part on property rights) in contrast to the lawless turmoil of a frontier where every individual is a stranger whose capacity for good or evil must be determined in never-ending face-to-face encounters.

Territorialism thus brings into play two antagonistic forces, one dynamic and centrifugal, the other stable and centripetal. The dynamic, expansive, gas-like force that disperses birds may shove some of them into frontiers where living is rough but where occasionally the species may "make its fortune." The stable, centripetal force that rivets a bird to its territory corresponds to the stay-at-home, property-owning conservatism that promotes comfortable living, reproductive success, and the preservation of family life. The poem, "To the Not Impossible Him" by Millay (1922)* touches on these two aspects of territorialism in man:

> How shall I know, unless I go
> To Cairo or Cathay,
> Whether or not this blessed spot
> Is blest in every way?

> Now it may be, the flower for me
> Is this beneath my nose;
> How shall I tell unless I smell
> The Carthaginian rose?

> The fabric of my faithful love
> No power shall dim or ravel
> Whilst I stay here,—but oh, my dear,
> If I should ever travel!

Snug in its home territory, the avian family is relatively secure, safe from want, safe from philandering adventurers—but it is just possible that a Carthaginian rose bush would provide a better nest site!

Finally, a territory confers remarkable psychological benefits on its owner. A bird changes its personality drastically when it sets foot off its own territory. The European Robin, *Erithacus rubecula*, defends its territory with song, posturing, and at times actual physical combat. The degree to which it employs these defenses depends on whether the bird is on its own territory or off. One of the male Robins studied by Lack (1943) was caught in a wire-cage trap in his own territory. Shortly after this his neighbor, a male called Double Blue (after the identifying rings on his legs) trespassed on the first bird's territory seeking food. The latter

* By permission of Norma Millay Ellis. Copyright 1922, 1950, by Edna St. Vincent Millay.

bird "at once postured violently and uttered a vigorous song-phrase from inside the trap, and Double Blue, who was one of the fiercest of all the robins, promptly retreated to his own territory, although the first male could not, of course, get out to attack him. I now caught the first male and moved him into a trap in the territory of Double Blue. The formerly timid Double Blue now came raging over the trap, posturing violently at the first male inside, while the latter, formerly so fierce, made himself as scarce as possible, and did not attempt to fight or posture back." This principle of belligerent aggressiveness in its own territory and shrinking timidity in its neighbor's territory has been seen in many species of birds. Several examples have been reported of birds which have died from ruptured hearts or aortas presumably as the result of the emotional excitement of territorial battles (Dilger, 1955). Even baby birds demonstrate the ego-puffing influence of territory possession. Downy chicks of Black-headed Gulls, *Larus ridibundus*, were observed by Kirkman (1937) to drive adult gulls away from their nests. The astonishing part about this is that "outside the nest, the chick is a hunted creature, pecked by every adult it passes and fortunate if it escapes with its life. Yet, inside the nest it opens its stubby wings, raises a small shrill voice, charges heroically, and the adult beats a retreat." A bird is ordinarily invincible in its own territory, or, as Lack puts it, victory "goes not to the strong but to the righteous, the righteous, of course, being the owner of property."

A rare demonstration of the operation of this principle occurred when two male Peregrine Falcons, *Falco peregrinus*, each independently acquired a proprietary interest in the same cliff-side eyrie (Peterson, 1948). Falconers had trapped and removed the original male owner of the territory and, a month later, thinking the eyrie still unoccupied, returned the bird to freedom. However, in its absence another male Peregrine had staked his claim to the cliff.

"Hardly had the tercel made a reconnaissance of his home cliff than another male streaked out of nowhere. There had been a replacement after all, . . . each of these birds, no doubt, felt itself to be the rightful owner. The greatest display of flying the falconers had ever seen took place—dog-fights in the air, plunges across the face of the cliff with only inches to spare, barrel rolls, all the maneuvers at their command. Twice the birds grappled on the ledge and tumbled to the wooded foot of the cliff. For three hours the battle lasted until the pale-breasted bird, the late-comer, departed."

In many species the possession of territory seems to be psychologically necessary for successful breeding. Lack (1940) kept two pairs of European Robins in each of two large aviaries, and in each instance the dominant, territory-owning pair bred, while the subordinate pair showed no traces of breeding behavior. Similar observations have been made on many other species. In the case of polygamous Redwinged Blackbirds, *Agelaius phoeniceus*, a dominant male owning an attractive patch of cattail marsh may acquire a harem of as many as six actively nesting females, while a subordinate male with a less desirable territory may have only one mate or none (Linsdale, 1938). Territory possession, at least in some species, also has a psychological effect on the pair bond of its owners. Lack (1943) tells of one of the rare instances in which a male Robin territory owner was bested in conflict by a vigorous interloper, and eventually chased away. "The hen took no part in this encounter, and after a while began to follow the newcomer about as if he were her mate ('None but the brave,' etc.)." The hen finally reared a family with the victorious male. In some species, the female will join her mate in repelling intruders on their territory. In such species territory ownership very probably helps to intensify the bond between the mated birds.

Probably one historical reason for the remarkably emphatic territorialism in birds is their superlative mobility. This brings about frequent contacts between individuals and therefore increases the probability that there will be contests over nest sites, conflicts for food, promiscuity

between mated pairs, and unstable family life. Territory ownership tends to put a brake on some of these volatile excesses made possible by flight, and restores some stability to the life of the individual and the family. At the same time, territory is a dynamic force that encourages speciation. The surprising fact is not that birds own real estate, but that, considering the numerous benefits of territory, some species are able to get along without it.

TYPES OF TERRITORY

In different species of birds, territories serve different ends. There have been many classifications of territory based on functions. The following is a modification of those of Mayr (1935) and Nice (1941).

The following seven general types of territory may be recognized:

1. Mating, nesting, and feeding territory.
2. Mating and nesting territory.
3. Mating territory.
4. Narrowly-restricted nesting territory.
5. Feeding territory.
6. Winter territory.
7. Roosting territory.

1. Mating, nesting, and feeding territories are probably the commonest sort. They are maintained by a great variety of birds, including many woodpeckers, shrikes, thrushes, icterids, warblers, sparrows, and others. When a territory is of this type, courtship, mating, and nest-building all normally occur within it, and after the young hatch, their food comes from it.

2. In mating and nesting territories, reproductive and nesting activities occur on the territory, but the food for the young is obtained elsewhere, often on neutral ground. Examples of such territory are found among some grebes, swans, harriers, the Redwinged Blackbird and several finches. The male Scarlet Finch, *Carpodacus erythrinus*, which defends its small territory with vigor, will feed amicably with its neighbors on neutral feeding

grounds 100 meters to a kilometer distant.

3. Territories restricted exclusively to courtship and mating are held by the males of many polygamous gallinaceous birds such as the Prairie Chicken, *Tympanuchus cupido,* Sharp-tailed Grouse, *Pedioecetes phasianellus,* and Capercaillie, *Tetrao urogallus,* as well as by males of the Ruff, *Philomachus pugnax;* some birds of paradise, bower-birds, some hummingbirds, and some manakins. In many of these species the males gather on special display grounds or *leks* where they call, "boom," dance, posture, or—rarely —fight, while the females look on and eventually make their choice of a mate. The male Sharp-tailed Grouse, for example, strut and boom on their traditional communal booming grounds, each male claiming and defending a particular spot in the area. The male bower-bird builds and decorates his bower, defends it from other males, and may even display in it, months before the breeding season begins. In the breeding season he displays there before a single female, and the pair may copulate there. The nest is located elsewhere, and the female is thought to receive no help whatever from the male in nest-building, incubation, or rearing the young. The male Golden-collared Manakin, *Manacus vitellinus,* presents most of his courtship display above the small court which he clears of leaves and other removable litter of the forest floor, and defends from others of his kind. The female builds her nest at a distance, and receives no help from him while she rears her young.

4. The fourth type of territory is found among those species which defend only the immediate surroundings of the nest. Many colonial water birds, such as penguins, pelicans, cormorants, shearwaters, gulls, terns, and herons, belong in this category, as well as a few of the solitary-nesting doves, swallows, and birds of prey. In many colonial birds, the limits of the nest territory are determined by the distance that the sitting bird can jab its beak. The nests of the Peruvian Brown Pelican,

Pelecanus occidentalis, are spaced about two per square meter; those of the Peruvian Guanay Cormorant, *Phalacrocorax bougainvillii,* about three per square meter. The burrow entrances of the Slender-billed Shearwater, *Puffinus tenuirostris,* may be as crowded as nine per square meter (Murphy, 1936). In a few colonial species such as the European Jackdaw, *Corvus monedula,* and the Australian Magpie, *Gymnorhina dorsalis,* the breeding territory is shared in common and defended by all the birds of the colony against intruders of the same species. In addition to cooperating in the defense of the colony, individuals often must also defend their own nests against other residents of the colony. This is shown by the fact that in many colonial-nesting species and even in some solitary-nesting species, the mutual pilfering of nesting materials is a common practice. Adelie Penguins, *Pygoscelis adeliae,* frequently steal stones from each others' nests. "Depredators, when conscious of detection or suspicion, make themselves look thin, sleek and small, and endeavor to lose themselves in the crowd. The offended birds, on the contrary, seem to swell with rage, for they erect their feathers when pursuing the thief, and the plumage at the back of the neck bristles out so as to form a crest and topknot" (Murphy, 1936).

5. Only a few species are known to have feeding territories separate from their nesting territories. The importance of food in a combined mating, nesting, and feeding territory is revealed by the fact that territory size, or its defense, often varies with the food supply. In 1953 the lemmings on which Pomarine Jaegers, *Stercorarius pomarinus,* preyed were abundant near Barrow, Alaska, and the Jaeger territories were each about 6 to 9 hectares in area, while in the preceding year, with a scarce lemming supply, the area of each territory averaged about 45 hectares (Pitelka *et al.,* 1955). Storks are reported to drive off newcomers when food in the neighborhood is scarce, but to let them remain when food is ample. Since

nuthatches make an investment in their year-round territories by storing seeds in crevices in bark, it is not surprising that both sexes defend the territory with vigor, especially in the autumn when juvenile males attempt to gain a foothold (Löhrl, 1957).

An example of a species that possesses a feeding territory isolated from its nesting territory is the Atlantic coast Seaside Sparrow, *Ammospiza maritima*, which defends both an area around its nest and a feeding strip along the ocean shore. The Hungarian Rock Thrush, *Monticola saxatilis*, also defends separate nesting and feeding territories; these may be several kilometers apart, and the territories of other pairs may lie between them (Farkas, 1955). An unusual example of feeding-territory defense is reported by Sprot (1937) in the case of Glaucous-winged Gulls, *Larus glaucescens*, which may lay claim to a small fishing boat and defend it "against all comers. Should the boat put to sea for several months, on its return to the harbor it will instantly be boarded by the same bird." Murphy (1936) likewise reports what might be called temporary feeding territories of Cape Pigeons, *Daption capensis*, at antarctic whaling stations where a single bird will claim for itself the carcass of an entire whale!

6. Many species of non-migratory birds are loosely associated with their territories throughout the year, but usually defend them only during the breeding season. But territory may be defended throughout the year by a few species such as the Plain Titmouse, *Parus inornatus*, of California, or the Great Gray Shrike, *Lanius excubitor*, of Europe. True winter territory, however, is an area separate from the mating and nesting territory. The California Loggerhead Shrike, *Lanius ludovicianus*, is reported to defend an individual winter feeding ground against all other shrikes; and in North Africa at least two winter visitors from Europe, the Robin, *Erithacus rubecula*, and Pied Wagtail, *Motacilla alba*, establish and defend winter feeding territories.

In Maryland, Kilham (1958) discovered that the Red-headed Woodpecker, *Melanerpes erythrocephalus*, has a special type of winter territory, in which it conceals stores of acorns in various cavities, and establishes a roost hole. These small storage and roosting territories (Fig. 12.1) are pugnaciously defended, not only against other woodpeckers and such potential acorn robbers as Blue Jays, *Cyanocitta cristata*, and Tufted Titmice, *Parus bicolor*, but also against Starlings, *Sturnus vulgaris*, which attempt to take over the roost holes. The defense is actively maintained from September until early May, when the Red-headed Woodpeckers depart for their mating and nesting territories.

7. Roosting territories are probably the least important and the least studied of all territories. Starlings, *Sturnus vulgaris*, show evidence of occupying the same individual perches night after night; and a European Tree Creeper, *Certhia familiaris*, that roosted in a small hole in the bark of a Sequoia tree, vigorously attacked

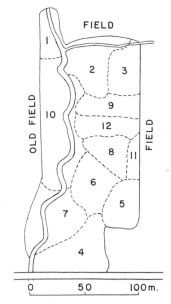

Figure 12.1.   Winter-time roosting and food-storage territories of 12 individual Red-headed Woodpeckers in a small bottom-land woodlot. Woodpeckers 1, 4, and 10 were immature; the others, adults. After Kilham.

a stuffed creeper placed at the entrance (Rankin, 1940).

There are, of course, species whose territorial behavior fits none of these categories exactly, and there are often individual departures from these standard types of territory tenure. Finally, there are birds like the Brown-headed Cowbird, *Moluthrus ater*, that claim no individual territory at all. Territorialism in the Orchard Oriole, *Icterus spurius*, must be extremely feeble or non-existent, since as many as five pairs (one author reported 20 pairs) have nested in a single tree with nests as close as one and one-third meters (Dennis, 1948).

FACILITIES PROVIDED BY TERRITORIES

Although spatial isolation is the irreducible common denominator of territories in general, territories must also be places of biological utility. They cannot be simply blocks of empty space. Therefore the biological uses to which a bird puts its territory determines its composition or general nature. The typical diet of a bird dictates that insects, worms, berry-bushes or the like be available in territories that embrace feeding activities. Each pair of the now probably extinct Ivory-billed Woodpecker, *Campephilus principalis*, was estimated by Tanner (1942) to require not less than 15.5 square kilometers (6 sq. mi.) of primeval wilderness. This species fed on the wood-boring grubs of trees that had been dead for two or three years. Its disappearance coincided with lumbering operations which eliminated the available habitats of required size.

For nesting territories, a suitable nest site, nesting materials, and possibly a singing post are required, depending on the species. In one locality in Panama, one-half of the failures of Rieffer's Hummingbird, *Amazilia tzacatl*, to rear broods were attributed by Skutch (1931) to the thievery of nesting materials. One female was observed to make twelve fresh attempts to build a nest, each of which was frustrated by the theft of material by hummingbirds of the same species or by birds of other species. Many species require nest cavities which they themselves are unable to make. How the availability of such cavities controlled the number of territories in a given area was revealed in an experiment in which 100 nesting boxes were hung in a German orchard (Creutz, 1949). In the first seven years with increased nesting facilities, the population of Pied Flycatchers, *Muscicapa hypoleuca*, rose from two to six pairs, but in the next five years it increased phenomenally to 45 pairs. Presumably something other than simple nest-hole availability operated here, or else the initial increase would have reached the maximum more quickly. A Peregrine Falcon, *Falco peregrinus*, commonly demands for its nest site a nearly vertical cliff with a narrow graveled ledge overlooking a wide span of lowland. Ledges high up on office buildings in large cities sometimes answer this requirement and are consequently chosen by Falcons for nesting sites. The territory of the female parasitic Old World Cuckoo, *Cuculus canorus*, is determined by the location of the nests she parasitizes. Shrike territories must include the thorny shrubs on which the birds may impale their hapless victims.

Scandinavian Black-headed Gulls, *Larus ridibundus*, are reported by Svärdson (1958) to have five requirements for their nesting territory: proximity to water; dry nest foundations; unimpeded view in all directions; isolation by water from terrestrial predators; absence of trees. Territories of American gulls are said by Peterson (1948) to require "a rock or piece of driftwood where the adults can stand and berate their neighbors; the nest; and a hiding place, a tuft of grass or a few weeds for the young to hide beneath." Occasionally there are species whose territorial requirements are quite extraordinary. In Switzerland, the Blue Rock Thrush, *Monticola solitarius*, is said to nest only in east-west oriented stone quarries 240 to 450 meters above sea-level, one pair to a quarry (Corti *et al.*, 1949). Farther south this species is not so particular in its demands. Some small passerine tropical birds choose nesting territories, possibly for protection, in trees which also hold nests of wasps or ants. If a given habitat has the optimum environmental ingredients required by a certain species for its territory, that habitat becomes magnetically attractive to unsettled birds. This was clearly revealed in Hensley and Cope's (1951) study already mentioned, in which 528 adult birds were removed in 49 days from a 16-hectare forest that originally held 154 territory-owning birds. As the replacement birds moved in, they established territories in the same places that had been occupied by predecessors of the same species.

SIZES AND SHAPES OF TERRITORIES

If space were the only consideration, territories would very likely be circular in shape, or perhaps hexagonal like the cells of a honey-comb, since the territory boundaries of one bird would flatten against those of his surrounding neighbors. The radius of each territory would be determined by the time and energy which

its owner could devote to defending his area. The geometry of areas tends to keep territories small, since the area that has to be defended increases as the square of its radius. Thus, doubling the radius of any territory quadruples the space to be maintained. The territory of the Chestnut-collared Longspur, *Calcarius ornatus*, approximates an ideal situation in the prairies of Manitoba. There each Longspur territory is approximately circular, with a radius of about 26 to 37 meters (Harris, 1944). However, in environments which are less homogeneous, the size and shape of a territory will vary with the surroundings. If a bird's territory abuts against a natural boundary that needs no defense, such as a river, the territory can be larger since there will be that much less boundary to defend. Should a territory characteristically follow a shoreline, it may be long and narrow as it is for some coots or for the West Coast Salt Marsh Song Sparrow, *Melospiza melodia*, whose territory averages 40 to 52 meters in length and only 9 meters in width (Johnston, 1956). Such long, narrow plots have more boundary to be defended than circular ones of equal area.

There are many variables that control the size of a bird's territory: the function of the territory; colonial or solitary habit of life; food; population density; foliage density; time of year; age of bird; its indi-

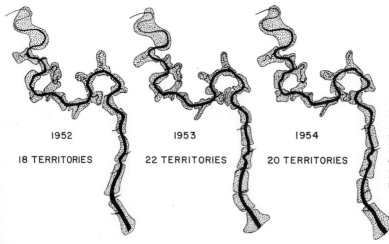

1952
18 TERRITORIES

1953
22 TERRITORIES

1954
20 TERRITORIES

Figure 12.2. Territories occupied in successive years by Salt Marsh Song Sparrows along a tidal slough, San Francisco Bay. Individual territories expand or contract in size according to population density. After Johnston.

Table 12.1. Territory Sizes

SPECIES	LOCALITY	SIZE OF TERRITORY (SQUARE METERS)	AUTHORITY
Black-headed Gull, *Larus ridibundus*	England	0.3	Kirkman
King Penguin, *Aptenodytes patagonicus*	Antarctica	0.5	Murphy
Least Flycatcher, *Empidonax minimus*	Michigan	700	MacQueen
Blackbird, *Turdus merula*	England	1200	Snow
Eastern Robin, *Turdus migratorius*	Wisconsin	1200	Young
Willow Warbler, *Phylloscopus trochilus*	England	1500	May
Redwinged Blackbird, *Agelaius phoeniceus*	Wisconsin	3000	Nero
Coot, *Fulica atra*	England	4000	Cramp
House Wren, *Troglodytes aëdon*	Ohio	4000	Kendeigh
American Redstart, *Setophaga ruticilla*	New York	4000	Hickey
Chaffinch, *Fringilla coelebs*	Finland	4000	von Haartman
Song Sparrow, *Melospiza melodia*	Ohio	4000	Nice
European Robin, *Erithacus rubecula*	England	6000	Lack
Oven-bird, *Seiurus aurocapillus*	Michigan	10,000	Hann
Hazel Grouse, *Tetrastes bonasia*	Finland	40,000	Pynnönen
Song Thrush, *Turdus ericetorum*	Finland	40,000	Siivonen
Black-capped Chickadee, *Parus atricapillus*	New York	53,000	Odum
Western Meadowlark, *Sturnella neglecta*	Iowa	90,000	Kendeigh
Great Horned Owl, *Bubo virginianus*	New York	500,000	Baumgartner
Mistle Thrush, *Turdus viscivorus*	Finland	500,000	Siivonen
Red-tailed Hawk, *Buteo jamaicensis*	California	1,300,000	Fitch *et al.*
Bald Eagle, *Haliaeetus leucocephalus*	Florida	2,500,000	Broley
Crowned Hornbill, *Lophoceros melanoleucos*	Africa	5,200,000	Ranger
Powerful Owl, *Ninox strenua*	Australia	10,000,000	Fleay
Golden Eagle, *Aquila chrysaëtos*	California	93,000,000	Dixon

One *hectare* = 100 meters square (or 10,000 square meters, or 2.47 acres)
One *square kilometer* = 1,000 meters square (or 1,000,000 square meters, or 0.386 square mile)

vidual aggressiveness, and others. The most important variable of all is the species of bird. In a very rough way there is a direct correlation between the size of a bird and the size of its territory. There also seems to be some correlation between voice and territory size, birds with loud or far-carrying songs having correspondingly large territories (Colquhoun, 1940). In colonial nesting species the individual territories are very small, even down to a matter of centimeters in the Bank Swallows, *Riparia riparia.* The Black Grouse, *Lyrurus tetrix,* which uses its territory only for display and coition, defends a tiny area of about 30 square meters (Lack, 1939). Predatory species are likely to have larger territories than non-predatory species;

birds living in sterile desert habitats, larger territories than those of more fertile habitats. Examples of approximate mean territory sizes for various species are given in Table 12.1.

VARIATIONS IN TERRITORY SIZE

Territories are of different sizes for a variety of reasons. As Table 12.1 shows, the Golden Eagle with its 93,000,000 square meters of territory occupies an area roughly 133,000 times as large as that of a Least Flycatcher with its 700 square meters. One can only guess at some of the factors responsible for this great contrast in size. Certainly the food resources of the territories cannot be the sole explanation. Even members of the same genus that have essentially similar diets show a striking difference in territory size: the Blackbird, *Turdus merula*, occupies 1200 square meters of space, and the Mistle Thrush, *Turdus viscivorus*, 500,000 square meters. The difference in size here may be mainly due to temperament, for the Mistle Thrush has an unusually peppery and aggressive disposition. Aggressiveness also differs among individuals of the same species, and varies seasonally in a given individual. Such changes are probably due to the concentration of sex hormones in the body, just as peck order aggressiveness depends on hormone balance. Castration of female lizards was found by Evans (1936) to heighten their territorial combativeness. The injection of male hormones into Blond Ring Doves, *Streptopelia risoria*, was found by Bennett (1940) to increase their territorial activity. The fact that in birds some of the most vicious fighting occurs during the height of the breeding season suggests a hormonal conditioning of territorial pugnacity and, accordingly, of territory size.

Individuals of the same species often show variations in territory size even in

the same habitat and at the same time of year. Territories of British Marsh Tits, *Parus palustris*, vary from 0.4 to 6.5 hectares; of Song Thrushes, *Turdus ericetorum*, in Finland, from 1.5 to 6 hectares; of American Redstarts, *Setophaga ruticilla*, from 0.06 to 0.4 hectares; of Song Sparrows, *Melospiza melodia*, in Ohio, from 0.2 to 0.6 hectares. In Algonquin Park, Ontario, territory held by the Ovenbird, *Seiurus aurocapillus*, varies in size from 0.32 to 1.74 hectares, depending on the type of forest cover in which the bird lives. The area is smallest in stands of aspen, intermediate in conifer-birch and mixed stands, and largest in maple stands. The size of the territory apparently increases with increasing height and density of the forest canopy, and with decreasing ground vegetation (Stenger and Falls, 1959).

Seasonal changes in territory size occur in many species and may be in part due to the waxing and waning of hormone levels in the blood. A study of territory size in the Ring-necked Pheasant, *Phasianus colchicus*, by Taber (1949) in Wisconsin showed a decline in territory size from about five hectares in April and May to two and one-half in mid-June. This change, however, was thought to be due primarily to increased numbers of birds in the region. Early arriving males of McCown's Longspur, *Rhynchophanes mccownii*, in Wyoming claim large territories which shrink progressively as other males arrive, until, later in the spring, a minimum is reached beyond which population pressure cannot compress territory size (Mickey, 1943). A number of species show a similar compressibility of territory size in response to population pressure: Little Ringed Plover, *Charadrius dubius*, House Wren, *Troglodytes aëdon*, European Robin, *Erithacus rubecula*, Field Sparrow, *Spizella pusilla*, Wood Warbler, *Phylloscopus sibilatrix*, and others. However, the Song Sparrow, *Melospiza melodia*, will not allow itself to be crowded. Territories in Ohio were found to be as large in a year of surplus population as in

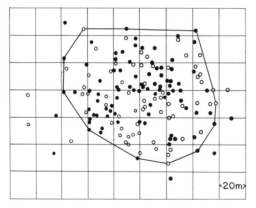

Figure 12.3.   The territory of a male Ovenbird in a conifer-birch forest in Ontario. Early morning observations, made once a week for eight weeks, determined the location of points in the territory actually frequented by the bird. Clear dots represent points occupied on the ground; black dots, above ground. Line encloses an area of 0.9 hectare. After Stenger and Falls.

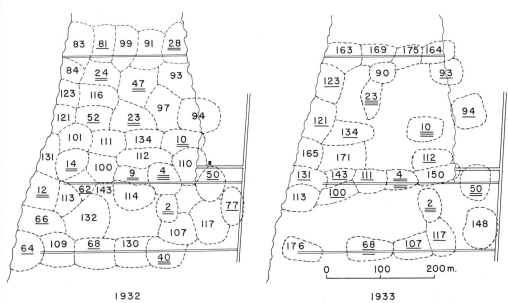

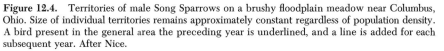

Figure 12.4.   Territories of male Song Sparrows on a brushy floodplain meadow near Columbus, Ohio. Size of individual territories remains approximately constant regardless of population density. A bird present in the general area the preceding year is underlined, and a line is added for each subsequent year. After Nice.

years of normal population density (Nice, 1937). Even birds of the same genus may show remarkable differences in regard to territorial compressibility. Territory size among the polygamous bishop birds of Africa was found to be almost indefinitely compressible in the Zanzibar Red Bishop, *Euplectes nigroventris* (from about 1000 to 8 square meters), but remained relatively fixed in the Crimson-crowned Bishop, *Euplectes hordacea* (Moreau and Moreau, 1938). Bishop birds occupying the smallest territories were as successful in reproduction as those having large territories. At times certain species, for example the European Robin and the Ring-billed Gull, *Larus delawarensis*, absorb part of an adjoining territory into their own when it is vacated by the death or disappearance of a neighbor.

Territory size is subject to still other modifying influences. The role of food supply has already been mentioned in connection with the Pomarine Jaeger, *Stercorarius pomarinus*. Geographical location is another factor: the territory of the Black Woodpecker, *Dryocopus mar-*

tius, varies in size from 120 to 180 hectares in Bohemia to 400 hectares in Germany, 850 hectares in the Netherlands, and 800 to 1800 hectares in Finland. A male Field Sparrow, *Spizella pusilla*, in Michigan increased the size of his territory with age and experience. In six consecutive summers, he controlled territories of the following sizes: 0.4, 0.5, 0.8, 0.8, 0.8, 0.8 hectare (Walkinshaw, 1945). Studies of birds nesting on small islands in Minnesota lakes showed that several species could successfully raise families on much smaller pieces of land than they required on the mainland; Song Sparrows, for example, repeatedly raised families on islands less than 0.4 hectare in area, and in one instance on one as small as 0.16 hectare (Beer *et al.*, 1956). Water surface itself may constitute territory. In three species of Australian ducks observed by Robinson (1945), the males defend certain areas of water, about three hectares or less in extent, which may change from day to day. They drive away other males of the same species, but will tolerate both sexes of other species. Facts such as these emphasize the importance in some instances of spatial isolation rather than the physical resources of the environment in determining territory size.

DEFENSE OF TERRITORY

Birds may defend their territories by voice, by threatening postures, by pursuit, or by actual physical combat. What the bird is defending in a particular territory is rarely apparent, and it may not become so even after prolonged study. And the object of a bird's defense may change with the seasons. It seems likely that the chief objects of territorial defense are the mate, the young, other members of a colony, a song or lookout post, a display ground, and food (Hinde, 1956). Ordinarily it is the male which arrives first in the spring and establishes and defends the territory while he waits for the female to arrive. Song Sparrows, Peregrine Falcons, *Falco peregrinus*, and many other species begin the breeding season in this way. Among species in which the birds are already paired when they arrive, for example, the Eastern Kingbird, *Tyrannus tyrannus*, the territory may be established by both sexes. In the polyandrous Chinese Pheasant-tailed Jaçana, *Hydrophasianus chirurgus*, and the Red-necked Phalarope, *Phalaropus lobatus*, of Greenland, it is the more energetic female which establishes and defends the territory while the drab male defends the nest, incubates the eggs, and takes care of the young. An unusual division of labor occurs in the Lucifer Hummingbird, *Calothorax lucifer*, of Mexico, in which the male and female stake out and defend separate territories, the male defending his territory from other males, and the female hers from other females. Only after the female completes the building of her elaborate nest does she seek union with a male (Wagner, 1946).

In typical territory establishment, however, the male chooses a territory and begins advertising his ownership of it by singing or by otherwise making himself conspicuous. If, in the course of territory defense, a male should chase an intruder across the territorial boundary into its own area, the roles of owner and intruder become reversed. The vociferous male which just five seconds before was burning with righteous wrath now suddenly becomes a silent, cowering intruder himself, and is quickly put to rout by his suddenly dominant neighbor. Territorial boundaries are frequently established by a delicate balancing of these see-saw reactions.

There is a great difference in the vigor with which different species defend their territories. A few kinds of tyrant flycatchers (Tyrannidae) are particularly bellicose, driving away not only other individuals of their own kind, but also dangerous birds of other species, small mammals, and even humans. At the other extreme are the mild-mannered Costa Rican Tityras, *Tityra semifasciata*, which seem to disdain physical combat and defend their nesting territories with long-drawn-out palavers and half-hearted feints (Skutch, 1946). Vigor of territory defense also varies seasonally, often being most intense early in the breeding season when boundaries are being established, and at low ebb after the young have fledged, as well as during the winter.

Birds probably use singing more than any other single means to defend their holdings against intrusion. A typical example of territory defense through song is described by Lack (1943) for the European Robin, *Erithacus rubecula*. In late May, a strange Robin invaded the territory of an established male. When the newcomer sang, the owner promptly replied from some distance away through the thick foliage. The newcomer, probably unaware that it was trespassing, sang again and was answered by the owner which had flown closer. When the strange bird sang again, the owner, still hidden by foliage, approached still more closely and sang more vigorously, finally venting a burst of violent song from some five meters distance. Upon this proclamation of ownership, the stranger fled and remained away, without having seen the owner and without either of them having struck a blow. While springtime singing in the Robin may serve the two functions of advertising for a mate and defending the territory against trespass, the vigorous singing of the autumn is exclusively territorial. Robins are not then courting, but do still hold territory.

Many other species use song in the defense of their territories. In a study of 12 species of wood warblers in New York, Kendeigh (1945) found that the males used song and chasing to protect their territories, but they rarely fought. Seaside Sparrows, *Ammospiza maritima*, defend both a nesting area and a shore feeding area by singing vigorously from an exposed perch, one male singing 395 songs in one hour (Woolfenden, 1956). The highly territorial Eastern Willet, *Catoptrophorus semipalmatus*, defends its territory with a spectacular ceremonial flight in which the male flickers its wings while circling higher and higher and calling "pill-will-willet" (Vogt, 1938).

Instead of singing, many species defend their territories with threat displays usually involving stereotyped postures or flights. In his well-known experiments with stuffed Robins, Lack (1934) discovered that the red breast of a trespassing bird had the same effect on a territory's owner as the proverbial red flag has on a bull.

In response to the invader's "red flag," the owner postures so as best to display his own red breast to the interloper. If this should not bluff the stranger into retreating, the owner may resort to physical attack. An interesting fact brought out by Lack's experiments is that the red breast feathers are themselves a releaser of an antagonistic response in another Robin. A mere tuft of red feathers placed in a bird's territory during the fighting season will suffice to bring on violent posturing and even battle, whereas an entire stuffed Robin colored brown (like an immature bird) may be ignored! Yellow Wagtails, *Motacilla flava*, similarly display aggressively in their border clashes by puffing out their bright yellow breasts at each other like miniature pouter pigeons (Smith, 1942). In other species, such as the Yellowhammer, *Emberiza citrinella*, or the American Sparrow Hawk, *Falco sparverius*, a stuffed dummy placed in a bird's territory is not enough to elicit defensive reactions from the owner. Experiments show that, for these species, form and color must be accompanied by movement, and perhaps by sound, before lively territorial defense will be released.

Instead of singing or posturing to display their red breasts, American Robins, *Turdus migratorius*, of both sexes threaten intruders by lifting their tails, crouching, and then making a series of short runs broken by brief pauses. Robin territories frequently overlap (Young, 1951). Accord-

Figure 12.5. Territorial threat display in male Yellow Wagtails. The birds follow this puffing of the bright, yellow breast feathers by swaying from side to side, then by a pecking and clawing combat or chasing flights. The female does not take part in these disputes. After Smith.

ing to Hailman (1960), the Mockingbird, *Mimus polyglottos*, establishes territorial boundaries by means of a hostile dance-display in which two birds, with bodies and tails erect, face each other across the boundary being established, and make short hops, advancing and retreating.

If an intruder enters the territory of a Herring Gull, *Larus argentatus*, the owner assumes a threatening attitude and starts walking slowly toward him. If the trespasser holds his ground, the owner bends down and tears out a large mouthful of grass and the intruder does likewise. Sitting opposite each other the birds attempt to pull the material from each others' beaks, and then try to take hold of a wing or beak and begin struggling. Other species, such as some grouse, some hummingbirds, the Great Tit, *Parus major*, the Field Sparrow, *Spizella pusilla*, the Lapwing, *Vanellus vanellus*, and the Phainopepla, *Phainopepla nitens*, use specifically patterned flights to intimidate territorial competitors. In addition to chasing each other through the air, two male Hazel Grouse, *Tetrastes bonasia*, may contest their territorial boundaries by running side by side on the ground for as long as 45 minutes at a time (Pynnönen, 1950).

Actual physical combat is resorted to in the defense of territory less often than song, posturing, flight, and other non-violent means of self-assertion. But when fighting does occur it may be lusty and even vicious. White Storks, *Ciconia ciconia*, may fight so vehemently over nest territory that eggs are crushed and sometimes one of the combatants is killed (Schüz, 1944). Penguins are particularly quarrelsome in protecting their tiny nesting territories, probably because the scarcity of suitable nesting sites heightens intraspecific competition. In a typical squabble, they beat one another with their flippers, and jab and bite with their formidable beaks. In describing fights between Peruvian Penguins, *Spheniscus humboldti*, Kearton (1930) remarks, "Combat over possession of burrows is also common between two or more pairs,

the fighting going on until all the participants are blood smeared." Mayaud (1950) estimates that territorial combat may be the chief cause of the high mortality among Emperor Penguins, *Aptenodytes forsteri*. Penguins frequently are seen with one eye missing as a result of either territorial or courtship battles.

Among the Falkland Flightless Steamer Ducks, *Tachyeres brachypterus*, both sexes defend their nesting territory. When one pair attempts to invade the territory of another, each bird attempts to seize its opponent by the neck and hold its head under water, meanwhile beating the bird with its hard wings. Murphy (1936) describes such an encounter: "The struggling birds spin round and round, making such a commotion in the water that the eye cannot follow their movements. If one succeeds in submerging the head of the other, the beating is redoubled and the water frequently reddened by blood. A defeated bird makes its escape as best it can, and the victor paddles off uttering growls of joy, while his mate expresses the same triumphant emotion by mewing like a cat." Kermadec Petrels, *Pterodroma neglecta*, of South Pacific islands, sometimes nest so close together in their colonies that the adults engage in territorial bickering to such an extent that their young are neglected and become "dwarfed starvelings" (Murphy).

In some species, such as the Herring Gull, *Larus argentatus*, or the European Robin, *Erithacus rubecula*, both the male and female help defend their territory against invaders of either sex, probably because in these species both sexes look alike. In many species with pronounced sex dichromatism, such as the American Goldfinch, *Spinus tristis*, and the Cardinal, *Richmondena cardinalis*, males defend the territory against males, females against females. In most wood warblers the male defends the territory proper, and the female defends a smaller area around the nest. Hens of the Hazel Grouse, *Tetrastes bonasia*, neither aid the cocks in defense of the territory nor observe territorial limits when wandering with their broods. In the semi-colonial and polygamous Redwinged Blackbird, *Agelaius phoeniceus,* the male defends a sharply defined and stable territory against intruding males but not against females. Each of the females nesting in his territory defends its individual nest against harem mates. In an experiment by Nero and Emlen (1951), males tolerated the introduction of alien nests, moved gradually with their supporting cattail clumps, and eventually accepted the females which persisted in following their moved nests. But the males would defend neither nests nor females of their harems if these were moved into neighboring territories. Male Redwings may cooperate, however, in driving a common enemy from the colony. Herring Gulls have been observed protecting not only their own nests, but those of their neighbors, by chasing away gulls from other colonies.

As a rule, a bird will tolerate birds of other species in its territory and drive out only birds of the same species, especially males. Sometimes as many as six different species of birds may be found nesting within a radius of 10 meters. A Bald Eagle, *Haliaeetus leucocephalus,* and a Great Horned Owl, *Bubo virginianus,* were found in a Florida tree incubating eggs less than one meter apart (Peterson, 1948). But occasionally territorial species are intolerant of other species. The European Fieldfare, *Turdus pilaris,* will drive from its territory jays, woodpeckers, and even Ravens, *Corvus corax.* The Wood Thrush, *Hylocichla mustelina,* repels Robins, *Turdus migratorius,* and Veerys, *Hylocichla fuscescens;* and the Alaskan Black Oystercatcher, *Haematopus bachmani,* will expel from its territory gulls, curlews, eagles, crows, and Ravens. It is probable that some of these birds are repulsed as egg robbers rather than as territorial intruders. Song Sparrows, *Melospiza melodia,* are known to drive away at least 16 species of birds (Nice, 1937). Occasionally titmice will attack birds of other species. Hinde (1952) is of the opinion that such attacks

represent the release of fighting behavior by a subnormal stimulus at a time when the threshold to the releasing mechanism is particularly low.

FAITHFULNESS TO TERRITORY

A question commonly raised is whether the Robins nesting in a particular yard are the same pair which nested there the year before. Until an individual bird could be positively identified after a long absence, such speculation was usually idle. The great increase in bird-banding since 1920 has permitted the positive identification of millions of individual birds by fastening numbered aluminum bands on their legs. A banding study of Robins by Farner (1945) in Washington state indicated that at least 70 per cent of the surviving young birds returned the next year to within 40 kilometers of their birthplace. A similar study of nation-wide banding returns by Hickey (1943) indicated that about 74 per cent of the Robins in various parts of the United States returned to within 16 kilometers of their original homes. The European Nutcracker, *Nucifraga caryocatactes,* is reported to mate for life and to keep the same territory year after year, one pair for as long as ten years (Swanberg, 1951). A survey of the records of 713 North American Bank Swallows, *Riparia riparia,* (out of 29,040 banded), which were recaptured a year or more later, showed that only seven of the birds were found more than 24 kilometers from the original nesting site where they were banded (Bergstrom, 1951). About 83 per cent of the recovered birds had been banded as adults, the remainder as immature birds.

This tendency of many migratory birds to return to their natal territory or its environs is called place faithfulness, site attachment, or, by its German name, *Ortstreue.* Commenting on the recovery of banded European Swallows, *Hirundo rustica,* Boyd and Thomson (1936) were of the opinion that "Adult Swallows that have nested almost invariably return to the same place in subsequent summers, and often to the same nest." In her study of Song Sparrows, *Melospiza melodia*, Mrs. Nice found that under favorable conditions over 60 per cent of the breeding males, and over 12 per cent of the fledged nestlings, returned to the home locality the following year. Birds show a striking ortstreue even for inhospitable antarctic homes. In the ten years between 1948 and 1957, some 7200 penguins, petrels, and other sea birds, 17 species in all, were banded in antarctic breeding colonies. In spite of wandering thousands of trackless kilometers over the world's oceans between breeding seasons, a great many of these birds returned to their former nest sites, often with their former mates (Sladen and Tickell, 1958). But very few of the birds banded as nestlings were recovered in subsequent seasons at their birthplaces. Carbon-dating of frozen mummies of Adelie Penguins, *Pygoscelis adeliae*, found in the ice at Cape Hallet, Victoria Land, indicates the continuous residence of a colony there for some 650 years (Austin, 1961).

Species, of course, differ in the degree to which they exhibit ortstreue. In her study of two species of European thrushes, Werth (1947) found that of 258 recovered Blackbirds, *Turdus merula*, which had been banded as nestlings, 72 per cent were retaken as adults at the breeding site; 21 per cent were recovered within eight kilometers, and 7 per cent were recovered beyond 8 kilometers from the breeding site. Of 249 Song Thrushes, *Turdus ericetorum*, originally banded as nestlings and recovered the next year, only 52 per cent were retaken at their birthplace, 31 per cent within eight kilometers, and 17 per cent more than eight kilometers away.

There are also sexual differences in site attachment. In a seven-year study of the Pied Flycatcher, *Muscicapa hypoleuca*, breeding in a nesting area of 3.9 square kilometers, von Haartman (1949) found that of 189 males banded as adults, 70 (37.0 per cent) returned to the nesting site, but that of 177 adult females, only 19 (10.7 per cent) returned. Some of the fe-

males seemed to possess ortstreue, while others were thought to be nomadic. In another study of the same species, von Haartman found that females which had lost a brood seldom returned to the same nesting territory.

The attachment which some species have for their nesting territories apparently increases with age and with each additional occupancy of the nest site. Extensive studies of ortstreue in the Common Tern, *Sterna hirundo*, by Austin (1940, 1949) have shown a remarkable tendency toward site attachment in this species. Of 2964 Cape Cod Terns that returned, subsequent to their banding, two or more times to the general location of their natal colony, 76.5 per cent returned to the same nest site on their second return; then, as adult birds returned to the colony in three, four, five, and more successive years, increasingly greater percentages of them returned to the same nest sites. One island that originally held a flourishing colony of Arctic Terns, *Sterna paradisaea*, became so completely overgrown with shrubs as to be unsuitable as nesting terrain. Nevertheless, a few of its oldest Tern inhabitants persisted in nesting there under conditions they would never have tolerated elsewhere.

A common pattern of ortstreue is for many adult birds to return to their nest territories in subsequent years, but for very few or none of the newly hatched young to return. This is due, no doubt, partly to the higher mortality among the young birds, partly to their greater tendency to wander, and partly to the greater attachment of the older birds to the nest territory, and to their territorial dominance over, and aversion to, any young which might attempt intrusion. A fourteen-year study of Tree Swallows, *Iridoprocne bicolor*, in Massachusetts by Chapman (1955) revealed that the percentages of adult swallows banded any given year and returning the next varied from 7 to 55 per cent and averaged 39.6 per cent. The percentage of nestlings banded any year which returned the next year varied from 0 to 5.0 per cent and averaged 2.4 per cent. A similar study of ortstreue in the House Wren, *Troglodytes aëdon,* in Ohio by Kendeigh and Baldwin (1937) showed that of 1831 banded, nesting adults, 631 (34 per cent) returned in subsequent years, and of 7375 banded young, only 152 (2.06 per cent) returned.

There are a few species that show a very feeble nest-territory attachment. Of 72 adult Cedar Waxwings, *Bombycilla cedrorum,* banded on South Bass Island in Lake Erie by Putnam (1949), only two

subsequently returned; and of 174 banded nestlings, none returned to its birthplace.

Birds also become attached to their winter territories, but probably not with the fervor that nesting territories command. A twelve-year study of winter territory ortstreue was made by Wharton (1941), who banded 9449 birds of 29 species in their South Carolina winter quarters and recorded the kinds and numbers that returned there in later years. Table 12.2 gives examples from his findings.

Table 12.2. Returns of Winter Residents

SPECIES	NUMBER BANDED	NUMBER RETURNED	PER CENT RETURNED
Eastern Robin, *Turdus migratorius*	172	0	0
Hermit Thrush, *Hylocichla guttata*	81	10	12.3
Cedar Waxwing, *Bombycilla cedrorum*	132	0	0
Myrtle Warbler, *Dendroica coronata*	39	3	7.7
Cowbird, *Molothrus ater*	89	0	0
Purple Finch, *Carpodacus purpureus*	101	1	1.0
Red-eyed Towhee, *Pipilo erythrophthalmus*	489	90	18.4
Savannah Sparrow, *Passerculus sandwichensis*	453	33	7.3
Slate-colored Junco, *Junco hyemalis*	347	8	2.3
Chipping Sparrow, *Spizella passerina*	3,753	738	19.7
White-throated Sparrow, *Zonotrichia albicollis*	3,112	570	18.3
Fox Sparrow, *Passerella iliaca*	56	0	0
Song Sparrow, *Melospiza melodia*	296	25	8.4

An experimental study of winter-territory ortstreue in gulls was made in Copenhagen by Petersen (1953). Black-headed Gulls, *Larus ridibundus,* and Common Gulls, *Larus canus,* were trapped, banded, and color-marked for sight identification, at their winter quarters in the lakes and parks of Copenhagen. Some were transported back to their breeding grounds, about 530 kilometers north in Sweden, and there released. Others were taken about 600 kilometers southward to Amsterdam, and still others were released at various directions and distances within Denmark. Of the Black-headed Gulls released in Sweden, 22 per cent returned to Copenhagen that same winter, as against 9 per cent from Amsterdam. Only 4 per cent of the Common Gulls returned.

The numerous advantages that a territory confers on its owner are reasons enough for a bird to become attached to

it. How the attachment becomes established is unknown, but it undoubtedly involves learning of some sort, and perhaps, for nesting-territory ortstreue, imprinting in the newly-hatched young. Whatever its origin, ortstreue plays an important, generally beneficent role in the lives of birds.

SUGGESTED READINGS

Howard's *Territory in Bird Life* is outstanding in this field. Armstrong's *Bird Display and Bird Behaviour* emphasizes the reproductive aspects of territory. For excellent studies of territorial behavior of specific birds see Nice, *Studies in the Life History of the Song Sparrow,* and Lack, *The Life of the Robin.* For definitions of territory and the history of the territory concept see Mayr, *Bernard Altum and the Territory Theory,* and Nice, *The Role of Territory in Bird Life.*

THIRTEEN

Courtship and Mating Habits

Each year, as the climbing spring sun brightens the landscape with a living coat of green, all nature prepares for a new generation. It is the mating season for birds. The warmth and light of lengthening days not only affect profoundly their plumage and sex organs, but also their behavior—especially behavior that has to do with reproduction. Male songbirds begin to sing, woodpeckers to drum, cock pheasants to strut in their colorful spring garments, and cranes to prance through their grotesque minuets.

Reproductive behavior in most birds can be divided into activities which are commonly rather stereotyped, discrete, and innate: territory establishment, court-ship, mate selection or betrothal, pair bond establishment, copulation, nest building, brooding of eggs and young, and the feeding or leading of young. There is, however, great diversity among species in the occurrence, timing, and duration of these breeding activities. Some birds stake no claims to territory; some choose their mates before they establish territory; some birds mate for life, others for ten minutes; some do not incubate their eggs or care for their young.

More is known, probably, about the life history of the Song Sparrow, *Melospiza melodia*, than about any other American species, thanks to the classic studies of Margaret Morse Nice (1937, 1943). This

228

strongly territorial sparrow may serve as an illustration of the breeding activities of a small passerine. In Ohio, the male acquires territory in late winter or early spring by singing, by posturing, and by fighting other males. He sings almost constantly until he attracts a mate; then he suddenly and almost entirely ceases singing. The male courts his mate by "pouncing" on her—that is, by flying down at her and colliding with her—and then flying away, singing loudly. Pairing or mate selection seems to be largely a matter of chance, the unpaired male pouncing on any female which happens to wander into his territory. If the female holds her ground and is not frightened away, the male changes his tactics and accepts her as his mate. The male may carry nest materials as a symbolic gesture, but the female constructs the nest by herself. Copulation occurs shortly before nest building begins, and continues at intervals until incubation starts. During nest building and incubation the male again sings, and defends both the territory and his mate, and later he attends the young. Incubation is performed by the female, who alone has incubation patches—bare skin on the belly—for warming the eggs. The eggs usually hatch in 12 or 13 days, and the young in the nest are cared for by both parents for about ten days. When they leave the nest they are also cared for by both parents, although the female gradually turns her attention to a new nest and begins preparations for a second brood. Between mated Song Sparrows there is a strong pair bond which usually persists throughout the breeding season of two or three broods. At the end of the season this bond dissolves, and each individual goes its own way. It is unlikely that the same pair will reunite the next year, even though both members may come back to the same general locality, chiefly because returning males have an opportunity to mate with resident females before their former mates return.

Sexual maturity is achieved at different ages in different species, usually at an earlier age in small birds than in large. In most small passerines, small owls, most gallinaceous birds, doves, many ducks, and others, sexual maturity is reached within nine to twelve months after hatching, and as early as six months in some weaverbirds. Some of the larger passerines, such as crows, many gulls, shorebirds, hawks, geese, and the males of some pheasants, first breed when they are two years old. Larger gulls, cormorants, boobies, and loons first breed at three or more years of age, and large eagles at the age of four, five, or six years. The male ostrich breeds at four years of age; the female, at three and a half. The Royal Albatross, *Diomedea epomophora*, first breeds when it is six or eight years old.

In some species, sexual maturity does not appear fullblown at a given age, but develops by stages. Yearling White Storks, *Ciconia ciconia*, commonly fail to migrate back to Europe, spending the summer in their African winter quarters. Second-year Storks migrate back and may visit nests, but do not breed. Third-year Storks may pair, copulate, and lay small clutches of eggs, but few of them successfully bring off young. Most White Storks first breed successsfully when they are four or five years old (Schüz, 1949). Similarly, first-year European Cormorants, *Phalacrocorax carbo*, show incipient sexual behavior; second-year birds generally pair and build nests but do not lay eggs, while third-year birds generally breed successfully (Kortlandt, 1942). Maturity in breeding behavior, like maturity in the physiology of the gonads, probably depends on the development of both endocrine and nervous systems and their influence on each other.

TYPES OF PAIR BONDS

The coming together of two birds for the procreation of young often originates a more or less durable bond between them: a "marriage" or pair bond that commonly results in monogamy. The duration of the pair bond varies greatly between species and between individuals. A mated pair may remain together for life, for several years, for one year, for one brood of young, or for even shorter periods. In birds the pair bond is probably more lasting than in mammals, because male birds often assist in rearing their young, which male mammals seldom do. Relatively few species of birds maintain a lasting pair bond. A long "engagement" period before the physical union seems in some species to promote an enduring conjugal state. According to Lorenz (1952), Bearded Tits, *Panurus biarmicus*, become engaged before their first molt, at about two and a half months of age, but do not breed until they are one year old. Jackdaws, *Corvus monedula*, and wild geese are betrothed in the spring following their birth, but do not become sexually mature until twelve months later. These species probably remain mated for life. On the other hand, ducks commonly form pairs in the autumn and winter in their winter quarters and do not breed until the following spring; yet in spite of this long betrothal the male and female usually separate when the eggs are laid or when they hatch. Among the flycatchers of Mexico, for example, the Black Phoebe, *Sayornis nigricans*, a male and female may associate for three months before starting a nest. In these flycatchers the long betrothal period is thought to be an adaptation to the variable time of the beginning of the rainy season (Wagner, 1941).

It is difficult to determine the nature of the psychological bond that holds a pair together. It may be common attachment to a territory; it may be "personal" recognition of each other or a comfortable familiarity with each other; or it may be something akin to human affection. That there may exist an affectionate bond between two birds is strongly suggested by the observations of Trautman (1947) on Black Ducks, *Anas rubripes*, during autumn courtship and pair formation. On two different occasions the partner of a shot bird refused to flush and leave its dying mate when the flock flew away from gunners. Color-banded pairs of Nuttall's White-crowned Sparrows, *Zonotrichia leucophrys nuttalli*, were observed by Blanchard (1936) to associate closely throughout the year, winter and summer, which indicated some sort of personal bond between them. Pairs of Adelie Penguins, *Pygoscelis adeliae*, likewise seem held together by personal bonds. Of ten pairs of birds banded at their nesting sites in the South Orkneys, twelve birds returned two years later, and five of the original pairs were still intact (Sladen, 1953).

Territory probably plays an important role in the pair bond of numerous species. A White Stork, *Ciconia ciconia*, fights viciously for possession of its nest, and once in possession it forges a stronger bond with the nest than with its mate (Schüz, 1938). Similarly, pairs of antarctic Wilson's Petrels, *Oceanites oceanicus*, return year after year to the same burrow, common ownership of the burrow presumably providing the attraction that holds the birds together (Roberts, 1940). If a Plain Titmouse, *Parus inornatus*, loses its mate, the survivor, whether male or female, remains in the nesting territory and secures a new mate (Price, 1936). Ortstreue is undeniably influential in the formation and maintenance of pairs. However, many species of birds pair before territories are set up; for example, Black-capped Chickadees, *Parus atricapillus*, and American Goldfinches, *Spinus tristis*.

Pair faithfulness also depends on the outward appearance of a bird's mate. Perhaps it is a simple matter of recognition. Ringed Plovers, *Charadrius hiaticula*, establish enduring pair bonds, but two birds which had each lost a foot were rejected by their former mates. Fortunately the two were of opposite sexes; they met, paired, and successfully raised normal offspring (Laven, 1940). Experiments by Noble and others (1938) on young Black-crowned Night Herons, *Nycticorax nycticorax*, showed that a pair of birds separated for 20 days, and then placed in a large cage with strange Night Herons, reformed their pair bond within three hours. Even when their beaks or legs were painted with brilliant colors, the paired Night Herons recognized each other; but when their crown plumes were covered, the birds became confused and no longer knew each other.

To determine the duration of pair bonds in wild birds is such arduous, time-consuming work that few authentic records are available for species reputed to mate for life. Records of lifetime matings of pairs living in cages or under other artificial conditions are, of course, of little value. Field studies of banded birds living under natural conditions indicate that relatively few species of birds mate for life, or even for several successive years. The Adelie Penguins with their apparently personal bonds are thought to pair for life in many instances. As a result of a ten-year field study of 292 matings of Yellow-eyed Penguins, *Megadyptes antipodes*, in New Zealand, Richdale (1951) discovered that 55 per cent of the mated pairs remained intact in the succeeding season; 33 per cent were dissolved because of the death or disappearance of one or both mates; and 12 per cent were "divorced" and remated with other individuals.

Most albatrosses and petrels are considered to have durable mating ties. From his 16 year study of the Royal Albatross, *Diomedea epomophora*, in New Zealand, Richdale (1952) concluded that this species normally mates for life. Two mated pairs were known to be intact after 15 years. Of 27 breeding Wilson's Petrels, *Oceanites oceanicus*, banded by Roberts (1940) in the antarctic in December 1935, 22 returned to their former nesting burrows in February 1937. Twenty of these birds had the same mates as before, and two birds had new, unbanded mates. Mated pairs of Manx Shearwaters, *Procellaria puffinus*, and Storm Petrels, *Hydrobates pelagicus*, were found by Lockley (Fisher and Lockley, 1954) to return to the same burrow year after year as long

as a given pair remained alive. A lifetime pair bond is thought to be the general rule for small petrels.

Many pairs of geese and swans raised as captives have remained mated for life, and many observers believe that the same condition holds among wild birds. Eagles are popularly considered to mate for life, and perhaps do; but reliable evidence for wild birds is lacking. Barn Owls, *Tyto alba*, and many parrots are known to establish long-enduring partnerships.

As a result of a six-year study of a colony of European Oystercatchers, *Haematopus ostralegus*, by Jungfer (1954), it was found that 24 pairs remained mated for two years, 10 pairs for three years, 3 pairs for four years, 2 pairs for five years, and 1 pair for six years. During five years, changes in mates occurred only 14 times. Whether the attachment was for the nest site or for the partner could not be determined.

A four-year study of pair bond persistence in Common Terns, *Sterna hirundo*, by Austin (1947) showed that of 122 mated pairs, 79.1 per cent of the time the original pair bond persisted from one season to the next. Gulls are believed to possess similarly firm pair bonds.

Enduring nuptial ties are found in many representatives of the Corvidae, including Ravens, *Corvus corax*, Carrion Crows, *Corvus corone*, Jackdaws, *Corvus monedula*, Magpies, *Pica pica*, Nutcrackers, *Nucifraga caryocatactes*, and others. In several non-migratory species of the Paridae, pairs hold together for two or more seasons.

By far the commonest mating arrangement among the small monogamous birds of the North Temperate Zone is pairing for one breeding season. Mrs. Nice, as already mentioned, found among her banded Song Sparrows, *Melospiza melodia*, only 8 cases of remating for a second season out of some 200 possible cases. A male Field Sparrow, *Spizella pusilla*, observed by Walkinshaw (1945), was faithful to his mate while they reared two or three broods each summer, but he had a different mate for each of six consecutive summers. A number of species such as the European Redstart, *Phoenicurus phoenicurus*, Chimney Swift, *Chaetura pelagica*, and Tree Swallow, *Iridoprocne bicolor*, show a somewhat higher degree of faithfulness. Of 67 pairs of Tree Swallows which were mated the previous year and returned to breed, 32.8 per cent of the original pairs remated and bred in the same nest boxes; 17.9 per cent remated and bred in nearby nest boxes; and 49.3 per cent were "divorced" (Chapman, 1955).

Unlike most small passerines, such species as the House Wren, *Troglodytes aëdon*, Bank Swallow, *Riparia riparia*, and several other hole-nesters normally remain united for only one brood. Usually in these species the male cares for the fledglings of the first brood while the female seeks another mate and begins a second brood elsewhere. Of 70 pairs of House Wrens that successfully reared one brood and then undertook a second brood the same season, the original pairs remained intact in 40 per cent of the cases (Kendeigh, 1941).

As the duration of a pair bond shrinks still further a point is reached where it is difficult to distinguish a brief pair bond from a casual or promiscuous union. The uniting of hummingbird pairs appears to be casual and short. A typical hummingbird union, as based on the close study of 14 Mexican species by Wagner (1954), occurs after the female has completed building her nest. The female mates with the first male of her species that she meets. He courts her briefly with display flights, songs, or sounds made by his feathers. They copulate and part after a very few hours, and she generally rears the brood single-handed while the male searches out other females.

Although it is not as common as monogamy, polygamy occurs in a wide variety of birds. It may occur in either of two forms: polygyny, in which one male is mated to several females, or polyandry, in which one female is mated to several males. Polygyny is the commoner form and is found regularly in many gallinaceous species, such as pheasants, including the Peacock, *Pavo cristatus*, and in ostriches, rheas, and several species of Icteridae—for example, the Redwinged Blackbird, *Agelaius phoeniceus*. In normal polygyny the male inseminates several females which incubate their eggs in separate nests and rear their young unassisted by him. A remarkable exception to this arrangement occurs in the South American Rhea in which several females lay their eggs, on occasion as many as 50, in one nest, where the male incubates them by himself. He also is responsible for the care of the young. Polygamy may be simultaneous as in these species mentioned, or successive, as in the African widow birds (Viduinae), in which the male, which is sexually active over a long interval, has a succession of wives during the breeding season. The females of this group are social parasites which lay their eggs in the nests of other species that raise their offspring for them. It is interesting that pair bonds may arise between a polygamous male and members of his harem. In a colony of Brewer's Blackbirds, *Euphagus cyanocephalus*, Williams (1952) found that of 70 matings, there were 45 cases in which both members of such pairs returned the following year; of these 45 possibilities for rematings, there were 42 (93 per cent) rematings and only three "divorces." In this species polygyny in a colony tends to increase as the ratio of females to males increases.

Occasional polygyny occurs in many species of birds that are normally monogamous, including swans, hawks, doves, sparrows, titmice, flycatchers, warblers, thrushes, and others. About six per cent of all House Wren matings are polygynous. In England and Holland about 50 per cent of all matings of European Wrens, *Troglodytes troglodytes*, are polygynous. But a strange state of affairs occurs on the isolated Scottish island of St. Kilda. Here a race of this Wren is strictly monogamous. This peculiar geographic variation in the nuptial habits of a single species is believed by Armstrong (1953) to be correlated with the availability of food during the breeding season. On bleak St. Kilda, food is scarce, the Wrens are monogamous, and both parents scurry to find enough food to feed their young. In English gardens, food is abundant, the Wrens are polygynous, and each female alone can find enough nourishment for her brood. Actually, the polygynous arrangement is biologically the more efficient one, since it enables a female to raise her brood regardless of the fate of her mate. The scarcity of food on St. Kilda requires a more costly investment in parental care for each successfully raised brood. Armstrong (1955) makes the additional point that polygyny "appears to accentuate competition and give selective advantage to the most vigorous males."

Polyandry, the reciprocal of polygyny, occurs mainly in those species in which the males incubate the eggs and rear the young: tinamous (Tinamidae), jaçanas (Jacanidae), painted snipe (Rostratulidae), phalaropes (Phalaropodidae), and button quail (Turnicidae). Through some evolutionary quirk in these birds, the role of the sexes has become largely reversed. The females are larger, have the brighter nuptial plumage, do the courting, and defend the territory, while the docile, drab males build the nest, incubate the eggs and rear the young. Polyandrous matings have been reported as occasionally occurring in species normally monogamous such as the White Stork, *Ciconia ciconia;* European Swift, *Apus apus;* Ovenbird, *Seiurus aurocapillus;* and Bluebird, *Sialia sialis*. There are also species that apparently practice social mating habits. The Formosan Babbling Thrush, *Yuhina brunneiceps*, has been observed in groups of five (two males and three females) feeding the young of one nest, while six different birds incubated eight eggs at another nest (Yamashina, 1939).

Sexual promiscuity occurs in those species which come together only for copu-lation and then see no more of each other. This form of mating is characteristic of the Ruff, *Philomachus pugnax;* many grouse such as the Prairie Chicken, *Tympanuchus cupido*, Sage Grouse, *Centrocercus urophasianus*, and Black Grouse, *Lyrurus tetrix;* manakins (Pipridae); many birds of paradise (Paradisaeidae); probably the bower-birds (Ptilonorhynchidae); and many hummingbirds (Trochilidae). A biological hazard in the fleeting unions of promiscuous species is the possibility of mating with a bird of another species and producing sterile hybrid offspring—if any. Natural selection has reduced this hazard of errors in species-recognition by developing almost incredibly spectacular plumes and colors, or strikingly distinctive calls and other sounds, or fantastic postures and dances, or, in the case of the relatively drab-colored bower-birds, the construction of distinctively shaped and decorated bowers.

Promiscuous polygyny also commonly occurs in the Boat-tailed Grackle, *Cassidix mexicanus*. The males display their charms at some distance from the nest colony, whence each female comes to copulate with the male of her choice. Several females commonly mate with a single male. Not only does the male take no part in building the nest or caring for the young; he kills and eats many of the nestlings in spite of the shrill protests of their mothers (McIlhenny, 1937).

The Magpie, *Gymnorhina dorsalis*, of southwestern Australia, probably represents a form of breeding intermediate between promiscuity and monogamy. A 12-year study of this species by Robinson (1956) showed that this bird lived in small groups of 6 to 20 individuals, among which sexual promiscuity was the rule. However, occasional pair bonds persisted and the males now and then helped to feed the nestlings. Sporadic promiscuity in otherwise monogamous species, such as swallows, swifts, wrens, and other birds, is probably biologically adaptive in that the casual mate may be available to take the place of a missing parent of half-grown young. Contrariwise, a bird that has lost its mate and young through predation may help a normal pair to rear its hungry brood. Inflexibly monogamous pair bonds would preclude such helpful arrangements. Occasionally, three or more adults of a monogamous species are seen feeding one brood of young. Unmated birds are also often available either as substitutes for a lost mate or as "baby sitters" to help a normal pair care for its brood. An experiment demonstrating the availability of such unmated birds is reported by Griscom (1947). The male of a wild pair of Indigo Buntings, *Passerina cyanea*, was shot and removed. The next day the female obtained a new mate. This second male was also shot, and the same process continued until nine different male buntings had been removed; the tenth was left undisturbed to help raise the family.

Sexual aberrations of various sorts occur in birds as in many other animals. Inbreeding is often biologically harmful and its rarity in the wild may be accounted for in part by such behavior mechanisms as the dispersal-encouraging intolerance of parent birds toward their grown young. Nevertheless, father and daughter matings have been reported for the Junco, *Junco hyemalis*, and Barn Swallow, *Hirundo rustica*; mother and son matings for the Barn Swallow and Tree Swallow, *Iridoprocne bicolor;* brother and sister matings for the Yellow-eyed Penguin, *Megadyptes antipodes*, Mallard, *Anas platyrhynchos*, Downy Woodpecker, *Dendrocopus pubescens*, Great Tit, *Parus major*, Yellow Wagtail, *Motacilla cinerea*, Junco, and Song Sparrow, *Melospiza melodia*. It is significant that brother and sister matings in the Bobwhite Quail, *Colinus virginianus*, reduce the hatchability of their eggs (Nestler and Nelson, 1945). Homosexual coition occurs occasionally between wild birds (e.g., the Ruff), and early imprinting has resulted in pair bonds between birds and humans, even to the extent of attempted coition with a human hand.

MEANING OF COURTSHIP DISPLAY

Just as the seasons swing back and forth between the bleak sterility of winter and the green fruitfulness of summer, so the lives of birds oscillate between the relative quiescence of the resting season and the impetuous excitement of the breeding season. The extravagant courtship displays that seem so absurdly exaggerated to human eyes are in part a reflection of the intense living of birds and in part a reflection of special needs resulting from their ways of life.

Courtship is ordinarily the province of the male. He shows his wares before the female with an astonishing assortment of tricks, varying according to species. He may posture so as to reveal his gaudiest nuptial plumage; spread his tail and erect his crest or inflate brilliantly colored pouches; parade, dance, fly with dizzying acrobatics; sing his most fetching love songs (which to man may be discordant squawks); bring tid-bits of food to his love —anything, it seems, to impress his mate-to-be. Very often these courtship displays are presented with dramatic suddenness. Almost always they are uniquely different from those of other species of the same region. That they consume a lot of energy is proved by the fact that the male Great Bustard, *Otis tarda*, weighs one-third more at the beginning than at the end of the courtship period; the male European Woodcock, *Scolopax rusticola*, sinks from a weight of 320 grams in April to 263 grams in July (Zedlitz, *in* Stresemann, 1927–1934). Like a lovesick swain who squanders his substance on his intended bride, a male bird almost bankrupts himself biologically in his courtship exertions.

Mate selection, or pair formation, is one of the functions of courtship in most species, but by no means the only one. At times the songs and displays of courtship serve also to warn away intruders and competitors from the owner's territory.

Figure 13.1. One of the functions of courtship activities in birds is to stimulate sex-readiness. In the European Redshank, courtship display is on the ground, and it involves bowing, bill-clicking, short bill-to-bill leaps in the air, and chasing. Here a male in sexual ardor is attempting coition with a stuffed bird. Photo by E. Hosking.

Another important function of courtship is the stimulation of ovulation. A virgin dove stroked on the back, or exposed to the sight of another dove in an adjoining cage, will often lay eggs. Courtship activities with their colorful drama undoubtedly affect other species in the same way. The laying of an egg is preceded by the bursting of an ovarian follicle, and this, in turn, coincides with the onset of a heightened receptivity in the female, preparing her for copulation (Stresemann, 1927–1934). In other words, courtship stimulates sexual readiness, not only in the bird being courted but also in the bird doing the courting, through self-stimulation. This reciprocal stimulation may be the chief function of the mutual courtship ceremonies of many colonial birds such as gannets, gulls, and penguins.

Courtship activities have the further function of regulating the timing of sex-readiness so that the reproductive physiology of a pair may be synchronized. This is particularly important in a flying animal, which cannot afford to carry indefinitely the extra ballast of greatly enlarged gonads. Prolonged courtship displays very likely serve to reinforce the pair bond between mated birds. Finally, courtship displays also function as species-recognition signs. This probably explains the striking peculiarity of many courtship calls, dances, postures, or morphological sec-

Figure 13.2. Courtship activities do not necessarily stop after coition. Fulvous Tree Ducks perform a stereotyped, postcopulatory dance on the surface of the water, rapidly treading with their feet while holding their bodies erect, breasts puffed out, necks arched, and their outer wings held high. Photo by B. Meanley.

ondary sex characters. The greater the courtship idiosyncracies in a given species, the more easily they are recognized by members of that species and the less intelligible they are to strange species. In this way the considerable erotic energy of the displaying bird is not wasted on an unsuitable partner, and the probability of hybridization is reduced (Stresemann, 1927–1934).

SEX DIMORPHISM AND COURTSHIP

Where both sexes of a species are externally similar in appearance, the male and female often take equal parts in courtship activities. In the nuptial display of the Gannet, *Morus bassanus*, the male and female stand facing one another, wings spread, tail depressed, beaks pointing skyward, heads wagging violently from side to side, while each bird gives off hoarse "urrah urrrah" calls (see the headpiece of this chapter). Often their beaks clatter together like castanets, or are stroked on each other like knives on whetstones. The display may be varied with elaborate bows of the head and neck or by the opening of mouths, displaying a wide, black gape. In general outline this form of mutual display is seen among many sea birds.

Among birds possessing no visible sexual dimorphism, courtship behavior provides a means of sex recognition. Penguins, for example, are apparently unable to determine sex visually, so they adopt a trial and error procedure to solve their problem. In a typical courtship performance, a male may place a pebble at the feet of another bird. If this second bird is a male, he may start a fight. If it is a female, she may be unreceptive and ignore the courting male; but if she is ready for courtship, the pair will go through various courtship ceremonies involving deep bowing, stretching their beaks skyward in the "ecstatic" posture, trumpeting, neck-twining, and other actions that eventually lead to coition. Courtship ac-

tivities may thus arouse sexual ardor, antagonism, or indifference, depending on the sex and physiological state of the partner.

In many species, however, sexual dimorphism provides striking differences between the male and female, especially in their nuptial plumage. The male, with his conspicuous coloration, undertakes the courtship activities. The less conspicuous female assumes the confining domestic duties of the nest, where her drab plumage affords some protection against predators. In those few species (phalaropes, painted snipe, and button quail) in which the male performs the domestic chores, it is, significantly, the female which takes the initiative in courtship, strutting her gaudier plumage, fighting with other females, and defending the home territory.

It seems probable that sex dimorphism first arose in birds as a "badge" for the quick and easy identification of sex. In some species it is still that and no more. To human eyes the only visible difference between a male Yellow-shafted Flicker, *Colaptes auratus*, and a female is the presence of small black "mustache" or "sideburn" marks on the sides of the male's head. This distinction is also the one the birds themselves use, for when Noble (1936) painted black mustache marks on a female, her mate immediately attacked her as though she were an intruding male. In some birds such as the Ruby-crowned Kinglet, *Regulus calendula*, and Goldcrest, *Regulus regulus*, the male makes the most of his modest adornments by "repeatedly raising and spreading out his crest sideways, forming a conspicuous flame-like patch of colour, with a vibrating movement as it reaches full expansion" (Delamain in *British Handbook of Birds*).

From such simple beginnings sexual dimorphism presumably evolved into the colorful and even grotesque ornamentations that the males of many species now use for all the various functions of courtship display, in addition to the primitive function of simply announcing their sex. It is significant that in many species the

Figure 13.3. Visible differences between the sexes may be large, as in peafowl, small as in the Yellow-shafted Flicker, or non-existent, as in penguins. The chief external evidence of sex in the Flicker is the black mustache mark, seen here in the male, but lacking in the female. If an artificial mustache be painted on a female, other Flickers will treat her as a male. Photo by G. R. Austing.

colorful feathers, and often other structures, used in courtship coincide in their periodic appearance with the appropriate period of the bird's breeding cycle.

Sexual dimorphism in color, or sexual dichromatism, occurs in variable degree. Many woodpeckers differ in sex coloration only in the presence of a small patch of red feathers on the head or nape of the male. Less colorful but more extensive is the dimorphism in the Kelp Goose, *Chloephaga hybrida*, in which the male is pure white all over and the female brownish black with white barring on her sides. In many species, however, nature has thrown restraint to the winds and developed in the male gorgeous colors, lengthened plumes, distinctive songs, bizarre behavior, and other theatrical effects that he may employ in his pursuit of a bride. Among families showing pronounced sex dimorphism in many of their species are ducks (Anatidae), pheasants (Phasianidae), hummingbirds (Trochilidae), trogons (Trogonidae), manakins (Pipridae), Cotingas (Cotingidae), birds of paradise (Paradisaeidae), sunbirds (Nectariniidae), wood warblers (Parulidae), tanagers (Thraupidae), and widow birds (Viduinae).

Among the 41 kinds of birds of paradise there are feathers of every hue of the rainbow as well as sparkling whites, dull browns, velvety blacks, and shimmering iridescent shades. Frequently the feather adornments of the gaudy male are modified in shape as well as in color. Some birds have central tail feathers two and three times as long as their bodies. Others, such as the Twelve-wired Bird of Paradise, *Seleucides ignotus*, have some feathers reduced to "wires" or simply elongated quills. In the Six-plumed Bird of Paradise, *Parotia* sp., the male possesses six barbless feathers projecting from the top of his head, each tipped with a small oval vane, the whole resembling a tiny racquet. In the excitement of courtship these racquets may be swung directly forward toward the observing female. Perhaps the most extraordinary courtship accessories in the world are the pair of long crown feathers trailing backward from the head of the male King of Saxony Bird of Paradise, *Pteridophora alberti*. Although the bird is no larger than a starling, each feather is about one-half a meter in length, with about three dozen tiny translucent flags or pennants arranged laterally on the shining white rachis. In past years, before the bird was protected, these feathers were also used for human ornamentation and were reputedly worth 280

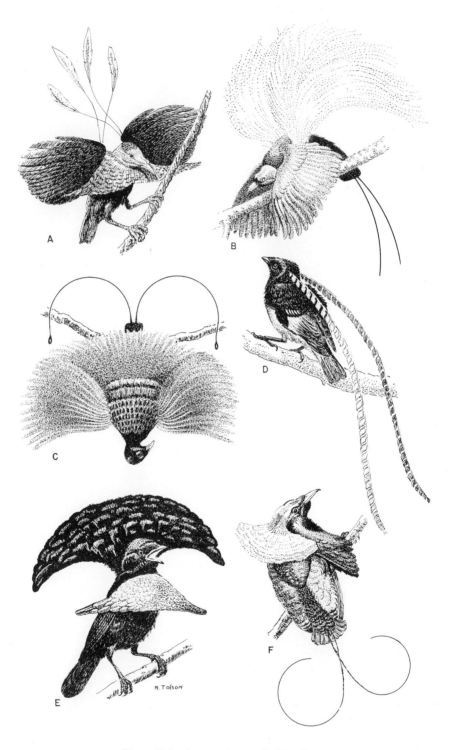

Figure 13.4. See opposite page for legend.

dollars a pair (Ripley, 1950). Other birds of paradise have feathers coiled into circles, twisted into corkscrews, or gathered into ruffs, capes, crests, false wings or "umbrellas." If an architect were to classify birds he would almost certainly place birds of paradise in the baroque category.

Among birds that have two molts each year, the change in appearance between the nuptial and resting plumages is often radical. The almost fluorescent red of the Scarlet Tanager, *Piranga olivacea*, in the breeding season changes to dull greens, yellows and browns in the winter. The loss of the ornamental central tail feathers of the Longtailed Widow Bird, *Diatropura procne*, reduces the total length of the bird from about 65 centimeters in the breeding season to only 22 centimeters during the rest of the year.

Structures other than feathers are used to impress the expectant female. Many species possess luridly colored patches of bare skin, or specialized combs, wattles, lappets, "horns," or pouches, which may be inflated either with blood or air and thus be made more conspicuous. During courtship display, the male Crimson Tragopan, *Tragopan satyra*, of Nepal, stands before the female with his two blood-inflated conical blue wattles erected on the crown of his white-spotted, black head. He makes the display more vivid by rapidly shaking his head and spreading his wings to show their crimson linings. The

male Umbrella Bird, *Cephalopterus ornatus*, has, in addition to his erectile "umbrella," a long, feathered, inflatable wattle, nearly as long as the bird himself, hanging in front of his breast. In courtship display the bird spreads his crest so that it overhangs his beak, inflates his dangling wattle with air, and emits a deep roaring call. The Magnificent Frigate Bird, *Fregata magnificens*, possesses during the breeding season a throat pouch of brilliant red skin, which he inflates with air into a bean-shaped balloon practically as large as his body. Similarly inflatable neck pouches appear during the breeding season in several grouse such as the Sage Grouse, *Centrocercus urophasianus*. The pouches function both in display and as sounding boards for calls or "booming." The capacities of the esophageal pouches in two mature Sage Grouse were measured by Clarke and others (1942) in May at the height of the breeding season, and were found to have volumes of 4000 and 5400 cubic centimeters as compared with autumn measurements of 90 and 100 cubic centimeters. Histological studies of the walls of these pouches showed large quantities of elastic fibrous connective tissue.

Sometimes ordinary structures become brightly colored and are used in courtship display. During the breeding season the male Blue-footed Booby, *Sula nebouxii*, sticks up his tail and goose-steps in front

---

Figure 13.4. Male birds of paradise, showing examples of the spectacular plumage which they display in courtship. A, Wallace's Standard-wing Bird of Paradise, *Semioptera wallaceii*. The bib of breast feathers is metallic green, and the crown of the head is violet. The four white wing feathers may be raised or lowered at will. B, The Greater Bird of Paradise, *Paradisaea apoda*, is a brown, crow-sized bird with a yellow crown, glittering green throat, and soft, golden wing plumes which are held erect and vibrated for courtship display. A dozen or more males may display simultaneously and energetically in one tree. C, The Blue Bird of Paradise, *Paradisaea rudolphi*, displays his bright blue plumes while hanging inverted, slowly swinging his body sideways, and singing in a monotone. D, The King of Saxony Bird of Paradise, *Pteridophora alberti*, has two crest feathers in the form of long shafts lined with small blue and white pennants. E, The Lesser Superb Bird of Paradise, *Lophorina superba*, is a small black bird with two sets of erectile plumes: a velvety black cape and an iridescent green bib. In addition, during courtship the male exposes the bright green lining of his mouth cavity. F, The Magnificent Bird of Paradise, *Diphyllodes magnificus*, has bright yellow cape feathers and a metallic green bib, both of which it can erect in display. The two coiled tail "wires" are greatly prolonged feather shafts. After Ripley, and paintings by W. A. Weber.

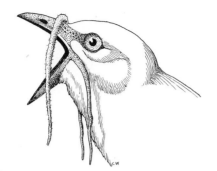

Figure 13.5.   In addition to brightly colored feathers, some birds possess other accessories used in courtship. The Central American Three-wattled Bellbird, *Procnias tricarunculata*, in the excitement of courtship display, erects its whip-like wattles and exposes its wide gape. The bird gets its name from its bell-like call.

of his prospective mate, lifting each bright blue foot as high as he can. The mouth cavities of many birds are strikingly colored and are prominently displayed in courtship ceremonies, sometimes by the male, sometimes mutually, as in sea birds. Here again, the colors vary widely: the Gannet, *Morus bassanus*, black; Razor-billed Auk, *Alca torda*, yellow; Common Puffin, *Fratercula arctica*, orange; Black Guillemot, *Cepphus grylle*, red; Lesser Superb Bird of Paradise, *Lophorina superba*, bright green; Sickle-bill Bird of Paradise, *Epimachus fastosus*, yellowish green; Rifle Bird, *Craspedophora magnifica*, white. Such gape displays are particularly effective in courtship because they can be made with striking suddenness merely by opening the mouth.

Not all secondary sex characters are externally visible. In numerous ducks—for example, the Rosy-billed Duck, *Metopiana peposaca*, of South America—there may be enlargements in the syrinx and trachea of the male. The Trumpeter Manucode, *Phonygammus keraudrenii* (Paradisaeidae), gets its name from sounds made possible by the enormously long trachea of the male coiled under the skin of his breast. In addition to this adaptation, which gives him a trumpeting voice, the bird has a collar of narrow, iridescent feathers which he can erect into a fan-like

disc through which he thrusts his head while displaying. The trachea of the female is of ordinary length.

VARIETIES OF COURTSHIP DISPLAY

Song may be employed in lovemaking as well as in war or in territorial defense. Its importance in courtship can be judged in some species by the amount of time the male devotes to song before and after he secures a mate (see p. 190). In some species, like the Prairie Chicken, *Tympanuchus cupido*, certain courtship sounds, such as "booming," are restricted to the breeding season because the structures necessary for them exist only at that time of the year. In most species, however, it seems likely that courtship song is largely controlled by hormonal and psychic conditions. Very often the injection of male hormones in a bird, even in a female, will bring on courtship song and behavior.

The lovemaking male serenades his would-be mate not only with calls and songs, but with a great variety of other sounds, according to species. The tom Turkey, *Meleagris gallopavo*, rattles his quills; hummingbirds, snipe, and nighthawks in flight make assorted humming, buzzing, singing, bleating, or roaring sounds as specialized feathers vibrate in the passing air; woodpeckers drum on dead limbs and tin roofs; displaying manakins, probably by striking their specially stiffened wing quills together, produce noises like the snapping of fingers or like a pencil dragged over the teeth of a comb; voiceless storks clapper their mandibles together, and some pigeons and owls clap their wings over their backs. Nature utilizes whatever resources are at hand to heighten the charms of the wooing male.

Another form of courtship activity involves contact. This type is common among birds lacking sexual dimorphism, particularly sea birds. Such courtship may involve sparring with bills, "kissing," caressing, entwining necks, nibbling at each other's feathers, or simple side-by-side bodily contact. The so-called "love birds" or Budgerigars, *Melopsittacus undulatus*, provide an example of courtship based largely on the sense of touch.

Very rarely does a brightly colored male bird merely stand where the female can see him. Usually he postures or moves about so that his brightest adornments are clearly revealed. There is a high correlation between courtship movements and the particular structures that are the male's showiest ornaments. The Peacock, *Pavo cristatus*, for example, spreads his fan-like tail-coverts and approaches the female obliquely with the drab rear-side of his fan exposed to her. At just the right distance, he suddenly swings himself around and dazzles her with every one of the hundred or more shimmering "eyes" vibrating and every quill rattling. To climax the performance, he screams with demonic ardor and then settles back to let his theatrics sink in. The male Golden Pheasant, *Chrysolophus pictus*, stands broadside to the female and spreads his beautiful black and gold collar sideways so that she may absorb its full splendor. The Ruff, *Philomachus pugnax*, lowers his head nearly to the ground before the female and extends his large Elizabethan ruff. The male Blue Bird of Paradise, *Paradisaea rudolphi*, hangs upside down on an exposed branch, the better to reveal his magnificent breast plumage. It seems altogether possible that the bird of paradise hanging upside down before his intended mate, and a small boy "skinning the cat" on a tree limb in front of his best girl, are both expressing the same deep ancestral urge. Other paradise birds, some parrots, and some oropendolas also display while inverted. The dramatic effects of courtship displays in nearly all birds are enhanced by their strangeness and frequently by their suddenness.

Courtship display may also take the form of dance rituals. Cranes perform different forms of solemn and stately dances, sometimes in mixed pairs, or in pairs of males with the females looking on, and sometimes in large mixed flocks. A description of the dance of a pair of Sandhill Cranes, *Grus canadensis*, is given by Nelson (*in* Armstrong, 1942).

> "Another pirouette brought him facing his charmer, whom he greeted with a still deeper bow, his wings meanwhile hanging loosely at his side. She replied with an answering bow and hop, and then each tried to outdo the other in a series of spasmodic hops and starts, mixed with a set of comically grave and ceremonious bows. The pair stood for some moments bowing right and left, when their legs appeared to become envious of the large share taken in the performance by the neck, and then would ensue a series of skilled hops and skips, which are more like the steps of a burlesque minuet than anything else I can think of. Frequently others join, and the dance keeps up until all are exhausted."

Some birds become so absorbed in their dancing that men may approach closely, or even kill some of the dancers, without disturbing the rest. The ancients, according to Robert Graves (1948), knew how to take full advantage of this habit. Moreover:

> "In the mating-season they used to put a decoy cock-partridge in a cage at the end of a long narrow winding brushwood tunnel and gave it corn to eat. Its lonely cry, combining the call to love with the call to food, attracted the hens along the tunnel, and when they reached the cage and it uttered its usual challenge call, other cocks would come running up, only to be knocked on the head with sticks by the waiting hunters as soon as they emerged from the tunnel."

This sport is said to be still practiced in Mediterranean countries.

The Black-crowned Night Heron, *Nycticorax nycticorax*, in his courtship overtures lowers his head and wings and

> "executes a queer sort of courting dance on the spot of the future nest, treading from one foot to the other with a peculiar weaving action. From time to time he suddenly lowers his head and neck vertically, while his shoulders lift as in a hiccough, and he utters his courting cry. This cry is very deep and quite low, sounding like steam escaping through the safety-valve of a boiler" (Lorenz, 1938).

It is significant that the legs of the Night Heron develop their bright rosy tinge during the breeding season. Should a female approach a courting male, he lowers his head with one cheek parallel to the ground, at the same time uttering a guttural greeting call.

"The head is then raised and the feathers on the crown, neck and back are raised. At the same time the pupil is contracted and the eyeball actually protruded from its socket, exposing the red iris to its maximum extent. The plumes are erected and may even fall forward over the head as the male bows again to the female and either repeats the greeting or turns his partly open mouth toward her" (Noble *et al.*, 1938).

The courtship ceremony of the Night Heron illustrates how a variety of resources may be employed in impressing a potential mate: dancing, leg color, plume erection, eyeball protrusion, calls, and still others.

The polygynous and promiscuous jewel-like manakins (Pipridae) of Central and South America perform astonishing courtship dances and flights. Sometimes the males dance in pairs, sometimes in groups; but frequently they perform on or over dance areas which are floors of the tropical forest where the birds have cleared away all litter. The Long-tailed Manakin, *Chiroxiphia linearis*, of Costa Rica is described by Slud (1957) as performing two kinds of dances. In one dance, two males perch crosswise, facing the same direction, on a horizontal branch or vine near the ground. Each bird rises alternately straight into the air about half a meter, and then descends to the starting point. At the top of each fluttering rise the bird hangs suspended "as though attached to a rubber band" and exposes his conspicuous red cap, fluffed sky-blue back, long arching tail and bright orange legs. Each bird gives a guttural, cat-like *"miaow-raow"* as he rises. Gradually the alternating flights into the air increase in frequency and decrease in height until the two birds seem to be caught in an uncontrolled epileptic frenzy—and suddenly the dance is over. To perform the other dance, the two males perch lengthwise on a branch, both facing the same direction and about half a meter apart. The bird in front gives his cat-like call and rises into the air. As he hangs hovering at the crest of his rise, the second bird with flicking wings hitches himself forward on the branch accompanied by low, ticking sounds, until he is directly under the hovering bird. The bird in the air then descends diagonally backward and alights on the spot just vacated by the second bird. The second bird, now in the forward position, rises into the air and hovers while the first bird begins hitching forward on the limb. This continues, and the two males "replace one another with cyclic regularity . . . like balls in a juggling act." All the while the modestly colored female may be observing them from the sidelines. Stereotyped acrobatic courtship dances such as these are characteristic of many tropical species. The male Standard-wing Bird of Paradise, *Semioptera wallaceii*, even performs a backward somersault from his perch, landing on the ground with his wings closed (Armstrong, 1942).

Courtship displays in numerous species are performed in groups. A small group of Yellow-thighed Manakins, *Pipra mentalis*, each male on his own horizontal limb, will act like whirling dervishes whenever a female approaches their assembly in a tropical rain forest. First, a given male stretches high on his legs to expose his bright yellow thighs. He holds his deep black body horizontal, and his scarlet head bent downward. With his wings partly open, each bird then reverses his position on the limb in rapid sequence, facing first forward and then backward, so that his conspicuous head describes fiery circles about the pivot of his gaudy legs. In another type of dance each male, again stretched high on his yellow legs and with his wings held overhead, slides rapidly backward on a horizontal limb for about 30 centimeters and then jumps forward to the starting place and repeats his stiff-legged, backward fox-trot over and over. Along with this bizarre dance, each manakin gives off loud buzzings and sharp snapping sounds, probably made with the specially modified wing feathers.

Even more social are the courtship dances of many Galliformes. Very often the birds dance and posture on traditional courting grounds called *leks*, on which each male defends his special display territory. In the polygamous Black Grouse, *Lyrurus tetrix*, of Europe, a group of males will gather on their lek each spring, and at about sunrise begin calling, dancing, and posturing to defend their individual mating territories and to attract the females. Each male holds his head upright, spreads his bow-shaped tail, droops his wings, inflates his fleshy red "eyebrows" with blood, and begins jumping and fluttering over his chosen spot. Should another male approach his territory, the owner will quickly thrust his head and neck forward and perhaps run a few steps toward the intruder and then retreat. Fighting is highly formalized and is usually restricted to threats. If a female approaches a male, he will circle around her with quick steps, often tilting his body and tail toward her. If she crouches and they copulate, other males may try to interfere.

Not surprisingly, many savage tribes throughout the world perform dances clearly derived from those of courting or fighting birds. The Blackfoot Indians of the Northwest mimic the foot-stamping, bowing, and strutting of the Sage Grouse, complete with a costume imitating the spread tail of the grouse. According to Armstrong (1942) the Jivaro Indians of South America mimic the dance of the Cock-of-the-Rock; the Chukchee of Siberia, the dance of the Ruff; the Monumbo of New Guinea, that of the cassowary; the Australian aborigines, the Emu; the natives of New Ireland, the hornbill; the Maidu of California, the tree-creeper; and the Tarahumare Indians of Mexico, the Turkey. Armstrong is of the opinion that both in birds and in man, dances have similar functions for self- and corporate-stimulation (for either love or war) and also for the release of excess energy. Of course, human dances also have intellectual functions such as the propitiation of harmful spirits, the promotion of fecundity in crops, or success in hunting. According to Plutarch (*ca.* A.D. 46–120) the ancient Greek hero Theseus introduced into Delos a Crane Dance which was performed around an altar and must have had

religious significance: the crane was sacred to Apollo the sun-god (Graves, 1948).

Social courtship is practiced not only by numerous species of gallinaceous birds but also by that extraordinary shore bird the Ruff, *Philomachus pugnax*. In this species, the males and females are reported to live in separate flocks throughout the year and to come together only for a few minutes during the spring courtship dance for coition. Then they separate once more until the next breeding season. During the mating season the male has a ruff of prominent neck feathers and exaggerated ear tufts. His courtship dance consists of an excited running about the lek with wings fluttering, head and neck held horizontally and ruff expanded. Suddenly the bird stops, lowers his head until the bill touches the ground, and then freezes into a rigid posture with the spectacular ruff expanded, wings spread and tail depressed. Shortly the bird will shiver his wings and either become quiescent, sometimes even apparently taking a nap, or begin his wild scurrying about once more. If a female approaches a male and perhaps nibbles at his ruff or head feathers, coition ensues. Then the two part, probably never to see each other again.

Courtship dancing is not necessarily limited to land. A variety of water birds perform the equivalent of dancing on and in water. In a stereotyped courtship ceremony, the male and female Great Crested Grebe, *Podiceps cristatus*, swim toward each other on the surface of the water and touch beaks. Then they dive and emerge facing each other, each with a bit of water weed in its beak. Next, in their well-known "penguin dance" the grebes rise upright in the water with their pure white bellies exposed to one another, and while maintaining this position weave their bodies back and forth. In some species of grebes and loons, the pair will actually patter ecstatically and with extraordinary speed over the surface of the water while in this same upright, penguin-like position, sometimes for as far as half a kilometer, only to turn around and skitter

Figure 13.6. European male Ruffs in communal courtship display. Note the great individual variation in the coloration of ruff feathers. Photo by C. C. Doncaster.

back again. Among other forms of display that involve diving, splashing, and pattering over the surface of the water, the Red-throated Diver, *Colymbus stellatus*, rolls over in the water, belly uppermost, kicks and splashes with its legs in the air, and then dives, emerging upside down and repeating the strange performance.

Many birds conduct their courtship activities in the air. In some species, courtship consists merely in a flight that exposes the more colorful markings of the male to the eyes of the female. Daily, during the nest-hole construction period, the Great Spotted Woodpecker, *Dendrocopus major*, hovers moth-like in the air with his tail raised to expose the fiery red underparts. Just before coition the male Snow Finch, *Montifringilla nivalis*, flies in circles about his mate, exposing the white feathers of his wings and tail. As discussed earlier, many species, such as goatsuckers, snipe, and hummingbirds, combine remarkable aerial acrobatics with unusual

sounds caused by the rushing of air across specially adapted feathers.

Among the more spectacular courtship flights are those of some snipe, herons, hawks, doves, hummingbirds, swifts, and Corvidae. In its display flight the male Lapwing, *Vanellus vanellus*, rises slowly from the ground, then speeds up his wing beats and rises at a steep angle. Suddenly he plunges toward earth, turning and twisting and somersaulting "as though out of control" and then "sweeps off with erratic flight tilting from side to side and producing a quite loud humming throb with its wings" (Tucker, 1943). The male Marsh Hawk or Harrier, *Circus cyaneus*, along with numerous other hawks, plunges directly earthward from a great height, turning somersaults and uttering shrill cries during his descent. At other times, he impresses the female by performing an up and down roller-coaster flight, rising only a few meters above the ground and looping the loop and screeching on each downward plunge. Among the ducks, finches, weaver finches, sylviid warblers, and others, there occur reckless courtship flights in which the male pursues the female. In some swifts the chase will climb high in the heavens where it abruptly ends as the pair "lock in a copulatory embrace and fall a thousand feet, their wings flailing the air like a pin-wheel" (Peterson, 1948).

Fighting between males is accepted courtship practice in many species. The fighting not only decides which males "deserve the fair" but it also undoubtedly stimulates sexual ardor in many of the combatants. Often, of course, it is difficult to distinguish courtship fighting from territorial fighting or from display to impress the female. Occasionally male Ruffs will seize one another's ruffs and hold on for several minutes. One of the chief mating-season activities of the gregarious Avocet, *Recurvirostra avosetta*, is formalized fighting by both sexes. Often, at the height of battle, a bird will put its head under its wing as though going to sleep. Such in-

congruous action is probably a displacement activity brought on by the intensified emotions aroused by combat. Male penguins engage in courtship fights of impressive vigor, sometimes emerging from conflict minus a tongue or an eye. Rival Adelie Penguins, *Pygoscelis Adeliae*, begin fighting with their beaks, "but they soon resort entirely to blows of the flippers and end by leaning against each other in a sidewise position and battering away with the 'outside' wings, like clinched pugilists, raining blows until the battering sounds a tattoo." (Murphy, 1936). The female Adelie seems no less belligerent. When a male suitor approaches her expectantly, she jabs at him with her powerful, sharp beak. This abuse the male meekly accepts, upon which the female refrains from further attack and both birds assume the widespread "ecstatic" posture, crossing their upstretched beaks and weaving their heads from side to side, while uttering their unmusical calls. Unless another male waddles in to interrupt this love making, the pair may copulate and establish a pair

Figure 13.7. Courtship "billing" in the Adelie Penguin. In many species of sea birds the sexes are visually indistinguishable. In such species, the sex of a given bird may be revealed by its response to courtship activities. Photo by Expéditions Polaires Francaises.

bond for the season or for longer. Love and war, eroticism and aggression, are closely allied partners in the breeding behavior of many birds, and it is likely that both of these seemingly antithetical activities promote the psychic and physiological functions necessary for race survival.

A special category of courtship display is provided by the bower-birds (Ptilonorhynchidae) of Australia and New Guinea. These relatives of crows and birds of paradise are not conspicuously ornamented, but the males make up for their lack of nuptial finery by constructing bowers and display grounds which serve the same functions as secondary sex characters in other birds. This conclusion is supported by the fact that males of the least colorful species of bower-birds build the most elaborate and highly ornamented bowers, and vice versa (Gilliard, 1958).

Among bower-birds a common type of bower is constructed by the male in the form of two parallel hedges of interlaced grasses or twigs stuck in the ground. In the space between the hedges is an avenue in which the male may do some of his displaying. This is the "avenue" type of bower. In another type of construction the bower may be in the form of a stack of

Figure 13.8. The maypole bower of the Brown Gardener Bower-bird.

twigs erected around a vertical sapling, or arranged in the form of an open-sided tepee or hut whose roof-center is supported by a sapling. These are the "maypole" bowers, some of which may be as high as three meters. The floor under and in front of them is cleared of all litter by the males and decorated with collections of colorful objects neatly piled and, in the case of perishable leaves, flowers, and fruits, often replaced daily, even for months on end. The clear space adjoining each bower is known as the display area.

Among the objects commonly collected and spread out on the display area are bleached bones, snail shells, parrot feathers, seeds, colored fruits, bits of colored glass, colored paper, bright metallic objects, and even jewelry. The Brown Gardener Bower-bird, *Amblyornis inornatus*, builds an open-sided maypole bower that looks very much like a thatched hut. Incorporated in the walls of the hut may be living orchids. In front of the hut the display area may have neatly piled "gardens" of mushrooms, flowers, cartridge shells, colored fruits, or stones of a given color, one kind of object to each pile.

A few species of bower-birds even paint the walls of their bowers. They make their paint by mixing saliva with chewed-up fruits, grass, rotten wood, or charcoal, and then smear the paste on the sticks of the bower. Two species, of which the Satin Bower-bird, *Ptilonorhynchus violaceus*, is one, manufacture wads of fibrous bark which they use as paint brushes to apply the colors (Marshall, 1954). This represents one of the extremely rare instances of tool-using by an animal.

As the reproductive season opens and hormones begin to flood the tissues of the male bower-bird, he begins to decorate his bower and to display "energetically and noisily," often holding a display object in his beak. The display ground, according to Marshall, is the focal point of the male's territory and the chief agent that attracts the female's interest, keeps rivals away, and helps stimulate and synchronize the male and female reproductive machinery.

At least in some species, coition occurs in the bower. After fertilization, the female builds her nest at a distance from the bower. There she incubates the eggs and rears the young, unaided by the male. After the young have fledged, the female may bring them to the bower, where the family engages in communal display—possibly an imprinting exposure which may educate the young in the intricacies of display etiquette for that species.

Some bower-birds show remarkable discrimination in their selection of ornamental objects to display in their bowers. The Stagemaker Bower-bird, *Scenopoeetes dentirostris*, with its toothed mandibles laboriously chews or "saws" off green leaves of shrubs and trees and then carries them to its display ground where they are neatly arranged with their paler undersides up. When Marshall turned all the leaves in one bower right side up, the bird soon flipped them over again to suit his own avian esthetic notions. Withered leaves are removed each morning and replaced with fresh ones.

Experimenting with the bird's esthetic preferences, Ripley (1947) placed a few flowers of different colors on a Brown Gardener's display area. When the bird returned it cast out all the flowers but one orchid.

"Last of all the bower-bird picked up the pretty red orchid. This time it seemed to be in two minds. It would hop this way and that from one pile of fruit or flowers to another. Finally, with many darts and flourishes the orchid was placed on top of the pink flowers. The two colors swore a bit, but under the circumstances it was certainly the best matching job that could be done."

The Satin Bower-bird has intensely blue eyes and favors blue display ornaments: flowers, berries, bits of paper, or bits of glass, all blue. The driving urge of males to secure blue articles for their display grounds was studied by Marshall through the ingenious expedient of placing many fragments of broken blue glass bottles, each piece numbered with a diamond pencil, near known bowers over an area of about 130 square kilometers (50 sq. mi.).

Within seven days, 34 per cent of the glass fragments appeared at the bowers, and a month later, 79 per cent. Weekly inspection of the bowers during the next two years showed Marshall that these bits of glass migrated continuously between bowers, in consequence of perpetual raiding and counter-raiding. The more aggressive the male, the bigger the share of these glass jewels he possessed.

One amazing characteristic of the avenue-bowers of the Satin Bower-bird is their orientation. Of 66 bowers examined by Marshall, the deviation of the axis of the central avenue from true north and south was never more than 30 degrees. When the bower of a male in an aviary was experimentally shifted from its original orientation of 15 degrees (east of north) to 310 degrees (northwest by southeast), the bird re-oriented the walls one twig at a time to approximately the original bearing. This north and south bearing of avenues is thought by Marshall to be a

Figure 13.9.   A Satin Bower-bird at its avenue bower. This blue-eyed bird collects blue ornaments to decorate his bower. Photo by the Australian News and Information Bureau.

response to natural lighting. An early morning display performance in an east-west oriented bower might lose its effectiveness on a female staring into the glare of the rising sun.

A bird with a penchant for accumulating bright shiny objects is the Spotted Bower-bird, *Chlamydera maculata*. It will even enter tents and houses to pilfer cutlery, coins, thimbles, nails, screws, lead bullets, and pieces of glass and tin. Marshall relates the story of a car owner who, noting the disappearance of the ignition keys from his car, and familiar with the habits of this bird, walked about a kilometer to the nearest display ground and retrieved his keys!

When alone, the male of this species displays moderately and intermittently, but should a female approach his bower, he immediately throws himself into a frenzied performance. He alternately lifts and lowers his lilac mantle feathers; he contorts his body into strange postures and frequently leaps into the air. He may attack objects on the display floor and fling them about with vigorous abandon. After some twenty minutes of such effervescence, the male may copulate with the passive female outside the bower and then return for additional violent display, after which he calmly tidies up his bower. In this species, as also in the Satin Bower-bird, the male displays around the bower for weeks and even months before coition occurs, and continues to display after the female leaves and begins to incubate. It seems that the long maintenance of sexual activity and display by the male—sometimes four to five months—is an adaptation to ensure the readiness of the male for the sudden, brief, and unpredictable period when the female becomes sexually active. The female's reproductive activity seems to be triggered by some as yet undiscovered environmental factor which precedes that time of year when protein food, mainly insects, will be most abundant for raising young. And in most bower-bird country this does not occur every year on the same date.

SYMBOLIC COURTSHIP RITES

Many necessary, every-day activities may become formalized and adapted to functions quite different from their original ones. Among these symbolic formalities is courtship feeding, which occurs in species that feed their young by regurgitation, or with their beaks, or with food carried in their talons. It is commonest in species in which the male and female remain together for the breeding season. It rarely occurs in species like ducks and game birds which do not feed their young. In a review of this subject, Lack (1940) lists 14 orders of birds, including 17 families of the Passeriformes, in which courtship feeding is known to occur. Whenever courtship feeding does occur, the male nearly always feeds the female, with the significant exception of the button quails in which the male incubates and rears the young. In the usual situation the female may beg her mate for food with much the same posture, wing fluttering, and even infantile calls that the young birds use in importuning their parents for food. In a few species such as terns, either sex may beg food from the other, and in waxwings the male and female may pass the food back and forth from bill to bill. Courtship feeding and related formalities, such as billing and gaping, are, according to Armstrong (1942), sexual ceremonies that have evolved from the parental habit of feeding young birds—latent activities that reappear in the adult in a new context. Often courtship feeding continues and becomes "real" feeding by the male of the incubating female. Very rarely does the male feed the female only during the incubation period.

Nutrition is not the reason for courtship feeding. This is easily seen in such species as the Atlantic Common Murre, *Uria aalge*, which carries fish to the nest site and holds them in its beak for several hours. The female European Robin, *Erithacus rubecula*, may beg her mate for food even though she is standing in a dish full of meal worms, or, later in the breeding

Figure 13.10. Courtship feeding in European Crossbills. The male is passing regurgitated seeds from his crop into the mouth of the female. Photo by E. Hosking.

cycle, beg him for food when her own mouth is full of worms to feed the young (Lack, 1943).

In some species, courtship feeding is associated with coition and may function as a releaser for that behavior. Courtship feeding occurs just prior to coition in pigeons and Rooks, *Corvus frugilegus;* it occurs during copulation in the Yellow-billed Cuckoo, *Coccyzus americanus,* and Galapagos finches (Geospizinae); and after copulation in Starlings, *Sturnus vulgaris,* and terns. The male Roadrunner, *Geococcyx californianus,* holds a lizard in his beak during coition and feeds it to the female immediately afterward. Experiments by Mason (1945) on the Corncrake, *Crex crex,* showed that males would display in front of a dummy, and attempt copulation with it. After 23 such attempts at coition one bird disappeared, only to return with a green caterpillar, which it offered to the stuffed bird before it resumed its futile attempts. In some species courtship feeding seems primarily to cement the pair

bond: for example, in European Robins and hornbills.

Food is passed from the male to the female in various ways. Most commonly the male places it in the female's gaping mouth. In many finches, gulls, and doves, the male regurgitates the food for the female. Among hawks, the food may be passed from the talons of the male to the female in mid-air, the latter turning upside down to accept the symbolic gift. Tengmalm's Owl, *Aegolius funereus,* calls and repeatedly flies to his nest hole, and finally persuades his mate-to-be to enter the nest, where she finds a freshly killed mouse awaiting her. The barnyard rooster will call a hen to a real or imaginary bit of food by means of a formalized "tid-bitting waltz," and the Adelie Penguin, *Pygoscelis adeliae,* will "feed" his spouse with pebbles or bits of snow.

Related to courtship feeding are the stylized ceremonies of billing, fencing, gaping, and similar forms of lovemaking. Billing is common among water birds such as penguins, cormorants, gannets, grebes, puffins, and herons, as well as among some of the parakeets, doves, corvids, and finches. The King Shag, *Phalacrocorax albiventer*, woos his mate by holding "her head gently in his large open bill, and the two will sway from side to side. The birds will then bow, kiss and nibble each other about the head, and utter sundry grunts and coos and a blowing sort of whistle" (Cobb, *in* Murphy, 1936). Courting Ravens, *Corvus corax*, will hold on to each other's beaks in a prolonged kiss. The brightly colored mouth cavities are exposed in ceremonial courtship gaping by the males and sometimes by both sexes of certain cormorants, guillemots, gulls, terns, storks, birds of paradise, thrushes, and other species.

Although in the normal sequence of events courtship precedes nest-building, symbolic or mock nest-building may be

Figure 13.11. Courtship in the European Common Heron involves neck-stretching, bill-snapping, feather-fluffing (as shown here), and symbolic nest building in which the male passes to the female a stick which she builds into the nest. Photo by E. Hosking.

employed as a mode of courtship. A great many species handle bits of nesting material as part of the courtship routine. The Black Skimmer, *Rhynchops nigra*, gently passes a stick to the female just before coition; and the Roseate Spoonbill, *Ajaia ajaja*, presents sticks to his mate with much head-bobbing and bill-rubbing to reinforce the pair bond. In the pair formation ceremonies of the Yellowhammer, *Emberiza citrinella*, both sexes fly to the ground to pick up and drop pebbles and bits of vegetation (Diesselhorst, 1950). Breeding synchronization in Bullfinches, *Pyrrhula pyrrhula*, is accomplished by the mated pair showing nesting material to each other (Nicolai, 1956).

During the mating season, a Gannet, *Morus bassanus*, may "pretend" to receive imaginary nesting material from an invisible mate and build it into a fictitious nest (Lorenz, 1937). Also during the courtship period, female skuas will drop grass before the males; grebes will dive and bring up water weeds in their beaks; and Moorhens, *Gallinula chloropus*, will engage in symbolic nest-molding. For some species, the building of the actual nest provides courtship stimulation. The male Phainopepla, *Phainopepla nitens*, begins a nest, and if he acquires a mate, she helps to complete it. If, however, the male finishes the nest without securing a mate, he starts another, dismantling the first to get material for the second (Rand, 1943). There is some evidence that the completed nest built by the male serves in some species to put the female into the mood for breeding. This seems to be the case for some weaver birds (Ploceidae), the Penduline Tit, *Remiz pendulinus*, and the Australian Magpie-lark, *Grallina cyanoleuca*. A completed nest or nest site may have a magnetic attraction for an unattached female bird. Males of several species use their nests to "seal the wedding compact": among them are owls, woodpeckers, European flycatchers, wrens, and others. The male Collared Flycatcher, *Muscicapa albicollis*, demonstrates his nest hole to passing females with a special call and a slow flight near the hole, exhibiting all his conspicuous plumage characteristics. His urge to display the nest hole is so consuming that he displays to strangers even while his mate is busy carrying nesting materials into the hole. So strongly attractive is the nest hole display that, should the male display at another nest hole while his mate is incubating eggs in the first-chosen nest, she may desert the eggs and start afresh in the new, empty nest hole (Löhrl, 1951).

In all these strange and wonderful fashions male birds court their mates. They use the limited materials and talents they have at hand to win their brides, but they use them in distinctive and striking ways, often with dramatic suddenness. In fundamentals, avian and human courtship patterns are not widely divergent. A young man stepping out with his girl may put on his best suit of clothing (breeding plumage), and set forth with a box of chocolates (courtship feeding) under one arm and a bouquet of roses (bower-bird display) under the other. Before taking his girl to a dance (courtship dancing), the two of them may listen to a record of highly rhythmic jazz and join in on the chorus (courtship singing). During the evening the young man may pull from his pocket a blueprint of their dream home (nest display), while the young lady repairs her make-up with lipstick (gape display). At the end of the evening it is not unlikely that the young couple will indulge in a courtship activity known in both classes of vertebrates as billing and cooing. The hot-springs of love run deep and pervasive in the clay of all vertebrates. It is not surprising that their external bubblings appear to be much the same, whether in a university graduate, an Australian bushman, or a lowly sparrow.

SUGGESTED READINGS

A very full and delightfully written treatment of courtship display is found in Armstrong's *Bird Display* and its later revision, *Bird Display and Behaviour*. For a scholarly and entertaining account of the astonishing courtship displays of bower-birds, see Marshall's *The Bower-Birds*. Wallace's *An Introduction to Ornithology* contains a brief, well organized survey of mating habits. A thorough study of reproductive behavior in a limited group is found in Richdale's *Sexual Behavior in Penguins*.

FOURTEEN

Nests

*Yea, the sparrow hath found an house,
and the swallow a nest for herself, where
she may lay her young.*
Psalm 84:3

A great variety of animals build nests, but of them all—insects, fish, amphibia, reptiles, mammals, and others—birds are by far the most expert and most industrious nest-builders. They build nests of many different materials and in a bewildering variety of forms, and locate them in more varied sites than do any other animals.

FUNCTIONS OF NESTS

Birds use their nests chiefly to protect themselves, their eggs, and particularly their developing young from predatory animals and from adverse weather during the breeding season, the most vulnerable period in the life cycle. For protection against predators, birds rely mainly on nests that are inaccessible, camouflaged, or built in colonies which provide the safety of numbers.

For inaccessibility, nests are commonly constructed at the tips of tree branches, on ledges of cliffs, in burrows or cavities, on isolated islands, and on or over water. Several species build floating nests, and others construct nests propped up on reeds like the homes of the ancient Swiss

Figure 14.1. One of the chief functions of a nest is protection. The floating nests of grebes, built of aquatic plants, protect them from many terrestrial predators. Shown here is a European Little Grebe and its two young. Photo by E. Hosking.

lake dwellers. Each of these varied building sites rules out whole classes of potential predators.

For camouflage, nests are often built of materials found in the immediate vicinity, and therefore inconspicuous. Nests in grassy habitats are often made of grass; in reed beds, of reeds; in trees and shrubs, of twigs or branches. Sometimes the outsides of nests are covered with such disguising materials as mosses (by kinglets) or lichens (by hummingbirds) which decrease their visibility. The acme of inconspicuousness is achieved in some species (plovers, goatsuckers) by the simple expedient of building no nest at all and laying the eggs (often concealingly colored) directly on the bare ground. Although in such cases the "nest" matches its environment perfectly, other useful functions of a nest may be lacking.

Either through their construction or placement, many nests protect their inhabitants from rain, floods, drifting sand, or the burning rays of the sun, as well as from the eyes of predators. Many ground-dwelling species, such as the Eastern Meadowlark, *Sturnella magna,* and Ovenbird, *Seiurus aurocapillus,* and great numbers of tropical tree-dwellers build roofed-over nests. Nests of many desert species are commonly built in the lee of a sheltering rock or in the shade of some shrub.

A second major function of a nest is to maintain the warmth which promotes incubation of the eggs and the rapid development of the young. The sheltering warmth of the nest, in conjunction with the heat supplied by the brooding parent, parallels the warm protection of the uterus for an embryo mammal. Since warm young birds develop and reach maturity more quickly than young with less warmth, nests reduce the length of their period of highest vulnerability to exposure and predation, and thereby lengthen their life-expectancy.

Nests have the further function of supplying a supporting platform so that the eggs and young may be situated in trees, or on soggy ground, or even floating on water like the nests of grebes. Frequently the base of a nest is composed of coarse sticks or twigs which provide anchorage and support, while the superstructure is made of the finer and warmer materials which provide warmth, protection, and camouflage.

Finally, the construction and possession of a nest satisfies some of the deepest innate urges that a bird has—nest-building, brooding, and the care of young—all in one compact package. For species whose young remain in the nest several days or weeks after hatching, nest life enhances family solidarity and increases opportunities for educating the young.

EVOLUTION OF NESTS

One can only guess at the evolutionary origin of birds' nests. So much diversity is shown in nest-building behavior, even between close relatives, that patterns of nest building have relatively little taxonomic or evolutionary significance. Among flycatchers of the family Tyrannidae, for example, the Eastern Kingbird, *Tyrannus tyrannus*, builds a nest of weeds, grasses, moss, and plant-down, often at the extremity of a tree branch; the Crested Flycatcher, *Myiarchus crinitus*, lines a tree cavity with grasses, twigs, and rootlets, and often garnishes it with a cast-off snake skin; the Phoebe, *Sayornis phoebe*, constructs a bulky nest of mosses and mud, lined with grass or hair, typically on a beam under a bridge; the Yellow-bellied Flycatcher, *Empidonax flaviventris*, builds its nest of moss and grasses on the ground; the Tody Flycatcher, *Todirostrum cinereum*, builds a hanging, purselike nest of grasses and other fibers that has its entrance in the side.

Variability is found as well among the nests of auks, boobies, plovers, gulls, terns, doves, finches, and other birds. Perhaps the group showing the greatest diversity in nest types is the family of ovenbirds or Furnariidae of Central and South America. Within this family there are some species that nest in rock crevices or tree

cavities; some drill tunnels in banks or in dead trees; some build nests of twigs or branches in a tree; others make globular two-chambered, oven-shaped nests of mud; and in one species several pairs cooperate to build a communal apartment house of sticks (Gilliard, 1958).

Since birds have descended from reptiles, it is conceivable that their earliest nests were similar to those of some contemporary reptiles, that is, the eggs were laid in a pit in the ground and then covered over with earth or vegetation. The megapodes or "incubator birds" of Australasia and the Black-backed Coursers, *Pluvianus aegyptius*, of Egypt, also bury their eggs in the earth; and numerous other species (e.g., grebes, ducks, eagles) cover their eggs at times with vegetation or down feathers.

Another explanation advanced to account for the origin of birds' nests relates nest building to courtship and mating behavior. Elaborating the ideas of Selous, Darling, Coward, and others, Armstrong (1942) suggests that nest-building behavior may have originated in emotional responses associated with courtship ceremonies or copulation. When a courting male tern, bearing a fish, approaches the female on the ground, she depresses her head and breast while raising her wings and tail, and meanwhile kicks sand rearward with her feet. As the male circles the female she rotates so as to continue facing him, thus making a saucer-shaped depression or "scrape." She may pick and jerk toward her bits of nesting materials as she keeps rotating on the scrape. Many other species show similar scrape ceremonies during courtship: plovers, curlews, the ostrich, nightjars, grouse.

The female Red-throated Diver, *Colymbus stellatus*, lies in a grassy depression near the water's edge during copulation with the male. Immediately after the act, in an instinctive frenzy, she tears out beakfuls of moss and grass which she aimlessly throws behind her without attempting to arrange the material into a nest. Nevertheless, she makes a rude, cup-

Figure 14.2. A European Nightjar on its nest. The eggs are laid on the bare ground, usually near dead wood. Note that the bird enhances its inconspicuous coloration by flattening itself against the ground and by closing its eyelids. Photo by E. Hosking.

shaped depression in which she lays her eggs. The behavior involved in such haphazard domestic arrangements may in time become perfected through natural selection into the building behavior of such elaborately specialized nests as the hangnests of the orioles and caciques. Even the crudest saucer-shaped depression may increase the chances of egg survival, and therefore species survival, by preventing the eggs from rolling away and by holding them together in a warm, compact mass.

Successive steps in the evolution of birds' nests have been postulated by Makatsch (1950) to have occurred somewhat as follows. From a primitive scraped depression in the ground—a nest form still used by many ground dwellers—there probably evolved a simple nest of scrape-plus-vegetation. By the turning movements of the incubating bird, the twigs or grasses may have become molded into a shallow cup. By adding building materials

to the rim (a consequence that might be expected from the position of the incubating bird's bill) the nest cup may have become deepened. It is but a small step from a deep cup-shaped nest to a roofed-over nest. A ground-nester might pull grass tufts together and into the side walls of the nest, making an oven-shaped nest. Such a covered nest in a tree might next evolve into the simpler types of hangnests supported from above by a rope of interlaced fibers; this last form might quite naturally develop into the most complex sleeve-shaped hangnests with side entrances and other refinements.

CHOICE OF NEST SITE

Simply because they can fly, birds are practically unlimited in their choice of nest sites even though they may range from oceanic islets to alpine precipices, from polar ice-fields to "impenetrable" jungles. In this regard, birds have no peers. Coupled with their unexcelled mobility, birds seem to exercise an instinctive talent for seeking out sheltered niches in which to build their nests: in crevices, under overhanging ledges, deep in shrubs, even behind waterfalls.

It is often the male which chooses the nest site and the female which does the nest building. In the Domestic Chicken the rooster may enter the nest box and, by clucking, entice a female to begin laying her eggs there. Among migratory species in which the male arrives first in the spring, the male commonly establishes the territory and sometimes locates the nest site within it. The male House Wren, *Troglodytes aëdon*, and the male Phainopepla, *Phainopepla nitens*, begin building their nests before their mates arrive, and the male Prothonotary Warbler, *Protonotaria citrea*, picks out a cavity in a dead willow and begins lining it with mosses before his mate appears. In many species the choice of a nesting place becomes a part of the courtship ceremony. This is well illustrated by the Collared Flycatchers, *Muscicapa albicollis*, as described in the preceding chapter.

Among polygamous species such as grouse and pheasant, it is ordinarily the female who chooses the nesting place. In some of the polygamous weaverbirds of the genus *Euplectus*, the male chooses the territory for his entire harem while the females select their individual nesting sites within it. Great variation, however, occurs in site selection, even among close relatives.

In selecting the nest site, a bird may show anticipatory nest-molding or brooding behavior in a spot completely devoid of nest materials. A female American Robin, *Turdus migratorius*, may crouch and slowly spin around in a suitable tree crotch for several days before she begins building her nest there; and a female European Mistle Thrush, *Turdus viscivorous*, may "brood" a bare nest site for two or three weeks before nest construction begins.

Although the capacity for flight opens up to birds as a class almost unlimited site possibilities, there are anatomical and ecological limitations for different species that prevent a completely free choice of nest locations. Swallows with their weak wide bills could not possibly chisel out nest cavities in solid wood as do woodpeckers, and heavy-footed ground-nesters like the pheasants could not exploit soggy marsh habitats for nests as successfully as long-toed jaçanas or web-footed grebes.

In addition to such structural limitations and adaptations, there are undoubtedly psychic factors that influence a bird's choice of a nest site. Of several hundred nests of the Ruffed Grouse, *Bonasa umbellus*, observed by Edminster (1947), two-thirds were placed at the base of fairly large tree trunks, and the majority of the remainder were at the base of stumps. Phoebes, *Sayornis phoebe*, typically build on girders under bridges, and the Prothonotary Warbler, *Protonotaria citrea*, prefers a dead tree stub overhanging water. Foliage density may be important to some species. In studying a nesting colony of Common Crows, *Corvus brachyrhynchos*, in a California walnut orchard, Emlen (1942) found that nests built early in the season before the leaves were fully out were located a mean distance of 12.2 trees from the edge of the orchard, while later nests were built a mean distance of 8.8 trees from the edge. Peregrine Falcons, *Falco peregrinus*, are strongly attracted to ledges on cliffs for their eyries, and will use such reasonable substitutes as high office buildings or cathedral spires. Since 1940, Peregrines have raised young on a ledge at the 20th story of the Sun Life Building in Montreal, and a pair has nested for so many years in the spire of Salisbury Cathedral that they have become special wards of the Dean. The magnetism of a suitable nesting site was attested by the construction by a Rufous Ovenbird, *Furnarius rufus*, of its globular mud nest on the axle of a windmill. The nest of course went round with each rotation of the axle, but the bird

Figure 14.3.   A pair of Ospreys at their nest. Ospreys feed on fish, and consequently build their nests near water. The nest, which is usually lined with grasses, is often used for many years. Photo by M. D. England.

entered its nest to incubate only when the wheel stood still (Makatsch, 1950).

Frequently a species will adapt itself to non-typical nest sites. The Peregrine, for example, will nest in trees where cliffs are unavailable, and on the ground where both cliffs and trees are lacking. In the Baltic countries, about half of its nests are on cliffs, while the remainder are about equally divided between tree and ground sites. The Black Kite, *Milvus migrans*, which typically nests in large trees, is forced by the lack of them near Brienzer See, Switzerland, to become exclusively a cliff nester. Mallards typically nest on the ground, but occasionally one will nest as high as 10 to 15 meters above ground in the branches or hollow cavity of a tree. Abnormal nesting sites may be chosen because of individual variations in instinctive response, or they may be explained by a dearth of normal sites. In eastern Romania the House Sparrow, *Passer domesticus*, has preempted all nesting places under eaves and in barns. As a consequence, the Tree Sparrow, *Passer montanus*, has taken to nesting between the stones of village wells, as many as five nests to a well, and from one-half to five meters below ground level (Frank, 1944). Similarly Chimney Swifts, *Chaetura pelagica*, have nested in wells in Nova Scotia.

That a lack of suitable nest sites may be a critical limiting factor in bird popu-

lations is revealed by such studies as that of Creutz (1944), in which the placing of 100 nest boxes in a German orchard increased the number of resident, nesting Pied Flycatchers, *Muscicapa hypoleuca*, from 6 to 45 pairs in five years. In like manner, the extensive rubble areas in German cities left by World War II provided excellent nest sites for Black Redstarts, *Phoenicurus ochruros*, whose numbers accordingly increased strikingly.

Birds may become habituated to nest sites that at first would appear quite unsuitable. Wild ducks, turkeys, swallows, and shore birds have all been known to nest within a meter or two of railways where trains thunder by every few minutes. Tree Swallows, *Iridoprocne bicolor*, Barn Swallows, *Hirundo rustica*, Robins, *Turdus migratorius*, and Phoebes, *Sayornis phoebe*, have all raised successful broods on moving ferry boats. A European Robin, *Erithacus rubecula*, once built its nest in a wagon that travelled about 320 kilometers shortly after the young birds hatched. One of the parents accompanied

Figure 14.4.   A pair of Reed Warblers at their cup-shaped nest in a reed bed. The nest is constructed by the female alone. The male is shown swallowing a fecal sac from one of the young. Photo by E. Hosking.

the wagon the entire distance, feeding the young en route (Lack, 1946). In a similar instance, a pair of White Wagtails, *Motacilla alba*, built their nest on a tank truck that made frequent long trips away from a garage in Westphalia, Germany. Incubation was maintained during these trips, the pair changing off upon each return of the truck. Four young were successfully fledged (Lokietsch, 1957).

While birds normally nest near their chosen habitat—water birds near water, forest birds in the forest, and so on—this is not always the case. The Peruvian Gray Gull, *Larus modestus*, is an ornithological enigma in that it makes its living in the rich coastal waters of Peru and Chile but nests on flat, rock-strewn deserts from 35 to 100 kilometers inland (Goodall *et al.*, 1945). The White Pelicans, *Pelecanus erythrorhynchos*, of Great Salt Lake nest on isolated islands where food is lacking. They must fly from 50 to 160 kilometers to obtain food for themselves and their young.

A dearth of normal nesting sites may force birds to inhabit distinctly unsuitable sites. The Magnificent Frigate-bird, *Fregata magnificens*, normally nests atop dense cactus thickets, as at Bimini in the Bahamas; but on Little Swan Island it nests at the tops of trees ten meters high where the birds lose their balance on the unstable twigs. Often the birds will fall, get caught by the neck in a tree fork and hang there until they die (Murphy, 1936).

HEIGHT OF NESTS ABOVE GROUND

Some species of birds normally nest on the ground: loons, grouse, turkeys, pheasants, most ducks, geese, cranes, rails, shore birds, gulls, larks, and many more. Other species typically nest at different heights above ground. The Nightingale, *Luscinia megarhynchos*, usually nests about one meter above ground level; the

American Robin, *Turdus migratorius*, two to three meters. A species preference for a relatively fixed nesting height was nicely illustrated by observations on the nest sites of Kingbirds, *Tyrannus tyrannus*, by Mayfield (1952). In northern Michigan this species often nests on the intersecting corner braces of steel electric-transmission towers. These braces, which occur at heights above ground of about 2, 7, 9, 11, 13 meters and so on to the top of the tower, appear to human eyes to be equally suitable for nesting sites. Yet, of 16 occupied Kingbird nests found on these towers, 15 were on the 2-meter braces and only one on the 7-meter brace, and in this case a nearby hill reduced the apparent height of the brace. When nesting in wooded habitats, this species prefers sites

six to seven meters above ground. A study by Young (1955) of 202 American Robin nests near Madison, Wisconsin, showed a range in heights from 0.6 to 9 meters with an average height of 2.3 meters. A study of 398 Robin nests in Michigan by Nickell (1944) gave extreme heights of 0.3 to 20.0 meters and an average of 3.1 meters. When a suitable nesting site at a normal height is lacking, a given bird may select one at a very different height. Nests of Barn Swallows, *Hirundo rustica*, are commonly built on low rafters in barns, but one was observed by Hickey (1955) in a Minnesota observation tower 32.6 meters (107 feet) above ground. Other examples of nesting-height variations are given in Table 14.1 taken from Cruickshank (1956).

Table 14.1. Heights of Wood Warbler Nests at Hog Island, Maine

SPECIES	TOTAL NESTS	LOWEST NEST (METERS)	HIGHEST NEST (METERS)
Parula Warbler, *Parula americana*	71	1.5	16.5
Magnolia Warbler, *Dendroica magnolia*	33	0.3	4.2
Myrtle Warbler, *Dendroica coronata*	44	1.8	13.2
Blackburnian Warbler, *Dendroica fusca*	7	13.2	23.2
American Redstart, *Setophaga ruticilla*	50	0.3	15.9

The same bird may build its nest at different heights above ground according to the season. In Michigan, June nests of the Field Sparrow, *Spizella pusilla*, average 15 centimeters above ground; July nests, 34 centimeters; and August nests, 43 centimeters (Walkinshaw, 1939). Similarly, Mrs. Nice (1937) found for the Song Sparrow, *Melospiza melodia*, that nine-tenths of the first nests built each season were constructed on the ground, and two-thirds of the second, but only one-third of the third. The majority of the third nests each season were built higher, generally in bushes. In both species, the seasonal rise in nest altitude paralleled and probably was stimulated by the rising growth of grasses and other vegetation. There are

also geographical and ecological variations in nest height. In the eastern United States, the Brown Thrasher, *Toxostoma rufum*, commonly builds in low shrubs, but in its western range it builds on the ground.

COLONIAL NESTING

Colonial-nesting species present a special case of site selection in which one bird requires a nest site that is surrounded by nests of other similar birds. In certain cases large aggregations may not be true communities, but represent association forced by a lack of suitable nest sites. In most colonial species, however, the birds are probably brought together through some form of gregarious appetite. Such an instinctive response could easily have arisen through natural selection because of the advantages of cooperative defense of nests against predators. As a general rule, the larger the colony, the more successful this defense is. In all true colonies, however, each nesting bird owns and defends a small territory around its nest—a territory whose radius usually corresponds to the reach of its owner's wings or beak. An incipient social tendency in nesting appears in some species such as the Linnet, *Carduelis cannabina,* which at times nests socially and at other times nests in isolation, or in the Great Crested Grebe, *Podiceps cristatus,* which breeds in colonies in northeast Europe and Macedonia but is a solitary nester in central Europe.

Colonies in some species are small groups with perhaps a few dozen nests: for example, those of herons, storks, doves, accipiters, swifts, and a few passerines. Other species may nest in colonies totaling hundreds or thousands of birds: penguins, petrels, gannets, pelicans, flamingos, gulls, terns, and auks. On Macquarie Island south of New Zealand, there formerly existed single colonies of King Penguins, *Aptenodytes patagonicus,* each including millions of birds, and covering 12 to 16 hectares. Hunters killed hundreds of thousands of these birds each year for their oil, until the total island population was estimated to be 7000 birds. Since 1933, the birds have been protected and their numbers somewhat restored.

Ordinarily, colonies are made up of a single species of bird, but sometimes two or more species may compose a nesting aggregation. This is particularly true of related species that require similar nesting sites: gulls and terns; herons, egrets, spoonbills, and ibises; guillemots, auks, and puffins; Jackdaws and Choughs. Occasionally in a large colony of one species there may be one or a few pairs of birds of another species. A small scattering of ducks, grebes, or shore birds may nest in a large breeding colony of gulls and terns. Heron colonies often attract falcons, kites, or hawks. Among 13 east European heron colonies, 11 included the nest of a Peregrine Falcon, *Falco peregrinus,* and in one other instance a Falcon nested only 150 meters from the colony. In five cases the herons and Falcons nested in the same tree! (Makatsch, 1950.) In such associations, the Falcons seem to be attracted not to the herons but to their old tree-top nests, which the Falcons adopt as their eyries.

Some aggregations of birds are based on a predator-prey relationship. The Falkland Skua, *Catharacta skua,* is not primarily a colonial nester, but the easy living made possible by preying on a penguin or gull colony attracts sufficient numbers to make a small adjoining colony of skuas.

In a few colonial species, especially

Figure 14.5. A nesting colony of Cliff Swallows at Deerfield, Wisconsin. These once-abundant mud-nest builders have been eliminated from most of their former range because House Sparrows evict them from their completed flask-like nests. Photo by J. Emlen.

Figure 14.6. The nest of the Social Weaver, Transvaal, Africa. The underside of a nest with its individual entrances is shown at the right. Photos by H. Friedmann.

among the Ploceidae, individual nests are built so closely together that they combine to form a large apartment house or arboreal warren. Each nest, however, is independent of the others and has its own entrance. In the case of the Social Weaver, *Philetarius socius*, the pairs in a colony work together to build a large thatched dome of grasses in an isolated tree in the African veldt. Then, on the under side of this roof, the pairs build their individual flask-shaped nests with downward-directed, pipe-like entrances. Several hundred individual nests may be accommodated under one thatched roof. At times these community nests weigh enough to cause large branches to break.

A somewhat different form of community nest is built by babbling thrushes (Timaliidae) and anis (Cuculidae, subfamily Crotophaginae). Among these birds as many as ten pairs may join forces to build a single nest in which several females will then lay their eggs. The eggs are incubated and the young are fed com-

munally. Although the Groove-billed Anis, *Crotophaga sulcirostris*, are apparently monogamous, Skutch (1959) believes that their habit of communal nesting arose from a strong sense of social attraction and an absence of territorial defense.

PROTECTIVE NESTING ASSOCIATIONS

There are times when even the cleverest placement of a bird's nest will be unavailing against the designs of a persistent predator. Though the bird may locate its nest on a quagmire, in a thorny shrub, at the tip of a willowy branch, in a hollow limb, or on the face of a precipitous cliff, some predatory fish, snake, weasel, or hawk may find the nest and destroy its eggs or young. Many more eggs and young meet this fate than grow to successful maturity. As a result of this high susceptibility to predation, some species, aided by years of natural selection, have adopted extraordinary means of protecting this most vulnerable stage in the bird's life cycle. One of the most striking of these means is the choice, by defenseless birds, of a nesting site in the vicinity of a large, aggressive species. Very commonly small passerine birds, such as sparrows, grackles, weaver birds, and even birds as large as night herons, will build their nests in the edges and undersides of nests occupied by storks, owls, ospreys, hawks, or eagles. In Macedonia, for example, the nests of Imperial Eagles, *Aquila heliaca*, often contain in their fringes the nests of Starlings, *Sturnus vulgaris*, or House Sparrows, *Passer domesticus* (Makatsch, 1950). In such situations the larger, more aggressive bird acts as the "lord protector" of the smaller species by keeping away possible predators, but like a human feudal overlord, it may occasionally exact tribute from the lowly serfs. In the main, however, the larger predatory bird seems to tolerate its smaller tenants, perhaps because it has learned that the quickly darting smaller bird is uncatchable. In British Guiana, small tyrant flycatchers and tanagers characteristically nest around the nest of a large aggressive flycatcher, *Pitangus*, whose noisy intolerance of other predatory birds protects both its own nest and those of its satellites.

In a similar way, many birds have become hangers-on of human communities, profiting from the relative absence of hostile predators near man-made dwellings. In the Cameroons, the Masked Weaver, *Ploceus cucullatus*, builds its nests along the village streets with the heaviest traffic (Stresemann, 1934). In Europe, the Serin, *Serinus canarius*, seems to nest along congested streets in preference to those with less traffic. Among the species more commonly associated with human communities are storks, pigeons, Jackdaws, *Corvus monedula*, Rooks, *Corvus frugilegus*, swallows, swifts, weaverbirds, sparrows, robins (both American and European), and starlings. There are, of course, other advantages to living in human communities, such as protected nesting sites and unusual food sources.

Even more curious is the pronounced tendency of many small, inoffensive tropical birds to build their nests in the vicinity of nests of aggressive insects. In Australia, the Black-throated Warbler, *Gerygone palpebrosa*, is called the "hornet-nest bird" because it so commonly nests beside hornets' nests (Chisholm, 1952). The South American Cacique, *Cassicus cela*, commonly builds its flask-shaped hangnest near the nests of arboreal wasps. As many as eight or ten Cacique nests may be clustered about a wasp nest, often so close that the birds' nests rub each other in the wind (Beebe, *in* Stresemann, 1927–1934). Frequently the species that associate with ants, bees, and wasps are community nesters. Evidence indicates that in most if not all of these associations, the birds seek the insect's nest and not vice versa (Hindwood, 1955). As a rule, the insects do not bother the nesting birds but do attack humans and other animals that come too close.

Most remarkable of all are those tropical birds which make their nests *inside* the nests of stinging or biting insects. The woodpecker, *Micropternus brachyurus*, regularly nests in the center of the spherical, papier-mâché tree-nest of ants of the genus *Cremastogaster* (Stresemann, 1934). The Ruddy Kingfisher, *Halcyon coromandus*, of Borneo lays its eggs "in the pendulous nest of a peculiarly vicious bee" (Pycraft, 1910), while Australian kingfishers of the genera *Halcyon* and *Tanysiptera* prefer to excavate their homes in the occupied nests of tree termites, as do several Papuan and Brazilian parrots. In Australia, three species of parrots and five of kingfishers regularly excavate their nest-burrows in termites' nests (Chisholm, 1937, 1952). In many of these odd partnerships the insects neither bother the birds nor seem to benefit from the birds' presence. The birds, on the other hand, are protected, at least by the ants, bees, and wasps, from predators, and in some cases eat the insects and their young.

Tropical birds are so abundantly surrounded by tree-dwelling predators—insects, snakes, lizards, monkeys, and other birds—that defenseless species are hard put to lay their eggs and raise their young in security. This no doubt accounts for the fact that while in the temperate zone most nests are open cups, in the tropics over one-half of all bird nests are covered over on top, with the entrance at the side or bottom where access by predators is difficult. Tree-cavity nests in the tropics offer safety as long as the birds occupy them. Once they are abandoned, bees and wasps soon take them over. In Southern Rhodesia one ornithologist erected 23 nest boxes to attract hole-nesting birds. The first year over half of the boxes were occupied by bees and wasps, and the second year all of them. "It therefore seems likely that small birds such as pygmy parrots which drill their nest holes in swarming termite houses, actually play one kind of insect against the other" (Gilliard, 1958).

FORMS OF NESTS

Birds' nests appear in an almost infinite variety of forms, ranging from a mere depression in the ground to the most intricately woven, multi-chambered hangnest. Ordinarily the character of a nest is determined by heredity, the raw materials used, the site chosen, the experience and adaptive intelligence of the builder, and possibly by imprinting or imitation. In a large number of species the nest-building instinct has been lost completely, although it may persist among some of their near relatives.

Among birds that build no nest there are those like many sea birds, shore birds, goatsuckers, and vultures that lay and incubate their eggs on the bare ground or some similarly unprepared place. The Fairy Tern, *Gygis alba*, lays and incubates its single egg on the bare branch of a tree. The subspecies *candida*, of Cocos Keeling Island, lays its egg in the angle between two leaflets of a horizontal frond of the coconut palm. As the frond matures it droops and withers until it eventually falls. Among settlers discovering a Tern incubating on a withering leaf "it is an object

of keen betting . . . whether the young bird will be hatched out before the leaf falls" (Pycraft, 1910). A remarkable substitute for a nest is contrived by the King and Emperor Penguins, *Aptenodytes patagonicus* and *A. forsteri*, which hold their solitary eggs off the antarctic ice on top of their webbed feet and envelop them in a warm fold of belly skin. The penguins are even able to waddle about while thus incubating their eggs.

Other birds that build no nests are those species which use the abandoned nests or burrows of other birds or mammals, or such species as may forcibly evict the rightful owner from its nest, or nest parasites, such as many cowbirds and cuckoos, which lay their eggs in the nests of other species, abandoning them to the care of the foster parents. Often hawks, kites, falcons, and owls use abandoned nests of herons, crows, magpies, and rooks. Shearwaters often use old rabbit burrows. Many small passerine species, such as the Tree Swallow, *Iridoprocne bicolor*, the Bluebird, *Sialia sialis*, and Crested Flycatcher, *Myiarchus crinitus*, will nest in old woodpecker holes, supplying them, however, with soft lining materials. Species that forcibly expropriate other birds' nests include the House Sparrow, *Passer domesticus*, Starling, *Sturnus vulgaris*, and the Piratic Flycatchers, *Legatus leucophaius*. The Burrowing Owl, *Speotyto cunicularia*, of California, takes over the holes of ground squirrels. After campaigns of ground squirrel extermination, the Burrowing Owl population drops accordingly. A study of Australian birds by Roberts (1955) revealed 80 species that use the nests of other birds.

For many ground nesters, such as ostriches, sand grouse, some petrels, falcons and vultures, and many shore birds, a slight depression in the soil serves as a nest. Some gannets, terns, gulls, or puffins may add a modest amount of vegetation or feathers to the scrape; some penguins, plovers, and terns may collect stones as nesting material. Many ground nesting birds such as ducks, pheasants, grouse, and sparrows build well formed cup-

Figure 14.7.   The nest of the European Stone Curlew is merely a shallow depression on the ground where small stones or rabbit droppings (shown here) may be present. Both the egg and the newly-hatched young show obliterative coloration. Photo by E. Hosking.

Figure 14.8.   A Bank Swallow colony. The burrows are dug horizontally from two-thirds to a full meter in depth, ending in a small nest chamber. Photo by E. Hosking.

shaped nests of grasses and other vegetation. Some water birds, such as coots, rails, jaçanas, and grebes, build floating or shallow-water nests of reeds, rushes, and other aquatic vegetation.

One of the more secure forms of nest is that made in a cavity. Birds may dig their own holes or use ready-made ones. Excavated cavities may be made in the ground (by most of the smaller Procellariiformes), in vertical banks (by kingfishers, motmots, bee-eaters, some swallows), or in living or dead trees (by woodpeckers, some titmice, some trogons). The Rhinoceros Auklet, *Cerorhinca monocerata*, of British Columbia, has been observed nesting underground in holes 8 meters long, bee-eaters in holes 3 meters long, and kingfishers in holes 2 meters long—all dug by the birds themselves. The Burrowing Owl, *Speotyto cunicularia*, uses only its feet in digging its burrow, but the kingfishers, bee-eaters, and swallows dig with their beaks and eject the loose earth with their feet somewhat like a digging dog. A pair of small Asiatic kingfishers, *Ceyx tridactylus*, dug a hole one-quarter meter deep in 40 minutes. Typically, in these earthen burrows, the eggs are laid in a chamber at the inner end, either on the bare ground or in the midst of some nesting materials. Birds that live in lands lacking in trees are likely to be burrowing species.

Most woodpeckers chisel out their own nest holes, generally in sound wood, while the few species of titmice that dig in trees must excavate in pulpy, partially decayed wood because of their weak bills and light skulls. Some species that use ready-made tree cavities may partially close the nest entrance with pitch or clay as nuthatches do, or with mud and droppings as hornbills do. The nest opening of hornbills is made so small that the female must remain a prisoner within the cavity from one to four months, depending on the species, until she and the young break out. In some species, the female leaves before the young, and recloses the entrance. This imprisonment keeps out monkeys and snakes, but it means that the male often must feed the female and young singlehanded. Should the entrance rim be accidentally broken, the unfledged young will instinctively repair it by trowelling fresh "mortar" into place with their bills.

Open nests built above the level of the ground are ordinarily attached to branches or twigs of trees and bushes, and are built of locally available materials such as twigs, leaves, grasses, mosses, mud, plant down, animal hair, feathers, and spider-webs. Often the nest material is intercrossed with the surrounding branches to provide firm attachment to the tree.

Birds of most orders build simple, primitive nests that consist of little more than a platform of sticks and twigs. The weight and activities of a bird near the center of its nest cause the nesting material to pack down and be lower than the rim—a for-

Figure 14.9. The nest and eggs of a Cooper's Hawk. This species instinctively lines its rather primitive stick nest with flakes of bark. Photo by G. R. Austing.

tunate thing for the safety of the eggs. Birds building relatively primitive nests are the cormorants, darters, frigate-birds, herons, bitterns, storks, some accipiters, many pigeons and doves, some cuckoos, and a very few passerine birds—for example, the Rose-breasted Grosbeak, *Pheucticus ludovicianus.* The nests of some of these birds, for example, a frigate-bird, or a Mourning Dove, *Zenaidura macroura,* are so skimpy that the eggs may be seen from below through the bottom of the nest. Eggs sometimes roll off the nest of a frigate-bird when it takes flight. The loose sticks of the frigate-bird's nest may become more securely cemented together with droppings after the young hatch. Occasionally some of the above-mentioned birds build up the rims of their nests with twigs or branches, and thus improve the security of the nest for eggs or young.

Somewhat more elaborate is the cup-shaped nest characteristic of most passerine birds in the temperate zone. Typically a cup nest is composed of a base or platform of coarse materials, a cup of grasses, moss, or some similar fine materials, and a soft, warm lining of fine grasses, hair, plant down, or feathers. Mud, spider webs, or saliva may be used to cement some of these materials together.

The nest of the American Robin, *Turdus migratorius,* provides an example of a moderately well finished cup nest, typical of thrushes. The nest is usually straddled on the limb of a tree or braced in a fork. Its base and outside are composed of coarse grasses, leaves, rootlets, and at times shreds of paper or rags. The inner wall is plastered with mud, and the cup lined with fine grasses. Craft in nest construction progresses by almost imperceptible degrees from such a nest to the exquisitely fashioned cup nests of such species as the American Goldfinch, *Spinus tristis,* which builds its nest externally of fine grasses and moss, and lines it inside with thistledown. So firmly are Goldfinch nests put together that at times they hold water and drown the young. The nest of

the Blue-gray Gnatcatcher, *Polioptila caerulea,* is a beautifully constructed cup of fine grass, moss, plant fibers, and plant down, felted and woven together with spider webbing and covered on the outside with lichens which help to conceal its location. The inside of the cup is warmly lined with hair, thistledown, and other plant floss.

Many species of birds build covered nests. The Magpie, *Pica pica,* both in Eurasia and North America, erects a large dome of thorny sticks over its bulky nest, leaving an opening on one side. One of the ant-thrushes, *Thamnomanes caesius,* fastens over the top of its nest a large leaf that serves as a sun and rain shield. Wrens and dippers commonly build covered nests with side entrances.

Probably the most elaborate of all nests are the covered, pendent nests of various small passerine birds. These hangnests are especially abundant in the tropics, where they help to outwit tree-dwelling predators. It is here that the building of pensile nests has reached its highest perfection, particularly so among the caciques, oropendolas, troupials and orioles—all members of the blackbird family or Icteridae. Hangnests of the polygamous Montezuma Oropendola, *Gymnostinops montezuma,* of tropical America are normally built in colonies of up to 100 nests, all hanging from the tops of tall trees. Each nest is a tubular sac, often as much as two meters in length, with the opening near the top and the nest chamber near the bottom. To leave or enter its nest the owner must crawl up or down this long sleeve. Even such apparently secure nests are occasionally robbed by snakes (Skutch, 1954). Some nests have hidden nest chambers and false entrances, apparently evolved as devices to frustrate predators. The Baya Weaverbird, *Ploceus philippinus,* builds a pensile gourd-shaped nest with two chambers, the lower one for eggs, the upper, an entrance tunnel. The tubular side entrance of the felted, spherical nest of the titmouse, *Anthoscopus caroli,* may be closed each time the bird leaves the nest.

Figure 14.10. One of the more elaborate covered nests is that of the Long-tailed Tit of Europe. It is made of moss, cobwebs, and hair, and covered externally with lichens. Inside, it is warmly lined with as many as 2000 feathers. Photo by E. Hosking.

Figure 14.11. Hangnests of the Central American Oropendola provide security against enemies both by their colonial grouping and by their pendent construction. Photo by A. F. Skutch.

Hangnests are frequently suspended at the tips of slender branches, and quite commonly they hang over water.

MULTIPLE NESTS

In addition to their breeding nests, some species build extra nests that are variously called incomplete nests, dummy nests, cock nests, play nests, or sleeping nests. The variety of names given these nests shows that their significance is not completely clear. A common example of this type of nest-building is provided by the House Wren, *Troglodytes aëdon*. Each season before the female arrives, the male will build several globular masses of twigs in sheltered places, some of them nearly complete, some unfinished. When the female arrives, the male will sing and display before a nest, and creep in and out. If his advertising is persuasive enough, the female will adopt one of the nests, line it with soft materials, and lay her eggs in it. In a three-year study by Kluijver *et al.* (1940) of the European Wren, *Troglodytes troglodytes*, groups of 10, 7, and 8 color-banded males built 58, 57, and 40 nests in three successive years, or an average of 6.2 nests per bird each year. Although some of the males remained unpaired, half of them were polygamous, some having as many as three mates at once. Inasmuch as the most zealous builders were the most successful in attracting females, it may be that in this species multiple nest building represents exaggerated courtship activity. After the young leave the nest they may be led by the male to these extra nests for overnight shelter. A male Long-billed Marsh Wren, *Telmatodytes palustris*, will usually build about six more or less complete nests within his territory. In Australia, the equally industrious Spotless Crake, *Porzana plumba*, builds four to ten extra nests, some of which may be used for brooding the young. The European male Moorhen, *Gallinula chloropus*, sometimes assisted by the female, builds nest platforms or bases on which the

young may later be brooded. Extra nests built by the African Cape Weaverbird, *Hyphantornis capensis*, are used as dormitories both by the male during the incubation period and by the female after the young are large enough to crowd her from the brood nest. Probably as a consequence of the vigor of his building instinct, the male may demolish one of the nests he had built only three or four weeks earlier and use the materials to build a new one. A variation of this activity is seen in the energetic building of the Yellow-tailed Thornbill, *Acanthiza chrysorrhoa*, of Australia. In this species, both sexes build an oblong nest with several chambers inside, one of which is used for rearing the young, and the others possibly as sleeping chambers for the male or possibly for frustrating predators or nest parasites such as cuckoos. The male may continue adding to the nest long after it is functionally complete.

A special case of multiple nest building is found in numerous species whose low intelligence, coupled with their highly developed nest-building instincts, leads them into difficulties. For many species an "ideal" nesting site may prove to be irresistibly magnetic. In nature such sites are ordinarily rare, and a given bird is lucky to find even one. But man's repetitious artifacts at times create an embarrassing wealth of desirable nesting sites. The American Robin, *Turdus migratorius*, has been reported several times to build numerous nests in between the rungs of horizontally hung ladders, or in the corners of steps of fire escapes. Herrick (1935) tells of one Robin that started five nests on different fire escape steps, completed two of them, and laid two eggs in one nest and one in the other. In incubating, it divided its time between the two nests, and after five days abandoned them both. In Ohio, another Robin began 26 separate nests on a wooden girder in the spaces between the roof rafters it supported. Workmen erecting this building supplied the bird with pans of wet clay to line its nests, and placed bets on the location of the final, functional nest. After a week of confused effort spread over these delectable multiple niches, the bird settled on one nest, laid eggs in it, and hatched them. Parallel stories of multiple nestings are told of the Robin's close European relative, the Blackbird, *Turdus merula*. One Blackbird built parts of nine nests between the rungs of a hanging ladder; another built ten nests, of which two were completed (Makatsch, 1950). A pair of European Robins, *Erithacus rubecula*, started to construct 23 different nests in a stack of pipes laid on their sides, while another started 12 nests in a series of pigeon-holes (!) in a workshop (Lack, 1946). It is not always a matter of mistaken orientation among successively repeated nest sites that prompts multiple nest building. One Song Thrush, *Turdus ericetorum*, built five nests one year and six the following year, all in natural, non-repetitive sites. Here, apparently, the bird possessed an abnormally active nest-building instinct.

SIZES OF NESTS

As a rule, birds' nests vary in size with the size of the builder; but this is by no means always true. Very probably the hummingbirds build the smallest and lightest nests, while eagles and storks build some of the largest and heaviest. Nests of White Storks, *Ciconia ciconia*, have measured over 2 meters deep and 1.7 meters in diameter and weighed over a ton. Probably the largest recorded nest of a Bald Eagle, *Haliaeetus leucocephalus*, was one near St. Petersburg, Florida, which was 6.1 meters deep and 2.9 meters wide. These enormous nests are largely the result of years of accumulation of nesting materials at the same site. Sea Eagles, *Haliaëtus albicilla*, have been known to breed annually in the same nest for as long as 60 years. One such nest that crashed down in a storm weighed two tons (Makatsch, 1950).

Perhaps the largest nest in the world is that built by the hen-sized megapodes or "incubator birds" of Australia. The earthen mounds which these birds scratch together with their feet, and in which their eggs are incubated by the heat of decomposing vegetation, may be added to, year after year, until they become 4.2 meters high and 10.7 meters wide (Wetmore, 1931). The nest of the African Hammerhead, *Scopus umbretta*, is remarkable not only for its large size but for its architecture. Although this stork-like bird stands about 30 centimeters tall, it builds a large ball-shaped, clay-lined nest of sticks up to two meters in diameter and firm enough to hold a man on its domed roof. As described by Lydekker (1901) the nest has an entrance on one side so small that the bird must creep in. Inside, the nest contains three chambers: an upper sleeping and incubation room, a middle chamber for the young when they are too large for the upper chamber, and a vestibule or look-out chamber. The nest is usually placed in the fork of a tree near the ground.

Even small passerines may construct massive nests. The Rock Nuthatch, *Sitta neumayer*, of the Balkan peninsula, is a sparrow-sized bird that weighs about 40 gm. Both sexes build the nest in a rock cranny and plaster the opening with a funnel-shaped entrance made of mud mixed with leaves, twigs, and other debris. This earthen nest, including the mortar spread on the rock and in its crevices, may weigh up to 38 kilograms, or about 950 times the weight of one bird (Mayaud, 1950). American nuthatches have lost this Old World trait of building ramparts around their castles except for a vestige retained by the Red-breasted Nuthatch, *Sitta canadensis*, which smears pitch about the entrance to its tree cavity home.

MATERIALS USED IN NEST BUILDING

When one considers the multitude of materials used for building nests, one naturally wonders how a given species knows which materials to select. What causes the Cliff Swallow, *Petrochelidon pyrrhonota*, to select mud for its nest, and the Wood Pewee, *Contopus virens*, to decorate the outside of its nest with lichens? Undoubtedly the majority of such choices are ordered by instinct, but other factors play important roles. Without its abundant down feathers the duck could not line its nest with warm down, and without copiously flowing salivary glands most swifts would be unable to cement other materials together to make their nests. Obviously, the size of a bird limits the size of the building materials it uses. A hummingbird could not use crow-sized sticks for its nest. Further, the habits and habitat of a species restrict its choice of building materials. Water birds are likely to use aquatic vegetation for their nests; meadow birds, grasses; and woodland birds, forest materials.

Modes of transport also influence the choice of nest materials. Most birds carry nesting materials in the beak, but accipiters carry their materials in their talons, while the parakeet *Agapornis* has the remarkable habit of flying to its nest with grass stems, leaves, and woodchips tucked under its rump feathers, which have specially adapted hooklike appendages for this function. While many species carry their twigs, grass, or mud from considerable distances, most ducks, geese, and swans have lost the instinct to carry nest materials, and pull in what leaves, grasses, moss and other plants they can reach with their bills while sitting on the nest site. A short-legged swift which spends its waking hours in flight cannot forage on the ground or in trees for suitable materials, but must snatch its twigs on the wing.

Without doubt the availability and abundance of nest materials have a bearing on their choice by a bird. Nests of the Gentoo Penguin, *Pygoscelis papua*, are built of woody twigs and stalks in the Falkland Islands; of grass, moss, and bits of seaweed at South Georgia; and, still farther south in the Antarctic Archipelago

where terrestrial vegetation disappears, of molted feathers and the bleached bones of their dead relatives. The Chipping Sparrow, *Spizella passerina*, used to be called the Hairbird because it lined its nest mainly with horsehairs. But with the gradual disappearance of the horse in rural America, it has substituted fine grasses for its nest lining. A Chaffinch, *Fringilla coelebs*, which normally coats the outside of its nest with lichens, once used paper confetti instead because it was locally abundant; and doves have been observed using short pieces of rusty wire when these were more easily to be had than the conventional twigs. A Carolina Wren, *Thryothorus ludovicianus*, built its nest of hairpins; and a pair of crows in Bombay once built their nest with 25 pounds worth of gold spectacle frames which they stole from an open shop window (Herrick, 1935).

Materials used in nest construction may be animal, vegetable, or mineral, or various combinations of these. Plant materials are more commonly used than any others. One of the most common types of nests is that made of a cup of interwoven coarser grasses lined with fine grasses, moss, or plant down, and resting on a platform of twigs. Fibers of bark are used in the nests of some vireos, and most woodpeckers use as a nest lining the wood chips left behind from their labors. The tailorbirds of southeast Asia stitch the edges of broad green leaves together to make a funnel-shaped receptacle for their nests. Dippers and hummingbirds often use moss as the main ingredient of their nests. Yellow Warblers, *Dendroica petechia*, and American Goldfinches, *Spinus tristis*, use large amounts of cottonwood- and thistle-down for their nests, while the European Goldfinch, *Carduelis carduelis*, employs slender fir twigs, fine roots, and wool. The Song Thrush, *Turdus ericetorum*, may line its grassy cup with a plaster made of saliva, rotten wood, or dung. The cave-dwelling Oilbird, *Steatornis caripensis*, constructs its heavy, crater-shaped nest with a plaster made of regurgitated seeds and its own excrement. Many sea birds construct their nests of marine algae, which stiffen upon drying. The Parula Warbler, *Parula americana*, typically builds in a hanging clump of the lichen *Usnea*, or the "Spanish moss" *Tillandsia*.

Many birds decorate the outsides of their nests with lichens: several hummingbirds, gnatcatchers, titmice, the Eastern Wood Pewee, *Contopus virens*, Chaffinch, *Fringilla coelebs*, and others. Such a covering, which often matches the surroundings, helps make the nest less conspicuous. Perhaps a latent esthetic sense resides in some species, for they seek brightly colored or shiny objects to decorate their nests. The Moorhen, *Gallinula chloropus*, occasionally places flowers or pieces of paper on the outside of its nest, and various flycatchers, sparrows, finches, and starlings have been observed placing flowers or flower petals in their nests. The fondness of crows and eagles for brightly colored objects in their nests is well known. Gannets, *Morus bassanus*, have adorned their nests with such objects as golf balls, blue castor-oil bottles, strings of onions, and even a clockwork toy steamer (Armstrong, 1942). Red-backed Shrikes, *Lanius collurio*, were found by Shreuers (1941) to be particularly attracted to rags and strings of all colors except green as nesting material, even though the resultant nests were more conspicuous and less stable than those made of the usual native materials. Several sea and shore birds may decorate the edges of their nests with empty mollusc shells and some European nuthatches embellish their nests with sparkling green stones or colored beetle wing-covers.

Some birds are veritable junk collectors. One Red-tail, *Cercomela familiaris*, used in the base of its nest two kilograms of odds and ends, including 361 stones, 15 nails, 146 pieces of bark, 14 bamboo splinters, 3 pieces of tin, 35 old pieces of adhesive tape, 103 pieces of hard dirt, 30 pieces of horse manure, several pieces of rags and bones, 1 piece of glass, and four pieces of old inner tubes (Makatsch, 1950).

During World War II many species of birds collected for their nests the fine strips of aluminum foil dropped by bombers to confuse ground radar stations.

Animal products used in nest building are mainly the wool, hair, and feathers used by many species as warm nest linings. However, cast-off snake skins are used by at least 31 species of birds, notably the Crested Flycatcher, *Myiarchus crinitus*, which commonly drapes such a skin half in and half out of its nest cavity. Bones may be used as nesting materials by owls, kingfishers, penguins, petrels, terns, and others. Spider webbing is many times used by hummingbirds, titmice, white-eyes, flower-peckers, and spider-hunters in nest building, either to bind materials together or to suspend the nest from above. Some hummingbird nests are made of a firm felt compounded of

Figure 14.12. A Lammergeier beside its nest of sticks and sheep wool, in a small mountain cave in Spain. To get at the marrow inside, the species has the habit of dropping large bones on rocks. Hence its ancient name of "Ossifragus." Photo by E. Hosking.

plant down and spider silk. Sometimes these felted nests are suspended from leaves or branches or even from the roofs of caves by thin single cords made of spider webbing. One such nest built by hummingbirds of the genus *Phaethornis* apparently defies gravity in that the nest-cup rides in mid-air in the normal horizontal position, and yet its rim is fastened to the supporting cord on only one side. The mystery of its equilibrium is solved by an ingenious bit of engineering: the bird fastens counter-balancing lumps of clay on the appropriate side of the cup so that it does not tip and spill its inmates.

One animal product that some birds use in their nests is their own saliva. Some swifts, hornbills, and hummingbirds secrete unusually abundant amounts of mucilaginous saliva and use it to cement twigs, grass, feathers, plant down, clay,

and other ingredients into nest forms, and also to glue their nests to supporting branches or walls. The San Geronimo Swift, *Panyptila sancti-hieronomyi*, builds its tubular pendent nest of floss-borne seed collected in mid-air and cemented together with saliva. The Cayenne Swift, *Panyptila cayennensis*, makes its tubular, felted nest of feathers and saliva, and the Chimney Swift, *Chaetura pelagica*, cements together twigs to make its half-cup nest and to glue it to the inside of a chimney or hollow tree. Most exceptional is the Palm Swift, *Cypsiurus parvus*, which fastens its simple, bracket-shaped nest of saliva, feathers and plant fluff on the under side of a withered, hanging palm leaf. The two eggs are cemented to the nest shelf with saliva and therefore cannot be rolled around during incubation as is typical procedure in most incubating birds.

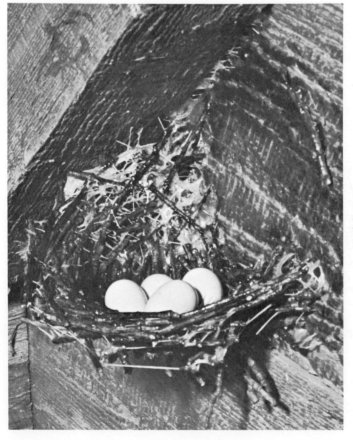

Figure 14.13. A Chimney Swift's nest showing the sticky salivary mucus which cements the twigs together and to the wall. Photo by R. B. Fischer.

Probably the swaying of the leaf in the wind substitutes for this necessary movement. One of the smallest and most delicate nests in the world is that of the Crested Tree Swift, *Hemiprocne mystacea,* of southeast Asia, whose thin, parchment-like nest of saliva, bark-strips and down is glued to one side of a horizontal branch, and is just large enough to hold the bird's solitary egg. While incubating, the bird sits crosswise on the branch so that its weight is supported by the branch and not by the flimsy nest.

Climaxing all of these saliva-containing nests are the nests of the Edible Swiftlets of the genus *Collocalia.* The nests of some of these birds are composed entirely of dried salivary mucus, and are in the form of a small translucent quarter-sphere attached to the face of a rock wall. These are the nests that are prized by the Chinese for making birds'-nest soup. As many as three and one-half million nests have been exported from Borneo in a single year for this purpose. One Javanese species, *Collocalia gigas,* nests regularly behind waterfalls; and another species, *C. francica,* has achieved what is probably the zenith of nest-site security by building its mucus nests in grottoes which can be reached only through an entrance which, at least during high tide, requires diving under the sea! (Stresemann, 1927–1934.)

The salivary glands of some swifts and swallows enlarge greatly during the nesting season. Even so, the Edible Swiftlet that makes its nest exclusively of saliva requires from 33 to 41 days to make one nest. In one night a single Swiftlet deposited a strip of dried salivary mucus 45 mm. long, 8 mm. high, and 2.5 mm. thick (Stresemann, 1927–1934).

Mineral materials used in nest building are largely restricted to stones and mud, although many species make nest scrapes on rock, earth or sand, and others burrow in soils of various sorts. Stones to make nest platforms are gathered by several species of penguins, petrels, plovers, terns, and larks. The Black-necked Stilt, *Himantopus mexicanus,* often paves its scrape with mussel shells. Several species of ground-nesting larks—for example, the Horned Lark, *Eremophila alpestris*—typically build at one side of their grass-cup nest a courtyard paved with small flat stones. Desert larks may erect stone walls around their nests. These may function to shelter the nest from wind or from the eyes of predators. In Spain, the Black Wheatear, *Oenanthe leucura,* has been known to place as many as 76 small stones under its nest and to arrange 282 stones into a sheltering wall 22 centimeters long and 6.5 centimeters high (Makatsch, 1950).

Mud is used extensively and in a wide variety of nests. It may be used alone or mixed with various sticks, pebbles, or fibers. In Australia, the Mudlarks, *Grallina cyanoleuca,* and Apostle-birds, *Struthidea cinerea,* balance their symmetrical bowls of dried mud high on horizontal branches. The mud that is used to build these pottery-like nests is reinforced with horsehair and wool. The nest is lined with soft feathers and grass. Mud nests resembling large inverted pails are built in shallow water by the flamingos (Phoenicopteridae). They scoop together enough mud to erect a mound about 40 centimeters across the top and 50 centimeters high. The Yellow-nosed Albatross, *Diomedea chlororhynchos,* builds a similar nest mound about 30 centimeters high and composed of mud mixed with vegetation. Several species of swallows build their nests largely of mud. The Cliff Swallow, *Petrochelidon pyrrhonota,* builds its retort-shaped nests of mud pellets, and locates them in colonies on cliffs or under eaves of barns (Fig. 14.14). The quality of the mud used may vary locally; nests made of clay are much stronger than those made of sandy silt. In Wyoming and Wisconsin, Emlen (1954) found that Cliff Swallows' nests constructed too rapidly or in humid weather often collapsed before completion. Even nests a month old, and containing well developed young, disintegrated during a prolonged rainy spell.

A much more resistant mud nest is that built by the Rufous Ovenbird, *Furnarius*

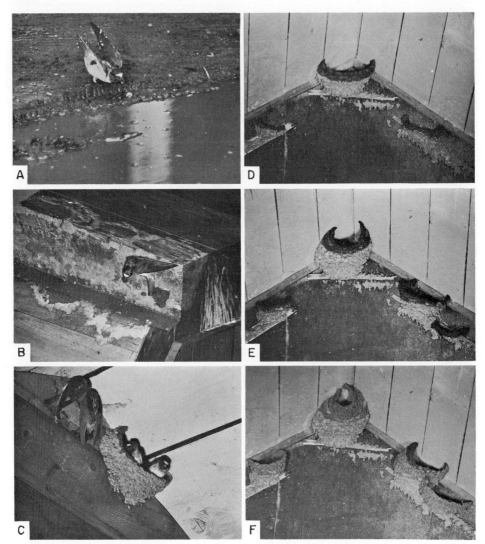

Figure 14.14. Cliff Swallow nest construction: *A*, A Swallow gathering a pellet of mud. *B*, Applying a pellet to a horizontal beam. *C*, Two Swallows in a half-finished nest. *D, E, F*, Successive stages in nest construction. Freshly added mud appears dark. Photos by J. Emlen.

rufus. This species erects its two-chambered, ball-shaped nest on horizontal limbs, or on telephone pole cross-arms, where it withstands all kinds of weather. The Ovenbird is destined to become famous as the bird whose formula for mud saved thousands of human lives. In South America, a trypanosome blood infection called Chagas' disease afflicts estimated millions of humans. It causes severe debil-

itation in adults and is often fatal in children. This incurable disease is transmitted by the bite of an insect, the "barbeiro," which flourishes in the cracks of native mud huts. The simplest way to prevent the disease is to build crack-free houses. Pondering this problem, Dr. Mario Pinotti, head of Brazil's National Department of Endemic Diseases, recalled that as a boy he threw rocks at Ovenbird nests but that

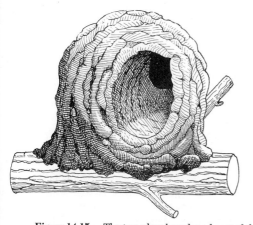
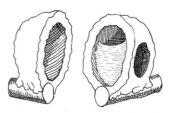

Figure 14.15. The two-chambered mud nest of the Rufous Ovenbird, constructed of a mortar made of sand and cow-dung. The diagram at the right shows a vertically sectioned nest with the entrance vestibule at the right, separated by a partial partition from the egg chamber at the left. After Pycraft.

they never cracked. Research showed that the Ovenbird compounded its house mortar of sand and cow-dung. Following this lead, government health workers plastered 2000 huts with the Ovenbird's odorless cow-dung formula. After six months, every house was free of cracks and free of the barbeiro, although 98 per cent had been infested previously. In 1958, 200,-000 homes were plastered. It is hoped that within a generation 2,500,000 homes will be plastered with the Ovenbird's beneficent mortar and that Chagas' disease will be no more (Time, 1958).

NEST BUILDING BEHAVIOR

Problems of nest construction do not exist for those birds that use abandoned nests of other birds or mammals, or for those that forcibly appropriate occupied nests. By far the majority of species, however, build their own nests. Typically, they build a nest for each brood of young, or, less often, for the successive broods of one season, although some of the larger species, such as storks and eagles, may use the same nest for decades, adding new nesting material each year. Although building a new nest for each generation

of young is expensive in labor, it minimizes the chances of disintegration of a nest while it is sheltering eggs or young, and it reduces the possibility of the accumulation of nest parasites. Also, the experience gained in building several nests rather than one may enable the individual bird to do a better job both in site selection and in nest building.

There can be little doubt that nest-building is primarily an instinctive activity. This interpretation is strongly supported by the simple fact that birds of the same species build nests that conform closely to a given pattern. Over a century ago, Charles Darwin (1845), in his *Journal of Researches,* described the automatic, instinctive nature of nest building in one of the ovenbirds, *Geositta cunicularius,* which normally digs a horizontal nesting burrow about two meters long in a vertical earthen bank.

"Here [at Bahia Blanca] the walls round the houses are built of hardened mud, and I noticed that one, which enclosed a courtyard where I lodged, was bored through by round holes in a score of places. On asking the owner the cause of this, he bitterly complained of the little casarita, several of which I afterward observed at work. It is rather curious to find how incapable these birds must be of acquiring any notion of thickness, for although they were constantly flitting over the low wall, they continued vainly to bore through it, thinking it an excellent bank for their nests. I do not doubt that each bird, as it came to daylight on the opposite side, was greatly surprised at the marvellous fact."

Like the building of multiple nests by robins and other species, this futile digging by the ovenbird illustrates what today is considered a stereotyped, instinctive response to a strong releaser situation —in this case, the mud wall. Even under natural conditions, instinctive nest building can misfire and produce non-adaptive results. When a gull is prevented by its mate or by circumstances from brooding its eggs or young, it commonly indulges in an instinctive displacement activity— in this case, fetching building materials. As a consequence, the size of a gull's nest may be determined by the number of times the bird is prevented from sitting on it (Kirkman, 1937). Oversized nests may become convenient storehouses from which other gulls may pilfer building material. In Norway, so much material, often stolen from such accumulations, is brought to the nests of Black-headed Gulls, *Larus ridibundus*, that eggs, and at times even newly hatched young, are covered over and perish (Ytreberg, 1956). A similar non-intelligent behavior was observed by Roberts (1940) among Wilson's Petrels, *Oceanites oceanicus*, in Antarctica. When surplus moss was placed in front of the nest burrows of these birds, they carried it inside in such quantities that "there was hardly room for the birds to get in," and Roberts had to remove some of the moss. On occasion, the nest-building instinct may operate at the wrong time. A pair of Carolina Wrens, *Thryothorus ludovicianus*, were raising a brood of six-day-old young in a nest box when another male began courting the female and building a "courtship nest" of twigs on top of the nestlings. Neither parent attempted to remove the nesting material on top of the young, but continued feeding them and removing their excrement as best they could. Eventually the intruding male was deported 30 kilometers away, and the brood was successfully raised (Laskey, 1950). Apparently when the time is ripe

for the nest-building instinct to operate, it does so regardless of appropriateness or external adaptability. In his study of the Tricolored Blackbird, *Agelaius tricolor*, Emlen (1941) found that eggs or young experimentally introduced into an unfinished nest would not interrupt the normal course of nest-building activity.

In common with other instinctive acts, nest building sometimes appears in an incipient or "slumbering" form. An eagle bringing food to its young may feed them and then pick up a stick from the nest, carry it a few steps, and put it down. This form of half-hearted playing with nesting materials appears in many species. In the European Wren, *Troglodytes troglodytes*, the male normally builds the shell of the nest and the female lines it with soft feathers and wool. Occasionally the female helps with the male's job of nest construction, and sometimes the male demonstrates feeble nest-lining behavior (Armstrong, 1955).

In an attempt to discover to what extent instinct controlled nest building behavior, Marais (1937) reared four generations of weaverbirds completely divorced from nesting materials. The descendants of these birds wove perfect examples of this species' elaborate nests. Many more experiments of this sort need to be done before one can say with much assurance to what extent nest-building is an instinctive and to what extent a learned performance. It seems very unlikely that young megapodes or "incubator birds" (Megapodiidae) learn much about nest building from their parents. When they burst out of their underground nests they head for a completely independent existence in the brush. Yet, when they reach breeding age, they build nests that are typical of the species.

It is certainly true that birds of many species build better nests as they grow older. Mature female Tree Swallows, *Iridoprocne bicolor*, for example, build better nests, and line them with more feathers, than do year-old females. But whether this is the result of experience or an expression of physiological or psychological maturation, it is at present impossible to say. The diversity of nest-building habits within closely related groups such as the Tyrannidae or Paridae indicates clearly that the instinctive element in their nest-construction behavior is relatively labile and subject to rapid evolution.

That birds are not complete automata in their nest building is suggested by their adaptability to unusual conditions. When half of the nest of a House Martin, *Delichon urbica*, was destroyed by water, the adults repaired the nest, making roughly alternate trips bearing mud for the nest and insects for the young (Rivière, 1940). Other species show similar adaptability.

NEST CONSTRUCTION

In the construction of nests, the sexes may play different roles. Van Tyne and Berger (1959) distinguish six ways in which the labor may be divided between them.

1. Both sexes share more or less equally in building the nest: kingfishers, woodpeckers, swallows.

2. Both sexes gather material for the nest, but the female builds it alone: Rooks, *Corvus frugilegus*.

3. The female builds the nest alone, but the male brings the building materials: doves and pigeons.

4. The female constructs the nest entirely unaided by the male: hummingbirds, manakins, Red-eyed Vireo, *Vireo olivaceus*.

5. The male builds the nest, but the female brings the materials: frigate birds.

6. The male builds the nest entirely unaided by the female: some shrikes, the Philippine Weaverbird, *Ploceus philippinus*.

There are probably about as many different techniques used in building nests as there are species of birds. Only a few examples of the different methods used can be given here. For most species the beak and the feet are the principal tools used.

Birds building nests of grasses and weeds more often work hardest early in the morning, partly, perhaps, because at this time of day the building materials are more moist and pliable. The Great Reed Warbler, *Acrocephalus arundinaceus*, will at times soak a mouthful of dry nesting material in water before weaving it into its nest. Many birds, in constructing the common cup-shaped nest, first build the supporting platform of coarse materials and then build a rim of finer materials to make the bowl.

The shaping of the cup as done by thrushes illustrates a procedure common to many species. The following account is based on the performance of the European Blackbird, *Turdus merula*, as described by Stresemann (1927–1934). The thrush presses its body into the nest mold for about four seconds, then rises for about five seconds, and then presses again. With each successive down-pressing, the bird rotates its body about 36 degrees from the previous position. After about ten down-pressings, the bird makes two to three complete rotations in the same direction. At its next visit to the nest, it may turn in the opposite direction. Should any loose ends of grass stick out, the bird will pull them out and tuck them back into the walls of the nest.

A 17-day-old fledgling Olive-backed Thrush, *Hylocichla ustulata*, will go through these movements. One held in cupped hands by Dilger (1956) snuggled down and "simultaneously kicked backward with both feet and forcibly thrust its breast against the side of the cup. The wings were held rather high on the back but not unfolded and the tail was rather depressed. The bird would perform a few rapid thrusts and kicks and then turn slightly in the cup and repeat these acts." Increased pressure by the edge of a hand against the pushing breast provoked an increased pressure by the bird at this point, suggesting that irregularities in the ring-shape of the cup stimulate compensating thrusts by the bird.

The weaving of a hangnest requires a

Figure 14.16. Hangnest construction by the Baya Weaverbird of India. Upper, A male, on an initial "wad" stage of the nest, is giving the invitation display to a prospecting female arriving in the colony. Lower, Half-built nests at the left. In the lower nest a male is displaying to a female who has just appropriated the nest at the "helmet" stage of construction. When the nest is finished, the lower chamber will be closed to form the egg chamber; the upper chamber will be accessible from the outside only by means of a long, sleeve-like tube directed vertically downward, with the entrance hole at the bottom. Photos by Salim Ali.

more complex performance, and this varies considerably according to the type of nest made. Generally such a nest is started by the bird's hanging several long plant fibers over a branch. To ensure that a given fiber will cling to the branch, the Red-billed Weaverbird, *Quelea quelea*, holds one end of it under its foot and then, with its bill, winds the loose end several times around the branch, as well as around the end of the fiber it is holding

with its foot. It then ties a knot in the fiber by drawing the free end through the narrow space between the branch and that portion of the fiber held under its foot. This stereotyped performance is repeated until there are several dangling fibers, each firmly tied to the branch. The bird then flutters or crawls among the hanging fibers while holding one of them in its beak. Repetition of this movement results in the plaited or woven cord that suspends the nest. Other fibers are next woven into the lower ends of this cord by pushing and pulling them through the slowly developing fabric, and occasionally tying knots in them. Gradually the dangling cord is fashioned into a wreath, a hammock, or a cup, and eventually into the hangnest characteristic of the species.

Actual sewing is performed by the famous Tailorbird, *Orthotomus sutorius*, of southeast Asia. With its sharp bill this small bird pierces holes in the edges of large green leaves and then stitches them together by pulling plant fibers through the holes, making a green funnel-shaped receptacle for its nest.

The use of mud in forming a nest involves either scooping it together in a mound or carrying it a mouthful at a time to the nest site, where the soft pellets are pressed together into the specific nest form. With much ceremonious bowing and braying, the male Black-browed Albatross, *Diomedea melanophris*, brings mud and moss to the nest where the female, with similar ceremony, accepts it and treads it into a large cylindrical mound. Both sexes of the Cliff Swallow, *Petrochelidon pyrrhonota*, carry in their mouths soft pellets of mud to the nest site, where they deposit them in long superimposed rows to form their flask-shaped nests.

For digging holes in wood, woodpeckers have several serviceable adaptations. Their beaks are often chisel-edged at the tip instead of pointed, and their skulls are unusually heavy. To grip the tree they have strong feet, commonly with two opposed toes (instead of one), and stiff tail feathers to brace the hammering body. In

Figure 14.17. The nest of the Long-tailed Tailorbird, showing the stitched leaves which make the container for its fluff-lined nest. The bird first pierces holes in the edges of large leaves with its beak, and then draws plant fibers through, knotting them on the outside so that the stitches will hold. There are 9 species of tailorbirds in southeast Asia. Photo by Loke Wan Tho.

pecking at firm wood they do not strike their blows blindly, but aim them from alternating directions as does a wood-chopper.

In digging its nest hole in a vertical bank, a bee-eater, *Merops apiaster*, first flies repeatedly at the wall with a partly opened beak, sometimes from a distance of several meters, sometimes in rapid forward and backward flights from a distance of only 25 to 30 centimeters. When the hole is deep enough to provide a foothold, the digging pace is accelerated, and when the hole is about 10 centimeters deep the bird works inside it and kicks out the loose soil with its feet.

Some indication of the amount of labor involved in building a nest is provided by the weights of some of the larger nests mentioned previously. The South American Rufous Ovenbird, *Furnarius rufus*, weighs about 75 gm., but its spherical mud nest weighs 3.5 to 4 kg.—perhaps 50 times the weight of the bird. A young, inexperienced Chaffinch, *Fringilla coelebs*, was estimated by Marler (1956) to average

1300 building visits for one nest. Barn Swallows, *Hirundo rustica*, have been estimated to make over 1200 mud-carrying trips to construct one nest. A Long-tailed Tit, *Aegithalos caudatus*, has built into one nest as many as 2457 feathers. A series of nest dissections by Wing (1956) revealed that the nest of the Black-throated Oriole, *Icterus gularis*, contained 3387 separate pieces of grass and plant fibers, some of them as long as 125 centimeters; the nest of the Rose-throated Becard, *Platypsaris aglaiae*, 1844 pieces of leaves, twigs, and grasses; and that of a Purple Finch, *Carpodacus purpureus*, 753 pieces, mostly grass.

With so many pieces and so much weight to carry for one nest, it is not surprising that some species have resorted to pilfering and even outright robbery of nesting materials. Such behavior could easily have stemmed from the habit some birds have of tearing apart one of their old nests to build a new. The Puerto Rican Honeycreeper, *Coereba flaveola*, may tear materials out of her nest while it still contains young, to build a new nest for the next brood. She may also steal materials from the nest of a brooding neighbor (Biaggi, 1955). The Mexican Violet-eared Hummingbird, *Colibri thalassinus,* may line its nest with plant down stolen from the nest of the White-eared Humming-bird, *Hylocharis leucotis,* sometimes to such an extent that the latter's nest is com-pletely destroyed (Wagner, 1945). Oppor-tunities for thievery of nest materials are particularly good among colonial nesters. Mutual pilfering of nest materials is quite common among penguins, cormorants, pelicans, and storks. At times kleptomania may become infectious, as it sometimes does in colonies of Rooks, *Corvus frugi-legus,* and crescendo into wholesale free-for-all plundering. Nest thievery is so uni-versal among the Antarctic Blue-eyed Shags, *Phalacrocorax atriceps,* that one member of a pair stands guard at the nest while the other sets forth to filch bones, feathers, stones, and seaweeds from its neighbors' nests (Murphy, 1936).

The time consumed in building a nest depends on a number of variable factors such as the size of the nest and its com-plexity; the materials used and the dis-tance they are carried; the species build-ing the nest; whether one or both mem-bers of the pair do the building; the age and experience of the builder; the time of year and the weather; and the geographic latitude.

Birds that lay their eggs on the bare ground require no time to prepare their nest. The larger and more elaborate the nest, the more time required to construct it. It is often difficult to say that a given nest requires a given number of days to be built, because the bird building it may work very energetically at first and then slow down to a leisurely pace. A Kirtland's Warbler, *Dendroica kirtlandii,* observed by Van Tyne (*in* Bent, 1953), made 131 trips the first day, bringing materials to the nest and arranging them, and 59 the second day, completing the body of the nest. The third day she made 7 trips, and the fourth day 6 trips to bring lining for

the cup. Several species are persistent builders, adding materials to the nest throughout the incubation period, and in some birds such as Allen's Hummingbird, *Selasphorus sasin,* the Osprey, *Pandion haliaetus,* and Honey Buzzard, *Pernis apivorus,* materials may be added to the nest up to the time the young leave it.

As a rule, small passerines build their nests in a few days. The Corn Bunting, *Emberiza calandra,* requires only two days; the Field Sparrow, *Spizella pusilla,* 3 days; Red-eyed Vireo, *Vireo olivaceus,* 5 days; American Robin, *Turdus migra-torius,* 6 to 20 days; Carrion Crow, *Corvus corone,* 9 days; Dipper, *Cinclus mexi-canus,* 15 days. The male Long-tailed Tit, *Aegithalos caudatus,* takes about 9 days to build the nest proper, and the female takes 9 days more to line it. The Golden Eagle, *Aquila chrysaëtos,* may build a complete nest in two months, and the African Hammerhead, *Scopus umbretta,* in four months. Large nests such as these last, however, may be used in successive years with or without annual additions of nesting materials, depending on the spe-cies.

The Rufous Ovenbird, *Furnarius rufus,* may require several months to build its nest if dry weather interferes with its mud-gathering. Some tropical humming-birds need green moss to build their nests and in dry years may omit nest building altogether. Species that breed two or more times a year generally build their second nests faster than their first. The American Goldfinch, *Spinus tristis,* takes about 13 days to build a nest in July as against 5 or 6 days in August; and the Prothonotary Warbler, *Protonotaria citrea,* requires about 5 days to build a nest in late May as against 2 days in June.

Geographically, several species have been shown to build their nests with more deliberation in the tropics than their near-est relatives do in temperate regions. Whereas the Kiskadee (Derby) Fly-catcher, *Pitangus sulphuratus,* and Ver-milion-crowned Flycatcher, *Myiozetetes similis,* of Mexico require about 24 days to build their nests, their tyrant flycatcher relatives in temperate North America take only from 3 to 13 days (Pettingill, 1942). This is in spite of the fact that in Mexico both sexes of *Pitangus* work on the nest, while among their northern relatives only the females build. It seems likely that natural selection has accelerated nest-building behavior in birds of temperate regions where the breeding season is shorter.

The survival of any species of animal depends primarily on reproductive success. In the millions of years during which they have been evolving, vertebrates have taken two diametrically opposed paths toward breeding efficiency. One path, followed by the lower vertebrates, has emphasized the production of great numbers of eggs. A fish may lay hundreds of thousands of eggs per year, but may give them absolutely no care. The other path, followed by mammals and birds, emphasizes superlative care of the eggs and young, but of necessity gives that care to very few of them. One of the chief ways in which birds provide that care is by their varied, warm, and wonderfully ingenious nests.

SUGGESTED READINGS

Although they are old books, *Birds' Nests,* by Dixon, and *A History of Birds,* by Pycraft, still have much valuable information on nests. Both Van Tyne and Berger's *Fundamentals of Ornithology* and Wallace's *An Introduction to Ornithology* have good sections on this subject. Barruel's *Birds of the World* gives a brief treatment of nests, and Gilliard's *Living Birds of the World,* although it has no special section or chapter on nests, gives very interesting material on the subject and many striking photographs of different kinds of nests. A very complete, illustrated treatment of nests is given in Makatsch's *Der Vogel und Sein Nest.*

FIFTEEN

Eggs

. . . an egg is full of meat.
Shakespeare

A primitive vertebrate, such as the codfish, may lay as many as 10,000,000 tiny, jelly-like eggs at one spawning, and then abandon them in the ocean to an almost certain death. The few eggs which escape the normal hazards of their environment and grow to maturity require four or five years to become full-sized fish about a meter long. Because of this long, dangerous period of immaturity, the codfish *must* lay a great number of eggs or the species will perish.

This "slaughter of the innocents" is greatly reduced among the reptiles by the use of a more highly developed egg. In contrast to the codfish, a somewhat less primitive tortoise lays only about 100 eggs in an excavated hole in the ground, and leaves them to their fate. The greatly increased probability of survival which is reflected in the relatively small number of eggs is mainly due to two evolutionary innovations. First, the reptile eggs have a tough, water-resistant outer membrane which makes possible their development on land, where food and oxygen are more abundant and where the eggs are inaccessible to a great many aquatic predators and diseases. Second, each egg is large, and stored with enough nourishment to give the hatchling tortoise a rapid and vigorous start in life.

Birds, far less primitive than the tortoise, have carried this principle of a protected, terrestrial development still further. Not only do they lay their large eggs in sheltering nests which are often built in sites inaccessible to most predators, but they hasten the development of the embryo within by warming it with the heat of their own bodies. Moreover, after the young bird hatches, they feed it and protect it until it is able to fend for itself. As a consequence of this painstaking care, a newly hatched bird, in contrast to an infant codfish, may race through the period of vulnerable infancy in a matter of a few weeks instead of months or years, and is sooner able to reproduce and replenish its species' numbers. Since the incubating bird must be able to warm the eggs with its own body, the number of eggs that can be covered is naturally more limited than the numbers of fish or even reptile eggs in one clutch. But this limitation is compensated for, both by the accelerated rate of development made possible by incubation, and by the superlative care most birds give their newly hatched young. A bird that lays only one or two eggs a year may be more efficient reproductively than a fish that lays millions.

FORMATION OF THE EGG

A complete egg is composed of the yolk or ovum, formed in the ovary, and a series of enveloping layers of albumen, shell membranes, and the shell proper, which

are added to the yolk as it descends the oviduct. The following account of egg development is based largely on the egg of the Domestic Hen as described by Sturkie (1954).

The funnel-like infundibulum of the oviduct grips the ripe ovum shortly before it bursts from the ovary (see Fig. 8.3). The ovum remains only about 18 minutes in the infundibulum and is then passed on by peristalsis to the magnum of the oviduct where, in about three hours, it receives its layer of albumen. The egg next passes to the isthmus where it remains about an hour and receives its shell membranes. Next it passes to the uterus where it may remain about 20 hours while receiving its shell and pigment. Finally, the completed egg quickly passes through the muscular vagina and is laid.

When first secreted by the magnum, the albumen or white of the egg is in the form of a single, dense, jelly-like layer; but by the time the egg is laid, four distinct regions of albumen are visible. Innermost is a thin, watery layer within which the yolk may freely rotate. Outside of this layer is a thicker, middle layer of albumen, which, in turn, is surrounded by the thin, outermost fluid layer. The fourth region runs through the other three. It is the chalaza, a pair of dense, twisted cords of albumen attached to opposite ends of the yolk and coincident with the long axis of the egg. The yolk is so centered and suspended in the inner layer of thin albumen

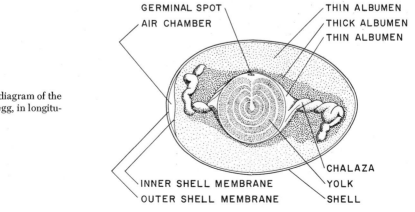

Figure 15.1.   A diagram of the Domestic Hen's egg, in longitudinal section.

GERMINAL SPOT
AIR CHAMBER

THIN ALBUMEN
THICK ALBUMEN
THIN ALBUMEN

INNER SHELL MEMBRANE
OUTER SHELL MEMBRANE

CHALAZA
YOLK
SHELL

by these twisted strands of the chalaza, that it may rotate so that its animal pole is always up and the heavier vegetal pole always down, no matter what the position of the egg in the nest. The chalaza probably arises from protein fibers of mucin of the inner albumen as a consequence of the rotation of the egg as it descends the oviduct.

Egg albumen is composed of three types of protein: mucin and globulin make up about 5 per cent each, and albumin makes up about 90 per cent. Mucin gives the thicker layer of egg white its viscosity. Globulin is most concentrated in the inner thin layer and least concentrated in the outer thin layer. The highest amount of albumin is found in the outer thin layer.

Experiments have shown that the mechanical stimulus of the yolk pressing against the walls of the magnum causes it to secrete albumen. Almost any solid, rounded object inserted in the magnum will become covered with egg-white. However, yolkless eggs show that other stimuli must also be involved.

Two fibrous shell membranes are formed by the isthmus—a thick external membrane and an internal one about one-third as thick. The two membranes separate at the blunt end of the egg to form an air chamber. Both membranes are made of the tough protein keratin.

The shell proper is secreted in the uterus and is composed of a light protein framework similar to collagen, and a heavy deposition of inorganic minerals. The minerals, mainly calcium carbonate, are arranged in the protein matrix as vertical crystals separated by minute pores through which oxygen and carbon dioxide may pass. The shell of a typical hen's egg is composed of about 94 per cent calcium carbonate, 1 per cent magnesium carbonate, 1 per cent calcium phosphate, and 3 to 4 per cent protein. About two-thirds of the calcium used in secreting the shell comes from ingested food, and one-third from calcium stored in the large bones of the body.

Egg shells may be thick or thin depending on the species of bird and the way it treats its eggs. The heavy-footed African Francolins, *Francolinus* spp., have thick-shelled eggs that one "can practically bounce off a wall" (Heinroth and Heinroth, 1958). The heaviest shell known is that of *Francolinus coqui*; the shell amounts to an amazing 28.1 per cent of the total egg weight (Makatsch, 1952). Light-footed ducks, sandpipers, and doves, on the contrary, have thin-shelled eggs. Doves incubate their eggs almost constantly, and hence expose them to few mechanical hazards. Certain species of Indian woodpeckers, which inhabit ants' nests, are reputed to lay eggs with abnormally soft and transparent shells, probably because the woodpeckers' diet of ants is rich in formic acid (Moreau, 1936).

The composition of the entire hen's egg is given by Romanoff and Romanoff (1949) as being made up of 65.6 per cent water, 12.1 per cent proteins, 10.5 per cent lipids, 0.9 per cent glucides, and 10.9 per cent minerals.

Birds' eggs vary greatly in the amount of yolk they contain. By weight the yolk may vary from 15 per cent in some cormorants to about 50 per cent in some ducks (Heinroth and Heinroth, 1958). As a general rule, eggs which hatch out into naked, blind, helpless young (altricial species such as the passerine birds), contain about 20 per cent yolk; those which hatch into immediately active young (precocial species such as the gallinaceous birds and ducks) have about 35 per cent yolk.

SIZE, SHAPE AND TEXTURE OF EGGS

An egg is more than a mere package of food to provision the developing embryo for its start in life. The size, shape, surface, and color of an egg often have additional value for a species. Reasonably enough, large birds lay large eggs, small birds, small eggs. The largest known egg is that of the extinct "elephant bird," *Aepyornis*, of Madagascar, whose eggs,

known only as fossils, held about two gallons and measured 34 by 24 cm. (13.5 x
9.5 in.). Shells of this egg were heavy
enough to be fashioned into eating bowls
by the former aborigines of Madagascar.
At the other extreme is the tiny Vervain
Hummingbird, *Mellisuga minima,* of Ja-
maica, whose egg is less than 10 mm. long.
One egg of *Aepyornis* could hold the contents of about 33,000 eggs of this small
hummingbird.

As a rule, the larger the bird, the
smaller its egg is in relation to the parent's
size. The big ostrich lays an egg which
weighs only 1.7 per cent of its body
weight, while the tiny wren lays an egg
that equals 13 per cent of its body weight.
Among the Procellariiformes, the large albatrosses lay eggs that equal about 6 per
cent of their body weight, the medium-
sized fulmars, eggs 15 per cent, and the
smallest petrels, eggs 22 per cent of their
body weight. Similar studies of related
species of European birds by Makatsch
(1952) revealed the same relationship. The
Black Woodpecker, *Dryocopus martius,*
for example, weighs 300 gm. and lays an
egg that weighs 11 gm. or 3.7 per cent of
its body weight, while the Lesser Spotted
Woodpecker, *Dendrocopus minor,* which
weighs only 21 gm., lays an egg weighing
2.1 gm. or 10 per cent of its body weight.
In comparing in this way the eggs of a
series of large and small related species
within such groups as owls, ducks, falcons,
doves, and gulls, Makatsch found that the
egg-to-body weight ratios of the large
birds averaged only 41 per cent of those
of the small birds. Probably the species
that holds the record for laying the relatively largest egg is the kiwi (*Apteryx* sp.),
a hen-sized bird weighing about 1.8 kg.
Its enormous egg weighs about 420 gm.,
or about one-fourth of its body weight.

There are other weight relationships
that occur fairly systematically. Precocial
species, whose young hatch out alert and
active, usually lay larger eggs than do
altricial species whose young are born
naked and helpless. A 5-kg. precocial
crane, for example, lays an egg which

Figure 15.2.   The Greenshank, an Old World sandpiper, whose four large eggs hatch out into precocial
young. Photo by E. Hosking.

weighs 4 per cent of its body weight;
while the 5-kg. altricial eagle lays an egg
which is only 2.8 per cent of its body
weight. The egg of the precocial Guillemot, *Uria aalge,* is about twice as large as
that of the altricial Raven, *Corvus corax,*
although the two birds are of equal size.
Birds which lay large clutches of eggs
usually lay smaller eggs than do their relatives who lay fewer eggs. Lastly, young
birds commonly lay smaller eggs than
older birds of the same species, and sometimes the younger birds' eggs lack yolks.
There are, however, exceptions to all these
general rules. A special case of adaptive
egg size is found in the European Cuckoo,
Cuculus canorus, whose unusually small
eggs match in size those of the hosts
whose nests the Cuckoo parasitizes. Even
within a single species, eggs may vary in
size. The eggs of the White Heron, *Cas-
merodius albus,* are regularly larger in
Europe than those of the same species in
India. Whether this is caused by an environmental or hereditary influence has
yet to be determined.

The shape of a bird's egg is probably
acquired while it is in the magnum of the
oviduct. The diameter and muscular ten-

sion of the walls of the oviduct, as well as the distribution or packing of visceral organs, probably play a part in determining an egg's shape. There is evidence that the shape of the pelvic bones is related to the shape of a bird's eggs: birds with deep pelves are likely to lay eggs that are nearly spherical in shape, while birds with dorso-ventrally compressed pelves incline toward elongated eggs (Rensch, 1947).

Probably the shapes of birds' eggs are of little significance except for the pyriform or top-shaped eggs of shore birds, auks, or guillemots. These eggs, rather pointed at one end and broad at the other, will roll in a small circle on the ground rather than in a straight line—a valuable feature for the guillemots whose one or two eggs are laid on bare rock ledges on ocean cliffs. A further advantage in such eggs is found in the compact way they pack together when there are three or four in a nest—common numbers for many shore birds. If the four eggs in the nest of a Killdeer, *Charadrius vociferus*, are disarranged, the bird will rearrange them with pointed ends inward much like the

slices of a pie. Not only is the parent better able to cover its eggs, but the heat they receive from its body is dissipated less rapidly, thanks to their compact positioning.

Most birds' eggs have the familiar oval shape of the hen's egg, slightly broader at one end than the other. In some species, such as doves and goatsuckers, the two ends of the egg are equally rounded and the general egg shape approaches an ellipsoid. Among many hawks and eagles the egg is a short oval approaching the nearly spherical egg laid by owls, kingfishers, and bee-eaters. Long, elliptical eggs are characteristic of the stream-lined, rapidly-flying swifts, hummingbirds, and swallows.

In surface texture most birds' eggs are smooth and have a dull matte finish like the egg shell of the Domestic Hen. Different textures are found, however, in numerous species. The eggs of the ostriches, storks, and toucans are deeply pitted, while those of the emu, cassowaries and chachalacas, *Ortalis* spp., are rough and corrugated on the surface. Also rough-

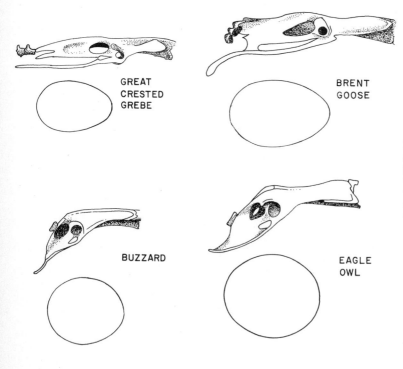

GREAT
CRESTED
GREBE

BRENT
GOOSE

BUZZARD

EAGLE
OWL

Figure 15.3. In some birds the shape of the egg correlates with the shape of the pelvis, especially with the position of the backward-bending ischial bones: the deeper the pelvis, the rounder the eggs. After Rensch.

surfaced are the eggs of grebes, boobies, flamingos, and certain cuckoos. Anis have eggs with a chalky surface layer which easily rubs off and exposes a bluish or greenish deeper layer. In the spectacular egg of the Guira Cuckoo, *Guira guira*, the white chalky layer is deposited in the form of a coarse lattice or network which overlays a deep blue background layer. Another striking variation is found in the tinamous' eggs with their glossy, porcelain-like finish. Woodpeckers also have glossy eggs, and the eggs of many ducks have a greasy, water-repellent surface.

COLORS OF EGGS

Studies of the chemistry of egg pigments indicate that they are mainly derived either from the blood pigment hemoglobin or from bile pigments which are decomposition products of hemoglobin. According to Völker (*in* Makatsch, 1952) there are two chief egg pigments: porphyrins, derived from hemoglobin, which are responsible for the brown and olive colors, and cyanin from the bile, which makes blue and green pigments. Pigments may appear singly or together in an egg, or not at all. They may occur in different layers, or penetrate throughout the shell as in tinamou eggs. In the cassowary egg, the outside of the shell is uncolored; the inside layer is green. In certain hawks and passerines, only the very outside of the shell is pigmented. All pigments are secreted by the walls of the oviduct, particularly in the region of the uterus.

In many species, the egg is of a uniform color or tint: blue or greenish blue in many cormorants, thrushes, herons, and starlings; ivory in the ostrich; pale green in many ducks; dark green in the emus; olive brown in some bitterns, and nearly black in the tinamou *Notoprocta perdicaria*. Solidly black eggs have been collected in northeastern South America for many years, but the identity of the bird laying them remains a mystery. In Europe, Cetti's Warbler, *Cettia cetti*, lays eggs that are colored a deep brick-red. The eggs of many birds are white or nearly so. Some birds occasionally forsake their characteristic egg color and lay reddish eggs, only to return to the usual color later. This inexplicable aberration is known as erythrism and is seen in the eggs of the Red-backed Shrike, *Lanius collurio*, and other species.

On these various ground colors—usually white, gray, cream, brown, red, blue, or green—there are arranged in many species blotches, specks, or streaks of brown, red, lavender, gray, black, and other colors. Or, as in the beautiful egg of the Kingbird, *Tyrannus tyrannus*, the spotting may be made of combinations of different colors. The spots may be large or small, many or few. Often, as in the eggs of many sparrows, the spots are concentrated in a wreath around the larger end of the egg. Spots apparently result if the egg stands still while small pigment glands in the wall of the uterus apply the color. If, on the contrary, the egg moves, lines of various shapes—spirals, rays, or random scrawls—result. The blue egg of the Redwinged Blackbird, *Agelaius phoeniceus*, is marked with dark purple or black scrawls which indicate that the egg moved about erratically in the uterus while the pigment glands secreted their color.

Ordinarily, the eggs of a given kind of bird are sufficiently uniform and fixed in coloration so that a student can tell a species by its eggs. However, variations do occur within species and genera that are at times more extreme than the fluctuations between the familiar white and buff eggs of the Domestic Hen. The highly burnished eggs of the several species of South American tinamous vary "from pale primrose to sage-green or light indigo, or from chocolate-brown to pinkish orange" (Newton, 1896). The Bluebird, *Sialia sialis*, which normally lays blue eggs, shows a modest variability in color. Of 774 eggs laid in nest boxes in a Nashville, Tennessee park in 1952, 71 (9.1 per cent) were white, the rest, blue (Laskey, 1943). Probably the most extreme intraspecific variability in egg color is found in the Guillemot, *Uria aalge.* This species lays a large, pyriform egg whose ground color may be "deep blue-green, bright reddish, warm ochreous, pale bluish, creamy or white, usually marked richly or sparingly with blotches, spots, zones or intricate patterns of interlacing lines which vary in color from light yellowish-brown to bright red, rich brown or black, sometimes quite unmarked" (Jourdain *in* Witherby *et al.* 1949). Since these birds nest in enormous colonies where each female lays her single egg on an exposed rock ledge, this color variability is apparently an adaptation to help a given bird identify its own egg or nest. Extensive experiments by Tschantz (1959) showed that a bird could be induced to accept a strange egg only if the color and pattern were similar to its own. A different color or pattern caused the egg to be rejected.

Even an individual bird may lay eggs of different colors. Sometimes such a change may occur with age, but in some instances eggs of the same clutch may vary in color. A captured bird will at times lay an egg deficient in coloration, indicating either that disturbance and captivity have arrested the secretion of pigment, or that the egg, laid prematurely, did not remain in the uterus long enough to receive its full quota of pigment.

Originally bird eggs were probably white, as reptile eggs now are. With time, natural selection may have favored colored bird eggs because of their inconspicuousness. This explanation gains support from the fact that white eggs are generally restricted to hole-nesters (swifts, owls, most petrels, some doves, parrots, woodpeckers, kingfishers, bee-eaters, rollers, and others); or to open-nesters which begin incubation after they lay the first egg (some doves, herons, hummingbirds, owls, grebes); or to those open-nesters which cover their eggs with down or vegetation when they leave the nest (some ducks, geese, grebes, and many gallinaceous species) (Stresemann, 1927–1934). Most other open-nesters, particularly those laying their eggs on the bare ground

(excepting those like the Guillemot which nest on inaccessible ledges), lay concealingly colored eggs. In an analysis of egg color in birds of the thrush family (Turdidae), Lack (1958) discovered that egg color was of no taxonomic significance, but that it showed a relationship with the type of nesting site: hole-nesting species tended to have immaculate white eggs; shallow-hole and niche nesters, speckled white, immaculate blue, or speckled blue; ground-nesters surrounded by vegetation, obscured brown, gray, or olive eggs; those nesting in forks of branches, eggs with blotches or shadow-marks on a white or blue background. The white eggs of hole-nesters "Perhaps result merely from the absence of selection by predators, but more probably are adapted to increase the visibility of the eggs to parents in dim light." In western India occurs the Yellow-wattled Lapwing, *Lobipluvia malabarica,* whose eggs closely match the color of the bare ground on which they are laid. One region along the Malabar Coast has a brick-red, sandy, laterite soil, scattered through which are black nodules of ironstone. In this particular region the Lapwings lay red eggs with brownish specks "exactly like the ground on which they are deposited" (Baker, 1923). Probably the most highly adaptive egg coloration in the world is that found in the European Cuckoo, *Cuculus canorus.* Different races of this species lay eggs whose colors and markings match, often with astonishing fidelity, the eggs of the host species whose nests they parasitize.

THE TIME OF LAYING

The laying of eggs is of course part of the reproductive cycle which, as shown in Chapter 8, is under the close control of the endocrine glands. The activity of the glands, in turn, is responsive to a variety of environmental stimuli: length of day, precipitation, temperature, food availability, psychic stimuli, and perhaps others. Long continued natural selection, working through such influences on the breeding cycle, has caused each species to lay its eggs at such a time that the young will hatch when conditions are most favorable for rearing them. In species with a long incubation period, this may mean that the eggs must be laid during an inhospitable season, as is the case with the Great Horned Owl, *Bubo virginianus*, which in Florida lays its eggs in mid-December, and in Pennsylvania and Iowa lays them in mid-February. By the time the eggs hatch, the spring crop of rodents is becoming available as food for the hungry young owls. Similarly, the Emperor Penguin, *Aptenodytes forsteri*, lays its single egg in late June or July in the depth of the dark antarctic winter. When the young hatch out 53 days later, it is still bitter winter, with temperatures as low as −50° C. In the relatively mild spring and summer days that soon follow, the young are able to fatten up on the abundant food of polar waters, but barely in time to reach independence by the onset of the next winter. That the time of egg laying and the advance of spring are nicely synchronized is seen in the nesting records of the British Trust for Ornithology for the Meadow Pipit, *Anthus pratensis*. At sea level, the bird lays its eggs an average 3.8 days earlier in the south of Britain than in the north, and it begins laying one day later for each 40 meters rise in elevation (Coulson, 1956). However, the advance of spring is not rigidly controlled by the calendar, and it may vary from year to year. In their study of the Alpine Swift, *Apus melba,* Lack and Arn (1947) discovered that the species began nesting around May 17 during 9 years of good spring weather, and around May 31 in 8 years of cold, wet weather.

Much later than other falcons, the Eleanora Falcon, *Falco eleonorae,* begins laying its eggs around the first of August on the Cyclades Islands off Greece. Here the timing is dictated by food availability. Until late in the summer, small birds, the preferred food of this falcon, are very scarce on the Cyclades; but in the early fall, hordes of small migrating passerines throng the island and furnish food at just the right time for the growing young falcons (Stresemann, 1927–1934).

Not only may environmental stimuli initiate egg-laying in birds, but they may cause a suspension of laying. If, in the course of laying, the nest of a Serin, *Serinus canarius*, is destroyed, the bird will cease laying until a new nest is constructed (Benoit, 1950).

Like the Domestic Hen, most passerine species lay their eggs at one-day intervals until the clutch is completed. Usually larger species require longer intervals between eggs than smaller species. Since an ovum will not ordinarily be released by the ovary and enter the oviduct until the previously formed egg has been laid, the egg interval of a species depends chiefly on the time it takes the oviduct to secrete the various egg layers around the ovum. Often the last eggs of a clutch come at greater intervals than the first ones. The European Oystercatcher, *Haematopus ostralegus*, for example, lays its second egg a trifle more than 24 hours after the first, but the third and fourth eggs come at intervals of 48 hours or more. Cold, wet weather, as well as psychic influences, may delay the normal pace of egg laying. The egg interval may on rare occasions be shortened, as was the case with the Yellow-shafted Flicker, *Colaptes auratus*, which laid two eggs within 13 hours (Sherman, 1910). The examples of egg intervals which follow are taken from Stresemann (1927–1934) and Makatsch (1952).

Table 15.1. Intervals Between Successive Eggs in a Clutch

---

24 hours: most passerine birds, many ducks, some geese, woodpeckers, rollers, the smaller shore birds and smaller grebes.

38 to 48 hours: ostriches, rheas, larger grebes, some ducks, swans, herons, bitterns, storks, cranes, bustards, doves, some accipiters, owls, some cuckoos, hummingbirds, swifts, kingfishers.

62 hours: some cuckoos and goatsuckers.

3 days: emus, cassowaries, penguins (*Pygoscelis*).

4 to 5 days: Lammergeier, *Gypaëtus barbatus*, Spotted Eagle, *Aquila clanga*.

5 days: condors, kiwis.

5 to 7 days: Booby, *Sula cyanops*, some hornbills.

4 to 8 days: some megapodes.

Eggs are laid by many species early in the morning, even before sunrise, but there are many deviations from this schedule. The Ringed Plover, *Charadrius hiaticula*, lays its eggs at all hours of the day and even at night. The European Cuckoo, *Cuculus canorus*, seems to prefer the afternoon. Many pheasants and the Common Gull, *Larus canus*, may lay their eggs in the evening; the American Coot, *Fulica americana*, shortly after midnight. Painstaking studies by Skutch (1952) of Central American birds showed that tanagers, finches, wood warblers, honeycreepers, wrens, and hummingbirds usually lay early in the day, from before sunrise to soon after. Tyrant flycatchers often lay later in the forenoon. Salvin's Manakin, *Manacus aurantiacus*, and two species of Crotophaga lay around midday, and the goatsucker, *Nyctidromus albicollis*, late in the afternoon. For a species whose egg interval does not correspond with the 24-hour solar day, the time of laying on successive days will vary. The Domestic Hen and the Bobwhite, *Colinus virginianus*, lay their eggs somewhat later each day until laying occurs in the evening. Then the birds skip a day and lay the next egg in the early morning.

To lay a single egg requires only a few seconds in the case of brood parasites like the Cowbird, *Molothrus ater*, or the European Cuckoo; but three to ten minutes for the Bobwhite, and an hour or so for geese. In the act of laying, a bird typically raises the front end of the body, opens its mouth and breathes rapidly, spreads and vibrates its wings and then drops them. Finally it opens its beak wide, and, with obvious straining, lays the egg (Makatsch, 1952).

CLUTCH SIZE

A curious fact, and one difficult to explain satisfactorily, is the great variation in the number of eggs that different birds lay. Some lay but a single egg: the larger penguins, petrels, albatrosses, guillemots, some large vultures, most puffins, the larger doves, several swifts and goatsuckers. Two eggs per clutch are laid by the kiwi, most penguins, loons, boobies, many eagles, cranes, some auks, most pigeons and doves, some goatsuckers and hummingbirds, and many passerines in the tropics; three eggs: most gulls and terns; four eggs: most snipe, plovers and sandpipers; four to six eggs: most passerine species at higher latitudes; eight to twelve eggs: ducks, gallinaceous birds, titmice. One might expect those species that lay many eggs to be more successful in reproducing their kind than those that lay few eggs, but this does not seem to follow.

Certainly, for most species, clutch size is determined by heredity, probably as a consequence of years of natural selection —selection for the optimum number of eggs per nest for a given species and its way of life. For some species, such as the extinct Passenger Pigeon, *Ectopistes migratorius*, many petrels, shearwaters and albatrosses, clutch size is constant. In other birds it may be more flexible. A study by Burns (*in* Bent, 1939) of 169 nests of the Yellow-shafted Flicker, *Colaptes auratus*, revealed clutches varying in size from 4 to 14 eggs each, although the larger sets may have been the product of two females.

Certain regular patterns in clutch-size variation suggest a number of factors, chiefly environmental, which may influence the number of eggs a given bird or a given species may lay. Birds in northern latitudes, for example, often lay larger clutches than their relatives in the tropics. The factors in variation may either be ultimate factors which operate through natural selection on the hereditary control of clutch size, or proximate factors which operate more directly on the physiology of egg production. Among factors which have been suggested as having some control over clutch size are the following: size of bird; age of bird; size of nest; size of eggs; the number of eggs the bird can successfully incubate; the number of young that can be successfully raised; the number of broods per season; intensity of predation; population density; geographic distribution; migration; time of year; length of daylight; climate and weather; type of habitat; food: its nature, abundance, and availability; the number of parents caring for the young. Subtle mixtures of these variables make it extremely hazardous to say with much certainty which factor has how much influence in determining the clutch-size of a given bird or species. Nevertheless, certain correlations seem quite apparent, and probably represent cause-and-effect relationships.

In many instances, larger species lay fewer eggs than their smaller relatives. For example, the Goshawk, *Accipiter gentilis*, lays three or four eggs per clutch while the smaller Sparrow Hawk, *Falco sparverius*, lays five to seven. The large Black Woodpecker, *Dryocopus martius*, lays an average of 4 eggs, and the Lesser Spotted Woodpecker, *Dendrocopus minor*, 6. Possibly this relationship reflects the inability of smaller birds to combat predators as successfully as larger species, and therefore represents an adaptive compensation in clutch-size for a heavier loss of young. In Africa, Moreau (1944) found that within a given family the tendency is for larger birds to have smaller clutches.

Nest size in itself may limit the size of a clutch. Perhaps as a means of concealment from predators, the nest size of some Old World flycatchers and cuckooshrikes has been reduced to such an extent that the incubating female completely hides the small nest. Of birds belonging to the genera *Microeca* and *Lalage* (Campephagidae), those species laying and hatching only one egg build tiny nests that are much more difficult to discover than those species laying two eggs (Stresemann, 1927–1934).

Clutch size and egg size seem to be related in a complementary fashion, but the significance of the relationship is not clear. Of two related goatsuckers in India, the larger species, *Batrachostomus javen-*

sis, lays two eggs; the smaller, *B. moni-leger*, lays one, which, however, is considerably larger than one egg of *javensis* (Stresemann, 1927–1934). Here the primeval dilemma of race survival—whether to devote more care to fewer but larger eggs, or to dilute the care and gamble on greater numbers of young—seems to have been resolved by natural selection through pushing close relatives in contrary directions.

It is obvious that there must be some limit to the number of eggs a given bird can lay, cover, and successfully incubate. However, this limit does not seem to have been reached, at least in some species. Wagner (1957) demonstrated experimentally that two species of Mexican finches could successfully incubate and rear clutches of four or five, instead of two or three eggs, suggesting that, in these species, clutch size was determined by other factors.

Lack (1954) holds the opinion that clutch size depends on the largest number of young that the parents can successfully feed. While this theory seems to be supported by observations on temperate zone swifts, experiments by Skutch (1949) with tropical tanagers showed that larger than normal broods of nestlings could be successfully fed by parent birds who adjusted their rate of feeding to the increased demands of the brood.

Geographic variation in clutch size is known for many species. As one moves away from the tropics toward the poles, the clutch size of geographic races of a given species (or of species of a given genus) increases strikingly. This has been found to be true for birds of various orders; passerines, gallinaceous birds, owls, hawks, rails, gallinules, herons and others. Many tropical American tyrant flycatchers, troupials, tanagers, and finches lay only two eggs, but their temperate zone relatives lay four to six eggs (Skutch, 1949). The European Robin, *Erithacus rubecula*, lays average clutches of 3.5 eggs in the Canary Islands, 4.9 in Spain, 5.8 in Holland, and 6.3 in Finland (Lack,

1953). This widespread and striking increase in clutch size with increase in latitude seems to be due, in part, to two influential factors: latitudinal differences in mortality and in day-length. For birds residing in temperate and arctic zones, the hazard of winter climate must increase the mortality rate; if the birds migrate south for the winter, the sometimes greater hazards of migration do the same. Clutch sizes in European titmice seem to bear this out. The sedentary Marsh Tit, *Parus palustris*, Willow Tit, *P. atricapillus*, and Crested Tit, *P. cristatus*, generally have one brood a year and average 8 eggs per clutch. The migratory Great Tit, *Parus major*, Blue Tit, *P. caeruleus*, Coal Tit, *P. ater*, and Long-tailed Tit, *Aegithalos caudatus*, commonly have two broods per year and average about 12 eggs per clutch (Steinfatt, 1938). In contrast to the dangers of a northern winter, the benefits of a northern summer are equally great. Birds breeding in northern latitudes are assured abundant food, particularly protein-rich insect food, and daylight up to 24 hours in length, for feeding their augmented broods. Birds settled throughout the year in the tropics are exposed neither to the catastrophes of winter nor of migration, and accordingly have less need for large clutches or a high reproductive rate. Nature seems rarely to push a species' reproductive performance much beyond a comfortable "live and let live" level.

An unintentional experiment that supports this day-length, clutch-size argument arose from the transplantation of the European Goldfinch, *Carduelis carduelis*, to Australia about 100 years ago. Today, in Australia, this species averages 3.7 eggs to a clutch; in ancestral Britain, the species averages 5 eggs. This shrinkage in the clutch size of the Australian Goldfinch is thought by Frith (1957) to be due at least in part to the shorter day-length in Australia for food collecting, which in turn reduces the number of young that can be raised. From extensive studies of equatorial African birds representing 22 families, Moreau and Moreau (1940) reported that during the breeding season these birds had "a working day more than 30 per cent shorter than the average in the British nesting season" and that "practically without exception African broods run smaller in number than those of allied Temperate Zone birds."

Long days in the northern regions not only provide more hours in which small birds can hunt food for their young, but they also give diurnal predators more time for finding and killing the young birds—a further evolutionary incentive toward large clutches. There is reasonably convincing evidence that the larger clutches of temperate zone species are an adaptation to the selective forces of higher mortality due to the rigors of winter, migration, and increased hours of predation in the nesting season, coupled with the opportunities that longer days afford for raising larger broods. There are, of course, numerous exceptions to this general tendency, particularly among those species having a constant clutch size. Against this principle of larger broods in long-day regions, one must balance the fact that in many species an *increase* in latitude brings a *decrease* in the number of clutches per season. In Tennessee, the Prothonotary Warbler, *Protonotaria citrea*, rears two broods a year; in Michigan, one. In Mediterranean regions, the Nightingale, *Luscinia megarhynchos*, typically has two broods; in central Europe, one. Nevertheless, the evidence now available supports the general principle that most temperate zone birds lay more eggs per season than their tropical relatives.

Regional variations in clutch size also occur among populations of the same species living at the same latitude. In southern Africa the Palm Swift, *Cypsiurus parvus*, lays 2 eggs; but in Madagascar, 3. Contrariwise, the average clutch of many passerines, hawks, owls, and gallinaceous birds in central Europe is about one-half an egg larger than the average clutch of the same species in England. This is thought by Lack (1954) to be due to a difference in food supply, especially in insects, which are probably more abundant in drier central Europe than in rainy England.

Climatic conditions influence clutch size in certain species, probably in most instances through controlling their food supply, but also probably through the direct influence of weather on egg-laying. Cold, humid weather may cause a reduction or even a complete suspension of laying. Swifts and swallows which feed on air-borne insects lay larger clutches in fine sunny seasons than in cold, wet ones. The weather in the Canton of Vaud, Switzerland, in 1948, was unfavorable and the mean clutch size of 40 nests of the Barn Swallow, *Hirundo rustica,* was 4.0 eggs. In the favorable summer of 1951, the mean clutch size for 70 nests was 4.6 eggs (Nicod, 1952). In a contrary way, wet seasons in dry regions may bring more food, and with it, larger clutches. A four-year study of the Horned Lark, *Eremophila alpestris,* in Montana, showed that this species laid larger clutches in wet years than in dry (Dubois, 1936). In Tunisia, a severe drouth in 1936 reduced the average clutch size of three species of larks from the normal 5 or 6 eggs to 2 or 3 (De Guirtchitch, 1937).

Among certain species, more food definitely means more eggs. Snowy Owls, *Nyctea scandiaca,* lay twice as many eggs in good lemming years as in poor years. Hawks and owls generally have larger clutches in years when mice are abundant. In Europe, Magpies, *Pica pica,* may increase their clutches by an egg or two in years when June beetles are abundant; and the Nutcracker, *Nucifraga caryocatactes,* lays 4 eggs in Sweden when pine seeds and hazel nuts abound, but 3 eggs in lean years. In Western Australia there has been an increase in the average clutch size of the Little Eagle, *Hieraëtus morphnoïdes,* Wedge-tailed Eagle, *Uroaëtus audax,* and Australian Goshawk, *Accipiter fasciatus,* ever since the introduced rabbit spread into their range (Ser-

venty and Whittell, 1951). It also seems likely that the type of food a bird eats may influence its clutch size. The corn-eating Scaled Quail, *Callipepla squamata,* of Mexico, normally lays 10 to 13 eggs, while the Spotted Wood Quail, *Odontophorus guttatus,* which searches all day for insects, worms, and the like, has a clutch of 4 to 6 eggs (Wagner, 1957).

It seems improbable, in these correlations between clutch size and food supply, that there is necessarily a direct physiological causal connection between the two. In some instances, the larger clutches are already laid before the abundant food is at hand. Most likely the birds respond to anticipatory stimuli which in some manner presage an increase in food abundance. A seven year study of British titmice, by ornithologists of the Edward Gray Institute of Field Ornithology at Oxford, has shown that not only do clutches increase in size in those years that caterpillars are more abundant, but that the young titmice appear each year just as the caterpillars emerge in numbers. These two events may vary from year to year as much as a month, and yet they always occur in synchrony. These parallel happenings both correlate with and possibly are set in motion by early spring temperatures (Lack, 1955).

Great Tits, *Parus major,* feed their young mainly on leaf-eating caterpillars which are abundant early in the season when first-brood young hatch out, but are scarce later when second-brood young appear. Second broods are attempted only about 7 per cent of the time. First clutches average about ten eggs; second clutches, about seven. Of hatched nestlings, 95 per cent flew from first broods, but only 37 per cent from second broods, the majority of the young starving (Lack, 1954). The rarity, small size, and high mortality of second broods in this tit make clear the kind of selective pressures that dictate the size and timing of bird clutches.

Anticipatory weather stimuli are not invariably dependable. Central European

Swifts, *Apus apus*, may lay a typical clutch of 3 eggs early in the summer, but if the weather should turn cold and rainy and reduce the numbers of flying insects, the parent birds will remove 1, 2, or 3 eggs from the nest—"the worse the weather the more eggs"—and drop them to the ground (Koskimies, 1950). This heroic trimming of clutch size is probably an adaptive instinctive act of whose significance the bird is unaware.

A perplexing problem in clutch size is presented by those species that lay more eggs than normally hatch and develop into mature birds. For example, the Brown Booby, *Sula leucogaster*, normally lays two eggs, the second about seven days after the first, but begins incubation with the first egg. As a consequence, the first chick to hatch monopolizes the food and its parents' care, and the second chick, if it ever hatches, dies of starvation, neglect, trampling, or cannibalism. In a large colony of Boobies in the Bahamas, Chapman (1908) found that less than one per cent of the occupied nests contained two live chicks. A similar fate awaits the last-born young of many penguins, pelicans, storks, herons, eagles, hawks, owls and other species in which the young hatch out at different times. Schifferli (1949) showed that in the Swiss Barn Owl, *Tyto alba*, all the eggs hatched in clutches of 4 or less, but in larger clutches there were frequently one or more unhatched eggs. When larger broods of 5 to 7 young did hatch out, there was a tendency for the youngest birds to die of cannibalism or starvation. Some observers consider this infanticide a wasteful maladaptation, or at least a Malthusian mechanism to prevent overpopulation. It may, however, be quite the contrary. Lack (1954) makes the point that the staggered hatching of eggs, which results in young of different sizes, may be an adaptation to bring family size into close adjustment with food supply. He says, "In such species the normal clutch tends to be somewhat larger than the parents can raise in an average year, the extra

egg or eggs being a reserve that can be utilized in good years." Since many species seem unable to anticipate an especially bountiful year and to adjust their clutch size accordingly, they do the second best thing and lay extra eggs that represent a premium paid toward a "race insurance policy." In groups like ducks and gallinaceous birds, all of whose eggs hatch at the same time, there is no preferential treatment of certain young, and the entire brood may die in a bad year.

Still another important factor that probably influences the evolution of clutch size is the intensity of predation that is focused on a species. Young of open-nesting birds are generally subject to heavier predation than those of hole-nesting species. One way to reduce the predation on open-nesters is to shorten the highly vulnerable nestling period. In Europe, the average nestling period of open-nesting passerines is around 11 days, while that of the more protected hole-nesters is about 19 days—undoubtedly a difference promoted by natural selection. Since a given amount of food will permit either a few young to grow rapidly or more young to grow slowly, it is not surprising that open-nesters average smaller clutches (5.1 eggs) than hole-nesters (6.9 eggs) (Lack, 1954).

A further extension of this principle is illustrated by the open-nesting Anseriformes and Galliformes whose precocial young, even though they leave the nest the day they hatch or the day after, nevertheless have a longer period of dependent infancy than do most altricial, nest-dwelling young. As a consequence they are subject to more hours of predation and other environmental dangers than are altricial young. Accordingly, such birds as ducks, geese, pheasants, and grouse lay unusually large clutches, as if to anticipate the expected losses.

Clutch size may also vary seasonally. In many species that lay two or more clutches per year, the first clutch may be larger than later ones. First clutches of the Blue-winged Teal, *Anas discors*, in Iowa, average about 9 eggs; second clutches, about 4 eggs. April clutches of the Great Tit, *Parus major,* in Holland, average 10.3 eggs in early April, 7.4 eggs in early June (Kluijver, 1951). A study in southern Michigan of seasonal variation of clutch size in 71 nests of the Field Sparrow, *Spizella pusilla,* gave the following: in May, 3.77 eggs; June, 3.69; July, 3.14; August, 3.0 (Walkinshaw, 1939). Almost identical results were obtained for the Chipping Sparrow, *Spizella passerina.* In a few species, it has been observed that clutch sizes are largest in the latter part of June, and smaller both before and after that time. In such species, clutch size may be primarily adapted to day length.

MULTIPLE AND REPLACEMENT CLUTCHES

If, in the midst of their laying, one should remove an egg from the nest of a Crow, *Corvus brachyrhynchos,* or of a Barn Swallow, *Hirundo rustica,* the birds will remain satisfied with the remaining eggs and incubate their clutches of less than normal size. Or, if one should add extra eggs to their nests, the birds will each still lay the normal number of eggs for a clutch (5 for these species) and try to incubate the abnormally large clutch. Similar experimental manipulations of egg-number in the clutches of doves, shore birds, large birds of prey, many passerines, and other species, have failed to change the characteristic number of eggs laid. Even the hatching of previously introduced eggs, or the presence of nestlings being fed by the male, have no effect on the rigidly fixed number of eggs laid by a female Tricolored Blackbird, *Agelaius tricolor* (Emlen, 1941). These species which have fixed clutch sizes are known as *determinate* layers. Apparently the number of oocytes in the ovaries which ripen into ova is predetermined for a given season or period of laying, and cannot be modified by external stimuli.

On the other hand, some species are *indeterminate* layers: some penguins, ducks, gallinaceous birds, some woodpeckers, some passerines, and others. In a noted experiment by Phillips (*in* Bent, 1939), a Yellow-shafted Flicker, *Colaptes auratus,* which normally lays 6 to 8 eggs, was induced to lay 71 eggs in 73 days by removing the eggs as rapidly as they were laid but always leaving one "nest egg." A similarly treated Wryneck, *Jynx torquilla,* whose normal clutch is 7 to 10 eggs, laid 62 eggs in 62 days; and an ostrich, whose normal clutch is less than 20 eggs, laid 65 eggs in three months in the Marseilles Zoo. The Willow Ptarmigan, *Lagopus lagopus,* normally lays 8 or 9 eggs, but 11 hens, whose eggs were experimentally removed daily, averaged 16.8 eggs per clutch, and one of them laid 27 eggs before stopping (Höst, 1942). This capacity of indeterminate layers to make up losses in egg-number has, of course, been artificially selected by man in domestic fowl. The artificially propagated Quail, *Coturnix coturnix,* in Japan has been induced to lay 365 eggs in one year (Meise, 1954), and Domestic Hens, descendants of the Jungle Fowl, *Gallus gallus,* have laid up to 352 eggs in 359 days.

Even though indeterminate layers can lay more eggs than the normal clutch, under natural conditions they all automatically stop laying when the standard number of eggs has been laid. It is thought that the feel of the "proper" number of eggs against the abdominal skin of the bird is somehow relayed to the endocrine glands which cause cessation of ovulation. This problem needs further experimental study.

The great advantage in indeterminate laying is that it enables the bird quickly to replace lost or stolen eggs and build its clutch up to full size. When an *entire* clutch is destroyed or removed, most birds, with the possible exceptions of large birds of prey and albatrosses which have long incubation periods, will produce a second replacement or substitute clutch. This, however, may be a slow process and usually involves repeating all the breeding cycle preliminaries: courtship, perhaps nest building, copulation, and then egg laying. Even so, pigeons may begin the new cycle half an hour after the loss of their clutch, and the first egg of the replacement set will appear in about 5 days. This interval between the loss of a clutch and the first egg of its replacement clutch varies with species. In the Song Sparrow, *Melospiza melodia,* the interval is 5 days; in the Starling, *Sturnus vulgaris,* 8 days.

Although many species have but one clutch per year, many others have two, and some have even more. In temperate latitudes the Mourning Dove, *Zenaidura macroura,* commonly attempts 5 clutches per summer. Sometimes, in doves and in certain passerines, the broods follow one another so closely that the eggs of one brood are laid in a second nest before the young of the preceding brood have flown from the first. In some species, like the Great Reed Warbler, *Acrocephalus arundinaceus,* the male builds a new nest while the female feeds the young, which do not leave the old nest until several days after the second clutch is started. Whatever the method—whether by large clutches, small clutches with better care, numerous clutches or overlapping clutches —natural selection has provided every species, except those on the verge of extinction, with enough replacements to balance mortality.

SUGGESTED READINGS

The most exhaustive treatment on birds' eggs is found in Romanoff and Romanoff, *The Avian Egg.* The physiology of egg production is well treated in Sturkie's *Avian Physiology.* Lack's *The Natural Regulation of Animal Numbers* contains excellent material on clutch size. The natural history of birds' eggs is well treated in Makatsch, *Der Vogel und Sein Ei.*

SIXTEEN

Incubation and Brood Parasitism

I know a Wizardry
Can break a speckled egg-shell,
And shake thrushes out of it, in every hawthorne tree.
Alfred Noyes, *Wizards.*

Incubation in a bird is the rough equivalent of pregnancy in a mammal. The parent in either case provides warmth and protection for the developing embryo. Whereas in mammals foods are supplied to the embryo and wastes removed from it via the blood stream of embryo and mother, in birds, food in the form of a highly specialized "infant formula" is stored in the egg by the walls of the uterus before the egg is laid, and embryo wastes either accumulate in the embryo's allantois or are given off through the egg shell in gaseous form. While avian "pregnancy" has its shortcomings, it also has several advantages. For one thing, both parents may share in its duties. This not only reduces the wear and tear on one parent but it helps hold the pair together so that they both may help raise the young—an arrangement practically unheard of in mammals, excepting some carnivores like the wolf, and, of course, man. Another advantage is that in birds, the incubating individual, unlike the pregnant mammal, may in cases of dire

297

emergency desert the eggs and escape to live and breed another day.

INCUBATION BEHAVIOR

Many birds begin incubation with the laying of the first egg: loons, grebes, pelicans, herons, storks, eagles, hawks, cranes, many gulls, cuckoos, parrots, owls, swifts, hummingbirds, hornbills, and a few passerine species. Early incubation of the clutch provides greater protection for all the eggs from storms and enemies. It results, however, in young that hatch out at different times and therefore are of different ages. In a brood of 6 young Barn Owls, *Tyto alba*, the first to hatch will be about 15 days older than the last. This has its disadvantages. The parents may start feeding the first-hatched young while other young or the eggs need brooding; or the older nestlings may abuse or even eat their younger brothers; or the parents may kill and tear the youngest

nestling to bits, as is regularly done by the Lammergeier, *Gypaëtus barbatus* (Stresemann, 1927–1934). As Lack (1954) has suggested, this form of incubation may be a method of adjusting the brood size to conform with food supply. The fact that large birds of prey usually lay 2 or 3 eggs but rarely raise more than one fledgling was known even to Aristotle, who, coupling the fact with the then popular notion that eagles were warm, courageous creatures, wrote: "Often one of the two eggs becomes rotten, and the third practically always, for being of a hot nature they make the moisture in the eggs to over-boil, so to say" (*De Generatione*, Platt, 1912. Quoted in Nice, 1954).

Ducks, geese, gallinaceous birds and most passerines hold off incubating the clutch until the last egg is laid, and even 10 days beyond that in the Rock Partridge, *Alectoris graeca*, or the Bobwhite Quail, *Colinus virginianus*. This makes it possible for all the young to hatch within a short interval, and for the parent bird

Figure 16.1. Young Barn Owls, showing differences in age caused by incubation beginning with the first egg laid. Ages, left to right, youngest, oldest, second youngest, second oldest. Photo by E. Hosking.

to shift completely its behavior from incubation to the care of the young. After 28 days of incubation, the dozen or so eggs of the Mallard, *Anas platyrhynchos*, generally all hatch out within a period of about two hours. If any of the ducklings hatch half a day or so later, the female leaves them behind to die as she shepherds her brood to open water. In still other species—ostriches, rheas, rails, and woodpeckers—incubation begins shortly before the completion of the set.

How does a bird know that a clutch is complete and that it is time to change its behavior from laying to brooding? Egg removal experiments show that for many species the number of eggs in a full clutch is not the maximum number the bird can lay. Very probably the feel of enough eggs against the belly tells the bird that it is time to incubate. This tactile stimulus seems to cause the pituitary gland to secrete prolactin, which has the function both of suppressing the output of its follicle-stimulating hormone and therefore suppressing ovulation, and of initiating broodiness or incubating behavior. Other stimuli undoubtedly bring on broodiness in species which begin incubation with the first egg laid. In the Jackdaw, *Corvus monedula*, the mechanism of brood initiation is not precise, for some individuals begin incubation with the first egg, some when the clutch is complete, and others at an intermediate point.

A bird's behavior also alters as incubation progresses. A noisy nuthatch becomes secretive and quiet. If a Great Tit, *Parus major*, is removed from her eggs at certain stages of incubation, she will almost invariably desert the nest, but at other stages she can be picked off the nest and returned, and will continue to brood. Brooding owls tend to become more belligerent toward intruders as incubation progresses. When gulls hear the peeps of unhatched young through the egg shell they shift their behavior markedly, and excitedly begin to call, preen, and move about.

Hatching of the eggs generally stimu-

Figure 16.2. Ring-necked Pheasants just hatched. In precocial species with large broods, incubation is delayed until the last egg is laid. As a consequence, all young hatch at about the same time. Photo by E. Hosking.

lates a rapid shift, especially in precocial parents, from brooding to care of the young. The eggs of European grebes (*Podiceps* spp.) hatch at different times. When the first eggs hatch, the feeding instincts of the parents seem to overpower the brooding instincts, with the result that the remaining eggs may be left to their fate. Out of a clutch of 4 or 5 eggs only 2 young are typically raised (Stresemann, 1927–1934). On the other hand, a female Spotted Flycatcher, *Muscicapa striata*, may at times interrupt incubating a second clutch of eggs in order to feed the young of her first brood.

A veritable passion for incubating eggs is seen in some species, notably penguins, which, lacking eggs, will "incubate" stones and even lumps of ice. In the antarctic penguins this heightened instinct is understandably a good thing, but at times it is carried to excess and eggs and young are crushed in disputes over their ownership. The immediate stimulus that awakens the incubation response may be the egg, or for some species may be the nest itself. For many species, the egg has significance only within the nest, and if it is removed a short distance from the nest, the bird will ignore it. Many species have been observed incubating empty nests after their eggs have been stolen; others (eagles, owls) may brood the empty nest before their eggs are laid.

There are a number of species, particularly those that build scrapes of shallow nests on the ground, which will attempt to retrieve eggs displaced short distances from the nest. Among such species are grebes, gulls, terns, shore birds, gallinaceous birds, and those hawks, owls, and doves that nest on the ground. Birds like the passerines, which build deep cup-nests, or which nest in trees, will not attempt to retrieve eggs (Poulsen, 1953).

Substitution experiments have shown that many species will incubate almost any object placed in the nest: light bulbs, golf balls, mollusc shells, watches, dice, garishly painted cubes and other strange objects. Experiments by Tinbergen (1951) have shown that certain objects will act as hypernatural releasers of incubating behavior. A European Oystercatcher, *Haematopus ostralegus*, will try to incubate an impossibly large egg in preference to its own. Geese have tried to incubate ostrich eggs and artificial models even larger.

Such experiments as these raise the question: to what extent do birds recognize their eggs? Obviously those host species that throw out cuckoo's eggs which do not match their own must be able to tell some difference between them. Natural selection has probably heightened the sensitivity for egg recognition in those species commonly parasitized by other birds. A keen ability to discriminate its own eggs from others is found in the Atlantic Common Murre, *Uria aalge*, probably because the species nests in large colonies with similar nest sites and lays eggs with extremely variable markings. An individual Murre not only recognizes its own egg but will roll a displaced egg back to the nest from distances of up to 5 meters. So attached are these birds to the appearance of their own eggs that they will brood half egg-shells and even broken eggs whose bloody embryos stain their feathers (Johnson, 1941). For other species, the "feel" of

the egg is more important. Experiments by McClure (1945) revealed that the Mourning Dove, *Zenaidura macroura*, would without hesitation accept eggs colored red, green, black, blue, orange, and other colors, but if an egg were cracked or punctured the dove would either remove it or abandon the nest. For many species, it is probably the combination egg-plus-nest that evokes normal incubation behavior. The fact that many species will continue to incubate infertile or addled eggs long past their normal incubation period shows that the egg itself is an important stimulus. A female Black-capped Chickadee, *Parus atricapillus*, has been known to incubate its eggs 11 days beyond the normal hatching time; a European Robin, *Erithacus rubecula*, 35 days; a Black-headed Gull, *Larus ridibundus*, 50 days; a Ring-necked Pheasant, *Phasianus colchicus*, 72 days.

BROOD PATCHES

A bird sitting on its eggs is not necessarily incubating them. Feathers are very poor heat conductors. Incubation depends on the copious transfer of heat from the brooding bird to the developing egg, and this requires close contact between the blood stream of the bird and the shell of the egg. Brood or incubation patches achieve this end. These are areas of bare skin on the belly of the bird which develop shortly before the complete set of eggs has been laid. A bird may have a single median brood patch, as in many passerines, birds of prey, grebes, and pigeons; two lateral brood patches, as in auks, skuas, and shore birds; three brood patches—one median and two lateral—as in waders, gulls, gallinaceous birds, and others; or none at all, as in ducks, geese, cormorants, gannets, and penguins (Tucker, 1943). There is little correlation between the size of a brood patch and the size of a bird's clutch. In general, brood patches arise only in the sex which incubates the eggs: for example, only in male phalaropes. If both sexes incubate, both usually have brood patches,

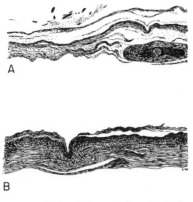

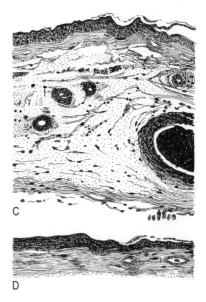

Figure 16.3. Cross-sections of the abdominal skin of a Red-winged Blackbird at successive stages in the incubation cycle: *A*, Non-breeding stage. Down-feather papilla at right. *B*, After laying the first egg. *C*, Early incubation stage, showing the abundant and large blood vessels. *D*, After the young have just left the nest. Magnification 140X. After Bailey.

but a number of male passerines cover the eggs although they lack a brood patch.

A brood patch undergoes two main changes just before incubation starts. It loses its feathers—chiefly down feathers—and the dermis of the skin becomes spongy and richly supplied with large blood vessels so that the skin looks inflamed. Studies by Baldwin and Kendeigh (1932) indicated that a House Wren, *Troglodytes aëdon,* was able, through shedding its feathers, to apply to its eggs a temperature 5.6° C. higher than would otherwise have been possible. Hormones initiate the development of brood patches. Pellets of the female sex hormone estradiol, implanted into White-crowned Sparrows, *Zonotrichia leucophrys,* produced incubation patches in non-breeding males and females, and injections of prolactin speeded the process (Bailey, 1952).

Ducks and geese create a brood patch by plucking down feathers from their breasts and using them to make a warm nest lining. When the female leaves the nest to feed, she covers her eggs with the down. Open-nesting ducks generally have dark colored down which matches the surroundings, while hole-nesters, such as the tree ducks, have white down (Stresemann,

1927–1934). On leaving their eggs unattended, grebes cover them with wet vegetation; the Patagonian Seed-snipe, *Thinocorus rumicivorus,* scrapes dry earth over them; and European Wood Pigeons, *Columba palumbus,* unlike other doves, cover them with small twigs. These actions serve more to protect the eggs from the eyes of predators than to warm them.

Boobies and gannets warm their eggs by standing on them. The webs of their feet are heavily vascularized with vessels that by-pass the capillaries and thus allow a faster, warmer circulation. Murres and penguins have similarly warmed feet but incubate their eggs by holding them on top of the feet. In addition, some penguins have evolved a muscular brood pouch or fold of belly skin which envelops and warms the egg as it rests on top of their feet.

INCUBATION TEMPERATURES

One of the marvels of bird life is the fact that the Emperor Penguin, *Aptenodytes forsteri,* successfully incubates its egg in the midst of antarctic winter temperatures as low as −60° C. (−77° F.). This means that the penguin must maintain a temperature in the egg of approximately 34° C. (93° F.) day and night, without a break, for 8 or 9 weeks. It is small wonder that these polar birds are avid and close incubators. Actual temperatures of antarctic penguin eggs undergoing incubation were determined by Eklund and Charlton (1959) for the summer-breeding Adelie Penguin, *Pygoscelis adeliae,* by inserting within an egg a miniature electronic telemetering instrument whose broadcast impulses could be received and converted into degrees of temperature. While the average body temperature of the Adelie Penguin was 40° C., fluctuating from 38° to 41.5° C., the average temperature of the incubating egg was 6 degrees less or 34° C., fluctuating from 29° to 37° C.

Using thermocouples inserted into incubating eggs of 37 different species of birds representing 11 orders, Huggins (1941) determined that the average egg temperature was about 34° C. With the incubating bird on the eggs, the average temperature was 34.3° C.; for periods when the bird was off the eggs, the temperature was 33.4° C. Eggs in the center of a nest were warmer than the others. Baldwin and Kendeigh's (1932) pioneer studies in this field showed that eggs in the center of a nest fluctuated between 34° and 37° C. A parallel study by Westerkov (1956) of incubation temperatures for the Ringnecked Pheasant, *Phasianus colchicus,* gave a bare brood patch temperature of 39.5° C., an air temperature at the top of the eggs under the sitting hen of 35.1° C., and at the bottom of the eggs, 25° C. In this species, ground temperatures greatly affected egg temperatures. The fact that incubating birds usually turn eggs in the nest is probably an adaptation directed toward providing all the eggs in a nest with more even temperatures. A pheasant will turn her eggs about once every hour; the European Sparrow Hawk, *Accipiter nisus,* about once every twenty minutes; and the American Redstart, *Setophaga ruticilla,* about once every 8 minutes. This periodic moving of the eggs not only provides

equal heating throughout the eggs, but prevents embryonic membranes from adhering to the shell. If Domestic Hens' eggs are turned in the incubator only twice daily, only 58 per cent of them hatch; when they are not turned at all, only 15 per cent. The eggs of the Palm Swift, *Cypsiurus parvus,* are firmly cemented into its nest with salivary glue, but possibly the swinging of the palm leaf to which the nest is attached provides the equivalent of egg rotation. How megapode eggs, buried in the earth, are able to develop successfully without movement is a problem yet to be solved.

Eggs which rest in spots exposed to full sunlight must sometimes be kept cool. In hot summer weather many incubating birds will protect their eggs from direct sunshine by standing over them, using the body and wings to make a shading canopy. A Common Nighthawk, *Chordeiles minor,* nesting on a flat roof was thus able to hold the temperature of her eggs to 46° C. although the temperature of the surrounding roof rose to 61° C. (142° F.) (Weller, 1958). The Osprey, *Pandion haliaetus,* is known to shake water from its wet feathers over its eggs in warm weather. This action may function both to cool the eggs and to prevent excessive water loss.

The temperature at which an egg is incubated has a profound effect on the rate of development of the chick embryo within, and therefore on the time of its hatching. Like all metabolic processes, embryonic development, within limits, proceeds more rapidly the higher the temperature. Investigations by Kendeigh (1940) of the metabolic rate of the growing embryo of the House Wren, *Troglodytes aëdon,* showed that at the normal incubation temperature of 35° C. the egg required 13 days to hatch; and that at 37.8° C., heightened metabolism so accelerated development (126 per cent) that, theoretically, an egg should hatch in 10 days although no bird's egg is known to do so. Conversely, a sub-normal incubation temperature of 32.2° C. lowered metabolism sufficiently (to 72 per cent of normal) to require 18 days for hatching. Similar studies by Romanoff (1934) on the Bobwhite, *Colinus virginianus*, showed that at an egg temperature of 36.7° C., eggs required 5 or 6 more days for hatching than at 38.9° C. Of course, factors other than speed of development are involved in the natural selection of optimum incubation temperatures—for example, the temperature under which the highest percentage of eggs hatch, or the resistance of the embryo to environmental stresses. Nevertheless, considering the weighty survival advantages of a short incubation period, it is not to be wondered at that the high normal body temperatures of birds closely approach the lethal limit.

Eggs of most wild birds tolerate a considerable degree of chilling—an adaptation, no doubt, to the absences of the incubating bird for feeding. Ring-necked Pheasants, *Phasianus colchicus*, typically leave their nests for an hour or so each day, during which the eggs cool to air temperatures. Crane eggs may be uncovered an hour at 0° C. without killing the embryo. Eggs of Manx Shearwaters, *Procellaria puffinus*, may be deserted in their burrows for 7 days and still contain living embryos. Eggs of this species survived as long as 13 days exposed to normal laboratory air temperatures (17° to 24° C.) (Matthews, 1954). Eggs of Storm Petrels, *Hydrobates pelagicus*, have hatched after 2 or 3 successive days of chilling, and one egg still hatched after a cumulative total of 11 days of parental absence, involving one spell of 5 successive days of chilling. In this last instance, the egg required 50 days for hatching rather than the normal 41 days (Davis, 1957). Tolerance for low temperatures was also found by MacMullan and Eberhardt (1953) in the Ring-necked Pheasant eggs. Exposure of incubating eggs to a steady shower of water at 16° C., or soaking the eggs in water at 20° to 22° C. for periods of less than 10 hours, resulted in no significant mortality. In general, it was found that eggs are more tolerant of low temperatures early in incubation than late, and that occasional chilling of the eggs to 7° C. does no great harm, although high mortality occurs among eggs exposed to 0° C. for 5 or 6 hours. Newly hatched chicks were much more vulnerable to low temperatures than eggs at any stage of incubation.

INCUBATION PATTERNS

Great diversity in incubation patterns is found among birds, indicating that there are no weighty advantages in any particular variety. Usually both sexes take part in incubating the eggs, particularly in those species lacking pronounced sex dimorphism. A survey by Van Tyne and Berger (1959) of some 160 families, representing the majority of living birds, showed that both sexes usually incubated the eggs in about 54 per cent of the families, the female alone in 25 per cent, the male alone in 6 per cent, and the male, female, or both, in 15 per cent. For those species in which one sex is more conspicuously colored than the other, the drab, less conspicuously marked partner usually takes over the incubation chores. But this is not invariably true. For example, the colorful male Rose-breasted Grosbeak, *Pheucticus ludovicianus*, shares with his mate the brooding of the eggs. Incubation by both sexes is considered the primitive pattern. The following discussion is based on a classification of incubation patterns by Skutch (1957).

INCUBATION BY BOTH PARENTS

Although in the majority of species both sexes take part in incubation, the male often takes a minor part. When the female is the chief brooder, as in most passerines, the male often brings food to her. In many of the water birds the sexes share about equally in incubation. In the Double-crested Cormorant, *Phalacrocorax auritus*, the parents relieve each other at the nest at 1 to 3 hour intervals. Among fulmars, shearwaters, and many petrels, each parent takes a turn incubating for 1 to 5 days at a stretch while its partner is away at sea feeding.

Often the two parents will observe a strict incubation schedule. Among doves and pigeons the female sits on the eggs from about 5:00 in the afternoon until about 9:00 the next morning; the male from 9:00 A.M. to 5:00 P.M. The female Black Swan, *Cygnus atratus,* likewise incubates most of the day and all of the night, the male warming the eggs only between about 10:00 A.M. and 5:00 P.M. In the Starling, *Sturnus vulgaris,* and Mexican Trogon, *Trogon mexicanus,* both sexes incubate by day but only the female by night. In reverse fashion, among woodpeckers the male incubates by night and both sexes by day. In the Ostrich, *Struthio camelus,* the darker colored male incubates the clutch by night and the gray female by day—an arrangement that aids concealment from foes.

There are a few species in which both sexes incubate simultaneously. In the African savannas, both the male and female Common Waxbills, *Estrilda astrild,* sit together in their dome-shaped nest incubating their numerous eggs, both day and night (Stresemann, 1927–1934). Simultaneous incubation, but in different nests, is achieved by the European Red-legged Partridge, *Alectoris rufa.* The female builds two nests and then fills the first nest with eggs. These eggs remain unincubated for about 14 days while she lays another 10 eggs in the second nest. She now returns to the first nest to incubate those eggs while the male incubates the second clutch. Each parent cares for its own covey of young; a union of the two groups does not occur (Portal, *in* Stresemann, 1927–1934).

The instinctive urge to incubate is at times so great that the parent on the nest may be reluctant to be relieved of his or her duties. Often a male goatsucker must gently push his mate off the eggs in order to take her place. If an incubating Magpie-lark, *Grallina cyanoleuca,* is unwilling to leave the eggs, its mate administers a peck

(Roberts, 1942). In other species, a formalized nest-relief ceremony takes place at the change-over. In the case of the Brown Pelican, *Pelecanus occidentalis,* the returning bird alights near the nest and walks slowly toward it with its bill directed vertically and its head weaving from side to side. The sitting bird

"sticks its bill vertically into the nest, twitches its half-spread wings, and utters a low, husky, gasping *chuck.* ... After 5 or 6 wand-like passes of its upraised head, the advancing bird pauses, when both birds, with apparent unconcern, begin to preen their feathers, and a moment later the bird that has been on duty steps off the nest, and the new comer at once takes its place"
(Chapman, 1908).

Terns, herons, cranes and many other species also use nest relief rituals.

INCUBATION BY ONE PARENT

While there are disadvantages in reducing the number of egg-caretakers to one, there is the advantage that the fewer birds there are around the nest the less conspicuous it is to predators. In this connection, it is significant that one-parent incubators are common among birds which nest in the open, but not among those which nest in holes, where protection against predators is more assured.

The female alone incubates the eggs among many passerines (manakins, tyrant flycatchers, buntings, sparrows, most crows and jays), many ducks and geese, hawks, eagles, most owls, hummingbirds, those gallinaceous birds with pronounced sex dimorphism, and, so far as known, in all polygynous species except the rheas and certain tinamous. In many instances, the male feeds the female and guards her and the nest, keeping watch from some inconspicuous nearby perch. Among several species of hawks and harriers, the female rises from the nest and flies out to receive food from the male in mid-air, either talons to talons, or by catching it in the air as he drops the prey. Female hornbills (Bucerotidae) are imprisoned in tree cavity nests by the mortaring of most of the entrance with mud, regurgitated food, and droppings, leaving only a small hole through which the males pass fruits, whole or regurgitated. After an imprisonment of 1½ to 4 months the female emerges fat and healthy with her young, but the hard-working male is thin and bedraggled. In the genus *Lophoceros*, the female emerges first, and the young close themselves in the nest hole for a while longer.

In only a few species does the male alone incubate: kiwis, tinamous, rheas, emus, cassowaries, painted snipe, button quail, and the Emperor Penguin, *Aptenodytes forsteri*. In the polyandrous phalaropes and button quail, it is the female which is the larger, more brilliantly colored sex and the one which does the courting. The drab males not only stay at home and incubate the eggs, but singlehanded they raise the young. A most unusual incubation pattern is shown by the Chinese Pheasant-tailed Jaçana, *Hydrophasianus chirurgus*. The female lays as many as 10 successive clutches of 4 eggs each, and a different male incubates each of the clutches and rears the young by himself (Hoffman, 1949). Another unusual pattern is demonstrated by the polygynous South American rheas. One male makes a nest in which all the members of his harem will lay their eggs—from 20 to as many as 50—which the male then incubates in solitude.

Nest Attentiveness

Many kinds of birds incubate their eggs almost constantly, day and night: penguins, woodpeckers, doves, trogons, hornbills, hoopoes, antbirds, and others. On the other hand, several tyrant flycatchers and swallows are inconstant in brooding, sitting on their eggs only half of the daylight hours and spending the rest of their time away from the nest. The majority of birds in which one sex alone does the incubating spend from 60 to 80 per cent of the day on the nest (Skutch, 1945).

The term *nest attentiveness* refers to the time the incubating bird is on the nest; *in-attentiveness*, the time when it is off. Attentiveness varies greatly, depending on such fluctuating influences as species, sex, individual, geography, season, weather, stage of incubation, type of food eaten and its abundance, disturbance by other animals, and other factors. In some species, such as the Palm Swift, *Cypsiurus parvus*, the incubation schedule is very erratic; in others, such as the European Redstart, *Phoenicurus phoenicurus*, attentiveness is regular and almost rhythmic. The female of this species alternates about 15 minutes on her eggs with 8 to 25 minutes off. The number of times daily that one female spent off her eggs for the 12 days of incubation was 23, 24, 27, 32, 28, 27, 28, 29, 30, 29, 32, 30 (Ruiter, 1941).

Table 16.1 gives examples of nest attentiveness for selected small species of birds, mostly passerines. Since the data given represent birds living in different climates and at different stages of incubation, they are valid only for very general comparisons. Most of the figures are rounded off and in some instances represent averages from two different sources.

Knowing that in Finland the Pied Flycatcher's incubation period was longer in May than in June, von Haartman (1956) investigated the effect that nest box temperatures might have on the species' brooding rhythm. By using thermostatically controlled nest boxes he discovered that the warmer the box the shorter the individual brooding period. The length of periods off the nest was not affected by outside temperatures. In the European Wren, *Troglodytes troglodytes*, cooler weather calls for more time on the eggs. Attentive periods were found by Armstrong (1955) to average 29 minutes at outside temperatures of 21° C., and 33 minutes at temperatures of 18° C. Inattentive periods for these temperatures were 14 and 11 minutes, respectively.

A hummingbird may leave its eggs 140 times in one day; a Robin, 20 times; a Domestic Hen, once or twice. Some albatrosses incubate steadily, day and night, for three weeks; and a male Emu in a zoo re-

Table 16.1. Nest Attentiveness of Small Bird Species in Which Only the Females Incubate

SPECIES	AVERAGE TIME ON NEST (MINUTES)	AVERAGE TIME OFF NEST (MINUTES)	ATTENTIVE PERIODS PER DAY	DAYTIME ATTENTIVENESS (PER CENT)
Allen's Hummingbird				
Selasphorus sasin	4.6	1.3	140	78
Barn Swallow				
Hirundo rustica	7.2	2.5	79	70
Streaked Flycatcher				
Myiodynastes maculatus	30.3	12.6	13	71
Black-capped Chickadee				
Parus atricapillus	24	7.8	34	76
Pied Flycatcher				
Muscicapa hypoleuca	86.7	4.7	11	95
Carolina Wren				
Thryothorus ludovicianus	58	33.5	11	64
American Robin				
Turdus migratorius	44	11	20	80
Red-eyed Vireo				
Vireo olivaceous	29	10	28	75
American Redstart				
Setophaga ruticilla	25	3.3	37	88
Ovenbird				
Seiurus aurocapillus	105	19	9	82
Bullfinch				
Pyrrhula pyrrhula	111	12	9	90
Song Sparrow				
Melospiza melodia	25	7	34	75

fused to leave his eggs for 60 days, fasting all the while. Because the hummingbird is so very small it loses body heat rapidly and must therefore leave its nest to seek food many times a day to make up this energy loss. It is more difficult to see why so many large sea birds remain on their eggs for long periods without eating, particularly when in many species both sexes incubate and can relieve each other of the duties of incubation. Among petrels and shearwaters the two sexes share incubation, each bird attending the eggs from 2 to 4 or 5 days without relief, while its mate is away

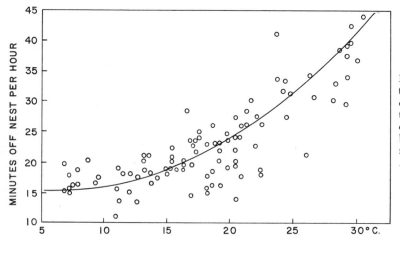

Figure 16.4. A curve showing the relationship between mean daily air temperatures and mean time spent away from the nest during an active day of an incubating European Wren. Circles represent individual records. After Armstrong.

at sea feeding. Albatross pairs likewise share incubation, and among the different species the attentive period by one parent on the egg varies from 6 to 30 days (Richdale, 1952). Some penguins also refrain from eating during incubation. Within a day after she lays her egg, the female Emperor Penguin, *Aptenodytes forsteri*, turns it over to the male, who incubates it alone for 62 to 64 days, fasting the while (Prevost, 1953). All this time he is living on stored fat. Adelie Penguins, *Pygoscelis adeliae*, may fast as long as four weeks while incubating, with a consequent weight loss of over 25 per cent. Large birds with their low rate of heat loss are able to store sufficient fat in their bodies to tide them over long incubation periods even in cold climates.

OTHER PATTERNS OF INCUBATION

As discussed previously, there are species that build community nests and practice communal incubation. The anis (*Crotophaga* spp.) are highly gregarious birds which cooperate to build a shallow cup of sticks, lined with green leaves, in which several of the females will lay their eggs—as many as two dozen—which several birds then incubate simultaneously. The Babbling Thrush, *Yuhina brunniceps*, of Formosa is another communal breeder. At one nest, 6 birds were observed incubating 8 eggs; at another, 2 males and 3 females fed 5 young (Yamashina, 1938). Without question the most remarkable form of incubation is that of the Megapodiidae of Australia and the Dutch East Indies. These birds, known as mound birds, incubator birds, or megapodes (from their big, powerful feet), use other than animal heat to incubate their eggs. For incubation they exploit heat from three sources: the sun, subterranean volcanism, and fermenting vegetation. The account that follows is largely after Frith (1956, 1957).

The Maleo, *Megacephalon maleo*, of the hill forests of the Celebes, migrates on foot as far as 32 kilometers (20 miles) to the nearest ocean beaches having black sand. There pairs dig holes to bury their large eggs (10 x 6 cm. or 4 x 2½ inches). The black sand absorbs sufficient solar heat to incubate the eggs. Many females may lay their eggs in one communal hole about 30 to 60 centimeters deep. This same species also lays eggs in the warm soil next to hot springs or volcanic steam fissures.

Another megapode, the Brush Turkey, *Alectura lathami*, lives in the steaming rain forests of Australia and New Guinea. Here, where little sunshine reaches the forest floor, the birds heap up piles of rotting vegetation (Fig. 16.5) and let the heat of fermentation incubate their eggs. These mounds are often 3 meters high; those of a near relative, the Scrub Fowl, *Megapodius freycinet*, are reported to be

Figure 16.5. A Brush Turkey of Australia and its mound. Fermenting vegetation in the mound furnishes the heat to incubate the eggs. Photo from Australian News and Information Service.

as high as 6 meters (20 ft.) and as wide as 15 meters (50 ft.). The same mound may be used year after year, each female burying in its compost 7 to 12 eggs, usually with the large end up. When the precocial young hatch, they dig their way up to the surface and immediately begin an independent existence, some of them being able to fly the first day.

In the Mallee Fowl, *Leipoa ocellata*, of the semidesert regions of southern Australia, the female lays eggs at 4- to 8-day intervals, and may produce as many as 35 in one season. Accordingly, the egg-laying period is unusually long, extending from mid-September to late February. For the hard-working male, who prepares and attends the mound, the season is even longer, since the construction of the mound begins in May (Australian autumn), 4 months before the first egg is laid, and the eggs require approximately 2 months to hatch. So for approximately 11 months of the year he is busy either building or tending the mound to control its temperature.

In this arid climate, fermentation alone is not enough to provide adequate incubation temperatures throughout the long nesting season, nor is solar heat always sufficient. If, in the spring, the fermenting vegetation raises the temperature of the mound above 33° C. (92° F.), the male laboriously opens the mound in the cool mornings to let heat escape. When the midsummer sun beats too warmly on the mound, he adds more soil on top to provide an insulating layer to keep the eggs from cooking. In dry autumn weather, when the heat of fermentation is gone, he uncovers the mound enough to let the sun's noon heat penetrate to the eggs, and then scratches back on top of the mound the sun-warmed earth to keep the eggs warm overnight. Certainly, this substitution for normal incubation is no labor-saving arrangement. By observing birds from blinds for hundreds of hours, Frith learned that the average male Mallee Fowl worked 7 hours per day in the spring, 13 in summer, and 10 in the autumn; and that throughout all three seasons he averaged 5.3 hours per day of actual digging!

By means of experimental manipulation of mound temperatures (electric heating cables, etc.) Frith proved that the male Mallee Fowl was able to detect internal variation in mound temperatures, by sampling beakfuls of earth, and to take proper action to cool or warm the mound as needed. In one mound, for example, which a male had been visiting daily to release heat, Frith removed all the organic matter so that the temperature quickly dropped to 16° C. On the bird's

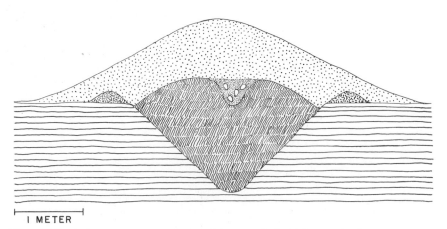

I METER

Figure 16.6. A diagrammatic cross-section of the mound of a Mallee Fowl. The pit contains fermenting compost, with the eggs laid in a depression on top, and the whole covered with sandy soil. After Frith.

next visit, he detected the lower temperature and began his autumn routine of opening the mound in the heat of the day, while all the other males in the vicinity were busy cooling theirs. In nature, this species is able to maintain the temperature of the egg chamber in each mound at an even 33° C., with not more than a degree or two of fluctuation.

Aside from the megapodes, at least one other species is known to use other than animal heat for incubation. The Egyptian Plover, *Aegyptius pluvialis*, buries its eggs in sandy islands of the Nile and broods them only at night when the sun's heat fails. This plover may also shade the eggs by day to avoid excess heat.

BROOD PARASITISM

Another substitution for the usual pattern of incubation, and one much lazier than that the incubator birds use, is brood parasitism or nest parasitism. This method involves an escape from the chief duties of raising a family—building the nest, incubating the eggs, and rearing the young —through the simple expedient of imposing them on another bird, usually one of another species. This characteristic, a nasty and subversive one by human standards, but perfectly natural and biologically "moral" by avian standards, is practiced by representatives of five families: Anatidae, Cuculidae, Indicatoridae, Icteridae and Ploceidae. Birds of various genera among these families lay their eggs in nests of other species and abandon them to the care of their foster parents.

No one knows quite how this behavior originated. Possible steps toward brood parasitism are suggested by some of the activities of non-parasitic species. Many species use old or abandoned nests of other birds instead of building their own. Owls often nest in old crow nests, sparrows in swallow nests, and starlings and flycatchers in woodpecker holes. Many species that normally build their own nests and incubate their own eggs will occasionally lay their eggs in other

birds' nests—a common happening in duck marshes. It is significant that the non-parasitic Yellow-billed Cuckoo, *Coccyzus americanus*, now and then lays in strange nests. It is possible that the loss of territorial defense as seen among the cowbirds (Friedmann, 1929) may have led to loss of the nest-building instinct and subsequently to brood parasitism. Many brood parasites are either polygamous or promiscuous, and such breeding habits tend to weaken the pair bond and territory defense by the male. These weaknesses in turn create problems easily solved by brood parasitism.

Another line of reasoning, advanced by Herrick (1935), suggests that different parts of a bird's reproductive cycle may be interrupted or delayed with a resultant lack of a harmonious relation in successive parts of the cycle. For example, a bird may be ready to lay its eggs before it finishes the nest—a situation that apparently occurs frequently among Redwinged Blackbirds, *Agelaius phoeniceus*. In such a dilemma, a bird might easily be tempted to lay its egg in any convenient nest—a plausible prelude to habitual and eventually instinctive brood parasitism. Whatever its origins, brood parasitism is a widely spread, successful way of life for several species.

One of the commonest and most highly evolved brood parasites is the European Cuckoo, *Cuculus canorus*, various races of which parasitize over 125 other species of birds. At the onset of the breeding season, the female Cuckoo seeks out and intently observes a host bird actively building a nest or laying eggs. Apparently the sight of an appropriate host stimulates the Cuckoo to ripen an egg follicle and lay an egg, because the time interval between such a psychic stimulus and the subsequent laying of the egg is 4 or 5 days, an interval corresponding to that in many small birds between the time of the destruction of a clutch and the laying of the first egg of the replacement clutch (Stresemann, 1927–1934). The Cuckoo lays usually one egg to a nest at 48 hour intervals. The egg is quickly laid, often in as little time as 5 seconds, and ordinarily between 2:00 and 6:00 P.M. when the owner of the nest is likely to be away. Normally, the Cuckoo will remove one of the host's eggs while visiting the nest. As many as 25 eggs may be produced by one Cuckoo in a season, but about 12 seems to be the usual number.

Ordinarily, the female Cuckoo lays her egg in an incomplete clutch of the host species, or in a freshly completed clutch. Her sharp discrimination in choosing nests at the proper stage is indicated by Capek's observations (*in* Stresemann, 1927–1934). Of 273 nests containing Cuckoo eggs, 130 contained incomplete host clutches, 68 held fresh, complete clutches, 20 contained incubated complete clutches, 5 were occupied, but contained no eggs, and 13 were abandoned.

Host species react to the Cuckoo egg in their nests either by accepting it and incubating it with their own eggs, or by removing it from the nest, or by abandoning the nest completely. Some species are much more sensitive than others to the presence of Cuckoo eggs. In Germany the Wood Warbler, *Phylloscopus sibilatrix,* is very likely to desert its nest

if it finds a Cuckoo's egg there, while the Redstart, *Phoenicurus phoenicurus,* is more prone to accept the egg.

A great many birds react to strange objects in their nests by throwing them out. If the Cuckoo egg does not resemble the host's eggs in size and color, the host may remove it. This is not necessarily because a given bird knows the color of its own eggs and objects to anything different. Rensch (1925) removed 3 eggs from an incompleted clutch of the Garden Warbler, *Sylvia borin,* and substituted three of the Lesser Whitethroat, *Sylvia curruca.* The next day, when the bird laid her fourth egg, she promptly threw it out of the nest since her own egg was "strange" with reference to the other three!

In many instances, the egg of the European Cuckoo strikingly resembles that of its favored hosts. In Finland, the Cuckoo lays bright blue eggs, and its chief hosts are the Redstart and Whinchat, *Saxicola rubetra,* both of which lay blue eggs. In Hungary, the Cuckoo lays greenish eggs boldly blotched with brown and black, and so does its chief dupe, the Great Reed Warbler, *Acrocephalus arundin-*

GARDEN
WARBLER   CUCKOO

GREAT REED
WARBLER   CUCKOO

REDSTART   CUCKOO

WHITE
WAGTAIL   CUCKOO

Figure 16.7. Eggs of four European passerines, each paired with the type of Cuckoo egg most frequently found with it in the nest. This mimicry shows clearly the evolutionary ecological adaptation in the eggs of different races of the European Cuckoo. Magnification 1.2X. After Rensch.

aceus. Throughout Europe and Asia, there are races of the Cuckoo whose eggs very closely resemble those of its selected fosterers. In southern England, however, the Cuckoo victimizes a variety of wagtails, pipits, warblers, and other species which lay very dissimilar eggs. Probably as a consequence, the Cuckoo lays an egg with generalized coloration that matches the eggs of no single host species very closely.

In a study of the Khasia Hills Cuckoo, *Cuculus canorus bakeri,* in India, Baker (1942) found that normal hosts, whose eggs matched the Cuckoo's eggs in coloration, deserted their nests only 8 per cent of the time when parasitized, but abnormal fosterers with discordant eggs deserted 24 per cent of the time. Such rejection of the Cuckoo's eggs has doubtless been the factor that produced races of Cuckoos whose eggs match so closely those of their favored hosts.

Cuckoo eggs are adaptive in other ways also. Although the various species of cuckoos are generally larger than the birds they parasitize, their eggs are small, about like those of their hosts. Where cuckoos parasitize larger birds, such as crows, their eggs are larger, again matching those of their hosts. The shell of the European Cuckoo egg is thick and strong, weighing about 25 per cent more than shells of other eggs the same size. Above all, the Cuckoo egg hatches in about 12½ days, whereas the eggs of most host species require 13 or 14 days. This gives the young Cuckoo the enormous advantage of a head start over its foster brothers in growth and in claiming food from the host parents.

When the young Cuckoo hatches, it is blind, naked, muscular, and able to gape for food like most altricial young. When it is about 10 hours old, an instinct appears that is one of the wonders of the

Figure 16.8. A blind young Cuckoo ejecting the eggs from a Tree Pipit's nest. Young nest-mates are thrown out in the same fashion. Photo by E. Hosking.

animal kingdom. If any solid object, such as an egg, young bird, or even an acorn, touches the sensitive shallow depression on the little Cuckoo's back, the blind bird manipulates it to the rim of the nest and shoves it overboard. The young Cuckoo persists in this behavior until it has cleared the nest of all objects but itself. This "overboard" instinct disappears in 3½ or 4 days. The perhaps overly-adaptive urge of many breeding birds to brood and feed almost anything within, and to ignore anything outside the nest, powerfully furthers this murderous instinct of the young Cuckoo. The host parent will usually ignore her own starving and dying young even when they are just outside the nest cup, and instead of caring for them will feed and brood the rapidly growing, parasitic foster child.

In the Anatidae, only the Black-headed Duck, *Heteronetta atricapilla*, of South America, is a true brood parasite; it regularly lays its eggs in the nests of other species of ducks, coots, gulls, and even a hawk. A strong parasitic tendency is found in the North American Redhead Duck, *Aythya americana*, which frequently lays its eggs in nests of other ducks and leaves them to be incubated by the nest owner.

Brood parasitism is also practiced by the honey-guides or Indicatoridae, so called because of their famous habit of leading man and other animals to nests of bees, where man and bird share spoils.

Figure 16.9. Even after the young Cuckoo has grown nearly to full size, the duped foster-parent still feeds it, so blind is its instinct to place food in a gaping mouth.

These birds, largely natives of Africa, all lay their eggs in the nests of other species, particularly their relatives, the barbets and woodpeckers. The nestling of the Greater Honey-guide, *Indicator indicator*, is known to eject its foster brothers from the nest, but probably a more effective means of eliminating its nest-mates is provided by the remarkable, needle-sharp mandibular hooks on the beaks of the blind nestlings of at least two species of *Indicator* (Fig. 16.10). These weapons are used in a "ferocious, relentless gripping and biting" attack on their foster brothers until they die and are presumably removed from the nest by their uncomprehending parents (Friedmann, 1955). These hooks drop off when the honey-guide nestlings are about 2 weeks old.

A wide range in stages of parasitism is found among the Icteridae in the New World. Most of the numerous species are not at all parasitic, while some, like the Bay-winged Cowbird, *Agelaioides badius*, of South America, may build their own nests, but more often use the nests of other species for laying and incubating their eggs. A complete brood parasite is the Brown-headed Cowbird, *Molothrus ater*, of North America. This familiar bird lays its eggs in the nests of over 250 other species of birds and abandons them to their host's care.

Compared with the European Cuckoo, the Cowbird is not particularly specialized for parasitism (Chance and Hann, 1942). It has not evolved races that specialize in parasitizing certain host species. Its eggs, unlike the Cuckoo's, are of normal size and shell-thickness, and show no mimicry of the host's eggs. Cowbird's eggs, however, hatch with a day or two less incubation than the typical host's eggs. The young Cowbird does not evict its nest-mates, although in many cases it is larger and stronger than they are, and may crowd some or all of them from the nest, or it may usurp the lion's share of food so that the host's young starve. According to Hann (1941), the Cowbird

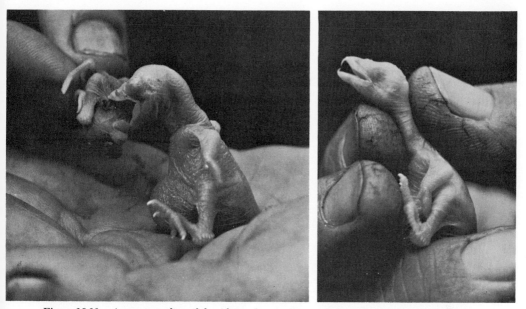

Figure 16.10. A young nestling of the African Greater Honey-guide. Left, attacking its nest-mate, a young barbet. Right, the sharp mandibular hooks drop off after the Honey-guide is about two weeks old and presumably has the nest to itself. Photos by G. Ranger, courtesy of H. Friedmann.

parasitizes the nest of an Ovenbird, *Seiurus aurocapillus*, by furtively entering the nest about 20 minutes before sunrise, taking a few seconds to a minute to lay its egg, and then departing. Either later that day, or on the preceding day, it normally removes one egg of the host species (Fig. 16.11) by piercing it with its mandibles. The European Cuckoo removes an egg, unpierced, at the time it lays its own egg.

A favored host of the Cowbird is the Song Sparrow, *Melospiza melodia*. Mrs. Nice (1937) found, in central Ohio, that for each female Cowbird there were, in different years, from 8 to 15 pairs of Song Sparrow hosts. Studies by Hicks (1934), Nice (1937), and Norris (1947) revealed that from 26 to 78 per cent of the nests of Song Sparrows were parasitized by the Cowbird. Mrs. Nice found that successful non-parasitized nests each raised an average of 3.4 Song Sparrows, while successful parasitized nests raised only 2.4 Song Sparrows. Of the Cowbird eggs laid in Song Sparrow nests, 32 per cent hatched

and fledged, as against 36 per cent of the Song Sparrow eggs.

Most weaverbirds (Ploceidae) raise their own young, but a few have become parasitic, especially the polygynous forms. The widow birds (sub-family Viduinae) are all brood parasites, and some of the waxbills (Estrildinae) construct no nests but use those of other species for incuba-

Figure 16.11. A female Cowbird removing an egg from the nest of an Ovenbird. Photo by H. W. Hann.

ting their own eggs. Not only do the eggs of widow birds resemble those of their favorite hosts, but the plumage of the nestling widows often resembles that of their step-brothers. Most astonishing of all is the striking resemblance between the so-called "feeding targets" or brightly colored gapes of such parasitic nestlings as *Vidua serena* and its host nestling, the Common Waxbill, *Estrilda astrild.* These mimetic resemblances disappear when the young leave the nest. Needless to say, both species of nestlings remain in the nest and grow up together. Otherwise the mimicry would be of little if any use.

INCUBATION PERIODS

Assuming normal, undisturbed incubation, the average time interval between the laying of an egg and the emergence of the young bird from the shell represents the *incubation period* for that species (Heinroth, 1922). The time that an adult bird sits on the eggs does not necessarily coincide with the incubation period. Studies with thermocouples have shown, for example, that some doves may sit on their eggs without heating them, and that at times male goshawks, lacking an incubation patch, will also apparently incubate but not warm the eggs. For practical purposes a species' incubation period may be defined as the time interval between the laying of the last egg of a clutch and the hatching of the last egg (assuming that all eggs hatch).

Great variety is seen in the incubation periods of birds, extending from 11 or 12 days in the Brown-headed Cowbird, *Molothrus ater,* and the white eyes, *Zosterops* spp., to 81 days in the Royal Albatross, *Diomedea epomophora.* Most small passerine species have incubation periods of 12 to 14 days: the American Robin, *Turdus migratorius,* for example, averages 13 days, but the Common Crow, *Corvus brachyrhynchos,* and many other Corvidae require 18 to 20 days. The incubation period of the Domestic Hen,

Gallus gallus, averages 21 days; that of various species of owls, 26 to 36 days; hawks and eagles, 29 to 45 days; most petrels, 38 to 56 days; and albatrosses, 63 to 81 days. The land bird with the longest incubation period is probably one of the megapodes: the Scrub Fowl, *Megapodius freycinet,* whose eggs require 63 days to hatch.

As a very rough general rule, the eggs of large birds have longer incubation periods than those of small species. Surprisingly, however, the tiny hummingbirds require about 16 days, while the much larger Yellow-shafted Flicker, *Colaptes auratus,* hatches its eggs in 11 or 12 days; and the Diving Petrel, *Pelecanoides urinatrix,* incubates its 15 gram egg for 56 days, while the much larger Ostrich, *Struthio camelus,* incubates its 1500 gram egg in only 42 days.

Various naturalists have searched for general principles which might explain the wide diversity found in incubation periods among different species, but thus far no universally valid rule has been discovered. In general, birds of high evolutionary rank like the passerines have relatively short incubation periods, while those of low rank have relatively long ones. This is partly explained by the fact that the more highly evolved species have higher body temperatures. However, the Ruddy Quail-dove, *Geotrygon montana,* which has a low taxonomic rank, hatches its eggs in 12 days. So many variables besides species are involved in incubation times that it is very difficult to know what influence a given factor has. The proximate cause determining the length of incubation is, as Mrs. Nice (1954) makes clear, the rate of development of the embryo within the egg. But the ultimate causes underlying the variable rates of embryonic development are much more difficult to determine.

Ecological factors undeniably have an effect on the incubation period. Among tyrant flycatchers in the tropics, Skutch (1945) found that those that build pensile, relatively inaccessible nests had longer

Table 16.2. Incubation Periods of Hole-Nesting as Compared with Open-Nesting Birds

	PLACE	NUMBER OF SPECIES	AVERAGE DURATION OF INCUBATION	AUTHORITY
Hole-nesters	Europe	18	13.8 days	Lack, 1948
Hole-nesters	Europe	12	13.8	von Haartmann, 1954
Hole-nesters	U.S.A.	10	13.8	Nice, 1954
Open-nesters	Europe	54	13.1	Lack, 1948
Open-nesters	Europe	13	12.2	von Haartmann, 1954
Open-nesters	U.S.A.	11	12.0	Nice, 1954

incubation and nestling periods than did the open-nesters. A comparison of the incubation periods of hole-nesting versus open-nesting birds shows this same relationship (Table 16.2).

Even more striking, once the eggs have hatched, is the variation in duration of the nestling period among tropical American tanagers. Skutch (1954) reported that species which habitually nested low had short periods of 11 to 13 days; those which built open nests higher up had periods averaging 14 to 20 days, while those which built roofed-over nests had nestling periods of 17 to 24 days. A fair assumption is that the shorter periods of open-nesters represent a selective adaptation to higher losses from predation. Heinroth (1938) points out that in Africa, swarming with beasts of prey, the ostrich incubates his 1500 gram egg only 6 weeks, while in Australia, which is poor in predators, the much smaller Emu, *Dromiceius novaehollandiae*, sits on his 600 gram eggs for 8 weeks!

Still other environmental influences may effect incubation periods. Among tanagers and warblers, Skutch (1954) found that incubation periods were longer in the tropics than in the temperate zone. In a seasonal study of the European Wren, *Troglodytes troglodytes*, Kluijver *et al* (1940) discovered that average incubation periods steadily decreased in length as spring progressed: April, 17.5 days; May, 16.3; June, 15.3; and July, 14.5 days. Further, there is

great variation in incubation attentiveness. Some species like the pigeons incubate almost constantly, while many others like the flycatchers are off their nests nearly half of the daylight hours. Such absences probably lengthen appreciably the incubation time. Finally, loosely built nests probably mean greater heat loss and therefore slower incubation.

Much research remains to be done before all these varied factors can be properly assessed. Without question the dominating factor is heredity, which controls the rate of embryonic development and the time of hatching. All of these other influences are either secondary modifiers of the innate clockwork within each egg, or are selective forces that imperceptibly shift the basic hereditary incubation rate.

HATCHING

As the process of incubation goes on, an egg steadily loses weight. Part of this loss represents evaporated moisture, and part of it gaseous metabolic waste from the respiring embryo within. The average weight loss of 24 eggs of the Bluebird, *Sialia sialis*, during the 13 day incubation period was 12.6 per cent (Hamilton, 1943). Whether an egg hatches properly or not may depend, among other things, on its treatment during incubation. Eggs of the Mallard, *Anas platyrhynchos*, were incubated under experimentally controlled conditions of moisture by Mayhew (1955). The best hatching success was obtained from eggs dipped in water once a day and incubated at 65 per cent relative humidity. This relationship explains why ducks nesting in fields far from water have poor hatching success in dry summers.

Many birds, particularly those that lay eggs at about sunrise, are fairly constant in their hour of laying. The hour at which eggs of a given species hatch, however, is much more variable. Painstaking observations by Skutch (1952) of the time of hatching of eggs of Costa Rican passerines showed that of 26 hatchings of 2 species of flycatchers of the genus *Myiozetetes,* 11 occurred at night, 14 in the forenoon, and only 1 in the afternoon. This non-random distribution of hatching hours was explained by Skutch as apparently due to a diurnal rhythm in the efforts of the young bird to break out of the shell. Records of 93 hatchings among 11 species of finches, tanagers, and wood warblers gave 27 at night, 51 in the forenoon, and 15 in the afternoon. Here the time of hatching was thought possibly to be determined by the hour of laying and a constancy in the rate of embryonic de-

velopment. In either case, the adaptive "advantage of hatching early in the day is that the nestling can be promptly fed; whereas if it hatched late in the afternoon or after nightfall it might have to wait many hours for its first meal."

The chief role in hatching is played by the chick itself. In preparation for liberation from its limestone prison, the maturing chick develops two tools. One is a short, pointed, horny "egg-tooth" at the tip of its upper mandible. The other is a set of prominent hatching muscles located largely on the upper side of its neck and head, and apparently used to force the head and egg-tooth upward against the inside of the egg shell. Both of these structures are transitory and disappear shortly after hatching. It is significant that the hatching muscle in the domestic chick reaches its highest state of development the day before the chick breaks out of its shell (Fisher, 1958).

Sometimes, a day or two before hatching, the young chick inside the egg makes itself known by peeping. This anticipatory conversation with the world is particularly common in gallinaceous birds. On hearing their eggs peep, incubating birds often become excited and may even fetch food as though anxious to get on with the next phase of the domestic cycle.

The first step in hatching is the puncturing, or "pipping," of the shell by the chick with its outwardly-pressed egg tooth. For most young birds the escape from the egg is a methodical, laborious process. Normally the head of the chick lies toward the blunt end of the egg near the air chamber. For a day or two, the chick hammers at its shell with its egg tooth. Then, as described by Allen *in* Bent, 1923) for the chick of the Black Duck, *Anas rubripes,* it chips its first hole about one-third of the distance from the end of the egg.

Figure 16.12.   Curlew chicks hatching. Note the egg-tooth on the tip-end of the beak of the upper bird. Photo by E. Hosking.

". . . then came a second or two of rest, followed by what felt like a scramble inside; then a second of quiet, and the horny little knob on the end of the bill was driven through the shell one-eighth of an inch to the right of the first puncture. This routine was re-

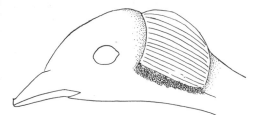

Figure 16.13. The hatching muscle in the domestic chick as it appears at the time of hatching. Diagrammatic. After Fisher.

peated over and over until some 25 or 30 punctures had been made, completely encircling one end of the egg . . . The efforts seemed stronger as it started around the same circle again, and the cap of the shell would be lifted a little each time showing that it was attached by little more than the tough membrane beneath the shell. Before the second circle was half completed, it tore the cap loose so that it could be raised like the lid of a box, with one inch of the membrane acting as a hinge. In freeing itself from the shell the neck was stretched out and the little one breathed for the first time. Then the shoulders were pushed out into my hand, free of the shell, . . . while the bird lay gasping and gaping widely with its bill. In half a minute more it was entirely free from the shell and lay weak and helpless in the sun . . ."

Other Black Ducklings "went through the same procedure, invariably breaking the shell from left to right." One can see in this performance the significance of rotation of the eggs in the nest during incubation. Neglect of this instinctive behavior by the parent would result in the adhesion of the chick to the inside of the shell and hence allow no chance for the chick to cut its liberating circle of punctures.

Not all birds hatch with equal facility. Young of the Wood Thrush, *Hylocichla mustelina,* take from 5 to 22 hours between the first chipping and emergence from the shell; the European Wren, *Troglodytes troglodytes,* 2 days; the Royal Albatross, *Diomedea epomophora,* 3 days; Sooty Shearwaters, *Puffinus griseus,* at least 4 days.

Parent birds rarely assist their young to emerge from the shell, but merely stand by as interested observers. Once the young have freed themselves, the parents either eat the shells or carry them some distance from the nest, where they will not reveal its location to predators. Young flamingos are said to eat their own egg shells, possibly as a mineral supplement to their first meal.

Precocial birds do not bother about the shells if, like the ducks and pheasants, the parent leads the young from the nest within a day or so after they hatch out. Since such precocial species do not feed their young but merely lead them to food, it is essential that all eggs hatch out at about the same time. The synchronous hatching of the dozen eggs of the Greater Prairie Chicken, *Tympanuchus cupido,* is described by Gross (*in* Bent, 1932) as:

"remarkably uniform, and in some instances the time elapsed from the time of the hatching of the first to the last egg is less than an hour. In cases where incubation started before the last one or two eggs were laid, the latter may be delayed, and in several cases . . . they failed to hatch in time, and the contained young were left behind when the brood left the nest."

Those young that survive the ordeal of hatching emerge into a world which presents them with two immediate problems: to find food, and at the same time to avoid becoming food for some other animal. A high proportion of young birds meet this unhappy fate before they become independent of parental care.

SUGGESTED READINGS

For general treatment of the broad field of eggs and incubation, see Davis, *Breeding Biology of Birds,* in Wolfson's *Recent Studies in Avian Biology,* and Kendeigh, *Parental Care and its Evolution in Birds.* Good introductions to the problem of brood parasitism are found in Chance, *The Truth about the Cuckoo,* and Friedmann, *The Cowbirds.*

SEVENTEEN

The Care and Development of Young

Soon as the little ones chip the shell,
Six wide mouths are open for food;
Robert of Lincoln bestirs him well,
Gathering seeds for the hungry brood.
William Cullen Bryant, *Robert of Lincoln.*

The rearing of young birds follows a general pattern: they hatch out, are fed by the parents, are protected from enemies and from the elements, and finally are feathered and fly off to live their own lives. But there are two distinct types of newly hatched birds, and they fit the pattern in quite different ways.

One type, the *precocial* bird, hatches out covered with down, legs well developed, eyes open and alert, and soon able to feed itself. Because it is usually able to leave the nest and to run after its parents shortly after hatching, it is also called a *nidifuge* or nest fugitive. The young of the American Golden Plover, *Pluvialis dominica*, leave their arctic nest within two hours after hatching. Nidifuges are often ground-nesting species that, as adults, are good runners or good swimmers and feed either on the ground or in the water. These precocial birds include such forms as the ostrich and its relatives, loons, grebes, ducks, geese, swans, gallinaceous birds, marsh birds and shore birds. Some semi-precocial young, such as those of flamingos, coots, and some gulls and terns, may remain at the nest for a few days after hatching and be fed by their parents, but these are exceptional.

The other type, the *altricial* bird, is born naked, or nearly so, is usually blind, and is too weak to support itself on its legs. About the only thing it can do when newly hatched is to hold up its unsteady, gaping mouth for food. It may be able to do that very soon. A nearly naked young Wood Thrush, *Hylocichla mustelina*, four minutes after it frees itself from its shell, can call and gape for food. Altricial parents supply all food until the young are nearly adult in size. Naturally, such birds remain confined to the nest for some days or weeks. They are therefore called *nidicoles* or nest-dwellers. These helpless, altricial nidicoles are found among the pelicans, hawks, pigeons, parrots, cuckoos, owls, swifts, hummingbirds, kingfishers, woodpeckers, and passerine birds.

An interesting relationship between egg type and precocity in young birds has been pointed out by Heinroth (1938). In a precocial species the egg is about 35 per cent yolk by volume, and in many ducks may be as much as 50 per cent. But in altricial species such as the eagle, the yolk makes up only about 20 per cent of the egg. Not all of the yolk in eggs of precocial species is consumed by the time of hatching. From one-third to one-seventh of it remains in the belly of the newly hatched offspring. The greater the proportion of yolk in the fresh egg, the more there remains in the hatched youngster. An altricial bird normally uses up its yolk before hatching, and therefore has less reserve food to sustain its first days of life. Accordingly, the altricial nidicole is more dependent on parental feeding. The nidifugous or precocial domestic chick, on the other hand, has a generous 5.3 grams of yolk left in its belly 12 hours after hatching; 3.3 grams a day later; 2.5 grams at 3 days, 0.6 gram at 3 to 4 days, and 0.05 gram 5 to 6 days after hatching, according to Stresemann (1927–1934). This explains why it is that, on a two or three day trip from hatchery to farmer, young chicks need not be fed. In general, the weight of a hatched bird is about two-thirds that of the fresh egg from which it came. The

Figure 17.1. Left, the one-day-old precocial, or nidifugous, chick of the Ruffed Grouse, eyes open, alert, and ready to run. Right, the one-day-old nestling of the House Sparrow, naked, blind, helpless.

evaporation of water and the loss of gases and feces from the metabolizing embryo account for the difference.

The most precocious species of bird known, and the one that is most like the reptiles in hatching from its eggs completely independent young, is the Australian megapode, or incubator bird, a member of the Galliformes. The young of this bird, on hatching from the buried eggs, are reported to scramble to the surface sufficiently feathered to be able to fly several meters, and to begin a completely independent life.

A highly significant difference between precocial and altricial birds, as Portmann (1950) makes clear, is one of organ proportion and development. In the altricial nidicoles the organs of metabolism are enlarged at the expense of the rest of the body, above all at the expense of the nervous system, the sense organs and the locomotor organs. The young nidicole "is a veritable growth machine permitting prodigious metabolism of an efficiency not found elsewhere among the higher vertebrates." For example, a Cuckoo that weighs but 2 grams at hatching will, in only three weeks, attain the adult weight of 100 grams—a multiplication of 50 times its original weight. Such fantastically rapid growth is completely unknown in mammals. But some birds, particularly the nidicoles, have achieved it at a heavy price in nervous development, as the following table illustrates:

Table 17.1. A comparison of recently hatched nidicole and nidifuge young,
to show the proportions of eyes, brains, and intestines to body weight
(after Portmann)

| TYPE | SPECIES | PERCENTAGES OF TOTAL BODY WEIGHT | | |
		EYES	BRAIN	INTESTINES
Nidicole:	Swift, *Apus melba*	6.1	3.1	14.6
	Starling, *Sturnus vulgaris*	4.0	3.2	14.1
Nidifuge:	Quail, *Coturnix coturnix*	5.5	6.2	9.7
	Pheasant, *Phasianus colchicus*	4.2	4.2	6.5

As an example of localized emphasis in nidifuge development, Sutter (1951) notes that the brain of a newly hatched Quail, *Coturnix coturnix*, "has only to increase its weight three times to reach adult size, while the body weight increases as much as twenty-one times." On the other hand, the cerebellum of the just-hatched altricial Starling is no further advanced than that of the half-incubated (12 day) domestic chick embryo still in its shell. It should be made clear, however, that once the nidicole begins its rapid growth, it soon outstrips the average nidifuge in mental endowment.

One further distinction between nidicole and nidifuge relates to the development of nerve fibers in the brain. The growth of myelin sheaths—a sign of maturation—is at hatching much farther along in nidifuge young than in nidicoles. In the evolutionary race for survival, the nidifuge species have gambled on a longer infancy, tempered however with alert senses and athletic locomotor equipment. The nidicoles on the other hand are born stupid and sluggish, but hurry through the vulnerable period of infancy by eating and growing at a furious tempo.

FEEDING THE YOUNG

As soon as they emerge from the shell, young birds are brooded by the parents to dry their down, if they have any, and to warm and shelter them against the elements. If the young are precocial they are soon led away from the nest to a suitable spot where they shortly learn to feed themselves. In precocial species such as the Domestic Fowl and many ducks, the female takes complete charge of the brood from this time on, leading the young to food, but not feeding them directly. In altricial species the young are fed by the parents, normally from the first day on.

Among most hummingbirds, and other species which are polygamous, the male does not aid in caring for the young; and of course in brood parasites, such as the cuckoo or cowbird, neither parent ordinarily shows any concern for its offspring. But in many of the precocial shorebirds and in the majority of passerines both sexes take some part in rearing the young. In many instances the female spends more of her time brooding the delicate young than feeding them, and the male devotes himself to finding food for them. In other cases the female feeds young more assiduously than the male. The female Red-eyed Vireo, *Vireo olivaceous*, has been observed to do about 75 per cent of the feeding of the young; the female Arctic Warbler, *Phylloscopus borealis*, does about 74 per cent of the feeding, but the male brings more food per trip, as is often the case in such situations.

In some species, such as the English Robin, *Erithacus rubecula*, or the House Wren, *Troglodytes aëdon*, the female may desert her young and begin laying eggs for the second brood, leaving the male alone to finish feeding the first brood. In the Snowy Owl, *Nyctea scandiaca*, the female broods the young constantly while they are small, and the male brings all the food. Many doves run their household duties on a regular shift, the male feeding the young from mid-morning to late afternoon, and the female taking charge the remainder of the 24 hours. The male European Chiff-chaff, *Phylloscopus collybita,* does not help feed his young; he spends his time in the treetops singing and defending the territory. Here seems to be an instance where natural selection favored territory defense over the feeding of young.

KINDS OF FOOD

The kind of food fed the young varies with species. For nearly all species, whether the adults eat fruits, seeds, insects or other animal food, the young commonly eat a diet high in protein. Such a diet most effectively promotes the rapid multiplication of cells in the growing young bird. An analysis of the stomach contents of Ruffed Grouse, *Bonasa umbellus,* chicks in Virginia, by Stewart (1956) showed a gradual change in diet with age. In late May and early June they ate 91 per cent insect and 9 per cent plant food; in August, 1 per cent insect and 99 per cent plant food. A study of the stomach contents of 4,848 grain-eating adult House Sparrows, *Passer domesticus,* by Kalmbach (1958) revealed a diet of 3.4 per cent animal matter, and 96.6 per cent vegetable; the stomachs of 3,156

young, on the contrary, contained 68.1 per cent animal and 31.2 per cent vegetable matter. The fruit-eating Quetzal, *Pharomachrus mocinno,* of Central America, Skutch (1945) found, fed its young almost exclusively on insects for the first ten days.

That the adult bird has at least a dim awareness of the appropriateness of animal food for the growing young, was observed by Van Tyne (1951) in Michigan. An adult male Cardinal, *Richmondena cardinalis,* en route to its nest of young with a beakful of worms, stopped at a feeding shelf, put down the worms to eat a few sunflower seeds for himself, then picked up the worms again and flew on to the nest, presumably to feed them to the young. The young themselves seem instinctively to prefer an animal diet to a vegetable diet when given a choice. Young incubator-raised ducklings, when presented with a mixed meal of duckweed and small invertebrates, will pick out the animal food.

METHODS OF FEEDING

Great variety is shown in the ways young birds get their food. In many precocial species, such as the Domestic Hen, the adult merely points out the food to the young, who pick it up off the ground. This technique is followed by the gallinaceous birds and many other nidifugous species whose young soon become able to distingush palatable from unpalatable in-

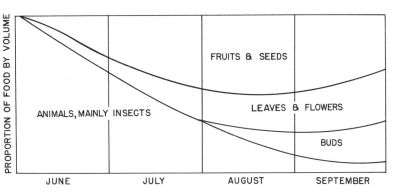

Figure 17.2. A generalized diagram showing the seasonal changes in diet for young Ruffed Grouse. After Edminster.

PROPORTION OF FOOD BY VOLUME

FRUITS & SEEDS

ANIMALS, MAINLY INSECTS

LEAVES & FLOWERS

BUDS

JUNE   JULY   AUGUST   SEPTEMBER

sects. By far the majority of young, particularly the passerines, woodpeckers and cuckoos, are fed directly from the beak of the parent in the way familiar to anyone who has watched a robin feed its babies.

Many parent birds swallow the food as they find it, and later regurgitate it at the nest. This method of feeding has two advantages. The adult can carry more food per trip, and the digestive juices, regurgitated with the food, aid the digestion of the food in the stomachs of the young. Gulls and storks regurgitate their food in front of the nestlings, who then pick it up from the ground or the nest-rim. Young penguins and pelicans plunge shoulder-deep into the gullets of their parents and feed on the shrimp and fish the parents have caught. The Diving Petrel, *Pelecanoides urinatrix,* has been observed by Richdale (1943) feeding its young at night in its underground burrow. The young petrel places its slightly open beak crosswise within the beak of the parent just in from the sea. The adult regurgitates a red, creamy ribbon of food "as if from a tube of toothpaste," which the young bird seizes with the tip of its rapidly vibrating mandibles. Adult spoonbills and albatrosses likewise take the bills of their young crosswise between their own beaks and direct the vomited food by means of their tongues into the young birds' mouths. Heron young, on the contrary, take their parents' beaks crosswise within their own

Figure 17.3. Young pelicans plunge deep into the adult bird's gullet to feed on regurgitated fish.

Figure 17.4. A male Little Bittern regurgitating food into the mouth of a nestling. The young bird seizes and tugs the mandible of the parent. Photo by E. Hosking.

when feeding. Many finches thrust regurgitated insects and seeds into the gaping beaks of their young, the hummingbird even thrusting its sword-like beak two-thirds its length down the gullet of its young, almost far enough to pierce the stomach.

All pigeons and doves regurgitate "pigeon's milk," a creamy substance very like rabbit's milk in its protein, fat and ash content. Even more remarkably, as Lewis (1944) has revealed, the same endocrine mechanisms are involved in each animal. The milk of pigeons and mammals comes from fatty cells shed from the epithelial tissues in either the bird's crop or the mammal's mammary glands. If prolactin from the anterior pituitary gland is injected experimentally into these animals, both crop and mammary glands will begin producing milk. Not only will the crop walls of the pigeon begin functioning, but the pigeon will exhibit broodiness and protective care of eggs and young. The young domestic pigeons feed on pigeon's milk some five days; then, for up to 18 days, they eat a mixture of pigeon's milk and crop-softened grain.

Predatory birds bring food in their beaks or talons, and feed it, torn to bits, to their

Figure 17.5. The Short-toed Eagle of Europe feeds its nestlings bits of snakes, amphibians, and lizards. When older, the young bird will begin to tear apart the prey brought to it. Photo by E. Hosking.

small young. They do not tear the food when their offspring are older. In the European Kestrel, *Falco tinnunculus,* the female takes the prey brought to the nest by the male, and tears it into small pieces and feeds the young. Should the female die (Heinroth, 1938) the young may also die, since they are unable to swallow the entire prey tendered them by the uncomprehending male, who lacks the instinct to tear the meat into bits. When the young are older and stronger, they are able to tear up the prey themselves.

TIMING OF THE FEEDING INSTINCT

The urge to feed their young is deepseated in most birds. It rises to the surface and will not be denied when the clockworks of the reproductive cycle reach the proper time. In fact, the instinct appears even in young birds themselves, so that the young of the first brood of the summer may help in feeding their younger brothers and sisters of the second brood. This incipient parental care has been observed in coots, tanagers, fairy wrens, swallows, bluebirds, and other species. It is possible that the habit of young birds feeding later broods may be of evolutionary significance in the development of social life and communal nesting, as in the tropical Smooth-billed Ani, *Crotophaga ani.*

Sometimes the reproductive clockworks, like man-made clocks, lose time, and the parents raise their young later than normally. In such cases the instinct to care for their young may be superseded by the stronger urge to migrate south, and the hungry young are abandoned and die. This occasionally happens in swallows and martins, when an early autumnal cold spell makes food scarce. Or the urge may appear in an adult before the young are born, in which case anticipatory food-bringing occurs. Adult Starlings may bring insects to the nest a week before the eggs hatch (Schüz, 1943); but the insects are not fed to the mate. Anticipatory "feeding" of this sort has been reported in wood warblers, tanagers, and other species. Skutch (1942) relates, contrariwise, how the instinct to feed its young dawned tardily in a male Mexican Trogon, *Trogon mexicanus*. Although the female began feeding the young as soon as they hatched, the male would fly to the nest cavity with an insect in its beak, sit there stupidly observing the hungry, clamoring young, and then fly off with the insect undelivered. Two or three days after the young hatched out, the male made five successive trips to the nest with food, but fed the young on only one of them. Two days later, how-

ever, he fed them regularly on every trip. In some species, such as the Common Nighthawk, *Chordeiles minor*, the young may not eat until they are two days old (Bent, 1940), living on stored yolk up to that time. If, in such species, the parents are ready to feed the young before they are ready to accept the food, this hereditary disparity in timing could have been the evolutionary beginning of the habit of regurgitation. Finally, the instinct to feed young seems to achieve in the adult bird a momentum that carries on when the reason for its existence ceases. Common Murres, *Uria aalge*, that have lost their young frequently return and offer food to the empty nest for two or three days following the loss. It may be that the numerous cases reported of birds feeding foster children of the same or of other species result from loss of their own young coupled with strong momentum from the feeding instinct. An amusing tale is told by Southern (1952) of a pair of Spotted Flycatchers, *Muscicapa striata*,

Figure 17.6. A European Nightjar feeding one of its chicks regurgitated insects. The large eyes of the adult are correlated with its crepuscular habits. Photo by E. Hosking.

Figure 17.7. Sometimes the urge to feed transcends species, and here, even class boundaries. This Cardinal was discovered feeding an adopted "brood" of goldfish. Photo by Paul Lemmons, Shelby, N.C.

whose nest with eggs was destroyed in a storm. They were observed the next day energetically stuffing butterflies down the throats of week-old Blackbirds, *Turdus merula*. When the rightful parents of the Blackbirds attempted to approach their young, the Flycatchers viciously drove them away. However, once the young Blackbirds were fledged, their own parents took full charge of them.

Perhaps the zenith of interspecific feeding of young is represented by a North Carolina Cardinal, *Richmondena cardinalis*, that was observed for several days feeding goldfish in a garden pool. As the goldfish crowded to the edge of the pool with their open mouths, the Cardinal, standing on the pool's edge, expertly delivered mouthfuls of worms to them! One can only guess how such a strange association arose, but it seems likely that the Cardinal, bereft of its young, approached the pool to drink, and was met by gaping goldfish accustomed to being fed by humans. The two instinctive appetites, one to feed, the other to be fed, magnetically

attracted each other; and a temporary, satisfying bond was set up.

THE STIMULI FOR FEEDING

Such peculiar happenings raise the question: What stimulus excites the feeding responses in birds? The young of some species will gape spontaneously. Newly-hatched Starlings kept in a dark, vibration-free room were observed by Holzapfel (1939) to gape without apparent external stimuli up to four or five days in isolated birds, and eleven days in broods where one bird stimulated another.

In nature, quite a variety of stimuli can elicit gaping in the young. The light-colored swollen flanges at the angles of the jaws of many altricial young are highly supplied with tactile nerve-endings (Herbst corpuscles). When these flanges are touched, the nestling's beak suddenly and vigorously springs open as though activated electrically. A slight shaking of a nestful of very young birds will often cause them to gape. When adult Bank Swallows, *Riparia riparia,* enter the nest burrow to feed their young they usually give a series of high-pitched notes, but if these fail to arouse the proper response, they gently trample on the young until they gape and are fed. Air currents are the tactile stimulus used to elicit the begging response in Chimney Swifts, *Chaetura pelagica,* a response no doubt based on the wing-flapping descent of the parents in the chimney.

Acoustic stimuli are used by the Chough, *Coracia pyrrhocorax,* and even a crude human imitation of their feeding call will arouse the gaping response. Clapping of the hands will cause some young cuckoos to gape. Many altricial young, after several days in the nest, respond to special feeding notes of the parents.

Since altricial young are commonly born blind, visual stimuli are not at first effective, although the young of woodpeckers and other species will often gape when the opening to the nest hole is quietly darkened. When such nestlings grow older and gain their sight, tactile and acoustic stimuli (except feeding-calls) lose their meaning, and the young respond to visual stimuli. Experiments with crude cardboard models of their parents' beaks show that the pattern and color of the beak are remarkably potent releasers of the begging response. The chick of a Herring Gull, *Larus argentatus,* as Tinbergen (1953) discovered, will respond again and again, up to hundreds of times, to a crude model of its parent's beak, in spite of the fact that the dummy never provides it with food. The chick simply cannot resist the stimulus. In similar experiments by Collias and Collias (1957) on incubator-raised chicks of the Franklin Gull, *Larus pipixcan,* the chicks pecked at a cardboard model of a red (parental color) bill seven times as often as at a white bill, and five times as often as at a green bill. In all species, the gaping response of the young probably depends both on the hunger of the young and on the external releasing stimuli.

Just as young birds need signals to set off their begging response, so adults need stimuli to release their feeding behavior. Here again, feeding "in vacuo" or without apparent external stimuli occasionally occurs. A caged Song Thrush, *Turdus ericetorum,* for example, if given a worm at the proper stage in its reproductive cycle, will kill it, hop about restlessly giving its nest call, and finally attempt to stick the worm in a crack (Heinroth, 1938)! The instinct will not be denied.

Normally, of course, the hungry young attract and stimulate the feeding adults with their cries and twitters, their vehement head waving and their wide-open mouths. The young of many altricial species also display remarkable "targets" at which the parents direct their food. Most nidicole young possess gaudy mouth linings, the preferred colors being yellows, reds, or oranges. Moreover, the flanges at the margins of the jaws are bright yellow

Figure 17.8. Young Bearded Tits, showing in their gaping mouths the conspicuous white "targets" which are thought to stimulate and direct the feeding behavior of the parent bird. Photo by E. Hosking.

or white, particularly so in young that live in dark, covered nests (hole-dwelling passerines, Picidae and Coraciidae). Even more striking are the bizarre structures in the mouths of such species as the desert Horned Lark, *Eremophila alpestris,* with jet-black spots and bars on the tongue and bright orange roof of the mouth. The young Bearded Tit, *Panurus biarmicus,* is described by Pycraft (1910) as possessing a brilliant carnelian-red roof to its mouth, supplied on either side of its mid-line with symmetrical rows of glistening white conical processes. Nestlings of the Gould-ian Finch, *Poephila gouldiae,* not only have the roof of the mouth marked with five black spots symmetrically disposed, and a black bar crossing the tongue, but have at each angle of the jaws three "re-flection pearls," bead-like bodies brilliantly opalescent in emerald green and blue. These reflective spheres, found in many Ploceidae, glow like small lamps in the gloom of the covered nest and help the parents find the open mouths of the young. Evidence that all of these extravagant structures function to arouse and direct the feeding response of the adult is borne out by the fact that they are quite transitory, disappearing entirely when the young ma- ture into adults.

A question naturally arises regarding the equal sharing of food among the young in a nest. Is it a matter of intelligent judg- ment on the part of the parent birds? Do they take care to see that all young are fed in turn, or that an underfed weakling gets preferred attention? This, too, seems to be a purely mechanical, instinctive business. When a young bird has just swallowed a worm, its swallowing reflex ceases to func- tion again for some moments. So, when the adult comes to the nest and blindly thrusts some food in the nearest or most attractive gaping mouth, the youngster will swallow the food if it is hungry, but will not if it is sated. If the food is not swallowed, the parent takes it out and thrusts it into other mouths until it goes all the way down. Thus, instinctive responses normally assure an equal distribution of food.

Does instinct explain the apparently in- telligent reaction to brood-size: larger and older broods needing and getting more food per day than smaller and younger broods? Or, for example, the remarkable adjustment by a female flycatcher to the emergency needs of her brood when the male parent dies? In such a situation the female, with a great burst of energy, be- gins feeding her offspring with as much food as the two parents together did pre- viously. In a series of ingenious experi- ments with the Pied Flycatcher, *Musci-capa hypoleuca,* in Finland, von Haart-

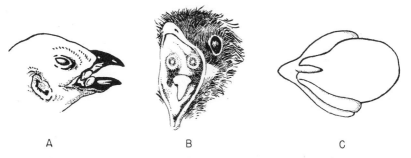

A   B   C

Figure 17.9. *A,* "Reflection pearls" at the angle of the jaws of an oriental parrot-finch. These light-reflecting bodies aid the parent in directing food into the nestling's mouth. After Sarasin. *B,* The attractive targets on the palate of the young Crested Coua of Mada-gascar are in the form of a raised bulls-eye and outer ring of glistening white, separated by a bright red ring. After Bluntschli. *C,* Dorsal view of a young Starling's head, showing the swollen, sensitive mouth flanges. When these are touched, the nestling's mouth springs open. After Portmann.

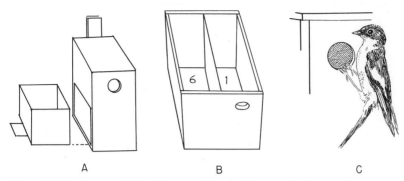

A   B   C

Figure 17.10. Experimental nest boxes used by von Haartman to discover the stimulus that controls the amount of food which adults bring to their broods. *A,* A nest box with a drawer-like bottom that permits the rapid and unobtrusive changing of nestlings. *B,* A double nest box (with top removed) showing the thin cardboard partition between chambers. The parent flycatchers could hear the six hungry young in the closed, left-hand chamber, but could see and feed only the single nestling in the right-hand one. *C,* An adult Pied Flycatcher. *A* and *B* after von Haartman.

man (1953) analyzed such behavior and determined that here also the adjustment of the parent bird is instinctive and not intelligent.

By means of mechanical registering devices at 35 nest boxes, von Haartman established the fact that large broods of Pied Flycatchers received food more often than small broods. When he removed five young from a brood of seven, leaving but two in the nest, the number of feeding visits from the adults gradually decreased. If the number was reduced to one, the feeding visits fell off even more. By using young from other nests, and a nest box with a drawer-like bottom, sated young could quickly and unobtrusively be removed and replaced with hungry young in the experimental nest. When five of a brood of seven young were removed from the nest and the two remaining young fed, then shortly replaced with two very hungry young from another nest, and as soon as these were fed they too were replaced by two other hungry substitutes, and so on, it was found that the parent birds lavished practically as much food on the transient brood of two as they had previously fed to all seven. It was the reaction of the young that stimulated the parents to bring food, and not their number.

To determine whether the parents re-

acted to the appearance of the gaping young or to their cries, von Haartman arranged a double nest box with one youngster in the normal side with an entrance, and six hungry brood-mates in the other side, invisible and inaccessible to the adults and separated from the normal side by a cardboard partition. Thus the

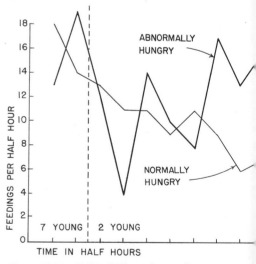

Figure 17.11. If 5 Pied Flycatcher nestlings are removed from a brood of 7, the 2 remaining birds ("normally hungry" in chart) are fed a decreasing number of times per half-hour by the parents. But if the two that remain in the nest box are continually and surreptitiously replaced with abnormally hungry young, the feeding rate increases sharply. After von Haartman.

parents could hear the hungry six but neither see nor reach them. The hungry, clamoring six in the hidden side stimulated the parents to feed the single accessible bird with more than twice its normal budget of food; and when it was so stuffed that it could swallow no more, the parents would urge it to accept more food with their feeding call, upon which the hunger-concert in the adjoining chamber would be redoubled, and to no avail! In fact, their piteous cries even attracted strange adults to perch on the roof of the box; they, of course, could not feed the clamoring young any more than could their own parents. So, in this species, it is the hunger cry of the young that provides the most effective stimulus to feeding behavior in the adults.

FREQUENCY AND AMOUNT OF FEEDING

Precocial young soon learn to feed themselves, usually under parental guidance, but altricial young must be fed for

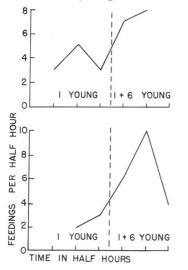

Figure 17.12. Parent birds feed a single nestling at an accelerated rate when they are stimulated by the hunger cries of 6 other invisible, inaccessible young. Left of the dotted line in each curve is shown the rate of feeding for the single nestling by itself; right of the line, the rate for the same bird while 6 hungry young are clamoring in the adjacent chamber. After von Haartman.

a period of days, weeks, or even months. Food is ordinarily brought to the altricial young fairly regularly, but the frequency of the trips varies according to species, the number of young, the age of the young, the method of carrying food, the time of day, the season, and the weather. Young of the Golden Eagle, *Aquila chrysaëtos,* are fed a hare or a grouse twice daily; those of a Bald Eagle, *Haliaeetus leucocephalus,* receive food about four or five times daily. Half-grown young Barn Owls, *Tyto alba,* are brought prey about ten times a night. Sooty Shearwaters, *Puffinus griseus,* feed their young every other night on the average, but bring single meals that often weigh about as much as the nestling.

At the other extreme are small insectivorous birds such as the Great Tit, *Parus major,* which has been reported making as many as 900 feeding visits to the nest per day, or 60 per hour. These species bring small amounts of food each trip. Among those species that regurgitate food, larger and hence less frequent loads are brought to the nest. An African swift, *Apus caffer,* that carries food in a sublingual pouch, feeds regurgitated insects to its young about once each hour; but the Pied Flycatcher, which brings insects in the tip of its bill, feeds the nearly-fledged young 33 times an hour, or a total of some 6200 feeding trips during the nest life of the young. During cold, wet weather, when insects are not flying, the European Swift, *Apus apus,* may not feed its young for many days. The young live on their stored fat and may lose as much as one-half their weight, but by reverting to reptilian cold-bloodedness, they may survive as long as 21 days without food—a thing completely unheard of in other small altricial young.

The rate of feeding normally increases with the growth of the young. At first, most nestlings eat *relatively* more food (often as much as their own weight per day) and grow more rapidly than they do later on. As they approach fledging, they eat absolutely more but relatively less per

Figure 17.13. A House Wren may make as many as 500 trips a day, bringing food to its young. Photo by G. R. Austing.

day—perhaps one-fourth of their body weight per day. For example, a brood of five young Ovenbirds, *Seiurus aurocapillus,* was found by Hann (1937) to receive 27 feedings the first day out of the shell, and 123 feedings the last day before leaving the nest. Bussmann (1943) reported the mechanically recorded daily feedings of a nestful of six young European Nuthatches, *Sitta europaea,* as follows:

DAYS AFTER HATCHING:	FEEDING TRIPS PER DAY:	DAYS AFTER HATCHING:	FEEDING TRIPS PER DAY:
2	119	14	263
4	166	16	276
6	255	18	353
8	263	20	335
11	215	22	270
12	287	24	(Leave nest)

These are rather typical figures for a small hole-nesting passerine; and they reveal not only the increase in daily feedings with an increase in age and appetite of the young, but also a decline in the frequency of feedings shortly before the young leave the nest. This, too, is typical of many species and may reflect the fatigue of the overworked parents, or a naturally evolved device to encourage the nearly-fledged young to leave the nest and seek their own food. As a possible example of the latter function, the Manx

Shearwater, *Procellaria puffinus,* requires about 72 days to fledge, the last 12 of which are spent without food. After about six foodless days, deserted by their parents, the fat chicks come to the mouth of the burrow a short while each night and exercise their wings. After about a week of this, they leave the burrow, make their way to the sea, plunge in and begin an independent life.

It sometimes happens that the parent bird cannot secure enough food to feed the full brood, in which case the weaker individual of the family starves, or, in predatory species, may be eaten by the parent or by his brothers. In the nests of Golden and Bald Eagles ordinarily only one eaglet grows up to leave the nest, although two eggs may have hatched out. The younger, weaker eaglet becomes a meal for his older, stronger brother or sister.

Work Expended by Parents in Feeding Young

When one considers the energy required to raise a brood of demanding young birds, it is not surprising that the parents show fatigue at the end of the nesting period. Some species travel great distances to gather food for a single meal for the young; the White Pelicans, *Pelecanus erythrorhynchos*, of Great Salt Lake go as far as 160 kilometers (100 miles), and Flesh-footed Shearwaters, *Puffinus carneipes*, of the South Atlantic, 136 kilometers. A pair of Blackfooted Albatrosses, *Diomedea nigripes*, spend as much as six months feeding their single youngster. North of the Arctic Circle many species put in a long day caring for their broods. Several twenty-four-hour

observations have shown that a female Arctic Warbler, *Phylloscopus borealis*, fed her young steadily for an 18-hour day; a pair of Pied Flycatchers fed theirs for 19.6 hours, and in Lapland an adult male Bluethroat, *Cyanosylvia svecica*, began feeding his young at 3:00 A.M. and retired for the night at 11:45 P.M., nearly a twenty-one hour working day! It is small wonder that the female Pied Flycatcher loses 17 per cent of her weight by the end of the feeding period in Finland.

NEST SANITATION

Most passerine nidicoles will tolerate eggs or young birds in their nests, but no foreign objects. In a small nest crowded with six or eight young birds, the need for scrupulous sanitation seems clear. The nest must be kept dry and warm, and it should not afford a breeding site for insect and other parasites, nor should the careless disposal of feces betray its location to predators. To these ends many altricial species, especially passerines and woodpeckers, instinctively remove the fecal sacs of the young immediately upon their discharge. Since the sacs are en-

Figure 17.14. A Barred Warbler removing a fecal sac from the cloaca of one of its nestlings. Photo by P. O. Swanberg.

veloped in a clean, tough mucus membrane, the task is simple. In many species the feces are expelled by the young bird as it is fed, are immediately seized by the parent and either (in the first few days) eaten or (later) carried away from the nest site. Of 112 removals of fecal sacs of the Brown Thrasher, *Toxostoma rufum*, observed by Gabrielson, 104 sacs were taken from the nestling that was being fed on that visit. Excreta are taken away from the nest by passerines on an average of about one trip in four.

When adult birds eat the feces of nestlings, they probably make use of the same kind of digestive economy that occurs in rabbits and hares. These animals have a large caecum in which cellulose foods are partly digested by bacteria. Two kinds of feces are formed: the common, small, brown droppings, and a larger, softer, lighter type which comes from the caecum, and which the rabbit eats directly from the anus. By passing this food through its digestive tract a second time, the rabbit brings about its more complete digestion (Schmidt-Nielsen, 1960). It seems probable that food passing through the very young nestling still retains some undigested remnants which provide nourishment for the parent bird, who is often too busy feeding the young nestlings to seek food for itself.

In disposing of fecal sacs, swallows and martins may drop them over water; wrens and nuthatches deposit them on tree branches away from the nest. As young swallows grow strong enough, they back up to the edge of the nest and defecate in a location more convenient for fecal removal. Some kingfishers possess an unusually muscular cloaca, and the older young turn their bodies around and discharge the fecal mass out of the tunnel opening. Young White-rumped Swifts, *Apus affinis*, defecate through the nest hole even before their eyes are open.

Birds whose nests are in no need of concealment, such as eagles, usually shoot the liquid feces over the edge of the nest, marking the ground beneath with a white circle. Trogons, motmots, hoopoes, and many pigeons are representative of species that practice no nest sanitation. The nest of the filthy Wood Pigeon, *Columba palumbus*, becomes such a culture medium for vermin that in one nest 6573 individual insects and other invertebrates of 58 species were found in one liter of nest-bottom material. However, the Ruddy Quail Dove, *Geotrygon montana*, keeps its nest scrupulously clean by eating the feces.

Many species also remove from the nest the egg-shells remaining after the young hatch. These are often eaten (Tree

Figure 17.15. A Greenshank (left) and a Bullfinch (right) removing egg-shells from their nests. Photo by E. Hosking.

Sparrow, *Passer montanus,* Yellow War-bler, *Dendroica petechia*) or carried away (Golden Plover, *Pluvialis dominica,* Cur-lew, *Numenius arquata*). Bobwhite Quail, *Colinus virginianus,* however, leave them in the nest. Sometimes Great Horned Owls, *Bubo virginianus,* accumulate so many dead rabbits and other rodents in the nest that the young die from the ef-fects of the insanitary mass. A Brewer's Blackbird, *Euphagus cyanocephalus,* on the other hand, removed its own dead young from the nest and deposited them in the place regularly used for fecal sac disposal.

Probably the most striking witness to the strong urge of most altricial birds to keep their nests clean is the experience many bird-banders have had in banding nestlings. Sometimes the young in the nest are banded with colored bands, or even colored tags, but normally with bright aluminum bands. To the adult bird a band is often a foreign object that has no business in the nest, so out it goes. The fact that the baby bird is attached to the band does not seem to matter. In at least three instances on record, the parent bird tugged vigorously enough to break the young bird's leg. Grinnell and Storer (*in* Bent, 1949) tell of a young American Robin, *Turdus migratorius,* whose parent had fed it a piece of meat too large for it to swallow immediately. The parent bird, obeying the instinct for cleanliness, re-moved the offending piece of meat with the young bird dangling beneath—a per-fect example of throwing the baby out with the bath!

BROODING THE YOUNG

When the infant bird hatches from its shell it is brooded by the parent. This dries it out and helps to maintain suffi-cient warmth to promote metabolism and growth, since the young bird is born cold-blooded or poikilothermal. Different spe-cies require different times to establish warm-bloodedness or homothermism.

Closely adapted to the gradual develop-ment of temperature control in the young is the instinctive reduction in the daily time devoted by the parent to brooding. In Laskey's (1948) study of the Carolina Wren, *Thryothorus ludovicianus,* she found that the female brooded 68 per cent of the daytime the first or hatching day, 65 per cent the second, 15 the third, 10 the fourth, 11 the fifth, and not at all thereafter. At night she brooded con-stantly. Lack and Lack (1952) deter-mined that the Swift, *Apus apus,* brooded its young 98 per cent of the time when they were under one week old, 52 per cent the second week, and only 7 per cent after that. For the European Wren, *Troglodytes troglodytes,* Armstrong (1955) found that the average brooding time was reduced daily by six to eight per cent. In nearly all species the amount of brooding given the young increases in cold or wet weather, decreases in warm or dry. The female Lucifer Hummingbird, *Calothorax lucifer,* of Mexico, sometimes broods its young so constantly in wet weather that they die of starvation.

Mourning Doves, *Zenaidura macroura,* brood almost constantly, and nearly up to the time when the young leave the nest. Lawrence (1948) observed on different days a nest of Nashville Warblers, *Vermi-vora ruficapilla,* in Ontario, and noted the time spent brooding the young and the number of feeding trips made to the nest. On the first day (Fig. 17.16) there were in the nest a one-day-old Cowbird, *Molo-thrus ater,* two just-hatched warblers, and one warbler egg. Five days later a six-day-old Cowbird, and three warblers, five and four days old, occupied the nest. The change both in time spent brooding and in the frequency of feeding trips shows very clearly in the graphic record of these observations.

When birds rear their young in unu-sually cold environments, they meet diffi-cult problems that require special solutions. One adjustment to the perpetual cold of the antarctic is the irresistible urge to brood, found in parent birds. Murphy

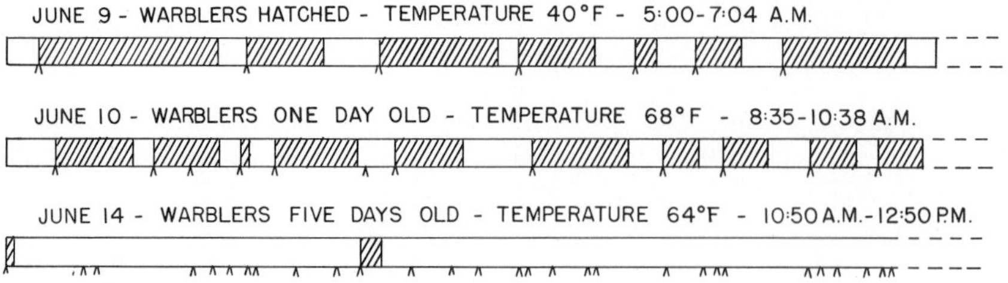

JUNE 9 - WARBLERS HATCHED - TEMPERATURE 40°F - 5:00-7:04 A.M.

JUNE 10 - WARBLERS ONE DAY OLD - TEMPERATURE 68°F - 8:35-10:38 A.M.

JUNE 14 - WARBLERS FIVE DAYS OLD - TEMPERATURE 64°F - 10:50 A.M.-12:50 P.M.

Figure 17.16.   Nest-attentiveness in the Nashville Warbler. Two-hour samples taken from observations on three different days. Shaded portions of bars represent periods when the female was on the nest brooding the young; clear portions, when she was off the nest. Each dart under a bar indicates a feeding visit by one of the parents. As the young grow older they are brooded less often and fed more. After L. de K. Lawrence.

(1936) observed a pair of Giant Fulmars, *Macronectes giganteus,* that brooded for a week over a chick "which had been crushed as flat as a pancake." Some penguins are such avid brooders that they may fight for the privilege of mothering the chicks—to the detriment of the latter. A special adaptation to antarctic cold is seen in the Emperor Penguin, *Aptenodytes forsteri.* When their downy young are old enough to waddle about, they gather in crèches, or kindergartens, where they huddle together, surrounded by a watchful "snow fence" of adults. During storms, these crèches of chicks may be completely covered with snow, but the fat young emerge undamaged.

This irresistible instinct to brood even transcends species barriers. Flickers sometimes raise young Starlings; some ducks are notorious for the mixed flotillas of ducklings in their care; a young eagle slipped into a chicken's nest will be solicitously brooded. Three hen's eggs were substituted by Dubois (1923) for those in the nest of a Short-eared Owl, *Asio flammeus.* The altricial owl hatched the eggs into precocial domestic chicks, brooded the downy young, and quite naturally brought them dead mice and decapitated birds to eat. The owl and the chicks got along amicably together for five days, the chicks being surreptitiously fed corn meal by the observer. Then two of the chicks died from overeating, but the other chick survived the owl's care for five days more

and then was abandoned by its foster mother. Such widely unrelated species do not always get on as well as this. A captive Eagle Owl, *Bubo bubo,* incubated and hatched domestic chicken eggs, but when the young chicks failed to eat the animal food the foster mother offered them, she ate them.

DEFENSE OF YOUNG

Practically the only defense the young bird itself has against enemies is to crouch in the nest as quietly and inconspicuously as possible, or, if it is able, to flee from the nest and hide in the surroundings. Parent birds may meet predatory threats by directly attacking the predators, by distracting them from the young, or, less commonly, by leading or moving the young to a safer site. The vigor with which the parent defends its young is, according to Nice (1949), greatest in precocial species at the time the eggs hatch or shortly after, and in altricial species shortly before the young leave the nest. Anyone who has observed young birds extensively has been swooped at and screamed at by outraged parents, and occasionally even struck by their beaks or claws. Some species, if the threat to their young persists, change their tactics and perform what for many years has been called "injury feigning" or the "broken-wing ruse." Today ornithologists usually

Figure 17.17.   A crèche of young Emperor Penguins, in Antarctica, still blanketed with snow from a recent storm. The adults protect the huddled young both from predators and from the sharpest blasts of the wind. Photo from Expéditions Polaires Francaises.

Figure 17.18.   The so-called "injury-feigning" display of a Ringed Plover. Photo by E. Hosking.

call this behavior *distraction display*, placing the emphasis on its demonstrated effectiveness rather than on the conjectured intent of the bird. No one can deny the effectiveness of the performance once he has been its object. Not only humans, but cats, dogs, snakes, and many other predatory animals, including birds, have been "lured" away from nests or young birds by the persuasive drama. The parent bird flutters on the ground as though crippled, and utters piteous cries in its extremity, but it seems always to flutter just beyond reach of the disturbing intruder. In his efforts to catch the apparently incapacitated bird, the intruder is led farther and farther away from the nest, until suddenly the bird "recovers" normal mobility and flies away. Both the stereotyped nature of the performance and its occasional non-adaptive application (for example, by a Ringed Plover, *Charadrius hiaticula,* to a strange egg in its nest) argue against its being interpreted as an intelligent, purposive act. Perhaps the best current interpretation of distraction display is that it originated in the bird's inability to react simultaneously to two great drives: one to protect the nest or young, and the other to flee from the predator. The result is a frenzied compromise refined in its more convincing aspects by years of natural selection into what today appears to be "injury feigning."

Parent birds may also protect their young by carrying them away from danger on their backs (grebes, Common Scoter, *Oidemia nigra*), with their feet (Red-tailed Hawk, *Buteo jamaicensis,* Moorhen, *Gallinula chloropus*), with their beaks (Franklin Gull, *Larus pipixcan,* Water-Rail, *Rallus aquaticus*), or with beaks and feet together (American Woodcock, *Philohela minor*). More effective protection is the instinctive response of nidifugous young to warning cries of their parents. Dawson (1909) describes such a response in young Western Gulls, *Larus occidentalis:*

"The danger sign had, of course, been passed around, and not a youngster on the island but froze in his tracks, no matter where he happened to be. It was pathetic to find . . . babes soaking heroically in the filthy green pools . . . rather than attract attention by scrambling out. One youngster had evidently been nibbling playfully at a bit of driftwood cast up high, for I found him with a stick between his mandibles as motionless as a Pompeian mummy."

Young Ruffed Grouse, *Bonasa umbellus,* are described by Edminister (1947) as instinctively responding in different ways to four different calls of the mother when a hawk threatens her brood. At one call the young freeze; at a second, more violent call, they scatter and freeze; another call keeps them immobile; and a final "all clear" call brings them back to her. Young Turnstones, *Arenaria interpres,* and other species are reported by Bergman (1946) to freeze at parental warning even before they hatch from the egg.

While instinctive solicitude is normally shown by nearly all species of birds for their young, there are times, especially among colonial nesters, when protective instincts are imperfectly developed, or else are nullified by competing instincts. Every large colony of Herring Gulls, *Larus argentatus,* is strewn with murdered young that have been killed by breeding gulls other than their parents. A gull cherishes its own young in the nest, but treats all other young as strangers and trespassers to be driven away. Many lost and wandering chicks are killed by the vicious blows of nest-defending adults. The remarkably automatic shift from one instinct to another was observed by Peterson (1948) when a lost downy chick ran up to the wrong parent. The adult jabbed at the young but missed it, so the baby continued running toward the old bird until it touched its breast. "Immediately the reaction switched from infanticide to brooding," and the young chick was temporarily accepted as her own. Of all the young hatched in a colony of Ring-billed Gulls, *Larus delawarensis,* on Green Island in Mackinac Straits, Michigan, in 1952, Emlen (1956) estimated that only 31 per cent survived to fledging, primarily because of such infanticide.

Young male White Storks, *Ciconia ciconia,* in their first year of breeding are said by Schüz (1943) to pick up and shake their own young as if they were prey, sometimes even eating them. Here, apparently, the instincts for rearing and protecting the young have not matured sufficiently to supplant those directed toward protecting the nest against predators.

DEVELOPMENT OF YOUNG

As a general rule, those species that have a short incubation period show rapid cell multiplication and rapid growth in their young; those with a long incubation period show slower growth. Likewise, those young fed by their parents grow rapidly and those that feed themselves grow slowly. The incubation period of the House Wren, *Troglodytes aëdon,* for example, is 14 days, and the young reach their maximum weight in 12 days. The Alpine Swift, *Apus melba,* requires 19 to 20 days for incubation, and reaches adult weight in about 27 days. Generally, large species grow more slowly than small; the Field Sparrow, *Spizella pusilla,* reaches adult weight in 8 or 9 days, the Sparrow Hawk, *Falco sparverius,* in about 20 days, the Yellow-billed Tropic-Bird, *Phaethon lepturus,* in 41 days, while the California Condor, *Gymnogyps californianus,* reaches only two-thirds its adult weight when 100 days old. Even species of the same adult size show great variation in growth rate, as is seen in the growth curves of the White Pelican, *Pelecanus erythrorhynchos,* and Mute Swan, *Cygnus olor* (Fig. 17.19).

Before they leave their nests, many young birds weigh more than their parents. Sixty-three days after hatching, the White Pelican weighs 13,850 grams while

as an adult it will weigh 10,000 grams. A 40-day old Leach's Petrel, *Oceanodroma leucorhoa,* weighs 69.5 grams as against an adult weight of but 43 grams. The chick of Wilson's Petrel, *Oceanites oceanicus,* just before its starvation period, weighs twice as much as an adult. This type of excess weight development, characteristic of penguins, albatrosses, shearwaters, petrels, parrots, owls, kingfishers, swallows and other birds, represents fat storage that enables the young birds to survive periods of food shortage and also gives them energy to use when they begin to grow feathers and to exercise their muscles. Stresemann tells of a captive albatross that refused to eat, yet survived over 29 days.

Other young, such as the Bluebird, *Sialia sialis,* Yellow Warbler, *Dendroica petechia,* McCown's Longspur, *Rhynchophanes mccowni,* and Field Sparrow, *Spizella pusilla,* increase in weight rather steadily until they reach adult weight, at which point they level off. The growth weights of all species are subject to decline when adverse weather influences feeding frequency.

In different species not only does absolute size increase at different rates, but

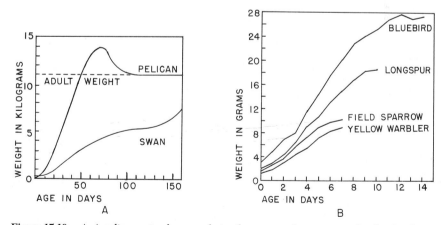

Figure 17.19. *A,* A pelican not only grows faster than a swan, but, two months after hatching, it exceeds its own adult weight by nearly 3 kilograms. After Portmann. *B,* Most young passerine birds reach mature weight quickly, and without greatly exceeding their adult weight. Curves end on the day the young typically leave the nest. After data from Hamilton, Mickey, Walkinshaw, and Schrantz.

different parts of the body grow and mature at different rates. This has already been pointed out for the growth rates of the alimentary canal and nervous system of altricial and precocial young. Quite often those organs which are soonest needed by the growing young develop first. Heinroth (1948) has shown that although both the precocial crane and the altricial stork grow up and are capable of flight in about 70 days, the ground-dwelling crane's legs grow most rapidly (7 mm. per day) between the 8th and 16th days of life, and those of the nest-dwelling stork most rapidly (5 mm. per day) between the 20th and 38th days. It would be hazardous for the roof-top stork to walk too early in life. This type of locally emphasized growth in a bird shows other ecological relationships. Young ground-dwelling Bobwhites and other quail are able to fly when less than two weeks old. Their legs are too short for effective escape from predators by running. The young Japanese Paradise Flycatcher, *Terpsiphone atrocaudata*, able to fly from the nest when ten days old, has fully developed wing feathers while the

rest of the body is still covered with down. This type of localized development represents a physiological economy that permits the young to reach independence early, and shortens the extremely vulnerable period of nest life.

Birds still show a relationship to ancestral reptiles in that the young, especially of altricial species, are born cold-blooded. Species vary considerably in the time they require to develop homothermism or warm-blooded temperature control. The antarctic Wilson's Petrel, *Oceanites oceanicus,* understandably in a greater hurry than most species, attains temperature control in two days; the Field Sparrow, *Spizella pusilla,* in about 7 days; the House Wren, *Troglodytes aëdon,* 9 days; and the Cliff Swallow, *Petrochelidon pyrrhonota,* about 21 days.

As young birds develop, in and out of the nest, they achieve increasingly complex behavior, some innate, some learned. Part of the development of the young bird is a simple maturation of structures or of instincts. A bird cannot use its eyes until they are open, or its wings until they are fully feathered. While there are num-

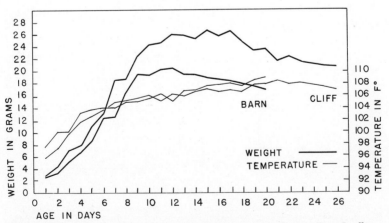

Figure 17.20. Growth and temperature development curves of young Barn Swallows and Cliff Swallows. In each species, maximum weight is achieved before complete temperature regulation. Food must first be made available before physiological processes can draw on it for the maturation of structures and functions. After D. Stoner.

berless variations of the scheme presented here, the day-by-day development of a typical small, open-nesting, altricial bird will be about as follows:

DAYS AFTER HATCHING:	CHARACTERISTIC BEHAVIOR:
1.	Raises head and gapes at any disturbance. Evacuates in the nest.
2.	Eyes begin to open. (Primary feathers show through the skin.)
3.	Eyes open. Uses wings as props. Evacuates at edge or door of nest.
4.	Beginning of most rapid growth. Begins to use legs. Voice stronger. (Primaries pierce skin.)
5.	Bird faces opening of nest or the feeding parent. Temperature control nearly established.
6.	Shows better muscular coordination. Shows fear and responds to alarm note of parent.
7.	Exercises neck, wings and legs. Relative growth rate begins to decline. (Primary feathers unsheathing.)
8.	Alert to sights and sounds outside nest.
10.	Preens unsheathed feathers. Stretches wings and legs. Pecks at objects.
13.	Acquires fluttering flight. Leaves nest.

Some altricial species develop much more slowly than this. The hole-nesting African Lesser Honey-guide, *Indicator minor*, for example, is still blind and nearly naked when 11 days old, and does not leave its tree-cavity nest until it is about 35 days old (Friedmann, 1955). Typical hole-nesting birds can fly well when they leave the nest at about 16 days of age. A precocial bird, on the other hand, is endowed with most of the above accomplishments on the day it hatches. In a sense, it passes its nestling stage in the egg.

DURATION OF THE NESTLING PERIOD

Not only is the length of time that the altricial young stay in the nest correlated with the length of the incubation period (long incubation, long nestling period) but also with the size of the species, larger species having longer nestling periods. Furthermore, birds such as the American Robin, *Turdus migratorius*, that nest in the open and whose eggs and young are accordingly exposed to many environmental hazards, have shorter nestling periods than cavity nesters such as woodpeckers. For 54 European open-nesting species, Lack (1948) determined that the average nestling period lasted 13.2 days, while for 18 hole-nesters it lasted 17.3 days. Nice (1957) found that the corresponding figures for United States species were: 11 species of open-nesters, 11.0 days; 10 species of hole-nesters, 18.8 days. Obviously, natural selection has shortened the nestling period for species that are the most susceptible to disaster.

In addition to the primary factor—an instinctive maturation of behavior that, at a specific time, stimulates the young bird to leave the nest—such factors as the weather, hunger, accidents, and parental nudgings influence the departure from the nest. As was observed earlier, the amount of food brought the young is often reduced, or even completely cut off, during the last few days of nest life.

Many birds apparently entice their young from the nest by holding food so far away that the hungry youngster will have to leave the nest to reach it. With drastically reduced diets, the Bald Eagle, *Haliaeetus leucocephalus*, starves its young into leaving the nest. The Japanese Paradise Flycatcher has been observed by Jahn (1939) feeding two young that had already left the nest, 30 times in one hour; but it completely ignored the begging nestling left behind until it, too, left the nest. Tree ducks entice their cavity-dwelling children to leave the nest en

Figure 17.21.   A Chipping Sparrow feeding its young. The eyes of the nestlings are just beginning to open, but they have not yet learned to gape toward the feeding parent. Their beaks still show the touch-sensitive flanges. Photo by G. R. Austing.

masse by calling them from the ground below. The young tumble out in a torrent, flap their stubby wings ineffectually in their downward plunge, bounce off the earth and waddle after their mother to the nearest water. The Chachalaca, *Ortalis vetula*, is reported by Farmer (*in* Bent, 1932) to carry her precocial young from the tree nest down to the ground, one at a time, clinging to her legs. The Pygmy Nuthatch, *Sitta pygmaea*, has been observed by Law (*in* Bent, 1948) tugging a recalcitrant young one from the nest hole and allowing it to flutter to the ground.

EDUCATION OF THE YOUNG

After leaving the nest the young bird still has much to acquire in the way of behavior: skill in finding and eating suitable food, skill in flight, in song, in social relationships and other functions. Some of these skills are a matter of the maturation of instincts. Many young birds will go through bathing movements the first time they see water, or will perform nest-molding or copulation movements without having observed them in older birds, and before they are themselves old enough to breed. Experience soon teaches a young chick which specks are pebbles and dirt and which are palatable food.

Sometimes enticement from the nest and education of the young in food capture are combined in one operation. Swallows and martins have occasionally been observed feeding their young, late in the nestling period, by flying back and forth in front of the nest with insects in their beaks which the young seize without leaving the nest. A similar technique was reported by Bralliar (*in* Bent, 1940) for the Eastern Belted Kingfisher, *Megaceryle alcyon*, which beat a small fish into sluggishness and then dropped it into the water, where the young found it easy prey for their first inexpert dives for food. The young also practiced fish-catching by diving to retrieve small twigs from the water. Marsh Hawks, *Circus cyaneus*, and others give their newly-fledged young practice in catching prey by dropping a mouse, for example, in mid-air; the young bird catches it with its talons after it has fallen only a few feet. Many observers tell of the play of young hawks and eagles which prepares them for the serious duties of making a living. Cade (1953) recounts the play of a young Prairie Falcon, *Falco mexicanus*, with a bit of dried cow manure which it swooped on, picked up with its talons and dropped, only to swoop, pick up and drop, again and again. Herrick (1924), in his notable study of the Bald Eagle, *Haliaeetus leucocephalus*, tells how the young play in their eyrie with sticks, much as a kitten does with a ball.

Imitation plays a role in the education of the young. A domestic chick raised with an African gosling, *Anser cygnoides*, soon took on some of the gosling's behavior such as grass-eating, and even mimicked the phraseology and modulation of the gosling's voice (Klopfer, 1956).

Flight exercises are performed by many young before they leave the nest. Young eagles and hawks will stand on their nest rim and practice flapping their wings with daily increasing skill until they finally take off into the air. Many swifts and swallows, on the contrary, have no opportunity to practice wing-strokes in their cavity nests, and yet are able to fly expertly on their first attempt, sometimes as far as a half kilometer. Turkey Vultures, *Cathartes aura*, that have been confined in cages too small to allow wing motion are unable to fly even when three months old, because of lack of exercise.

SUGGESTED READINGS

Examples of the care and development of the young of many species are given in Pycraft's *A History of Birds*. For works treating the biological principles of this subject, see Wallace, *An Introduction to Ornithology*, and the Heinroths' small book, *The Birds*. For a modern, thoroughly documented treatment of the care of young, see Kendeigh's *Parental Care and its Evolution in Birds*. Nice's *Development of Behavior in Precocial Birds* presents the results of much study and first-hand observation by one of America's foremost ornithologists.

EIGHTEEN

The Numbers of Birds and Their Regulation

He clasps the crag with crooked hands;
Close to the sun in lonely lands,
Ringed with the azure world, he stands.

The wrinkled sea beneath him crawls;
He watches from his mountain walls,
And like a thunderbolt he falls.
Alfred Tennyson, *The Eagle*

A favorite pastime of biologists is to compute the total number of descendants left by a single animal or a pair of animals, carried through several generations, assuming that all young live to maturity to reproduce as did the original parents. An oyster, for example, that lays over a million eggs at one spawning would, if all young survived to breed, beget sufficient offspring in only seven generations to make a heap of oysters greater than the mass of the earth. Many organisms are wastefully lavish when it comes to reproducing their own kind. A carp lays two to four million eggs a season; a tapeworm, 120,000 eggs a day. Even the American Robin, *Turdus migratorius*, which commonly produces, in one season, two modest broods of four young each, will leave a spectacular 19,500,000 descendants in ten years—if one makes the superficially plausible assumption that all

342

young survive at least ten years and reproduce the same number as the original pair. The British scientist MacBride carried this kind of reckoning to a total of 30 years—not a long time in the evolutionary history of Robins—and discovered that the original pair of birds would produce by that time 1200 million million million descendants. There would be room, he says, for only 1/150,000 of these birds on the entire surface of the earth even though they stood jammed shoulder to shoulder.

Such intellectual exercises as these merely underscore the reproductive potential of a species. Common sense quickly tells us that this potential is never realized. Nonetheless, certain species of birds sometimes achieve almost incredible populations. In 1871 the Passenger Pigeon, *Ectopistes migratorius*, concentrated in a "great nesting" in central Wisconsin where an estimated 136 million birds bred within an area of 2,200 square kilometers (850 square miles) (Schorger, 1937). Another flock of this species was estimated by Alexander Wilson to contain over 2000 million birds. The Guanay Cormorant, *Phalacrocorax bougainvillii*, congregates in flocks of four or five million on a single island off the coast of Peru. The Mutton Bird, or Slender-billed Shearwater, *Puffinus tenuirostris*, flies at dusk to its home islands in immense river-like streams. One such stream observed in 1909 required the better part of a night to pass a given point, and another flock observed in 1798 by Flinders (Murphy, 1936) took only an hour and a half to fly by, but was estimated to contain more than 1.5 million birds. In 1906, nine million Jackass Penguins, *Spheniscus demersus*, bred on Dassen Island off the Cape of Good Hope (Pycraft, 1910).

Not all great concentrations of birds have occurred in the distant past. In the bitterly cold winter of 1946–1947, a flock of Bramblings, *Fringilla montifringilla*, estimated to total 11 million birds, roosted in a small valley near Porrentruy, Switzerland (Gueniat, 1948). This single flock consumed an estimated 10 to 12 tons of beechnuts daily.

The total numbers of birds in different parts of the world can only be very roughly approximated. From scores of breeding bird censuses taken by the Audubon Society, Peterson (1948) estimates that there are about 7600 million breeding birds in the United States (or about five birds per hectare), and that between two-thirds and three-fourths of them are land birds. For the North American continent north of Mexico he estimates that there are between 12,000 and 20,000 million birds. For the entire world, Fisher (1951) estimates that there are in the neighborhood of 100,000 million birds. This number is only one-third as many as a single pair of Robins might leave as descendants in 16 years, if we apply the original assumption that all offspring live to reproduce 8 young each year!

Obviously, something kills off most of these hypothetical offspring before they reach breeding age. Even so, the reproductive potential of a species is occasionally allowed to express itself with considerable effectiveness. When a species is introduced into a new and favorable habitat, its numbers increase phenomenally at first, and then level off at a population far under theoretical possibilities. This has been the history of the House Sparrow, *Passer domesticus*, and Starling, *Sturnus vulgaris*, in North America, the latter species increasing, in less than 60 years, perhaps a million-fold over the 120 birds introduced into New York City (Peterson, 1948). In 1937, two male and six female Ring-necked Pheasants, *Phasianus colchicus*, were introduced on Protection Island off the coast of Washington. Six years later these eight birds had increased to 1898 (Einarsen, 1942).

Reproductive potential in a given species depends chiefly on the number of eggs laid in a clutch, the number of clutches in a season, the age at which the bird begins breeding, and the bird's longevity. For most species the chief element in breeding potential is the number of eggs laid per year, and in this characteristic there is wide variation.

LONGEVITY

Here again, one must distinguish between potential longevity, as realized by captive birds protected from predators, adverse weather, starvation, accidents, and other environmental hazards, and the actual longevity achieved by birds in the wild. Records of longevity of caged birds are relatively easy to get, but for wild birds the problem is more difficult. The wild bird must be caught, individually marked —usually with a numbered aluminum leg band—released to live a normal wild life, and then subsequently recovered, usually at the time of its death. Ideally the bird should be banded as a nestling so that its complete life span may be known, but many longevity records are for wild birds that were caught and banded when already adults. For example, the oldest known captive Herring Gull, *Larus argentatus*, died at 49 years of age (Mayaud, 1950). Of 3806 American Herring Gulls banded as young and recovered after death, the oldest bird was 19 years old (Marshall, 1947). The European record for a banded wild bird of this species is 28 years. Probably the world record for longevity in the wild is held by a Curlew, *Numenius arquata*, which was banded as a chick in Sweden on July 4, 1926, and shot "in perfect condition and full vigour" at Norfolk, England, 31½ years later, on January 25, 1958 (Kuhk, 1960).

In Table 18.1 are given the maximum ages currently attained by banded wild birds as reported chiefly in the journal *Bird-Banding*. About one-half of these records represent the maximum longevities of birds recovered from the approximately 8,000,000 banded wild birds recorded in the files of the U.S. Fish and Wildlife Service. The majority of the remainder represent similar records from European banding programs. It should be emphasized that the table gives the extreme old age attained for each species, usually by only one bird out of thousands banded. For instance, out of 21,715 Purple Finches, *Carpodacus purpureus*, banded by Magee (1940), there were subsequently 1746 recoveries, among which only one bird lived as long as 10 years, 6 as long as 8 years, and 18 as long as 7 years. Similarly, out of 4469 Purple Finches banded by Groskin (1950), there were 95 recoveries, among which only one each lived as long as 5, 6, and 7 years beyond the original banding date.

Numerous records of longevity in captive birds have been published. A compilation of such records was made by Flower (1938) from 35 published sources covering over a thousand species of birds. Representative examples from Flower's list include the White Pelican, *Pelecanus onocrotalus*, 51 years; Canada Goose, *Branta canadensis*, 33; Condor, *Vultur gryphus*, 52; Bateleur Eagle, *Terathopius eucaudatus*, 55; Australian Crane, *Grus rubicunda*, 47; Eagle Owl, *Bubo bubo*, 68; Domestic Hen, *Gallus gallus*, 30; Domestic Pigeon, *Columba livia*, 30; Cockatoo, *Cacatua galerita*, 56; Raven, *Corvus corax*, 24; Starling, *Sturnus vulgaris*, 17; Garden Warbler, *Sylvia borin*, 24; House Sparrow, *Passer domesticus*, 23; Cardinal, *Richmondena cardinalis*, 22; European Goldfinch, *Carduelis carduelis*, 27.

POPULATION STABILITY

Even the most casual observer realizes that the number of robins about his home does not change drastically from year to year. Careful yearly observations of conspicuous species confirm the fact of their relative stability in numbers. Since 1928 the number of Herons, *Ardea cinerea*, in various English rookeries has been carefully counted each year, and although there may be a reduction in their numbers after a severe winter, the population quickly returns to its former level and remains stationary until the next adverse season (Lack, 1954). Unless environmental

Table 18.1. Maximum Known Ages of Banded Wild Birds

SPECIES	MAX. AGE (YEARS)	WHERE BANDED	BIRD-BANDING (VOL. AND PAGE)
Yellow-eyed Penguin, *Megadyptes antipodes*	18	New Zealand	°
Chinstrap Penguin, *Pygoscelis antarctica*	11	Antarctic	29:23
Red-throated Loon, *Colymbus stellatus*	23	Sweden	24:70
Cormorant, *Phalacrocorax carbo*	17	England	29:112
Heron, *Ardea cinerea*	20	Sweden	26:75
White Stork, *Ciconia ciconia*	19	Hungary	7:89
Canada Goose, *Branta canadensis*	23	Michigan	†
Mallard, *Anas platyrhynchos*	16	U.S.S.R.	29:112
Teal, *Anas crecca*	20	U.S.S.R.	29:112
Golden Eagle, *Aquila chrysaëtos*	20	Germany	9:206
Buzzard, *Buteo buteo*	24	Germany	24:83
Peregrine Falcon, *Falco peregrinus*	14	Germany	24:71
Osprey, *Pandion haliaetus*	21	New York	7:42
Black Vulture, *Coragyps atratus*	11	Louisiana	21:14
Coot, *Fulica atra*	19	Switzerland	25:114
Oystercatcher, *Haematopus ostralegus*	27	Germany	27:86
Curlew, *Numenius arquata*	31	Sweden	‡
Woodcock, *Scolopax rusticola*	12	Germany	2:43
Herring Gull, *Larus argentatus*	28	Denmark	27:128
Arctic Tern, *Sterna paradisea*	27	Germany	23:72
Caspian Tern, *Hydroprogne caspia*	26	Michigan	23:72
Puffin, *Fratercula arctica*	21	Norway	31:92
Mourning Dove, *Zenaidura macroura*	9	Mass.	17:67
Barn Owl, *Tyto alba*	10	California	8:56
Swift, *Apus apus*	17	Germany	28:168
Yellow-shafted Flicker, *Colaptes auratus*	12	Michigan	10:165
Crested Flycatcher, *Myiarchus crinitus*	6	Penna.	8:58
Skylark, *Alauda arvensis*	6	Italy	19:23
Barn Swallow, *Hirundo rustica*	16	England	24:20
Common Crow, *Corvus brachyrhynchos*	14	Manitoba	13:112
Blue Jay, *Cyanocitta cristata*	15	U.S.	9:104
Black-capped Chickadee, *Parus atricapillus*	9	Mass.	17:39
House Wren, *Troglodytes aëdon*	5	Ohio	8:60
Catbird, *Dumatella carolinensis*	9	Ohio	8:60
Brown Thrasher, *Toxostoma rufum*	13	N. Carolina	10:42
Blackbird, *Turdus merula*	9	Germany	22:35
American Robin, *Turdus migratorius*	10	Tennessee	14:77
European Robin, *Erithacus rubecula*	11	Ireland	14:150
Starling, *Sturnus vulgaris*	16	Ohio	5:142
Yellow Warbler, *Dendroica petechia*	7	Michigan	10:165
Cowbird, *Molothrus ater*	8	Texas	8:62
Redwinged Blackbird, *Agelaius phoeniceus*	14	New York	21:115
Common Grackle, *Quiscalus quiscula*	16	S. Dakota	13:40
Scarlet Tanager, *Piranga olivacea*	9	Penna.	29:43
Cardinal, *Richmondena cardinalis*	13	Tennessee	8:128
Slate-colored Junco, *Junco hyemalis*	11	Mass.	14:46
Song Sparrow, *Melospiza melodia*	8	Mass.	14:77

° Richdale, L. E. 1957. *A Population Study of Penguins.* Oxford.
† *Auk*, 74:510.
‡ *Die Vogelwarte*, 20:233.

conditions change abnormally, most bird populations remain remarkably constant despite the potential which all species possess for almost unlimited increase. This stability can only mean that birth rate equals death rate; that natality matches mortality. This balance between life and death is convincingly demonstrated by investigations of different geographic populations of the Blue Tit, *Parus caeruleus*, by Snow (*in* Lack, 1954). In England this bird lays an average clutch of 11 eggs, and its annual adult mortality is 73 per cent; in Spain and Portugal the average clutch is 6 eggs and adult mortality 41 per cent; in the Canary Islands the clutch drops to 4¼ eggs and mortality to 36 per cent. Similar studies in other species give similar results. Such a hand-in-glove fitting of birth rate with death rate raises an intriguing question: Has natural selection increased the reproductive potential of a species to compensate for an increased death rate in certain environments, or does a higher breeding rate automatically result in higher mortality? Students of animal populations disagree on their answers to this question, and this indicates that more research on the problem is required. Whatever the reasons for the rather precise balance between natality and mortality, it is true that both rates vary greatly among different species and in different habitats.

POPULATION DENSITIES

Habitat makes a great difference in the numbers of birds found in different parts of the world. Just as plant abundance varies from sterile deserts to lush tropical jungles, so bird abundance varies geographically and regionally. Since all food eventually comes from the chlorophyll of green plants, birds are generally more numerous where vegetation is thick and varied. This relationship holds not only on land but also in the ocean where microscopic plant life, or plankton, uses sunlight to convert nitrates, phosphates and

other nutrients into food. In the northeast Atlantic, where plankton is abundant, one may see from the deck of an ocean liner over 100 sea birds each day, but in the plankton-poor equatorial Atlantic one will see only one or two birds a day (Jespersen, 1924). The teeming flocks of sea birds that nest in dense colonies do not, of course, find their food in the immediate neighborhood of their nests, nor do colonial-nesting swifts and swallows which feed on flying insects.

Although food is by far the most important element in the habitat which controls population density, it is by no means the only one. Nesting sites, nesting materials, singing posts, the general vegetational appearance of the habitat, and probably other subtler factors play a role. In a Maryland chestnut orchard, about one hectare in area, there were no hole-nesting birds until 98 bird houses were installed. A three- to four-fold increase in the total bird population resulted from the newly available nesting sites (McAtee, 1940). The effect of cattle-grazing on bird densities was studied in Canada, New York and Ohio by Dambach (1941), who found that in ungrazed woods there were, on the average, 299 adult birds of 17 species per 40 hectares, while in grazed woods there were only 137 birds of 10 species. Even related species with similar nesting and feeding habits may differ markedly in population density in an identical habitat. In a large deciduous forest tract in Louisiana, Tanner (1941) found only one (now extinct) Ivory-billed Woodpecker, *Campephilus principalis*, to 36 Pileated Woodpeckers, *Dryocopus pileatus*, to 126 Redbellied Woodpeckers, *Centurus carolinus*.

Many studies of avian population densities in different habitats have been made in Europe, Africa, and North America. One cannot compare their findings very closely because the censuses were made by using different techniques, which yielded varying degrees of accuracy. However, the studies agree in broad outline, and show in general that the richer and more varied the plant food resources of

Figure 18.1. Sea birds commonly gather in dense nesting colonies, as shown in this aggregation of Gannets. Mutual stimulation in breeding activities, and common defense against enemies, probably more than compensate for the disadvantages of congested living. Photo by E. Hosking.

an environment, the denser its bird population. They also show that for each habitat there is an optimum number of birds which can be supported, and that if the bird population presses beyond this limit, mortality is increased or fecundity diminished. Every habitat has its rather precisely limited "carrying capacity"—a concept considered in a later chapter. Table 18.2 gives representative examples of population densities in various habitats as reported by different observers.

To a given bird, death may appear in many forms. It may pounce suddenly with red fangs or talons, or it may creep in slowly and agonizingly in the form of a fungus infection of the lungs, a dwindling food supply, a freezing rain, a drying pond, or a strong headwind during migration. What may be a common cause of death for one species may be quite uncommon in another. But whatever guise death may take, it increases its toll as an animal population grows. When the breeding potential of a species creates increasing pressure against the carrying capacity of its habitat, environmental resistance in various lethal forms reacts with counterpressure which trims down the excess population. In the great majority of birds, 80 to 93 per cent of the eggs fail to develop into breeding adults. High as this proportion may seem, it is extremely low compared with that of many lower animals. Of the millions of eggs a mackerel lays, 99.9996 per cent will die as eggs or larvae in the first 70 days of life (Sette, *in* Lack, 1954).

Table 18.2.   Densities of Breeding Birds in Different Habitats

HABITAT	LOCALITY	NO. ADULT BIRDS PER 40 HECTARES (OR 100 ACRES)	AUTHORITY
Desert, Tundra			
Salt marsh fill	New Jersey	6	Hickey '39
Alpine zone	N. Finland	9	Granit '38
Desert steppe	Colorado	10	Bourlière '50
Rock tundra	Canada	44	Soper '40
Grass tundra	Canada	84	Soper '40
Prairie, Savanna			
Rough grazing land	England	70	Fisher '51
Grassland	Michigan	112	Kendeigh '49
Prairie	Washington	246	Wing '49
Dry grass veld	S. Africa	65	Winterbottom '47
Savanna	Tanganyika	96	Winterbottom '47
Scrub brush	N. Rhodesia	310	Winterbottom '47
Dense scrub bushveld	E. Cape Prov.	1150	Winterbottom '47
Tropical grassland	Tanganyika	4000	Winterbottom '47
Forests			
Burned over forest (winter)	Finland	2	Lehtonen '43
Dwarf forest	Lapland	36	Bourlière '50
Sub-alpine birch forest	N. Finland	35	Granit '38
Pine forest	N. Finland	120	Granit '38
Aspen-red maple forest	Michigan	118	Kendeigh '49
Cedar-balsam forest	Michigan	292	Kendeigh '49
Bog forest	Ohio	130	Hickey '37
Flood-plain deciduous forest	Illinois	216	Fawver '47
Second-growth hickory forest	Ohio	536	Hickey '37
Young deciduous forest	W. Virginia	522	°Audubon F.N. '48
Mature deciduous forest	W. Virginia	724	Audubon F.N. '48
Young spruce forest	W. Virginia	690	Audubon F.N. '48
Virgin spruce forest	W. Virginia	762	Audubon F.N. '48
Mixed forest	Holland	896	Tinbergen '46
Oak-hornbeam forest	Slovakia	816	Turcek '51
Forest bird sanctuary	Germany	5600	Bruns '55
Cultivated Lands			
Bare, fallow land	England	200	Fisher '51
Cereals, root crops, clover	England	200	Fisher '51
Scrubby pasture	Hungary	328	Udvardy '47
Orchard, DDT-sprayed and mowed	Maryland	76	Audubon F.N. '48
Orchard, unsprayed, unmowed	Maryland	468	Audubon F.N. '48
Village with many trees	Holland	936	Tinbergen '46
Golf links	England	1000	Fisher '51
Park (zoological garden)	Germany	1170	Steinbacher '42
Farm yard	Germany	1840	Mildenberger '50
Gardens	England	3000	Fisher '51
Bird sanctuary (Whipsnade)	England	5800	Huxley '36

° *Audubon Field Notes.*

PREDATION

Several different kinds of predation may affect a single species of bird. In his long-continued banding studies of the Common Tern, *Sterna hirundo,* on Cape Cod, Austin (1946) found that the worst predator was the common rat, which ate the eggs and young. In 1932 the entire crop of several thousand chicks was destroyed by rats that invaded the colony. Owls attacked the adult terns; in a single night one Great Horned Owl, *Bubo virginianus*, might decapitate 15 or 20 adult terns, although it would eat only one of them. Foxes, skunks, and weasels sometimes killed hundreds of tern chicks, and the adult terns themselves occasionally pecked and killed stray young that invaded their nesting territories.

A 17-year study of 820 unsuccessful nestings of the Wood Ducks, *Aix sponsa*, in Illinois showed that 51 per cent of the nests were destroyed by fox squirrels, 37 per cent by raccoons, 10 per cent by snakes, and 2 per cent by opossums. One-third of all adult Wood Ducks killed by predators were victims of raccoons (Bellrose, 1953). Snakes are common despoilers of birds' nests not only in the tropics but, for some species, also in the temperate zone. Of several hundred nests of the Bluebird, *Sialia sialis*, in Tennessee, 23 to 40 per cent were probably destroyed by snakes each year (Laskey, 1946).

Of course, birds are preyed upon by other birds, especially such raptors as eagles, hawks, owls, jaegers, skuas, and shrikes. But species not particularly adapted to a predatory way of living may at times prey on other birds. The toucan robs the nests of many tropical birds; House Wrens, *Troglodytes aëdon*, frequently destroy the eggs and young of Bluebirds and other passerines; some ducks and oystercatchers have been observed eating the eggs and young of terns; and grackles often kill the young and adults of smaller passerine species. Although the Blue-footed Booby, *Sula nebouxii*, and Kelp Gull, *Larus dominicanus*, of South America are primarily fish eaters, they are also inveterate enemies. The Gulls stealthily rob the Booby nests of eggs and young. In bloody reprisal the Boobies will attack any wandering Gull chicks that misguidedly approach them, and while "the poor victim cries out in terror, the furious Camanay [Booby] may thrust its saw-edged beak into its open mouth and out through the back of its skull. More than

once I have seen young gulls so impaled by the lower mandible of a Camanay that the latter had to shake its bill violently to get rid of the burden" (Murphy, 1936).

As discussed earlier, infanticide serves as a further brake on the reproductive rate of certain eagles, hawks, and owls. In what Wendland (1958) calls "Cainism," the first hatched young of the Lesser Spotted Eagle, *Aquila pomarina*, often tramples and kills the later hatching young in the nest. In unfavorable years for food, over one-third of the young of European Buzzards, *Buteo buteo*, may die from this cause alone.

Animals which are normally inconsequential as enemies of birds may, in times of abundance, become serious predators. In 1937 when the wood mouse population in the Rhineland was unusually high, Mildenberger (1940) found that 19 of 26 nests of ground-nesting warblers, especially Chiffchaffs, *Phylloscopus collybita*, were destroyed by mice.

While birds, mammals, and reptiles are the chief vertebrate predators of birds, fish may at times levy a heavy toll on them. Post mortem studies on northern pike in Saskatchewan showed that 7 out of every 100 taken during the nesting season contained ducklings (Sprungman, 1941), and stomachs of goosefish have been found to contain loons, grebes, cormorants, widgeon, scaup, scoters, mergansers, gulls, auks and guillemots (Bigelow and Welsh, 1924). Crabs in tropical regions are known to be severe predators of young birds, especially ground-nesting terns; and in the southern United States, biting ants prey on quail chicks. Occasionally turtles, frogs, spiders and praying mantises catch and kill birds, but ordinarily they are not important predators.

A moot point among ornithologists is the degree to which predators regulate bird population levels. Some consider predation a relatively negligible factor in regulating population density, while others think it is highly important. Undeniably, predation exerts varying degrees of influence on different species. About

40 per cent of the eggs of the Jackass Penguin, *Spheniscus demersus,* are reported by Kearton (1930) to be devoured by gulls and ibises. Of 186 nests of the Blue-winged Teal, *Anas discors,* studied in Iowa, 100 (54 per cent) were destroyed, largely by skunk, mink, fox, and raccoon (Glover, 1956). Similar stories have been reported for many other species. In the Sacramento Valley of California, 52 per cent of 333 duck nests and 54 per cent of 150 coot nests were destroyed by mammalian predators (Anderson, 1957). On occasion the intensity of predation rises to heights that would seem impossible for a prey species to sustain. Predation, mainly by skuas, causes the destruction of 70 per cent of eggs and young of Adelie Penguins, *Pygoscelis adeliae,* at Adelie Land in the antarctic (Sapin-Jaloustre and Bourlière, 1951). Skuas and fulmars were reported by Comer in 1895 to kill 95 out of every 100 young Wandering Albatrosses, *Diomedea exulans,* on Gough Island in the South Atlantic (Murphy, 1936).

Even predatory birds are victims of predation. In England, of 24 nests of the Short-eared Owl, *Asio flammeus,* observed by Lockie (1955) only five survived to hatch young, and only two raised young to fledging age, as a result of predation by foxes and crows. Predation may have been particularly severe in this case because it occurred at a time when meadow mice were scarce.

Several experimental attempts have been made to assay the effect predators have on wild bird populations. In 1936, skunks destroyed 30 per cent of 351 duck nests on the Lower Souri Refuge in North Dakota; but in 1937, after 423 skunks had been trapped and removed, the survivors destroyed only 6.4 per cent of 566 nests (Kalmbach, 1938). The experimental removal of predators from New York habitats of the Ruffed Grouse, *Bonasa umbellus,* resulted in 24 and 39 per cent destroyed nests, whereas in control areas where predators were not removed, the nest destruction was higher: 51 and 72 per

cent. However, mortality of young grouse chicks in the contrasted areas was nearly identical: 57 and 54 per cent in the experimental areas and 67 and 55 per cent in the control areas. Paradoxically, adult losses were largest in the experimental (predator-removed) areas, and smallest in the control areas, at least during years of grouse abundance (Edminster, 1939).

Such results as these indicate that predator-prey relations are not simple problems in arithmetic. Undoubtedly numbers play a role in predation. The more animals there are to prey upon in a given area, the more easily they are found by predators and, in all probability, the more intense the predation. For 15 years a local population of Bobwhite Quail, *Colinus virginianus,* in Wisconsin was counted each April and November by Errington (1945). Using Errington's figures and assuming a reproductive potential of 18 eggs per pair of adults, Lack (1954) showed that the greater the summer population the higher the per cent loss of birds by autumn (Fig. 18.2).

On the other hand, in some species, the denser the population the higher its fecundity. On Cape Cod in 1934, a colony of 13,000 adult Common Terns, *Sterna hirundo,* raised 12,498 young, whereas a neighboring colony of 1600 adults raised only 649 chicks (Austin, 1949). Of course, other factors than size of colony may have entered in here. These phenomena illustrate what are known as *density dependent* influences in the life cycles of animals. Population densities, in short, affect intensity of predation, as well as such things as the spread of disease, malnutrition and starvation, competition for territory, perhaps the rate of reproduction, and other elements which, in complex and often subtle combinations, control the numbers and survival of animals. Much research is needed to unravel the skein of relationships between these elements.

One method some species have evolved to reduce predation involves timing. The Antarctic Whale Bird, *Pachyptila desolata,* comes ashore at night to dig its nest burrow and to raise its family while skuas

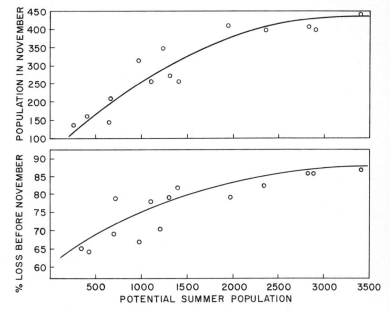

Figure 18.2. Density-dependent mortality in the Bobwhite Quail: the denser the population, the higher the death rate. The upper curve shows the actual autumn population, plotted against the potential summer population. The lower curve shows the calculated summer and early autumn percentage of birds lost, plotted against the potential summer population. After Lack, based on data from Errington.

and other predators are asleep. Early the next morning it leaves for the open sea where it feeds in safety. Predation is also lessened through seasonal timing of the life cycle. On a German island where there are nesting colonies of Common Gulls, *Larus canus*, Red-breasted Mergansers, *Mergus serrator*, and Mallards, *Anas platyrhynchos*, the gulls prey mainly on the Merganser eggs, probably because the Mergansers are still incubating their eggs when the gulls are feeding their young. The eggs of the Gulls and Mallards hatch at about the same time (Reinsch, 1953). Normally the Bluebird, *Sialia sialis*, nests two or three weeks earlier than the House Wren, *Troglodytes aëdon*, but occasionally a late spring freeze will destroy the eggs of the Bluebirds and cause them to lay replacement clutches at about the time the migrating Wrens arrive. This results in competition between the two species, and greater than normal destruction of Bluebird eggs by the aggressive Wrens (Musselman, 1946). A species may, of course, have different predators at different stages in its life cycle. The eggs of the Red-footed Falcon, *Falco vespertinus*, are eaten by Rooks, *Corvus frugilegus*, and

Tawny Owls, *Strix aluco*, while the young are killed by the Goshawk, *Accipiter gentilis*, (Horvath, 1955).

Birds react in a variety of ways to combat losses from predation. First, they must be able to recognize enemies. Many passerine birds instinctively recognize an owl as an enemy (Hartley, 1950). In some species the parent birds apparently educate their young to recognize enemies, as was described for the Jackdaw, *Corvus monedula*, in Chapter 11. Perhaps the most common reaction to the approach of a predator is to fly away or to dive under the water. The next most common reaction is immobility or "freezing," particularly in species with concealing coloration, or in birds brooding their eggs or young. Some of the larger, better armed birds, such as hawks, owls, and swans, will fight back, as will some passerines of pugnacious disposition like the jays. A few species practice a form of group defense. When a hawk dives toward a flying band of Starlings, *Sturnus vulgaris*, the latter bunch together into a dense flock, and the hawk, unable to single out an individual bird, flies off frustrated. Coots, floating on the water, thwart eagles in the same way. In general, defensive reactions toward predators are heightened during the breeding season.

A further factor in the complex equation involving predator and prey is the presence or absence of alternative prey. Foxes in the Hudson Bay region prey on Canada Geese, *Branta canadensis,* somewhat more heavily in years of mouse and lemming scarcity than in normal years when these rodents are abundant. The rodents act as *buffers* to absorb some of the predation that might otherwise be directed toward the geese (Hanson and Smith, 1950). In similar fashion the Giant Fulmar, *Macronectes giganteus,* is a destructive predator in antarctic penguin colonies, but farther north at the Falkland Islands, where more food is available, the bird is mainly a harmless scavenger (Murphy, 1936).

Predation is not necessarily an undiluted evil for the species preyed upon. Although exact quantitative studies seem to be lacking, it is probable that predators often act as sanitary police in catching and removing aged, diseased, abnormal, or crippled birds from a prey population. Further, even widespread, indiscriminating predation on a prey species may hold its numbers in check and prevent it from snowballing into destructive overpopulation. This has been demonstrated in the case of the Kaibab Deer of Arizona whose predators, pumas and wolves, were removed in a misguided attempt to increase the deer population. The experiment succeeded too well, and the deer population rose from about 4000 to 100,000, which exceeded by far the carrying capacity of the environment. As a result, the deer "ate themselves out of house and home" and starved in wholesale numbers until the population dropped to around 10,000 animals. Without much doubt the same sort of checks and balances operate between birds and their predators to establish a relatively stable population equilibrium.

A somewhat unexpected benefit from predation by crows on the eggs and young of ducks has been suggested by Cartwright (1944). He reasoned that such single-brooded birds, undisturbed by predators, would produce synchronized early nestings which would be disastrously vulnerable to late spring freezing, flooding, or similar calamities. Predators provide insurance against such mass catastrophes by destroying many of the first nestings of the ducks, forcing them to lay replacement clutches and thus stagger their nestings through a longer period of time. In the light of present knowledge, it is extremely hazardous to claim that one species is "detrimental" because it preys on another.

To sum up, the role of predation in controlling bird populations seems largely to depend on the number of predators and their selectivity in choice of prey, the number and health of prey animals, their rate of reproduction, their instinctive or learned reactions to predators, including emigration, and the carrying capacity of the prey species' environment, especially its food and cover.

MAN'S INFLUENCE ON BIRD NUMBERS

Man's use of the land has caused great changes in its character, and most of them have been detrimental to bird life. Some species such as the House Sparrow, *Passer domesticus,* Barn Swallow, *Hirundo rustica,* and Robin, *Turdus migratorius,* are more or less human satellites and have increased in numbers as the result of man's conversion of wild land into cities, farms, and parks. But for many species man's changes have reduced the populations of native birds, some of them to extinction. In the last 60 years, for example, some 2,400,000 hectares of Iowa prairie, with potholes and marshes suitable for duck nesting, have been reduced by drainage to about 20,000 hectares. Deforestation has greatly reduced the available habitats for tree-nesting species.

Many of the tools of civilization have had peculiarly destructive effects on bird life. High towers and monuments, telephone wires, and electric transmission wires kill many nocturnal migrants. In

Denmark 35 per cent of all the banded White Storks, *Ciconia ciconia*, that were recovered between 1952 and 1954 were found dead near high-tension transmission lines. Under certain atmospheric conditions, airport ceilometers possess a destructive magnetism for many small nocturnal fliers. About 50,000 birds of 53 species were killed by crashing into the ground around a Georgia Air Force base ceilometer on the night of October 8, 1954. While man-made hayfields offer attractive nesting sites for many gallinaceous species, the attraction is usually fatal. A study by Yocum (1943) of the Hungarian Partridge, *Perdix perdix*, in Washington, showed that 63 per cent of its nests were located in hay fields. Of those nests (61 per cent) which were unsuccessful in raising young, 85 per cent were destroyed by farming activities, mainly mowing. Automobiles kill many roadside nesters, such as woodpeckers. Oil pollution from steamships annually kills thousands of sea birds. On the Netherlands coast alone, the annual toll from oil pollution is estimated to be between 20,000 and 50,000 birds (Bruijns, 1959). In many communities where trees are sprayed with toxic chemicals for protection against insects, native songbirds have practically disappeared.

As a hunter, man is an active predator against all species shot as game, and also against many other species simply because they present a moving target. Not only are millions of birds killed directly, but probably even more are crippled and die later, or else they suffer poisoning from the effect of eaten or imbedded lead pellets. A tally of the 4700 sportsmen who hunted geese on Horicon Marsh, Wisconsin, in 1952, showed that it took the average hunter 36 shots to bag one goose! Fluoroscopic examination of 735 Canada Geese, *Branta canadensis*, in the Mississippi Valley revealed that 44 per cent of them carried lead shot; and a parallel study of the Pink-footed Goose, *Anser brachyrhynchus*, in England, disclosed an incidence of 41 per cent (Elder, 1955).

Formerly protected by their isolation, many species living on oceanic islands have later succumbed to the invasion of domestic animals such as cats, dogs, pigs, goats and sheep, as well as rats, mice, rabbits and other hangers-on of civilization. In 1918 a shipwreck deposited rats on Lord Howe Island off Australia, until then a bird paradise. Since then the rats have completely exterminated five species of native birds. The island of Herokopare near New Zealand had a population of 400,000 sea birds until 1931 when cats were introduced. Now only a few thousand birds remain. The same sorry story can be told for hundreds of islands all over the world. Mayr (1945) states that "more kinds of birds have become extinct on the islands of the Pacific than in all the rest of the world put together." The disturbances caused by man need not be drastic to have an adverse effect on bird populations. Sometimes the mere appearance of a man in a colony of sensitive birds such as spoonbills will cause them to desert their nests en masse and permanently.

THE ROLE OF COMPETITION

Most of the things that birds require of an environment are limited in quantity— food, territory, nesting sites, dust baths, singing posts, and so on. Since birds of the same species make the same demands on their habitat, the more birds in a given locality, the less there is of any given requirement for each. Eventually the carrying capacity of the environment acts as a brake on population increase. Usually one element required of the habitat occurs in short supply before others, and this one then becomes the "critical limiting factor" which either holds down the population or causes the surplus birds to emigrate. This phenomenon is particularly evident among species whose numbers fluctuate widely, often in cycles, through the years.

Competition occurs between birds of different species that live in the same habitat. Hole-nesting birds frequently compete for nesting sites. Starlings, *Sturnus vul-*

garis, often steal nests from woodpeckers; and House Sparrows, *Passer domesticus,* often forcibly eject Cliff Swallows, *Petrochelidon pyrrhonota,* from their mud-flask nests. Even the Bald Eagle, *Haliaeetus leucocephalus,* is not immune to nest robbery. Within a period of six years in Florida, Broley (1947) found 31 out of a total of 619 eagle nests usurped by the Great Horned Owl, *Bubo virginianus.* In Michigan where the Prothonotary Warbler, *Protonotaria citrea,* and House Wren, *Troglodytes aëdon,* compete for nest sites, only 25.7 per cent of the eggs in 121 Warbler nests survived to fledge, whereas in Tennessee, where the Wren is not a competitor, 56.1 per cent of the eggs in 30 nests produced fledged young (Walkinshaw, 1941).

Quantitative studies on competition for food among wild birds are difficult to make, but such phenomena as infanticide and cannibalism, which are so common among boobies, pelicans, gulls, terns, owls, hawks, and eagles, probably have their root in food shortage. Lack (1954) is of the opinion that closely related species which live in the same habitat have evolved different diets and thus have avoided direct competition for food. However, as a result of studying mixed flocks of African birds, Winterbottom (1950) finds evidence of food competition between close relatives. Further study is needed to resolve this problem.

THE ROLES OF CLIMATE, WEATHER, AND ACCIDENTS

Climate has its greatest influence on bird numbers through the indirect means of controlling growth of the plants and plant foods on which birds depend. However, climate does have a direct influence on bird survival, especially on the tender young, mainly through its extremes in temperature and rainfall. Perhaps the best evidence of climatic control of bird populations is found in the fact that long-range gradual changes in mean annual temperatures are paralleled by the gradual exten-

sion or regression in the geographic ranges of many species. This topic will be considered further in Chapter 20.

However, nature periodically performs a dramatic experiment showing that even moderate climatic changes may have profound effects on bird numbers. About once every seven years the Pacific Equatorial Counter-Current swings southward off the coast of Colombia head-on into the north-flowing Peru Current. It is then called "El Niño" and it sets into play the following events: A band of coastal waters extending about 2000 kilometers in length from Ecuador to southern Peru becomes about 5° C. warmer than normally. This causes the death of the usual plankton and the death or disappearance of the teeming fish life characteristic of the Peru Current. Finally, hundreds of thousands of cormorants, boobies, and pelicans, which normally feed on Peru Current fishes, sicken and die (Murphy, 1936). The precise reasons for the deaths of so many birds remain to be discovered, but the change in seawater temperature is probably the inciting force behind the catastrophic drama.

Weather, as distinct from climate, has short-range but often similarly drastic effects on bird numbers. It, too, may affect a species indirectly through regulating its food supply, as, for example, by a late spring freeze, which kills a crop of wild berries, or a drought, which prevents the maturing of seed crops. More dramatically, weather may kill birds directly by swinging to extremes beyond their limits of tolerance. After the unusually severe winter of 1946-47, the occupied nests of Herons, *Ardea cinerea,* in Britain, were reduced 40 per cent in numbers (Alexander, 1948). In 1941, a combination of a cold wet spring followed by a drought in May caused 55 per cent of the 1830 pairs of White Storks, *Ciconia ciconia,* in Schleswig-Holstein to raise no young, whereas in favorable years the proportion was as low as 13 or 14 per cent (Emeis, 1942). When such adverse weather reduces the food supply so that the young starve, the parent storks generally eat the smaller young and throw the larger ones out of the nest.

Numerous accounts have been published of the disastrous effects on bird life of sudden, brief cold spells or storms. After an early spring snow-and-ice storm near Quincy, Illinois, Musselman (1941) estimated that about one-half of all Bluebirds, *Sialia sialis*, in that region were destroyed. In southern Louisiana in 1940, a late January ice storm coated the ground and vegetation with a thick layer of glare ice. This resulted in widespread destruction of birds. Speaking of one species alone, McIlhenny (1940) wrote that the Woodcocks, *Philohela minor,* "got no protection from man, and were slaughtered by the tens of thousands with sticks, .22 rifles, and shotguns. They were sold openly on the streets of the towns . . . at fifty cents to a dollar a dozen, but very few were taken by buyers on account of their being so thin." Many birds, of course, perished directly from starvation. Two July hailstorms in Alberta in 1953 were estimated by Smith and Webster (1955) to have killed over 148,000 waterfowl; and a heavy, wet snowstorm in March, 1904, killed millions of Lapland Longspurs, *Calcarius lapponicus*, in western Iowa and Minnesota, an estimated 750,000 lying dead on the frozen surfaces of two small lakes alone (Roberts, 1932). Facts such as these indicate that many species live dangerously close to their limits of environmental toleration. They apparently possess what an engineer would call a very low safety factor for meeting wider than normal fluctuations in environmental conditions.

The resilience with which a population recovers its numbers after heavy destruction by storms seems to depend chiefly on a species' breeding potential. The year after the destruction of so many Longspurs, Roberts reported that there was no apparent reduction in their numbers. British Herons require four or five years after a hard winter to regain their former numbers; kingfishers perhaps four years; European Crested Larks, *Galerida cristata*, two years.

At times weather conditions may decimate bird populations in unexpected ways. Persistent high winds may blow thousands of sea birds far inland where many of them die of fatigue or starvation. Gentle rains may turn clayey soil into such consistency that it clings to birds' feet causing "mud-balling," which weights down the victims. Young gallinaceous chicks often succumb to mud-balling (Yeatter, 1934). In 1945–1946 about 500 ducks on a Texas wildlife refuge died from exhaustion by becoming shackled to sticky balls of mud, a typical Mallard, *Anas platyrhynchos*, acquiring about 400 gm., and a Pintail, *Anas acuta*, about 750 gm. (1 lb., 11 oz.) of mud on its feet (O'Neill, 1947). Fog sometimes causes birds to lose their way and fly into trouble. In 1889 Stevens (*in* Bent, 1932) told of an immense flock of young Passenger Pigeons, *Ectopistes migratorius*, flying across Crooked Lake, Michigan, in a fog, becoming confused, and descending on the water. Thousands drowned and "the shore line for miles was covered a foot or more deep with them."

In addition to weather, birds are subject to a wide variety of natural accidents that injure and kill them. At times they become entangled in, or strangled by, horse hairs or other fibrous nesting materials. Bird banders frequently trap birds with amputated feet or crooked legs which testify to past fractures. Of 6212 bird skeletons ex-

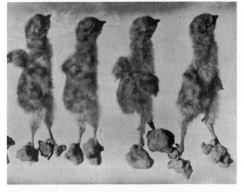

Figure 18.3. Young Hungarian Partridge killed by mud-balling. Wet, clayey soils, under certain conditions, will cling to birds' feet and cause their death through exhaustion, exposure, and starvation. Photo by R. E. Yeatter.

amined by Tiemeier (1941), 4.5 per cent showed healed injuries, 11.78 per cent of which were the result of gunshot wounds. In passerine birds, 75 per cent of the injuries were of the clavicle.

The eruption of Mt. Pelée exterminated three species of birds on Martinique. Falling trees and rocks may destroy whole families of birds. At times birds fly into lethal situations as a result of intoxication from eating fermented or narcotic fruits. On all sides and at all times, birds are surrounded by threats to their lives.

PARASITES AND DISEASES

Western civilized man lives such a sheltered, antiseptic existence that he finds it difficult to comprehend the high incidence of disease in wild creatures. The probabilities are that any wild bird selected at random can be shown to be infected with one or more forms of parasites or disease organisms. Of 112 Crows, *Corvus brachyrhynchos*, collected in Wisconsin and Iowa by Morgan and Waller (1941), 81 per cent were found to be parasitized with one or more of 17 species of parasites. An examination of 1525 birds of 112 species and subspecies in the American Southwest by Wood and Herman (1943) revealed that 23.4 per cent were infected with blood parasites alone; and a study of Redwinged Blackbirds, *Agelaius phoeniceus*, on Cape Cod by Herman (1938) showed that 60 per cent were infected with avian malaria. The subject of bird parasites and diseases is such a large and complex one that only its bare outlines can be considered here. Birds seem to be subject to the same general types of diseases and functional disorders as man, and probably, if the truth were known, to as many different varieties.

ECTOPARASITES. The chief external parasites of birds include biting lice, fleas, calliphorid flies, hippoboscid flies, mosquitoes, black flies, ticks and mites. With the exception of some of the biting lice (Mal-

lophaga) and mites, which live on skin and feathers, these are all bloodsucking parasites. A list of 198 different species of ectoparasites, taken from 255 species and subspecies of birds in states east of the Mississippi River, was compiled by Peters (1936). Some of these individual parasites may attack a variety of hosts, the tick *Ixodes brunneus*, for example, having been found on at least 64 species of birds (Boyd, 1951). Others, such as the Mallophaga and certain mites, are highly host-specific, a given parasite generally being restricted to a single species or genus of birds. Blowflies of the genera *Protocalliphora* and *Apaulina* lay their eggs in birds' nests, particularly those of hole-nesters, and the maggots feed on nestling birds, sucking the blood from their feet and legs and occasionally entering ear cavities and nostrils, or burrowing under the skin. An examination of 162 cavity-nests by Mason (1944) revealed *Protocalliphora* nest-infestations of 94 per cent for Bluebirds, *Sialia sialis*, 82 per cent for Tree Swallows, *Iridoprocne bicolor*, and 47 per cent for House Wrens, *Troglodytes aëdon*. From one to 86 maggots infest a single nest. Hippoboscid or louse flies are flat flies that live among a bird's feathers and suck blood from its skin. They, and black flies, mosquitoes and ticks are known to transmit infectious diseases, particularly of the blood, from one animal to another.

Ticks are likely to infest ground- or bush-nesting birds, or carnivorous birds that feed on tick-infested rodents. Of 944 birds banded by Wharton (1931) in 1930, 8.7 per cent were infested with ticks. Of these birds, the brush-dwelling White-throated Sparrow, *Zonotrichia albicollis*, and Rufous-sided Towhee, *Pipilo erythrophthalmus*, were 11.7 and 47.1 per cent infested, respectively. Ticks often attack the soft tissues around a bird's eyes, sometimes causing blindness and on occasion causing death in young birds. The fact that a nest-dwelling, well-fed tick may survive 3 or 4 years on one meal, suggests a possible reason why Cliff Swallows, *Petrochelidon pyrrhonota*, and similar colonial hole-nesters may change nest-sites every few years.

One function of preening must certainly be the removal of ectoparasites. Passerines of three different species, whose upper mandibles were mostly gone and therefore useless for preening, were found to be very heavily infested with Mallophaga. Dust and water baths, and possibly anting, probably reduce the numbers of parasites in a bird's plumage.

It seems quite possible that the rapid development of nestlings is in part an adaptation to ectoparasite infestation, because the less time a young bird remains in the nest, the fewer parasites it is likely to acquire. Because several kinds of ectoparasites accumulate in nest litter, the young birds of second broods are more likely to become heavily infested than those of first broods. Since certain ectoparasites, such as ticks, are transmitted by bodily contact, they are commoner in gregarious species than in non-gregarious.

ENDOPARASITES. Among the commoner internal parasites are the Trematoda or flukes, Cestoda or tapeworms, Nematoda or roundworms, and the Acanthocephala or spiny-headed worms. While some kinds of parasitic worms may be transmitted directly from one bird to another, more commonly one or more alternate hosts are involved in a worm's life cycle. Thus the adult that lives in a bird is acquired through eating a fish, tadpole, snail, crustacean, earthworm, mole, or some other animal that contains a larval form of the parasite. Small numbers of parasitic worms in a bird do not ordinarily seem to affect its health or vigor, but large numbers may cause emaciation or death. At times, many young storks die from heavy infestations of intestinal flukes; and Eider Ducks, *Somateria mollissima*, on both sides of the Atlantic, die in great numbers from infestations of spiny-headed worms. As many as 1600 tapeworms of 6 different species have been found in a single duck, and a survey in Washington of 3400 Mallards, *Anas pla-*

tyrhynchos, showed that 94.7 per cent of them contained internal parasites. The variety of internal parasites which may infect birds is not generally appreciated. In her monograph on nematode parasites of birds, Cram (1927) describes approximately 500 species, without including the numerous microscopic forms.

Specific parasitic worms usually attack certain organs or tissues in the body, such as the intestines, lungs, liver, trachea or blood. A study of pheasants in Nebraska showed that 40 per cent were parasitized with roundworms which infected their eyes. Ten per cent of a flock of wintering Canada Geese, *Branta canadensis,* in North Carolina died of gizzard worms. These nematode worms caused little damage when there were fewer than 150 in each gizzard, but more than that caused denuded gizzard linings and death (Herman and Wehr, 1954).

In a survey of the parasites of the Ruffed Grouse, *Bonasa umbellus,* Edminster (1947) mentions 14 species of roundworms, 7 of tapeworms, 5 of flukes, as well as numerous protozoa and bacteria. As a small sample of the variety of parasites that attack a single species of bird, data from Edminster on only one-half of the roundworms which parasitize Ruffed Grouse are tabulated on the following page.

MICROSCOPIC ORGANISMS. The commoner microorganisms which infect birds are protozoa, fungi, bacteria, and viruses. A listing of only the parasitic blood protozoa of birds by Herman (1944) included 47 different species. Various studies of thousands of birds of scores of species show that from one-fourth to one-third of all wild birds have blood parasites.

Among the protozoa which infect birds, the commonest are probably the sporozoa which cause avian malaria: *Plasmodium, Haemoproteus,* and *Leucocytozoon.* These three genera of parasites, all of which destroy red blood corpuscles, are transmitted by the bites of *Culex* mosquitoes, hippoboscid flies, or black flies. In California Quail, *Lophortyx californicus,* the per-

Table 18.3. Seven of the 14 Roundworms Known to Parasitize
Ruffed Grouse (after Edminster, 1947)

NAME	DESCRIPTION	PRODUCES	NO. PER BIRD	INCIDENCE
Stomach worm *Dispharynx spiralis*	12 mm. long. White. In pro-ventriculus.	Swelling of proventriculus, emaciation, death.	Avg. 3–12. Up to 228.	Varies greatly from 0–28% Common in domestic chicken.
Intestinal worm *Ascaridia bonasae*	50–100 mm. long. Yellowish. In intestines.	Emaciation in heavy infections.	Avg. 1–15. Up to 200.	Ontario—21% Minn.—37% Mich.—20–37% N.Y.—9–71%
Gizzard worm *Cheilospirura spinosa*	30–40 mm. long. Slender, white. In gizzard lining.	Thickens gizzard walls. May cause death.	Avg. 12–16. Up to 40.	Mich.—42% Minn.—21% Penna.—22% Wis.—19% Ontario—0–14%
Eye worm *Oxyspirura petrowi*	12–18 mm. long. Lives under nictitating membrane of eye.	Conjunctivitis	1–17 per eye.	Mich.—15–28%
Blood worm *Microfilaria* spp.	Microscopic. In blood.	Emaciation.	Millions.	N.Y.—0–11%
Gape worm *Syngamus trachealis*	15–20 mm. long. Red. Attacks windpipe.	Causes bird to choke and gape.	Dozens.	N.Y.—1% Common in domestic chicken.
Larval muscle worm *Physaloptera* spp.	2–3 mm. long. Encysted in muscles of breast and legs.	No apparent damage.	1 to many dozens.	Minn.—3%

centage of wild birds infected with malaria has been as high as 97 per cent; this sometimes causes widespread mortality. *Leucocytozoon* infections may also cause severe losses in grouse, turkeys, and ducks. Experimental exposure to this parasite of young domestic ducks in northern Michigan by Chernin (1952) revealed a significant seasonal relationship: few birds exposed in late June and early July became infected, and none died of the disease; 90 to 100 per cent of the birds exposed to the sporozoa in late July and early August became infected, and of these, 14 to 83 per cent died; after mid-August the ducks were immune to infection. This type of relationship between season and infectiousness has important bearings on epidemic or, more properly, epizootic infections which sporadically kill great numbers of wild birds. Such epizootics are more com-

mon among terrestrial colonial birds than among non-colonial species because of the greater opportunities for contagion in colonies. Likewise, epizootic infection is generally higher in dense populations—among grouse, for example—than in scattered populations. Colonial seabirds seem relatively immune to epizootic outbreaks, probably because of the slight traffic between colony nests and because the ocean, where the birds feed, is a poor culture medium for the infective organisms.

Other protozoan parasites of birds include trypanosomes, coccidia and trichomonads. The trypanosomes are not of common occurrence. They are extra-cellular blood parasites, not particularly pathogenic in birds, and are transmitted by mosquitoes. Nine species of coccidia are known to infect wild birds, the genus *Eimeria* attacking the lower orders of birds and *Isospora* the higher. These organisms cause the destruction of the intestinal lining, loss of appetite, emaciation, diarrhea, and, in heavy infections, hemorrhage and death. *Eimeria* has caused enormous losses in the poultry industry. In wild birds the incidence of infection averages around 31 per cent in Europe, and is highest in summer and autumn.

Trichomonas gallinae, a flagellated protozoon, infects the throats of doves, pigeons, hawks and domestic fowl. It stimulates a growth which obstructs the esophagus and thus causes starvation. An epizootic outbreak of trichomoniasis occurred among the Mourning Doves, *Zenaidura macroura,* in Alabama in 1951, killing an estimated 25,000 to 30,000 birds. It has been suggested that the extinction of the Passenger Pigeon, *Ectopistes migratorius,* was hastened by a similar epizootic plague.

A great variety of birds, particularly aquatic species, are occasionally infected with the mold *Aspergillus* which attacks the wind-pipe, lungs, and air-sacs, but may occur throughout the body. Epizootic outbreaks of aspergillosis have occurred among ducks, especially during prolonged periods of wet weather.

Bacteria cause relatively few diseases in wild birds, possibly because many of the microorganisms cannot multiply successfully at birds' high body temperatures. Pullorum disease, or bacillary diarrhea, is a common and devastating malady in young chickens, and has been suspected as the cause of death of thousands of young terns. Other avian bacterial diseases include tetanus, diphtheria, tuberculosis, cholera, tularemia and botulism. Botulism results from the eating of decaying vegetation in which the anaerobic bacterium *Clostridium botulinum* has grown. The virulent toxin given off by the bacterium, and consumed by the bird with the food, affects the nervous system, causing paralysis and, eventually, death. Botulism has killed millions of waterfowl and shore birds in the United States in recent years.

Virus diseases include a contagious "foot pox" which causes wart-like growths on the feet and at the base of the bill. It is common in sparrows and may result in the loss of toes or feet. Ornithosis, or psittacosis, is one of the few avian virus infections which may be transmitted to man. It causes in man an infection resembling pneumonia, and is occasionally fatal. Several epidemics of ornithosis have occurred among employees of fowl processing plants; in one such firm in Pennsylvania, 12 out of 89 employees contracted the disease in 1957 (Boyd, 1958). Birds also occasionally act as reservoirs of encephalitis or inflammation of the brain, which may be transmitted from them to men and farm animals through insects. Migrating herons were thought to spread a virulent strain of this virus in the Far East, causing the deaths of 2800 humans in Japan and Korea in 1958 and of 500 in Korea in 1959.

Still other lethal agents affect birds. Tumors, muscular dystrophy, uremic poisoning, convulsions, arteriosclerosis, aortic rupture, and various genetic structural and functional abnormalities have been found in birds. Arteriosclerosis has a very high incidence in Domestic Chickens: 45 per cent in birds over one year old (Dauber, 1944). Even "smog" takes its toll. In February, 1959, a persistent smog caused asphyxia in 250 to 300 Starlings, *Sturnus vulgaris,* on the main street of Sleaford, in Lincolnshire, England (Peet, 1959). A "red tide" of marine microorganisms caused the deaths of many marine birds on the Washington coast in 1942 (McKernan and Scheffer, 1942). Between two and three per cent of the North American waterfowl population is probably killed each year by lead poisoning, and the rate will undoubtedly increase as duck hunting increases.

Death in birds may come not only from the presence of lethal agents, such as storms, predators, parasites, and diseases, but also through the absence of certain requirements, such as food, vitamins, trace minerals, oxygen, and others. And, of course, various decimating agents may work in combination. A bird even slightly weakened by parasites is that much less agile in escaping a predator. Since birds

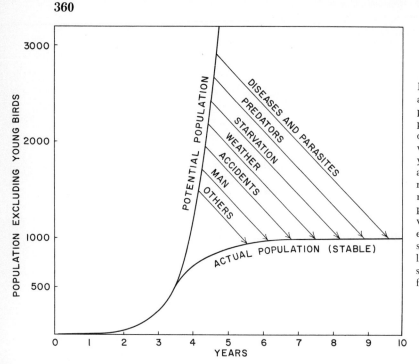

Figure 18.4. The counteracting forces that produce population equilibrium. One pair of Robins could have over 19 million descendants within ten years if all the young survived that long and all pairs of descendants raised 8 young per year. In nature such population explosions are prevented by a variety of forces and influences which cause the "steel spring" of unimpeded population increase to stabilize at supportable levels. Adapted from Leopold.

apparently live so close to their limits of toleration, even small differences in health may have fatal consequences.

Surrounded as birds are by death in so many forms, one begins to understand why so many species have high reproductive potentials. The stable population level which characterizes most wild birds is thus the result of an equilibrium between a species' breeding habits and its living conditions. The agents responsible for this equilibrium have been compared by Leopold (1933) to two antagonistic forces. One of them, which represents the theoretical force of unlimited reproduction, acts like a steel spring always tending to curve upward. This force is counteracted by various strings pulling downward which represent the environmental forces which collectively keep the population leveled off at supportable numbers. These leveling forces are of two kinds: those, like predators, which kill directly, and those, like poor food and water, which reduce the breeding potential. Some forces, like parasites, may do both. Figure 18.4 assumes that one pair of Robins, capable of rear-

ing 8 young per year, is installed on a natural area capable of supporting about 1000 Robins. The actual population curve has been smoothed and does not show the annual saw-teeth of spring and summer rise when young hatch out, nor the fall and winter decline as the young and older birds die.

CHANCES OF SURVIVAL

Since different species of birds enjoy different breeding potentials and live under very different environmental conditions, one would expect them to show different rates of mortality, as they do. Whatever their rate of death, however, most populations remain constant. This means that, ordinarily, deaths in a given species are matched by replacement; but there are two instructive exceptions to this principle. One occurs when a species is introduced into a new and suitable habitat, as the Starling, *Sturnus vulgaris*, was in North America, and the Skylark, *Alauda arvensis*, in New Zealand. Such a species may increase in numbers spectacularly for a few years or decades, but eventually it levels off at a stable population density. The other exception occurs in species that fluctuate in numbers from year to year, sometimes periodically. In either case, these birds increase in numbers until food, predators, disease, or some other density-dependent element in the environment keeps the population in check.

There are many difficulties hampering the study of vital statistics of bird populations. Even though a bird may be banded and its identity thus fixed for life, it may not be banded as a young bird of known age. Most banded birds, once released, are not subsequently captured, or if they are, may not be recovered at the time of their death. The great majority of wild birds die only to decay or be eaten, unobserved by human eyes. Moreover, various statistical biases may attach to the small percentages of dead birds which do come to human attention. Nevertheless, many studies of bird survival, mortality rates, mean longevity and similar vital facts have been undertaken, and much important information obtained.

These studies employ diverse techniques of varying reliability, but most of them rely on population sampling devices similar to those used in public opinion polls. In its simplest form, such a population study has been compared to a counted handful of black beans (banded birds) inserted into and mixed with a jar full of more numerous but uncounted white beans (an unbanded, wild population of birds). The study of a handful of the mixed black and white beans (the later recovery of banded and unbanded birds) enables one to make quantitative predictions about the whole population, based on the assumption that the same statistics apply to the white beans (unbanded wild birds) as to the black beans (banded and counted birds about whose life span something is known).

In the case of small populations of relatively sedentary birds, more direct and precise studies of population statistics may be undertaken. An example of the facts obtained in such investigations may be furnished by Johnston's (1956) study of the salt marsh Song Sparrows, *Melospiza melodia*, of San Francisco Bay. Of every hundred eggs laid by this species, 26 per cent were lost before hatching, leaving 74 live nestlings. Mortality of nestlings was 30 per cent; as a result only 52 fledglings left the nests. Of these young birds, 80 per cent died the first year, leaving only 10 as adults to breed the following season. During the next year there was 43 per cent

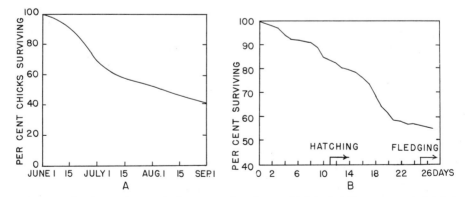

Figure 18.5. Curves showing the heavy mortality of young birds in their first summer. A, Survival curve of precocial young Ruffed Grouse between hatching and the first autumn. After Edminster. B, Survival curve of 261 eggs and the subsequent hatched altricial young of the Bronzed Grackle. After Petersen and Young.

mortality among these one-year olds, leaving only six out of each original hundred to carry on the following year; and each subsequent year mortality among the survivors amounted to 43 per cent.

High mortality is the normal fate of all young birds. For a colony of 9000 to 10,-000 Emperor Penguins, *Aptenodytes forsteri,* in Adelie Land, Antarctica, Sapin-Jaloustre (1952) estimated that, from the time the egg was laid until the molt of the young, mortality was between 80 and 90 per cent. Quite clearly, the high mortality of eggs and young must be compensated for if a population is to maintain its numbers. High losses can be replaced either by laying large numbers of eggs, by increasing mean longevity, or both.

Mortality rates vary not only between species, but at different periods in the life cycle. Since the eggs and young are particularly vulnerable to weather and predators, their mortality rate is almost invariably higher than that of adults. Therefore,

the longer the duration of the egg and nestling stages of a species, the greater the probable mortality. This is particularly true of altricial species whose eggs and young reside in open nests. A survey of various American and European studies of nesting success of both open- and hole-nesting altricial species has been made by Mrs. Nice (1957). A few representative results from this survey appear in Table 18.4.

The data in the table show clearly the superior success of cavity-nesting altricial species, both in hatching eggs and in fledging young. They also show wide variation in the nesting success of such closely related species as sparrows. The great discrepancy in fledging success for the same species (Bluebird), as determined by different workers in different parts of the country, suggests that caution should be used in applying such statistics to general principles of population survival. These and similar figures do not, of course, tell what percentage of the fledged

Table 18.4. Nesting Success of Altricial Species (after Nice)

SPECIES	EGGS LAID (NUMBER)	EGGS HATCHED (PER CENT)	EGGS FLEDGED (PER CENT)	AUTHORITY
OPEN-NESTING BIRDS				
Mourning Dove, *Zenaidura macroura*	8018	54.6	46.6	McClure
American Robin, *Turdus migratorius*	548	57.8	44.9	Young
Redwinged Blackbird, *Agelaius phoeniceus*	1140	72.2	59.2	Smith
American Goldfinch, *Spinus tristis*	696	65.3	48.6	Stokes
Chipping Sparrow, *Spizella passerina*	277	66.8	61.4	Walkinshaw
Field Sparrow, *Spizella pusilla*	1738	51.1	35.7	Walkinshaw
Song Sparrow, *Melospiza melodia*	585	66.5	41.5	Nice
26 studies	21,040	59.8	——	Nice
29 studies	21,951	——	45.9	Nice
HOLE-NESTING BIRDS				
Tree Swallow, *Iridoprocne bicolor*	1123	83.4	61.0	Chapman
Pied Flycatcher, *Muscicapa hypoleuca*	3724	70.7	62.2	Creutz
Great Tit, *Parus major*	45,466	——	64.9	Kluijver
House Wren, *Troglodytes aëdon*	6773	82.3	79.0	Kendeigh
Bluebird, *Sialia sialis*	6260	63.0	44.5	Laskey
Bluebird, *Sialia sialis*	1290	——	65.0	Musselman
Starling, *Sturnus vulgaris*	10,557	——	75.1	Lack
23 studies (8 species)	34,000	77.0	——	Nice
33 studies (13 species)	94,400	——	66.0	Nice

young survive to independent breeding existence. Most altricial young after leaving the nest are still dependent on their parents for at least a few weeks.

Precocial or nidifugous young generally leave the nest a few hours after hatching and usually remain in the care of one parent for several days or weeks. It is extremely difficult to follow the fates of either altricial or precocial wild young during this period of youthful wandering, but Lack (1954) in summarizing some 60 studies of survival in various species, both altricial and precocial, estimates that probably "less than one-quarter of the eggs laid give rise to independent young."

One can easily see that this high but variable mortality in young birds plays an important role in shaping the character of a population. The saw-tooth character of the annual population curve has already been mentioned. Age characteristics of any population will naturally depend on the relative gains and losses of young and old birds each year. Species, for example, with pronounced natural longevity or with high first year mortality will tend to show a preponderance of adult birds in their populations, as seems to be the case

in many sea birds. Computations by Austin and Austin (1956), based on 6965 recoveries of Common Terns, *Sterna hirundo,* banded as chicks, indicate that 90 per cent of the breeding population on Cape Cod is composed of birds three to ten years old. Birds one and two years old rarely return to the colonies to breed. An example of age-structure of a population of California Quail, *Lophortyx californicus,* is shown in Figure 18.7 taken from Emlen (1940).

Once a bird survives its risk-laden first year, the mortality rate for its remaining years remains more or less constant. That is, the expectation of further life in an adult bird remains the same regardless of its age. In the European Oystercatcher, *Haematopus ostralegus,* life expectancy seems even to improve with age, according to observations on banded birds by Drost and Hartmann (1949). This apparent absurdity, so different from human experience, probably derives from the fact that, as a bird ages, its growing senility is counterbalanced by its accumulating experience in meeting the problems of survival. Further, in spite of their potential longevity, most birds die long before

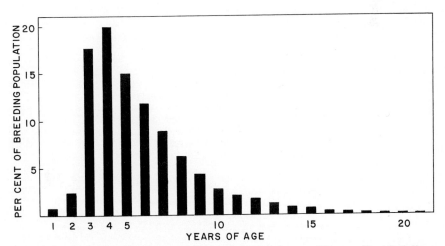

Figure 18.6.   Age composition of a breeding population of Common Terns on Cape Cod. From the 4th year upward, annual mortality averages 25 per cent per year. Birds 1 and 2 years old rarely return to the colony to breed. After Austin and Austin.

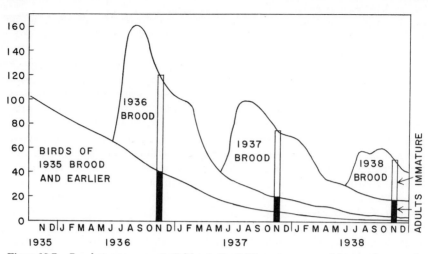

Figure 18.7. Population turn-over in California Quail. The age structure of the population each November is shown by the vertical bar: Black = Adult birds; White = Immature. Eggs and chicks are not shown in the diagram. After Emlen.

old age weakens their faculties seriously, so that death from old age is essentially unknown among wild birds. An analysis, for example, of 5448 recoveries of banded Mourning Doves, *Zenaidura macroura*, in southeastern United States showed a mortality rate of 70 per cent for the first year and 55 per cent each year thereafter (Anonymous, 1957). In Table 18.5 representative examples, taken from Lack (1954), give adult survival statistics for different kinds of birds. The reciprocal relation between adult annual death rate and life expectancy is obvious. The luxury

of a low annual death rate can be enjoyed only by those species demonstrating a high life expectancy.

FLUCTUATIONS IN POPULATIONS

While the great majority of bird populations seem to remain relatively constant in number except for seasonal fluctuations, there are certain species, especially non-migratory birds of northern regions, whose populations may increase by several hundred per cent over a few years,

Table 18.5.   Annual Adult Survival in Various Species of Birds
(after Lack, 1954)

SPECIES	MEAN ANNUAL ADULT MORTALITY (PER CENT)	MEAN FURTHER LIFE EXPECTANCY (YEARS)	AUTHORITY
Blue Jay, *Cyanocitta cristata*	45	1.7	Hickey
American Robin, *Turdus migratorius*	48	1.6	Farner
European Robin, *Erithacus rubecula*	62	1.1	Lack
Common Swift, *Apus apus*	18	5.6	Weitnauer
Royal Albatross, *Diomedea epomophora*	3	ca. 36.	Richdale
Yellow-eyed Penguin, *Megadyptes antipodes*	10	9.5	Richdale
Night Heron, *Nycticorax nycticorax*	30	2.8	Hickey
California Quail, *Lophortyx californicus*	50	1.5	Emlen
Herring Gull, *Larus argentatus*	30	2.8	Paynter

and then abruptly decrease to their original numbers. These fluctuations may show cyclic, repetitive patterns or may be irregular in nature. When one considers the variety and instability of the factors which cause death in birds, it seems surprising that there are not more disturbances of population equilibrium.

There is not much doubt that food abundance is an important regulator of bird abundance, especially in those species whose diet is narrowly limited in variety. A given species of bird may increase its numbers phenomenally following two or three successive seasons of good food crops. Then, should the crops fail for one year, the birds either die in great numbers or, because of their superior mobility, invade new regions. These mass invasions of exceptional range are called *irruptions*. They have been recorded for certain owls, woodpeckers, nutcrackers, jays, waxwings, titmice, crossbills, grosbeaks, and other species.

In 1863, 1888, and 1908, the Sand Grouse, *Syrrhaptes paradoxus*, emigrated from its normal range in Asia Minor and southern Russia and spread in enormous numbers throughout Western Europe and the British Isles. In Britain in 1888 a special Act of Parliament was passed for their protection, in the hope that the species would establish itself, but by 1892 the birds had completely disappeared. In 1939 there was an irruption of Purple Finches, *Carpodacus purpureus*, and in 1941, one of Black-capped and Boreal Chickadees, *Parus atricapillus* and *Parus hudsonicus*, in northeastern United States, the latter species even invading the skyscraper canyons of New York City. Between 1896 and 1939 there were 16 winter invasions of Germany by the Siberian Nutcracker, *Nucifraga caryocatactes*. These invasions seemed always to be correlated with years of poor pine seed crops (the bird's chief food) in the home range of the species.

This same irruptive phenomenon has been observed in mammals, as in squirrels when an acorn crop fails, and even in man, as in the case of the massive Irish emigration that followed the potato famine in 1846.

It is unlikely that birds emigrate from regions of food scarcity because they "recognize" that they will starve if they remain there. A more probable explanation is that dense populations of birds, built up during years of abundant food crops, are themselves the immediate stimulus for irruption. Such mass emigrations, set off by sheer numbers, probably represent an adaptive response to sporadic famine, built up through thousands of years of natural selection. In this sense, food lack is the ultimate cause of irruptive behavior. Among species that show sporadic irruption, e.g., the Siberian Nutcrackers, it is likely to be the young birds rather than the old which emigrate. This is probably because the older birds are more attached to the home territory and have peck-order seniority, while the young have been naturally selected as more vigorous exploiters of strange regions.

This correlation between food-lack and mass movements of birds is a demonstrable fact as shown by Reinikainen (1937). Every March for 11 years he covered the same region of Finland on skis for about 120 kilometers, and recorded both the number of Red Crossbills, *Loxia curvirostra*, he encountered and the abundance of spruce cones, the seeds of which are the staple diet of these birds. Where cones were plentiful, birds were also plentiful, and where the cone crop failed, birds were rare or absent. In contrast to the geographic fixity of most species, the nomadic habit of the Crossbill, coupled with its restricted diet, enables the species to survive even though its food crop should fail over wide areas.

Cyclic fluctuations in bird populations are largely restricted to predatory and gallinaceous species distributed between 30° and 60° north latitude, where food supplies are less varied, and climate less regular, than farther south. There are two rather well-defined cyclic patterns in North America: a 10-year cycle charac-

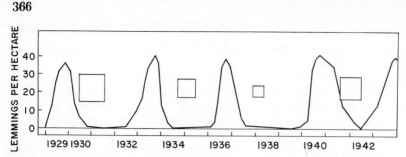

Figure 18.8. The relation between Snowy Owl irruptions and lemming abundance. The curve shows the cyclic abundance of lemmings for different years at Churchill, Manitoba. The squares indicate the times and relative abundance of Snowy Owls invading New England. After Shelford.

teristic of populations of Ruffed Grouse, *Bonasa umbellus*, Goshawks, *Accipiter gentilis*, and Great Horned Owls, *Bubo virginianus*, as well as the Varying Hare, *Lepus americanus;* and a 4-year cycle found in the Snowy Owl, *Nyctea scandiaca*, Rough-legged Hawk, *Buteo lagopus*, and Northern Shrike, *Lanius excubitor*, and also the lemmings, *Dicrostonyx* spp. To say that these animals exhibit population cycles of 10 and 4 years does not mean that their population peaks come precisely at those intervals. However, the phenomenon is regular and striking enough to have caused much study and speculation.

To account for these cycles, a great variety of explanations have been suggested, ranging from sunspot and climatic cycles through predators, food-lack and epizootics, to over-hunting, in-breeding and lack of cover. In the case of cycles and irruptions of predatory birds, the explanation is simple and direct. Snowy Owl irruptions into the northern United States coincide very closely with precipitous declines in the numbers of lemmings, their preferred food (Fig. 18.8). The same correspondence exists between fluctuations in populations of the Varying Hare and those of Great Horned Owls and Goshawks.

Less evident is the basic cause of cycles in gallinaceous birds. Lack (1954) is of the opinion that a producer-consumer, density-dependent oscillation is set up between rodents and their vegetable food. When, for example, the lemmings be-

come too populous, their food plants suffer and decline, and this reduction is followed by a "crash" year of lemming decline. With the lemming population reduced drastically, plants again have a chance to regain their abundance; then the lemming population builds up again until the next crash. When foxes, hawks, and other predators are faced with the disappearance of lemmings, they turn with greater intensity on alternate prey, such as grouse and ptarmigan, thus initiating in these birds a cyclic population oscillation. Nearer the equator, where animal communities are more complex, and where numerous alternative foods are available when a preferred type fails, food relationships are sufficiently elastic to dampen population oscillations to the vanishing point.

Still another explanation of cyclic irruptions is proposed by Svärdson (1957) who points out that 60-year records for the fruiting of Swedish spruce trees show that a heavy seed crop appears every third or fourth year. This may be a plant adaptation which ensures a higher total number of seeds produced and germinated through the years because the staggered years of production prevent the building up of a large, sedentary population of seed-eating birds and other animals. In seedless years the birds must move elsewhere and possibly eat a substitute diet. The spruce trees, in essence, have evolved a mechanism which, to their benefit, drastically reduces the carrying-capacity of the birds' environment, and yet allows the trees sporadic bursts of seed production great enough to surmount the destruction of seeds by a reduced population of birds. Nomadic wanderings and irruptions of birds may represent a complementary adaptation. Whatever the ultimate explanation, cycles in avian populations are a well-established fact, and further research will probably clarify the mechanisms responsible.

SUGGESTED READINGS

Lack treats the subject of population in simple and clear language in *The Natural Regulation of Animal Numbers.* For a brief review of population problems, see Gibb's chapter on *Bird Populations* in Marshall's *Biology and Comparative Physiology of Birds.* For excellent technical discussions of the subject, see Hickey's *Some American Population Research on Gallinaceous Birds,* and Farner's *Bird-banding in the Study of Population Dynamics,* both found in Wolfson's *Recent Studies in Avian Biology.* In the same volume is a brief treatment of *Diseases of Birds* by Herman.

NINETEEN

The Ecology of Birds

It is interesting to contemplate a tangled bank, clothed with many plants of many kinds, with birds singing on the bushes, with various insects flitting about, and with worms crawling through the damp earth, and to reflect that these elaborately constructed forms, so different from each other, and dependent upon each other in so complex a manner, have all been produced by laws acting around us.

Charles Darwin, *The Origin of Species*

Ecology is the study of the relationships between organisms and their environments, or between organisms and what Darwin called the conditions of their struggle for existence. This is a deceptively simple statement, for ecology covers an unusually broad spectrum of natural phenomena. It is concerned with organisms and their adaptations in structure, physiology, and behavior. It is concerned with all aspects of the environment which may affect organisms: the soil they walk on, the air they breathe, the food they eat, the weather they endure, and all interacting organisms, whether plants or animals.

Ecology is a young, rapidly growing science, and it contains some of the uncertainties, contradictions, and even adolescent jargon of youth. It may be studied from the standpoint of a given organism as related to its environment (autecology), or from that of groups of organisms in an environment (synecology).

Emphasis may be placed on habitat—for example, the ecology of caves—or on the distributional or geographic effects of selected environmental factors—for example, the effects of rainfall on animal distribution. Throughout this book thus far, emphasis has been placed on the adaptations of birds to their conditions of existence. In this chapter an attempt will be made to list and analyze some of these interrelationships between birds and their environments, starting with the physical factors in the environment (soil, water, temperature, and light), progressing through the biological factors (plants and animals), and ending with a study of the more comprehensive fabrics that these threads of influence weave—the ecology of major habitat types such as lakes, forests, and grasslands.

Because no environment is entirely static, perfect adaptation cannot exist in any animal; for if the animal were perfectly adapted to its surroundings today, it would not be so tomorrow when the weather changes or the season advances, let alone through longer spans of time when more substantial changes may occur in the habitat. Further, a creature of high mobility, like a bird, is unlikely to adapt very closely to a given habitat when one of the chief advantages of mobility is the capacity to exploit diverse habitats. Even so, birds show a surprising variety of adaptations to their various conditions of existence. These adaptations, of course, must at times be restricted by the limitations imposed on birds by their one supreme adaptation, the power of flight. This fact illustrates the ecological principle that specialization in one direction often closes doors to the possibility of other adaptations. A flying machine such as a bird cannot, for example, don the protective armor-plate of a turtle, desirable as such protection might be at times.

PHYSICAL FACTORS OF ENVIRONMENT

Every bird lives in an environment composed of two fundamentals: matter and energy. Matter provides the medium (air) within which the bird lives, a substrate (ground or water) on which it walks or swims, and the materials of which the bird's body is made. The energy of the environment, which is absorbed by the bird for its own needs, comes ultimately from sunlight, via foods eaten by the bird.

THE SUBSTRATE

Although some birds may be air- or water-borne for days on end, they must sooner or later come to earth, if for nothing else than to breed. The physical character of the ground on which a bird typically walks is commonly attested to by the bird's feet and legs (Fig. 19.1). Birds adapted to relatively firm, flat, open country typically have long, powerful legs, with short toes which are often reduced in number—a characteristic paralleled by the hoofed mammals of similar habitats. Among the long-legged, short-toed runners are ostriches, emus, rheas, coursers, bustards, tinamous, and a ground-dwelling bird of prey, the Secretary Bird, *Sagittarius serpentarius*, of Africa, whose toes are only about one-fifth as long as those of a comparably large hawk, but whose legs are perhaps three times as long.

Birds that do much scratching of the ground in seeking food (Galliformes) or in building mounds (Megapodiidae, Menuridae) have powerful legs and feet with heavy, blunt claws. Birds that frequent marshy ground are apt to have long legs and compensating long necks (herons, bitterns, cranes, storks), or lobate-webbed toes (grebes, coots, phalaropes, finfeet) suitable both for walking on mud or for swimming. Another adaptation for a soft substrate is found in the jaçanas, shore birds whose extremely long toes enable them to walk on floating aquatic vegetation such as water lily pads, and thus exploit a habitat which attracts few, if any, avian competitors.

As a substrate, snow presents serious problems of both temperature and support,

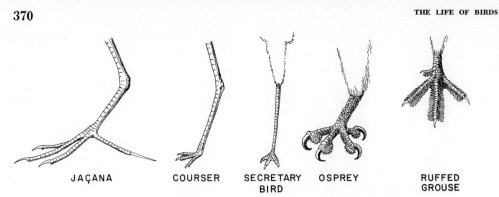

JAÇANA   COURSER   SECRETARY   OSPREY   RUFFED
                             BIRD   GROUSE

Figure 19.1. Examples of adaptations of feet to different substrates. The jaçana and the courser both belong to the Charadriiformes, but the jaçana, with its exceedingly long toes, walks about on floating vegetation, while the short-toed courser lives typically on hard desert soils. The Secretary Bird and Osprey are both falconiform birds, but the former has given up its strong legs and sharp talons for short-toed stilt legs, more suitable for stalking prey on the ground. Under each toe, the Osprey has pads with sharp spicules which help it to grasp the fish on which it feeds. The comb-like fringes on each toe of the Ruffed Grouse serve as snowshoes in winter.

which many birds avoid through migration. Several species of the grouse family solve the problem of locomotion by growing fringe-like scales along the side of each toe for the winter season only; in the spring these "snowshoe" fringes are molted. The feet of the Scottish Ptarmigan, *Lagopus mutus*, are relatively unfeathered in summer, but in winter each toe is so heavily feathered that the bird walks on feathers—an adaptation which provides both support and insulation. The remarkable change in the plumage of several species of ptarmigan from white in winter to brown in summer was discussed earlier. Another type of adaptation to snow is found in the antarctic Adelie Penguin, *Pygoscelis adeliae*, whose nostrils are so feathered over as to keep snow out of its air pasages. Other species of this genus which live in warmer climates have exposed, unfeathered nostrils (Murphy, 1936).

The topography of the substrate is of ecological significance to many species, particularly during the nesting season. Many swallows, kingfishers, bee-eaters, South American ovenbirds, motmots, todies, and jacamars require vertical banks of soil into which they dig their nest burrows. The Peregrine Falcon, *Falco peregrinus*, prefers as a nest site a ledge on a vertical cliff. Most gulls normally nest on shores which slope gradually to the water's edge. If overpopulation forces some gulls to nest on steep shores, they lose many young by drowning, because the latter rush to the water when disturbed, and are unable to clamber back up the steep slopes.

Recent studies have shown a relationship between the mineral content of soils and the ecological distribution of birds. In New York, the Hungarian Partridge, *Perdix perdix*, is restricted to soils of limestone origin (Wilson, 1959). Both field observations and laboratory feeding experiments show that calcium is required in the diet of the Ring-necked Pheasant, *Phasianus colchicus*. In two comparable field areas, the presence or absence of calcium was the only variable discovered which could explain the heavy population of pheasants in a limestone region and their scarcity in a non-calcareous area (Dale, 1955). Birds lacking calcium in their diet are unable to produce more than a very few eggs.

Adaptations apply not only to finished structures and their functions, but also to the way in which structures grow. As described earlier, the precocial young of ground-nesting cranes leave the nest and follow their parents shortly after hatching. For over two months the young depend entirely on their legs for locomotion. Accordingly, their wings develop slowly and their legs very rapidly: the legs achieve

Figure 19.2. Ecological adaptation in the growth of legs and wings. *A*, A young crane 2 days old is able to run, and at 32 days its legs have almost finished growing. Its wing feathers, however, have scarcely sprouted. *B*, A stork at 1½ days is blind and helpless. At 29 days its wing feathers are well along toward maturity, but its legs are still poorly developed. Adapted from Heinroth.

their most rapid growth between the 8th and 16th days of life. Storks have a body architecture similar to that of cranes, but they raise their young not on the ground but high in roof- or tree-top nests. This ecological difference in nest sites is correlated with a striking difference in leg and wing development of the young. Sturdy, rapidly growing legs would not only be useless in the young stork's nest habitat but positively dangerous. Accordingly, its legs develop slowly, growing most rapidly between the 20th and 38th days of life. Its wing feathers, however, sprout much earlier than those of the crane, and the young stork makes its first venture from the home nest into the world by means of its wings and not its legs (Heinroth, 1938).

Water is frequently a substrate for many water birds, and it may become a medium for a short while when a bird dives into it. Many of the adaptations of birds to an aquatic life are obvious and well known: webbed feet, powerful leg muscles, large uropygial glands, and dense water-proof plumage. In many ducks the oily flank feathers form pockets on each side into which the folded wings fit, dry and ready for instant action. Expert divers, such as the loon, have marrow-filled bones rather than the usual hollow bones—an adaptation promoting more efficient under-water swimming. Different species of penguins are known to swallow stones, presumably as ballast which would serve the same end. Penguins spend more time in water than any other birds, and they are well adapted to such an existence. Their bodies are smoothly streamlined and covered with small, hair-like feathers. Their wings have developed into powerful flippers which can propel them through the water at speeds of up to 36 kilometers per hour. Their bodies are thickly covered with blubber for insulation against heat loss. Their eyes are so well adapted for vision under water that the birds are notoriously myopic on land.

Different kinds of water birds show distinct preferences for different kinds of aquatic habitats. Some species are exclusively fresh water birds, others salt water, and still others are able to live in either type of habitat. The saltiness of sea water, when swallowed, causes the dehydration of body tissues and, in most animals, eventual death. This obstacle to the invasion of the sea by birds has been overcome by petrels and other sea birds through the development of nasal or salt glands, which are many times more efficient than the kidneys in removing salt from body fluids. The remarkable ecological plasticity of a single species in adapting to this problem is demonstrated by the Mallard, *Anas platyrhynchos*, which in most parts of the world is a fresh water dweller and possesses ordinary-sized nasal glands. In Greenland, however, is a race of Mallards which has become semi-marine and whose salt glands are roughly ten times as large as those of fresh water Mallards (Fig. 6.4). This one ecological adaptation in water birds makes possible an enormous extension in the range of aquatic habitats open to them. It is very likely that similar structural and functional adaptations, as yet undiscovered, underlie such preferences and capabilities as those of the Snow Petrel, *Pagodroma nivea*, for cold water; the tropic birds, Phaëthontidae, for clear, saline, moderately warm water; the Laughing Gull, *Larus atricilla*, for warm water, and the Brown Pelican, *Pelecanus occidentalis*, for silt-free salt water (Murphy, 1936).

CLIMATE AND WEATHER

Climate, more than any other physical factor, determines whether or not a given species will live in a given region. Climate is largely a matter of rainfall and temperature, and its effects may be felt by the bird directly, or indirectly through the influence of climate on vegetation and other environmental features. The twice-a-year global surge of migration shows to what extent temperature change alone requires adaptive adjustments in billions of birds. At all stages of their life histories, from eggs to adults, birds exhibit a tremendous variety of adaptations to temperature. Only a few representative examples of these adaptations can be given here.

Within vital limits, *change* in temperature works a greater hardship on an organism than a steady hot or a steady cold temperature. The Emperor Penguin, *Aptenodytes forsteri*, goes through the most exhausting stage of its life cycle, the breeding period, during the antarctic winter when temperatures range as low as $-60°$ C. The Snow Petrel, *Pagodroma nivea*, nests atop mountains only $10°$ or $11°$ in latitude from the south pole. However, when a number of Magellanic Penguins, *Spheniscus magellanicus*, migrate north each winter (July, August) and settle on the sandy beaches of Uruguay, the birds sicken and die by the hundreds as the air and water warm up with the advance of spring (Murphy, 1936). Whether the warmth causes its harmful effects directly or indirectly is unknown. The remarkably lethal effect of a $5°$ increase in water temperature has already been discussed in connection with the Peru Current and "El Niño." More familiar are the disastrous effects of unusually cold weather on the survival of birds in temperate regions.

An indirect way in which cold weather limits a species' activities and distribution is through the freezing of water. Birds of northern lakes and streams must be able to migrate south as soon as ice covers the water where they make their living. The Belted Kingfisher, *Megaceryle alcyon*, which fishes for its food by diving under water, is forced to fly south in the autumn ahead of the ice, and it migrates back north in the spring as soon as thaws open its feeding territories. Sea birds do not have to face this sudden metamorphosis of their habitat. As winter closes in, the sea never freezes solidly over wide areas, but leaves open waterways between ice floes through which sea birds may travel equatorward without flying. These facts possibly explain why there are flightless sea birds, but no flightless fresh water birds except in ice-free climates (Allen, 1925).

Through years of natural selection, temperature fluctuations have brought about adaptive changes in the structure, physiology, and behavior of birds. Feathers probably evolved primarily as heat-conserving devices and were later adapted for flight. A further adaptation to heat conservation is the increase in the number of feathers that many birds of cooler latitudes wear in winter. Layers of body fat are also used for insulation against cold. Fat is particularly well developed in birds inhabiting cold waters, and, of course, birds of polar regions. Since large bodies have relatively less heat-radiation surface than small bodies (p. 92), large birds can tolerate cold climates better than small birds can. This explains why birds of high latitudes have, as a rule, larger bodies than their warm climate relatives.

An ingenious adaptation that keeps the feet of ducks and geese from freezing while they stand on ice consists of a direct connection between the arteries and veins of the feet. This arrangement, found also in the beaks of some cold climate birds, provides for a by-passing of much of the capillary circulation, thus allowing a more rapid circulation and therefore a more rapid replacement of lost heat. In warm weather, air sacs promote the rapid cooling of the body as well as efficient respiration.

Chief among the physiological adaptations to temperature is thermoregulation, or warm-bloodedness, which enables birds to remain active day or night, winter or summer, in habitats spread over the surface of the entire earth. The complete absence of cold-blooded reptiles from high latitudes suggests the great ecological value of this adaptation. Birds are able to maintain relatively constant body temperatures throughout a wide range of environmental temperatures, cooling themselves by sleeking their feathers and panting when external temperatures exceed their own, and generating more body heat and fluffing their feathers when cold air temperatures cause greater heat loss. As animals of incomparably high metabolism, birds maintain resting body temperatures ranging from 37.8° C. to 44.6° C. and averaging about 40.5° C. (Man = 37.0° C.). This temperature presses close to the lethal maximum body temperature of 46.7° C., but is quite far from the lethal minimum

of 21.7° C. (Bourlière, 1950). The efficiency of temperature regulation is seen in the fact that, within vital limits, for every rise or fall of 10° C. in environmental temperature, a small bird's body temperature rises or falls only 0.1° C.

As in all animals, there are extremes in environmental temperatures beyond which birds cannot survive. These limits vary with species, health, age and other factors. Even closely related species may exhibit widely different temperature tolerances. The European Yellowhammer, *Emberiza citrinella*, is a non-migratory species able to endure winter temperatures as low as −36° C. The Ortolan Bunting, *Emberiza hortulana*, which breeds in the same parts of Europe, tolerates a minimum of only −16° C., and consequently must emigrate south for the winter. Such factors as fat storage, metabolic efficiency, preferred diet, habitat choice, roosting habits, and thickness of plumage —all amenable to selective adaptation— determine a species' temperature tolerance, and its limits of geographic dispersal. The length of cold winter nights during which birds must fast, and of short winter days, during which they must eat, are also important considerations in the ecological distribution of cold climate species (p. 130).

As a means of stretching their energy resources over cool periods of enforced fasting, a very few species have adopted a form of dormancy similar to mammalian hibernation. These periods of lowered body temperature (which greatly reduce the rate of heat loss and therefore postpone starvation) range from overnight in some hummingbirds, through a week to nine days in young swifts, to a few months in some goatsuckers. To combat unusually high temperatures, many species begin panting when their body temperatures reach a certain threshold temperature. In the California Quail, *Lophortyx californicus*, this temperature is 43.5° C. An ability to tolerate a body temperature of as much as 4° C. above normal is probably an adaptation to life in hot climates (Bartholomew and Dawson, 1958).

Physiological adaptation to chilling is found to a surprising degree in the embryos of incubating eggs. This tolerance of occasional interruptions in the incubation heat is very likely an adaptation to the food-hunting absences of the incubating parent (p. 303). At the other extreme, the eggs of the Ostrich, *Struthio camelus*, are able to withstand high desert temperatures that would be deadly to eggs of other species. The rate with which the hatched young develop is also adapted in some species to thermal requirements. The large Emperor Penguin, *Aptenodytes forsteri*, hatches its chick in the coldest period of the antarctic winter, and broods it assiduously until warmer weather arrives. The far smaller Adelie Penguin, *Pygoscelis adeliae*, living at the same latitude, hatches its chicks in the summer time. These young grow and mature with astonishing speed and reach relative independence, along with the more slowly developing young Emperors, by the time the next winter arrives.

Numerous adaptations to temperature extremes are found in the behavior of birds. To avoid intolerable cold, many species migrate to warmer climates for the winter. Diurnal birds are almost all inactive at night, and this fact, coupled with a slightly lowered body temperature, greatly reduces their heat loss in cold weather. Many species form roosting or sleeping aggregations, some small species huddling together so tightly as to form feathered balls (Fig. 7.8). In the most bitter antarctic weather, incubating male Emperor Penguins huddle together for protection. Weight loss per day among these birds is only about one-half that of penguins kept isolated (Prevost and Bourlière, 1957). Since these birds fast during the incubation period, the metabolic economy of this behavior is doubly adaptive in that it conserves heat and it also stretches energy reserves over the period of continuous, uninterrupted incubation which is essential in polar climates.

When sleeping during cold weather, most birds fluff their feathers, thus creating a thicker, warmer layer of insulating air. Most birds also tuck their beaks under their feathers, thus providing themselves with pre-warmed air to breathe and reducing the body surface area much as does a human who hugs himself to keep warm. The Snow Bunting, *Plectrophenax nivalis*, and several grouse escape the most extreme cold of winter by plunging into snow banks where the temperature is relatively mild. Many other species seek the thermal protection of dense thickets, natural cavities, and other places where the immediate temperature and wind are less severe than in the open. Atmospheric conditions in these localized environments are known as *microclimates*, and they are widely exploited by birds living under extreme climatic conditions. In extremely cold weather, for example, the air temperature above the snow surface in Alaska may be $-50°$ C., but only 60 centimeters below the surface the temperature may be a relatively warm $-5°$ C. Microclimates often figure in the selection of nesting sites. At altitudes of 1500 to 1700 meters in the Alps, birds build their early season nests on southern exposures; but by June, as the season advances, many birds change to northern exposures (Heilfurth, 1936). Desert birds commonly build their nests in the shade of bushes or on the east sides of rocks and bushes where they will avoid the sun during the hottest part of the day. In very hot weather birds largely restrict their activity to the morning and evening hours when the air is cooler. In caring for their eggs and young, parent birds will ordinarily brood them more attentively in cold weather, and in hot weather protect them from the sun by spreading their wings over them. In these and numberless other ways, bird adaptations serve as homeostatic agents to reduce the impact of temperature extremes in environments which would otherwise be intolerable.

The influence of precipitation and humidity on birds is largely indirect, through their control of the growth and distribution of vegetation and food. There are, however, some direct effects of ecological consequence. Prolonged cold rains are much more destructive of bird life than prolonged dry cold, because the insulating value of plumage deteriorates as it becomes wet. Deep snows cover the food of many species of birds and may cause widespread hardship or death. The heavy snows of 1946–1947 in Europe caused Carrion Crows, *Corvus corone,* and Magpies, *Pica pica,* to attack cattle, pecking through their hides to feed on their flesh (Bourlière, 1950). As described earlier, the reproductive cycle in many arid land species is stimulated by rainfall, long before the rain could have any effect on vegetation or food supply. The Red-backed Shrike, *Lanius collurio,* is reported to prefer sunny, dry areas for breeding, and to avoid cloudy or rainy regions. While it is difficult to separate other characteristics of a habitat from humidity and rainfall, it seems likely that for some desert species dryness in itself is an ecological requirement. Certainly the eggs of a desert lark require less moisture for successful incubation than the eggs of a grebe. The California Quail, *Lophortyx californicus,* intro-

duced into New Zealand, favors regions where rainfall averages less than 150 centimeters annually (Williams, 1952).

Since climate is made up predominantly of temperature and precipitation, attempts have been made by game managers to increase the success of game bird introductions by planting an exotic species in a region whose climate matches that of its optimum native habitat. Two such climates are quickly compared by scrutinizing climographs of the two regions: graphs in which mean monthly temperatures are plotted against the ordinate, and total monthly rainfall against the abscissa. Introductions of the Hungarian Partridge, *Perdix perdix,* have been attempted in various parts of the United States. In Missouri and California, where the climographs show a wide deviation from that of the bird's optimum European habitat, introductions failed. But in Montana, where the two climographs showed greater agreement, especially during the crucial breeding season months, the introductions succeeded (Twomey, 1936) (Fig. 19.3).

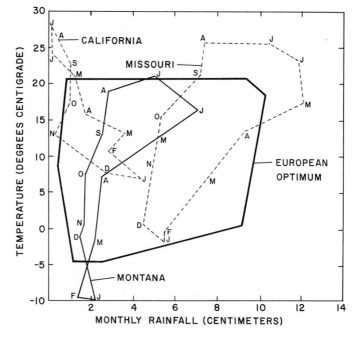

Figure 19.3. The Hungarian Partridge, transplanted from central Europe to America, has successfully established itself in Montana, but has failed conspicuously in California and Missouri, whose climates do not agree closely with the climate of the species' ancestral home. After Twomey.

Wind intensifies the ecological effects of temperature and precipitation. A driving rain or a blizzard is much more dangerous to birds than a gentle rain or snowfall. Regions with prevailingly steady winds present birds with distinctly different environments from less windy regions with the same climographs. Wind inhibits singing and other activities of birds. In strong winds, many birds fly near the earth where wind velocity is lessened. Other species, on the contrary, use winds for soaring, particularly in regions where hills or mountains create updrafts. Wind also serves as a vehicle for bird distribution. Birds are more likely to disperse in directions that prevailing winds carry them than in contrary directions. The circumglobal Blue Petrel, *Halobaena caerulea,* is limited in its oceanic wanderings by the northern edge of the belt of the Roaring Forties to the north, and by pack ice to the south (Murphy, 1936).

Nest sites are often chosen with reference to prevailing winds. Many of the larger procellariiform sea birds locate their nests on cliffs or slopes on the windward sides of islands where taking off in flight is facilitated by updrafts of air. Woodpeckers living in exposed regions, such as mountain heights, are likely to dig their nest holes on the sides of trees away from prevailing winds. Many smaller birds of exposed regions in deserts and steppes build their nests on the lee sides of rocks, shrubs, or other windbreaks to avoid the full effect of wind storms. Desert larks and wheatears often erect walls of small stones beside their nests. This behavior probably represents an age-old adaptive response to wind.

LIGHT

As an ecologic factor, light influences birds mainly through its intensity and duration, and to a lesser extent through its wave-length (color) and direction. Eyes of nocturnal birds are usually larger than those of diurnal species. The partly noc-turnal Red-footed Booby, *Sula sula,* which feeds on night-surfacing squids, has apparently the largest eyes of any members of its family. Other boobies are more strictly diurnal (Murphy, 1936). Whereas the retinas of nocturnal species are rich in rods, those of diurnal species are rich in color-sensitive cones. The ability of most birds to discriminate colors undoubtedly influences their search and selection of food. The variously colored oil droplets in the retinal cells of many birds may well be an adaptation for the precise detection of small objects (insects, worms, berries, seeds) of the same or complementary colors.

The two great natural rhythms of light— daily and yearly—have profound effects on birds: on their anatomy, physiology, behavior, and distribution. The daily rhythm of light and darkness has impressed on birds a daily rhythm of activity and rest, inverted, of course, in nocturnal species. Diurnal birds are more active, and have higher temperatures and higher metabolism, by day than by night. The close correspondence of their activity with light, rather than with temperature or some other environmental factor, is seen, for example, in the close relationship between sunrise and awakening song (p. 202). The annual cycle of change in day-length in all parts of the world excepting equatorial regions inaugurates the global cycle of the seasons with all the profound and widespread effects they have on birds and plants. The many deep-seated adaptive responses of photoperiodism—courtship, mating, territorial battles, nest-building, egg-laying, incubation, plumage molt, migration—are, in hordes of birds, set into motion by changes in day length. These have all been treated in more detail elsewhere. It is enough here to emphasize the fact of their ecological connection with sunlight. Without the eons of fine polishing by natural selection, some birds might today wear their dullest colors for their courtship dances, lay their eggs in sub-zero weather, or migrate north rather than south in autumn. For most species the great clock of changing day-length sets off all these activities and keeps them synchronized with the best times of year for their fruitful functioning.

BIOLOGICAL FACTORS
OF ENVIRONMENT

The basic difference between plants and animals is that only plants can manufacture food from inorganic raw materials. This means that all animals, birds included, depend ultimately on sunlight and the food-manufacturing photosynthesis of green plants for their food. "All flesh is grass." Plants are of ecologic importance to birds, not only as sources of food but also for nesting materials, nesting sites, lookout posts, singing stations, and protective cover. Plants probably satisfy some psychological needs in birds as well, but food is of primary importance.

Adaptations to food show most obviously in the structure of birds' beaks. While there is wide diversity in the shapes and sizes of beaks, their adaptations seem to tend either toward a generalized bill suitable for eating a variety of foods, or toward a highly specialized bill suitable for eating foods of a restricted type. Species ecologically tolerant of a wide variety of foods are said to be *euryphagous*. Crows and gulls, with their straight, simple beaks, eat fish, birds, eggs, invertebrates, fruits, vegetables, seeds, carrion and other foods. Birds limited to a restricted diet are said to be *stenophagous*, or, if they are restricted to a single type of food—a very rare occurrence—*monophagous*. The Everglade Kite, *Rostrhamus sociabilis*, is reputed to be monophagous, feeding only on snails. With their long beaks and brushy-tipped or tubular tongues, hummingbirds are rather closely restricted to nectar and insects as food. The long, sensitive beaks of snipe and woodcock limit their diets to the worms and other invertebrates they can find by probing soft earth. Crossbills find their peculiarly asymmetrical beaks most useful in extracting the seeds of pine and spruce cones. Many species of ducks employ their fringe-edged beaks for sifting seeds and small animals from muddy water, while the Broad-billed Whalebird, *Pachyptila forsteri*, uses the whalebone-like fringes of its upper mandible for filtering plankton from sea water. Other examples of adaptations in beaks are given in Chapter 6.

Adaptations to food are also found in internal organs such as the food-storing crop of pigeons, the seed-grinding gizzard of the Turkey, and the cellulose-digesting caeca of the Domestic Fowl. In general,

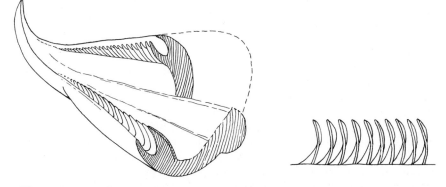

Figure 19.4. Maxillary lamellae of the Broad-billed Whalebird. There are about 150 of these fringe-like keratin plates along each margin of the upper jaw, and they grow as long as 3.5 mm. tall at the inner end of the mouth. At right is a series of plates as seen from the mid-line of the mouth. After Murphy.

seed eating birds have muscular, grinding gizzards, while meat eaters have glandular stomachs that digest food almost entirely by enzymes. But even in an individual bird there may be adaptations to changes in diet. The stomachs of some gulls are thin-walled and richly supplied with digestive glands while they feed on fish, but in the autumn when gulls may move inland and feed on grain, their stomachs gradually change into muscular gizzards capable of crushing corn (Beebe, 1906). A corresponding increase in the musculature of the gizzard occurs in the Redwinged Blackbird, *Agelaius phoeniceus*, when it seasonally shifts its diet from insects to seeds (Allen, 1914). An ability to adjust to a different kind of diet at different times of year is a valuable adaptation for a bird living in a region with pronounced seasonal changes, for food availability may change from insects in spring and summer to fruits in the fall, and to seeds in winter.

Too narrow a specialization in diet can be dangerous to a species, because some natural catastrophe may destroy the one or several foods on which the bird depends. This nearly happened in 1931–1933 when a blight killed most of the eel-grass which Atlantic Brant, *Branta bernicla*, ate as their preferred food. Apparently unable to turn to substitute foods, about 80 per cent of the Brant population disappeared (p. 96). Whatever a bird's feeding adaptations and habits may be, it must live in those regions where its preferred foods are found. It follows, therefore, that slight adaptive changes in the structure of a bird's beak, or in the chemistry of its digestive enzymes, might so change its diet as to cause definite changes in its geographic distribution. These latter changes in turn might require new adaptations in limits of toleration for temperature extremes, rainfall, nest sites, and other environmental conditions. Ecologic adaptations may thus be either balanced or pitted one against the other.

Among the other needs supplied to birds by vegetation, one of the most important is a secure and effective nesting site. Some species show pronounced preferences for specific types of nest-site vegetation. Ring-necked Pheasants, *Phasianus colchicus*, choose hayfields, preferably older ones, for nesting. In its breeding ground the Rockhopper Penguin, *Eudyptes crestatus*, tolerates no vegetation larger than grass, while the Jackass Penguin, *Spheniscus demersus*, will nest either among tufts of tussock grass or in the midst of thickets of brush. Vesper Sparrows, *Pooecetes gramineus*, or Horned Larks, *Eremophila alpestris*, are likely to build their nests in a meadow with short grass; but if the grass grows half a meter or more, Bobolinks, *Dolichonyx oryzivorus*, are more likely to nest there.

Not only the height, but also the density and character of vegetation often determine its nesting population. Some species, like the Myrtle Warbler, *Dendroica coronata*, typically nest in conifers, while others, like the vireos, nest in deciduous trees. Some, like the Wood Thrush, *Hylocichla mustelina*, nest in dense woods; others, like the Robin, *Turdus migratorius*, in more open, park-like locations. Birds living in dense vegetation, for example the Tufted Duck, *Aythya fuligula*, generally have louder voices than those which frequent more open habitats, like the Common Eider, *Somateria mollissima*. Seasonal changes in the character of a stand of vegetation may affect its suitability as a habitat. The Ruffed Grouse, *Bonasa umbellus*, prefers coniferous woods as cover in the winter, and deciduous woods in summer. It seems, as a general rule, that dense vegetation discourages the flocking habit in birds, while more open plant formations, such as prairies, steppes, or savannas, encourage flocking.

Birds are not only affected ecologically by vegetation, but, on occasion, they reciprocate and affect the vegetation. The Bigua Cormorant, *Phalacrocorax olivaceus*, of Patagonia, and the Red-footed Booby, *Sula sula*, of the Caribbean, sometimes nest in such dense tree-top colonies that their guano kills the trees, and thus ruins their habitat for further residence. On the other hand, the Rock-hopper Penguins, *Eudyptes crestatus,* on the South Atlantic island of Tristan da Cunha, fertilize with their droppings the tall tussock grass, which responds with vigorous growth and shelters the Penguins from wind, rain, and predators (Murphy, 1936). Herons and other fish-eating birds of Tampa Bay, Florida, used to be killed as competitors of human fishermen. After 12 years of protection, however, their rookeries grew so large that they dropped an estimated 50 tons of guano each day into the bay, with the result that mullet fishing became better than at any time in the last half century (Peterson, 1948)! This example of food ecology illustrates how minerals and living organisms participate in ongoing cycles of energy and materials. The manure of birds supplies the nutrients for microscopic plankton organisms in the water which provide food for the fishes that are eaten by the birds. Sunlight falling on the plankton provides the basic energy that runs this cycle, and the guano provides some of the chemicals which are assembled in energy-storing combinations as food. Similar food cycles exist all over the world, on land and in water, but ordinarily they do not occur in such a compact and obvious form.

Other forms of bird-plant interdependence are seen in the pollination and distribution of plants by birds. Ornithophilous plants are those whose flowers are so constructed that they can be pollinated only by birds of certain special habits and with beaks of highly specific shapes which fit the flower's structure (p. 107). In some instances the mutual interdependence is very close. A mistletoe (*Loranthus*) of India will not fruit unless its flowers are pollinated by sunbirds of the genus *Cinnyris.* Birds which feed on and pollinate ornithophilous plants belong chiefly to the families Nectariniidae, Meliphagidae, Drepanididae and Trochilidae. The geographic dispersal of plants by birds is relatively common and does not require highly specialized adaptations either in the bird

or the plant. The European Mistle Thrush, *Turdus viscivorus,* is well known for its role in spreading the parasitic mistletoe.

Part of every bird's biological environment is composed of other animals. These other animals may be mates, offspring, predators, prey, competitors, parasites, or symbionts. Many of the relationships between birds and these other animals have been considered earlier under such topics as courtship, care of the young, predation, and parasitism. In every instance, these relationships can be classified as being either beneficial, neutral, or harmful to the bird in question. Sometimes the relationships may be individually harmful but racially beneficial, as in the exhaustion of a parent bird feeding its brood of young.

Beneficial relationships are of two kinds: those beneficial only to the bird, and those mutually beneficial to both the bird and its partners. Among the latter type are many family and colony relationships which often demonstrate positive cooperation between individuals. The colonies may be composed of a single species or of several. Benefits to the members of a colony are obtained by the many eyes alert to detect danger, the strength in numbers for defense against predators, opportunities for mutual education, cooperative nest building, the advantages of synchronized breeding (p. 143), and, occasionally, cooperative food finding.

In many instances, mutually beneficial relations occur between birds and mammals. A typical example is furnished by the African tick birds of the genus *Buphagus,* which groom buffalo, rhinoceros, giraffes, and other mammals, removing their ticks and other vermin.

Other interspecific relationships that are primarily beneficial to the bird alone are, among others, predator-prey relations where the bird is the predator, and brood parasite-host relations where the bird is the parasite. In the case of bird nesting-associations with ants, bees, wasps, and termites, what is beneficial to the bird may be harmful to the insects. Other examples of unilateral benefits to birds include associations such as those of ant-birds which feed on the insects stirred up by army ants; ptarmigan which follow caribou and benefit from the food they dig up in winter; the Rough-legged Hawk, *Buteo lagopus,* which follows the arctic fox to feed on the mice it stirs up; and the great variety of birds, such as egrets, bee-eaters, anis, starlings and cowbirds, that follow herds of antelopes, cattle and other ungulates, using them as beaters to raise up insects. Ducks frequently nest in or near colonies of gulls or terns, and profit from the latter species' aggressive attacks on nest robbers such as crows. A variety of small birds build their nests near or in the edges of the larger nests of hawks and eagles, where they obtain immunity from predation by other birds but seem to suffer few, if any, attacks by their host.

Among the more passive interspecific relationships are those of birds which inhabit the nest burrows of other species. The Elf Owl, *Micrathene whitneyi,* nests in saguaro cactus cavities excavated by woodpeckers; the Peruvian Inca Tern, *Larosterna inca,* sometimes nests in a little vestibule cavity that it scratches out in the occupied burrow of a penguin; the Flesh-footed Shearwater, *Puffinus carneipes,* occasionally shares a burrow with the lizard *Sphenodon* of New Zealand; the Snow Finch, *Montifringilla taczanowskii,* of Tibet sometimes sleeps and eats in the burrows of pikas. Completely neutral relationships within monospecific aggregations are probably unknown in nature simply because birds of the same species require the same kinds of food, nesting sites, dust baths, look-out perches and so on, and the supply of these is always limited, so that competition is inevitable. Neutral heterospecific groups of birds are more likely to occur, but even among them it is probable that one or more of the demands which different species make on the environment may coincide, especially in dense populations.

Competition, then, is the rule most likely to govern relations within aggregations of birds, particularly if the different individuals require the same essential and exhaustible elements from the habitat. Predation and cannibalism do occur in such groups, but only to a minor degree; otherwise they would be self-eliminating processes. The keenest competition occurs between birds of the same species because of the identity of their requirements.

Whenever problems of existence become widespread and persistent, natural selection usually provides solutions more or less effective. In this regard, the problem of competition is no exception. As breeding potential increases populations, and competition for life-needs intensifies, different problem-solving mechanisms come into play.

The establishment of territory is an intraspecific competition-reducing mechanism. As discussed earlier, it is essentially a device which ensures the efficient exploitation of food and other requirements, and also limits population to numbers which a given habitat can support. Those birds unsuccessful in establishing territories either become reserve individuals ready to replace territory owners that die, or are forced to disperse into new regions outside the normal range of the species. Massive dispersal in the form of irruption seems to be a competition-easing mechanism which follows periods of extreme overpopulation.

Another way in which competition may be reduced within a species is by ecologic diversification in habitat preferences. In the eastern United States there are two ecologic races of the Savannah Sparrow, *Passerculus sandwichensis,* one inhabiting salt marshes, the other, dry hillsides; in Puerto Rico, two races of the Yellow Warbler, *Dendroica petechia,* inhabit gardens and mangrove swamps, respectively; in the western United States there are numerous races of the Song Sparrow, *Melospiza melodia,* which inhabit a great variety of environments ranging from hot deserts to foggy arctic shores, from salt marshes to mountain meadows. The sort of adaptability that makes such biological adventuring profitable is illustrated by the

Black-shouldered Kite, *Elanus caeruleus.* A small population of this species has adapted itself to life on the desert island of Masirah, off Arabia, by substituting fish for rodents as its main food, caves for trees as nesting sites, and small broods for large (Green, 1949). Intraspecific competition, in short, stimulates individuals to explore, penetrate, and adapt to marginal and eventually new and different habitats.

Competition between different species living in the same habitat may be lessened if the two or more species require different things from the environment, particularly food. One would expect Cormorants, *Phalacrocorax carbo,* and Shags, *Phalacrocorax aristotelis*, which nest on the same cliff and feed in the same waters to be keen competitors. On the contrary, a study by Lack (1945) showed that the Shag ate mainly free-swimming fish and eels while the Cormorant fed on bottom-dwelling flat-fish and crustaceans. For many kinds of birds it seems true that related species living in the same habitat do not eat the same foods unless the latter are unusually abundant, as, for example, mice and grasshoppers in plague years. This is known as Gause's Rule, and it has been found to apply to European birds of prey, titmice, and other species. The explanation seems to be that if two species compete for food, it is very unlikely that both are equally well adapted in feeding habits; therefore one will sooner or later eliminate the other.

In North America the Black-capped Chickadee, *Parus atricapillus,* covers an extensive range where it has no closely related competitors and where it inhabits a variety of wooded environments: wet woods and dry, coniferous woods and deciduous, mountain woods and valley forests. In Europe, however, where this same species lives among six different species of small titmice of the identical genus, its range is largely restricted to swampy forests, while the other titmice occupy the other types of forest which the Chickadee inhabits in North America. The reverse of this situation occurs in Tenerife, Canary Islands, where the Chiffchaff, *Phylloscopus collybita,* is the only representative of its genus; here it occupies, in addition to its own habitat, those of its European congeners, the Wood Warbler, *Phylloscopus sibilatrix,* and the Willow Warbler, *Phylloscopus trochilus* (Svärdson, 1949).

These facts illustrate the principle that competition within a species encourages the dispersal of a population outward, both ecologically and geographically, from its optimum habitat (as with the Chickadee in America). Competition between species, on the contrary, encourages each species to seek out its optimum habitat (as shown among the various European titmice). Figure 19.5, from Svärdson, illustrates these two tendencies diagrammatically.

Figure 19.5.   The effect of competition on habitat selection. The peak of each curve represents optimum habitat conditions for any particular species; the descending arms, the less desirable, marginal conditions. Strong intraspecific competition causes a population to spread out into marginal habitats, while strong interspecific competition causes each species to retreat to its optimum habitat where it is best able to meet the competition of other species. After Svärdson.

NICHES

The habitat of any given bird may be considered from three different standpoints: Where is it? What is it? Why does this particular species of bird live there? The first or spatial standpoint is a simple question of geography. The second or structural standpoint is more complex and concerns such things as the geology, topography, chemistry, meteorology, botany, and zoology of the habitat. The third or functional viewpoint is the most complex of all and concerns the intimate give and take between the bird and its environment. It attempts to determine why Species A rather than B is located there. Considered from this dynamic, functional aspect, an environment becomes a *niche*, or, as Odum (1959) puts it, a bird's habitat is its address; its niche is its profession.

A bird's adaptations in structure, physiology, and behavior have been molded through years of natural selection to fit, more or less closely, a combination of the physical and biotic characteristics of its typical environment. Every species seems to recognize its peculiar niche instinctively. When Hensley and Cope (1951) removed 528 birds of 42 species from a 16 hectare spruce-fir forest, each niche that became vacated was occupied, usually by the next morning, by a bird of the same species as the original owner. The remarkably specific attraction that a given niche sometimes has for a given bird is seen in the attachment of Peregrine Falcons, *Falco peregrinus*, to eyries on vertical cliffs overlooking plains or bodies of water. At one eyrie all sets of eggs for ten years were robbed, yet the adult birds failed to desert the site (Hickey, 1942). One would scarcely expect such a magnificently wild bird as the Peregrine to select an automobile-choked city as its habitat; yet so closely does a ledge on a tall skyscraper fit its niche requirements that this bird has nested in the midst of many great cities. Similar ecologic attraction was reported by Rowan (1921) to exist between a patch of old heather and

pairs of Merlins, *Falco columbarius*, which used this location as a nesting site for 19 consecutive years, despite the fact that every year both birds occupying this niche were shot before they could hatch an egg.

Birds of many kinds demand highly specific types of niches and are intolerant of even slight deviations from the standard form. The Nicaraguan Seed-Finch, *Oryzoborus nuttingi*, for example, is found only in reed beds along rivers. Many other species, however, show great ecologic tolerance for deviations from the optimum niche. The American Robin, *Turdus migratorius*, is found breeding from Mexico to the Canadian tundra, from sea-level to mountain snow-lines, and from deserts to rain-forests. The Ring-necked Pheasant, *Phasianus colchicus*, introduced into Hawaii in 1865, now ranges from sea-level to altitudes of 3700 meters, from subtropical to occasionally freezing temperatures, from lands with less than 25 centimeters rainfall to those having over 750 centimeters, from recent lava soils to deep loam soils. It is associated with all sorts of vegetation: forests, grassland, deserts, and cultivated fields (Schwartz and Schwartz, 1951).

It is difficult to discover why some species are so strictly limited to certain narrowly prescribed niches while others, perhaps close relatives, tolerate such widely varied niches. For some species it is clearly a matter of food. For others it may be temperature, or rainfall, or even a psychological matter of the way the landscape "looks." In any case, birds of wide ecologic tolerance are likely to show widespread geographic distribution, those of narrow tolerance, narrow distribution.

CARRYING CAPACITY AND LIMITING FACTORS

Man's first dim awareness of the ecologic interplay between animals and their environments probably arose as a consequence of failing supplies of game. When a short hunting trip no longer yielded enough game to feed his family, primitive man usually began to ask himself questions. Have we offended the supernatural guardians of the animals? Is there less game because of some sickness? Is it starvation? Too many predators? As human populations increased and the hunting problem became more acute, man began to apply tribal taboos, and later game laws, to conserve game. Perhaps the earliest such law on record is that from Moses:

> If a bird's nest chance to be before thee in the way, in any tree or on the ground, whether they be young ones, or eggs, and the dam sitting upon the young, or upon the eggs, thou shalt not take the dam with the young: but thou shalt in any wise let the dam go, and take the young to thee; that it may be well with thee, and that thou mayest prolong thy days.
>
> Deuteronomy 22:6.

Here, quite obviously, is a law intended to conserve breeding stock.

When the principal game bird of Britain, the Red Grouse, *Lagopus scoticus*, began to decrease in numbers, the traditional and obvious control measures were invoked: restrictions in hunting, predator control, the establishment of reservations and refuges, game farming—all to no avail. The grouse population steadily decreased. Finally an intensive, ecologic study of the problem was undertaken to seek out actual limiting factors that affected the population. As a result of the information obtained, several unorthodox control measures were applied: patches of heather were burned; many older, breeding grouse were removed; predators were controlled; grit provided; wet places drained. As a consequence of these measures, the grouse population increased 30-fold, chiefly, in all probability, because of the first two controls (Leopold, 1933). This historically important experiment in game management revealed that the *critical limiting factors* which held down the grouse population were not the apparent and obvious ones such as over-hunting, or starvation, or even heavy predation. More subtle limiting factors were involved, but they were the more significant ones. Burning the heather provided variety in habi-

tats and created open sunning-yards where young chicks could dry themselves after rain and fog and thus reduce mortality from respiratory diseases. Removing the old breeders opened up their territories to younger, more productive birds. Scattering grit, a dietary necessity, was required because the native grit was too deeply covered with years of peaty accumulations of organic matter. All these and other limiting factors exercised a quantitative control of the number of grouse a given area of land could support—that is, its *carrying capacity*. Every habitat thus has a carrying capacity which, of necessity, varies with the different species of birds living there. Grit, so important to grouse, would be of no use whatever to a hummingbird.

Among all the limiting environmental factors which surround and influence birds —food, vegetation, precipitation, temperature, sunlight, soil, secure nest sites, predators, diseases, and others—certain ones will pull down more powerfully on the steel spring of population increase than others. The critical factors that limit population density may be very different for different species of birds. These facts underlie the principle proposed by Liebig in 1840 as the "law of the minimum," later revised by Shelford in 1911 as the "law of toleration." These laws hold that the survival of any organism, plant or animal, depends on that environmental factor whose presence in minimum (or maximum) amount immediately exercises a controlling or limiting effect on its life, despite the favorable condition of other environmental factors. For example, a well-fed grouse, disease free, supplied with a safe nesting site, exposed to optimum climate, and protected from predators, will still weaken and die if the grit available to it falls below a certain critical minimum. Similarly, too much of certain environmental elements—high temperature, sunlight, rain, calcium in the soil—may operate as limiting factors. These influences may reduce a population either by causing the death of individuals or by reducing their reproductive potential—for example, by causing infertility of eggs.

In nature it is probably true that the complex interrelations of factors make it exceedingly difficult to identify a single environmental agent or material as *the* limiting factor. The minimum lethal air temperature for a bird varies, for example, with duration of exposure, season of the year, age of the bird, condition of plumage, amount of fat stored in its tissues, amount of food in the digestive tract, and other factors. So one cannot say without qualification that a given air temperature is the lethal minimum for a given species. Nevertheless, the principle has enough validity to be useful in ecologic studies.

MAJOR TYPES OF HABITATS

Although there is an almost limitless variety of natural habitats, the more prominent kinds can all be classified in about a dozen major classes. These broad categories, such as evergreen forests, deserts, or the seas, are easily recognized even by the uninitiated. The chief distinctions between them are based on the kind and amount of vegetation they possess, and vegetation is largely determined by temperature and rainfall, although soil, day-length, altitude, wind, and other influences play roles of varying importance. Animals, of course, are important components of any habitat, but plants are considered the key to habitat type because they do not move; they are generally the dominant form of life, and they are the food source on which animals depend for their energy. Plant distribution, therefore, normally determines animal distribution.

Different attempts have been made to identify and describe with some precision the major habitat types in North America. In the late 19th century, C. Hart Merriam proposed a series of great transcontinental *life zones* based primarily on latitudinal temperature differences. These life zones, a series of broad bands, each running roughly east and west across the continent,

he called, in sequence from north to south, the Arctic, Hudsonian, Canadian, Transition, Upper Austral, Lower Austral, and Tropical Zones. Because of pronounced differences in precipitation between the eastern and western halves of the United States, Merriam called the Transition Zone in the moist east the Alleghanian Zone, and called the Upper and Lower Austral zones in the drier west the Upper and Lower Sonoran Zones. This division of habitats, in spite of its defects, won wide acceptance from naturalists, and life zones are still occasionally used in descriptive ecologic work.

More recently, Clements and Shelford (1939) proposed a system of *biomes* in which each major habitat was defined according to its dominant form of vegetation. These great areas of vegetation are believed to be climaxes, or stable forms of vegetation, climatically determined, and capable of maintaining themselves indefinitely if undisturbed. Examples of major biomes in North America are Tundra, Coniferous Forest, Deciduous Forest, Grassland, and Desert. Should a biome be disturbed or destroyed by man or by some natural catastrophe, it would eventually revert to its original state if left to itself. With time, the disturbed area would pass through a series of characteristic vegetation types, or successions, until it again reached the climax form, at which stage it would again become stabilized. Since these and other schemes of habitat classifications depend largely on individual judgment, their application to natural situations is never perfect.

One biome does not stop at a sharp boundary where another begins. Instead, a region or transition known as an *ecotone* occurs between them, as, for example, between the coniferous forest and grassland biomes. Smaller subdivisions of biomes and ecotones also occur, all the way down to such units as individual thickets or small woodland pools.

A given species of bird may be restricted to a minor subdivision of a biome; it may range throughout a biome; or it may be distributed over several biomes. Even closely related species vary markedly in this regard. The Song Sparrow, *Melospiza melodia,* breeds throughout North America; but the Ipswich Sparrow, *Passerculus princeps,* breeds only on Sable Island, Nova Scotia. The Sharp-tailed Sparrow, *Ammospiza caudacuta,* breeds across Canada and the United States from British Columbia and southern Mackenzie to the St. Lawrence valley and North Carolina; while its close relative, the Cape Sable Sparrow, *Ammospiza mirabilis,* is restricted to a coastal fringe in Florida about 95 kilometers long.

Every major habitat presents special conditions of life and, usually, peculiar problems of existence for birds living there. Birds occupying a given habitat, as a rule, are adapted to exploit these conditions and to meet these problems, at least sufficiently well to meet local competition of other species. In the brief survey of major habitats which follows, only a few of their special conditions and problems can be given, as well as only a few of the avian adaptations which relate to them.

POLAR REGIONS.   These regions of eternal ice and snow present drastic problems of low temperatures, long winters, no land plants, and practically no cover. Very few birds are able to tolerate such extreme conditions. The antarctic penguins have evolved the most effective adaptations to this harsh environment. They combat the low temperatures by accumulating great reserves of insulating body fat, huddling together in storms, and occasionally burrowing in the snow. They have a remarkably strong urge to brood eggs and young, and have developed warm feet and special brood pouches for this function. All food in this habitat comes from the sea, and penguins are fitted to capture fish, prawns, and other sea animals by such adaptations as eyes accommodated for underwater vision, fish-holding tongues, streamlined bodies, reduced feathers, and powerful flippers instead of wings.

TUNDRA.   The vast, circumpolar belt of mosses, sedges, grasses, lichens, flowering perennials and dwarf shrubby alders, willows, and conifers is called the tundra. It extends across the northern parts of North America, Europe, and Asia, just south of the perpetual snows and north of the tree line. A short distance below the surface the ground is permanently frozen. In the brief summers of 24 hour days and no nights, the ground becomes wet and boggy; wild flowers and insects appear in profusion; and many ponds and streams arise. Because of the impossibility of hibernation, predatory reptiles are completely absent in the tundra, and the widespread interspersion of land and water gives nesting birds added security from the few predatory mammals present. Great numbers of shore birds and waterfowl breed in the tundra in summer, as well as a lesser number of hawks, ptarmigan, cranes, owls, larks, and finches. Practically all of these birds escape the rigors of the tundra winter by migrating south in the fall. As an adaptation to the brief summer season, birds exhibit strikingly accelerated reproductive cycles: quick nest building, short incubation periods, rapid molting, and rapid development of precocial young. Were it otherwise, the closing in of winter would cause the deaths of myriads of young birds unable to migrate or to care for themselves. The abundant insects, coupled with the long northern days, enable most tundra species to raise larger broods than their relatives of temperate or equatorial regions.

Ptarmigan are year-round residents of the tundra. They change their plumage from an inconspicuous white in winter to an inconspicuous brown in summer. They can sustain themselves on a vegetable diet in winter, and they survive the bitterest cold by burrowing under the snow. By means of fringed scales or heavy feathers on their feet, they are able to walk on soft snow. The Snowy Owl, *Nyctea scandiaca,* also has heavily feathered feet, and it feeds throughout the year on the usually abundant lemming. Resident birds of the tundra and other cold habitats commonly have larger and more compact bodies than their temperate and tropical zone relatives. This conserves heat because a large body has relatively less heat-losing surface than a similar small one.

ALPINE REGIONS.   In many ways, the alpine communities resemble the tundra. Vegetation is dwarf and scrubby; nights are cold, and the growing season short. However, compared with the tundra, drainage is much better; wind is usually stronger; the sun's rays, including the ultra violet, are more direct and intense; day-length is "normal," and the air is more rarefied. As in the tundra, ptarmigan change colors seasonally. Smaller birds avoid the wind by building their nests in the shelter of rocks, crevices, and vegetation. One would expect birds that do much flying in the high, thin air to have relatively larger wings and stronger breast muscles than lowland species, but this point has not been established. Birds of high altitudes do have relatively larger hearts (p. 111) which help to support the greater exertion characteristic of mountain-top living. To compensate for the low oxygen tension of mountain air, it is likely that the blood of alpine birds either contains more hemoglobin than that of lowland species, or possesses a more efficient oxygen dissociation curve for taking up oxygen more readily at low pressures, as is the case in developing chicks within the egg, and in llamas of the high Andes.

CONIFEROUS FORESTS.   These are the great evergreen forests of spruce, fir, and larch, found chiefly in Canada, northern Europe and Siberia, with occasional extensions southward along mountains, and isolated fragments in a few other parts of the world. The northern coniferous forest, or *taiga*, may have winter temperatures as severe as those of the tundra lying immediately to its north, but the summer growing season is warmer and longer. In the growth of organic matter the coniferous forest is 50- to 100-fold more productive than the tundra (Deevey, 1960) and there-

fore is better able to support a large year-round population of birds and other animals. Since most conifers retain their leaves over winter, they provide good shelter against the wind, and also prevent the wind-packing of ground snow which characterizes the tundra. The trunks and stems of conifers and other woody plants expose seeds, berries, nuts and fruits above the snow where they are available for winter feeding. Insects are abundant during summers in the taiga; reptiles are scarce, but mammalian predators more common than in the tundra. About 80 per cent of the birds that breed in the taiga in the summer migrate south for the winter. Among these are eagles, hawks, flycatchers, swallows, goatsuckers, thrushes, kinglets, vireos, warblers, and finches. Among the year-round residents are owls, grouse, woodpeckers, ravens, jays, nutcrackers, titmice, nuthatches, creepers, grosbeaks, and crossbills. The majority of these birds are either insect or seed and nut eaters, and various adaptations associated with these diets have been described earlier (p. 105).

DECIDUOUS FORESTS.   The typical forests of temperate Eurasia and North America are deciduous forests whose trees bear thin, flat leaves which are shed during winter. This biome demands a moderate amount of rainfall—75 to 150 centimeters per year. The larger deciduous forest regions are in the eastern United States, western Europe, eastern China, and Japan, with smaller areas in southern Africa, eastern Australia, New Zealand, and Patagonia. Deciduous forests contain a greater variety of trees, shrubs, and herbaceous plants than the coniferous forests. This provides a more varied vegetable diet for resident birds. The commoner trees in the deciduous forests of North America are the oak, hickory, beech, maple, elm, ash, sycamore, and poplar. Many of the trees and shrubs of this biome produce hard-shelled nuts— oak, hickory, beech, hazel—and many of the birds living here possess structural and functional adaptations for exploiting this nutritious source of food. A few species, such as jays, nutcrackers, woodpeckers, and nuthatches, have learned to hide stores of seeds or nuts for consumption in winter when other foods are scarce. Other species inspect crevices in bark for insects and their larvae, while woodpeckers dig them out of dead wood with their sharp beaks and extensible tongues. For permanent residents the diet may change from berries and insects in summer to nuts and seeds in winter. Other typical birds of the North American deciduous forest include hawks, quail, turkeys, doves, owls, crows, titmice, nuthatches, creepers, wrens, thrashers, thrushes, vireos, warblers, blackbirds, and finches. Many breeding birds of this biome nest in trees, some in cavities, some in open nests supported by branches. Species which nest or feed principally on the ground usually have inconspicuous coloration. Of the species which breed in the deciduous forests of North America, about three-fourths migrate south for the winter.

TROPICAL RAIN FORESTS. The rain forests of the tropics constitute the largest terrestrial biome on earth, covering some 20 million square kilometers. The air is constantly warm and moist, and the rainfall exceeds 120 centimeters and averages 225 centimeters per year. Tropical rain forests produce more organic material than any other type of biome: an estimated 24 thousand million tons of carbon per year as against 970 million tons for the deserts of the world and only 68 million tons for all tundra regions (Deevey, 1960). The main tropical rain forests occur in the lowlands of Central and South America, Africa, and the East Indies. The luxuriance of the rain forest vegetation is important to the animal residents, but probably more significant is its astonishing variety. While a dozen species of trees might be the maximum found in a deciduous forest, 400 to 500 species of trees and some 800 of woody plants have been identified in the Cameroon rain forest (Hesse *et al.*,

1937). Moreover, this tremendous variety of plant life is thoroughly intermixed: the trees do not normally grow in groves of a single species as is commonly the case with other forests. This fact places a premium on mobility in rain forest animals. Probably because of the great variety of plants and of the food and other necessities for birds that they produce, the rain forest harbors a greater variety of birds than any other biome.

The phenomenon of habitat stratification is well demonstrated in the rain forest. A series of different microclimates is arranged in horizontal strata as one descends from the sun-drenched forest canopy to the ground. The bright green crowns of the tall forest trees constitute the microhabitat where the sun shines the most intensely, and where the frequent tropical rainstorms beat most furiously; and it is the location of most flowers, fruits, and animals. The birds of this roof stratum include many brilliantly colored forms, such as parrots, macaws, toucans, trogons, and cotingas or chatterers, as well as several predatory hawks, eagles, and vultures. Midway to the ground is an understory of small trees, large shrubs, and lianas bedecked with orchids, bromeliads and other epiphytes. Here in subdued light and warm, humid, quiet air occur wrens, pigeons, curassows, woodcreepers, and other species. On the forest floor is relatively little vegetation because of the perpetual gloom. Air currents are negligible, and although the beating rains on the canopy produce no violence at this stratum, the humidity of the air is almost constantly at the saturation point. On this level are found the dull-colored partridge, rails, tinamous, antbirds, and in the Orient, colorful pittas. By adapting themselves to these different strata the different species of birds are able to avoid much of the competition for food, nesting sites, and territories.

Because of the scattering of the many types of plants, birds must keep moving, often in flocks, to obtain their preferred food. In most rain forests one can find trees budding, flowering, fruiting, and shedding their leaves at almost any time of year. This absence of accentuated seasonal reproduction of fruits makes possible the existence of stenophagous species, such as the fruit-eating pigeons or nectar-sipping hummingbirds. These latter often have bills whose shapes and lengths are remarkably adapted to the corollas of the flowers they visit.

Most birds of the tropical rain forests have loud calls which enable flocks to keep together even though individual birds are separated by dense foliage. Many tropical birds are active mainly in the morning and evening, and rest during the heat of the day. Many species build sleeve-like hang-nests which are less easily robbed than are open nests by the abundant snakes, lizards, and other predators. Open nests are usually small and inconspicuous as compared with nests in the temperate zones. Clutches of eggs are smaller than those of temperate zone relatives. This is perhaps an adjustment to the constantly available food, the shorter day-length, and the absence of the dangers of migration.

GRASSLANDS.   As a major habitat type, grasslands are distributed throughout the temperate and tropical zones. They vary from the tall-grass, park-like savannas of Africa and the pampas of Argentina through the prairies of midwestern United States to the almost desert-like, short-grass steppes of Asia. The dominance of grass in all these habitats is the result of insufficient rainfall to grow trees, but enough to prevent deserts. Rain, 30 to 100 centimeters per year, often comes in pronounced seasonal cycles which cause luxuriant vegetation and food in the spring and summer, followed by searing dry seasons which force many animals to emigrate. Grass fires may be a recurrent problem for animals. Grasslands are usually flat or slightly undulating open plains, lacking trees or rocks which might provide shelter against the sun, rain, or winter storms. The lack of natural cover and pronounced seasonal cycles have encouraged five major kinds of

adaptations in birds. Having very little incentive to leave the ground excepting for annual migrations, many birds, even though they may fly well, have adopted the cursorial habit: tinamous, bustards, quail, sand-grouse, the Secretary Bird, *Sagittarius serpentarius*, the Road Runner, *Geococcyx californianus*, larks, and others. In the emus, rheas, and ostriches, adaptations for running have been so adequate that their ability to fly has been lost. These large ratites or keel-less birds have long, powerful legs with reduced toes, long necks, and vestigial wings and feathers. The flocking habit, as seen in ostriches, certain grouse, longspurs, and buntings, is a common grassland adaptation. As a response to the lack of cover, several species either nest on the open ground (eagles, larks) or use underground burrows (Burrowing Owl, *Speotyto cunicularia*). In Tibet, three finches of the genus *Montifringilla* share burrows with native hares. Because of the absence of singing posts, many grassland birds give their territory and courtship songs while on the wing.

DESERTS.   Very little rainfall, very low humidity, and little or no vegetation are characteristic of deserts everywhere. The lack of cloud cover makes for extreme temperature fluctuations, often extending from freezing temperatures by night to intolerably hot temperatures by day. Air temperatures of 58° C. (136° F.) in the shade have been recorded in the Libyan desert, and soil surface temperatures were much higher. The desert substrate may be rock, shingle, or sand; the last type is the poorest in animal life. The rarity of drinking water practically excludes seed-eating birds from this biome, but not insect-eaters. As in the grasslands, many birds are cursorial in habit. Plumage commonly matches the sandy or stony ground; in the Sahara, 24 of 47 species showed homochromy, or ground-matching coloration (Bourlière, 1950). As protection against both the intense sun and violent winds, birds seek the shelter of shrubs and rocks for nesting and resting sites. They generally confine their activities to the cooler times of day. In Patagonian deserts, many ground dwelling birds possess horny opercula over their nostrils, presumably as an adaptation against inhalation of dust and sand. Earth burrows do not seem to be commonly used by desert birds, but cavities in cacti are occupied by some owls and woodpeckers. In both desert and steppe biomes, the reproductive cycle of birds is closely correlated with the season of rains; and when there is no rain at all, the birds ordinarily fail to breed. Characteristic birds of desert regions include hawks, doves, owls, woodpeckers, wrens, thrashers, shrikes, larks, and finches.

FRESH WATER LAKES, PONDS, AND STREAMS. Fresh water habitats are spread over the terrestrial world, particularly in regions of abundant rainfall. Lakes vary in size from the smallest ponds to the Great Lakes of North America. As a rule, the smaller, shallower lakes are much richer in plant and bird life than the larger, deeper ones. Water birds typically have larger-than-average uropygial glands and dense, oily plumage. Many of them have strong, short legs with webbed toes. Diving birds, such as grebes and loons, often have dorso-ventrally flattened bodies, and legs placed toward the rear. Their bones are generally less pneumatic than those of surface-feeding waterfowl. In taking off from the water in flight, birds of small bodies of water, for example "puddle ducks," rise directly into the air, while those of larger lakes and streams patter along the surface for some distance before they are airborne. Ducks adapted to feeding in shallow water tip their bodies vertically while remaining afloat on the surface and reach what submerged foods they can with their extended head and neck. Deep water ducks, on the other hand, dive for their food. Many kinds of feeding adaptations occur in the beaks of water birds: sifting devices for seeds and small animals; gaff-hooks, spears, serrated forceps for fish; and others. These are described in more detail in Chapter 6.

SHORES AND MARSHES. These are the amphibious environments, part land and part water, where vegetation and food are unusually abundant, but where problems of space, substrate, and seasonal food shortage affect bird residents. Shores and many marshes are fringe habitats, linear and narrow, so that gregariousness is forced on the birds which inhabit them. Long, wading legs and long, agile necks are common features of birds of these regions. The long legs of such birds as cranes, herons, and storks enable them to enjoy the advantages of both land and shallow water, while the shorter legs and webbed toes of coots and grebes fit them to exploit muddy shores as well as open water. Toes may be webbed fully, partly, or not at all, correlating in part with the swimming habits of the species, and with the firmness of its typical feeding ground substrate. The exceptionally long toes of the jaçana have already been mentioned. Certain of the sandpipers are typically found along muddy shores, others along sandy shores. Among shore birds, long, probing bills predominate, and many of them are heavily supplied with sensitive touch corpuscles which enable them to discriminate food particles from others in muddy water or soft earth. Correlated with the abrupt cessation of food supplies when, in colder habitats, the lakes and streams freeze over in autumn, is the strong migratory impulse found in most shore birds. Birds of sea coasts often show a daily behavior cycle, oscillating between land-feeding when the tide is in, and shore-feeding when it is out and many marine invertebrates are exposed.

THE SEAS. The oceans of the world make up a continuous, highly uniform habitat. Although they vary markedly in temperature and food resources, they are all flat, wet, salty, windy, and vast. The problems they present to birds are simple but formidable: no places to perch or to build nests, no cover for hiding, no fresh drinking water, a diet limited to sea food. The use by birds of a method of reproduction involving nests and eggs has prevented them from adapting completely to a marine existence. Even so, some species, such as penguins and albatrosses, are able to spend months away from land, completely dependent on the seas.

Sea birds show many of the same adaptations to an aquatic life as do freshwater birds: webbed feet, oily feathers, fish-eating adaptations in their beaks, and others. One peculiar adaptation in the beaks of Procellariiformes (albatrosses, shearwaters, fulmars, and petrels) is a pair of tubular projections covering their nostrils and apparently protecting them from salt spray on stormy days. More important are the nasal or salt glands in the heads of sea birds which make possible the drinking of sea water (p. 100). Without them it would be impossible for sea birds to explore the seas very far from land and fresh water. Long, narrow wings, the most efficient kind for gliding, are found in many sea birds, like the albatrosses, which spend much time on the wing. The distribution of sea birds follows closely the distribution of fish and other sea foods; these, in turn, reflect the concentration of nitrates, phosphates, and other nutrient chemicals in surface sea water. These nutrients are richest near the mouths of great rivers and in regions where deep ocean currents rise to the surface.

ALTITUDE AND LATITUDE

On a vegetation map of North America, the biomes of high (northern) latitudes extend southward along mountain ranges, and the biomes of low tropical latitudes extend northward along valleys. This is due to the fact that temperature is one of the main controlling factors of vegetation, and that a low mean annual temperature, whether at sea level in Alaska or on a mountain top in the Andes, will result in the growth of similar types of vegetation in both habitats. One can therefore cross a series of biomes extending from the tropical rain forest to the tundra either by journeying from the equator to the arctic circle, about 7000 kilometers north, or by ascending an equatorial mountain from sea level to an altitude of about four kilometers. For every 150 meters one climbs upwards, the air temperature drops approximately 1° C. On either trip one would pass over the same successive biomes, with differences in details caused by such factors as soil, wind, rainfall, exposure to sunlight, past geological history,

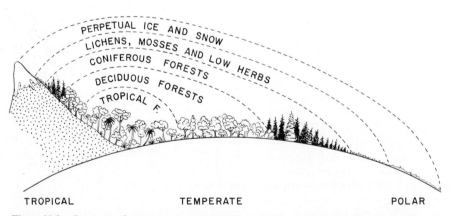

Figure 19.6. Starting in the tropics, one may travel across the major biomes of the earth either by climbing about 4 kilometers vertically on a mountain side, or by traveling about 7000 kilometers poleward at sea level.

and above all, the different annual cycles. Palm trees, for example, thrive in the temperate zone of tropical mountains, but not in the latitudinal temperate zone. In the former the temperature never drops to freezing, but in the latter it may fall many degrees below freezing.

An important advantage in comparing a series of biomes altitudinally (vertically) rather than latitudinally (horizontally) is the economy of time and effort required, and the opportunity for close comparisons of vegetation and animals of neighboring zones. An altitudinal study of the birds in the life zones (Merriam's) of Yosemite Park by Grinnell and Storer (1924) showed that species found in the Canadian zone high up in the Sierra Nevada mountains of Yosemite were also found near sea level in the same Canadian zone in Canada. The study also revealed that some species are multi-zoned, tolerating the varied living conditions of five different successive zones, while others, much less tolerant, were restricted to a single zone (Fig. 19.7). A study by Miller (1951) of the ecologic

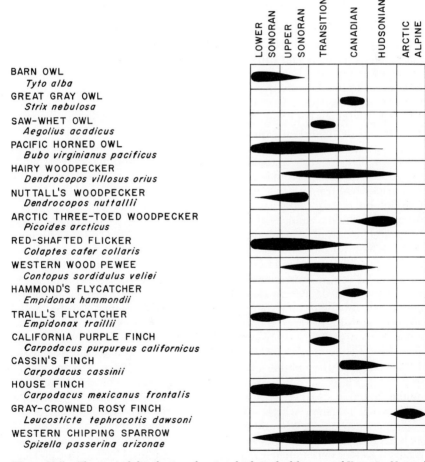

Figure 19.7. The vertical distribution of various birds in the life zones of Yosemite National Park. Some species are multi-zonal, while others are restricted to a single zone. The peculiar two-zoned distribution of Traill's Flycatcher shows that, for this species at least, habitat selection is more than a simple temperature response. After Grinnell and Storer.

distribution of California birds showed that there was a greater variety of birds in zones of lower altitude, as one would expect, than in the zones of higher altitude where living conditions are more rigorous. The study also revealed that of the 143 species of birds found, 54 species were restricted to one life zone, 89 species lived in two zones, 88 in three zones, 23 in four zones, 5 in five zones, and 1 species spread its residence over six zones. Such studies as these reveal the great difference between species in environmental tolerance.

HABITAT INTERSPERSION AND EDGE EFFECT

Every ornithologist soon learns that the best way to see a large variety of birds in a short time is to plan field trips to take in ecotones or margins between different types of habitats. A study by Lay (1938) in Texas revealed that the margins of clearings had 95 per cent more birds, representing 41 per cent more species, than comparable areas of the interiors of adjacent woodland. Birds commonly require more things for survival and reproduction than can be had from a single meadow or wood lot, but if their needs can be met by using both habitats, chances of successful living are increased. The meadow may furnish insects for food and grass for lining nests; the woods, twigs for a nest platform and cover for escape from enemies. This is why so many birds live on the edges of habitats. By mixing or interspersing habitats, the requisites of survival and population increase are made readily available to birds. In his study of edge effect, Beecher (1942) compared the number of nests per unit area of a large cattail marsh with the number found in equal areas of numerous small cattail marshes, which, of course, would have more edge per unit area than the large marsh. He found that nest densities were greater in the smaller marshes. A similar study of the breeding densities of the Ruff, *Philomachus pugnax*, in Denmark, by Andersen (1948) showed that nests in the center of a sanctuary averaged

2 to 11 per square kilometer, but along roads they averaged 236 per square kilometer. One reason why modern agriculture is so detrimental to wild birds is that it depends on large areas of homogeneous vegetation with little edge. Even in birds, mobility can become a problem if the necessities of life are spread too far apart. The chief reason for high population densities in parks and gardens (p. 348) is their rich interspersion of trees, shrubs, lawns, walks, flower beds, pools, and even buildings.

SUCCESSION

If one should fence off a square kilometer of flat, polished granite, and allow only natural forces and agents to affect it for many centuries, eventually there would be established on it a climax form of vegetation: a beech-maple forest, or a tundra, or a prairie, depending on the climate. Left undisturbed, the granite would have been successively covered with lichens, mosses, herbs, shrubs, trees, and finally beech and maple trees with their associated plants, assuming that this experiment took place in the climate now characteristic of northern Indiana. If, at the same time and in the same general location, one fenced off a square kilometer fresh water pond and left it undisturbed long enough, it too would eventually become a beech-maple forest, via submerged vegetation followed by floating plants, emergent marsh plants, shrubs, and finally trees, each growing on the accumulated organic debris of the previous generations. Such successions as these are constantly going on in nature wherever hurricanes, fires, glaciers, volcanic eruptions, landslides, epidemic plant diseases, or human agencies have disturbed the established climax succession. The time required for a complete series of succession from bare ground to climax varies in different parts of the world. The rapidity with which tropical woodland invades deserted plantations in humid regions is well known.

If climate changes, as it does, the climax

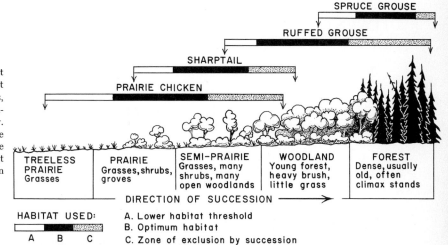

Figure 19.8. As plant succession brings about changes in habitats, changes in bird populations naturally follow. The bars indicate those habitats used during the year by four different species of Wisconsin grouse. After Grange.

SPRUCE GROUSE

RUFFED GROUSE

SHARPTAIL

PRAIRIE CHICKEN

| TREELESS PRAIRIE Grasses | PRAIRIE Grasses, shrubs, groves | SEMI-PRAIRIE Grasses, many shrubs, many open woodlands | WOODLAND Young forest, heavy brush, little grass | FOREST Dense, usually old, often climax stands |

DIRECTION OF SUCCESSION ⟶

HABITAT USED:
A. Lower habitat threshold
B. Optimum habitat
A   B   C
C. Zone of exclusion by succession

succession must also change. Lands which are now desert in the Near East were once thriving centers of human populations, luxuriant with vegetation and "flowing with milk and honey" when more rainfall was characteristic of the region. Man himself has been responsible for the development of extensive deserts in China, Arabia, Libya, Mexico, and elsewhere through his misuse of the land.

In regions of active plant succession, the bird population slowly changes its character to conform to change in plants and other animals associated with given forms of plants—insects, worms, snails, mice, and other birds. Woodpeckers, for example, not only require trees for their particular way of life, but wood-tunneling beetle larvae, acorns, and other such associates of trees. Some of these successional changes may be invisible to human eyes, but they may still involve critical limiting factors which determine whether a given species of bird will live in a given habitat. Sometimes the interrelations between birds and their environments are obvious and even dramatic. Elton (1927) tells how an Indian mynah bird and a Mexican lantana plant were introduced into Hawaii with the following results. Feeding on the lantana berries, the mynah and other birds caused the rapid spread of the plant. The mynahs also increased enormously in numbers. Although the lantana became a serious weed, the mynah was welcomed be-

cause it ate the army-worm caterpillars which periodically ravaged young sugar-cane plantations. To stop the spread of the lantanas, an agromyzid fly which ate its seeds was introduced. This control succeeded so well that the lantana decreased greatly in abundance, and as a result the mynahs also decreased to such an extent that there was a resumption of severe outbreaks of army-worms in sugar plantations. As the lantanas decreased, other species of introduced shrubs took their place and became serious weeds.

All of these multitudinous criss-crossing threads of relationship between birds, plants, insects, climate, and other environmental factors make up Darwin's web of life—a tremendously intricate, dynamic system, and one, for the moment, in equilibrium. But let one filament of the web be cut—let one tree die, or a new bird move in—and new adjustments are in order.

SUGGESTED READINGS

An exhaustive treatment of animal ecology is found in *Principles of Animal Ecology* by Allee *et al*. Briefer introductions to the subject are found in Elton's *Animal Ecology* and Odum's *Fundamentals of Ecology*. For the ecology of birds of specific habitats see Buxton's *Animal Life in Deserts* and Haviland's *Forest, Steppe and Tundra*. Kendeigh's *Animal Ecology* gives unusual emphasis to the ecology of birds.

TWENTY

The Geography of Birds

If we keep in view these facts—that the minor features of the earth's surface are everywhere slowly changing; that the forms, and structure, and habits of all living things are also slowly changing; while the great features of the earth, the continents, and oceans, and loftiest mountain ranges, only change after very long intervals and with extreme slowness, we must see that the present distribution of animals upon the several parts of the earth's surface is the final product of all these wonderful revolutions in organic and inorganic nature. . . .
Wallace, *The Geographical Distribution of Animals*

When birds took to the air, some 150 million years before the Wright brothers, or before Icarus, for that matter, they obtained a highway to every possible habitat on the earth's surface. Today, birds are at home in polar regions and in the tropics, in forests and deserts, on mountains and prairies, and on the oceans and distant islands. Yet, when one considers the superb mobility of birds and the eons of time they have had to populate the globe, it is surprising how few cosmopolitan species there are. Some shore and sea birds—sandpipers and plovers, petrels and gulls—are world-wide in their distribution. Representatives of grebes, herons, ducks, owls, ospreys, kingfishers, and swallows are at home on every continent. Ravens have inherited the entire earth except, for some obscure reason, South America. But these are exceptional. What one mostly sees, especially among land birds, is a picture of curiously limited and seemingly haphazard distribution.

Why should the birds of England and Japan be more alike, though 11,000 kilometers apart, than the birds of Africa and Madagascar, separated by a mere 400 kilometers? Why does South America have more than 300 species of hummingbirds while Africa, with very similar habitats, has not a single one? Why are the finches, found even on some of the most remote oceanic islands, not found in Australia? Why does the North American Turkey, *Meleagris gallopavo*, occur naturally nowhere else in the world?

In sharp contrast to birds with wide distribution are many species with very limited ranges. Oceanic islands commonly have endemic species with highly restricted distribution. The lark *Calandrella razae* is restricted to tiny Razo Island (8 square kilometers) of the Cape Verde Islands. The Atitlan Grebe, *Podilymbus gigas*, is known to occur only on Lake Atitlan in Guatemala. Kirtland's Warbler, *Dendroica kirtlandii*, nests in only a few counties of north central Michigan, and the Ipswich Sparrow, *Passerculus princeps*, nests only on Sable Island, Nova Scotia (about 50 square kilometers). Several South American hummingbirds have strikingly limited ranges. The Racket-tailed Hummingbird, *Loddigesia mirabilis*, is known to breed only in a tiny mountain valley in Peru, and *Oreotrochilus chimborazo*, just below snowline on the volcano Chimborazo in Ecuador. To the Laysan Teal, *Anas laysanensis*, belongs the perilous distinction of inhabiting perhaps the tiniest range of all, the shores of a marshy lagoon about five square kilometers (2 sq. mi.) in extent on the small Hawaiian island of Laysan. Such drastically limited geographic range often foreshadows extinction.

PRESENT WORLD PATTERN OF BIRD DISTRIBUTION

There are two ways of looking at bird distribution. The first and simplest is a de-

scription of the static, geographic location of the various species of birds. The second viewpoint recognizes the fact that bird distribution is a dynamic, constantly changing affair; that no species stays in one place forever. Intellectually a more lively approach, this second way of looking at bird geography attempts to explain why certain species live where they do. This can be done in two ways, one of which is ecologic. Water birds obviously do not live in deserts, nor woodpeckers in treeless steppes. But ecology does not explain why there are many hummingbirds in South America but none in similar rain forests in Africa; nor why the Red-breasted Nuthatch, *Sitta canadensis*, is found in the conifer forests of all North America, but in the Old World only in eastern Siberia, China, and on the mountain tops of Corsica in the Mediterranean. The explanation of riddles such as these depends on historical principles involving not only ecology but also geology and evolution.

Considering first the static, descriptive picture of bird distribution, one is impressed with the fact that the vast majority of birds live on only 29 per cent of the earth's surface—the land surface. Land provides a much greater variety of habitats than does the sea. As a consequence, the study of the terrestrial distribution of birds is a larger and more complex problem than the study of sea bird distribution.

Apparently, there is no place on earth so remote or isolated as to be completely deprived of bird life. A United States Air Force research party, drifting on a huge cake of ice within 240 kilometers (150 mi.) of the north pole, between the latitudes of 88° 01' and 88° 30' N., sighted birds described as "sea gulls" on eight different occasions between June 12 and August 15, 1952. The following year, birds were observed 15 times between 88° 15' and 86° 10' N. Latitude, ten of the observations being of small white birds which were probably Snow Buntings, *Plectrophenax nivalis*. One of the larger birds was collected, and proved to be an immature Kittiwake, *Rissa tridactyla* (Paynter, 1955). At the other end of the globe, South Polar Skuas, *Catharacta skua,* have been observed at 84°26′ S. Latitude (Murphy, 1936).

Relatively few breeding species are able to withstand the rigors of polar environments, although flocks of a given species may include tremendous numbers of individuals, as in the case of penguins, auks, and other sea birds. Breeding in the ecologically monotonous arctic tundras are many water birds and also a few land birds, such as ptarmigan, birds of prey, and a few finches. As one moves from polar regions toward the equator, the variety of bird life gradually increases until it reaches its maximum in tropical regions. This is probably because the tropics afford much greater habitat variety than polar regions. It also may reflect the fact that a larger portion of the earth was tropical, humid, and perpetually verdant during the Miocene and early Pliocene ages when modern bird families were evolving. Table 20.1, after Dobzhansky (1950), illustrates this north-south geographic gradient in the numbers of species. The relatively small number of species found in Florida is probably due to that state's physiographic monotony.

A closer look at the world distribution of birds reveals other geographic patterns. Whereas one species may spread over a broad, continuous geographic area, another may show a spotty, discontinuous type of distribution with unoccupied gaps between "islands" of residence. In certain regions a given species or family may be dominant; in another region it may be scarce. Certain regions may be characterized by the residence of many species or families peculiar to them, while other regions may possess not a single peculiar species.

Regional patterns such as these led Alfred Russel Wallace, building on the works of Sclater and others, to propose his well-known world plan of animal distribution. In his monumental work, *The Geographical Distribution of Animals,* published in 1876, Wallace divided the world into six great zoogeographical regions, each separated from the others largely by the peculiarities of its vertebrate fauna. Although no such scheme can have universal validity, Wallace's regions have enough natural reality that they are still widely used by zoogeographers. Figure 20.1 shows the world divided into Wallace's major zoogeographic regions. In the paragraphs that follow are sketched the avian characteristics of the six regions as based on information supplied largely by Barden (1941) and Darlington (1957).

The **Palearctic** region includes Europe, all of Asia except its southern projections, and northern Africa. The Palearctic, despite its vast size, is relatively poor in bird variety. Although 69 families breed within the realm, it possesses only one unique family, the Prunellidae or hedge sparrows. This region shares with the Nearctic region of the New World (the two areas together are called the Holarctic) 48 families of birds of which the following are

Table 20.1.   The Number of Species of Breeding Birds at Different Latitudes (after Dobzhansky, 1950)

LOCATION	NO. OF SPECIES	AUTHORITY
Greenland	56	F. Salomonsen
Peninsular Labrador	81	H. S. Peters
Newfoundland	118	H. S. Peters
New York	195	K. C. Parkes
Florida	143	S. A. Grimes
Guatemala	469	L. Griscom
Panama	1,100	L. Griscom
Colombia	1,395	R. M. de Schauensee

Figure 20.1. Wallace's zoogeographical regions of the world as seen on a polar projection map. Note that South America, Africa, and Australia are relatively isolated from the main land masses of the world.

found in no other regions:

      Gaviidae—Loons
      Tetraonidae—Grouse
      Alcidae—Auks
      Bombycillidae—Waxwings

Other characteristic birds of the Holarctic include hawks, owls, woodpeckers, swallows, thrushes, kinglets, titmice, crows, jays, and many northern-breeding shore and water birds. Additional birds characteristic of the Palearctic, but not exclusive to it, include larks, Old World flycatchers, Old World warblers, pipits, weaverbirds, and starlings. Most birds living in the northern parts of the Palearctic are migratory, and a great many are insectivorous.

The **Nearctic** region includes North America north of most of Mexico, and Greenland. In spite of the fact that 62 families of birds breed in the Nearctic, it, too, is poor in avian variety. At best, it possesses a single unique family, the Chamaeidae, or wren-tits, of the west coast of the United States; but some authorities dispute the claim. However, the turkey

family, Meleagrididae, is nearly restricted to the Nearctic area. In addition to those families shared with the Palearctic, the Nearctic is characterized by possessing the New World vultures, tyrant flycatchers, Mimidae, vireos, wood warblers, grosbeaks, finches, and Icteridae, all of which it shares with the following region. Here, too, typical birds are migratory and insectivorous.

The **Neotropical** region embraces South America, Central America, the lowlands of Mexico, and the West Indies. This is by far the richest of all realms in bird life, both in numbers and in variety. Yet, more primitive species live here than in any other region. Eighty-six families of birds, including over 1500 species, are known to breed in the Neotropical region. This represents about one fifth of all known species. Of these families, 31 are peculiar to the region. This is more than twice as many endemic families as are found in any other geographical division.

Whereas in every other region the songbirds or Oscines predominate in numbers, in South America they are in the minority; and the more primitive or sub-oscine passerines, especially the tyrant flycatchers, antbirds, ovenbirds, woodcreepers, manakins, and cotingas, are the dominant forms. Other characteristic, but not unique, families include herons, storks, ducks, rails, hawks, owls, cuckoos, pigeons, parrots, goatsuckers, trogons, swifts, hummingbirds, barbets, woodpeckers, swallows, thrushes, vireos, wood warblers, Icteridae, tanagers and finches. Among the 31 Neotropical families that are endemic, or nearly so, are the following:

> Rheidae—Rheas
> Tinamidae—Tinamous
> Anhimidae—Screamers
> Cracidae—Curassows
> Opisthocomidae—Hoatzin
> Psophiidae—Trumpeters
> Eurypygidae—Sun bitterns
> Thinocoridae—Seedsnipe
> Steatornithidae—Oilbirds
> Nyctibiidae—Potoos
> Todidae—Todies
> Momotidae—Motmots
> Galbulidae—Jacamars
> Bucconidae—Puffbirds
> Ramphastidae—Toucans
> Dendrocolaptidae—Woodcreepers
> Furnariidae—Ovenbirds
> Formicariidae—Antbirds
> Pipridae—Manakins
> Cotingidae—Cotingas
> Phytotomidae—Plant-cutters

The **Ethiopian** region is made up of Africa south of the Sahara, southern Arabia, and Madagascar. This part of the world lacks the climatic variety which the three previous regions display. Sixty-seven families of land and fresh water birds breed here, but only six of these families are peculiar, or nearly so, to the region:

> Struthionidae—Ostrich
> Scopidae—Hammerhead Stork
> Sagittariidae—Secretary Bird
> Coliidae—Mousebirds
> Musophagidae—Touracos
> Prionopidae—Helmet Shrikes

In addition, there are six sub-families essentially peculiar to the Ethiopian region: Guinea fowl, tree hoopoes, bush shrikes, buffalo weavers, widow birds, and tick birds. Characteristic birds which are shared with other regions include herons, storks, Old World vultures, sand grouse, pigeons, owls, bustards, cuckoos, cranes, goatsuckers, trogons, kingfishers, bee eaters, rollers, hornbills, honey-guides, pittas, larks, swallows, shrikes, Old World orioles, drongos, starlings, cuckoo shrikes, bulbuls, Old World flycatchers, thrushes, wagtails, sunbirds, finches, and weaverbirds. As one might expect, birds of the Ethiopian region show strong affinities with those of the Oriental region; 30 per cent of the Ethiopian genera occur also in the Oriental region. However, agreement at the species level drops to 2 per cent, which suggests a long period of independent evolution in the two areas (Moreau, 1952).

The **Oriental** region includes India, Burma, Indo-China, Malaya, Sumatra, Java, Borneo and the Philippines. Of the 66 families of land and fresh water birds resident in this region, only one, the Irenidae, or fairy bluebirds, is endemic, and the Eurylaimidae, or broadbills, is nearly so. All the other families are also represented in one or more of the other geographic regions. Birds of the Oriental region resemble those of tropical Africa more than those of any other region, but they also show affinities with those of the Palearctic and Australian realms.

Characteristic birds of the Oriental region include many pheasants and pigeons, some owls, parrots, woodpeckers, pittas, babblers, corvids, shrikes, hoopoes, honeyguides, sunbirds and finches. Less common are megapodes, fruit pigeons, frogmouths, wood swallows, flowerpeckers, honey eaters, lories and cockatoos. Many migratory northern birds spend the winter in the Oriental region.

The **Australian** region is limited to Australia, Tasmania, New Zealand, the Celebes, the Moluccas, New Guinea, and the smaller islands of this general area of the East Indies and Polynesia. When Wallace studied the animals of this part of the world, he was impressed by the striking differences between the faunas of the Australian and Oriental regions. In setting a line of demarcation between the two faunas (now called "Wallace's Line"), he judged that the sharpest differences between them were observable between Bali and Lombok of the Lesser Sunda Islands, and between Borneo and the Celebes to the north. While this line makes sense for some vertebrates, such as the freshwater fishes, it is highly artificial for others, such as the birds. Among birds in this part of the world a gradual transition occurs. The Oriental species gradually give way to the Australian as one moves from Sumatra and Java across Bali and Lombok toward Australia. Nevertheless, if there are to be two geographic realms, a line has to be drawn somewhere, and Wallace's Line seems to be as good as any other.

There are 58 families of terrestrial and freshwater birds in the Australian region of which the following 15 are essentially unique:

Casuariidae—Cassowaries
Dromiceiidae—Emus
Apterygidae—Kiwis
Megapodiidae—Megapodes
Rhynochetidae—Kagu
Aegothelidae—Owlet Nightjars
Xenicidae—New Zealand Wrens
Menuridae—Lyrebirds
Atrichornithidae—Scrub-birds
Cracticidae—Bell Magpies
Grallinidae—Magpie Larks
Paradisaeidae—Birds of Paradise
Ptilonorhynchidae—Bower-birds
Meliphagidae—Honey-eaters
Dicaeidae—Flowerpeckers

In addition to these exclusive families, the Australian region has many characteristic pigeons, parrots, frogmouths, wood swallows, cuckoo shrikes, and wren warblers.

Bird geography may be studied from this standpoint of geographic regions, or equally well from the standpoint of the distribution of families of birds. Such a study, conducted by Barden (1941), revealed that of 144 families (the widely ranging sea birds and several other families were not considered), 33 or almost one-fourth of them were each represented in every one of Wallace's six geographic regions. Table 20.2, based on Barden and on Bartholomew's *Atlas of Zoogeography* (1911) gives, in order of decreasing ubiquity, examples of the geographic range of various families.

DYNAMIC BIRD GEOGRAPHY

A restless world of heaving earthquakes, wandering shorelines, shifting climates, and changing coats of vegetation can scarcely be expected to have sedentary tenants. A given bird's geographic range is not likely to stand firm before the chilling, grinding advance of a glacier. Consequently, as the environment changes, a species must respond either by adapting to the changed conditions or by moving into a more suitable range—or by dying. Wallace, as the co-author with Darwin of the theory of natural selection, was well aware of these facts. His map of animal distribution is only a single frame from a motion picture film—an arrested moment in the long and disturbed history of animate nature.

Birds must be reasonably well adapted to their habitats, or they will lose out in the relentless, competitive struggle for existence which envelops all organisms. But ecologic fitness is not the only explanation of their distribution. The successful transplantation of exotic species, such as the Starling, *Sturnus vulgaris*, to North America, or the Skylark, *Alauda arvensis*, to New Zealand, proves that other factors must be considered. Very often, similar ecologic niches in different parts of the world are occupied by quite unrelated species of birds. The nectar-feeding niche occupied by the hummingbirds (Trochilidae) in South America is filled by the sunbirds (Nectariniidae) in Africa, and the honey-eaters (Meliphagidae) in Australia. The insect-eating niche of the tyrant flycatchers

Table 20.2. The Geographic Distribution of Selected Bird Families (after Barden, 1941, and Bartholomew, 1911).

FAMILY	NEOTROPICAL	NEARCTIC	PALEARCTIC	ETHIOPIAN	ORIENTAL	AUSTRALIAN
Anatidae—Ducks, Geese, Swans	x	x	x	x	x	x
Accipitridae—Hawks, Eagles	x	x	x	x	x	x
Charadriidae—Plovers, Turnstones	x	x	x	x	x	x
Cuculidae—Cuckoos	x	x	x	x	x	x
Strigidae—Owls	x	x	x	x	x	x
Caprimulgidae—Goatsuckers	x	x	x	x	x	x
Apodidae—Swifts	x	x	x	x	x	x
Alcedinidae—Kingfishers	x	x	x	x	x	x
Corvidae—Crows, Magpies, Jays	x	x	x	x	x	x
Gruidae—Cranes		x	x	x	x	x
Burhinidae—Thick-knees	x		x	x	x	x
Laniidae—Shrikes		x	x	x	x	x
Paridae—Titmice		x	x	x	x	x
Fringillidae—Finches, Grosbeaks	x	x	x	x	x	
Otididae—Bustards			x	x	x	x
Trogonidae—Trogons	x	x		x	x	
Muscicapidae—Old World Flycatchers			x	x	x	x
Troglodytidae—Wrens	x	x	x		x	
Upupidae—Hoopoes			x	x	x	
Bucerotidae—Hornbills				x	x	x
Capitonidae—Barbets	x			x	x	
Pittidae—Pittas				x	x	x
Gaviidae—Loons, Divers		x	x			
Tetraonidae—Grouse		x	x			
Podargidae—Frogmouths					x	x
Trochilidae—Hummingbirds	x	x				
Indicatoridae—Honey-guides				x	x	
Tyrannidae—Tyrant flycatchers	x	x				
Dicaeidae—Flowerpeckers					x	x
Thraupidae—Tanagers	x	x				
Struthionidae—Ostriches				x		
Rheidae—Rheas	x					
Dromiceiidae—Emus						x
Coliidae—Colies				x		
Ramphastidae—Toucans	x					
Pipridae—Manakins	x					
Menuridae—Lyre birds						x
Ptilonorhynchidae—Bower-birds						x
Irenidae—Fairy bluebirds					x	
Prunellidae—Hedge sparrows			x			

(Tyrannidae) of the New World is occupied by the flycatchers (Muscicapidae) in the Old World. Penguins (Sphenisciformes) in the antarctic are represented by the auks (Alcidae) in the arctic. Complete perfection in ecologic fitness probably never occurs in nature, partly because the environment never stands still, and partly because birds continue to evolve. As the genetic complexion of a bird population changes, the species may be forced to seek a new habitat—a change in geographic range. Such a species finds itself in the position of a man who has inherited a fortune and subsequently moves into a more desirable neighborhood. Of course, a species may also lose its fortune. The Ascension Man-O'-War Bird, *Fregata aquila*, although a superbly flying sea bird, is rarely seen out of sight of land. The oil from its very small preen gland is inadequate to waterproof its feathers. As a result, the bird cannot alight on the ocean or be caught in a sudden rainstorm without becoming waterlogged. This greatly restricts the potential of the species for geographic spread.

Animal distribution, then, is the result of the interplay of two great dynamic agents: the perpetually changing environment and the continually evolving bird. Furthermore, the very geological and climatic changes which shift and isolate existing species over the face of the earth become agents of natural selection through which new species evolve and old species die out. While ecologic fitness furnishes the clue to many of the problems of animal distribution, especially on the local level, the historic forces of geology, climatology, and evolution must be invoked to explain many of the large-scale patterns of bird distribution.

Now and then nature performs an experiment through which man can observe in a relatively short time some of these forces at work. In 1883 the East Indian island of Krakatoa was overwhelmed by a tremendous volcanic eruption. Heat and volcanic ash sterilized the island of all life. After three years, ferns and flowering plants, about two dozen kinds, had established themselves on the island. After 14 years there were 12 ferns and 50 flowering plants. Twenty-five years after the eruption, 240 species of invertebrate animals, mostly insects, were found living on the island, and 16 species of birds. By 1921, 38 years after the explosion, 573 species of animals had become established there, including 26 species of breeding birds. The nearest land from which these plants and animals might have come was 18.5 kilometers away (Hesse, Allee and Schmidt, 1937).

Invasion of new territory is only a part of the story; withdrawals from previously occupied range probably occur just as often. A given species' geographic distribution, seen as a time-lapse motion picture—that is, the dynamic view of a species' range—would through the years appear something like a gigantic ameba extending and retracting its lobes as it slowly crawls over the surface of the earth. This way of looking at bird geography focuses attention on the forces which cause these motions. Seen from the viewpoint of the bird itself, the forces may be roughly classified as either active or passive. A species may change its geographic range as a result of its own activities, or it may be shoved about by environmental forces. Clean-cut distinctions between the two methods of dispersal are difficult to make, but abundant evidence shows that the present map of global distribution is the result of the long-continued operation of both.

ACTIVE BIRD DISPERSAL

As used here, the word dispersal means both the outward spread of birds from an established area of residence and also the withdrawal from such an area. Mobility itself is one of the chief forces promoting the wide and rapid geographic dispersal of birds. No other class of animal can match birds in the speed, ease, and efficiency of their flight—flight which may make accessible even the remotest areas.

Birds, however, vary greatly in the exercise of their powers of flight. In California, both adults and young of the salt marsh Song Sparrow, *Melospiza melodia,* are remarkably sedentary. Thirty-four banded nestlings established their first breeding territories an average distance of only 185 meters from their natal homes (Johnston, 1956). At the other extreme are such earth-girdling species as the albatrosses. A nestling Wandering Albatross, *Diomedea exulans,* banded at Kerguelen Island, was found dead one year later, 13,000 kilometers westward in Chile. A Black-browed Albatross, *Diomedea melanophris,* was shot near Spitzbergen in the Arctic Ocean some 11,000 kilometers out of its usual range. Another bird of this species settled in a colony of Gannets, *Morus bassanus,* on the Faeroe Islands, and lived among them for 34 years until shot and preserved for a museum (Murphy, 1936). Such birds as these may be the pioneers which open up new range for a species. This tendency toward wide roving appears to be genetically a very plastic trait, at least in albatrosses. Murphy describes three sub-species of the White-capped Albatross, *Diomedea cauta,* one of which is sedentary and remains in the vicinity of the Chatham Islands, another which roams the seas of the Australian-New Zealand region, and the third which is circumglobal in the southern seas.

Population pressure is another powerful force which may cause changes in the range of a species. Particularly in species which show territorial behavior, the birds living on the periphery of a species' range may be forced into new areas (p. 212). Contrariwise, in a species whose numbers are declining, there will be a recession from parts of the originally occupied range.

Withdrawal from a formerly occupied range is commonly forced on a species either through competition with a more successful species or through some change, either in the environment or in the species itself, which may reduce the bird's ecologic fitness for that particular area. Birds live constantly under such threats of dispossession in their home ranges. Consequently, any mechanisms which may promote dispersal into new and untried ranges are of great benefit to a species.

Irruption is one such mechanism. As discussed earlier, certain species resident in the north temperate boreal zones burst out of their traditional range in years of high population and low food supplies to invade new areas. The Snowy Owl, *Nyctea scandiaca,* has repeatedly irrupted southward into the United States in winters of lemming scarcity. In the 1945–1946 invasion, ornithologists counted 13,502 Snowy Owls in the United States. They were observed in a band extending the entire width of the continent, and as far south as Oregon, southern Nebraska, central Illinois, Pennsylvania, and Maryland. Twenty-four were observed on ships in various parts of the Atlantic, several birds landing on ships hundreds of kilometers from the nearest land (Gross, 1947). Siberian Nutcrackers, *Nucifraga caryocatactes,* have invaded Germany 15 times between 1896 and 1933, each time when the pine-seed crop failed in their home range. Similar irruptions have been recorded for the sandgrouse, titmice, crossbills, and numerous other species.

In these irruptions one sees a temporary surmounting of the normal barriers of a species' range through an increase in population pressure. Invasions provide a mechanism for the sampling of new ranges, and although they do not normally result in establishing new permanent homes for the species, even rare and sporadic successes can be of enormous significance in the long-range history of a species. As a result of irruptions from the continent, the Crossbill, *Loxia curvirostra,* established itself in Ireland in the 19th century and in England in the 20th (Thomson, 1926). Invasions of the Pied Flycatcher, *Muscicapa hypoleuca,* in England in the late 19th and early 20th centuries have resulted in its establishment there, and since 1901 it has been gradually spreading its range (Campbell, 1955).

Population pressure also promotes range expansion through what seems to be an in-born tendency in the young of many species to strike out and explore the world in all directions. Every new generation puts some added strain on the traditional habitat for food, nesting sites, and territory; and the younger birds find themselves in unequal competition with the entrenched older ones. The wanderlust of first-year birds is apparently an adaptive device whereby natural selection has met this contingency. This trait appears in both ir-ruptive and non-irruptive species. In the 1953 irruption of Crossbills into Europe, young birds predominated. Of 179 birds captured in Mecklenburg, Germany, only 20 were in adult plumage (Bub and Ku-merloeve, 1954). In Switzerland, the band-ing of young Barn Owls, *Tyto alba*, showed that in years of high nestling productivity 57 to 68 per cent of them dispersed 50 kilometers or more from their natal nests; in years of normal productivity the per-centage was only 37 (Schifferli, 1949).

Similar results were obtained by Gross (1940) from a banding study of over 23,000 Herring Gulls, *Larus argentatus*, on Kent Island, New Brunswick. In this species there is an almost explosive dispersal of young birds at the end of the breeding sea-son. Subsequent recoveries of 773 (3.3 per cent) of these gulls revealed that the younger birds flew greater distances to their recovery points than the older ones. First year birds were recovered an average distance of 1380 kilometers from Kent Is-land; second year birds, 695 km.; third year birds, 465 km.; fourth year and older birds, 467 km. (Fig. 20.3). Recoveries of 1409 Herring Gulls previously banded in rookeries in northern Lake Michigan by Wilson and Lyon gave average recovery distances for first, second, third, and fourth year and older birds of 690, 515, 350, and 289 kilometers respectively. The young of numerous other species of birds show a similar nomadism. Very probably the year-ling birds of a given species are ecologi-cally more adaptable than the older ones, and hence are better equipped to go traveling, to withstand different climates, eat strange foods, and, probably, to exploit new range. Older birds, once they have

Figure 20.2. Young Herring Gulls banded as nestlings at Beaver Islands, Michigan, dis-persed during their first year of life as shown by the radiating lines. Older gulls are much more likely to remain sedentary. After Lincoln.

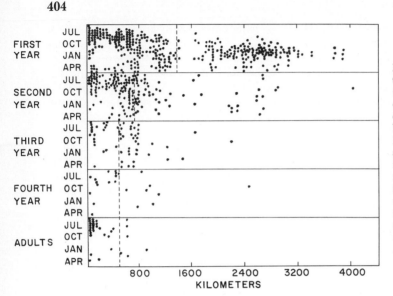

Figure 20.3. The dispersal tendency of young Herring Gulls is shown by this scatter diagram based on the recapture of 773 out of 23,434 birds banded as nestlings in New Brunswick. Each dot represents a recaptured bird plotted against its age, the season of the year recaptured, and the distance from its natal colony to the place of recapture. The mean distance of the recovery points from the colony for each age group is indicated by the broken line. Adapted from Gross.

nested in a given location, are more likely to be tied to it by habituation, ortstreue, and peck-order seniority.

Seasonal migration is quite different from youthful nomadism, but at times it undoubtedly encourages the extension of range. Long-distance migrants are in a better position to discover new habitats, and they are naturally more tolerant of diversity in the environment than are sedentary species. In the mountains of Colombia, such winter visitors from North America as the Yellow-billed Cuckoo, *Coccyzus americanus,* the Rose-breasted Grosbeak, *Pheucticus ludovicianus,* and several warblers have been observed ranging freely through the temperate, sub-tropical, and tropical life zones, whereas the permanent residents are more rigidly confined in zonal boundaries (Chapman, 1917). Numerous wood warblers (Parulidae) breed in the boreal and temperate zones of the New World and migrate to the tropics for the winter. A number of species belonging to the genera *Parula, Geothlypis, Dendroica, Vermivora,* and others have developed both migratory and resident races, the latter living permanently, for example, in Central America, South America, or the islands of the Caribbean. Whether these sedentary populations are descendants of

northern migratory species, or vice versa, it is impossible at present to say, but migration has undoubtedly played a role in the establishment of these parallel races.

Migration may, on the contrary, restrict the dispersal of a species. Darlington (1957) makes the point that much bird migration is an orderly, north and south, annual movement which, as an instinctive routine, prevents certain species from the random scattering in other directions which might otherwise increase opportunities for dispersal.

PASSIVE BIRD DISPERSAL

As air-borne creatures, birds are at times passively displaced from their usual haunts by prevailing winds and hurricanes. For birds, as for airplanes, the flight eastward across the Atlantic is much easier than the return westward flight in the teeth of the prevailing westerly air currents. Forty-eight species of North American land birds have been recorded in western Europe, usually during the spring or fall migration periods and often during or at the end of periods of strong westerly winds. Less than a dozen European land birds have been known to cross the Atlantic to North America (Alexander and Fitter, 1955).

Ornithological literature abounds in references to land birds observed from ships far at sea. A record of such sightings, kept over a period of 22 years by naturalists aboard research vessels of the Woods Hole Oceanographic Institution, listed 54 species of land birds. Most of these birds were observed within 320 kilometers of the nearest land, but several of them were seen as far out as 640 kilometers (Scholander, 1955). As a rule, these birds were observed during migration periods, particularly in the fall, and generally at times when there were strong offshore winds. Many of the birds alighted on the ships, exhausted. Between September 15 and 19, 1959, during a period of strong offshore winds, two Ruddy Turnstones, *Arenaria interpres,* two Kestrels, *Falco tinnunculus,* and 16 passerine birds of eight species appeared near or on a weather ship anchored in the Atlantic 640 kilometers west of Ireland and 1300 kilometers south of Iceland. One of the Kestrels remained on board for three days, during which it ate at least five of the passerine migrants (McLean and Williamson, 1960).

There is persuasive evidence that such wind-driven birds may at times enlarge a species' range. The island of South Georgia is 1600 kilometers due east and leeward of Tierra del Fuego, in the belt of the Roaring Forties. There are two endemic land birds there: a pipit, *Anthus antarcticus,* and a teal, *Anas georgica,* whose nearest relatives live in Argentina directly to the windward (Murphy, 1936). The West Indies are leeward of the Cape Verde Islands during the period of late summer cyclones—a fact probably accounting for the presence in both regions of one species each of tropic bird, frigate bird, and booby. Thirteen species of passerines introduced into New Zealand and Australia have established themselves on nine islands lying between 160 and 880 kilometers off shore. It is thought that strong winds were largely responsible for their dispersal (Williams, 1953).

Wind storms are notorious transporters of birds. Hurricanes often carry sea birds

far out of their normal ranges. During the winter of 1954–1955, severe Atlantic storms carried great numbers of Kittiwakes, *Rissa tridactyla,* into Germany and Switzerland. The Atlantic hurricane of September, 1938, deposited living White-tailed Tropic-birds, *Phaëthon lepturus,* whose normal range is the West Indies, as far north as Maine and Vermont. Other Atlantic hurricanes have driven tropical petrels as far inland as Rochester, N.Y., Ottawa, Ontario, and Montreal, Quebec.

In April, 1947, an intense low pressure area moved from Kansas into the Great Lakes area, bringing with it strong southeasterly winds. As a result, many migrating warblers and vireos arrived in Ontario an average of 32 days earlier than their mean arrival dates, and they were accompanied by numerous abnormally rare species (Gunn and Crocker, 1951).

At least one historic range expansion can be attributed to a specific storm. On the night of January 19, 1937, a flock of European thrushes known as Fieldfares, *Turdus pilaris,* was migrating from Norway toward England, probably to escape

Figure 20.4. The European Fieldfare, a close relative of the American Robin, was, in a 1937 storm, driven from Norway to Greenland, and has since established a colony there. It seems very possible that in future years this species may invade the North American continent. Photo by E. Hosking.

a sudden cold spell. They were caught in mid-course by strong southeasterly gales and carried to Jan Mayen and the northeastern coast of Greenland. At both places, the birds were observed and collected on January 20. By the end of January, the birds on Greenland had moved to its southern tip, where they have since established a sedentary population (Salomonsen, 1950).

There is little evidence that water currents assist in the distribution of birds, but the possibility should not be ruled out. Penguins are typically antarctic birds, but the Galapagos Penguin, *Spheniscus mendiculus*, lives on the equator at the northern extremity of the cold, north-flowing Peru Current. In this case, the temperature of the water and its food resources were probably more responsible for this penguin's unorthodox distribution than the current itself.

Man himself has been an important agent in the passive dispersal of birds. The imported European House Sparrow, *Passer domesticus*, Starling, *Sturnus vulgaris*, and Chinese Ring-necked Pheasant, *Phasianus colchicus*, have succeeded phenomenally in establishing themselves in North America. In the late 19th century, there were many "acclimatization societies" in the United States, dedicated to the importation and release of exotic bird species. One such group in Cincinnati liberated 3000 birds of 20 species between 1872 and 1874, but without success. Peterson (1948) estimates that many hundreds of thousands of birds, representing over 100 foreign species, were released in America in this period, and that the great majority of them failed to establish themselves. In the Hawaiian Islands, however, some 50 introduced species have established themselves, unfortunately at the expense of about two-thirds of the original native species.

BARRIERS AND ROUTES OF DISPERSAL

In spite of their superior powers of flight, warm-bloodedness, and high reproductive potential, certain birds do not exist everywhere on earth that conditions are ecologically tolerable for them. Obstacles of different sorts and of variable powers of exclusion prevent a species from expanding its range into ecologically suitable regions. These barriers may be physical, spatial, biological, psychological, or chronological. A mountain can be a barrier to a plains bird, an ocean to a land bird, a continent to a sea bird, and a prairie to a forest bird. A high mountain is a stronger barrier than a low one, a broad ocean stronger than a narrow strait. Wallace's zoogeographical regions are all surrounded by major physical barriers such as the oceans, the Sahara desert, the Himalayan mountains.

High mountains are very obvious barriers to bird dispersal. Their crests frequently offer obstacles in the form of cold, thin air, little oxygen, snow and ice, or rocky soil, little food and cover, and vertical height itself, which requires great exertion to overcome. Very commonly high mountain ranges mark the distributional limits of bird populations.

As physical barriers, deserts offer such obstacles to dispersal as rapid and extreme temperature fluctuations, lack of water, a high rate of evaporation, lack of food and cover, dust storms, and intense insolation. Such a sterile complex of ecologic factors offers little attraction to a species to enlarge its territory.

Since very few barriers are absolute, their effects on bird distribution are selective and retarding rather than completely prohibitive. Only the more vigorous, mobile, adventurous, lucky, or ecologically tolerant species or individuals are able to surmount certain barriers to achieve an enlarged range. Thus, barriers commonly act as filters. Since some of the more difficult barriers may be overcome only on rare occasions when all contributing conditions are "right," it may be thousands of years before a given species may leap a given barrier and appropriate a new range. This is illustrated by the fact that

Figure 20.5. The Collared Turtle Dove, a species that has recently been expanding its range in Europe with unmatched speed. Photo by E. Hosking.

few land birds reside on isolated oceanic islands, but even more significantly by the fact that no habitable oceanic island is so remote that some species of land bird cannot reach and colonize it (Darlington, 1957).

Of the great physical barriers, the oceans are probably the most effective in restricting land birds within their home ranges. Until man intervened, it was the Atlantic Ocean which kept the House Sparrow, *Passer domesticus,* from the Americas. Like other successful invaders of new territory, the House Sparrow increased its numbers and its range slowly when first introduced, but later increased markedly the pace of its invasion. Between 1870 and 1875 it expanded its American range by 1300 square kilometers, but in the single year of 1886 it is estimated to have added 1,340,000 square kilometers to its range (Bent, 1958).

During the past quarter century the Collared Turtle Dove, *Streptopelia decaocto,* has expanded its range with explosive speed, spreading some 1900 kilometers northwest across Europe from the Balkans to Great Britain and Scandinavia, sometimes advancing as much as 240 kilometers per year. The species seems spectacularly well adapted for exploiting its new range, and breeds within a year or two of its arrival in new regions. It has been breeding in Britain since 1955. Few, if any, other species have ever been known to take over new range as rapidly. It is not known what barriers restrained this species from its dramatic dispersal until so recently. Mayr (1950) suggests that this expansion in range was initiated by genetic changes in peripheral populations of the species.

Another species currently engaged in extensive range expansion is the Old World Cattle Egret, *Bubulcus ibis.* Perhaps carried by the northeast trade winds, or by some tropical hurricane, this bird made its way across the Atlantic from Africa to British Guiana, late in the nineteenth century. This hypothesis is supported by the fact that recently a Cattle Egret banded as a nestling in Spain was recovered a year later in Trinidad (McKean, 1960). The species has multiplied its numbers and spread its range so successfully that it reached Florida in 1942, Massachusetts by 1952 (Sprunt, 1955), Wisconsin by 1960, and central Canada by 1961. The Cattle Egret and Fieldfare are the only species of birds known historically to have established themselves in the New World as breeding birds without human help. The Egret is also currently expanding its range in South Africa and New South Wales.

Without question, the surmounting of barriers and the invasion of new ranges will continue indefinitely as long as birds evolve and environments change. For certain species one can anticipate possible fu-

Figure 20.6. The Cattle Egret is currently invading and establishing new range in North America. It and the Fieldfare are the only Old World species known to have established themselves in the New World within historic times without man's aid. Photo by E. Hosking.

ture changes in residence. The larks (Alaudidae) of North America, dwellers of plains and open country, have begun to filter into South America via the Andean paramos. If some of them can cross either the great Brazilian rain forests or the high Andes mountains, and reach the extensive pampas of Argentina, they should find an ecologic paradise awaiting them (Barden, 1941). The Brown Pelican, *Pelecanus occidentalis,* of the Caribbean is a sea bird that does not venture far from shore. It feeds on fish which it sights from the air and then seizes in plunging dives. The muddy waters pouring out the mouths of the Amazon make this method of feeding fruitless, and have prevented the extension of the pelican's range southward. Murphy (1936) hazards the guess "that if 50 adult pelicans from the West Indies were set free along the coast of southern Brazil, the birds would take to their new home as rabbits did to Australia." Rivers can be bar-

riers in other ways. The right-bank tributaries of the Amazon have cut the forest bordering the river into great "islands," in each of which distinctive but related species of birds are isolated.

Even to a sea bird the ocean presents barriers to dispersal. The story of El Niño, related earlier, reveals the striking effect that temperature may have on bird distribution. There are warm water species and cold water species. The Royal Tern, *Thalasseus maximus,* a warm water bird, is bottled up in the Pacific Ocean within 30 degrees of latitude, between the cool south-flowing California Current and the chilly north-flowing Peru Current. But in the Atlantic, thanks to the warm Gulf Stream and Brazil Current, its range covers 70 degrees of latitude, extending from Florida to Argentina (Fig. 20.7). The Shoemaker Petrel, *Procellaria aequinoctialis,* on the other hand, is tied to cold surface waters and is sandwiched between the antarctic pack ice and the Equatorial and Brazil Currents. Similarly, the antarctic Snow Petrel, *Pagodroma nivea,* is a bird of ice floes and cold water. The 12° surface water isotherm marks both the northern limits of its range and that of the opossum shrimp, its most abundant food source (Murphy, 1936).

Although some species seem to be directly limited by temperature boundaries, temperature is probably of greater importance indirectly, through controlling the food supplies of a given range. According to Stresemann (1927–1934) the decisive factors in determining the geographic distribution of birds are usually climate and the nature of the soil, these two elements accounting for minerals, food, vegetation, cover, nesting sites, and other requirements.

As described earlier, the interplay between birds and climate involves many and diverse ecologic relationships, most of which are important for distribution. The effects of winds have already been mentioned. Of other climatic factors important in distribution, only a few examples can be given in the space available.

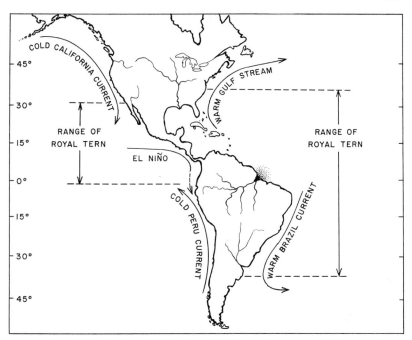

Figure 20.7. Warm water birds like the Royal Tern are restricted to a narrow range along the Pacific shores of the Americas because of the flow of cold ocean currents toward the equator. The outward flowing warm currents in the Atlantic more than double the width of this species' range. The turbid water at the mouth of the Amazon restricts the Brown Pelican to the Caribbean Sea. Periodic invasions of warm water by "El Niño" along the west coast of South America have disastrous effects on fish and water birds. Adapted from Murphy.

Fifty years ago in southern Sweden, the Hooded Crow, *Corvus cornix,* and the Blackbird, *Turdus merula,* were migratory harbingers of spring. Today they are both all-year residents. This change in status is due to the warmer springs and milder winters which this Scandinavian peninsula has undergone since the 1880's. This warming trend, paralleled in many other parts of the North Temperate Zone, is attributed to changes in the Azores high pressure area and the Icelandic low pressure mass, which permit an increased northward flow of warm air. As a consequence, there has been in recent years a striking northward expansion of range by resident and migratory birds (Hustich, 1952).

A survey of resident species by Kalela (1949) showed that of the 25 species of birds the northern limits of whose ranges were in southern Finland, 11 (44 per cent)

have expanded their ranges northward while 6 (24 per cent) have decreased somewhat in numbers since 1950 (Fig. 20.8). In the United States, the Cardinal, *Richmondena cardinalis,* is now a common resident in northern states where it was unknown a half century ago; and the Robin, *Turdus migratorius,* formerly only a summer resident in Pennsylvania and corresponding latitudes, is today increasingly common as a winter resident.

In arid regions, such as South Africa, rainfall may occur in spotty patterns. Many breeding birds will shift their residence from year to year to coincide with the more humid regions where vegetation and food are more abundant. Among the birds of Nepal, Ripley (1950) found that many species existed in two races, an eastern and a western Himalayan race, respectively, and that the line separating

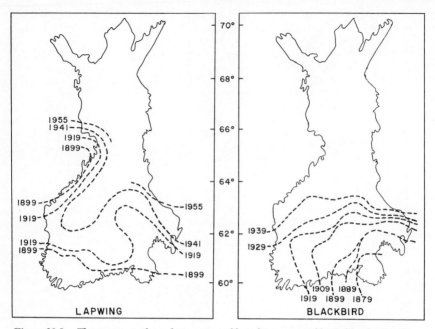

Figure 20.8.   The recent northward expansion of breeding ranges of birds like the Lapwing and Blackbird in Finland is correlated with the gradually warming climate, especially of winters and springs, in northern Europe. After Kalela.

these close relatives was probably the isohyet near the eighty-seventh degree of longitude, east of which the annual rainfall is about 190 centimeters and west of which it is only 125 centimeters.

Even fog may determine the geographic range of a species. Investigations by Hawksley (1957) of breeding colonies of Arctic Terns, *Sterna paradisaea*, in the Bay of Fundy, showed clearly that young chicks gained weight on clear days but generally lost weight on foggy days which restricted the ability of adult birds to provide food. The absence of this species as a breeding bird on the Bering Sea shores of Siberia is probably due to the frequent fogs there.

Weather disasters may remove a bird from part of its established range. Persistent cold rains in 1903 practically eliminated Purple Martins, *Progne subis,* from

northern New Jersey to southern New Hampshire, and this lost range was not recaptured for many years (Griscom, 1941). A population of Carolina Chickadees, *Parus carolinensis,* in central Tennessee was killed off by an ice storm in January, 1951, and even four years later the population had recovered only about one-half its former numbers (Goodpasture, 1955).

Length of day, which becomes progressively more variable as one moves away from the equator, probably influences the geographic breeding ranges of many species. The assumption of breeding plumage and behavior, and the timing of the sex cycle in many species are closely related to day length. This relationship seems to be a hereditary matter originating in an adaptation to a specific latitude and seasonal light pattern. The possession of relatively fixed photo-periodic breeding

Figure 20.9. An Emperor Penguin and its chick. This largest and most southerly of penguins lays, incubates, and hatches its single egg in the frigid depths of the antarctic winter—a physiological feat without parallel in the animal kingdom. Photo by Expéditions Polaires Francaises.

Figure 20.10. Hairy Woodpeckers of Canada (left) and Costa Rica (right) illustrate Bergmann's Rule that warm-blooded animals living in the cooler, higher latitudes are likely to have larger bodies which conserve heat more effectively than small bodies.

responses very likely prevents the successful spread of some species into latitudes with pronouncedly different daylight patterns.

A wide-spread, continuous population of a given kind of bird may, through many years of natural selection by physical factors, be broken up into geographic populations of graduated types. This is particularly true for the climatic factors of temperature and humidity. Species and races of birds which live in colder climates commonly have larger bodies than their relatives living in warmer climates. For example, the largest penguin is the Emperor, *Aptenodytes forsteri*, of Antarctica, while the smallest species are those living in Australia and the Galapagos Islands. A large body is advantageous in a cold climate because of the thermal economy of its more favorable surface-volume ratio. This principle is known as Bergmann's Rule, and it has been found by Rensch (1936) to hold true for about 90 per cent of the geographic races of non-migratory Palearctic species. As an example, autumn weights of the European Wren, *Troglodytes troglodytes*, vary from 9.0 to 11.0 gm. in southern England, through 10.1 to 15.1 gm. on Fair Isle, Scotland, to 13.5 to 20.0 gm. on Iceland (Armstrong, 1955).

For the Chickadee (or Willow Tit), *Parus atricapillus*, Rensch (1947) found that the geographic distribution of body size paralleled very closely the mean January isotherms of western Europe, with larger bodies correlating with lower temperatures. January is the most critical month of the year for the survival of small species such as these. Presumably birds with relatively smaller bodies are the first to die of exposure to cold in bitter winter months, leaving the increasingly larger types to populate the increasingly colder zones. Bergmann's Rule does not apply with equal faithfulness to migratory species, since they are not subject to this extreme form of selection.

Geographic gradients are found in other attributes of widely distributed species. Allen's Rule states that birds that live in colder regions generally have relatively shorter beaks, legs, and wings than their nearest relatives in warmer regions. Such projections lose heat more rapidly than the main bulk of a bird's body. A difference of one per cent in wing-length corresponds to a difference of 2° north latitude in Redpolls, *Carduelis flammea*, of just over 1° in Puffins, *Fratercula arctica*, and a little over 0.5° in Wrens, *Troglodytes troglodytes* (Huxley, 1942).

Pigmentation likewise shows widespread geographic gradients. Gloger's Rule states that races of birds (and mammals) that live in warm and humid regions have darker pigmentation than races of the same species that live in cooler or drier regions (Fig. 20.11). Rensch (1936) compared climatic races of 16 species from the titmouse and nuthatch families and found that this rule applied in 15 of the species and was broken in one. As another general rule, birds with gaudy, metallic coloration are more likely to be found in humid tropical regions and those with much white plumage in polar regions.

Referred to earlier was the clutch-size rule which points out that races of a species which live at higher latitudes lay more eggs per clutch than races at lower latitudes (p. 291). In Finland, the European Robin, *Erithacus rubecula*, lays average

Figure 20.11. Gloger's Rule as illustrated by the Goshawk. At the left is the nearly white northerly race, *Accipiter gentilis buteoides*, from western Siberia; at the right, the heavily pigmented race, *A.g. melanoleucus*, from east Africa. After Kleinschmidt.

clutches of 6.3 eggs, and this number decreases gradually with decreasing latitude until the species averages only 3.5 eggs per clutch in the Canary Islands (Lack, 1953). In Britain, the European Goldfinch, *Carduelis carduelis*, lays a clutch of 5 eggs. About 100 years ago it was transplanted to Australia, where today it lays an average of 3.7 eggs (Frith, 1957). This change, of course, may be due to other influences than temperature. Rensch (1931) has discovered that omnivorous birds of temperate regions have relatively larger intestines, stomachs, and caeca than do related races in tropical climates. German titmice of the genus *Parus*, for example, have intestines 23.6 per cent longer than tropical races from the East Indies.

Races of birds living in cooler climates are more likely to be migratory than warm-climate relatives. For many species this is a simple matter of race-survival. Recalling the fact that many birds have more feathers in winter than in summer (p. 33), it seems logical to expect that sedentary cold-climate races should have a greater number of feathers per bird than their warm-climate relatives, but this point, apparently, has not been established. How-

ever, Irving (1960) has found that the tips of contour feathers of winter residents of arctic Alaska are fluffier than those of summer residents. In cold weather, when a bird erects its feathers, the soft tips interlock to imprison an insulating layer of warm air, whereas the stiff-tipped feathers of migrants readily separate and lose the insulating air.

BIOLOGICAL BARRIERS

Since green plants are the ultimate source of all food, the ranges of many birds depend almost entirely on the distribution of plants. In addition, birds commonly require nesting sites, nesting materials, song posts, and protective cover which are provided by plants. Of course the prey of insectivorous and predatory birds depend also upon plants.

Certain bird species are closely tied to one or a few plant species. Some hummingbirds have bills of such a shape that they can sip nectar only from particular flowers. Certain crossbills, nutcrackers, titmice, and kinglets are closely restricted to evergreen forests: for instance, the European

Nutcracker, *Nucifraga caryocatactes,* prefers conifer forests in which the Arolla pine occurs. The African vulture, *Gypohierax angolensis,* lives mainly on the fruits of the oil palm *Elaeis,* and consequently its geographic range coincides with that of the palm. The Palm Swift, *Cypsiurus parvus,* is chiefly limited to the range of the fan palm, *Barassus flabelliformis,* on whose leaves the bird cements its nest (Stresemann, 1927–1934). Narrow dependencies such as these are invitations to extinction.

Sea birds, no less than land birds, are limited in their distribution by food resources. The basic food stuff in sea water is the microscopic plankton, and plankton, in turn, reflects the abundance of mineral nutrients, such as phosphates and nitrates. Cold waters are generally much richer in plankton than warm waters; coastal waters, richer than pelagic. The concentration of plankton organisms in pelagic

south Atlantic sea waters was found by Hentschel (*in* Murphy, 1936) to vary from about 5000 per liter in equatorial waters to 100,000 per liter at 55° south latitude. The abundance of sea birds is more than seven times as great at 55° south latitude as at the equator (Fig. 20.12). A similar correlation between plankton abundance and sea bird abundance was found by Jespersen (1929) in the north Atlantic. In the plankton-rich north Atlantic between Iceland and England as many as 100 sea birds would be seen on a typical day, while in the almost barren waters of the equatorial Atlantic one bird or none might be seen per day.

Plants may either promote or hinder the dispersal of a species. Early in this century extensive fires in the western part of the upper peninsula of Michigan burned many openings in the solid growths of forest. The grass and shrubbery which soon clothed

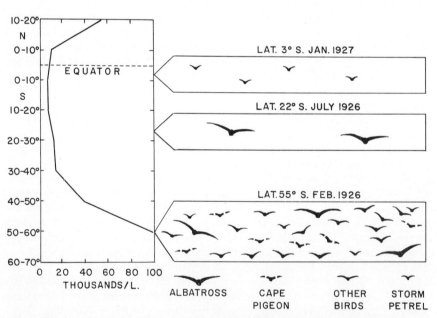

Figure 20.12. The relative abundance of sea birds at different latitudes in the pelagic South Atlantic as related to the abundance of plankton. The graph at the left shows the mean abundance of plankton in the upper 50 meters of the ocean in thousands of organisms per liter (after Hentschel). Relative bird abundance, at right, is after Spiess. Both diagrams are modified after Murphy.

these openings provided a suitable habitat for Sharp-tailed Grouse, *Pedioecetes phasianellus*, with the result that this species quickly expanded into this new range (Baumgartner, 1939). Changes in the general character of the vegetation of a given region almost inevitably are followed by changes in bird distribution.

Other animals likewise may affect bird distribution. As discussed in the previous chapter, many species of birds are associated with other animals as commensals, competitors, brood-parasites, predators, nest-cavity users, and so on. A tick bird species probably adjusts its geographic range to that of the ungulates it grooms; a cuckoo, to the range of its preferred host; a falcon, to the range of its preferred prey; an antbird, to the range of army ants which stir up the insects it feeds on. In Nebraska, competition between Ring-necked Pheasants, *Phasianus colchicus*, and Greater Prairie Chickens, *Tympanuchus cupido*, causes the elimination of isolated colonies of the latter (Sharp, 1957). There are no ducks whatever on Lake Edward in the Belgian Congo, and geese seem reluctant to swim there, probably because of the presence of large carnivorous fish (Lippens, 1938).

OTHER BARRIERS

In addition to the physical and biological barriers to bird dispersal, there seem to be psychological barriers. Lack (1937) has suggested that birds instinctively seek the visually prominent features of a habitat, and not necessarily the essential ones. Nesting sites are commonly chosen according to the density and height of forest vegetation rather than the species of trees involved.

Some land birds are capable fliers but are nevertheless stopped by moderate water gaps. The Central and South American cracids, puffbirds, toucans, ovenbirds, and manakins have failed to populate the West Indies; and the quail, trogons, and cotingas have reached only one or two is-

lands (Darlington, 1957). This fact may result simply from the reluctance of these birds to fly across water. Races of South American barbets are similarly isolated from each other by the broad tributaries of the Amazon. The reverse of this situation is seen in the fact that although the Isthmus of Panama is no barrier to many species of sea birds, it effectively separates two subspecies of the Brown Booby, *Sula leucogaster*, one on each side of the 80 kilometer land barrier (Van Tyne and Berger, 1959).

The lack of time can be a barrier to the dispersal of species. As a rule, the number of land bird species found on an oceanic island varies inversely as the island's remoteness from the nearest mainland center of dispersal. There are variables other than remoteness, of course, including latitude, wind direction, size of island, and habitat niches available. Although the Hawaiian Islands are some 3200 kilometers from the nearest mainland, Mayr (1943) estimates that they have been invaded and colonized by land or freshwater birds on 14 separate occasions.

Obviously, the longer time a species has at its disposal, the more opportunities it has for leaping such barriers as wide water gaps or high mountains. The past history of a species must therefore be taken into account in any attempts to explain present day avian geography.

HISTORICAL BIRD GEOGRAPHY

A ceaseless ebb and flow probably characterizes the range pattern of nearly every species of bird, particularly when it is considered over a long period of time. In the sometimes gradual, sometimes sporadic, shifting of bird ranges over the surface of the earth, changes of different sorts may occur. A species may extend its range or withdraw from a range previously occupied. It may increase its numbers or its dominance within its range, or decrease them. It may decrease its numbers to the vanishing point and become extinct.

Finally, a species may evolve into a different race or species, especially when it exists in small, isolated populations. Considering the constant interaction between evolving birds and changing environments, it is inevitable that geographic ranges change.

An exact study of historical bird geography is a practical impossibility because so many complex and unpredictable variables are involved: evolution, geologic change, climatic change, rapid dispersal, slow dispersal, ecologic adaptation, competition between species, barriers. The fossil record of ancient distributions of birds throws very little light on the subject, chiefly because of its incompleteness; fragile bird bones do not fossilize readily. Further, since birds often invade a new range with explosive rapidity—as measured in geologic time—their routes of dispersal cannot readily be reconstructed. Darlington (1957), speaking of the fragmentary record of fossil birds, points out:

"In no case do fossils clearly show the place of origin of a widely distributed family of birds. In some families the earliest known fossils arc in Europe or North America, but this probably reflects the distribution of paleontologists more than that of birds."

The fossil record does show that certain species once lived in areas outside their present range: for example, parrots in Nebraska, England, and Germany, and flamingoes in South Dakota. It also suggests that "certain groups of birds have always been confined to certain places: elephant birds to Madagascar, moas to New Zealand, penguins to southern and auks to northern parts of the world" (Darlington).

Beyond such facts as these, the past history of bird distribution must be reconstructed by the use of inferences based on present day distribution (remembering that the absence of certain bird groups may be as significant as the presence of others), and on the geologic history of changes in glaciation, climate, sea level, land-bridges, and water gaps between land masses.

One of the most striking facts revealed by Wallace's map of zoogeography is the correlation between the degree of unique-

ness of birds of certain continents and islands and the long-existing isolation of these pieces of land from the rest of the world. The northern hemisphere is roughly the land hemisphere of the world, and possibly the site of the origin of birds. The outposts of the great Eurasian and North American land masses, best seen on a polar projection map, are New Zealand, Australia, Africa, and South America. Each of these regions is noted for the large number of resident species which are found nowhere else on earth today. This fact is a logical consequence of the long-continued isolation of these regions either by climatic barriers, like that of the Sahara desert, or by broad water barriers.

A look at the history of American land mammals illustrates this point. Geologists believe that for perhaps 50 to 70 millions of years North and South America were separated by a water gap. The two continents were united by the Isthmus of Panama only a few million years ago. Until they were united, North America had 27 families of land mammals, South America 29 families; but the two Americas had only one or two of these families in common. After the rising isthmus joined the two continents, they exchanged mammals freely, so that by the Pleistocene epoch, a million years ago, they had 22 families in common (Simpson, 1940). Since many birds can and do fly across broad water gaps, they are not as hemmed in geographically as are mammals. Nevertheless, the distribution of birds in North and South America shows distinct similarities to that of mammals.

An interesting case study in the historical geography of North American birds has been made by Mayr (1946). Not only have North and South America been separated by water until recently, but North America and Asia were at several different times joined by a 2000-kilometer broad land-bridge across Bering Strait during the Tertiary Period (10 to 75 million years ago), during which time modern bird families were evolving. During much of the Tertiary, this land-bridge enjoyed a mild climate, which may have permitted even tropical species, such as parrots, to cross over into North America from the Old World.

As a consequence of past changes in climate and barriers, North America today has an avifauna which represents a variety of origins. Because of their wide distribution, or their antiquity in North America, the origins of some birds are at present indeterminable. In this category Mayr places 29 families, including sea birds, water birds, hawks, swifts, woodpeckers, swallows and others. Of the remaining birds, Mayr believes that nearly every temperate zone family of Old World birds has crossed over to North America. There is, significantly, a steady decrease in the percentage of Old World representatives as one travels from Alaska to Florida, where, even today, one-fifth of the residents are of Old World origin. Likewise, there is a progressive decrease in South American elements as one travels from Florida to Alaska. The traffic in this direction was much feebler, however. Not a single species of known South American origin has crossed over to Asia, and only a half dozen or so North American genera have done so.

As a rule, the Old World forms in North America tend to be non-migratory species, the South American forms migratory. Among the North American families that Mayr considers Old World immigrants are the pheasants, pigeons, cuckoos, owls, kingfishers, larks, shrikes, corvids, thrushes, titmice, nuthatches, creepers, and pipits. Among those invading North America from Central and South America are 15 families, including hummingbirds, toucans, manakins, cotingas, tyrant flycatchers, vireos, wood warblers, icterids, and tanagers. Forms that have originated within North America include perhaps 13 families, represented by American vultures, turkeys, motmots, waxwings, Mimidae, and wrens. Evidence indicates that European wrens and dippers originated in North America.

The study of long-term changes in sea level presents evidence of drastic, worldwide fluctuations. Between 17,000 and 6000 years ago, the melting of North American and Scandinavian glaciers poured sufficient water into the seas to raise the general level 100 meters, with upward surges of as much as 10 meters per century (Fairbridge, 1960). Such changes as these clearly must have flooded broad expanses of low-lying lands, and created new water gaps between formerly contiguous areas.

The islands of Sumatra, Java, and Borneo are separated from each other and from the mainland of Malaya by water less than 50 meters deep. When the seas were lower during periods of Pleistocene glaciation, these lands were all united into a single mass. As a consequence, the birds of all three islands today show considerable similarity, particularly the woodpeckers, barbets, cuckoos, and babbling thrushes. In the chain of islands east of Java, a deep but narrow strait (Wallace's Line) separates Bali from Lombok. Apparently this water gap is an ancient one that persisted even during periods of low sea levels. Consequently, birds to the west of this strait in Bali, Java, Sumatra, and Borneo have Asiatic affinities, while those of Lombok and islands to the east have progressively stronger Australian and Papuan relationships. Here the trogons, hornbills, barbets, woodpeckers, and broadbills of the western islands disappear, and the cockatoos, lorikeets, whistlers, and honey-eaters of the eastern islands take over.

Birds living on long- and widely-isolated oceanic islands illustrate a special aspect of zoogeographical adjustment. As a result of millennia of protective insulation from competition with large numbers of mainland birds, they have lost the genetic adaptability to cope with introduced species, and show a striking vulnerability to competition. Mayr (1954) points out that although island birds constitute less than 20 per cent of all species, yet of all the birds which have become extinct in historic times, over 90 per cent were island species. Apparently, the introduced species, which evolved on larger land areas amidst more rigorous competition, dominated and supplanted the island forms because of their superior evolutionary experience.

During the Tertiary and Quaternary

periods, earth climates fluctuated greatly. Periods of glaciation not only concentrated much of the earth's water in enormous continental ice masses and thus lowered sea level, but also caused many north temperate zone birds to shift their ranges southward toward the tropics. Other species were undoubtedly extinguished on a catastrophic scale. Later, as the climate moderated and glaciers melted, birds could either extend their ranges northward again, or upward on mountain ranges into corresponding life zones. That both types of range extension occurred is seen today in the discontinuous distribution of many species. The Azure-winged Magpie, *Cyanopica cyanus*, has one subspecies that lives in the mountains of Spain and Portugal, while another subspecies, its nearest relative, lives in brushy thickets along rivers of southeastern Siberia (Stresemann, 1927–34). In other words, certain species were left "high and dry" in the southern mountains as the glaciers withdrew to the north, pulling the lowland representatives north with them. Today, in the mountains of Guatemala, there are isolated populations of North American ravens, crossbills, flickers, creepers, bluebirds, and juncos left behind, in effect, by receding glaciers

(Griscom, 1945). Such isolated populations are known as *relicts*.

Discontinuous distribution may also result when a species surmounts a barrier that confines it. Aside from marine and seasonally coastal species, there are only two species of birds represented by breeding populations in both South America and Africa that are restricted to these two continents. These are two species of tree ducks of the genus *Dendrocygna*. Such a pattern of distribution can be explained only by assuming that these birds flew or were storm-driven across the south Atlantic (Friedmann, 1947).

A range of a species may also be fragmented into two or more isolated regions by movements of the earth's crust. The geologically recent upthrust of the Andes mountains has split apart numerous populations of tropical birds in Colombia and Ecuador, so that today their descendants occupy ranges on opposite sides of the mountains. With sufficiently long isolation from each other, such populations will eventually evolve into different races or species. The ornate Cock-of-the-Rock, *Rupicola peruviana*, is, for example, represented on the Pacific side of the Andes by the subspecies *R. p. sanguinolenta*, and on

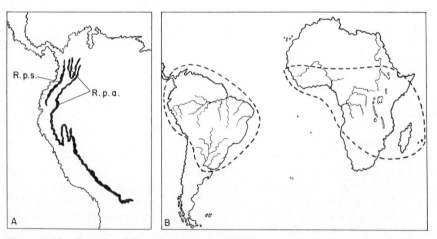

Figure 20.13. Examples of discontinuous geographic distribution. *A*, The Cock-of-the-Rock, a cotinga, has been split by the rising Andes Mountains into two sub-species: *Rupicola peruviana sanguinolenta* is restricted to regions west of the Andes, while *R. p. aurea* is found only in the central valleys and east slopes of the Andes. After Chapman. *B*, The White-faced Tree Duck, *Dendrocygna viduata*, a fresh water species, occurs only in the tropical regions of South America and Africa—a fact that can be explained only by assuming transatlantic dispersal. After Phillips, *in* Stresemann.

the Amazon side by *R. p. aurea* (Chapman, 1917). The fresh water fishes in the streams of the opposite sides of the Andes show similar affinities.

Although mountain ranges may isolate species, mountain passes may provide bridges to join them. Chapman describes a pass in the Andes at San Antonio, Colombia, where the tropical zone of the Cauca Valley practically reaches the divide. Here one can see a large reservoir of tropical bird species ready to spill over into a new and enlarged range as soon as the mountains sink a few hundred meters or climatic changes cause the tropical zone to rise an equal amount.

MAN'S INFLUENCE

Today, the environmental force that has the harshest and most far-reaching impact on bird distribution is man. In a very few instances man's cultural interference with the natural environment has encouraged the spread of species. His parks and lawns have increased the numbers and dominance of the American Robin, *Turdus migratorius;* his barns, for a time, the Barn Swallow, *Hirundo rustica;* his chimneys, the Chimney Swift, *Chaetura pelagica.* The spread of the Barn Owl, *Tyto alba,* throughout New York State, has been attributed to the adoption of mechanical refrigeration and the abandonment of old ice houses.

But in the main, man has been a force for restriction and extermination. Natural prairies, woods, ponds and streams, once teeming with bird life, have been converted into relatively sterile agricultural or urbanized environments, ecologically unsuitable for most native birds. In addition to the vast areas of virgin prairies and forests converted into cities and farms, additional land has been requisitioned for such arteries of transportation and communication as highways, railroads, electric power and telephone lines, and gas and oil pipelines. The amount of land in the United States devoted to rights-of-way for utility corporations alone has been estimated by Egler (1958) to be greater than the area of all six New England states!

Man's environment-modifying tools are powerful, pervasive, and destructive: gang-plows, power-reapers, ditch-diggers, earthmovers, paving machines, chain-saws, and power-sprayers. Forest fires, soil erosion, and water pollution contribute further to the destruction of natural habitats. Livestock and introduced pests also add to the deterioration of wild habitats. That byword for an extinct species, the flightless Dodo, *Raphus* sp., was sent on its way by the pigs, dogs, cats, and rats introduced by man on the Mascarene Islands.

Occasionally, man has tried to atone for his ecologic misdeeds by importing foreign species. Usually, only the less desirable species seem to establish themselves. The worst failures have been in experiments with introductions on oceanic islands. There used to be 68 species of native land birds on the Hawaiian Islands. Sixty per cent of these birds have become extinct since man and his camp followers have "civilized" the islands (Greenway, 1958).

Even without man, of course, the bright tapestry of bird geography will continue to be alternately torn and mended by the wearing and restorative forces of nature. But since man has willy-nilly taken a hand in the process, we must hope that he will acquire sufficient wisdom to provide refuge for the most threatened species before they, too, go the way of the Dodo.

SUGGESTED READINGS

Although published in 1876, Wallace's *The Geographical Distribution of Animals* still remains the classic in animal geography. For charts showing the world distribution of all the principal living families of birds, see Bartholomew's *Atlas of Zoogeography.* A splendid pictorial book with considerable geographic information is Gilliard's *Living Birds of the World.* An extensive treatment of threatened and extinct species is found in Greenway's *Extinct and Vanishing Birds of the World.* The best modern treatment of the principles of animal geography is probably Darlington's *Zoogeography: The Geographical Distribution of Animals.*

TWENTY-ONE

Flight

Birds are called Aves because they have no definite paths but wander through all pathless (avia) ways.

Isadore of Seville, *ca.* 570–636 A.D.

When the anthropologist Hortense Powdermaker recently surveyed native school children of Northern Rhodesia and asked them, given a free choice, what they most wanted to be, nearly half of the boys wanted to be birds. Almost half of the girls wanted to be boys, but about one quarter of the girls wished that they, too, might become birds (*Scientific American*, 196(1):60–62). This resounding vote of confidence in the avian way of life probably revealed a discontent with, and a desire to escape from, the lacks and tribulations of the youngsters' earth-bound lives.

The reptilian forerunners of birds, through the evolution of wings and feathers, achieved the children's goal of avoiding many problems that plague ground-dwellers. It seems reasonable to assume that food played a dominant part in the evolution of flight. Enlarged opportunities to secure food, particularly flying insects, and easy escape from hungry, earth-borne predators, very likely provided primitive flying birds with enough selective survival to bring about rapid evolutionary refinements in flight. These advantages, plus many others made possible through the conquest of air—rapid travel across great expanses and over otherwise impenetrable barriers, safer living and breeding quarters, seasonal migration—have made birds the lively, successful vertebrates that we know today.

ORIGIN OF FLIGHT

It seems a far cry from cold-blooded, groveling reptiles to warm-blooded, flying birds, but all evidence indicates that modern birds descended from reptiles. Fossil forms linking reptiles to birds have been too few to show exactly how the front leg of a lizard-like reptile became modified into the wing of a bird. The fossils of *Archaeopteryx*, the first known bird, show unmistakably that it walked on its large hind legs and balanced the fore part of its body with its long, bony tail. This stance released the smaller front legs from walking and enabled them to become modified into wings for use in flapping or gliding flight.

Two theories have been advanced to explain how this was brought about. Nopsca (1907) assumed that the reptilian proavian ran on the ground, flapping its front legs in the air, much as does a running and flapping barnyard chicken. The reptilian scales on the rear margins of the front limbs gradually lengthened and broadened into avian feathers, as natural selection, through many millenia, favored those individuals with longer, slightly airborne strides and, therefore, speedier locomotion. In time, according to this theory, the wings evolved sufficiently to bear the entire weight of the bird in the air. The other theory, proposed by Marsh (1880), Osborn (1900), Abel (1911), Heilmann (1927), and others, assumed that the bipedal reptile took to clambering about in the trees, leaping from limb to limb, gliding from one tree to another, and eventually perfected flapping flight. The prominent claws on the "fingers" of the front limbs or wings of *Archaeopteryx*, and the backward-directed hind toe on each of its feet suggest strongly that the bird was arboreal. However, it lacked the keel and breast muscles needed for sustained flapping flight, so the bird probably was able only to glide downward, as do flying squirrels.

PHYSICAL PRINCIPLES OF FLIGHT

The flapping flight of birds is exceedingly complex, and not well understood. However, the gliding flight of birds is much like that of the airplane, and both are subject to the same laws of aerodynamics. The following discussion of aerodynamic principles is based chiefly on Storer's (1948) *The Flight of Birds.*

When a drop of water or other fluid falls through the air, it is shaped by the friction and pressures of the resisting air into a "tear-drop" or streamlined form, a shape with less resistance or "drag" than an equal volume of some other shape. Forms with such contours—blunt and rounded in front and tapering, more or less, to a point in the rear—are found in the bodies of most birds. This is also true of fishes, which likewise face the problem of passing through a resisting, fluid medium. However, slipping through the air efficiently is not enough to make flight possible. The bird must also be supported by the air, and it must have "oars" or "propellers" to gain a purchase on the air to thrust its body forward. These are the functions of the bird's wings. Each wing, moreover, like a bird's body, is streamlined in cross-section.

When the leading edge of a streamlined form, such as a wing, cleaves the air "head on," it thrusts the air upward and downward so that the resultant movement of the air reduces its pressure equally on both the upper and lower surfaces of the wing. But if the contours on the two surfaces of a wing differ from each other, the air pressures against them will be unequal, because one air stream must travel farther and, therefore, faster than the other, and this will reduce its pressure on the wing surface. If, for example, the lower surface of the wing is flattened or made concave, and thus shortened in breadth, the air here will not be thrust aside as much as before, and therefore its pressure against the under side of the wing will be greater than that on the longer, convex, upper surface.

This difference in wing contours will result in an increased pressure against the under surface, and a partial vacuum over the upper surface, or in a net vertical lifting force at right angles to the surface of the wing. It is this lifting force that makes flight possible. Furthermore, if the leading edge of the wing is tilted upward with reference to its direction of forward motion (the angle of tilt being known as the "angle of attack"), lift will be increased. This results not so much from increased pressure on the lower surface of the wing as from decreased pressure on its upper surface. In a typical airplane wing the upper surface provides about three-quarters of the lift.

An inclined flat plane, moving through still air, will create some lift, and also some drag. If the plane is "cambered," or curved, so that it is concave below and convex above, it will create more lift. If it is both cambered and streamlined, it creates the greatest lift with the least drag (Fig. 21.1). Drag is, of course, the backward force opposing the wing's motion through the resistant air. Both lift and drag vary according to the wing's area, shape, velocity, and angle of attack.

As long as air flows smoothly over the longer, upper surface of a wing, it creates lift; and, within limits, the greater the angle of attack, the greater the lift, and also the greater the drag. At a given speed, a wing operates at maximum efficiency at that angle of attack which gives the highest lift-to-drag ratio. But when the angle of attack reaches about 15 degrees to the direction of the wing's motion through the air, it becomes too steep. Then the air stream begins to separate from the wing's upper surface and becomes turbulent, and

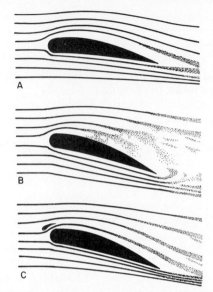

Figure 21.2. Smoke tunnel diagrams of a wing, or airfoil, at different angles of attack, moving through the air toward the left. *A,* In normal flight at a low angle of attack, the air streams smoothly over the upper surface of the wing and creates lift. *B,* At too steep an angle of attack, air passing over the wing becomes turbulent, lift disappears, and a stall develops. *C,* A wing-slot may prevent stalling turbulence by directing a layer of rapidly moving air close to the upper surface of the wing.

lift disappears. For a given wing, this point at which lift vanishes is known as its stalling angle.

Since lift also varies with speed, a given load can be carried at high speed with a small angle of attack, or at a lower speed with a larger angle of attack. Nevertheless, velocity may be reduced to a point below which the smooth airflow is disrupted, and stalling occurs regardless of the angle of attack. This speed is called the stalling speed. The stalling angle of a given wing can be increased somewhat, and hence the stalling speed can be lowered, if the air flow over the upper surface of the wing can be prevented from breaking away and creating turbulence. Wing slots achieve this effect. For example, an open slot along the front edge of a wing can be so designed as to direct, over the top of the wing, a stream of rapidly moving air, which will prevent break-away turbulence at the normal stalling angle of attack. The alula of a

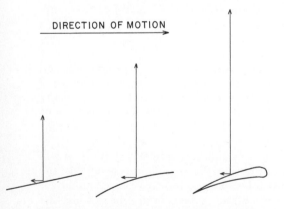

DIRECTION OF MOTION

Figure 21.1. Efficiencies of an inclined plane, a cambered plane, and an airfoil, moving through the air. Vertical arrows represent lift; horizontal arrows, drag. The cambered airfoil has by far the greatest lift-to-drag ratio. After Sutton.

bird's wing acts in this way. Flaps hanging diagonally downward from the trailing edge of a wing have the same function. Such accessories as these enable airplanes and birds to take off and land at steeper angles of attack, and therefore at slower speeds, than would otherwise be possible.

When the air on the under side of a wing slips out from under the trailing edge, it tends to swirl upward into the low pressure area above the wing and thus create a sheet of eddies, which disrupt the smooth flow of air across the wing's upper trailing edge. This lift-destroying, drag-creating turbulence is particularly strong and ex-

tensive near the wing-tips, where it is called tip vortex. One way of minimizing these disturbances is to lengthen wings so that the tip vortices are widely separated, since this makes a proportionately larger area of wing between them where the air can flow smoothly. Long wings are thus more efficient than short, stubby wings, but, naturally, not as strong. The ratio of the length to the width of the wing is known as its aspect ratio, long narrow wings having a high aspect ratio. Sailplanes and albatrosses may have aspect ratios as great as 18:1. The extreme efficiency of such long wings is seen in their high lift-to-

Figure 21.3. Long, narrow wings are efficient in producing lift with little drag, and are characteristic of rapid fliers. The bird shown is the European Sand Martin. Photo by E. Hosking.

drag ratio, which may be as high as 40:1. That is, for every 40 grams of vertical lift there is only one gram of resistance to forward motion (Jameson, 1960). Small wings are less efficient than large wings of the same design, because a larger proportion of the small wing's surface will be in the inefficient zones of edge and tip turbulence. Therefore, proportionately large wings are more necessary to small airplanes and small birds than to larger ones.

Another characteristic that influences a wing's performance is wing area in relation to the weight that must be carried. This area-to-weight ratio is known as *wing-loading* or span loading. In general, the larger this ratio (i.e., the larger the wings in proportion to the load carried), the less power needed to sustain flight. A light sailplane with large wings needs much less power to keep aloft than a heavy, small-winged, fighter plane.

BIRD AS A FLYING MACHINE

In Chapter 1 it was pointed out that, in order to fly, a bird must solve two basic problems: the reduction of weight and the increase of power. There is more to flight than this, of course. A bird must have wings for support and propulsion through the air. However, most of the anatomical and physiological differences that set birds apart from other vertebrates seem to be adaptations devoted to the solution of these two problems. These adaptations were considered in more detail earlier. It is enough here to list the most important ones.

WEIGHT-REDUCING ADAPTATIONS

Thin, hollow bones.
Extremely light feathers.
Elimination of most skin glands.
Elimination of teeth and heavy jaws.
Elimination of tail vertebrae and some digits.

Extensive bone fusion, especially in the pectoral and pelvic girdles and vertebral column.
A system of branching air-sacs.
Oviparous rather than viviparous reproduction.
The atrophy of gonads between breeding seasons.
The eating of concentrated foods.
Rapid and efficient digestion.
The excretion of uric acid instead of urine.

POWER-INCREASING ADAPTATIONS

Warm-bloodedness.
Heat-conserving plumage.
An energy-rich diet.
Rapid and efficient digestion.
High glucose content of the blood.
A four-chambered heart which provides double circulation.
Rapid and high-pressure circulation.
A highly efficient respiratory system.
Breathing movements synchronized with wing beats.
A high rate of metabolism.

In addition to these adaptations, there are others that conserve power through promoting clean aerodynamic design in the bird's body; this design permits the bird to pass through the air smoothly with little friction, and with a high degree of stability. The streamlining of the body, wings, and even the individual primary wing feathers contributes greatly toward this end. Most organs and the heaviest muscles are centrally placed between and beneath the wings, providing an automatic stability which requires little muscular correction. For example, one muscle that flexes the wrist keeps its weight near the body by originating above the elbow but inserting its tendon beyond the wrist where the action takes place. The supracoracoideus muscle, which elevates the wing, is not situated (as is the corresponding muscle in a reptile or mammal) beside the backbone. Instead, it is inserted ventrally on the sternum, and produces its lifting action through a pulley-like slip high in the shoulder girdle. Similarly, many of the muscles of the legs are concentrated near the body and carry out their functions by means of long, string-like tendons which activate the extremities. Such central placement of the heavy muscles of the wings and legs greatly reduces their moment of inertia and, therefore, the work required to move them.

Various skeletal adaptations related to flight have already been mentioned. Probably one of the earliest modifications was the development of bipedal locomotion, which released the fore-limbs for flight. This required a shortening of the long reptilian body axis so that the hind feet could be placed under the center of gravity. The long and heavy reptilian tail was reduced to a tiny vestige—the pygostyle. The pelvic girdle was lengthened and fused to the vertebral column so that it protects and supports the visceral organs, provides mechanically advantageous sites for the origin of heavy leg muscles, and gives strength and rigidity for withstanding the shocks of leaps and landings.

The sternum, as remodeled, now provides similar protection and support on the under side of the body, and its keel furnishes ample room and suitable leverage for attachment of the breast muscles. The powerful, wing-flapping contractions of these muscles might crush the rib cage were it not for the development of stout coracoid bones, which brace the wings and shoulder girdles against this compressive force. The neck in birds has become highly mobile, taking over several functions of arms and hands. These and many less profound modifications in the skeleton have kept pace with the most fundamental adaptation of all, the development of the forelimbs into wings.

ADAPTIVE STRUCTURE OF WINGS

Relieved of their ancestral job of walking on the ground, the forelimbs of birds have become strikingly modified for supporting the body in air. Their attachment to the body has been moved dorsally and posteriorly so as to be located nearly over the body's center of gravity. The new motions required for flight have resulted in several major changes. The humerus is oriented in its shoulder socket so that the wing's chief movement is up and down rather than forward and backward, although it is still capable of considerable rotation. At rest, the wing can be folded into a compact Z against the body, out of harm's way. The elbow joint has become a hinge joint which permits movement of the forearm only in the plane of the wing. This stiffens the entire extended wing into a plane, which resists twisting when exposed to air pressures. The total length of the wing has been increased to accommodate enough flight feathers to support the bird in the air. However, in different birds the various segments of the wing are not lengthened proportionately. In the hummingbird, the bones of the hand are longer than those of the upper arm and forearm together; in the frigate bird, all three segments of the arm skeleton are about equal in length; in the albatross, the humerus, or upper arm, is the longest segment. These varying proportions in wing length are associated with different modes of flight. The ulna of the forearm, in all birds but the kiwis, is now a stout bone on whose posterior margin the secondary wing feathers are attached.

The hand, no longer concerned with walking, climbing, or manipulating objects, has been drastically changed. It supports the large primary feathers, whose chief functions are to propel and maneuver the bird in flight. The almost fleshless hand has been simplified through a reduction in the number of its bones and a fusion and flattening of those remaining. The carpal bones of the wrist have been reduced from 5 to 2; the digits, from 5 to 3; the thumb has disappeared completely. The second digit supports the alula and is independently movable. The third and fourth digits, which support the primary feathers, are partly fused together, and their segments or phalanges flattened, fused, and reduced in number. The hand bones, in short, are nearly reduced to a rigid, flat paddle on whose rear margin are supported the all-important flight primaries.

Stretching along the front edge of the wing, from the shoulder to the wrist, is a triangular elastic membrane, the patagium. This tough membrane acts as a gliding plane, and also partly controls the movements of the larger wing feathers. A similar flat membrane extends along the rear of the wing from the shoulder to the elbow.

As seen earlier on page 92, when any object increases in size, its surface increases as the square, and its mass as the cube, of its linear dimensions. This means that large, heavy birds should have proportionately larger wings, or more efficient wings, than small birds. As a bird increases in size, wing area does not keep up with weight. Because of the great moment of inertia in large wings, and the problem of making them strong enough for flight without making them too heavy, flying birds much larger than a condor are probably a physical impossibility.

One might suppose that in an ideal bird, regardless of its size, there should be a fairly constant wing-loading ratio. This is far from true. Wing-loading among the different species of birds may vary by a factor of as much as 19. This is not surprising when one considers the variable size and efficiency of wings, the variation in wing-beat frequency and amplitude, the different types of flight (flapping, soaring, hovering) and the periodic variations in the weight of a given bird. Table 21.1, taken from Poole (1938) gives wing-loading data for representative North American species. Wing areas are based on the two outstretched wings but not the tail.

The table clearly shows that the heavier birds have a higher wing-loading (fewer square centimeters of surface per gram weight) than the lighter ones. This probably means that the larger birds approach the absolute limit of wing-loading. Because of the anatomical and physiological extravagance of extremely large wings, large birds cannot afford the luxury of the generous margin of safety that small birds can. The large wings of small birds also

Table 21.1. Wing-Loading in Representative North American Birds
(after Poole)

SPECIES	WEIGHT (GMS.)	WING AREA (SQ. CM.)	WING AREA PER GM.
Ruby-throated Hummingbird, *Archilochus colubris*	3.0	12.4	4.2
House Wren, *Troglodytes aëdon*	11.0	48.4	4.4
Black-capped Chickadee, *Parus atricapillus*	12.5	76.0	6.1
Barn Swallow, *Hirundo rustica*	17.0	118.5	7.0
Chimney Swift, *Chaetura pelagica*	17.3	104.0	6.0
Song Sparrow, *Melospiza melodia*	22.0	86.5	3.9
Leach's Petrel, *Oceanodroma leucorhoa*	26.5	251.0	9.5
Purple Martin, *Progne subis*	43.0	185.5	4.3
Redwinged Blackbird, *Agelaius phoeniceus*	70.0	245.0	3.5
Starling, *Sturnus vulgaris*	84.0	190.3	2.2
Mourning Dove, *Zenaidura macroura*	130.0	357.0	2.4
Pied-billed Grebe, *Podilymbus podiceps*	343.5	291.0	0.8
Barn Owl, *Tyto alba*	505.0	1683.0	3.4
Common Crow, *Corvus brachyrhyncos*	552.0	1344.0	2.4
Herring Gull, *Larus argentatus*	850.0	2006.0	2.4
Peregrine Falcon, *Falco peregrinus*	1222.5	1342.0	1.1
Mallard, *Anas platyrhynchos*	1408.0	1029.0	0.7
Great Blue Heron, *Ardea herodias*	1905.0	4436.0	2.3
Common Loon, *Gavia immer*	2425.0	1358.0	0.6
Golden Eagle, *Aquila chrysaëtos*	4664.0	6520.0	1.4
Canada Goose, *Branta canadensis*	5662.0	2820.0	0.5
Mute Swan, *Cygnus olor*	11602.0	6808.0	0.6

compensate for the relatively large proportions of their wing areas devoted to inefficient margins. For these two reasons, small birds tend to have large wings and light wing loads. If a Mute Swan, *Cygnus olor,* had the same wing-loading as a Barn Swallow, *Hirundo rustica,* its two wings would have 81,000 square centimeters of surface instead of an actual 6800. If these giant wings were designed with the same aspect ratio as those of the swallow (figured at the conservative ratio of 6:1), each wing would be seven meters long, and the bird's total wing span would be over 14 meters (46 feet)! The structural, mechanical, and physiological absurdity of such wings is evident.

FUNCTIONS OF WINGS

Wings of birds vary in shape as well as in size, and both characteristics are intimately related to function, habitat, and niche. Wings have been classified under four major types by Savile (1957). *Elliptical* wings are found on birds adapted to forested or shrubby habitats where birds must maneuver in close quarters. Such wings have a low aspect ratio and a somewhat reduced tip vortex. Associated with the slow flight that is often advantageous in such habitats, many elliptical wings have a high degree of slotting, especially in the form of separated primaries. Elliptical wings are found in most gallinaceous species as well as in many doves, woodpeckers, and passerines, especially the Corvidae. *High speed* wings are characteristic of birds that feed on the wing or make long migrations. Such wings have a low camber (flattish profile) and a fairly high aspect ratio. They taper to a rather slender tip, without slots; and they show the sweep-back and "fairing" to the body of modern fighter-plane wings. Such wings are found in shore birds, swifts, hummingbirds, falcons, and swallows. Savile's third type is the *high-aspect ratio* wing, most commonly found in such soaring sea birds as albatrosses and frigate birds. These long

and narrow wings rarely have wing-tip slotting. The *slotted high-lift* wing is the fourth type. It possesses a moderate aspect ratio, deep camber, and marked slotting. Characteristic species are terrestrial soaring birds, such as vultures and hawks, owls, and predators which carry heavy loads.

To illustrate one way in which different types of wings suit different ways of living, Storer (1948) compares two birds of roughly equal weight but different ways of life. A Great Blue Heron, *Ardea herodias,* uses its long legs to wade in marshes where it stalks its prey. In alighting, it must take care to land slowly and carefully to avoid damaging its legs. The wings of the heron are deeply cambered and, for such a large bird, generous in size, with a cm.-per-gm. value of 2.3. The Common Loon, *Gavia immer,* on the contrary, is a heavy diving bird of open lakes. Large wings would only be a mechanical embarrassment under water. However, with its extremely small wings, giving it a wing-loading value of 0.6, the Loon must fly rapidly to sustain itself in air. Hovering to a gentle landing is out of the question. In alighting, the bird must dissipate the momentum of its flight in a long, splashing glide over the surface of the water.

To perform its two basic functions, propulsion and lift, the typical wing must drive the body through the air and must also support it there. Its construction is adapted to these requirements. It is thickest at its leading edge, and tapers to a thin edge at the rear. At the wing's leading edge, bones give it rigidity and strength, while covert feathers, standing perpendicularly to the wing's surface, give the wing a rounded and smooth streamlining. The upper surface of the wing is convex in cross-section; the lower surface is concave, like the cambered wing of an airplane. In flight, this shape causes a partial vacuum above the wing and pressure below, creating lift. Such cambering is especially pronounced in slow fliers. Since the trailing edge of a wing is more flexible than the leading edge, it bends upward under air pressure from below, resulting (as in a propeller blade) in *pitch*, which drives the bird forward with each downward wing beat.

Flight feathers are also streamlined in cross section, particularly those primaries that meet the air on edge. The stiff quill or rachis of each feather lies not in its middle but toward the leading edge. The leading vane is thicker and narrower, and the trailing vane thinner and wider.

Feathers overlap each other somewhat like the shingles on a roof, so that the firm, leading edge of one feather lies above the more flexible trailing edge of the feather in front. This arrangement provides a surface relatively impermeable to air on the down stroke, but one that may open like a venetian blind on the upstroke to let air slip through.

Unlike the wing of an airplane, the wing of a bird is both a wing and a propeller. The hand, with its large primaries, does most of the propelling; the forearm, with its secondaries, provides most of the lift. In flight, the hand is the most active member, moving through a slanting oval, or a figure 8, while the upper arm and forearm move very little. As a rule, propelling force is developed only during the approximately vertical movements of the wing.

The relative importance of the hand and its primaries was revealed by an experiment of Chapeau (Stresemann, 1927–1934) in which the removal of only a small portion of the tips of its primaries prevented a dove from flying. On the contrary, removing enough of the arm or secondary feathers to reduce the area of the entire wing by 55 per cent (from 547 square centimeters to 248 square centimeters) still did not keep the bird from flying! This experiment illustrates the extreme importance of the outer ends of the primaries in propelling the bird.

Secondary feathers are characteristically smaller than primaries; otherwise the wing would be too bulky to fold compactly. The number of flight feathers carried by a wing varies. Most birds have 10 primaries on each hand, the outermost usually reduced

in size. Finches, wood warblers, swallows, honey-guides, and others have only nine primaries, while herons, ducks, geese, gulls, and terns have 11, and grebes, storks, and flamingos usually have 12. Greater variability occurs in the number of secondaries carried on the forearm. Most passerines have nine secondaries, but swifts and hummingbirds have only six or seven. Large soaring birds with elongated forearms may have about 20 secondaries, and the Wandering Albatross, *Diomedea exulans*, has 32.

In addition to the primaries, the hand also supports a few small feathers on the thumb or first digit. These constitute the alula or "bastard wing," and function to produce a wing slot during slow, labored flight (Fig. 21.4).

Because of its stiff but elastic construction, a feather under stress does not have the same shape it has while at rest. The relative size and rigidity of different parts of the barbs, which make up the vanes, and of the rachis and quill stiffening the center, provide a remarkably responsive structure for exploiting the air. Air striking an isolated or projecting feather from different directions and with different velocities will cause it to bend up or down or sideways, or to twist on its axis. Ordinarily, the broader, more flexible vane on the trailing edge of a feather bends up more easily than the leading vane when subjected to air pressure from below. This twists the leading edge of the feather downward, producing a propeller pitch, which results in the feather's forward motion with each downstroke.

Barbs of a contour feather are normally inserted on the rachis at an angle slanting outward. Feather resistance against an air stream moving in a direction from the quill toward the tip will cause the linked barbs to bend inward toward the rachis, thus narrowing the vanes. Air moving either crosswise on the feather, or from the tip toward the quill, will cause the barbs, particularly those of the wider, trailing edge, to swing outward and widen the vanes. Barbs are so constructed that they do not

Figure 21.4. An American Robin in slow flight. Note the projecting alula. Photo by G. R. Austing.

easily bend at right angles to the plane of the feather vanes. This mechanism usefully insures that feather vanes will be their widest when wings are outstretched, as in soaring flight or when birds are alighting, and, on the contrary, their narrowest and least air-resistant when wings are partly folded as in rapid flight.

Birds with high-lift, slotted wings have primaries that separate from each other at their outer ends when the wing is under pressure from below, and in this way produce a series of slots. Each projecting feather twists under pressure and acts as an individual propeller blade, or acts as an efficient, narrow wing capable of flight at a high angle of attack. Hawks, owls, ravens, and many other birds have primaries whose veins are narrowed or notched along their outer ends, making feather separation and slot formation easier when required.

Not all the work of flying is done by the wings. Since wings are generally attached slightly in front of a bird's center of gravity, the body tends to trail downward. In flight, the lowered tail is acted upon by the horizontal air stream and is lifted in a compensating fashion. This arrangement constantly provides the tail with a firm "grip" on the air stream for quick maneuvering actions (Stresemann, 1927–1934).

Various actions of the tail—raising, lowering, twisting, opening, and closing—aid the wings in supporting, balancing, steering, and braking the body in flight. Birds with short tails and small wings, such as ducks, are unable to make sharp turns in the air. As a rule, rapid fliers have short tails. Some aquatic birds, such as auks, loons, and grebes, have such stubby tails that their webbed feet are substituted for steering. Stresemann points out that broad-tailed predatory birds, such as eagles and hawks, carry their prey in their talons, posteriorly, under the tail, whereas birds like the pelican, cormorant, or albatross, with well developed wings but meager tails, carry their booty in the beak or esophagus.

GLIDING AND SOARING FLIGHT

In all likelihood, gliding was the original form of bird flight, and it is still the simplest. It requires no propelling energy from the bird itself. It is the form of flight used by an airplane coasting to a landing. The two chief forces acting upon a bird in flight are the pull of gravity on its mass and the resistance of air to its passage. A gliding bird, coasting downward, is simply using its weight to overcome the air resistance to its forward motion.

A soaring bird is one that maintains or even increases its altitude without flapping its wings. It can do this either by gliding in rising currents of air (static soaring), or by exploiting adjacent air currents of different velocities (dynamic soaring). The three chief requirements for successful soaring are large size, light wing-loading, and maneuverability. Large size gives a bird sufficient momentum to carry it through small, erratic air currents without loss of stability or control. Stability and maneuverability, however, are antagonistic qualities, and perfection in both cannot be found in a single bird. The relatively small breast muscles of soaring birds prove that this is an economical method of flying. Some species, such as the vultures and albatrosses, have become so highly adapted to soaring that they fly almost exclusively by this means.

As soaring flight evolved, there developed two distinct types of wings, which function in different ways and are adapted to different habitats. On the one hand are the slotted, high-lift wings of land birds such as condors. These are adapted to slow speed, high altitude, static soaring. On the other hand are the high-aspect ratio wings, represented by those of the albatrosses. These are adapted to high speed, low altitude, dynamic soaring. The line between the two types is not always hard and fast,

and some hawks, for example, practice both types of soaring.

Soaring land birds, static soarers, keep aloft mainly by seeking out and "riding" rising air currents. Of these there are two sorts: *obstruction currents* and convection currents or *thermals*. Obstruction currents are up-drafts caused when a steady or prevailing wind strikes and rises over such objects as hills, buildings, or ships at sea. A wind coming down the lee side of a mountain may strike the plain and rebound in a series of "standing waves," each with an up-draft component.

Thermals are up-drafts caused by the uneven heating of air near the surface of the earth. The air over cities or bare fields heats more quickly than that over forests or bodies of water. Since warm air expands and is therefore lighter, it rises above cooler air. Thermals are generally local disturbances in the form of slender columns or huge "bubbles" of rising air. Extrapolating results of laboratory experiments with convection currents of hot gases, and fluids of different densities, Cone (1962) suggests that these bubbles on which soaring birds fly are slowly rising vortex rings, or doughnut-shaped "thermal shells," similar to the smoke rings that sometimes accompany gas explosions. He postulates that each ring is a circulating mass of air with movement upward through the center of the ring and downward on the outside. Thermals may also occur when an advancing cold front slides under and lifts a mass of warm air. As a rule, thermals rise to greater heights than obstruction currents. Although owls have slotted, high-lift wings, they are not soaring birds, because thermals and dependable winds rarely occur at night when owls are active.

Maneuverability is particularly important to land soarers since the thermals on which they rise are often small and undependable pillars of warm air. In order to circle in tight spirals within these pillars, the birds need short, broad wings—short wings for low inertia and quick, sensitive response to capricious air currents; broad slotted wings for high lift capacity. It is essential, of course, that the rate of gliding

Figure 21.5. The Red-tailed Hawk has the broad, slotted wings characteristic of static soarers. Photo by G. R. Austing.

descent, or *sinking speed*, be no greater than the rate of air rise in the thermal.

Observations from distances as close as five meters, made from a motorless sailplane, showed that the Turkey Vulture, *Cathartes aura,* has a minimum sinking speed of 0.61 meter per second (2.28 kilometers per hour), and the Black Vulture, *Coragyps atratus,* one of 0.79 meter per second (2.83 km./hr.) (Raspet, 1950). For a Turkey Vulture weighing 2.5 kg., such a sinking speed means that either the rising air or, in a calm, the bird itself, must expend 0.017 horsepower in work to keep it aloft. These different sinking speeds of the two species of vultures depend, of course, on differences in wing-loading. These apparently slight differences have striking geographic consequences. The range of the more buoyant Turkey Vulture extends as far into the cool north as southern Canada, but the aerodynamically heavier Black Vulture is restricted to the southern half of the United States and to tropical regions where the warm sun generates many and vigorous thermals.

A bird soaring in tight spirals cannot fly at high speeds. To fly slowly and yet provide enough lift to avoid sinking requires a high angle of attack, and to achieve this without stalling is the land soarer's problem. The efficiency of deeply slotted wings makes possible the combination of low speed and high lift. Each separately extended primary feather acts as a narrow, high-aspect wing set at a very high angle of attack. Such wing construction greatly reduces tip vortices, but the high angle of attack increases drag. However, since drag increases as the square of air speed, it is not a very great problem for slowly flying birds. In that accomplished soarer, the California Condor, *Gymnogyps californianus,* 40 per cent of the wing span is occupied by slots (Storer, 1948). The deeply slotted wings of a Condor, however, would be useless for oceanic flying, because wet feathers could not be smoothly or quickly manipulated.

To suit the demands of the moment, a soaring bird can alter the shape and expanse of its wings by fanning or folding its feathers, by changing the wing-spread, camber, sweep-back or angle of attack.

Such changes allow the bird to select the optimum lift-to-drag ratio for any given speed.

Updrafts occur even over large bodies of water. The rising currents of air formed on the windward sides of waves and swells are used by shearwaters and other small species for water-level soaring and gliding. Gulls commonly soar on the rising obstruction currents caused by ships or seaside cliffs. The ease of soaring and gliding contrasted with the work of wing-flapping seems to have made some gulls lazy. At Woods Hole, Massachusetts, there is a windward embankment which creates updrafts and is used by Herring Gulls, *Larus argentatus*, to glide directly windward to an island two-thirds kilometer off shore where they roost.

"It is amusing to note that, upon failing to reach the roosting place on the first trial, the birds will return to the region of the up-flow (while they still have enough altitude for a quick down-wind glide), rather than flap their wings for the last few hundred feet of the flight. Apparently several minutes of extra soaring time are preferable to a few seconds of wing-flapping" (Woodcock, 1940).

Thermal updrafts occur over water only when the air temperature is colder than the underlying water temperature—a condition likely to occur in the North Atlantic in winter. Under such conditions, gulls may be seen far from land, soaring high in the air. But should a warm front bring in a mass of air warmer than the sea water, convection stops, and the gulls can soar only on obstruction currents or fly by the laborious flapping of their wings. In relatively calm, cold air, these sea thermals are thought to occur in roughly hexagonal, vertical cells, with the updraft in the center and the downdraft around the edges, or *vice versa*. Under these conditions, gulls soar in circles around the edges of the updrafts and glide from one thermal cell to another.

However, with surface winds of about 25 to 40 kilometers per hour, these cells are laid down parallel to the sea's surface, and thus change from columnar cells to linear "strip" or "roll-convection" cells. At these wind velocities, gulls cease to soar in circles and begin soaring in straight lines along the up-welling air currents of adjoining strip cells. At wind velocities of over 45 kilometers per hour, all soaring stops, probably because the pattern of strip cells is destroyed (Woodcock, 1942).

On the seas, thermals are too unreliable, and wave-deflected updrafts too small, irregular, and too near the surface, to sustain a large bird in soaring flight. Fortunately, over wide stretches of the ocean, another and more reliable source of energy is available. Steady winds, such as the trade winds or the "Roaring Forties," blow across the ocean surface. Their friction with the waves causes the lower levels of air to move more slowly than those higher up. As a result, wind velocity gradients are set up: wind just above the waves may be moving at a speed of 32 kilometers per hour, whereas that 20 meters above the surface may be moving at twice that speed.

Soaring sea birds, such as the albatrosses, have learned to exploit this velocity gradient. By gliding sharply downward *with* the wind, from upper, high speed levels to lower, low speed levels, the bird acquires momentum which it applies, after wheeling head-on *against* the wind, toward climbing back up. It is much like a man hopping off a moving bus and using his bus-acquired momentum to run up a slope at the edge of the road. As the climbing bird applies its momentum against the wind, the ever-increasing velocity of the wind, as the bird continues rising, acts, by increasing the bird's air speed, to extend the drive of its momentum until it reaches its original height, circles leeward, and repeats the cycle. This type of flight is known as dynamic soaring. Albatrosses fly almost exclusively by this means, and therefore are most commonly found in the great oceanic wind belts.

The special requirements for dynamic soaring are light wing-loading, low drag, and a relatively high but variable speed. Long, narrow wings with high aspect ratio meet these requirements. The Wandering Albatross, *Diomedea exulans*, with an aspect ratio of about 18 to 1, and a lift-to-drag ratio of about 40 to 1, is reputed to have the greatest wingspread of any living bird—as much as 3.65 meters (12 feet). Although such wings are adapted to rapid flight, they are somewhat less maneuverable than the wide, slotted wings of land soarers, but this slight lack is compensated for by the reliability of sea winds.

FLAPPING FLIGHT

Perhaps one of the most remarkable things about flapping flight is the fact that an inexperienced fledgling can leave the nest and fly successfully on its maiden attempt, although it uses a form of flight so complex as to defy precise analysis. The young of some birds, such as hornbills, swifts, swallows, and wrens, are raised in small, crowded cavities, where flapping their spread wings is out of the question. In spite of this, they are able to fly considerable distances on their first flights. On its first attempt, a young African Bank Martin, *Psalidoprocne holomelaena,* flew continuously for at least six minutes (Moreau, 1940). The young of many burrowing petrels fly with great skill on their initial attempts. Without previous practice, young whale birds and diving petrels leave their burrows and fly as far as 10 kilometers on their maiden flights (Murphy, 1936).

On the other hand, the young of many other species practice flapping their wings before trying true flight. The young Wandering Albatrosses unsteadily hop into the air, flailing their wings, while instinctively facing windward. The young of Gannets, *Morus bassanus,* reared on narrow ledges of precipitous seaside cliffs, sensibly face away from the sea when practicing their wing-flapping. Young Turkey Vultures, *Cathartes aura,* kept in cages too small to allow wing-stretching, were unable to fly at the normal age for lack of practice, or perhaps because captivity prevents normal development.

The difficulties of understanding flapping flight are apparent when one considers the variables involved. A beating wing is flexible and yields under pressure. The shape, expanse, camber, sweepback, and even the positions of individual feathers may change pronouncedly. Not only are the frequencies and amplitudes of wingbeats subject to change, but different parts of the wing change in velocity and angle of attack even during a single beat. Further, the forces of inertia and air pressure change as a bird accelerates in taking off, or brakes in alighting. All told, this is a formidable list of variables. Nevertheless, some of the principles of flapping flight have been discovered, largely through high speed photography.

The popular notion that wing-flapping is a sort of swimmer's breast stroke pushing downward to support the bird in the air, and pushing backward to propel it forward, is not true. When a small bird takes off, the wing moves downward and *forward* on the downstroke. Since the trailing edge of the wing is less rigid than the leading edge, it bends upward under air pressure and forms the entire wing into a propeller which pulls the bird forward through the air, the wing feathers biting the air with their under surfaces. On the return stroke, upward and *backward,* the wing does little or no propelling. It is partly folded against the body, and the hand primaries twist open, much like jalousies, so that the rising wing meets a minimum of air resistance (Fig. 21.6). The upstroke is largely a passive recovery stroke. The wing is then extended and makes another downstroke.

In larger birds, with their slower wing action, the time consumed by the upstroke is too long, and too precious, to waste in neutral "idling." The heavier wing-loading and the greater body inertia to be overcome in taking off require work to be done on both wing strokes. In rising, the wing bends slightly at the wrist and elbow, and the whole arm (humerus) rotates backward at the shoulder joint to such a degree that the all-important primary feathers now push against the air with their upper surfaces and drive the bird forward. At the

Figure 21.6. A Black-capped Chickadee in flight. During the upstroke of the wing, the primary feathers twist and open in a venetian-blind fashion which allows them to slip through the air with little effort. Photo by H. C. Johnson, Hart, Mich.

end of the upstroke the partly flexed arm is rotated forward and extended, producing a rapid backward snap of the primaries, restoring them to the proper more elevated position for the downstroke. The downstroke, as in smaller birds, is a downward and forward pulling action. The entire excursion of the wing tip in a completed down and up beat may be in the form of an oval or a figure 8, slanted down-

ward and forward in the direction of flight. During the hard work of taking off, the wings will beat more vigorously in greater arcs, and in ovals more inclined toward the horizontal. Not only are the wing slots likely to be opened at this time, but the alula is commonly extended and it reduces air turbulence over the unslotted secondaries, creating even more lift. Some birds are said to be unable to take off if their alulas are removed. In taking off, the somewhat vertical position of the body enables the wings to beat in a more nearly horizontal plane and thus produces a more nearly vertical thrust for leaving the ground.

The rate at which birds flap their wings varies inversely with their size. Large vultures flap their wings about once each second. Medium sized birds, including ducks, small hawks, shore birds, doves, and crows, beat their wings two or three times a second (Blake, 1947). Chickadees beat with a frequency of about 30 times per second, an average-sized hummingbird about 40 times, and the smallest hummingbird perhaps 80 times per second (Greenewalt, 1960).

Large birds, whether they flap, glide, or soar, face special launching problems because of their heavy wing-loading and the high moment of inertia in their large wings. Unaided, their wings are incapable of initiating flight. Some birds, like the herons and storks, combine a launching thrust of their long legs with the potential energy afforded by their elevated nesting

Figure 21.7. On the recovery or upstroke the wings are flexed closely against the body, as shown by this Woodcock. Then, at the top of the stroke, they are fully extended to create as much lift and propulsion as possible on the downstroke. Photo by G. R. Austing.

sites. Others build up momentum by running windward on the ground like a condor, or pattering along the surface of the water like a coot or a goose. Albatrosses typically nest on the windward sides of islands where a short downhill run against the wind will see them air-borne. In emergencies, albatrosses, vultures, and other soarers may regurgitate recently eaten food before taking off. In South America, vultures and condors are trapped by baiting enclosures that are too small to provide a runway long enough for the birds to take off. Petrels are so named because, like St. Peter, they "walk" on the water. The smaller petrels head into the wind and glide over the waves, very near the surface, not by flapping their wings but by occasionally pushing against the water with one or both feet.

After a bird levels off in full flight, the wings do not beat as deeply as before, and the strokes are more nearly vertical. The arms become almost stationary, held out horizontally, and the hands do most of the flapping, bending at the wrists. It is now that the two functions of the wing become most obvious. The arm, with its secondary feathers, acts as the wing of an airplane and furnishes lift; the hand, with its primaries, acts as a propeller and provides forward drive, now, however, mainly on the downstroke.

There is great variation in the ways of flying. Some birds fly easily, from the first wing beat, while others labor greatly to gain the air. Some fly with straightforward flapping, while others alternate short periods of flapping with gliding. Woodpeckers exhibit an undulating flight, flapping a few times on the up-curve, and diving on the down-curve with the wings tightly closed against the body. Many birds, in their bizarre courtship flights, gyrate through the air as though intoxicated (perhaps with love). Some loop-the-loop and somersault; others zoom back and forth in arcs like a swinging pendulum; still others essay breath-taking power dives, pulling up abruptly before the object of their attention. A few birds, notably the hum-

Figure 21.8.   While hovering or flying backward, a hummingbird applies power and lift on both up- and downstrokes of the wings. The extreme rotation of the wings at the shoulder sockets makes possible the use of their upper surfaces to provide lift on the upward or recovery stroke. After C. H. Greenewalt.

mingbirds, are able to fly backward a short distance, or to hover in a fixed spot in mid-air.

Hovering flight makes such special demands on the wings that, in the hummingbird, drastic modifications in wing structure have occurred. In its bony structure the wing is almost all hand; the upperarm and forearm are extremely short. The elbow and wrist joints are practically rigid; they make a permanently bent, inflexible framework which can be moved only at the shoulder, but there very freely and in almost any direction (Greenewalt, 1960). In proportion to the body, a hummingbird's wings are average in size; they are thin, flat, and pointed, with no slotting. The entire wing is essentially nothing but a variable pitch propeller.

In hovering flight, the hummingbird's body is slanted upward at about a 45 degree angle with the horizontal, so that the plane of the wingbeat is approximately horizontal. As the wing moves "up" (backward) and "down" (forward), its dorsal and ventral surfaces respectively face alternately downward. An extraordinary amount of rotation in the humerus makes this possible. The wing acts as an oscillating helicopter blade with a steep angle of attack, forcing the air downward with both up and down strokes. Each stroke, then, is a power stroke, which accounts for the fact that in hummingbirds the wing elevator muscles are about one-half as large as the depressor muscles, whereas in a non-hovering bird like the American Robin, *Turdus migratorius*, they are only one-ninth as large (Savile, 1950).

Compared to a rotating helicopter blade, the twisting, vibrating wings of a hummingbird are grossly inefficient and require great power. The comparatively enormous breast muscles and keel of the bird show this. Breast muscles may account for 30 per cent of a hummingbird's total weight. One happy circumstance which helps to alleviate the inefficiences of an alternating, helical flight mechanism is the fact that each wingbeat creates a trailing current of air against which every suc-

Figure 21.9. Like the hummingbird, the male European Nightjar holds his body nearly vertical in hovering flight. This permits using the wings in helicopter fashion. Photo by E. Hosking.

cessive reverse stroke moves, giving it the advantage of working in a higher air velocity, and hence with greater lift. In other words, with each stroke, the bird retrieves from the air some kinetic energy which was created by the preceding antagonistic stroke (Oemichen, 1950). Whatever the high metabolic cost of such flight, it provides superlative maneuverability.

Still another way of saving energy in flight is found in formation flying. Of the many species that fly in flocks of different kinds, a few have learned to fly in a way that saves them appreciable exertion. Pelicans, like many other birds, fly high when going with the wind, and, when flying against the wind, low and near the water where the wind velocity is reduced. But they also save much energy by flying in long files, each bird so spaced as to beat its wings against the rising, swirling wake of the bird immediately in front. They fly in such disciplined ranks that they even beat their wings in unison—the Germans call it "Resonanzflug"—like a line of aerial chorus girls. If the leader stops flapping and begins to glide, the others glide also. In the V-formations of ducks and geese, each bird rests only its inner wing-tip on the rising vortex of the bird in front. Although this is less efficient, it allows each bird better vision of what is ahead. Occasionally the leader of a V drops behind and lets another take its place, no doubt because the lead bird has the more fatiguing job.

For the bird in flight, landing is both more difficult and more dangerous than taking off. The great carnage that occurs, under certain atmospheric conditions, at radio and television towers, high buildings and monuments, and airport ceilometers, emphasizes the fact that abrupt landings can be as destructive to birds as to airplanes. Birds instinctively realize this, and they employ a variety of devices and actions to brake the momentum of their descent to earth.

Although some birds land vertically, helicopter fashion, the majority land obliquely, generally against the wind, and run on the ground or scud over the surface

Figure 21.10. A male European Whinchat alighting. In landing, many birds spread their tails and fan the **air** vigorously with their wings to arrest their momentum. Photo by E. Hosking.

of the water to dissipate harmlessly the kinetic energy of their momentum. Water birds need not land as skillfully as land birds, because the damaging consequences of a miscalculation on water are relatively minor. Some birds, like the woodpeckers, fly below their landing target and use up their kinetic energy in a final up-swing. Just before landing on the ground, a bird usually creates as much resistance against the air stream as it can. It erects its body nearly at right angles to the direction of flight. It opens its alula and creates other slots by spreading the wings and tail. In the last meter or so of flight, wings are vigorously fanned against the air. Water birds spread their extended webbed feet against the onrushing air. Among land birds, the legs are stretched forward to absorb the shock of first impact with the ground; and in larger species, the head may continue to move earthward so as to lengthen slightly the period of abrupt deceleration.

FLYING SPEEDS, DISTANCES AND HEIGHTS

Numerous tables have been compiled of the flying speeds of different birds, but often the data are unreliable because they have been gathered by imprecise methods, or the observer has not taken into account such modifying factors as assisting or hindering winds, age and health of bird, state of its plumage, and conditions of escape or pursuit. A rough estimate of the top speeds of many roadside birds can be made by "clocking" them with an automobile speedometer. On a calm day it is a rare bird that can match the cruising speed of a modern car. Most passerines probably fly under 80 kilometers per hour (50 MPH). The maximum speed of the Ruby-throated Hummingbird, *Archilochus colubris*, is nearly 43 kilometers per hour. The Peregrine Falcon, *Falco peregrinus*, perhaps the fastest bird alive, has been timed from an airplane at 290 kilometers per hour. Using stop-watches and telephonic communication over a measured course, Broun and Goodwin (1943) determined the ground speeds of 14 species of hawks and eagles during their southward fall migration, flying on the updrafts over Hawk Mountain, Pennsylvania. The average ground speeds of these birds varied between 42 and 67 kilometers per hour, most of them averaging about 48 kilometers. But these figures tell little of the actual air speed of the birds since they were all flying in variable up-drafts. Sixteen different records for Ospreys, *Pandion haliaetus,* ranged from 32 to 130 kilometers per hour. The speediest individual "was evidently making use of a very strong thermal so that the bird was in reality in steep diving flight without losing altitude." Air speeds of birds can of course be determined by following them in airplanes, but the presence of the airplane itself is a disturbing factor. Ducks so pursued have flown at air speeds of about 90 kilometers per hour. An airplane flying at 145 kilometers per hour

Figure 21.11. A Black-capped Chickadee launches itself with both its legs and its wings. If frightened in mid-flight, this tiny bird can begin to change its course within .03 second. Photo by H. C. Johnson, Hart, Mich.

was overtaken by a mixed flock of small sandpipers flying at an estimated 175 kilometers per hour (110 MPH) or more (McCabe, 1942).

The speed with which a bird can maneuver while in flight probably depends on its size and the rate of its wing beats. In any case, it can be astonishingly rapid. A Black-capped Chickadee, *Parus atricapillus,* was photographed in flight with a series of four stroboscopic flashes, each operating 30 milliseconds later than the one preceding. The first flash apparently frightened the bird, so that by the second flash, 30 milliseconds later, the bird had already begun to take evasive action (Greenewalt, 1955).

There is little point in a bird flying at high altitudes unless it can reap some advantage. The higher a bird flies, the more energy it requires to climb there, the colder it gets, the less air there is to support its wings, and the less oxygen there is to breathe. For most species, the rigorous demands of merely making a living preclude the physiological expense of high altitude flight. A few species, such as the hawks and vultures, fly at high altitudes in their sharp-eyed search for food. A very few species live in high mountains, probably driven there years ago by competition with lowland relatives. The Alpine Chough, *Coracia graculus,* has been found at altitudes around 8200 meters (27,000 feet) on Mt. Everest (Gilliard, 1958). Occasionally, certain birds like Jackdaws, *Corvus monedula,* circle high on rising thermals only to return to earth and repeat the performance over and over, as if playing a game.

In a series of observations from airplanes, Mitchell (1955) found that very few birds flew at altitudes greater than 150 meters. On the average, he encountered birds above this height only once in every 70 hours of daylight flying. Other observations of birds at high altitudes by Carr-Lewty (1943) showed Pink-footed Geese, *Anser brachyrhynchus,* flying at 2100 meters; Mallards, *Anas platyrhynchos,* 1900 meters; Swifts, *Apus apus,* 1000 meters; Wood Pigeons, *Columba palumbus*, 950 meters; and Eurasian Golden Plovers, *Pluvialis apricaria*, Starlings, *Sturnus vulgaris*, Barn Swallows, *Hirundo rustica*, and Rooks, *Corvus frugilegus*, all flying above 610 meters.

Radar scrutiny of nocturnal migrants showed that most passerine winter visitors in Britain fly below 1500 meters, although occasionally small passerines were seen flying at 4200 meters, and rarely at 6400 meters (21,000 feet). By day, the birds tended to fly somewhat lower (Lack, 1960).

Records of long-distance, sustained flying, under natural conditions, are practically impossible to obtain. However, numerous records of transatlantic flights by land birds incapable of resting on the water testify to remarkable flight endurance, even though the birds may have been aided by strong tail-winds. Some sea birds like the Sooty Tern, *Sterna fuscata*, seem unable to spend much time resting on the water without becoming waterlogged and unable to resume flight. Accordingly, their flight must be nearly perpetual except during the breeding season, since that is the only time they are ordinarily found on land. The spectacular overseas migrations of many shore birds, as well as the flights of small passerines across the Gulf of Mexico, are probably made without stopping. Swifts may spend the whole night in the air, flying out to sea to do so. Without question, birds have evolved a state of perfection in flight not yet achieved by man.

FLIGHTLESSNESS

Physiologically, flying is an expensive business, and when the advantages of flight no longer compensate for its cost, wings may atrophy or disappear. As a rule, flightlessness is associated with geographic isolation and the relative absence of predators. These factors probably accounted for the presence of the now extinct Great Auk, *Pinguinis impennis*, in arctic regions, and explain that of penguins in the antarctic.

Similar protective isolation occurs on oceanic islands where the majority of flightless grebes, cormorants, and rails exist. In New Zealand, where land predators were unknown until man introduced them, there is even a flightless Owl Parrot, *Strigops habroptilus*, and only recently the flightless wren, *Xenicus lyalli* became extinct. The dodos and Solitaire (*Raphus* spp.) of the Mascarene Islands were clumsy, flightless birds, and they, too, became extinct when man introduced predators. One species of duck has become flightless—the Flightless Steamer Duck, *Tachyeres brachypterus*, of Patagonia. Its powerful wings are too small for flight, but it uses them side-paddle fashion for swimming on the surface of the water.

A degree of isolation from predators can be secured by adopting nocturnal living, secretive habits, or fleet-footedness. The flightless Kagu, *Rhinochetus jubatus*, of New Caledonia, is active by night and sleeps in crevices or under tree roots by day. The famous wingless Kiwis (*Apteryx* spp.) of New Zealand likewise spend the day resting in their warren-like burrows, and by night wander through the dense forests sniffing out earthworms and insects. Many rails have become flightless, particularly those that have established themselves on oceanic islands. The typical rail is drab-colored, thin, and secretive, able to run like a mouse through reeds or marsh grasses rather than to take flight when alarmed. Many rails are also nocturnal. The large, flightless ratites—ostriches, rheas, emus, and cassowaries—probably survive in the face of moderate predation because of their large size, keen vision, rapid running, and aggressiveness. A New Guinea cassowary can easily disembowel a man or sever his arm with its powerful, kicking legs (Gilliard, 1958).

WALKING, SWIMMING, AND DIVING

Unlike most terrestrial vertebrates, birds are built for two forms of locomotion —walking and flying—and many species, such as the shore birds, have excellent equipment for both forms. They can run and they can fly—in either case skillfully and rapidly. However, as birds became molded to fit different niches, natural selection often specialized and refined the legs at the expense of the wings, or vice versa. This again seems to be a matter of anatomical and physiological economy. Why maintain splendid wings if the legs can do an adequate job? This principle may well explain why good runners fly poorly or not at all. Contrariwise, some of the best fliers, such as the hummingbirds, swifts, and swallows, are all but helpless on their feet.

Sometimes the specialization of legs for one habitat diminishes their usefulness for another. The duck with its widespread legs and webbed feet can only waddle ploddingly when on shore; loons and penguins, with their legs placed far back on the body, can swim and dive magnificently, but they can only walk slowly and awkwardly on land.

Ever since *Archaeopteryx*, most birds probably have been hoppers rather than walkers or runners. Certainly the majority of modern birds are perching birds—

that is, tree dwellers—and the quickest, most effective way to get about in a tree is to hop from one branch to another. The typical perching foot has four toes of medium length, three in front and an opposable single toe behind. The toe segments are about the right lengths to allow the toes to bend snugly around small branches. The tendons that flex the toes slip in grooves and sheaths, which are located outside (anterior to) the knee joint and outside (posterior to) the ankle joint. This guarantees that the tendon will be tightened and the toes flexed around their perch by the weight of the bird as it bends its legs in settling down to roost.

A remarkable device, which automatically maintains a sleeping bird's grip on its perch, is found in the tendons that flex the toes. In the feet, these tendons are located under the toe bones. On the lower surface of each tendon are located hundreds of tiny, firm, hobnail-like projections. When the bird perches on a branch, its weight forces these projections to mesh, ratchetwise, with hard ribs embossed on the inside surface of the adjacent tendon-sheath (Fig. 21.12). As long as the weight of the bird is opposed under its toes by the

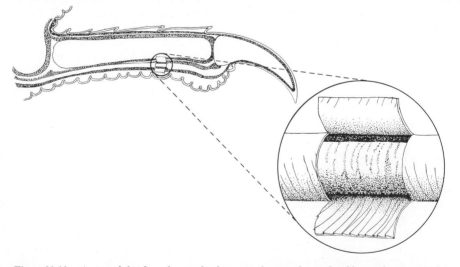

Figure 21.12.   A pigeon's hind toe, longitudinal section, showing the ratchet-like mechanism which holds a sleeping bird on its perch. The weight of the bird, pressing through its toe bones on the underlying tendons, locks them in place in their sheaths when numerous projections on each tendon engage the sharp ridges on the adjacent wall of the sheath.

branch, the tendons will remain locked in their sheaths and the toes will retain their grip.

Many birds have become specialized as tree-trunk creepers: nuthatches, creepers, woodcreepers, woodpeckers and others. These birds typically have short legs with strong, clinging toes, and, in the case of woodpeckers, generally two toes in front and two behind. The creepers, wood-creepers, and woodpeckers have stiff-quilled tail feathers, with acute tips which are used as a prop or third leg to brace the body against the pecking exertions of the head.

Parrots use their beaks as well as their feet in climbing, and, reciprocally, use their feet in eating. A study of 14 species in the National Zoological Park in Washington, D.C. revealed that the majority of the parrots were "left-handed," some of them exclusively so (Friedmann and Davis, 1938).

Walking and running birds, characteristic of steppes and similar open places, usually have long, powerful legs and very short toes. The toes are sometimes reduced in number: the ostrich has only two. Doves, gallinaceous birds, and rails normally accompany each walking step with a sudden forward jerk of the head. The head then remains fixed in space as the body moves forward, until the end of the step. Then the head is thrust forward before the next step is taken. This permits sharper vision than would otherwise be possible, for a steadily moving head cannot see objects—especially other *moving* objects—as clearly as can a head fixed in space (Stresemann, 1927–1934).

A ground-living bird usually has a light but strong pelvic girdle to absorb the shocks of jumping and alighting. Such birds living on soft, yielding earth often have very long toes like the jaçanas, or webbed toes like the coots. Ptarmigan grow special fringe-like scales on the edges of each toe in the winter-time only, when they function to support the bird on soft snow. Sandgrouse have short, thick toes adapted to walking on loose sand. Birds of marshes and shores have long, wading legs. These and many similar modifications show how natural selection has fitted birds' legs for locomotion in a variety of media and substrates.

Running speeds of birds cannot compare with flying speeds. However, an Emu, *Dromiceius novaehollandiae,* can run 50 kilometers per hour; a Ring-necked Pheasant, *Phasianus colchicus,* 34 kilometers per hour; and a Roadrunner, *Geococcyx californianus,* 32 kilometers per hour. Even a two-day-old Piping Plover, *Charadrius melodus,* can run 6.5 kilometers per hour for a distance of 25 meters.

A penguin is not ordinarily considered a land bird. It can travel on land or ice only by walking stiffly upright on its two short legs and tail prop, or by tobogganing on its belly. Nevertheless, penguins have been seen in Antarctica 110 kilometers from the nearest sea. Tracks of walking penguins, which were probably lost birds, have been found over 400 kilometers from the nearest rookery. The track of one small penguin (Adelie?) on the Ellsworth Highland, at an elevation of 1440 meters and over 300 kilometers from the nearest known coastline, was followed for two kilometers. The bird walked upright for two meters and then tobogganed the rest of the way. In the two kilometer path, the bird travelled a straight line, not deviating more than two degrees from a nearly due-south compass bearing (Sladen and Ostenso, 1960).

The adaptations required for swimming and diving are very different from those needed for flight. For paddling in water, legs should be located near the rear (like the engine and propeller of a boat), where the leg muscles interfere least with the streamlining of the body, and where they can best control steering. Legs are so articulated as to thrust easily backward, and their bones are flattened laterally so that they slip through the water with little resistance. Almost all swimming birds have webbed feet. Because of their hollow bones, air sacs, and light, air-imprisoning

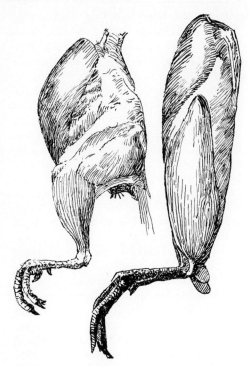

Figure 21.13. The plucked bodies of a pheasant (left) and a loon (right), showing the adaptations for underwater swimming in the latter. After G. Heilmann.

feathers, birds have very low specific gravities. Diving birds, however, are heavier than surface swimmers or good fliers. Penguins, loons, grebes, cormorants, and auks all have relatively solid bones and heavy bodies. Penguins' stomachs commonly contain stones, eaten, perhaps, as ballast to make their bodies heavier and more easily controlled under water.

The body of the typical flying bird is streamlined, broad and blunt in front, tapering to a slender tail. The typical diver's body, on the other hand, is long and cylindrical, with its center of gravity moved rearward. Water is a denser medium than air, and requires a different, more spindle-shaped form of streamlining. As insulation against the heat-absorbing water, many aquatic species have thick layers of subcutaneous fat and thick oily plumage on their ventral sides. Most water birds have large oil glands. Ducks and geese and other surface swimmers have a kind of pocket of waterproof flank feathers, which stick up on the sides of the body and in which the elbows and wrists of the wings may be kept dry while the bird paddles on the surface.

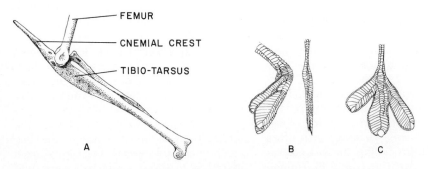

Figure 21.14. Structural adaptations for swimming and diving. *A*, Knee-joint and tibiotarsus of a Red-throated Diver (loon), showing the enormous development of the cnemial crest, on which are attached the powerful extensor muscles of the leg. After Pycraft. *B*, Side and front views of the lobate-webbed foot of the Great Crested Grebe, folded during forward movement in the water. *C*, Front view of the expanded foot during backward movement. Note the unusually thin silhouette of the shank and foot, which offer little more resistance to the water than a knife-edge. *B* and *C* after Barruel.

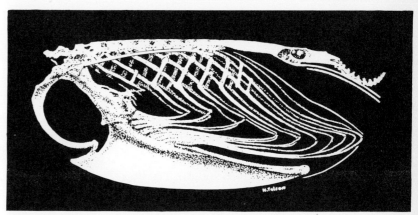

Figure 21.15. The trunk skeleton of a guillemot, showing the dorso-ventral compression of the body which is characteristic of diving birds. Protection against water pressure in deep dives is provided by the unusually long overlapping rib projections, or uncinate processes. After Pycraft.

Because of their buoyancy, some water birds have difficulty in getting below the surface to feed. Pelicans, gannets, terns, and others enter the water from the air in plunging dives. Gannets, which may dive from heights of 100 meters, lack external nose openings. This is probably an adaptation which protects the respiratory system from the effects of sudden impact with the water. Grebes seem to be able to squeeze air not only from their plumage but also from the air sacs of the body, and slowly sink into the water as their specific gravity increases. According to Stubbs (*in* Stresemann, 1927–1934), a Little Grebe, *Podiceps ruficollis*, with normally fluffed feathers, has a specific gravity of 0.66, but when the air is pressed from its feathers, its specific gravity rises to 0.84.

Geese, swans, and "surface ducks" feed in shallow waters, and tip their bodies head-down and tail-up to reach food on the bottom. "Diving ducks" submerge completely with quick, arching dives from the water's surface, and feed at various depths in the water. Once under water, they propel themselves with their feet, and hold their wings tightly against the body, although White-winged Scoters, *Melanitta deglandi*, swim with their alulae extended. Most divers, while submerged, paddle with both feet stroking simultaneously, but coots paddle alternately.

Among species that use their wings to swim under water are penguins, shearwaters, diving petrels, cormorants, auks, and guillemots. In good divers, large wings can be a handicap because of their friction with the water. As a consequence, the better divers have small, thin, but muscular wings. This means a heavy wing-loading, and poor flying ability. In all penguins, flight has completely disappeared, and the wings have become highly specialized, powerful flippers, capable of exceptional performance in swimming. The flippers may beat together or alternately. One may brake while the other beats forward, producing an extremely sharp turn. The surprising leaps that penguins can make from the water to ice shelves at least two meters high testify to the speeds they can develop under water. Several Gentoo Penguins, *Pygoscelis papua*, were timed by Murphy (1936), swimming under water at 36 kilometers per hour—a respectable flying speed for some birds.

Probably the majority of dives made by birds are under five meters in depth. Records of deep descents of diving birds are occasionally obtained when the birds become caught in fish nets or traps set at known depths. Loons have been taken in nets set 55 meters deep; cormorants, 40 meters; ducks, 36 meters; gannets, 26 meters; grebes, 23 meters. Under natural conditions, diving birds rarely stay under water more than a minute, although loons have been known to remain submerged for 15 minutes. Experimentally, ducks have remained alive under water for 16 minutes. This exceptional performance is probably due in part to the fact that ducks have proportionately about twice as much blood as do chickens. They also have a high concentration of hemoglobin in their blood, and of myoglobin in their muscles. Moreover, it is probable that the air sacs can work air back and forth through the lungs while the birds are submerged.

With all their many adaptations for movement in water, on earth, and in the air, birds are, in Walt Whitman's phrase, born

" . . . to match the gale,
To cope with heaven and earth and sea and hurricane."

SUGGESTED READINGS

An excellent, lucid, and brief account of bird flight is found in Storer, *The Flight of Birds*. Old, but still worth consulting, are Aymar, *Bird Flight*, and Horton-Smith, *The Flight of Birds*. Greenewalt's *Hummingbirds* has a section on hovering flight with many superb illustrations. For the more technical aspects of aerodynamics, see Sherwood's *Aerodynamics*, or the paper-bound book by Sutton, *The Science of Flight*.

TWENTY-TWO

Migration and Orientation

How oft against the sunset sky or moon
I watched that moving zigzag of spread wings
In unforgotten Autumns gone too soon,
In unforgotten Springs!
Frederick Peterson, *Wild Geese*

Animals, unlike green plants, cannot root themselves in one place and make their own food. They must move about and search for it, and as soon as they have exhausted the food in one place they must move on to another. With their unparalleled mobility, birds have explored almost the whole earth, searching not only for food but also for territory, nesting sites, and other necessities for survival.

Because of their high metabolism, birds must have abundant and unfailing sources of rich food. It commonly happens that, in regions with seasonal climatic changes, ecologic changes occur which may require the birds there to move away if they are to survive. In the temperate zones the deep chill of winter closes lakes and streams to water fowl, and so changes the land and its vegetation that most land birds must also leave for warmer regions. In the tropics, a dry season may so reduce the plants, berries, insects, worms, and other food, that the birds must emigrate to some more favorable place. These more or less regular, extensive, seasonal movements of birds between their breeding regions and their "wintering" regions are known as migration. This is simply a naturally selected tendency of birds to live the year through in places where conditions are optimum for them. Birds also make other rather extensive movements, such as the nomadism of crossbills, or the sporadic irruptions of Sand Grouse, *Syrrhaptes paradoxus;* but only the periodic to-and-fro movements between nesting and winter quarters are considered to be true migration.

Birds are by no means the only migratory animals. Among other periodic wanderers are some butterflies, squids, fishes, salamanders, reindeer, and bats. Some of these, like some birds, show remarkable capacities to "home" or to return to their birth places—for example, salmon and eels.

Some birds, of course, do not migrate at all. These are the sedentary or resident species which inhabit a given locality throughout the year. In the United States the House Sparrow, *Passer domesticus,* is sedentary, and in Britain, the Starling, *Sturnus vulgaris.* Even in the coldest climates, some birds remain sedentary. Year-around residents in the arctic and northern part of the temperate zone of North America include the Willow Ptarmigan, *Lagopus lagopus,* Snowy Owl, *Nyctea scandiaca,* Northern Three-toed Woodpecker, *Picoïdes tridactylus,* Raven, *Corvus corax,* Gray Jay, *Perisoreus canadensis,* Red-breasted Nuthatch, *Sitta canadensis,* Boreal Chickadee, *Parus hudsonicus,* and some Snow Buntings, *Plectrophenax nivalis.*

Certain species are neither completely settled residents nor regular migrants. The House Sparrow, for example, is migratory in China, and the Starling in central Europe. In England, the Heron, *Ardea cinerea,* is essentially sedentary, but in western Europe it is migratory, many individual Herons wintering in France, Portugal, Spain, and even northern Africa. In the United States the Barn Owl, *Tyto alba,* tends to be migratory in the northern part of its range and sedentary in the southern part (Stewart, 1952); and in central Ohio, Song Sparrows, *Melospiza melodia,* showed sex differences in migration: about one-half of the males and over two-thirds of the females migrated in the fall, while the rest of the population remained resident for the winter. Certain individual birds migrated one year but remained sedentary the next (Nice, 1937). Among North American Tree Sparrows, *Spizella arborea,* apparently a greater proportion of the females than of the males migrate south in winter (Heydweiller, 1936).

The migration-stimulating effect of seasonal change in climate is strikingly demonstrated even within a single species. The Red-eyed Vireo, *Vireo olivaceus,* is thought by Zimmer (1938) to have three different subspecies: one remains a year-around resident in central South America; the second migrates from North America, and the third from Argentina, on seasonal visits to the locale of the first.

There is little doubt that heredity plays an important role in determining migratory behavior. In some species, particularly long-distance migrants, the instinct to migrate is firmly implanted, while in others it is very weakly expressed, some individuals of a single brood migrating while others remain resident. In some species the immediate environmental stimuli play a determining role. Certain migratory ducks, for example, will abandon their normal fall migration journeys if open water and sufficient food are available throughout the winter season.

ADVANTAGES OF MIGRATION

On the long and arduous journeys from their homes or breeding territories to their winter quarters, birds expend much energy, and may encounter great dangers. The average small passerine crossing the North Sea between the British Isles and the continent loses about one-fifth of its weight. The windrows of dead birds that sometimes litter the beaches in various parts of the world bear testimony to the toll exacted of over-water migrants by adverse weather. In addition to the hazards of migration, a migrating bird normally gives up its hard-won territory once each year and must spend considerable energy to win a new territory again the following year. For species subjecting themselves to such an expensive activity as migration, there must be commensurate rewards; otherwise extinction would surely follow. Rewards there are, some of them immediate and obvious, some of them long-range and less apparent.

The advantages of migration are most clearly illustrated by long-distance migrants that move from arctic regions to tropical or subtropical regions for the winter. Species migrating shorter distances reap many of the same advantages, but often in a more dilute form.

The most obvious and perhaps the most important advantage provided by migration is the securing of a better climate for living. By flying hundreds and sometimes thousands of kilometers, birds can trade the bitter cold and long nights of northern winters for the gentler warmth and sunlight of southern climates. Conversely, in the summer they can escape the humid heat of the south and enjoy the long cool days of the northlands.

If all the birds that migrate should instead remain in their winter quarters the year around, they and the normally resident birds would make great demands on the food supply, and many birds might have difficulty in nourishing their young, while rich food resources in northern habitats remained untouched. However, by alternately exploiting two different habitats for food, more birds are able to exist. Very probably some species migrate for this one advantage. The Pennant-winged Nightjar, *Semeïophorus vexillarius*, breeds during the rainy season (September to November) in southern Africa from Angola to Damaraland, and from southern Tanganyika to the Transvaal. Then, in February, it follows the rains across the equator to "winter" quarters in Nigeria, Sudan, and Uganda. This periodic migration places the bird in each habitat at the most favorable time of year for feeding on its preferred food, flying termites (Stresemann, 1927–1934). Particularly in far northern habitats, insects are very abun-

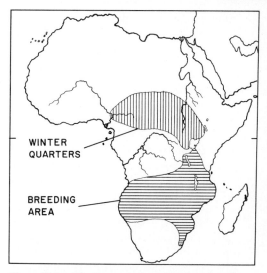

Figure 22.1. The Pennant-winged Nightjar breeds in southern Africa during the rainy season, and then migrates across the Congo basin to its winter quarters in the Sudan in time to enjoy the insect-rich rainy season there. The Nacunda Nightjar in South America makes a corresponding migration between Venezuela and Argentina. After Chapin, from Stresemann.

dant in summer, and they provide the rich protein food so necessary for young growing birds.

By changing their habitats twice each year, birds probably obtain benefits comparable to those provided by ecologic interspersion or "edge effect" that are so valuable to static populations. Certainly, geographic wandering makes possible greater variety in birds' diets, and probably more nourishing diets as well. This kind of interspersion occurs both in space and time: one diet in winter quarters, another in the summer breeding range. It may well be that certain elements in the summer diet, such as vitamins, minerals, and trace elements, are particularly valuable to the growing young. As deer sometimes travel considerable distances to find a salt lick, so, perhaps, some migrating birds unconsciously seek special dietary needs, which may be exposed and available in recently glaciated northern regions but buried under organic debris in warmer climates.

Especially in the far north, the long

summer days provide birds with longer "working hours" to gather more food to feed more young or possibly to raise them more quickly. In northern Alaska (69° N. Lat.) a female American Robin, *Turdus migratorius*, fed its brood approximately 21 hours each day (Karplus, 1952). As seen in Chapters 15 and 20, the farther north from the tropics a species breeds, the larger its brood generally is. Whether the enlarged broods are determined by heredity or environment, they are nicely adapted to the long days and abundant insects of northern summers.

Although the short duration of a far-northern breeding season creates problems for birds, it affords the tremendous advantage of concentrating the raising of all predator-vulnerable young into one brief period. The pressure of predation is thus divided among a greater number of eggs and young, and this results in a proportionately lower annual mortality. Further, the brief once-a-year appearance of young birds denies to their predators the sustained food they must have to build up populations large enough to decimate the birds on which they feed. Moreover, predators are strikingly few in the far north. The arctic fox is essentially the only predator on geese that nest on arctic islands, and only two species of reptiles are known to live north of the arctic circle. In the tropics, on the contrary, hosts of snakes and lizards, as well as monkeys, toucans, and other nest robbers, levy a huge toll on breeding birds, their eggs and young. A study of 35 nests by Skutch (1945) in a lowland forest in Panama showed that only five (14.3 per cent) were successful in raising any young, whereas at an elevation of 2500 to 2700 meters in the highlands of Guatemala, of 67 nests, 37 (55.2 per cent) were successful.

Somewhat similarly, it seems probable that parasites and infectious microorganisms are reduced in abundance in far northern habitats as a result of long, cold winters, shallow soil, frozen subsoil, and relatively small animal populations. At any rate, birds in the northern breeding zones reap some of the advantages that pigs,

chickens, and other domestic animals do when a farmer rotates the locations of their pens from time to time to reduce the chances of disease contagion from infected soil.

Migration furnishes another advantage in the vastly increased amount of space that it makes available to each breeding pair of birds. With more territory available, less time need be spent fighting to establish territory or nesting sites, and there is more space for the undisturbed rearing of the young. Population pressures are thus reduced at the most competitive time of the year. It may be that for some species, territorial aggressiveness is an ingredient in the forces responsible for migration.

Physiologically, migration makes possible a sort of external homeostasis, which enables birds, simply by traveling, to avoid some of the harsher extremes in the physical and biotic environment. Migration permits an economy of physiological adjustments to changing seasons—once the cost of travel itself is paid! It may be, too, that just as trout eggs develop best in cool waters, certain birds that breed in cool climates require a thermoneutral environmental temperature for the most efficient development of their young. This possibility, apparently, has not been investigated in birds. However, in Indiana, experimental pigs raised on refrigerated slabs of concrete breathed more slowly, and gained weight more rapidly, than control pigs raised under normal conditions.

Finally, migration provides certain genetic and evolutionary benefits. For one thing, it affords a very rigorous, three-pronged type of natural selection unknown to sedentary species. A long-distance migrant, especially, is subjected to different kinds of natural selection in its breeding quarters, its winter quarters, and while on the journey between the two habitats. Certainly, migratory species, subjected as they are to greater ecologic diversity, have a greater range of adaptability than resident species. This is illustrated by the fact, referred to in Chapter 20, that North American migrants, while in their Colombian winter quarters, tolerate a greater variety of altitudinal life zones than do native sedentary species. In addition, races of birds toughened—that is, selected—by the hardships of migration, should be better able to meet the arduous requirements of the breeding season than resident races.

As discussed earlier, migration undoubtedly promotes the geographic dispersal of birds. Insofar as dispersal may isolate small populations of a species from each other, it tends to increase the rate of evolution in that species because genetic variation, or mutation, makes a greater impression on a small population than on a large one. Very likely indigenous populations of land birds found on oceanic islands are descendants of birds that lost their way while migrating. The Arctic Tern, *Sterna paradisaea*, makes a migratory round trip from the arctic to the antarctic each year. In the antarctic exists another, relatively sedentary species, the Antarctic Tern, *Sterna vittata*, which closely resembles the Arctic Tern. It seems quite possible that years ago a few Arctic Terns remained behind in the antarctic winter quarters and began to breed there, and eventually evolved into the Antarctic Tern (Murphy, 1936).

In contrast to isolation, migration also permits the cross-breeding or hereditary mixture of populations residing in different geographic ranges. A special instance of this occurs in ducks: male ducks in their winter quarters will often pair with and follow females from birth places other than their own. This explains why Mallards, *Anas platyrhynchos*, exist as a single race throughout Eurasia rather than as a number of isolated subspecies. It is difficult to say which of these genetic influences of migration outweighs the other, but from the multiplicity of subspecies and the rarity of widely spread species, one might guess that migration favors genetic isolation.

ORIGINS OF MIGRATION

Considering the great benefits of migra-tion and the ease and perfection of bird flight, it would be one of the great mysteries of nature if birds did *not* migrate. Yet, when the average person looks at the streaming flocks of birds during a heavy migration movement, he is likely to pause and wonder, "When, and in what way, did this mysterious behavior begin?" Unfortunately, such a question cannot be answered simply and easily. Migration exists in great variety and complexity. It probably arose in different ways, at different times, and in different groups of birds. In fact, it is still arising—and disappearing —in different species today.

The wild canary or Serin, *Serinus canarius*, formerly a sedentary Mediterranean bird, has in the past century extended its range throughout continental Europe as far north as the North and Baltic Seas. Around the Mediterranean Sea the species is still sedentary, but in the new range the bird has become migratory, probably in response to the more rigorous climate (Dorst, 1956). A contrary situation occurred when a flock of migrating Norwegian Fieldfares, *Turdus pilaris*, was storm-driven to Greenland in 1937 (p. 405). Since that date these normally migratory birds have established a non-migratory population in southern Greenland. Apparently, when the hazards of migration are less than those of residence in a harsh winter environment, natural selection encourages migration in a species. But when the reverse is true, a species tends to remain sedentary.

Like most animals, including man, birds are inclined to be creatures of comfortable habit, and they will change their habits only under the whip of great necessity. Without question, ecologic stresses have been the most frequent cause of the migratory habit. Birds are driven out of their breeding areas by periodic climatic cycles, which bring on food shortages that are aggravated by the annual increase in bird population. Although the original impetus to migrate may be entirely external, the ceaseless repetition of seasons of famine, brought on by arctic frost or tropic drought, may eventually, through natural selection, winnow the sensitive protoplasm of a species until the urge to migrate at a particular time of year becomes innate, and comes into play at the appropriate season even in the absence of the original impelling threat of starvation.

In those tropical regions which have humid, warm climates throughout the year, birds may wander at random after the breeding season, but they do not travel widely. The chief exceptions to this are the fruit eaters and flower feeders—particularly the fruit doves, lories, and hummingbirds (Stresemann, 1927–1934). Such birds are unable to find enough food in a limited area and therefore must keep wandering. In the tropical rain forest there is a tremendous variety of plant life, but the plants are widely scattered, and rarely occur in solid stands of one species, as do plants of a temperate zone forest. Consequently, birds that feed on only a few plants are required to travel more extensively than birds with more catholic appetites. The examination of the stomach contents of two species of rain forest doves in Colombia revealed only five species of plants eaten by the Band-tailed Pigeon, *Columba fasciata*, a wandering species, whereas 19 species of plants and two of molluscs were eaten by the Eared Dove, *Zenaidura auriculata*, a sedentary species (Borrero, 1953). Food is apparently the key to the difference in mobility in these two birds.

Most birds and most humans live in the northern hemisphere, which is roughly the land hemisphere of the world. It is here that the great seasonal surges of periodic north- and south-bound migration are best developed. Although corresponding migratory movements occur in the southern hemisphere, they are very meager in comparison because of the relatively small amount of land available for breeding areas in the south temperate zone. The migratory movements, therefore, that most people know, are the preponderant south-in-winter and north-in-summer migrations of the northern hemisphere. The apparent simplicity of these movements has encouraged the appearance of several theories to

explain their origin, despite the fact that many other types of migration occur.

One of these theories is the Northern Home theory, which holds that the original home of birds was in the north temperate zone. Pleistocene (or earlier) glaciation forced the birds to seek the gentler climates to the south, according to this hypothesis, but they still return each summer to breed in the old homeland, only to be forced south again each autumn by the returning snows and food-lack of winter. A similar but contrasting Southern Home theory maintains that birds originated in the tropics, but that population expansion drove them to seek greener pastures, especially during the heavy food demands of the breeding season. Accordingly, many species developed the habit of pressing northward each summer into the food-rich lands released earlier by glaciers and now by the annual northward retreat of winter.

Still another theory maintains that the great north and south migrations originated in a hypothetical "drift" of the continents northward from Antarctica, and that migrations today are an attempt of various species to return to breed in their ancestral homelands, now much removed from their earlier, more southern location. The chief objection to this theory is that, had any such continental drifting ever occurred (and most geologists doubt that it has), it would have occurred millions of years before present day migration routes were established. Besides, there are many migration paths whose patterns cannot easily be accounted for by such a theory.

While it is unquestionably true that Pleistocene glaciation influenced migratory patterns in the past, it is even more certain that other influences are operating today to lengthen or shorten migration routes, to change their directions, or to eliminate them entirely in some birds and originate altogether new paths in others. The fact of multiple origins of migration is more easily comprehended when one realizes that the geographic range of any animal is not the static area that a map of its distribution indicates. As Darlington

(1957) makes clear, animal ranges are "inherently complex and unstable" and usually "change slightly with the animals' activities." At different times of the year animals may engage in different successive activities such as feeding, breeding, dispersal after breeding, and wintering. The niceties of ecologic adjustment will often require different ranges for each of these different activities, although all of them are contained within a "sedentary" species' gross range. If an animal can travel far and fast, these sub-ranges "can and sometimes do move far apart. This is what has happened in the case of strongly migratory birds."

Most bird migration today takes birds from a summer breeding area to a winter resting area. However, some species migrate between three different areas, each with a different function—a fact which gives force to the above argument. Several species of ducks, for example, make "molt migrations" by which they leave their breeding areas for a sheltered marshy place where they molt their flight feathers and grow new ones; then they fly to their winter quarters.

PATTERNS OF MIGRATION

Migration routes are probably determined more by climatic change, and its power to vary the food supply, than by any other environmental factor. This is why the majority of migration paths trend north and south. As a rule, the more rigorous the climate, especially in temperature extremes, the greater the percentage of birds that migrate. In Canada, the percentage of migrants is higher than in the United States. Still fewer of the Mexican birds migrate, and practically no birds migrate in the rain forests of the Amazon. About one-third of the breeding birds of Europe spend their winters in Africa south of the Sahara. Because the relatively small land areas south of the equator have much more uniform climates than those of the north temperate and boreal zones, very few southern hemisphere birds are strong migrants. In southern Africa there are about 20 species that move toward the equator to spend the winter, but not a single one migrates as far north as Europe (Steinbacher, 1951).

A migratory species often winters in a region ecologically similar to its breeding area. Birds that breed in forests seek forested winter areas; desert breeders will seek deserts. This is one explanation of the fact that shore birds breeding in the far north make such tremendous migrations to similar habitats in the far south. However, the longer the migratory journey, the more costly it is biologically. This may explain the year-around residence in arctic regions of several varieties of birds. The hardships of living in an austere habitat are weighed by natural selection against the hardships of long migration trips. As long as food is available, ptarmigan and a few other residents can tolerate the intense cold. Among arctic sea birds the Puffin, *Fratercula arctica*, and Black Guillemot, *Cepphus grylle*, regularly stay through the winter in Baffin Bay at about 77° north latitude, and, in mild winters, even at Amsterdam Island, north of Spitzbergen at 80° north latitude, feeding on littoral fish and invertebrates which they manage to catch, remarkably enough, in the darkness of the long winter nights. It is not the arctic cold, however, but the darkness that compels the Fulmars, *Fulmarus glacialis*, to migrate south in mid-November when the arctic night deepens. The first birds return in late January with the reappearance of twilight (Stresemann, 1927–1934).

Winter quarters are not always equatorward from breeding areas. If better feeding opportunities are to be found elsewhere, birds may migrate even in directions contrary to the seasonal trend. Thus, some albatrosses and guillemots migrate poleward after their breeding season to feed in cooler, more nutritious waters. Gulls whose breeding grounds are near Orlov, Russia (north of the Black Sea), winter to the west and southwest along the Mediterranean shores of Greece, Italy, Tunisia,

France, and Spain. Banding recoveries of Redhead Ducks, *Aythya americana*, which breed in the prairie states as far west as Utah, show that they migrate to the Atlantic coast in the fall. Likewise, Evening Grosbeaks, *Hesperiphona vespertina*, and Purple Finches, *Carpodacus purpureus*, banded in northern Michigan, have been recovered in numerous Atlantic coast states (Lincoln, 1950). The Rose-colored Starling, *Sturnus roseus*, which breeds in the Caucasian and Turkish steppes, spends its winters 3000 kilometers to the east in India; and Snow Buntings, *Plectrophenax nivalis*, which nested in northeast Greenland, have been recovered in northeast Russia.

Birds breeding in warmer climates are frequently rain followers, and rains do not always follow the sun in its annual movements north and south. In Madagascar there are five species of breeding birds that "winter" in Africa; one of them, the roller *Eurystomus glaucurus*, migrates as far eastward as the Belgian Congo (Rand, 1936). A much shorter east-west migration is that of the Mourning Chat, *Oenanthe lugens*, which breeds between the Nile and the Red Sea, and spends its winters on the fringes of the Sahara (Hartley, 1949).

The geographic location of continents, mountain ranges, great rivers, deserts, peninsulas, and islands creates opportunities and problems for migrating birds, and consequently helps to determine their migration paths. From this standpoint, the Old World and New World differ strikingly. In the New World the two continents are roughly north and south of each other. The great sierras run north and south, and there is a land connection, plus many islands, between the two continents. In North America, where migration predominates, the great Mississippi Valley runs north and south.

In the Old World, on the contrary, mountain ranges and great desert systems run east and west, creating barriers to north and south seasonal migration. Southern land masses suitable for wintering areas are displaced to the west (Africa) and east (East Indies and Australia) of the center of the great Eurasian breeding range of most Old World birds. Accordingly, many Eurasian birds are unable to pursue a north-south migration route to their winter quarters. Although many species that breed in east Asia winter in the Indo-Malayan regions, some of them winter far to the west in Africa. For example, the flycatcher, *Muscicapa striata neumanni*, which breeds east of Lake Baikal in Siberia, the swift, *Micropus apus pekinensis*, of northeastern China, and the Red-footed Falcon, *Falco vespertinus amurensis*, of southeastern Siberia, all winter in Africa, flying there by way of India, Baluchistan, and Arabia (Stresemann, 1927–1934).

Some birds, reluctant to cross deserts or large expanses of water, take long, circuitous routes to reach their winter quarters. Numerous central European species, for example, go around either end of the Mediterranean rather than fly across it to their African winter quarters. Some species trace an angular course around the eastern end of the sea in order to follow the Nile southward and thus avoid the sterile Sahara. Storks and other soaring birds must remain over land if they are to use terrestrial thermal currents for their long flights.

Most species, in their migrations, sweep across the land in broad paths or "fronts," and usually take a rather direct route from breeding to wintering areas. Whether a species travels in a broad or narrow path depends chiefly on the geographic extent of its breeding and wintering quarters and on the geographic and ecologic nature of the intervening route. The Ross Goose, *Chen rossii*, breeds in a very restricted area in northern Canada near Queen Maude Gulf and on Southampton Island, and winters in a small area in California; consequently it has a narrow migration path. Shore birds generally follow coasts of one sort or another to find food as they migrate, or else they migrate non-stop between summer and winter homes. Soaring birds, such as hawks and eagles, frequently migrate along very narrow corridors defined by mountains on whose flanks updrafts provide the motive force for their travels. The famous bird sanctuary at Hawk Mountain, Pennsylvania, is on such a migration highway.

Broad-front migrants are occasionally funneled into narrow paths by the nature of the territory over which they pass. The Scarlet Tanager, *Piranga olivacea,* nests from the Dakotas to the Atlantic Coast in a belt about 3000 kilometers wide. In fall migration it flies to the Gulf Coast, where its path narrows until it is about 1000 kilometers wide. From here it flies across the Gulf of Mexico to Central America where, in Costa Rica, its path narrows further to a mere 160 kilometers (Lincoln, 1950). Near the southeast shore of the Baltic is a long, narrow, off-shore island called the Kurische Nehrung. In the autumn, land birds, migrating southwesterly from the east Baltic countries and Russia, avoid the open water and become concentrated on this long, sandy ribbon of land. Sometimes as many as one-half million birds a day fly by. Until the end of World War II, the famous German ornithological research station, Vogelwarte Rossitten, was located here.

Such migration-diverting objects as sea shores, mountain ranges, large rivers, desert rims, or forest edges are called guiding lines, or in German, *Leitlinie*. It was long thought that most migrants flew in narrow paths along such guiding lines as, for example, the Mississippi River; but recent studies of migration, using observation by airplanes and radar, or by observing bird silhouettes against the full moon by telescope, have shown that the great majority of birds fly in broad fronts and are only rarely channeled into narrow paths by environmental guiding lines. Four such broad-front migration bands or "flyways" have been described by Lincoln for North America: the Atlantic, Mississippi, Central (or plains), and Pacific flyways. While there is a general consistency in the use of specific flyways by certain bird populations, birds are by no means rigidly re-

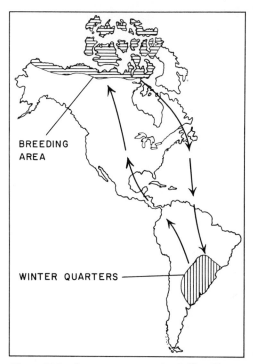

Figure 22.2. Loop migration in the Golden Plover. This species migrates south in the autumn via the Maritime Provinces and the Atlantic Ocean, but it returns north in the spring by a mid-continental route because ecological conditions there are more suitable for migration at that time. After Lincoln.

stricted to them. Ducks breeding in the Canadian prairie provinces may migrate along all four flyways.

There are certain deviations from the normal back-and-forth shuttling of most migration flights which throw further light on the origin of migration routes. The American Golden Plover, *Pluvialis dominica,* breeds from northern Alaska across arctic Canada to southern Baffin Island, and winters in southern South America. When migrating north in the spring, this species travels by way of Central America, Mexico, the Mississippi Valley and on through Canadian prairies west of Hudson Bay. However, to migrate south in the autumn, the majority of birds fly eastward to Labrador, Nova Scotia, and upper New England, where they strike out across the

Atlantic Ocean, non-stop, for South America. Thus the annual circuit describes a loop migration, or *Schleifenzug*. This particular loop migration is explained by Cooke (1915) as follows: Birds follow that route between summer and winter areas which provides the shortest path with adequate living conditions and food. The long Atlantic shore lines of Labrador, Nova Scotia, and New England provide both an ecologically suitable highway and a rich source of late summer berries, which the birds use to fatten themselves for the long trip across the open sea. To return by this same path would be fatal, because spring arrives late and foggy on the Labrador coast, and the still-frosty soil could offer no food to the exhausted oceanic fliers. But the trip up the Isthmus of Panama and the grasslands of mid-America is congenial, warm, and already producing food for the hungry migrants.

Another example of *Schleifenzug* is that of the Arctic Loon, *Gavia arctica*, which breeds in northern Russia and migrates south for the winter via the Black Sea to southern Europe. In spring, however, it makes an early return to its home by first flying northwest to the Baltic, and then northeast, and finally east to its breeding grounds. The loon is a large bird with heavy wing-loading, and it can alight and take off only from water; therefore it can migrate only where open water is available for landing, feeding, and taking off. Thanks to the Gulf Stream, the waters of the maritime Baltic countries thaw out earlier than those of inland Russia, thus encouraging this loop migration (Bodenstein and Schüz, 1944). Still other loop migrations are thought to be the result of strong, prevailing side-winds during one migration trip but not during the return trip, thus causing a lateral wind drift during the one flight but not during the other. This is possibly the reason for the numerous loop migration paths described by various European species migrating through North Africa.

"Leap-frog" migration aptly describes the pattern taken when races of the same species occupy two or more breeding areas (and also wintering areas) in the axis of migratory flight. There are six different races of the Fox Sparrow, *Passerella iliaca*, which breed and winter along the North American Pacific coast. One race both breeds and winters in the Puget Sound area. The races that breed progressively farther north along the coast, up to the outermost of the Aleutian Islands, winter progressively farther south in Oregon and California; each race on its southern migration passes over winter areas already preempted by the race that breeds south of it (Swarth, 1920). This type of migration, found also in other species, is probably an adjustment to mutual intolerance engendered by the sharpness of intraspecific competition. Many of the species and races that breed farthest north, winter farthest south.

Some migration paths seem to be remarkably crooked, illogical, out-of-the-way routes for connecting breeding and wintering areas. Careful studies show that

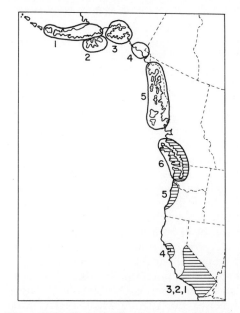

Figure 22.3. "Leap-frog" migration of the Pacific Coast Fox Sparrow. Breeding areas are encircled; winter quarters, shaded. The numbers refer to the different subspecies using the areas. After Swarth, from Lincoln.

these are not paths of biologic necessity, but are the fruits of tradition, much as the crooked streets of Boston trace their lineage to ancestral cow-paths. It is, of course, impossible to trace the historic causes behind all present day migration routes, but there is little question that past climatic changes, particularly glaciation, were responsible for the patterns many of them now display. In geologically recent times, birds of the boreal and north temperate zones have been shoved about, or exterminated, by extensive glaciation. The climatic changes wrought by glaciation caused wide-spread changes in the earth's vegetation and, therefore, in the birds' habitats. What is now the Sahara Desert was formerly a verdant winter refuge for birds from southern Europe. It takes very little imagination to realize the dislocations in migration routes that would be occasioned by the gradual drying up of the Sahara region, or by the slow shifting apart of any breeding and wintering areas.

As glaciers receded at the end of the last ice age, new northern and alpine habitats were opened up. These unoccupied habitats were ecologic vacuums into which various species extended their ranges, pushed from behind by population pressure. Range extensions were not always in the direction of the chief migration axis. But when the summer residents of these new habitats were ready to migrate "south" in the fall, it was only natural for them to join their relatives and fly with them along the ancestral pathway to their traditional winter quarters, rather than to strike out by themselves on a direct and shorter new path. As a species gradually extended its new range, more and more birds followed the illogical ancestral path to winter quarters. In some cases this happened because younger birds learned the way from their elders; in others the habit of following the crooked path became innate. This hypothesis clearly fits numerous present day migration paths, including the following.

As man and his agricultural activities spread westward in the United States, the Bobolink, *Dolichonyx oryzivorus*, followed from the Mississippi Valley prairies, and gradually established populations in Oregon, Nevada, and other western states. In migrating to South America each fall, these birds first return to the Mississippi Valley to join their cohorts, and then turn south and pursue the traditional pathway, rather than take a shorter, more direct route by themselves.

All along the arctic coast of North America breeds the Pectoral Sandpiper, *Erolia melanotos*. It has extended its range across Bering Strait into northern Siberia as far westward as the Taimyr Peninsula. When the Siberian population of these birds migrate to winter quarters, most of them do not fly directly south to an Asiatic refuge as one might expect. On the contrary, they first fly east across Bering Strait to Alaska, where they join the American birds and, with them, travel through North and South America to their winter quarters in Peru, Chile, Argentina, and Patagonia. In a reciprocal fashion, the Old World Ringed Plover, *Charadrius hiaticula*, has spread to Greenland, and to Ellesmere and Baffin Islands of the New World. The American population, instead of flying south along the shores of North America to its winter quarters, flies to Greenland, Iceland, and then down to its winter quarters along the shores of Britain, western Europe, and northwestern Africa.

Even more striking is the migration route followed by the Arctic Warbler, *Phylloscopus borealis*, of the Old World. This tiny bird presumably originated in northeastern Siberia. It has spread in two directions: eastward to northern Alaska, and westward across the entire breadth of the Siberian tundras to Finland and Norway. Its winter quarters are in southeastern China, Indonesia, the Philippines, Borneo, and adjacent islands. The Alaskan warblers cross Bering Strait and migrate south with the Siberian birds. But more astonishing is the long trip taken by the Norwegian and Finnish birds. When migrating to their winter quarters, they first fly east some 3000 or 4000 kilometers

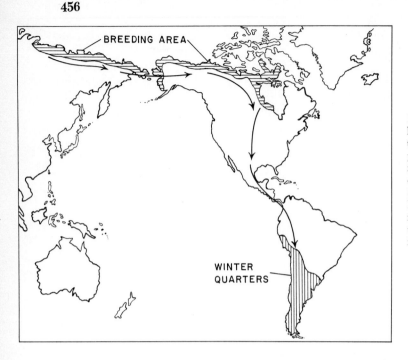

Figure 22.4. Many birds follow ancestral pathways to winter quarters. The Pectoral Sandpiper has extended its range from North America to north central Siberia. Each year, this Siberian population retraces its historic expansion path to join its American relatives when they migrate to South America for the winter.

across Siberia, and then go south with their relatives to the tropics. The total journey from Norway to southeastern Asia is probably about 12,500 kilometers—a long trip for a bird only 12 centimeters in length (Stresemann, 1927–1934)!

Evidence that these hereditary pathways are not of very ancient origin is seen in the fact that a bird of the identical genus as the Arctic Warbler follows a quite different migration route. The east Siberian population of the Willow Warbler, *Phylloscopus trochilus,* winters in east Africa; on its way there, it crosses the route of the Arctic Warbler at right angles.

The Wheatear, *Oenanthe oenanthe,* which breeds across the whole of northern Eurasia, has extended its range into North America both from the west, via Siberia into northern Alaska, and from the east, via Greenland into Labrador, northern Quebec, and the arctic islands to the north. Both of these American populations winter in tropical Africa, the birds from Alaska crossing Asia to reach the Cameroons and Tanganyika, and those from Labrador and Quebec flying across Greenland and Iceland to Europe and on to Morocco, Senegal, and Sierra Leone (Meinertzhagen, 1954).

Not all migratory birds are slaves to tradition. Stresemann (1927–1934) tells how the European Shore Lark, *Eremophila alpestris,* abandoned its ancestral migratory trail and set up a new one within historic times. This bird is widely spread across the Siberian tundras. It was unknown as a breeder in Scandinavia until 1837, when nests were first discovered there. At the same time the bird first appeared in Britain. Since then the bird has increased greatly in numbers in Norway and Sweden, and it regularly winters now along the east coasts of England.

Some birds reap the advantages of long distance migration with relatively little effort by migrating vertically instead of horizontally. Aristotle was aware of vertical, or altitudinal, migration:

"Among birds the more feeble of them descend to the plains in winter when it is cold because there they find the air more temperate; in summer when the plains are burning, they return to the heights." (Dorst, 1956).

This economical form of migration can be practiced only by a limited number of birds, because of the obvious limitations of alpine space. In the Rocky Mountains of Colorado, the following birds breed in the alpine or subalpine zones in summer and descend to lower levels in winter: Pine Grosbeak, *Pinicola enucleator;* Black-capped Rosy Finch, *Leucosticte australis;* Gray-headed Junco, *Junco caniceps.* A type of inverted altitudinal migration is found in the Blue Grouse, *Dendragapus obscurus,* which winters at high altitudes in the mountains of Idaho, where it feeds on needles and tree buds. The birds descend 300 meters or so in spring to feed on the earlier developing leaves and flowers, and the females with broods descend still farther in summer to feed their young on valley insects and berries (Marshall, 1946).

Oceanic birds also show migration movements correlated with the seasons. These are most sharply evident when sea birds come ashore to breed. Because of the lack of fixed observation posts in the open sea, students know much less about the movements of sea birds than about those of land birds. The surface of the ocean, which is the only part that birds inhabit, is a much more uniform environment than the surface of the land. It is flat, constantly wet, relatively uniform in its physical and chemical properties, and it varies in temperature throughout the world only about one-fourth or one-fifth as much as do land or air temperatures. As a result, sea bird migrations are probably less complex and varied than those of land birds. Sea birds have less need for wide movements to escape drastic seasonal changes in temperature. Nevertheless, some sea birds make remarkably long migration journeys. For example, the Slender-billed Shearwater, *Puffinus tenuirostris,* breeds on the coastal islands of southern Australia and winters throughout the Pacific Ocean as far north as the Aleutian Islands. More restricted, at least in latitude, and perhaps more typical of sea birds, are the seasonal movements of the Wandering Albatross, *Diomedea exulans,* as reported by Dixon (*in* Murphy, 1936). Observations during 2002 days in the

south Atlantic, between 20° and 60° south latitude, showed that this species was practically confined between 30° and 60° south latitude. In the winter, 96.9 per cent of the birds seen were between 30° and 50°, and only 0.1 per cent south of 50° south latitude, whereas in summer, 73 per cent were between 30° and 50°, and 26.5 per cent south of 50°. As with land birds, food is an extremely important factor in determining migration movements in sea birds. Ocean waters rich in fish and other foods are more heavily populated with birds than waters poor in food, whether the birds are migrating or in their winter or breeding areas.

MECHANICS OF MIGRATION

Migratory behavior is probably about as old as birds themselves. Even so, birds have not evolved into two distinct types, migratory and non-migratory. The many partial migrants living today—species in which some individuals migrate and others do not—suggest that migratory behavior is an evolutionary expedient, appearing or disappearing according to selective en-

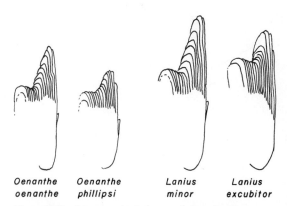

Oenanthe   Oenanthe   Lanius   Lanius
oenanthe   phillipsi   minor   excubitor

Figure 22.5. Migratory birds frequently have longer, more efficient wings than their non-migratory relatives. The Wheatear, *Oenanthe oenanthe,* migrates from Europe to central Africa; the species *Oenanthe phillipsi,* of Somaliland, is non-migratory. The Lesser Gray Shrike, *Lanius minor,* migrates from Europe to southern Africa; the Great Gray Shrike, *Lanius excubitor,* of Europe, is non-migratory. After Kipp.

vironmental pressures. Nevertheless, strongly migratory species usually have longer, more pointed wings than their sedentary relatives. As an example, the Wheatear, *Oenanthe oenanthe*, which migrates from Eurasia to Africa, has primary wing feathers that extend over twice as far beyond the secondaries as do those of the sedentary *Oenanthe phillipsi* of Somaliland (Kipp, 1958). Similar differences in wings occur between migratory and sedentary species of the same genus in genera of Old World warblers, shrikes, wrynecks, rollers, and nightingales. Kipp believes that these wing adaptations arose before the last glacial period. Of the 22 races of the Rufous-collared Sparrow, *Zonotrichia capensis*, of Central and South America, 20 are sedentary birds and have short, rounded wings. Of the other two races, both of which have long, pointed wings, one migrates 2900 kilometers each year and the other lives in the thin air of the high Andes (Chapman, 1940).

The great distances covered by migrating birds are frequently cited as one of the wonders of migration. Many shore birds, in their migrations, apparently fly thousands of kilometers without stopping for rest or food. Many small passerines cross the Gulf of Mexico from the Gulf Coast of the United States to Yucatan or Tabasco, probably in one long flight. With or without resting en route, many migrants make remarkably long journeys between breeding and wintering regions. Perhaps the longest migration trip is that of the Arctic Tern, *Sterna paradisaea*, which nests in circumglobal arctic regions and winters on shores in the sub-antarctic. From the North American arctic, this species crosses the Atlantic to follow the cooler, more nutrient waters of the west shores of Europe and Africa to the tip of South Africa, whence it crosses the south Atlantic to Antarctica or Patagonia—a trip of perhaps 18,000 kilometers. Shore birds that nest in the arctic make migra-

Figure 22.6. The champion long-distance migrant is probably the Arctic Tern, which may travel as far as 36,000 kilometers each year in migration flights. Photo by E. Hosking.

tions nearly as long. The Bristle-thighed Curlew, *Numenius tahitiensis*, of Alaska flies as much as 10,000 kilometers to reach its winter quarters in Polynesian islands.

The long land journeys of some passerines have already been mentioned. Remarkable as these trips are, they are no more surprising than the flights some birds perform in their daily activities. The European Swift, *Apus apus*, is estimated to fly at least 900 kilometers per day gathering insects for its young. This is probably an extreme, but it is likely that many species fly at least 100 kilometers per day in feeding activity. This same rate of daily travel would carry most of them fast enough to complete their normal migration flights with time to spare.

Accurate records of migration speeds are difficult to obtain. One dependable method of learning migration speeds is to observe the migratory movements of large flocks, which include so many birds that their progress across the country can be traced. For example, nearly every year there is one massed flight of waterfowl down the Mississippi flyway which exceeds all other flights in size. It is sometimes referred to as the "grand passage." By noting the beginning and ending of this great flight, and collecting records from many alerted observers both on the ground and in the air, one can gain a rather precise picture of its progress. In 1957, a grand passage of ducks began in eastern Saskatchewan and Manitoba on

October 23 and 24, and, on a broad front several hundred kilometers in width, proceeded in a south-southeasterly direction. About a half million ducks arrived at wintering areas in Louisiana on October 24 and 25. Careful analysis of this flight by Bellrose and Sieh (1960) indicated that the ducks leaving Saskatchewan made a continuous flight of some 2400 kilometers to Louisiana at an average ground speed of about 65 to 80 kilometers per hour, or 1600 to 1900 kilometers per day. A flock of Blue Geese, *Chen caerulescens*, and Snow Geese, *Chen hyperborea*, travelled, apparently without stopping, from James Bay, Canada, to Louisiana, a distance of 2700 kilometers, in 60 hours, or at the rate of 46 kilometers per hour or 1100 kilometers per day (Cooch, 1955).

Another way of determining the flight speeds of birds under semi-natural conditions is to displace a marked, breeding bird from its nest and see how long it takes to return. This technique does not reveal migration speeds, but at least it shows what a bird can do in natural flight. Table 22.1 gives flight speeds of various displaced birds that returned in the shortest times under such conditions. The birds listed in the table are all strong fliers. It is apparent that large size is not a requisite for flying either rapidly or far.

In Table 22.2 are given performances of marked birds made during actual migration flights. There is, of course, no guarantee that a banded bird will begin migrat-

Table 22.1. Flight Speeds of Experimentally Displaced Birds Returning to Their Nests

SPECIES	DISTANCE DISPLACED (KILOMETERS)	ELAPSED TIME OF FLIGHT (DAYS)	KM. PER DAY	AUTHORITY
Laysan Albatross, *Diomedea immutabilis*	5150	10	510	Kenyon and Rice, 1958
Manx Shearwater, *Procellarius puffinus*	5300	12.5	420	Mazzeo, 1953
White Stork, *Ciconia ciconia*	2260	11.9	190	Wodzicki, 1953
Herring Gull, *Larus argentatus*	1400	4.1	340	Griffin, 1943
Noddy Tern, *Anoüs stolidus*	1739	5.	350	Watson, 1910
Homing Pigeon, *Columba livia*	1620	1.5	1080	Allen, 1925
Alpine Swift, *Apus melba*	1620	3.	540	Bourlière, 1950

Table 22.2.   Flight Speeds of Banded Wild Birds Made Between Their
Release at One Point and Their Early Recovery at a
Distant Point, During Migration Season

SPECIES	DISTANCE COVERED (KILOMETERS)	ELAPSED TIME OF FLIGHT	KM. PER DAY	AUTHORITY
Slender-billed Shearwater, *Puffinus tenuirostris*	10,000	53 days	190	Serventy, 1957
Peregrine Falcon, *Falco peregrinus*	1600	21 days	76	Cooke, 1946
Turnstone, *Arenaria interpres*	800	25 hrs.	768	Armstrong, 1949
Arctic Tern, *Sterna paradisaea*	14,000	114 days	123	Lincoln, 1950
Lesser Yellowlegs, *Totanus flavipes*	3100	7 days	444	Cooke, 1938
Short-billed Dowitcher, *Limnodromus griseus*	3700	20 days	185	Cooke, 1938
Mallard, *Anas platyrhynchos*	890	2 days	445	Cooke, 1940

ing immediately upon its release, that it will fly directly to its recovery point, or that it will be recovered (if at all) immediately upon its arrival there. While these are maximum records, they very likely do not represent maximum potentialities of the species named.

The Shearwater listed in Table 22.2 was banded in its Australian burrow before it could fly. If it departed for Alaskan waters, where it was captured, at the time of year when most young departed, it must have migrated at a sustained speed of at least 625 kilometers per day for 16 days (Serventy, 1957).

One feature of the migratory movements of many species, as yet unexplained, is the greater speed of spring migration compared with that of autumn. It is as though birds were impelled much more strongly to reach their breeding areas than they are to reach their winter quarters. The Bar-tailed Godwit, *Limosa lapponica*, which breeds in Alaska and eastern Siberia, requires only one to one and one-half months to migrate north from New Zealand in the spring, but it takes two to three months to make the return trip in the fall. European Wood Warblers, *Phylloscopus sibilatrix*, travel northward from their African winter quarters in the spring at an average rate of about 180 kilometers per day, but return in the fall at the more

leisurely pace of 90 kilometers per day (Stresemann, 1955). Many other species show this same tendency.

Some birds migrate at a fairly uniform speed, if one can judge by the times of first spring arrivals at different latitudes. As a rule, early spring migrants advance northward more slowly than late migrants. The Black-and-White Warbler, *Mniotilta varia*, is a slow but early migrant, advancing northward across the United States at an average rate of about 32 kilometers per day. A more rapid migrant is the Gray-cheeked Thrush, *Hylocichla minima*, which migrates from Louisiana to Alaska at an average rate of about 210 kilometers per day. In this case, however, the bird does not travel at a uniform speed but flies about four times as far each day in Alaska as it does earlier in the spring near the Gulf Coast (Lincoln, 1950).

Birds generally migrate at moderate to low altitudes. In the "grand passage" of ducks mentioned above, the birds flew between 460 and 850 meters high by day and dropped to a minimum of about 150 meters by night. The Blue and Snow Geese migrating from James Bay to Louisiana were observed at night flying at an altitude of 2400 meters. A collision with one of these birds forced a commercial airliner to return to an airfield for repairs. Records of the United States Civil Aeronautics Administration show that over two-thirds of all collisions between birds and aircraft occur below 610 meters altitude, and practically none above 1800 meters (Williams, 1950).

Radar observations of migrating birds by Sutter (1956) in Switzerland showed that in clear weather and with tail-winds birds flew between 200 and 2000 meters above the ground. With head-winds, however, they flew nearer the ground where the wind velocity was lower. Lack (1959) observed emigrating birds by radar near the east coast of England in March, and discovered that by day migrants flew relatively low over land and were mostly out of radar range, but as they put out to sea they rose higher, into radar range (Fig. 22.7). By night, radar bird echoes were equally dense over land and over the sea, indicating that night-migrating birds rose high immediately on taking flight. Apparently, birds realize instinctively the dangers of flying at low levels in the dark. Large, almost invisible Japanese "mist nets" are used by ornithologists to catch birds for banding purposes. At Cape May, New Jersey, 18 of these nets, each about

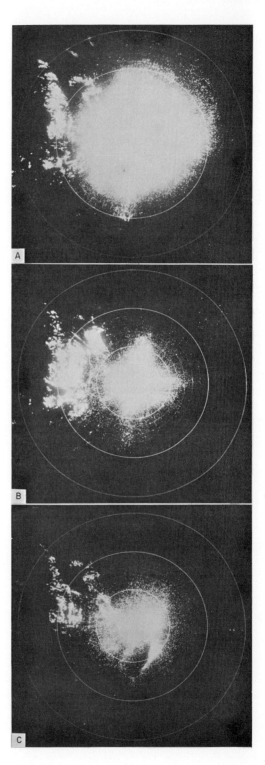

Figure 22.7. Three successive photographs of the same migration wave, as seen by radar from East Anglia, England. In each photo, the bright points of light represent radar echoes from birds. The larger patches of light to the left are chiefly high ground. North is at the top in each photo; the English Channel to the right, or East. The radar station itself is located in the center of the concentric circles, and the range from the station is shown by faint circles at 10-mile intervals, and heavier rings at 50-mile (80 kilometer) intervals.

A. shows the migration wave near the peak of nocturnal departures at 10:00 P.M. on March 11, 1957, with bird echoes extending northeastward from the station about 130 miles. By 4:00 A.M. the next morning, B, the nocturnal movement had dwindled to a moderate size, and by 6:00 A.M. the same morning, C, nocturnal emigration had nearly ceased and a moderate-sized morning emigration had begun. The sharp boundary crossing the 50-mile circle (in C) southeast of the radar station represents the seacoast. In the daytime the birds fly low over land, below radar range, and therefore show no echoes. But on reaching the coast and putting out to sea (right), they rise higher into radar range. After Lack. Photos courtesy of the Royal Radar Establishment. Crown Copyright.

10 meters long by 2 meters wide, did not catch a single bird during a night of heavy migration, but in less than an hour after sunrise they caught over 300 birds (Low, 1957).

Many species that show the aggressive intolerance of territorialism during the breeding season lose their mutual antagonism and become gregarious during migration periods. Preparatory to migration, many species gather in flocks, and often in flocks of several species. By traveling in flocks, young birds may learn the migration routes and successful migration behavior from older, experienced birds. These advantages do not apply, however, to species in which old and young migrate at different times of year. Flocks migrating at night are kept together by frequent chirps and calls that a listener on the ground can easily hear during a migration wave.

A popular misconception holds that migration is caused by a shortage of food. The supposition is that hunger drives birds to regions with more abundant food. While this idea does help to explain the long-range evolutionary origin of migration, it rarely accounts for present day migration movements. Baron von Pernau, aware of this fallacy, wrote, over two centuries ago:

"It is a very strange opinion if some believe the birds would emigrate, driven by hunger only. Instead they are usually very fat when about to leave us." (Stresemann, 1947).

WEATHER AND MIGRATION

Weather influences migration in at least three different ways. It controls the advance of the seasons, or the phenology of natural events, such as the date of the appearance of the first violet, or of the arrival of the first Robin. Secondly, it affects the migrating bird in flight, helping it, hindering it, or even at times crushing it to earth. Lastly, weather may be the stimulus that initiates the migration journey in a bird physiologically prepared for it.

The first, or phenological, influence of weather is essentially ecologic. Water birds gain nothing migrating north in spring if the lakes and streams are still frozen, nor can warblers and flycatchers survive if there are no insects awaiting them. There are early springs and late springs, and many species tailor their migration schedules to fit the season. Records by Saunders (1959) of the first arrivals among 50 different species in southern Connecticut showed that in late, cold springs, migrants on the average arrived later than in early, warm springs. In 1917, for example, the average of all arrival dates for 50 species was 5.38 days late, while in 1938 it was 6.15 days early, as compared with the 40-year mean arrival dates for all species (Fig. 22.8).

As spring advances northward each year, accompanying and successive waves of ecologic phenomena also march northward: the thawing of ice and snow, the first green blades, the emergence of insects and worms, the flowering of trees. Some birds migrate northward immediately on the heels of minimum spring conditions which allow their survival. The Canada Goose, *Branta canadensis*, pushes north roughly in step with the advance of the 2° C. isotherm; and in Europe, the Willow Warbler, *Phylloscopus trochilus*, migrates northward on a broad front which roughly parallels the progression of the 9° C. isotherm. Other species, such as the Gray-cheeked Thrush, *Hylocichla minima*, apparently wait in their winter quarters until ecologic conditions are suitable in the breeding zone; then they migrate north with a rush.

The ecology of changing seasons also influences the geography of migration pathways for some species. As mentioned above, the American Golden Plover, *Pluvialis dominica*, cannot retrace its fall migration route in the spring because the cold Labrador Current delays the arrival of spring along the northeast coast of North America. As a consequence, the birds fly up the center of the continent where conditions are more favorable.

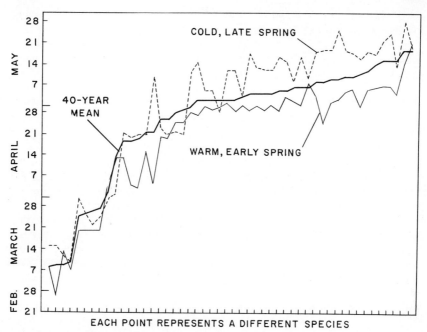

Figure 22.8. The arrival times of the first spring migrants vary with the weather. Each point on the thick line represents the 40-year mean of the first spring arrival-date for a given species in southeastern Connecticut. The species arriving earliest are shown at the left; those arriving latest, at the right. The solid light line shows the dates of the first arrivals of these same species during a warm early spring (1938) when most species arrived earlier than usual; the dotted line denotes arrivals during a late spring (1917). May, 1917, was especially cold and raw, and during this month the first arrivals averaged 8 days late. After Saunders.

Figure 22.9. In its spring migration, the Canada Goose advances northward roughly in step with the advance of the 2° C. isotherm. After Lincoln.

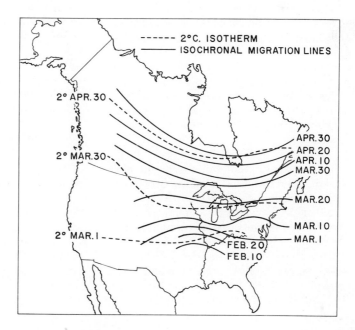

Swifts are extremely sensitive to weather conditions and frequently make migration-like massed flights to avoid cold, wet weather. Feeding, as they do, exclusively on air-borne insects, they require relatively fair weather if they are to avoid starvation.

Many studies have been made of the more direct influences of weather on birds while they are migrating. Attempts to correlate migration movements with barometric pressure, wind direction, precipitation, and temperature have resulted in conflicting conclusions. It seems clear, however, that the springtime waves of migrating birds in the eastern United States usually coincide with the flow of warm, moist, south winds from the Gulf of Mexico. These favorable winds characteristically occur in the gap between a high pressure anticyclone followed by a low pressure cyclone, as both slowly advance eastward across the country. There seems to be little doubt that adverse weather may impede migration and cause concentrations of birds to pile up. With the return of favorable weather, these birds move on in "waves" or "rushes." In southern Sweden in the autumn of 1952, 10 days of strong winds held up the migration of great numbers of birds. When favorable conditions returned, the birds moved south as in an avalanche (Mathiasson, 1957). At other times adverse weather may completely reverse the direction of migration and cause north-flying birds to fly south in the spring. Such reverse migration may continue for several hours or even several days, and involve flocks of many species of birds.

While head-winds may retard birds' flight speeds, and tail-winds increase them, wind direction itself has little to do with migration waves. A study by Dinnendahl (1954) of 241 waves of 13 species of nocturnal migrants passing through Helgoland in the North Sea showed no correlation with wind direction. However, migration waves rarely occurred when wind velocities, regardless of direction, exceeded about 50 kilometers per hour.

Side-winds may cause a lateral displacement of migrants, especially of young, inexperienced birds (Williamson, 1959). Many North American nocturnal migrants are deflected eastward by the prevailing westerly winds of the north temperate zone, to perish at sea when they become exhausted. The fact that many south-flying coastal migrants between Maine and Virginia are often seen flying west, or even north of west, in the fall, suggests to Baird and Nisbet (1960) that this may be an evolutionary adaptation to the off-shore drift caused by the prevailing winds. Whether this is an innate compensatory behavior or a simple response to wind direction and topography, it unquestionably prevents many fatalities.

The extensive literature on the influence of weather on migration has recently been reviewed by Lack (1960), who concludes that migration is relatively unaffected "by the general weather situation as such, or by barometric pressure, . . . or by wind direction . . ." However, more migration occurs in fine weather with clear skies and light winds than in rain, cloudy weather, or strong winds. Further, migration generally occurs in spring with warm weather and in fall with cold.

For many species, weather conditions may determine whether the birds will begin their migrations or not. But once under way, birds are deterred from migration only by extremely adverse weather. And weather as such cannot initiate migration in a bird physiologically unprepared for it.

TIMING OF MIGRATION

When a bird is internally prepared for migration, various external stimuli may trigger the beginning of migratory flight. Among these stimuli, weather plays an important role, not so much as weather itself, but more indirectly through the ecologic conditions it brings about. Even so, adverse weather may directly delay the departure of temperature zone species in the spring, or speed their departure in the fall. In the drier parts of Africa and Australia, certain species are rain followers, migrating to those regions where rain creates favorable conditions for raising young. Food failures may act as stimuli to initiate the migration of irruptive species like crossbills, while food abundance, on the other hand, may cause normally migratory species to become sedentary. Some species, for example, Lapwings, *Vanellus vanellus,* are thought to migrate south earlier in the fall if they suffer a nesting failure (Putzig, 1938).

The calendar-like regularity of the spring and fall migrations of many species is without doubt the consequence of the accumulated effects of millenia of climatic cycles impressed on the sensitive living cells of birds. There is great variation in the precision with which different species follow the calendar. The famous swallows of San Juan Capistrano Mission in California are not as precise in their timing as popular accounts might lead one to believe. Nevertheless, some species arrive and depart on their migrations with striking calendar regularity. Many pelagic sea birds, such as terns, boobies, and shearwaters, arrive at their breeding islands approximately the same week every year. The Slender-billed Shearwater, *Puffinus tenuirostris,* which winters in the Pacific up to the Aleutian Islands, arrives at its south Australian breeding grounds during the same eleven days every year (Marshall and Serventy, 1959).

Most species, however, show more diversity in their times of migration. Snow Geese, *Chen hyperborea,* have been known to arrive at their Delaware wildlife refuge as early as September and as late as November. A four-year study of migrating shore birds by New Jersey ornithologists showed that various species required as much as two to three months to pass through. As a rule, spring migration was of much shorter duration than fall migration, and young birds seemed to travel more leisurely than adults (Urner and Storer, 1949).

The apparent steady passage of migrant birds through a given region is not always the simple phenomenon it seems. The Yellow Warbler, *Dendroica petechia,* arrives in southern Arizona in mid-March, in northeastern Arizona in late April, and in Canada in May or early June. However, these dates alone give a misleading impression, for they do not apply to the same birds. The birds arriving in Arizona in mid-March are the resident race *sonorana;* more northerly races reach Arizona in late April; and the most northerly race, *rubiginosa,* does not enter Arizona until May, at which time it flies over the southern races on its way to Canada (Phillips, 1951).

Birds have their preferred times of day for migrating. The majority of small birds, including most passerines, feed by day and migrate by night, when they are safer from predators and when the air is generally more stable. Small birds, with their livelier metabolism, exhaust their energy stores in flight more rapidly than large birds do. Therefore, they must replace them quickly and effectively, and this can best be done by daylight. Furthermore, by migrating at night, they are less likely to be distracted by their surroundings and are better able to concentrate on covering distance. Larger birds, such as hawks, eagles, storks, herons, and crows, migrate by day and rest by night, as do also the insect-feeding swifts and swallows which sweep up their food as they migrate. Loons, ducks and geese, some shore birds, and auks may migrate either by day or by night.

Recent studies of nocturnal migrants by telescopes focused on the disc of the full moon (Lowery and Newman, 1955), and by radar (Lack, 1959), have shown that nocturnal migration begins soon after dark and builds up to a peak shortly before midnight, then gradually dwindles to essentially none by dawn. Spring emigration from England to the continent was found by Lack to be heavier by night than by day, but in the autumn, immigration was equally dense by night and by day. Radar echoes at present are unable to distinguish individual birds from small flocks. Nevertheless, the echoes show that nocturnal migrants generally fly on broad fronts and not in narrow paths or ribbons which follow guide-lines like rivers or coasts. Lunar observations corroborate this fact.

The time of year during which a migrant departs for winter quarters is related to its time of breeding. The European Swift, *Apus apus*, finishes nesting in Italy at the end of July, and leaves then for its winter quarters. In northern Germany it ceases breeding and departs around the first of August, and in mid-Finland, in late August and early September (Stresemann, 1927–1934). Conversely, the time consumed in flight by some long-distance migrants limits the time they have available for breeding. The Arctic Warbler, *Phylloscopus borealis*, mentioned earlier, winters in the Malay archipelago and arrives at its Norwegian breeding area, some 12,500 kilometers away, between June 18 and 25. It immediately starts breeding, and the young leave the nest at the beginning of August. Shortly thereafter they fly away with their parents for winter quarters. Stresemann points out that this species could not migrate much farther and have any time left for breeding! The fact that so many shore birds and waterfowl make such long migrations and have such short breeding seasons in the far north probably explains why some of them become paired in winter quarters rather than in the breeding area.

The times at which migration occurs may vary not only between different races of a given species but also between old and young, or between males and females of the same species. In many species, particularly among the passerines, the males often arrive at the breeding area before the females. In the northern United States, for example, the male Redwinged Blackbird, *Agelaius phoeniceus*, arrives in spring from one to five weeks before the female; and in Europe, the male Ortolan Bunting, *Emberiza hortulana*, precedes the female by one or two weeks. By arriving early in this way, the males have time to establish territory, so that when the females arrive, they can both proceed with breeding activities. Sexually segregated migration

of this sort may, in some species, postpone the stimulation that causes the maturation of the female sex organs. This would make possible a reduction in weight of the migrating female and ensure a more precisely synchronized sexual development of the two sexes.

Apparently, most young birds migrate to winter quarters with the adults, but in some species, such as the American Golden Plover, *Pluvialis dominica*, the adults migrate earlier in the fall than do the young, while in others, like the European Swift, *Apus apus*, the young often leave for winter quarters first. In some species, but certainly not in all, the time of migration seems to be related to the time of molting. In the European Red-backed Shrike, *Lanius collurio*, the adults have no post-breeding molt and are able to migrate south before the young have matured enough to accompany them. The White Wagtail, *Motacilla alba*, on the other hand, does have a complete post-breeding molt, and its young migrate from a week to ten days before the adults.

In some birds, sex and age may affect, in addition, the extent of migration. In some passerines, the males may remain sedentary while the females and young migrate to winter quarters. Among many of the shore birds and waders, such as gulls, terns, herons, and storks, the young disperse widely after leaving the nest. They may wander as vagabonds for from two to five years before maturing sufficiently to become regular, breeding migrants. All told, a considerable variety of influences bear on the timing of migration. It is usually very difficult, if not impossible, to say why a given species migrates when it does.

PREDISPOSITION TO MIGRATE

It is obvious that warmer weather, longer days, abundant food, or any other of the numerous stimuli that release the departure of migrating birds do not cause migration irrespective of the condition of the birds themselves. This is apparent from the simple fact that of two races of birds living under identical environmental conditions, one may be stimulated to migrate when spring comes, and the other may not. For example, the Oregon Junco, *Junco oreganus*, has both migratory and non-migratory races living in northern California. When both types of birds were simultaneously subjected to increases in day length, either natural or artificial, only the migratory race became restless and departed on its northward migration. The non-migratory race, subjected to identical conditions, remained sedentary (Wolfson, 1942).

It is clear that certain internal conditions predispose certain birds to migrate, and certain external conditions act on these birds as stimuli that release migratory behavior. In all migratory species, this predisposition seems to be a cyclic mechanism closely tied to reproduction, and it operates to ensure migration to the breeding area at the best time of year for raising the young. The mechanism is sensitive to a variety of external factors, such as length of day, temperature, rainfall, food abundance, and behavior interactions, which normally act to determine the time of migration either by stimulation or by inhibition.

Because of the intimate relation between migration and breeding, and particularly because, in early experiments, photo-periodism seemed to stimulate both sexual activity and migration, it was assumed that there was a causal connection between the two. This is not now thought to be the case. Arguing against such a connection is the fact that many sedentary species pass through their reproductive cycle without the slightest tendency to migrate. In addition, experiments by Putzig (1937) and others have shown that castrated birds are nevertheless able to migrate.

There seems to be general agreement that the predisposition to migrate involves fat accumulation and nocturnal restlessness, or *Zugunruhe*, at least in birds of the north temperate zone. Not only do migrants store generous amounts of peritoneal and subcutaneous fat in their bodies shortly before migration, but, should the fat be exhausted after a long migratory flight, they are able to replenish it with astonishing rapidity and then continue on their way. Natorp (*in* Stresemann, 1927–1934) found that the Wheat-ear, *Oenanthe oenanthe*, required only one week to fatten itself from the very lean condition at the end of molt to the plump condition it had on the day it left in migration.

A White-throated Sparrow, *Zonotrichia albicollis*, is a relatively short-distance migrant, breeding in Canada and wintering in the southern half of the United States. Fats extracted from 86 birds at different seasons of the year by Odum and Perkinson (1951) showed that just before spring migration fats accounted for 16.7 per cent of total body weight, and after migration only 6.9 per cent. The sedentary House Sparrow, *Passer domesticus*, on the contrary, shows a spring low ebb in total body weight which is about 8 per cent below the annual October maximum.

As a rule, the longer the migration flight, the greater the store of fat. Analyses of body-fat content of migrating birds killed in the autumn by collision with a television tower on the Gulf Coast of Florida showed that the average White-throated Sparrow had a fat content amounting to 6.2 per cent of its body weight, whereas 29 warblers of three species (Tennessee, *Vermivora peregrina;* Bay-breasted, *Dendroica castanea;* and Magnolia, *Dendroica magnolia*) averaged 30.1 per cent body fat, with extremes of 6.1 and 42.1 per cent (Odum, 1958). These warblers would normally have continued their migration across the Gulf of Mexico to Mexico and South America, and accordingly they needed greater stores of energy for migration than did the White-throats, which had essentially reached the end of their migration from Canada. There is suggestive evidence that a hormone from the anterior pituitary gland (Antuitrin G) stimulates fat deposition in juncos (Wolfson, 1945).

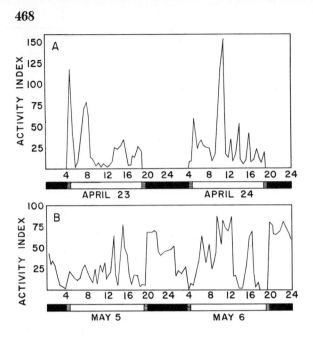

Figure 22.10. Forty-eight-hour records of the rate of activity of a first-year male White-crowned Sparrow. A, During the molting period just prior to the onset of *Zugunruhe*. B, After the onset of *Zugunruhe*. The black bar represents periods of darkness; the shaded bar, twilight; the open bar, sunrise to sunset. After Farner.

Zugunruhe is a twice-yearly cycle of nocturnal restlessness, which occurs in migratory birds during the migration seasons. Automatically recorded activity graphs of captive migrants show a daily rhythm in which the bird sleeps for a short period—15 minutes to two hours—after sunset, then awakens and hops and flutters in its cage with increasing vigor until shortly before midnight, after which the activity gradually dies down. This activity in captive birds closely parallels in time the nocturnal activity of freely flying migrants. In the springtime, warm weather will increase *Zugunruhe* in captive migrants, and cold weather will depress it, whereas in the autumn the exact reverse occurs. Non-migratory birds like the House Sparrow, *Passer domesticus*, show no night-restlessness at any season of the year.

The relation of day length to *Zugunruhe* was demonstrated by Lofts and Marshall (1960) on captive Bramblings, *Fringilla montifringilla*, which were kept throughout their normal springtime migration period under artificially shortened days as though it were winter. Neither *Zugunruhe* nor gonad enlargement occurred. At the end of the normal migratory period, the light dosage was increased to 14½ hours daily. The birds then developed *Zugunruhe* and the males responded with fat deposition and enlargement of testes. Experiments with castrates indicated that *Zugunruhe* and migration could occur in the absence of sex hormones.

A special feature of nocturnal restlessness in certain species is its compass orientation. Migratory White-crowned Sparrows, *Zonotrichia leucophrys*, kept in circular cages under the open California sky, showed a southerly orientation at night during the fall migration period in August and September, and a pronounced northerly orientation in *Zugunruhe* during the spring migration period in April and early May (Mewaldt and Rose, 1960). The birds demonstrated their tendencies to orient by perching on any one of 8 activity-sensitive perches symmetrically arranged around the periphery of a cage. In the nine-day period between April 23 and May 1, one male sparrow oriented at random by day, but by night chose the perch on the North side of the cage 5299 times (73 per cent), the Northeast perch 1053 times (15 per cent), the Northwest perch 411 times (6 per cent), and each of all other perches 2 per cent of the time or less.

Numerous experiments and much speculation have been devoted to the discovery of the basic causes of migration. As yet, there is no general agreement on the solution of the problem. For birds living in the north temperate zone, it seems likely that the predisposition to migrate hinges on a neuro-endocrine mechanism, which controls the timing and sequence of events in the annual cycle somewhat as follows (Farner, 1955): After a winter period of long nights and reproductive rest, the pituitary gland recovers from its refractory period (p. 153). The longer days and warm weather of springtime make possible increased feeding and less heat loss, and therefore a surplus energy balance. The increased day length stimulates the pituitary to secrete not only gonadotropic hormones which initiate the breeding cycle, but also other, unknown hormones which initiate rapid fat deposit and *Zugunruhe*. Once in this condition, a bird is easily induced to migrate by some external stimulus such as favorable weather.

This admittedly hypothetical explanation does not fit birds passing the winter, for example, in equatorial regions where day length does not change appreciably throughout the year. Without question, different migration-stimulating or inhibiting mechanisms exist for birds living under different environmental circumstances. Marshall (1961) makes the point that the neuro-endocrine machinery responsible for reproduction and migration is, week after week, under the influence of antagonistic sets of accelerators and inhibitors. Accelerators may be such influences as warmth, sunlight, territory, adequate food, the nest site, nest materials, and behavorial interactions. Inhibitors may include cold, inclement weather, hunger, fear, lack of nesting materials or of the traditional nest site.

ORIENTATION AND NAVIGATION

Probably the knottiest problem in all ornithology is how a bird finds its way home. Year in, year out, millions of migrating birds successfully travel hundreds and even thousands of kilometers, back and forth between their breeding and their wintering grounds, sometimes over what to man are featureless stretches of land or water, and very commonly by night. To do this successfully, a bird must know where it is; it must know the direction of its goal; and it must be able to maintain its course, or navigate, in that direction. Banded long-distance migrants have returned in successive years not only to the same pinpoint nesting site, but to the same restricted wintering area. Many individually marked birds have been experimentally displaced thousand of kilometers into completely strange areas, and yet have returned to their home nest sites, often with astonishing speed. For example, a Manx Shearwater, *Puffinus puffinus*, carried by airplane to Boston, over 5100 kilometers from its breeding island off Wales, was back in its nesting burrow 12½ days later (Mazzeo, 1953); and a Laysan Albatross, *Diomedea immutabilis*, experimentally displaced 6650 kilometers, returned to its nest in 32 days (Kenyon and Dice, 1958).

Homing ability is widespread in the animal kingdom. It is found in limpets, squids, lobsters, ants, bees, many fishes, salamanders, box turtles, bats, mice and many other mammals. Although the capacity for homing is best developed in birds, not all birds have equal facility in finding their way. Some wrens, titmice, doves, and sparrows are unable to return to their nests when experimentally displaced only a few kilometers. Homing ability is at least partly hereditary, as is shown by the fact that there are some breeds of homing pigeons which perform much better than others.

Whatever senses a bird may use to find its way, it still must recognize "home" when it arrives there. This recognition may be hereditary, or, more likely, acquired early in life, perhaps through imprinting.

ORIENTATION BY SPECIAL SENSES

Attempts to explain orientation are

usually based either on the use of known sense organs and their perception of "ordinary" clues in the physical or biotic environment, or on unknown sense organs which might extend the bird's range of perception. Because the traditional senses seem inadequate to account for many of the remarkable feats of bird orientation, many authors have postulated special senses, or special refinements of known senses.

This theorizing is not unreasonable if one considers some of the known sensory abilities of other animals: the exceedingly acute sense of taste in butterflies; the sharp olfactory sense of bloodhounds and moths; the ability of bees to see ultraviolet and to discriminate the plane of polarized light; the ability of pit vipers to perceive infra-red rays; the well-known capacity of bats and of at least two species of birds (the Oilbird, *Steatornis caripensis,* and Cave Swiftlet, *Collocalia brevirostris*) to avoid obstacles in the dark by echo-location (Griffin, 1953, and Novick, 1959). Even experimentally displaced blind newts are able to home, but by what sensory means is unknown (Twitty, 1959).

Among the theories involving special sense perception is the kinesis or retracement theory, which holds that a bird stores in its memory kinesthetic and semicircular canal impressions of every twist and turn of an outgoing journey, and recalls them, in reverse order, for guidance on the return trip. Numerous displacement experiments, with birds either anesthetized or constantly spun on turn-tables on the outgoing trip, showed no differences in homing ability between experimental and control birds. Moreover, a theory of this sort cannot account for orientation on the maiden trip of a young, unaccompanied, inexperienced bird.

Another hypothesis ascribes to homing birds an ability to sense the earth's magnetic field and thereby acquire a compass-like sense of direction. No one has yet convincingly demonstrated that birds are able to sense the earth's magnetism, however.

A third hypothesis, proposed by Ising (1946), suggests that, because of their motions over the surface of the earth, birds add to or subtract from the effects of the earth's centrifugal force, and that they are able to feel the gravitational differences in weight that result. In opposition to this, Griffin (1955) points out that a bird flying east along the equator at 65 kilometers per hour would find its weight increased by only 1 part in 2000 when it turned and flew west—hardly a detectable difference. Another force suggested as a possible clue to orientation—provided birds could sense it—is the Coriolis force. This is the lateral force generated in moving bodies that cross lines of latitude on the earth's surface: the force that causes the clockwise deflections of winds in the northern hemisphere. The almost infinitesimal value of Coriolis forces in a flying bird have discouraged wide acceptance of this means of orientation. A hypothesis advanced by Yeagley (1947, 1951), and based on experiments with homing pigeons, suggests that birds respond both to terrestrial magnetism and to Coriolis force, and that geographic gradients of the two forces create two sets of coordinates, something like the longitude-latitude grid, which birds unconsciously refer to while navigating. This theory has aroused much criticism and little support among ornithologists (Wynne-Edwards, 1948). The subtle nature of both forces involved, and the problematical character of bird receptors needed to sense them, make such a theory extremely difficult either to prove or disprove.

SENSE OF DIRECTION

The idea that birds possess an innate "sense of direction" cannot be as easily dismissed as some of the above theories. Rüppell (1944) captured 896 Hooded Crows, *Corvus cornix,* during their spring migration through Rossitten on the southeastern shore of the Baltic, and transported them by train to Flensburg (750 kilometers to the west), Essen (1025 kilometers west-southwest), and Frankfurt (1010 kilometers southwest), where they were released. Of these birds 176 were recaptured: 20 of them in their presumptive or traditional summer or winter ranges, but 156 of them in new and displaced summer and winter ranges, outside of and to the west of their normal ranges. The released birds had migrated in the traditional northeasterly direction, in a path parallel to their normal migration route but displaced to the west. This caused them to settle for the summer in Denmark and Sweden rather than in the east Baltic countries and Russia. The few displaced birds that returned to the normal breeding areas were probably older, experienced birds that had migrated there previously. Similar displacement experiments with Starlings, *Sturnus vulgaris*, and White Storks, *Ciconia ciconia*, showed that they, too, have an innate tendency to migrate in certain compass directions. Young White Storks from Rossitten, which normally migrate in a southeasterly direction toward the eastern end of the Mediterranean Sea, were transported to western Germany and released after the native Storks of this region had already departed for winter quarters. The young Storks flew in a southerly or southeasterly direction, as they would have flown from Rossitten, rather than in the southwesterly direction characteristic of west German White Storks (Schüz, 1949).

These and like experiments indicate that some species migrate according to an inner sense of direction, rather than an awareness of a distant goal. Possibly this same directional sense accounts for the results obtained by Kramer *et al.* (1956) with homing pigeons. Untrained birds were taken from their home cote in Durham, North Carolina, and released singly at ten minute intervals at places 26 and 28, 85 and 96 kilometers approximately due north, east, south, and west of Durham. Out of 675 flights, the largest number of successful returns, for both distance ranges, was from the south, and the smallest number from the north. A similar experiment in Germany gave similar results, but near Cambridge, England, pigeons returned to their cote more successfully from the north than from the south.

Radar observations of nocturnal spring migration of passerines across the North Sea from England indicated that the birds maintained a sense of direction but not a sense of position. With southerly winds, the flights headed north of east, and with northerly winds, south of east (Lack, 1960). Nocturnal migrants orienting only by means of a sense of direction would be at the mercy of drifting winds—in fact, they often are—until daylight permits visual correction of errors in navigation. An innate sense of direction may play a useful part in migration orientation for some species, but too great a dependency on it can be hazardous. Birds that follow

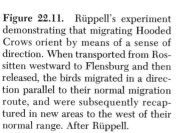

Figure 22.11. Rüppell's experiment demonstrating that migrating Hooded Crows orient by means of a sense of direction. When transported from Rossitten westward to Flensburg and then released, the birds migrated in a direction parallel to their normal migration route, and were subsequently recaptured in new areas to the west of their normal range. After Rüppell.

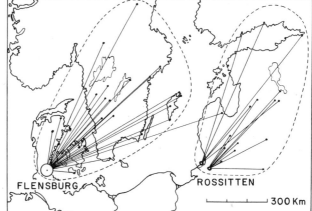

the crooked paths of "dog-leg" migration routes would need a series of different and precisely-timed direction senses if they were to arrive at their destinations. The development of new migration routes in historic times, and the obvious dangers of a petrified sense of direction in a constantly changing world, argue against its exclusive use as a means of bird orientation.

While no special sense organ has ever been proposed as the seat of the so-called sense of direction in birds, recent experiments by Gaultierotti *et al* (1959) have shown functional differences in the brains of migratory as compared with non-migratory pigeons. Birds with electrodes inserted in their cerebella were subjected to changes in velocity and plane of centrifugal rotation. After removal from the centrifuge, wild, migratory Turtle Doves, *Streptopelia turtur,* and Domestic Pigeons, *Columba livia,* of homing strains, produced characteristic electrical cerebellar after-discharges. There were no such discharges from the non-migratory Ringed Turtle Dove, *Streptopelia risoria,* and discharges from only 7 per cent of the Domestic Pigeons of non-homing stock. About one-half of the hybrids between homing and non-homing pigeons showed after-discharges.

VISUAL ORIENTATION

A sense of direction, or compass sense, is worthless unless a bird also possesses a sense of position—that is, knows where it is with reference to its goal. It needs, in effect, a compass, a chart, and knowledge of its map-location. It would be strange indeed if birds did not use their superior eyesight to aid them in navigation. Visual orientation is not incompatible with a sense of direction, but usefully supplementary to it. For example, a species may fly in a given direction until it reaches a seashore, and then follow that for the next leg of the journey. In some species, visual clues may be all that are required to guide birds on their migration travels. In the case

of birds following traditional migratory routes, which the young birds learn from their elders, the birds need only to remember the varied visual landmarks over which they fly: shores, islands, mountains, river valleys, prairies, deserts, forests. Young geese very likely learn their migration routes in this way. Stresemann (1927–1934) remarks that young geese are so dependent on the leadership of older birds that the young, in spite of a lively *Zugunruhe,* will remain and spend the winter at the breeding area if older birds are restrained from migrating by wing-clipping. It may be, too, that birds flying in flocks orient themselves better than birds flying individually, because of the possibilities of pooling navigational resources and of averaging out individual errors or deviations from the true path. In experiments with homing pigeons displaced to strange territory and followed by an airplane, Hitchcock (1955) found that pigeons released singly showed greater indecision and poorer homing ability than pigeons released in flocks.

Evidence that birds may rely on topographic memory to orient themselves is found in experiments such as that by Griffin (1943) in which three Herring Gulls, *Larus argentatus,* were experimentally displaced into presumably strange territory about 400 kilometers from their nests in two successive years. The second year the birds returned in approximately one-sixth the time they needed the first year, probably because they now recognized landmarks and could fly more directly back to their nests. Griffin also found that terns came back to their nests more promptly when released at points in their normal migration route, and thus, probably, a route familiar to them.

Strong, long-distance fliers probably combine several means of orientation to reach their goals: sense of direction, random search, topographic memory, and perhaps others. When one method proves to be inadequate, others may supplement it. The Gannet, *Morus bassanus,* is a highly marine species, rarely seen inland. When 17 marked Gannets were displaced

342 kilometers west-southwest from their nests on Bonaventure Island and released deep inland in Maine, they were observed by airplane to perform more or less random movements until they encountered the familiar Atlantic coast line, after which they made a more rapid and direct return home (Griffin and Hock, 1949).

In addition to topographic clues, birds may use ecologic and meteorologic clues for orientation. A migrating bird may well possess an inherited reaction to certain gross landmarks such as mountain ranges or forests, and also to certain finer details of landscape. The bird may prefer to fly over scrub desert rather than rock and sand desert, or over long-grass prairie rather than short-grass plains, or over oak-hickory forests rather than beech-maple woods. Still finer distinctions may be perceived by a bird whose eyes, supplied with colored oil droplets in many species, may discern otherwise invisible features of the landscape, as aerial cameras using special filters can detect features invisible to ordinary cameras.

The march of spring northward across the land provides seasonal phenologic clues to the migrating bird. One species may fly northward from a condition of early spring into late winter, while a more slowly moving species may progress northward at the same rate as spring itself. In the north temperate zone in April and May, spring advances northward about two degrees of latitude every week. Therefore, the difference that one week of spring sunshine would make in the appearance of a flower garden might be evident to a bird, and hence a clue to its direction of flight, if it flew due north or south two degrees in latitude or approximately 210 kilometers—not a strenuous day's flight for many migrants. Any bird flying even 100 kilometers in the "wrong" direction would soon see discrepancies between the landscape beneath it and the learned or innate image of the correctly unfolding migration path.

Although migrating birds do not ordinarily fly at great speeds or great heights, their flight makes possible a type of orientation clue denied to earth-borne travelers: the juxtaposition of landscape features both in space (through altitude) and in time (through rapid movement). Thus, birds can grasp larger configurations of the landscape and make meaning out of topographic and ecologic juxtapositions in somewhat the same way that the housewife can compare two color samples when they are side by side, but not when one is at the shop and the other at home. Ornithologists have perhaps been too prone to tackle the visual orientation problem analytically, looking for isolated clues when, possibly, birds recognize beneath them a terrestrial physiognomy much as a person recognizes the photograph of a friend, but would be at a loss to identify it if it were cut up and scrambled into jigsaw-puzzle pieces. If one person can recognize a friend among a thousand strangers, why should not a bird be able to recognize a "friendly" habitat or migration path among many similarly-appearing (to man) patches of the earth's surface? This does not deny the significance of prominent individual features of the landscape or face (mountain or wart) which might serve as visual clues to identity, but it helps to explain how a bird or a human may *unconsciously* use subtle differences in landscapes or faces to tell them apart. As Pascal remarked, "If the nose of Cleopatra had been shorter, the whole face of the earth would have been changed."

The fact that many migrants travel by night does not deny them the opportunity of inspecting the landscape by day. And even on moonless nights, the earth is by no means featureless. Rocks, trees, fields, rivers, and hills are clearly visible by starlight to dark-adapted eyes.

Visual orientation by features of the landscape does not seem particularly helpful to migrants crossing large stretches of the ocean. But even here there are a few clues to location or direction, some visual and others not: wind and wave direction (particularly in zones with relatively steady prevailing winds); islands, reefs, atolls; cloud formations over oceanic islands and over many cold waters such as the California Current; temperature and humidity differences in the air; temperature, color, and turbidity differences in the great surface currents of the seas and at the mouths of great rivers; fog belts where cold and warm currents come together, as on the Newfoundland Bank; the presence or absence of organisms visible from the air, such as dolphins, flying fishes, jellyfishes, whales, or, in the nighttime, glowing dinoflagellates; or accumulations of floating algae, as in the Sargasso Sea. These do not make an impressive list of road-signs in the vast reaches of the oceans, but they may nevertheless be useful clues to some wanderers.

One difficulty in the use of ecologic and phenologic clues for navigation is that they change with the seasons, and the changes do not always come in precisely predictable cycles. For example, an early autumn snow-storm can greatly change the appearance of the land. This may be one of the reasons the great majority of fall migrants move southward well ahead of the average time of the first snow-fall. Nor are ecologic clues generally available in the midst of the great expanses of desert or sea. It is difficult to see how they could be of any use to the New Zealand Bronzed Cuckoo, *Chalcites lucidus,* whose young, one month after their parasitic parents have preceded them, migrate about 1900 kilometers westward across the ocean to Australia, and then another 1600 kilometers northward over water to the Solomon and Bismark Islands, where they join their parents. This migration, one of the wonders of bird life, surely demonstrates the hereditary nature of some migration flights, but reveals, as yet, nothing of the means by which the young birds navigate successfully over relatively featureless water to a tiny wintering area.

Difficult to explain, also, is the attempted migration from Missouri of some 60 pinioned Canada Geese, *Branta canadensis,* which escaped from their pens in late May. These birds, unable to fly, walked or swam (until recaptured) toward their northerly breeding grounds as far as 40 kilometers, at the rate of 0.5 to 1.2 kilometers per day,

long after the normal time of migration. Other pinioned geese, experimentally released in Nebraska, North Dakota, and South Dakota, showed the same northward orientation. Very probably ecologic or phenologic clues did not operate in these cases (Hamilton and Hammond, 1960).

ASTRONOMIC NAVIGATION

One of the most dependable and changeless reference points a migrating bird could use in orienting itself is the sun —the same luminary that sailors use in their navigation. So it is not surprising that recent experiments have shown that some birds do use the sun in maintaining their migratory sense of direction. In the past decade, much research has been devoted to this intriguing approach to bird navigation, especially by Kramer (1957, 1961) and his students. Birds kept in circular cages during the migration season often show their restlessness by facing and fluttering in a direction conforming to that taken by migrating wild birds of the same species. Kramer placed Starlings, *Sturnus vulgaris,* in a cage exposed to sunlight, and observed that the birds fluttered on their circular perch in the normal migration direction as long as the sun shone, but on cloudy days their activity was disoriented. When the apparent position of the sun was artificially shifted by means of mirrors, the orientation of the birds shifted correspondingly. Since the direction of orientation of the Starlings remained constant for hours, this indicated that they made allowance for the normally changing position of the sun. That is, the birds possessed "internal clocks," which allowed them to maintain a compass direction sense by referring to the sun, regardless of the hour of day.

An experimental attempt was made by Hoffman (1954) to "reset" these inner clocks by subjecting Starlings for several days to an artificial light and dark cycle six hours advanced over the natural outdoor cycle. As a result, when the birds with their clocks reset were exposed to natural daylight, their direction of fluttering was shifted 90 degrees in a counter-clockwise direction. Birds whose clocks were retarded six hours, shifted their orientation 90 degrees in a clockwise direction. It was further found that the birds responded to the azimuth or compass bearing of the sun and not to its height above the horizon. This type of orientation is called *sun-azimuth* orientation.

Sun-azimuth orientation has also been demonstrated in the Eastern Meadowlark, *Sturnella magna*, Barred Warbler, *Sylvia nisoria*, Red-backed Shrike, *Lanius collurio*, and Domestic Pigeon, *Columba livia*. Homing pigeons whose internal clocks were shifted six hours, both forward and backward, were carried on a sunny day to various distances (9 to 161 kilometers) and in various directions from their home cote, and released. In their flight paths they showed corresponding mean deviations of roughly 90 degrees to the left and to the right, respectively, of the correct path, the one taken by the non-shifted control pigeons (Schmidt-Koenig, 1960). A few of the shifted pigeons were able to home rapidly in spite of their re-set clocks, which suggests that they oriented by means other than the sun-azimuth "compass."

Recent experiments with box turtles indicate that they too use the sun in orientation (Gould, 1957). The pioneer work on orientation in bees by von Frisch (1956) showed that they not only use the sun in navigation, but that scout bees inform workers in the dark hive just how far to travel and in what direction, with reference to the sun's position, to find a source of nectar. Interestingly, bees in the northern hemisphere compensate for clockwise azimuth shifts in the sun's position while orienting to their foraging plots; bees in the southern hemisphere, counter-clockwise. Inseminated queen bees shipped from the northern hemisphere to Brazil produced offspring compensated for azimuth changes in the northern, clockwise fashion, and therefore oriented falsely (Kalmus, 1956). Behavior such as this dem-

onstrates that the innate clock which compensates for the daily movement of the sun is an inherited mechanism in bees, as it must also be in birds.

Since birds are able to determine compass directions in the daytime with the help of the sun's position and an internal timing device, it is but a short logical step to assume that night-time migrants may be able to use the stars in the same way. This idea, in fact, appealed to the Scottish poet, John Logan, two centuries ago when he wrote, in his poem *To the Cuckoo*,

> What time the daisy decks the green,
>   Thy certain voice we hear;
> Hast thou a star to guide thy path
>   Or mark the rolling year?

Sauer's (1957) recent experiments with European warblers go far toward establishing the fact of navigation by the stars. During periods of spring or fall *Zugunruhe*, Sauer placed various European warblers in circular, rotatable cages exposed to clear, nighttime skies. The birds oriented in the direction taken by normal wild migrants for that place and time of year. Even when birds were turned away by having their perches rotated, they stubbornly persisted in facing and fluttering in the preferred migratory direction. On cloudy nights the birds showed no directional orientation. The cages were next placed under the dome of a planetarium. With the star images set for the local region (Freiburg, Germany), the birds oriented as they had under the natural sky. But when Sauer shifted the artificial sky so that it appeared as it would to a bird near Lake Baikal, Siberia, at that hour, (the birds' clocks were not shifted), the birds in the cage reacted by heading west as if to migrate back to Germany. Earlier experiments by von Saint-Paul (1954) had shown that the night-migrating Barred Warbler, *Sylvia nisoria*, could orient by the sun's azimuth. This suggests that some species are able to use both the sun and the stars for orientation.

The most remarkable of Sauer's experiments were done with a single Lesser Whitethroat, *Sylvia curruca*. This bird in its fall migration normally travels south-eastward from Germany across the Balkans and then heads straight south, flying up the Nile to its mid-African winter quarters. When the planetarium sky showed the south German latitude, the warbler oriented in the normal southeasterly migration direction; but when the sky was shifted to show its more southerly aspect of regions about 35 degrees south of Germany, the bird shifted its position and faced due south. Since this particular bird had been hand-raised and had never lived in the open, nor migrated to Africa, Sauer was convinced that it was born with a complete, innate navigation system— chart, compass, and chronometer! More experiments with more birds of different species need to be done before one can say with assurance that this theory of stellar navigation is correct.

Even should a navigation system of this kind be found to exist in many nocturnal migrants, it still would not explain some feats of bird migration. For example, a female Purple Martin, *Progne subis,* was removed from its nest containing young in northern Michigan and transported to Ann Arbor, 375 kilometers to the south, and released there at 10:40 P.M. The next morning at 7:15 the bird was back at its nest. The sky that night was completely overcast with a double layer of clouds, so it is unlikely that the bird used celestial navigation to find its way (Southern, 1959). It may be, as some authors suggest, that birds determine directions by reference to celestial bodies, and then, should the skies be clouded over and the reference points obscured, depend secondarily on substitute clues such as wind direction, topography, or ecologic patterns. But merely directional clues are of little value unless the bird knows where it is.

When a bird is transported in an opaque container into strange regions and released under cloudy skies, or at night, it is difficult to understand how the bird knows where it is, so that, even with an innate sense of direction, it knows in what direction it must travel to reach home. Many birds used in such experiments fail to return to their nests, but others do return, and their feat cannot be due to chance alone.

Even though all kinds of bird orientation and navigation cannot yet be explained in terms of known sense organs, it seems likely that the typical migratory bird depends, at least in part, on its ability to determine direction, perhaps by means of celestial bodies; an innate timing mechanism; possibly an inherited recognition of certain features of the earth's surface; and the capacity to learn migration routes by experience and remember them from year to year. But whatever the mechanisms may be, it is certain that they are constantly being sharpened and refined by natural selection. The longer the migration journey and the smaller its end targets, the more rigorous the selection and the more disciplined the bird's performance must be. Successful migration pays high rewards, but even slight errors in navigation may cost the bird its life.

SUGGESTED READINGS

The three chapters by Griffin, Farner, and Lowery and Newman in Wolfson's *Recent Studies in Avian Biology* give excellent reviews of recent knowledge on bird navigation, the stimuli for migration, and nocturnal migration. Another excellent account of the physiological preparation for migration is Marshall's chapter in his book *Biology and Comparative Physiology of Birds.* In the same book is a chapter on bird orientation by Kramer, who pioneered modern research in celestial navigation by birds. The classic reference for years has been Thomson's *Problems of Bird Migration;* his *Bird Migration* is briefer but more recent. A brief, well illustrated account of North American migration is found in Lincoln's *Migration of Birds.* Recent excellent summaries of the broad aspects of migration may be found in Van Tyne and Berger's *Fundamentals of Ornithology,* Wallace's *An Introduction to Ornithology,* and Hochbaum's *Travels and Traditions of Waterfowl.*

TWENTY-THREE

The Origin and Evolution of Birds

In the broad sweep of time between the present and that earlier era when the planet Earth had cooled sufficiently to cradle its first primitive organism, man has existed for only the briefest moment. If Mother Nature had kept a diary of the happenings on Earth since life first appeared, and if, unlike human diarists, she had written only one page every ten thousand years, her diary today would comprise over 300 volumes, each with 1000 pages. Somewhere near page 900 in the most recent volume she would have recorded the first appearance of man. Only on the very last page would she have made the observation that man had finally achieved the wit to record his own history. Small wonder it is that much of the history of life on earth is hidden from man, the naked, bipedal newcomer.

Man, however, has been able to reconstruct the broad outlines of much of the history of life on earth from the scraps of Nature's diary he. has found in the form of fossils and living vestiges. These show incontrovertibly that living organisms have

477

evolved, and that birds, for example, have evolved from reptiles.

At first glance, it seems unlikely that birds with their warm blood, easy flight, colors, songs, and lively actions could possibly have descended from the lethargic, cold-blooded, earth-grubbing reptiles. However, not only fossil birds but also many features of living birds testify to that relationship. Some of these reptilian affinities of birds have been mentioned earlier. The list that follows, assembled from Heilmann (1927), shows how impressive the resemblances are.

Many of the similarities between birds and reptiles are found in the skeleton. Both birds and reptiles have skulls that hinge on similar neck bones by means of a single condyle, or ball-and-socket arrangement. Their lower jaws are made of several bones, and articulate with the skull by means of a movable quadrate bone. The lateral brain-case (pleurosphenoid

bone) is much extended in each. There is a single sound-transmitting bone, or columella, in the middle ear. Ribs in birds and certain reptiles (*Sphenodon*) have overlapping tabs, or uncinate processes. The ankle joint in all birds and in several reptiles is intertarsal. Likewise in each, certain bones may be hollow, or pneumatic.

Birds possess scales on their legs which are remarkably similar to reptilian scales. Skin glands are practically absent in both animals. The pleural cavity in birds is very similar to that in crocodiles, and avian airsacs resemble those of turtles and chameleons. The brain of a bird is more like that of a crocodile than that of a mammal. Eyes of birds and of many lizards each contain a pecten. Both birds and reptiles have nucleated red corpuscles. Precipitin tests show that the blood proteins of birds are similar to those of turtles and crocodiles. Birds and reptiles lay similar eggs,

Figure 23.1. A cast of the first fossil of *Archaeopteryx* to be discovered. About one-fourth actual size. Photo courtesy of the American Museum of Natural History.

Figure 23.2. A restoration of *Archaeopteryx* based on the second specimen to be discovered. The body parts are arranged in the same position as the corresponding distorted bones of the fossil. Photo courtesy of the American Museum of Natural History.

and the hatching young of each often possess egg-teeth. In their embryonic development, birds and reptiles show many close parallels. On rare occasions vestigial or atavistic claws appear on the wings of such birds as ducks, hawks, cranes, rails, and crows. In the nestling Hoatzin, *Opisthocomus hoazin,* the ends of the second and third fingers have claws, which the young birds use in clambering about trees.

The differences between birds and reptiles are nevertheless pronounced. Birds are warm-blooded and have a double circulation, pulmonary and systemic, based on a four-chambered heart. Reptiles are cold-blooded and have a single circulation, put in motion by a three-chambered heart, although in crocodiles the heart approaches the four-chambered condition. Birds, and only birds, have feathers. It seems probable that feathers evolved to conserve heat and make homothermy possible, before they were used for flight.

ARCHAEOPTERYX

Some 150 million years ago, a flying reptile fell into the water of a tropical lagoon, drowned, settled into the fine silt at the bottom, and eventually became fossilized. If paleontologists had tried to draw up specifications for a missing-link between birds and reptiles, they could scarcely have improved on this fossil, called *Archaeopteryx lithographica,* which was uncovered in 1861 in a lithographic lime-stone quarry in Bavaria. The discovery of this Jurassic fossil was one of the most fortunate finds in the history of paleontology. It has settled once and for all any question regarding the reptilian ancestry of birds. Since the original discovery, two other fossils of *Archaeopteryx* have been found: one in 1877 and another in 1959, both in the limestone beds near Solenhofen, Bavaria.

Archaeopteryx possessed a shoulder girdle, pelvis and legs roughly similar to those of modern birds. Its feathers were, as far as can be told from fossil imprints, exactly like those of modern birds. On the other hand, most of its skeletal structures were decidedly reptilian—so much so that, were it not for its feathers, it would be classed as a reptile. It had a dinosaur-like skull with toothed jaws, a long bony tail, clawed fingers, and abdominal ribs, none of which are bird-like characters. Since this reptile-bird did not fit into any existing scheme of classification, a new taxonomic group was created for its solitary use: the subclass Archaeornithes of the Class Aves. All other birds belong to the subclass Neornithes. The following lists of details, based largely on Heilmann (1927), give some of the more important characteristics of this remarkable link between primitive reptiles and modern birds.

GENERAL CHARACTERS. *Archaeopteryx* was a lightly-built, crow-sized bird which may have weighed about 200 grams. The fossils show evidence of hollow bones. The trunk of its body was short and compact, as in modern birds. Its feathers seem to have differed from those of modern birds only in their symmetrical arrangement in pairs along the sides of the long bony tail, a pair to each vertebra. The head and upper neck were unfeathered.

Skull. The skull of *Archaeopteryx* resembled those of small dinosaurs of its time. The skull articulated with the neck by means of a single ball-like condyle. It had an expanded brain-case much like that of the pterosaurs (flying reptiles), had prominent dinosaur-like premaxillary and preorbital openings, and a somewhat larger than reptilian orbit surrounded by 14 squarish sclerotic plates, much as modern birds have. The facial bones were distinctly reptilian, although the snout was narrower than in most small dinosaurs. Both jaws carried socket teeth, another clearly reptilian character.

Backbone and ribs. The spinal column of *Archaeopteryx* was made of about 50 biconcave vertebrae. The long flexible neck was supported by 19 vertebrae and the trunk by 19 or 20. The sacrum was formed of 6 vertebrae, 5 of them fused together. This is a smaller number of sacral vertebrae than in any living bird, but is similar to the number found in some reptiles. The long tail contained 20 free vertebrae. There were 11 pairs of ribs, but unlike those of modern birds they were unjointed, lacked uncinate processes, and did not attach to the sternum. There was a series of slender abdominal ribs, a feature unknown in birds today.

Forelimbs. The arm of *Archaeopteryx* was rather long and strong. It supported 10 primary and probably more secondary feathers along its trailing edge as do the wings of modern birds. The ulna of the forearm was unusually stout for a bird. The hand had three freely mobile, clawed fingers, useful in climbing trees. The bones of the wrist and hand were not fused as in contemporary birds, but they showed a comparable reduction in numbers. The two clavicles fused to form a furcula—a modern feature. Since there was not a keeled sternum, the bird was either a weak flier or only a climber and glider.

Hindlimbs. The long bipedal hindlimbs of *Archaeopteryx* had four diverging toes, the first of which was turned backward and became a grasping opposable toe, extremely useful for climbing and perching. In this regard the leg was avian, but it was reptile-like in its fibula, which was as long as the tibia, and reptile-like also in the unfused metatarsal bones. As in reptiles, all three pelvic bones were separate, held together by ligaments rather than by fusion.

The long pubis, however, was directed backward, parallel with the ischium, as it is in birds.

FORERUNNERS OF ARCHAEOPTERYX

No fossil series has yet been discovered that links *Archaeopteryx* to the ancestral reptiles from which it must have emerged. The thousands of reptiles of the Mesozoic period were divided into five large subclasses, one of which, the Diapsida, was further divided into superorders. The first of these, the Lepidosauria, gave rise to three orders which included, among others, the lizards and snakes. The other superorder, Archosauria or ruling reptiles, gave rise to five orders, only one of which survives today—the Crocodilia. The other four orders were the Thecodontia (socket teeth) or ancestral archosaurs; the Saurischia (reptile pelvis), which gave rise to gigantic dinosaurs like *Tyrannosaurus* and *Brontosaurus*; the Pterosauria (winged reptile) archosaurs, which solved the problem of flight with huge bat-like membrane-wings supported chiefly by an enormous finger, some wings having a spread of 7.5 meters (25 feet); and the order Ornithischia (bird pelvis), which included bipedal herbivorous dinosaurs such as *Stegosaurus* and *Triceratops*.

Most authorities now agree that both dinosaurs and birds arose from a suborder of small thecodont reptiles known as the Pseudosuchia. Several genera of these primitive Triassic reptiles have been discovered which show structural leanings toward *Archaeopteryx*. Among them are *Euparkeria*, discovered in southern Africa, *Ornithosuchus* in Scotland, and *Aetosaurus* and *Saltoposuchus* in southern Germany. Similarities between these pseudosuchians and *Archaeopteryx* are particularly striking in the skulls (Fig. 23.3), but close agreement also exists in the fore- and hindlimbs, pectoral and pelvic girdles, ribs, and tail vertebrae. The epidermal scales of *Euparkeria* suggest a possible first step toward feathers in that they were

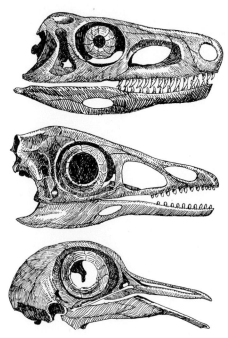

Figure 23.3. Skulls of *Euparkeria* (top), *Archaeopteryx* (middle), and a modern pigeon (bottom), showing the intermediate character of *Archaeopteryx*. *Euparkeria* and *Ornithosuchus*, (the latter shown in reconstruction at the beginning of this chapter), are representatives of the Pseudosuchian reptiles which are thought to be the ancestors of the first birds. After Heilmann.

about twice as long as wide, and had a central axis from which fine striations ran out on the two sides. No fossil intermediate between the pseudosuchians and *Archaeopteryx* has come to light, but Heilmann (1927) attempted the reconstruction of a hypothetical, missing-link "proavian," as shown in Figure 23.4.

FOSSIL RECORD SINCE ARCHAEOPTERYX

Compared with the fossil record of other vertebrates, that of birds is disappointingly incomplete and fragmentary. Birds are light-weight, fragile animals, easily destroyed or decomposed. When a bird dies and floats on some body of water, it is subject to destruction by aquatic predators and scavengers, and its buoy-

Figure 23.4.   A hypothetical ancestor of birds, intermediate between the Pseudosuchian reptiles and *Archaeopteryx*, as conceived by Gerhard Heilmann. From Heilmann, *The Origin of Birds*, courtesy of Appleton-Century-Crofts.

ancy usually prevents its settling into bottom sediments to become fossilized as was *Archaeopteryx*. Accordingly, there are many large gaps in the fossil history of birds, and even the relationships between many avian orders are still obscure because of these breaks in the continuity of the record.

There are, fortunately, certain localities where fossils of birds are found in relative abundance. These include such paleontologic sites as caves, dried-up lakes, diatomaceous earth strata, bogs, rock quarries, tar pits, and kitchen middens. In the United States, the most prolific source of avian fossils is California, which contains 44 different fossil localities, from which remains of over 220 species of birds have been found. By far the richest of these sites is in Los Angeles at Rancho La Brea, where several asphalt deposits ooze to the surface. Here, in the past, these tar pits acted as giant sheets of flypaper to trap unwary birds and mammals coming for drinks of water. Their struggles to free themselves from the sticky asphalt attracted predatory hawks, vultures, and even saber-toothed tigers, which in turn were trapped in the tar. From one La Brea pit alone were removed 30,000 fossil bird bones representing 81 species (Howard, 1955). In certain Pleistocene deposits in Wyoming, bird bones average 215 per cubic meter of material in an outcrop 30 to 100 centimeters thick and nearly a kilometer long. At Fossil Lake, Oregon, there have been discovered fossil fragments of 66 varieties of birds, 16 of which are extinct. Unfortunately, most of these rich deposits contain relatively recent fossils which tell little, if anything, about the descent of birds from reptiles. In 1952, Wetmore listed 787 known extinct species of birds. Table 23.1 attempts to give a brief over-all picture of the fossil record of birds. It has been adapted from material in Colbert (1955), Howard (1955), Rensch (1959), Storer (1960), and Wetmore (1952).

For all its gaps, the fossil record does furnish much important information about the history of birds. For example, it reveals that in the past certain birds lived outside their present ranges (parrots and hornbills in central Europe), and suggests that some groups have been permanently confined to specific places (moas to New Zealand and penguins to southern parts of the world) (Darlington, 1957). It should be made clear, however, that authorities sometimes differ widely in their interpretation of fossils, and that much present information is provisional in nature, awaiting further discoveries.

CRETACEOUS BIRDS. Thirty million years after *Archaeopteryx* appeared, birds had evolved into essentially the modern form. In the Cretaceous shales of Kansas,

Montana and Texas, six species of a gull-like bird of the genus *Ichthyornis* have been uncovered. In almost every detail these were modern birds. They had a deeply keeled sternum and modern bird wings, indicating strong powers of flight. The vertebrae were still biconcave as in reptiles, but the long tail of *Archaeopteryx* had disappeared. Although the brain was smaller than in contemporary birds, it was definitely larger than in reptiles of comparable size, and it had prominent optic lobes. A toothed lower jaw originally attributed to *Ichthyornis* has since been interpreted as belonging to a small mosasaur reptile. Numerous fish bones associated with the fossils indicate that the bird was a fish eater.

Three families of large, flightless diving birds have also been found in the Cretaceous. These include *Hesperornis* and related forms, some of them nearly two meters long. They were loon-like birds with vestigial wings, stubby tails, and powerful short legs placed far back on the body. There were conical teeth in both upper and lower jaws. The cerebrum and optic lobes of the brain were smaller than in recent birds, and the olfactory lobes were larger and more reptilian. The ribs had uncinate processes as in contemporary birds, and the sternum had no keel. The neck was long and flexible. In addition to *Ichthyornis* and *Hesperornis*, fragments of three other Cretaceous birds resembling geese, herons, and cormorants have been found.

One of the problems of ornithology concerns the origin of the flightless ostrich-like birds. Have they always been keelless (ratite), flightless birds, descended from flightless reptiles? Or are they the descendants of flying (carinate) keeled birds which secondarily lost the power of flight? The discovery of a fragment of a Cretaceous fossil called *Chaeagnathus*, with reduced wings, and a keel on its sternum, suggests that ostriches, emus, and other running birds may have had flying ancestors. The pelvis and vertebral column of an Eocene fossil, *Eleutherornis*, tends to confirm this

Table 23.1. A Brief Summary of the Fossil History of Birds (after Colbert, Howard, Rensch, Storer, Wetmore)

GEOLOGICAL ERA	GEOLOGICAL PERIOD		TIME IN YEARS SINCE BEGINNING OF PERIOD	IMPORTANT EVENTS IN THE HISTORY OF BIRDS	NUMBER OF NEW ORDERS APPEARING		
					Reptiles	Birds	Mammals
Cenozoic — Age of Birds and Mammals	Quaternary	Recent	10,000	Modern birds. 8600 species. Geographic races differentiated. Passeriformes dominant. Extinction of many island forms.			
		Pleistocene	1,000,000	All modern orders and families of birds represented. Many modern species represented. About 750 fossil species known. Ice age: period of great dispersals and extermination, especially of large ratites. The first men.			1
	Tertiary	Pliocene	10,000,000	Most modern bird genera probably in existence. Bird species probably reach their maximum numbers. Appearance of moas, ostriches, tinamous, goatsuckers. *Phororhacos* extinguished.			1
		Miocene	25,000,000	The majority of modern families probably in existence. Several modern genera of petrels, falcons, oystercatchers appear. A few extant passerine genera appear. Some families becoming extinct.			
		Oligocene	35,000,000	First appearance of albatrosses, shearwaters, boobies, grebes, storks, plovers, turkeys, pigeons, parrots, kingfishers, Old World warblers and sparrows. Phororhacoids in South America. Rise of modern mammals.		4	3
		Eocene	65,000,000	Probable period of major evolution in birds. First appearance of 27 families of modern birds, including penguins, pelicans, auks, loons, herons, ibises, rails, cranes, sandpipers, gulls, bustards, grouse, cuckoos, trogons, hornbills, shrikes, swifts, hawks, owls, and vultures. *Diatryma, Neocathartes, Gastornis* appear. *Eleutherornis* links carinate and ratite birds. Most mammals small and harmless.		16	21
Mesozoic — Age of Reptiles		Cretaceous	130,000,000	Toothed bird: *Hesperornis. Ichthyornis*, gull-like. First fossils of birds resembling cormorants, geese, and herons. Decline of dinosaurs.		6	2
		Jurassic	160,000,000	*Archaeopteryx*, the first bird. Flying reptiles. First primitive mammals.	4	1	2
		Triassic	200,000,000	Pseudosuchia, possible ancestors of *Archaeopteryx*. First dinosaurs.	10		2
Paleozoic — Age of Amphibians		Permian	230,000,000	Expansion of reptiles.	5		
		Pennsylvanian	250,000,000	Age of amphibians. First reptiles.	2		

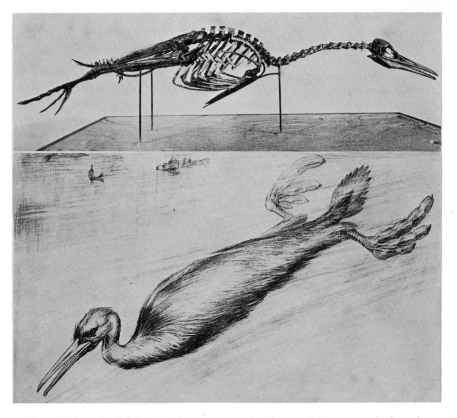

Figure 23.5. A fossil skeleton, and reconstruction by Gleeson, of *Hesperornis*, the large diving bird of the Cretaceous Period. Photos courtesy of the American Museum of Natural History.

conclusion, since the bones are intermediate between those of modern ostriches and flying birds.

EOCENE BIRDS. The beginning of the Tertiary probably saw the major blossoming, or peak radiation, of bird types. Certainly, by the beginning of the Eocene birds had acquired their basic forms as fliers, swimmers, and runners; and by the end of the period most modern orders of birds had made their appearance. The disappearance of the dinosaurs had opened many niches into which hordes of birds now moved. During the Eocene a few genera of Recent birds had already become established: *Milvus, Aquila, Haliaëtus, Phoenicopterus, Charadrius, Totanus, Numenius,* and others. In the Paris basin

there have been discovered 40 species of 25 genera of birds, including owls, vultures, secretary-birds, herons, partridge, sand grouse, swifts and trogons. The presence of trogons, which are now practically confined to the tropics, indicates that 60 million years ago France had a tropical climate.

Among early Tertiary fossils are three species having such generalized and intermediate characters that they throw light on the taxonomic relationships of several modern groups. *Romainvillia,* from France, links the ducks and geese. *Eostega,* from Hungary, is intermediate between boobies and cormorants. *Telmabates,* from Argentina, points toward a common ancestry for flamingos, ducks and geese (Howard, 1955).

Fossil penguins dating back to the Eocene have been found in New Zealand. Apparently they became differentiated into streamlined, submarine swimmers very early in bird history. They remain today the most highly specialized of all birds. Fossils of the largest penguins indicate that they were as tall as a man, standing one and one-half meters high and weighing approximately 120 kilograms.

Probably the most awe-inspiring bird to inhabit the North American Eocene landscape was the large, flightless *Diatryma*. This stout-legged giant stood over two meters high, was built somewhat like a stocky ostrich, and had a horse-sized head with an enormous hooked beak. In spite of its structural relationship to the cranes and rails, the bird was probably predatory. With some similar ground-dwelling relatives (*Gastornis* and *Remiornis*), it moved into the ecologic vacuum left by the dying predatory dinosaurs. It has been argued that the disappearance of these giant cursorial birds logically coincided with the appearance of the predatory placental mammals of the Oligocene. The argument gains force from the fact that in South America, which was geographically isolated from North America and its predatory mammals until the late Pliocene, flightless heavy-bodied relatives of *Diatryma* (*Phororhacos*, *Brontornis* and *Andrewsornis*) all survived in Patagonia until the end of the Pliocene, some 60 million years later. Although this may be true, the fact that rheas in South America and ostriches in Africa survive even today in the midst of predatory mammals suggests that they died out from other causes.

OLIGOCENE BIRDS. After the millions of years available for bird evolution in the Eocene, evolutionary inventiveness on the broad scale began to run out. In the Oligocene, fossils have been discovered of only four new orders and 16 new families of existing birds. These include albatrosses, shearwaters, boobies, grebes, storks, limpkins, plovers, stilts, thick-knees, turkeys, pigeons, parrots, kingfishers, Old World warblers, and sparrows (Storer, 1960).

Figure 23.6. Cast of a fossil skeleton of *Diatryma*, and its reconstruction. This predatory, flightless bird was taller than a man, and lived in North America during the Eocene Period. Photos courtesy of the American Museum of Natural History.

Several genera of Recent birds also appeared in the Oligocene period: *Sula, Pelecanus, Puffinus, Podiceps, Colymbus, Anas, Lanius,* and *Motacilla*. In South America, separated from North America's predatory mammals by a water gap, large flightless birds of prey persisted in the forms of *Brontornis, Andrewsornis* and *Phororhacos,* of which the last belonged to a group that contained three families and a dozen or more genera. *Phororhacos,* taller than a man, had rudimentary wings and a powerfully beaked head 65 centimeters long. Anatomic evidence suggests that the modern cariamas of South America are lineal descendants of *Phororhacos* and its allies.

MIOCENE BIRDS. By the end of the Miocene period, some 10 million years ago, probably the majority of avian families and many genera of contemporary birds were in existence. The earliest known fossils of storm petrels, falcons, and oystercatchers now appeared. Among the new genera were *Otis, Tringa, Uria, Ardea,* and *Apus*. *Phororhacos* was still living in Patagonia, and a new giant race, the moas, arose in New Zealand. An enormous flying sea bird, *Osteodontornis,* with a wing spread of 4.5 meters (15 feet) was found in the Miocene of California. Although it possessed tooth-like bony projections on each jaw, it seems to have been an early relative of the petrels and pelicans (Howard, 1957). Some of the complexities of tracing bird origins can be inferred from the fact that Miocene fossils excavated in South Dakota have included birds characteristic today not only of North America but also of South America and the Old World.

PLIOCENE BIRDS. The Pliocene, covering a span of about 9 million years, ended only one million years ago. Very probably, by its end, essentially all modern bird genera were established. Among the fossil forms that made their first appearance in this period were ostriches, tinamous, goatsuckers, larks, swallows, crows, nuthatches, creepers, thrushes, and pipits. In California, fossils of a flightless auk, *Man-*

Figure 23.7. The flightless giant *Phororhacos* lived in Patagonia during the Miocene. Drawing by C. R. Knight. Photo courtesy of the American Museum of Natural History.

calla, have been discovered, which show in the reduced wings a parallel adaptation to that of the Great Auk, *Pinguinus impennis,* which until recently lived on the north Atlantic coast of North America.

PLEISTOCENE BIRDS. The Pleistocene, covering the last million years of fossil history, was a period of drastic climatic change and widespread glaciation. Among the consequences of these global changes were great shifts in the geographic ranges of birds, and wholesale extermination of many species. According to Wetmore (1951), birds had reached their maximum abundance, and the genera and species of living birds had already evolved during the Miocene and Pliocene periods. If this is true, then the Pleistocene was a period of decline and extinction, with evolution limited mainly to the development of geographic races. From intensive studies of Pleistocene birds, Howard (1955) con-

Figure 23.8. The La Brea Stork, *Ciconia maltha*, is one of the 180 species of fossil birds found in the Pleistocene deposits of California. After Howard. Photo courtesy of the Los Angeles County Museum.

cludes that ". . . bird life as we know it today was essentially established some twenty-five to fifty thousand years ago." Of the approximately 180 fossil species discovered in Pleistocene deposits in California, 31 have left no descendants, and the remaining 150 or so species are practically identical with birds still in existence.

Even though the Pleistocene was a great dying-off period, it was also a period of expansion for some of the large flightless species, including the emus, cassowaries, moas, and elephant birds. In isolated New Zealand, there were between 14 and 20 species of moas belonging to the two families Dinornithidae and Anomalopterygidae. They varied in size from one-half meter to over three meters in height, and were constructed on the pattern of an enlarged kiwi, a bird to which they were related. Their legs were large and powerful, the largest species having tibiotarsal bones a meter in length. The moas, like the contemporary ostrich and emu, were ratites with a flat, keelless sternum. Instead of having vestigial wings, however, the moas lacked wings completely. Great numbers of moa skeletons, and also their egg shells, feathers, bits of skin and flesh, have been found in caves, bogs, and Maori camp grounds in New Zealand. One bog alone yielded 140 skeletons of four genera of moas. These birds appeared to be herbivorous.

On sheltered Madagascar lived another flightless group of Pleistocene giants, the elephant birds, or Aepyornithiformes. Although not as tall as the largest moa, the larger species of *Aepyornis* weighed more (up to 450 kilograms, or 1000 pounds) and laid larger eggs (7.5 liters, or 2 gallons, in capacity) than any other bird known, living or fossil. Like the moas, the elephant birds varied considerably in size, but all of them were stockily built with enormous legs and broad, heavy pelvic girdles. Their eggs had such stout shells that Madagascans used them for water containers and mixing bowls.

There were also aerial giants among the Pleistocene birds. Over 1000 bones of a large condor, *Teratornis*, have been recovered from the La Brea tar pits alone. A fragment of one teratorn found in a cave in Nevada represents the largest flying bird known. It was aptly called *Teratornis incredibilis*, and had a wing spread calculated to be 5 meters! (Howard, 1952).

RECENT BIRDS. The Recent period, which embraces the last 10,000 years, continues the Pleistocene motif in bird history. The major evolutionary innovations had long since occurred, and only minor subspecific variations were left to be incorporated in the family tree of birds. Ex-

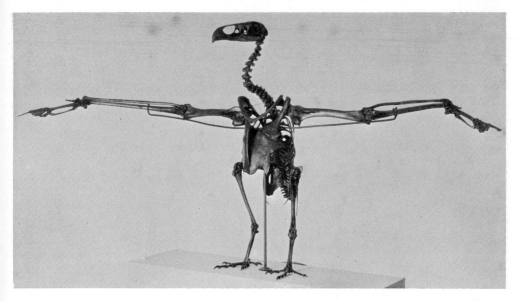

Figure 23.9. The Merriam Teratorn, *Teratornis merriami,* from the Pleistocene La Brea tar pits of California, was a vulture-like bird with a wing spread of about 3 meters. After Howard. Photo courtesy of the Los Angeles County Museum.

tinction of species continued until the number of birds throughout the world was reduced to its present level of about 8600 species. The dominant birds are now the Passeriformes, which outnumber all other orders combined.

Each of the glacial epochs of the Pleistocene undoubtedly caused widespread avian extinction, but the extreme specialization of some of the birds may have contributed largely to the disappearance of many species. Particularly in isolated or sheltered habitats, evolutionary adaptations tend to develop in exaggerated ways which quickly become harmful under changed conditions. The well-known inability of oceanic island birds to survive the competition and predation of rats, pigs, and other introduced human satellites is a case in point. Gigantism seems to have been one of these excessive developments, for the Pleistocene giants were prominent among those birds which suffered the evolutionary penalties of overspecialization.

Man himself has been one of the chief agents of bird extinction in the Recent period. He has exterminated species both indirectly by modifying their habitats through his cultural changes (including the introduction of competitors and predators), and directly by slaughtering them for food, feathers, or "sport." The majestic moas survived in New Zealand until Polynesians (later to become Maoris) immigrated there and began hunting them around 1350 A.D. Excavations of Maori kitchen middens have revealed burned fragments of the bones of 3 genera and perhaps 7 species of moas along with the bones and shells of other food animals. Included in the midden debris were also awls, fishhooks, and sartorial ornaments fashioned of moa bones (Buick, 1937). Radio-carbon dating of the crop contents of a moa indicated that it had died about 670 years ago. Buick estimates that the last moa probably died about three centuries ago, roughly a century before Captain Cook visited New Zealand.

Figure 23.10. The skeleton of a small New Zealand Moa, compared with its living relative, the Kiwi. Moas have become extinct within historic times. Photo courtesy of the American Museum of Natural History.

EVOLUTION OF BIRDS TODAY

During his five years' voyage around the world in H.M.S. *Beagle*, Charles Darwin was particularly impressed by the numerous and often bizarre fossils he saw in South America, and with the variety and peculiarity of organisms, especially birds, he found on the Galapagos Islands. In his *Journal of Researches*, Darwin (1845) wrote, with reference to these islands, the following prophetic words:

"The remaining land birds form a most singular group of finches, related to each other in the structure of their beaks, short tails, form of body and plumage. All these species are peculiar to this archipelago. . . . Seeing this gradation and diversity of structure in one small, intimately related group of birds, one might easily fancy that from an original paucity of birds in this archipelago, one species had been taken and modified for different ends."

Darwin's observation that species might not be forever changeless and immutable provided the germinal idea which grew into his book *On the Origin of Species by Means of Natural Selection* and shook the intellectual world. In its essence, Darwin's theory of evolution proposed that since all organisms vary, and since more individuals are born than can possibly survive, there is a competitive struggle for existence in which the fittest survive to propagate their kind. This principle of the survival of the fittest and the elimination of the less fit, or the principle of natural selection, has dominated biological thought ever since Darwin's day. But, like the organisms to which it applies, the principle itself has had to undergo some minor evolutionary changes.

Genetic Variation

Darwin was correct in assuming that all organisms possess more or less variability on which natural selection may operate to produce new races and species. He was impressed by the great reservoir of variability in the wild dove which enabled man to breed domestic pouters, fantails, trumpeters, homers, tumblers, runts, web-footed and even featherless pigeons. If artificial selection could develop such diverse types, why should not natural selection be able to produce an even greater array of forms, selected, however, for their capacity to survive rather than for their appeal to man's capricious fancy?

Darwin assumed that both acquired and genetic variations could be passed on from generation to generation. It was not until the rediscovery of Mendel's laws in 1900 that a clear distinction began to be drawn between genetic variations, or mutations, which are heritable, and acquired variations, or somatic modifications, which are not heritable. Today it is well established that only genetic variations—that is, those originating in the genes and chromosomes of the germ plasm—play a role in evolutionary change. The following list of a few of the many genetic mutations recorded for the Domestic Fowl, *Gallus gallus*, (Hutt, 1949), will give an idea of the variety and extent of the hereditary variations known to exist in a single species.

SKELETON. Rumplessness; short spine; twisted neck; crooked beak; missing mandible; shortened toes; shortened legs; extra toes; extra legs; crooked keels; no wings.

SKIN AND FEATHERS. Thickened epidermis; black, white, or yellow skin; extra lobes in comb; double spurs; naked (no feathers); woolly feathers; frizzled feathers; porcupine quills (no vanes on feathers); brittle feathers; feathers on feet; rapid feather growth; retarded feather growth; and a great variety of feather colors, shapes, and barrings.

NERVOUS SYSTEM. Congenital tremor; congenital loco (bird falls over backward); microphthalmia (half-sized eyeballs); blindness.

OTHER MUTATIONS. Absence of one kidney; body size; egg production; various mutations for egg size, shape, shell thickness, texture, color, and chemical composition; resistance to disease.

Many of these variant characters are due to mutations, or permanent changes, in single genes. Others, such as body size, are due to mutations in a number of genes which affect the same trait. As a rule, a single-gene mutation affects various structures and functions in the body, but it gets its name from its most apparent influence. For example, the mutation "frizzle," which changes normal feathers into ruffled curly feathers, also causes changes in metabolism and in the sizes of the thyroid gland, heart, gizzard, and other organs. Most of the genetic changes known for the Domestic Fowl are non-adaptive, or even definitely harmful; several result in death and are therefore known as lethal mutations. Many mutations, of course, produce changes in structure or function so slight as to escape casual scrutiny, yet they may affect the survival of the species, either by themselves or in conjunction with other mutations. Even though most mutations seem to produce non-adaptive characters, in a sufficiently long time adaptive mutations will occur in sufficient numbers to provide the raw materials for evolutionary change.

Speciation of Birds

Darwin believed, as do many persons today, that an adaptive variation in a single individual could, through sheer adaptive merit, assure that individual's survival, the eventual ascendancy of the adapted type in future generations, and thus the appearance of a new species. Recent work in genetics and evolution has shown that the production of new races and species in nature rarely, if ever, occurs so simply and directly. Instead of working on single hereditary factors in individuals, natural selection works on combinations of genes in populations of organisms. The population is the evolutionary unit, not the individual.

In order to understand how species evolve, one must first know what a species is. Until a few years ago, a species was defined by its morphological characteristics —its size, shape, and color. "Type" specimens were kept in museums as models or standards with which unknown forms were compared to determine their kinship. Today, species are defined as "groups of actually or potentially interbreeding natural populations, which are reproductively isolated from other such groups" (Mayr, 1942). This does not deny the fact that structural peculiarities characterize most species, but it places the emphasis on reproductive compatibility rather than on external appearance.

In simplest outline, the evolution of a new species of a sexually reproducing animal involves the following steps:

1. Geographic or ecologic isolation of one or more fragments of the population.

2. Genetic changes in the isolated populations, due to mutation, selection, and other forces, especially changes leading toward

3. The development of mechanisms for reproductive isolation and of ecologic divergence.

4. Development of sufficient genetic change to make the isolated and parent populations intersterile should they again meet, or at least to cause hybrids between them to be inferior to either in competition. In short, spatial isolation permits genetic divergence to continue until reproductive isolation is achieved. This is the simplest, most diagrammatic outline of species-forming. The separate elements in the process are worth examining in more detail. The discussion that follows is based largely on Mayr (1942, 1949).

ISOLATION AND EVOLUTION

The chief significance of isolation is that it prevents the flow of genes—the trading back and forth of hereditary factors—between the parent population and the incipient new-species population. Any mutations, new combinations of genes, or other hereditary novelties will be confined to the group in which they occur as long as it is reproductively isolated from the parent population. Genes provide the raw materials for creating differences between species. Therefore, the reproductive isolation of populations prevents them from having a common assortment of genes, and therefore a common heredity. By virtue of its superior gene combinations, each species fits a given ecologic niche, where it thrives better than its competitors. Isolating devices protect these superior gene aggregations.

Factors that promote reproductive isolation may be geographic (or spatial), temporal, ecologic, behavioral, physiological, anatomic, or genetic. The simplest of these, and the one most frequently in evidence as a species-promoting factor in bird evolution, is geographic isolation. The geographic range of a parent species may be fragmented by changes in climate, glaciation, rising mountains, shifts in sea level, or other physical alterations of the earth's surface, or by dispersal of a part of the population across normally separating barriers. The upthrust of the Isthmus of Panama, for example, created a barrier to sea birds which has resulted today in distinct Atlantic and Pacific subspecies of both the Masked Booby, *Sula dactylatra*, and the Brown Booby, *Sula leucogaster*. The marine fishes and invertebrates on the two sides of the isthmus show similar evolutionary divergences.

During the last glacial epoch, the southward advance of the glaciers against the Alps forced many species of birds into two or more refuges in the southeastern and southwestern parts of Europe. There the populations remained isolated from each other for several thousands of years. The post-glacial occupation of central Europe revealed distinct eastern and western species or subspecies of birds that were presumably monospecific before their southern fragmented residence. Thus, the Nightingale, *Luscinia megarhyncha,* of western Europe, and the Thrush Nightingale, *Luscinia luscinia,* of eastern Europe, are distinct species, thought to have arisen from a single pre-glacial parental species during their period of enforced geographical separation. Although today their ranges overlap, the two species do not interbreed. They are reproductively isolated from each other. The Icterine Warbler, *Hippolais icterina,* and the Olivaceous Warbler, *Hippolais pallida,* as well as other closely related pairs of species are presumed to have originated in the same way (Rensch, 1959).

The most instructive example of the influence of geographic isolation on species-formation is probably seen when a small population of a continental species somehow finds its way to an isolated oceanic archipelago. This is precisely what happened to Darwin's finches (Family Fringillidae, subfamily Geospizinae) when a small "seed" population of them, probably

storm driven, bridged the 950 kilometer water barrier between their ancestral home in South America and the volcanic Galapagos Islands. This group of more than a dozen islands opened up to the birds a whole series of unoccupied ecologic niches. The islands of the archipelago are so far apart that only on rare occasions could the finches disperse from one island to another. In time, however, most of the islands became occupied, and the various populations, isolated from each other, evolved into 14 distinct species. Undoubtedly descendants of a common finch-like ancestor, these birds now are adapted to an astonishing variety of niches. Some are still ground finches with heavy bills, feeding on seeds; some are tree dwellers specializing on insect food; one of the tree finches looks and behaves like a warbler, while another uses its bill as a woodpecker does to chisel out wood-boring insects. Lacking a long tongue, however, this woodpecker finch has developed a remarkable substitute: it breaks off a cactus spine and uses it as a probe to extract its insect prey! (Lack, 1947.)

This branching out of one type of bird into a diversity of ecologic niches is known

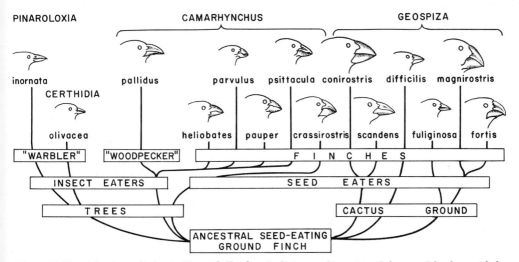

Figure 23.11. Adaptive radiation in Darwin's Finches. Isolation on the various Galapagos Islands provided evolutionary opportunities for the development of new varieties of birds from an ancestral seed-eating ground finch. Modified after Simpson *et al.,* from Lack.

as *adaptive radiation*. It has occurred many times in the evolutionary history of birds and other animals. Another striking example of adaptive radiation is seen in the sicklebills, or Drepanididae, of the Hawaiian Islands. These birds, originally honeycreepers from the American mainland, have evolved, on the various islands of the archipelago, into nectar, fruit, seed, nut, caterpillar and insect eaters (Amadon, 1950).

When a population of birds gains a foothold on a single isolated island, however, adaptive radiation does not occur even though a variety of unoccupied niches is available. That is because a single small island does not provide conditions for geographic isolation to occur within itself. The Geospizinae years ago made their way to Cocos Island, about 900 kilometers north-northeast of the Galapagos Islands, yet in spite of the presence of considerable ecologic variety in habitats the bird has remained a single species because of the impossibility of geographic isolation. A single island of an archipelago may, however, support two or more species descended from a common ancestor, as a consequence of successive invasions widely spaced in time. The first colonizers have time to evolve into a distinct species before the second immigrants arrive. Therefore they do not interbreed. Several of the Galapagos Islands, for example, harbor five or more species of Darwin's finches. Tiny Norfolk Island, about 1250 kilometers from Australia, supports three species of white-eyes: *Zosterops norfolkensis, Z. tenuirostris,* and *Z. albogularis.* Their only close relative is *Zosterops lateralis,* which lives on the Australian mainland. Stresemann (*in* Mayr, 1942) explains their presence on Norfolk Island by three widely-spaced waves of immigration. The first immigrants had evolved into a distinct and populous species by the time the second invasion of one or two pairs arrived, and the same process was repeated for the third wave. In each case, the earlier arrivals had become sexually isolated from the newcomers. If this had not been so,

the second invasion wave would have hybridized with the original colonists and would have been swamped into oblivion in a few generations. Alpine birds, living on isolated mountain peaks on continents, show this same phenomenon of double and multiple invasions.

Even small water gaps may effectively isolate geographic populations of land birds from each other. Mayr describes species and subspecies of the white-eye *Zosterops* which are separated from each other in the central Solomon Islands by water gaps of only 1.7, 2, 5, and 6 kilometers in width. Although the birds could easily fly across these straits in a few minutes, they do not do so, apparently because the water presents a potent psychological barrier.

Temporal isolation, like geographic separation, can effectively prevent the mixing of genes between two related populations of birds. A subspecies of the Australian roller, *Eurystomus orientalis pacificus,* winters with other subspecific relatives in the tropical East Indies. The birds do not interbreed because the Australian race is never in breeding condition while in its winter quarters (Mayr, 1942).

Numerous biologic influences bear on the isolation of avian populations. Instinctive behavior patterns often affect the fluidity of movement in a species. Migration and dispersion tend to prevent the isolation of small populations, while homing and ortstreue or territory faithfulness tend to reinforce isolation. Birds often show a psychic attachment to habitats of a certain appearance. For example, desert larks frequently choose to live on soils that match their plumage in color (p. 49).

More important than these influences, however, are the behavior patterns concerned with courtship and mating. All of the elaborate displays, dances, flights, songs, calls, and colors involved in courtship have an isolating function in that they tend to confine interbreeding to birds of a specific behavioral as well as morphologic type. If two birds pair and the responses of one sex to the courtship advances of the other are not "correct," copulation is unlikely to occur. Related species living in the same geographic locality (called *sympatric* species) are thus restrained from hybridizing and losing their genetic identity by the isolating effect of courtship behavior. Mayr makes the point that because of the need for complementary courtship behavior "wild hybrids are rare in bird species with definite pair formation and engagement periods, but fairly common . . . in genera and families without pair formation."

Social behavior coupled with mating habits may also affect the isolation of populations. Numerous species of ducks with circumpolar Holarctic distribution have few, if any, subspecies because in winter quarters a male and female from widely separated breeding ranges may pair. A drake from Maine, for example, may pair with a duck from North Dakota at their common winter quarters in Florida, and follow the female back to her North Dakota breeding grounds. Such a breeding pattern results in a thorough panmixia, or continuing exchange of genes on a broad geographic scale. As a result of this panmictic phenomenon, one species of Mallard, *Anas platyrhynchos,* lives in a broad band encircling the earth in the northern hemisphere. Geese, on the contrary, have a type of family organization that promotes inbreeding and hereditary isolation. Parents and young remain together as a family unit, migrating together both to their winter quarters and back the next spring to their breeding area. As a consequence, Canada Geese of the genus *Branta* have broken up into some 6 to 9 pronounced geographic races in North America (Mayr, 1942).

Ecologic barriers that isolate populations are numerous and varied, but often difficult to differentiate from geographic barriers. An ecologic barrier is sometimes met by the Great Reed Warbler, *Acrocephalus arundinaceus,* which normally builds its nest in marshy reed-beds. Some males establish territories in cattail marshes, but the females are then unable to build nests because the heavy weight of the wet material that they use cannot be supported properly (Kluijver, 1955). The cattail marsh thus acts both as a selective force, since birds attempting to nest there leave no offspring, and an isolating force, in that it restricts the geographic area in which the warblers may reproduce.

Competition between species also sets up barriers, but in this case it shuts a population out of a potential niche in which it might otherwise become isolated and evolve into a new subspecies or species. Mayr (1948) remarks that "there is no more formidable zoogeographical barrier for a subspecies than the range of another subspecies." Competition, therefore, is in this sense an evolution-retarding factor. Operating between sympatric species, on the other hand, competition may act to increase evolutionary divergence, as will be shown.

Physiological and morphological reproductive incompatibilities in birds have been poorly studied, but they are known to occur in other animals and to have isolating effects, and they no doubt occur also in birds. The non-synchronous response in the maturation of gonads in two races of a species exposed to the same photoperiod would cause a reproductive barrier between them. This occurs in two races of White-crowned Sparrows, *Zonotrichia leucophrys,* which occupy the same winter quarters in California.

Finally, isolation is promoted by gene mutations that lower fecundity or cause sterility or non-viability in hybrids of related populations. Since reproductive isolation is the goal of speciation, such mutations are at the same time both means and ends in the production of new species.

SELECTION AND EVOLUTION

Whereas new mutations increase the variability of a species, selection decreases variability by eliminating the poorly adapted variants. Variability, then, is increased by mutation frequency, decreased by selection pressure. The more rigorous the selection, the more rigidly specialize the resulting types of birds, and the less genetic resilience they retain for future evolutionary change.

Natural selection may operate through physical and biologic agents. Physical selective factors include such things as temperature, humidity, precipitation, sunlight, wind, density of air, chemicals in the soil or water, and topography. Biologic factors include food, predators, competition, mates, parasites, and diseases. Chance, or what is popularly known as "pure luck," operates at times in both the living and non-living worlds to shape the course of evolution.

The chapter on ecology outlined the many ways in which physical environmental factors influence birds. Insofar as a given factor determines whether an individual bird survives or perishes, that factor has a selective influence on the evolution of the species. Numerous examples were given earlier of *limiting* factors which acted in such a fashion: temperature, humidity, soil minerals, water salinity, daylength, and others. It will be enough here to give one more example, pointing out in this case some of the evolutionary consequences of a change in nesting substrate.

Most gulls nest on flat ground, but the Kittiwake, *Rissa tridactyla,* has abandoned this orthodox nesting behavior and shifted to nesting on narrow ledges of steep, seaside cliffs. Presumably this is a naturally selected anti-predator arrangement. With the change in nesting sites has come an array of correlated adaptations in structure, physiology, and behavior. Among some of those reported in an interesting paper on this species by Cullen (1957) are the following. The claws of the Kittiwake, longer and sharper than those of most gulls, give it a more secure footing on its narrow ledge. Using mud, it builds a nest more deeply cupped than that of other gulls. Correlated with the safety of the cliff-ledge location, the clutch has been reduced from three to two eggs. The adults do not carry away egg shells as do other gulls—a confirmation of the fact that such behavior is a naturally selected de-

vice to prevent advertising the nest site to predators. The adults give the alarm call less frequently than other gulls, and remain on the nest when predators do happen to approach, or make only weak attempts to fight the predators off. The young Kittiwakes have lost the cryptic coloration of other young gulls, and do not run from the nest when attacked. They sit close in the nest and face the cliff much of the time. Since the young are not in the habit of wandering about the colony as is commonly the case in other species of gulls, there is no need for the parents to know them individually. Whereas in other gulls the parents learn to recognize their own young in a few days, Kittiwakes are unable to do so until the nestlings are at least four weeks old. While some of these changes may not be hereditary, others unmistakably are, and all of the changes are clearly related to the nature of the nest site and to the accompanying pressure of predation.

Natural selection, acting through climatic factors, often produces heritable variations, which gradually change in magnitude or intensity over an extensive geographic area. Mention was made earlier (p. 412) of the gradual change in body size of the Chickadee, *Parus atricapillus,* correlated with the geographic distribution of mean January isotherms in western Europe. Species in which genetic characters vary in parallel with selective factors in the environment are said to form *clines* (Huxley, 1939). The gradual variation of species in such characteristics as body size, color, and size of clutch, in parallel with such factors as temperature, humidity, and altitude are the basis for the geographic rules of Bergmann, Gloger, Allen, and others, which were treated earlier.

Gradual or continuous changes such as these are characteristic of many species having a widespread, continuous geographic range. The changes illustrate the sensitivity with which adjoining populations of a given species respond to slight differences in climate (Mayr, 1942). Adjoining populations of such species commonly interbreed freely, whereas populations separated from each other by wide geographic gaps generally show more pronounced differences in hereditary traits. Such populations are called *allopatric* species, and are often incapable of interbreeding.

Continuously varying populations in a large, unbroken range show increasingly pronounced changes in character as one moves geographically outward from the center of the species' range. Often the terminal populations in such a series of interbreeding groups have become so different from each other that they cannot interbreed, although they are connected by a series of freely interbreeding populations. This form of "speciation by distance" is perfectly demonstrated by chains of grad-

ually varying subspecies of the Herring Gull, *Larus argentatus*, which form a ring in the northern hemisphere whose center of origin was presumably in eastern Siberia, and whose end-links overlap in western Europe. Here the extremely variant races coexist but do not interbreed (Mayr, 1942). Such rings of gradually varying races whose terminal points overlap but are inter-sterile are called *Rassenkreise*, or "circles of races." A situation similar to that of the Herring Gull has been found in titmice, kingfishers, white-eyes, babblers, warblers, wheatears, sparrows, and other species in various parts of the world. The different races of man show gradual genetic variations or clines, but they have not progressed far enough to produce a new species, since all human races are inter-fertile. If men had mating

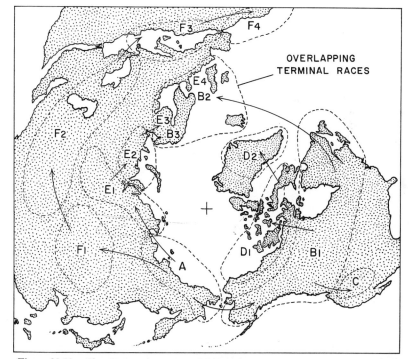

Figure 23.12.   The circumpolar ranges of different subspecies of the Herring Gull show an overlap in western Europe of the terminal links in a chain of intergrading races. The terminal races coexist without interbreeding, like genuine species. After Mayr.

standards as exacting as those of birds, *Homo* would consist of a number of species.

In the light of these examples, races or subspecies appear to be incipient species that may become full species if the gradually increasing divergences in character pass a certain threshold which confers reproductive isolation on the most extreme forms. Species that show such a multiplicity of variant forms are called polytypic species. The varying characters may correlate with selective environmental factors, or they may not. At times a given character change continues in a given direction through a geographic series of populations, which suggests that it, or some underlying related trait, may have adaptive value. In other cases the characters seem to vary geographically in a haphazard fashion, correlated with no known selective influence of the environment. Polytypic populations varying in this way may be explained as the result of chance genetic changes of no apparent adaptive significance—evolutionary accidents in mutation, or in the loss of genes, not very important to survival. Many tropical birds show polytypic variations of this sort, particularly in their coloration. Mayr estimates that at least 80 per cent of the birds of New Guinea, and 70 per cent of all Palearctic passerine species, are polytypic.

To find enough food for survival, and to avoid becoming food for some predator, are two of the most pressing problems that any bird faces. Therefore, food, competition, and predation are powerful biotic forces of selective importance in any bird's evolutionary history. Some of the many ways in which food brings selective pressures on a species have been treated earlier, in the chapter on ecology. It was there pointed out that related species with the same ways of life, especially identical feeding habits, cannot live indefinitely in the same habitat, because eventually one of them will prove to be superior to the other and crowd it out (Gause, 1934). There are, however, other possible solutions to the problem. The two species may divide the area geographically, one living in one part and the other occupying the remainder, or they may divide the habitat ecologically, feeding throughout the area but each on a different food. Cormorants, *Phalacrocorax carbo,* and Shags, *Phalacrocorax aristotelis,* solve the problem of coexistence by specializing on different foods (p. 381). In a

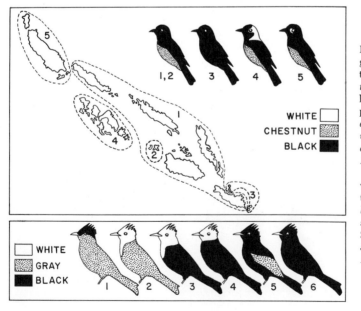

WHITE ☐
CHESTNUT ▒
BLACK ■

WHITE ☐
GRAY ▒
BLACK ■

Figure 23.13. (Above) Geographic variation in the polytypic flycatcher, *Monarcha castaneoventris,* of the Solomon Islands. The subspecies show 4 principal color patterns. *1, Monarcha castaneoventris castaneoventris. 2, M. c. obscurior. 3, M. c. ugiensis. 4, M. c. richardsii. 5, M. c. erythrosticta.*

(Below) Similar discontinuous variation is shown in races of the Asiatic bulbul, *Microscelis leucocephalus. 1,* lives in India and Burma, *2,* in Yunnan, *3,* in Szechuan, *4,* in southern China, *5,* in Formosa, and *6,* in Hainan. After Mayr.

detailed study of the food habits of 172 species of birds in Tanganyika, Moreau (1948) discovered that in 94 per cent of the cases in which two or more sympatric species belonged to the same genus, the different species were ecologically isolated by diet, habitat, or both, and thus avoided competing with each other. Wherever related species overlapped in range, they were either different in size of body or beak, or they used different methods of seeking food.

The avoidance of feeding competition may be more than a matter of the selection of certain foods and the rejection of others. At times it unquestionably involves physiological adaptations as, in an extreme case, the ability of honey-guides to digest beeswax. Sympatric species of flamingos show a structural difference in bills which enables them to feed side by side without competing. The Common Flamingo, *Phoenicopterus ruber,* has a shallow-keeled filtering bill, while the Lesser Flamingo, *Phoenicopterus minor,* has a deep-keeled type of filter.

Although competition reduces the range of genetic variation within a species by eliminating the less fit varieties, it has, paradoxically, the function of intensifying the divergence of related species that live in the same habitat. This happened to Darwin's finches in the Galapagos Islands. When two related species meet and compete for food on the same small island, they can both survive only if they evolve a measure of ecologic isolation. In both the tree finches (*Camarhynchus* spp.) and the ground finches (*Geospiza* spp.), the bills of two species inhabiting the same island differ more strongly than those of two species living on separate islands (Fig. 23.14). Competition has promoted increased specialization in their feeding tools; this in turn has brought partial ecologic isolation which has eliminated, or at least reduced, competition between the birds (Lack, 1947).

Species also compete for territory and nesting sites. In Europe, the Chaffinch, *Fringilla coelebs,* lives and nests in both deciduous and evergreen woods. On Gran

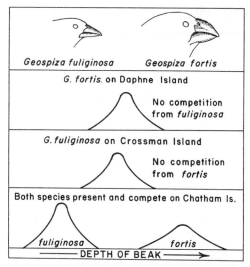

Figure 23.14.   Competition between species in the same habitat promotes evolutionary divergence. Species of *Geospiza* living on the same island show greater divergence in beak form than the same species living on isolated islands where they need not compete. After Simpson *et al.,* from Lack.

Canaria and Tenerife, of the Canary Islands, it does not nest in evergreen forests, for these are occupied by a related species, *Fringilla teydea,* which taxonomists consider a descendant of *F. coelebs* following an earlier invasion of the islands. On Palma, another island of the Canaries, *F. teydea* is missing, and *F. coelebs* breeds in both deciduous and evergreen trees. Obviously, the exclusion of *coelebs* from evergreens on Tenerife and Gran Canaria was brought about by competition (Lack, 1949).

To judge by the energy which most birds devote to courtship, one of the keenest forms of competition is that for mates. Darwin considered sexual selection, or assortative mating, an important form of natural selection. Certainly it can be a crucial form of selection, for the transmission of an individual's genetic peculiarities to the next generation depends on his securing a mate. Sexual selection is unquestionably responsible for much of the richness and variety of bird coloration, especially in the males, and for the elaborate displays, ritualized fighting, and profuse singing of many species. It is often difficult to decide whether a certain color pattern is used chiefly in courtship, hence may be attributed to sexual selection, or serves principally for species recognition or warning, hence has evolved by other means. But the fact that the most colorful plumage of the year appears in many species just before the breeding season, and that courting males usually expose their brightest adornments to their intended mates, indicates that sexual selection is a highly effective form of natural selection.

The bower-birds provide convincing evidence of the efficiency of sexual selection. In these birds the display function has been transferred from their plumage to inanimate eye-catching objects spread out in their bowers. The bowers represent "bundles of secondary sexual characters." It is significant that the least ornate of the male bower-birds, *Amblyornis inornatus,* "constructs the most complicated and highly ornamented bower known," while the male of *Amblyornis macgregoriae,* which "has by far the longest, most brilliant crest found in the genus" (with one exception, whose bower has not been discovered), builds the simplest bower known —a drab affair of short sticks, with colorless, inconspicuous display objects (Gilliard, 1956).

That birds really pay attention to the appearance of other individuals of their kind and make choices on that basis has been demonstrated by the experimental changing of plumage colors and patterns, and by the frequent rejection, among wild birds, of albinos, one-legged, or otherwise abnormal individuals. Kearton (*in* Murphy, 1936) tells of three abnormally pigmented African Penguins, *Spheniscus demersus,* (one an albino, one with a white head, and one with a black head) which were "friendless, shunned, and generally abused" by the other penguins of the rookery. The albino in particular "was snapped at by every other with which it came in close contact," and finally, when it lay dying on the shore, "it was abused by every passing penguin in its extremity." By human standards, this is deplorable behavior. But penguins are not human, and from the point of view of avian survival such behavior is highly "moral" in that it is functionally healthy, because it protects the genetic integrity of the species.

It is difficult to measure the selective pressures of predators upon prey species, but without question such pressures exist and have evolutionary consequences on such characters as coloration, sharpness of senses, "freezing" behavior, quickness and agility in flight. The remarkably close resemblance of the plumage of some larks to the soils they habitually frequent, of the mimetic resemblance of the frogmouths (Podargidae) to dead stubs of trees, must be due in large part to the millennia of unceasing elimination of the more conspicuous variants by predators. Penguins capture a higher percentage of conspicuously colored minnows in a swimming pool than of inconspicuously colored ones (p. 52). There is no reason to believe that predatory birds would do otherwise when preying upon other birds. Predation probably affects the length of incubation periods. Ostrich eggs in Africa have an incubation period shorter than that of emu eggs in Australia, very likely because predators are common in Africa and scarce in Australia (p. 315).

Apparently the incubation calendar of the Horned Lark, *Eremophila alpestris,* is fixed partly by weather and partly by predators. In the northern United States in April, many young Horned Larks succumb to late snows, cold rains, and food shortage; but late hatching is no cure for the trouble since "predaceous enemies cause a greater and greater loss as the season advances into June and July. The optimum season for the welfare of the young is shown to be May" (Bent, 1942). The fledglings are thus caught in a selective vise, one jaw of which brings biotic pressures, the other, physical pressures. It is reasonable to assume that the evolutionary adjustments made by many species are compromises between two or more selective pressures.

A special form of predation is the brood

parasitism of the European Cuckoo, *Cuculus canorus.* In southern England and other parts of Europe the Cuckoo lays, in nests of a variety of birds, eggs which do not closely resemble those of the host species. In the Khasi hills of India, however, the local race of Cuckoo lays eggs which are remarkably similar in size and coloration to those of its host or fosterer species. Baker (1942) observed the fate of Cuckoos' eggs deposited in 1642 nests of normal fosterers (where mimicry was very close) and in 298 nests of abnormal fosterers (where egg color agreement was poor). The incidence of nest desertion or other forms of Cuckoo-egg rejection by host species was only 8 per cent among the normal fosterers, but 24 per cent among the abnormal fosterers. This selective rejection of Cuckoos' eggs by fostering species depends both on the closeness of egg mimicry and the discrimination of the host species. Here is an example of natural selection clearly in operation. The Cuckoo is attempting to extend its parasitic sway over new species, and is meeting drastic selection in the higher percentage of rejections which it encounters.

It seems to be a reflection on the low intelligence of a tiny warbler or sparrow that it will continue to feed and protect a parasitic nestling Cuckoo even when it has grown to be ten or more times as large as its foster parent. The nestlings of most races of Cuckoos do not resemble the young of their hosts, even though the eggs of both species often agree closely in appearance. Once the feeding instinct has been awakened in the foster parent, the Cuckoo nestling's cry and open mouth prove irresistible, despite the lack of resemblance between the young Cuckoo and the fosterer's own nestlings. A few species, however, seem to be intelligent enough to distinguish the differences between the interloper and their own young. This dilemma has resulted in shifting the burden of adaptation back upon the Cuckoo. In Spain, both the eggs and the young of the Great Spotted Cuckoo, *Clamator glandarius,* resemble closely those of its host, the Magpie, *Pica pica.* A logical assumption is that the Magpie over many years exercised a form of intelligent selection by ejecting or abandoning young Cuckoos that looked "strange," and that natural selection reacted on the young Cuckoos by tailoring their appearance to match that of the host young (Cott, 1940).

Parasites and diseases have brought heavy selective pressures on birds through the years, and they have probably responded with the evolutionary development of various mechanisms of resistance and immunity. The Domestic Chicken, *Gallus gallus,* for example, is capable of producing a wide variety of microbial antibodies in its blood serum. But diseases are also important because of the role they play in aggravating population fluctuations. At the peak of a population cycle, intraspecific competition generates keen selective pressures. On the contrary, at the low ebb of population following an epizootic, so few animals remain that competitive pressures are negligible.

It is in such reduced populations that another evolutionary mechanism comes into play. Everyone is aware that in human affairs a sampling of public opinion is unreliable when it is based on a small sample. To attempt to learn who the next president will be by asking a dozen or a hundred persons is not a dependable procedure. Likewise, when a large population is reduced by disease to a small remnant, the remnant is very unlikely to have precisely the same genetic composition as the original population. In small samples, the genetic character may shift pronouncedly in one direction or another. This shift is known as "genetic drift." Since small splinter populations are often the ancestral stocks from which large populations grow, they provide an evolutionary mechanism known as "random race formation." The same phenomenon also occurs among the individual races of polytypic species, or, for that matter, in any small sample of a larger population which has become geographically isolated from the parent group. The small, storm-driven group of European Fieldfares, *Turdus pilaris,* which has recently established itself in southern Greenland (p. 405) very probably possesses a different combination of genes from its parental population.

Should a small population become isolated, as on oceanic islands, where there are numerous unfilled niches, it may exhibit "undirected" (i.e., relatively unselected) evolution, and branch out into extreme and often bizarre characters. This can occur because the effects of mutation frequency and isolation are stronger than selection pressure. Many mutations that would quickly be eliminated by selective pressures on the mainland are allowed to survive in the benign, selection-free island sanctuary. Under such conditions extravagant developments are possible, as, for example, the large size and flightlessness of the dodos (Raphidae) of the Mascarene Islands in the Indian Ocean. As long as no predators exist on such islands, the lack of wings, or the possession of excessive weight, carries no serious penalties. Extravagant developments may be expensive luxuries, but not so expensive as to bankrupt the species. But once man introduces predators or competitors to these islands, the highly aberrant species quickly becomes extinct. This has been a common fate of land birds isolated on oceanic islands.

To sum up, evolution is based primarily on isolation, variation, and selection. If isolation is too pronounced, gene mutations run on unchecked and produce excessive variation, which results in freaks and monsters. If selection is too rigorous, the result may be overspecialization, which makes the bird vulnerable to environmental change. The fact that such a rich and colorful variety of birds exists and is still evolving on earth today shows that there has been and continues to be a healthful balance between the forces of selection and mutation.

SUGGESTED READINGS

The standard reference on the ancestry of birds is the excellent and well illustrated book by Heilmann, *The Origin of Birds*. The paleontology of birds is well summarized in Storer's chapter in Marshall's *Biology and Comparative Physiology of Birds*, and a survey of recent fossil finds is given by Wetmore in Wolfson's *Recent Studies in Avian Biology*. A brief but well illustrated booklet dealing chiefly with La Brea Pleistocene birds is Howard's *Fossil Birds*. Greenway's *Extinct and Vanishing Birds of the World* treats that melancholy subject in an interesting fashion. For interesting and thorough discussions of the principles and mechanisms of evolution in the lives of birds today, read Mayr's *Systematics and the Origin of Species*, and Rensch's *Evolution Above the Species Level*. Lack's small book on *Darwin's Finches* gives a convincing account of the evolutionary history of the birds which first turned Darwin's thoughts toward the possibility of an evolutionary process.

References

A

Abel, O. 1911. *Die Vorfahren der Vögel und ihre Lebensweise.* Vienna.

Alexander, W. B. 1948. The index of Heron population, 1947. *British Birds, 41:*146–148.

Alexander, W. B., and R. S. R. Fitter. 1955. American land birds in western Europe. *British Birds, 48:*1–14.

Allard, H. A. 1930. The first morning song of some birds of Washington, D.C.: its relation to light. *American Naturalist, 64:*436–439.

Allee, W. C. 1936. Analytical studies of group behavior in birds. *Wilson Bulletin, 48:*145–151.

Allee, W. C., and N. Collias. 1938. Effect of injections of testosterone propionate on small flocks of hens. *Anatomical Record, 72* (4) plus *Supplement:* 60.

Allee, W. C., A. E. Emerson, O. Park, T. Park, and K. Schmidt. 1949. *Principles of Animal Ecology.* W. B. Saunders Company, Philadelphia.

Allee, W. C., and R. H. Masure. 1936. A comparison of maze behavior in paired and isolated Shell Parakeets. *Journal of Comparative Psychology, 22:*131–155.

Allen, A. A. 1914. The Red-winged Blackbird: a study in the ecology of a cat-tail marsh. *Proceedings of the Linnaean Society of New York, 24–25:*43–128.

Allen, D. L. 1954. *Our Wildlife Legacy.* Funk and Wagnalls Company, New York.

Allen, G. M. 1925. *Birds and Their Attributes.* Marshall Jones Company, Boston.

Amadon, D. 1950. The Hawaiian Honeycreepers (Aves, Drepanididae). *Bulletin of the American Museum of Natural History,* 95.

American Ornithologists' Union Committee. 1957. *Check-list of North American Birds.* Fifth Edition. American Ornithologists' Union, Baltimore.

Andersen, F. S. 1948. Contributions to the biology of the Ruff (*Philomachus pugnax* L.). *Dansk Ornithologisk Forenings Tidsskrift, 42:*125–148.

Anderson, A. 1957. A waterfowl nesting study in the Sacramento Valley, California, 1955. *California Fish and Game, 43:*71–90.

Anonymous. 1957. Mourning Dove investigations 1948–1956. *Technical Bulletin No. 1, Southeastern Association of Game and Fish Commissioners,* Columbia, South Carolina.

Armstrong, E. A. 1942. *Bird Display.* Cambridge University Press, London.

Armstrong, E. A. 1947. *Bird Display and Bird Behaviour.* Lindsay Drummond, London.

Armstrong, E. A. 1949. *Bird Life.* Lindsay Drummond, London.

Armstrong, E. A. 1950. The nature and function of displacement activities. In *Physiological Mechanisms in Animal Behaviour. Symposia of the Society for Experimental Biology. IV.* Academic Press, Inc., New York.

Armstrong, E. A. 1953. The history, behavior and breeding biology of the St. Kilda Wren. *Auk, 70:*127–150.

Armstrong, E. A. 1955. *The Wren.* Collins, London.

Armstrong, E. A. 1958. *The Folklore of Birds.* Collins, London.

Austin, O. L. 1940. Some aspects of individual distribution in the Cape Cod tern colonies. *Bird-Banding, 11:*155–169.

Austin, O. L. 1946. The status of the Cape Cod terns in 1944; a behaviour study. *Bird-Banding, 17:*10–27.

Austin, O. L. 1947. A study of the mating of the Common Tern (*Sterna h. hirundo*). *Bird-Banding, 18:*1–16.

Austin, O. L. 1949. Site tenacity, a behaviour trait of the Common Tern (*Sterna hirundo* Linn.). *Bird-Banding, 20:*1–39.

Austin, O. L., and O. L. Austin, Jr. 1956. Some demographic aspects of the Cape Cod population of Common Terns (*Sterna hirundo*). *Bird-Banding, 27:*55–66.

Austin, O. L., Jr. 1961. *Birds of the World.* Golden Press, New York.

503

Aymar, G. C. 1935. *Bird Flight*. Dodd, Mead and Company, New York.

B

Bailey, R. E. 1952. The incubation patch of passerine birds. *Condor, 54:*121–136.

Baird, J., and I. C. T. Nisbet. 1960. Northward fall migration on the Atlantic coast, and its relation to offshore drift. *Auk, 77:*119–149.

Baker, E. C. S. 1923. Cuckoos' eggs and evolution. *Proceedings of the Zoological Society, London:* 277–294.

Baker, E. C. S. 1942. *Cuckoo Problems*. H. F. & G. Witherby, Ltd., London.

Baker, J. R. 1938. The relation between latitude and breeding seasons in birds. *Proceedings of the Zoological Society of London,* 108, Series A: 557–582.

Baldwin, S. P., and S. C. Kendeigh. 1932. Physiology of the temperature of birds. *Scientific Publications of the Cleveland Museum of Natural History,* 3:1–196.

Bambridge, R. 1962. Early experience and sexual behavior in the domestic chicken. *Science, 136:*259–260.

Bancroft, W. D., *et al.* 1923. Blue feathers. *Auk, 40:* 275–300.

Barden, A. A. 1941. Distribution of the families of birds. *Auk, 58:*543–557.

Barruel, P. 1954. *Birds of the World*. Oxford University Press, New York.

Barth, E. K. 1949. Kroppstemperatur hos fugler og pattedyr. *Fauna och Flora, 4/5:*163–177.

Bartholomew, G. A. 1949. The effect of light intensity and day length on reproduction in the English Sparrow. *Bulletin of the Museum of Comparative Zoology at Harvard College,* 101:433–476.

Bartholomew, G. A., and W. R. Dawson. 1954. Body temperature and water requirements in the Mourning Dove. *Ecology, 35:*181–187.

Bartholomew, G. A., and W. R. Dawson. 1958. Body temperatures in California and Gambel's Quail. *Auk, 75:*150–156.

Bartholomew, G. A., T. R. Howell, and T. J. Cade. 1957. Torpidity in the White-throated Swift, Anna Hummingbird, and the Poorwill. *Condor. 59:*145–155.

Bartholomew, J. G., W. E. Clarke, and P. H. Grimshaw. 1911. *Atlas of Zoogeography*. John Bartholomew and Company, Edinburgh.

Baumgartner, F. M. 1939. Studies on the distribution and habits of the Sharptail Grouse in Michigan. *Transactions of the 4th North American Wildlife Conference, 1939:*485–489.

Bayer, E. 1929. Beiträge zur Zweikomponententheorie des Hungers. *Zeitschrift für Psychologie, 112:*1–54.

Beebe, C. W. 1906. *The Bird, Its Form and Function*. Henry Holt and Company, New York.

Beebe, C. W. 1908. Preliminary report on an investigation of the seasonal changes of color in birds. *American Naturalist, 42:*34–56.

Beecher, W. J. 1942. *Nesting Birds and the Vegetation Substrate*. Chicago Ornithological Society, Chicago, Illinois.

Beecher, W. J. 1951. Adaptations for food-getting in the American blackbirds. *Auk, 68:*411–440.

Beer, J. R., L. D. Frenzel, and N. Hansen. 1956. Minimum space requirements of some nesting passerine birds. *Wilson Bulletin, 68:*200–209.

Bellrose, F. C. 1953. Housing for Wood Ducks. *Illinois Natural History Survey Circular 45*, Urbana, Illinois.

Bellrose, F. C., and J. G. Sieh. 1960. Massed waterfowl flights in the Mississippi flyway, 1956 and 1957. *Wilson Bulletin, 72:*29–59.

Bennett, M. A. 1940. The social hierarchy in Ring Doves. II. The effect of treatment with testosterone propionate. *Ecology, 21:*148–165.

Benoit, J. *in* Grassé, P. 1950. *Traité de Zoologie, Tome XV, Oiseau*. Masson et Cie., Paris.

Benoit, J., and L. Ott. 1944. External and internal factors in sexual activity. Effect of irradiation with different wavelengths on the mechanisms of photo-stimulation of the hypophysis and on testicular growth in the immature duck. *Yale Journal of Biology and Medicine,* 17:27–46.

Benson, C. W. 1948. Geographic voice variation in African birds. *Ibis, 90:*48–71.

Bent, A. C. 1923. Life Histories of North American Wild Fowl. *U.S. National Museum Bulletin 126*. Washington, D.C.

Bent, A. C. 1932. Life Histories of North American Gallinaceous Birds. *U.S. National Museum Bulletin 162*. Washington, D.C.

Bent, A. C. 1937. Life Histories of North American Birds of Prey. *U.S. National Museum Bulletin 167*. Washington, D.C.

Bent, A. C. 1939. Life Histories of North American Woodpeckers. *U.S. National Museum Bulletin 174*. Washington, D.C.

Bent, A. C. 1940. Life Histories of North American Cuckoos, Goatsuckers, Hummingbirds and their Allies. *U.S. National Museum Bulletin 176*. Washington, D.C.

Bent, A. C. 1942. Life Histories of North American Flycatchers, Swallows, Larks, and their Allies. *U.S. National Museum Bulletin 179*. Washington, D.C.

Bent, A. C. 1948. Life Histories of North American Nuthatches, Wrens, Thrashers, and their Allies. *U.S. National Museum Bulletin 195*. Washington, D.C.

Bent, A. C. 1949. Life Histories of North American Thrushes, Kinglets, and their Allies. *U.S. National Museum Bulletin 196*. Washington, D.C.

Bent, A. C. 1953. Life Histories of North American Wood Warblers. *U.S. National Museum Bulletin 203*. Washington, D.C.

Bent, A. C. 1958. Life Histories of North American Blackbirds, Orioles, Tanagers, and their Allies. *U.S. National Museum Bulletin 211*. Washington, D.C.

Berger, A. J. 1953. On the locomotor anatomy of the Blue Coua, *Coua caerulea. Auk, 70:*49–82.

Bergman, G. 1946. Der Steinwälzer, *Arenaria i. interpres* (L.) in seiner Beziehung zur Umwelt. *Acta Zoologica Fennica, 47*:1–144.

Bergstrom, E. A. 1951. The South Windsor Bank Swallow colony. *Bird-Banding, 22*:54–63.

Biaggi, V. 1955. The Puerto Rican Honeycreeper, *Coereba flaveola portoricensis* (Bryant). *University of Puerto Rico Agricultural Station, Special Bulletin.*

Bigelow, H. B., and W. W. Welsh. 1924. Fishes of the Gulf of Maine. *Bulletin, U.S. Bureau of Fisheries,* 40, Part I:527.

Bissonnette, T. H. 1932. Light and diet as factors in relation to sexual photoperiodicity. *Nature, 129:* 613.

Bissonnette, T. H. 1937. Photoperiodicity in birds. *Wilson Bulletin, 49*:241–270.

Bissonnette, T. H., and A. G. Csech. 1936. Fertile eggs from pheasants in January by "night lighting." *Bird-Banding, 7*:108–111.

Blake, C. H. 1947. Wing-flapping rates in birds. *Auk, 64*:619–620.

Blake, C. H. 1956. Weight changes in birds. *Bird-Banding, 27*:16–22.

Blake, C. H. 1958. Respiration rates. *Bird-Banding, 29*:38–40.

Blanchard, B. D. 1936. Continuity of behavior in the Nuttall White-crowned Sparrow. *Condor, 38:* 145–150.

Blanchard, B. D. 1941. The White-crowned Sparrows (*Zonotrichia leucophrys*) of the Pacific Seaboard; Environment and annual cycle. *University of California Publications in Zoology, 46*:1–178.

Bodenstein, G., and E. Schüz. 1944. Vom Schleifenzug des Prachttauchers (*Colymbus arcticus*). *Ornithologische Monatsberichte, 52*:98–105.

Bond, R. M. 1942. Development of young Goshawks. *Wilson Bulletin, 54*:81–88.

Borrero, H. J. 1953. Notas preliminares sobre habitos alimenticios de palomas silvestres Colombianos. *Caldasia, 6* (27):75–80.

Bourlière, F., *in* Grassé, P. 1950. *Traité de Zoologie. Tome XV. Oiseaux.* Masson et Cie, Paris.

Boyd, A. W., and A. L. Thomson. 1936. Recoveries of marked swallows within the British Isles. *British Birds, 30*:278–287.

Boyd, E. M. 1951. The external parasites of birds; a review. *Wilson Bulletin, 63*:363–369.

Boyd, E. M. 1958. Birds and some human diseases. *Bird-Banding, 29*:34–38.

Bradley, O. C., and T. Grahame. 1950. *The Structure of the Fowl.* J. B. Lippincott Company, Philadelphia.

Brand, A. R. 1938. Vibration frequencies of passerine bird song. *Auk, 55*:263–268.

Braun, H. 1952. Über das Unterscheidungsvermögen unbenannter Anzahlen bei Papageien. *Zeitschrift für Tierpsychologie, 9* (1):40–91.

Brauner, J. 1952. Reactions of Poor-wills to light and temperature. *Condor, 54*:152–159.

Brodkorb, P. 1955. Number of feathers and weights of various systems in a Bald Eagle. *Wilson Bulletin, 67*:142.

Broley, C. L. 1947. Migration and nesting of Florida Bald Eagles. *Wilson Bulletin, 59*:3–20.

Broun, M., and B. V. Goodwin. 1943. Flight speeds of hawks and crows. *Auk, 60*:487–492.

Brown, G. 1937. Aggressive display of birds before a looking glass. *British Birds, 31*:137–138.

Bruijns, M. F. 1959. Stookolievogels op de Nederlandse kust. *De Levende Natuur, 62*:172–178.

Bub, H., and H. Kumerloeve. 1954. Die Fichtenkreuzschnabel (*Loxia curvirostra*) invasion in 1953 in Europa; mit besonderer Berücksichtigung Deutschlands. *Ornithologische Mitteilungen, 6:* 225–231.

Buick, T. L. 1937. *The Moa-Hunters of New Zealand, Sportsmen of the Stone Age.* Thomas Avery and Sons, Ltd., New Plymouth, New Zealand.

Burger, J. W. 1939. Some aspects of the roles of light intensity and the daily length of exposure to light in the sexual photoperiodic activation of the male Starling. *Journal of Experimental Zoology, 81:* 333–340.

Burger, J. W. 1949. A review of experimental investigations on seasonal reproduction in birds. *Wilson Bulletin, 61*:211–230.

Burrows, W. H., and S. J. Marsden, 1938. Artificial breeding of Turkeys. *Poultry Science, 17*:408.

Bussman, J. 1943. Beitrag zur Kenntnis der Brutbiologie des Kleibers (*Sitta europaea caesia*). *Der Ornithologische Beobachter, 40*:57–67.

Buxton, P. A. 1923. *Animal Life in Deserts.* E. Arnold & Company, London.

C

Cade, T. J. 1953. Behavior of a young Gyrfalcon. *Wilson Bulletin 65*:26–31.

Carlson, C. W. 1960. Aortic rupture. *Turkey Producer,* January, 1960.

Carr-Lewty, R. A. 1943. Reactions of birds to aircraft. *British Birds, 36*:151–152.

Campbell, B. 1955. The breeding, distribution and habitats of the Pied Flycatcher (*Muscicapa hypoleuca*) in Britain. Parts II and III. *Bird Study, 2:* 24–32; 179–191.

Cartwright, B. W. 1944. The "crash" decline in Sharptailed Grouse and Hungarian Partridge in Western Canada and the role of the predator. *Transactions of the 9th North American Wildlife Conference:* 324–329.

Cendron, J. 1953. La mue du manchot Adélie adulte. *Alauda, 21*:77–85.

Chance, E. P. 1940. *The Truth about the Cuckoo.* Country Life, London.

Chapin, J. P., and L. W. Wing. 1959. The Wideawake Calendar, 1953 to 1958. *Auk, 76*:153–158.

Chapman, F. M. 1908. A contribution to the life-histories of the Booby (*Sula leucogaster*) and Man-o'-War Bird (*Fregata aquila*). *Papers from the Tortugas Laboratory of the Carnegie Institution, Washington, D.C.,* 2:139–151.

Chapman, F. M. 1908. *Camps and Cruises of an Orni-thologist.* D. Appleton & Company, New York.

Chapman, F. M. 1917. *The Distribution of Bird Life in Colombia. Bulletin of the American Museum of Natural History, vol. 36.* New York.

Chapman, F. M. 1940. The post-glacial history of *Zonotrichia capensis. Bulletin of the American Museum of Natural History,* 77:381–438.

Chapman, L. B. 1955. Studies of a Tree Swallow colony. *Bird-Banding,* 26:45–70.

Chernin, E. 1952. The epizootiology of *Leucocytozoon simondi* infections in domestic ducks in northern Michigan. *American Journal of Hygiene,* 56:39–57; 101–118.

Chettleburgh, M. R. 1952. Observations on the collection and burial of acorns by Jays in Hainault Forest. *British Birds,* 45:359–364.

Chisholm, A. H. 1937. Bird-insect nesting associations. *Ibis,* Series 14:1:411–413.

Chisholm, A. H. 1952. Bird-insect nesting associations in Australia. *Ibis,* 94:395–405.

Clarke, L. F., H. Rahn, and M. D. Martin. 1942. Sage Grouse Studies II. *Wyoming Game and Fish Department Bulletin* No. 2:13–27.

Clements, F. E., and V. E. Shelford. 1939. *Bio-ecology.* John Wiley and Sons, New York.

Colbert, E. H. 1955. *Evolution of the Vertebrates.* John Wiley and Sons, New York.

Collias, E. C., and N. E. 1957. The response of chicks of the Franklin's Gull to parental bill-color. *Auk,* 74:371–375.

Collias, N. E. 1952. The development of social behavior in birds. *Auk,* 69:127–159.

Colquhoun, M. K. 1939. The vocal activity of Blackbirds at a winter roost. *British Birds,* 33:44–47.

Colquhoun, M. K. 1940. Visual and auditory conspicuousness in a woodland bird community. *Proceedings of the Zoological Society of London, series A,* 110:129–148.

Comar, C. L., and J. C. Driggers. 1949. Secretion of radioactive calcium in the hen's egg. *Science, 109:* 282.

Cone, C. D., Jr. 1962. Thermal soaring of birds. *American Scientist, 50:*180–209.

Cooch, G. 1955. Observations on the autumn migration of Blue Geese. *Wilson Bulletin, 67:*171–174.

Cooke, W. W. 1915. Bird Migration. *U.S. Department of Agriculture Bulletin 185:*1–47.

Corti, U. A., R. Melcher, and T. Tinner. 1949. Beiträge zur Biologie der Blaumerle, *Monticola solitarius* (L.). *Archives suisses d'Ornithologie,* 2:185–212.

Cott, H. B. 1940. *Adaptive Coloration in Animals.* Methuen, London.

Coues, E. 1903. *Key to North American Birds.* Page and Company, Boston.

Coulson, J. C. 1956. Mortality and egg production of the Meadow Pipit with special reference to altitude. *Bird Study,* 3:119–132.

Cowles, R. B., and A. Nordstrom. 1946. A possible avian analogue of the scrotum. *Science, 104:*586–587.

Cox, P. R. 1944. A statistical investigation into bird song. *British Birds,* 38:3–9.

Craig, W. 1908. The voices of pigeons regarded as a means of social control. *American Journal of Sociology, 14:*86–100.

Craig, W. 1918. Appetites and aversions as constituents of instincts. *Biological Bulletin, Woods Hole, 34* (2):91–107.

Cram, E. B. 1927. Bird parasites of the Nematode Suborders Strongylata, Ascaridata, and Spirurata. *U. S. National Museum Bulletin 140.*

Creutz, G. 1949. Die Entwicklung zweier Populationen des Trauerschnäppers, *Muscicapa h. hypoleuch* (Pall.), nach Herkunft und Alter. *Beiträge zur Vogelkunde,* 27–53. Akademische Verlagsgesellschaft, Leipzig.

Crew, F. A. E. 1923. Studies in intersexuality II: Sex reversal in the fowl. *Proceedings of the Royal Society, series B,* 95:256–278.

Cruickshank, A. D. 1956. Nesting heights of some woodland warblers in Maine. *Wilson Bulletin, 68:*157.

Cullen, E. 1957. Adaptations in the Kittiwake to cliff-nesting. *Ibis,* 99:275–302.

Cushing, J. E., and A. O. Ramsey. 1949. The non-heritable aspects of family unity in birds. *Condor, 51:* 82–87.

D

Daanje, A. 1941. Über das Verhaltung des Haussperlings, (*Passer d. domesticus* (L.)). *Ardea,* 30:1–42.

Dale, F. M. 1955. The role of calcium in reproduction of the Ring-necked Pheasant. *Journal of Wildlife Management,* 19:325–331.

Dambach, C. A. 1941. The effect of land-use adjustments on wildlife populations in the Ohio Valley region. *Transactions of the 5th North American Wildlife Conference, Washington:*331–337.

Danforth, C. H., and F. Foster. 1929. Skin transplantation as a means of studying genetic and endocrine factors in the fowl. *Journal of Experimental Zoology,* 52: 443–470.

Darling, F. F. 1938. *Bird Flocks and the Breeding Cycle.* Cambridge University Press, Cambridge.

Darling, F. F. 1952. Social behavior and survival. *Auk,* 69:183–191.

Darlington, P. J. 1957. *Zoogeography: The Geographical Distribution of Animals.* John Wiley and Sons, New York.

Darwin, C. 1845. *Journal of Researches into the Geology and Natural History of the Various Countries Visited during the Voyage of H.M.S. Beagle round the World.* Second Edition, Colonial and Home Library, London. 1902 Edition, P. F. Collier and Son, New York.

Darwin, C. 1859. *On the Origin of Species by Means of Natural Selection.* Various editions.

Dauber, D. V. 1944. Spontaneous arteriosclerosis in chickens. *Archives of Pathology,* 38:46.

Davis, D. E. 1940. Social nesting habits of the Smooth-billed Ani. *Auk,* 57:179–218.

Davis, D. E. 1942. The phylogeny of social nesting habits in the Crotophaginae. *Quarterly Review of Biology, 17:* 115–134.

Davis, D. E. 1955. Breeding biology of birds. *In* Wolfson, A., *Recent Studies in Avian Biology*, 264–308. University of Illinois Press, Urbana, Illinois.

Davis, D. E. 1957. Aggressive behavior in castrated Starlings. *Science, 126:* 253.

Davis, D. E., and L. V. Domm. 1941. The sexual behavior of hormonally treated domestic fowl. *Proceedings of the Society for Experimental Biology and Medicine, 48:* 667–669.

Davis, P. 1957. The breeding of the Storm Petrel. *British Birds, 50:* 85–101.

Dawson, W. L. 1909. *The Birds of Washington.* Occidental Publishing Company, Seattle.

Deevey, E. S. 1960. The human population. *Scientific American, 203* (3): 195–204.

De Guirtchitch, G. 1937. Chronique Ornithologique Tunisienne pour l'Année 1936. *L'Oiseau et la Revue Francais d'Ornithologie, 7:*450–472.

Deighton, T., and J. C. D. Hutchinson. 1940. Studies on the metabolism of the fowls. II. The effect of activity on metabolism. *Journal of Agricultural Science, 30:* 141–157.

Delacour, J. 1946. Les Timaliinés. *L'Oiseau et la Revue Francaise d'Ornithologie, 41:*7–36.

Dennis, J. V. 1948. Observations on the Orchard Oriole in lower Mississippi delta. *Bird-Banding, 19:*12–21.

Dice, L. R. 1945. Minimum intensities of illumination under which owls can find dead prey by sight. *American Naturalist, 79:*385–416.

Diesselhorst, G. 1950. Erkennen des Geschlechts und Paarbildung bei der Goldammer (*Emberiza citrinella* L.). *Ornithologische Berichte, 3:*69–112.

Dilger, W. C. 1955. Ruptured heart in the Cardinal, *Richmondena cardinalis. Auk, 72:*85.

Dilger, W. C. 1956. Nest-building movements performed by a juvenile Olive-backed Thrush. *Wilson Bulletin, 68:*157–158.

Dilger, W. C. 1962. The behavior of lovebirds. *Scientific American, 206* (1):88–98.

Dinnendahl, L. 1954. Nächtlicher Zug und Windrichtung auf Helgoland. *Die Vogelwarte, 17:*188–194.

Dixon, C. 1902. *Birds' Nests.* Frederick A. Stokes Company, New York.

Dobzhansky, T. 1950. Evolution in the tropics. *American Scientist, 38:*209–221.

Domm, L. V. 1955. Recent advances in knowledge concerning the role of hormones in the sex differentiation of birds. *In* Wolfson, A. *Recent Studies in Avian Biology.* University of Illinois Press, Urbana, Illinois.

Domm, L. V., and E. Taber. 1946. Endocrine factors controlling erythrocyte concentration in the blood of the domestic fowl. *Physiological Zoology, 19:*258–281.

Donner, K. O. 1951. The visual acuity of some passerine birds. *Acta Zoologica Fennica, 66:*1–40.

Dorst, J. 1956. *Les Migrations des Oiseaux.* Payot, Paris.

Drost, R. and G. Hartmann. 1949. Hohes Alter einer Population des Austerfischers. *Die Vogelwarte, 2:*102–104.

DuBois, A. 1923. The Short-Eared Owl as a foster-mother. *Auk, 40:*383–393.

DuBois, A. D. 1936. Habits and nest life of the Desert Horned Lark. *Condor, 38:*49–56.

E

Edminster, F. C. 1939. The effect of predator control on Ruffed Grouse populations in New York. *Journal of Wildlife Management, 3:*345–352.

Edminster, F. C. 1947. *The Ruffed Grouse.* Macmillan, New York.

Egler, F. E. 1958. Science, industry, and the abuse of rights of way. *Science, 127:*573–580.

Ehrström, C. 1956. Fåglarnas uppträdande under solförmörkelsen den 30 juni 1954. *Vår Fågelvärld, 15:*1–28.

Einarsen, A. S. 1942. Specific results from Ring-necked Pheasant studies in the Pacific Northwest. *Transactions of the North American Wildlife Conference, 7:*130–145.

Eisner, E. 1960. The relationship of hormones to the reproductive behaviour of birds, referring especially to parental behaviour: A review. *Animal Behaviour, 8:*155–179.

Eklund, C.R., and F. E. Charlton, 1959. Measuring the temperatures of incubating penguin eggs. *American Scientist, 47:*80–86.

Elder, W. H. 1954. The oil gland of birds. *Wilson Bulletin, 66:*6–31.

Elder, W. H. 1955. Fluoroscopic measures of shooting pressure on Pink-footed and Grey Lag Geese. *The Wildfowl Trust 7th Annual Report, London, 1953–54:* 123–126.

Elder, W. H., and M. W. Weller. 1954. Duration of fertility in the domestic Mallard hen after isolation from the drake. *Journal of Wildlife Management, 18:*495–502.

Eliassen, E. 1957, Right ventricle pressures and heart-rate in diving birds. *Nature, 180:*512–513.

Eliassen, E. 1960. (Yearbook for the University of Bergen, Mathematical and Natural Sciences Series, 1960, No. 12.)

Elton, C. 1927. *Animal Ecology.* Sidgwick and Jackson, Ltd., London.

Emeis, W. 1942. Über den ungünstigen Verlauf des Brutgeschäfts der schleswig-holsteinischen Störche (*Ciconia ciconia*) im Sommer 1941. *Beiträge zur Fortpflanzungsbiologie der Vögel, 18:* 153–155.

Emlen, J. T. 1937. Morning awakening time of a Mockingbird. *Bird-Banding, 8:*81–82.

Emlen, J. T. 1940. Sex and age ratios in survival of the California Quail. *Journal of Wildlife Management, 4:*92–99.

Emlen, J. T. 1941. An experimental analysis of the breeding cycle of the Tricolored Red-wing. *Condor, 43:*209–219.

Emlen, J. T. 1942. Notes on a nesting colony of Western Crows. *Bird-Banding, 13:*143–154.

Emlen, J. T. 1954. Territory, nest building and pair formation in the Cliff Swallow. *Auk, 71:*16–35.

Emlen, J. T. 1955. The study of behavior in birds. *in* Wolfson, A., *Recent Studies in Avian Biology.* University of Illinois Press, Urbana, Illinois.

Emlen, J. T. 1956. Juvenile mortality in a Ring-billed Gull colony. *Wilson Bulletin, 68*:232–238.

Emlen, J. T., and F. W. Lorenz. 1942. Pairing responses of free-living valley quail to sex-hormone pellet implants. *Auk, 59*:369–378.

Errington, P. L. 1945. Some contributions of a 15-year local study of the Northern Bobwhite to a knowledge of population phenomena. *Ecological Monographs, 15*:1–34.

Evans, F. C., and J. T. Emlen. 1947. Ecological notes on the prey selected by a Barn Owl. *Condor, 49*: 3–9.

Evans, L. T. 1936. Territorial behavior of normal and castrated females of *Anolis carolinensis*. *Journal of Genetic Psychology, 49*:49–60.

F

Fabricius, E. 1951. Zur Ethologie junger Anatiden. *Acta Zoologica Fennica, 68*:1–175.

Fabricius, E. 1959. What makes plumage waterproof? *Report of the Wildfowl Trust, 10*:105–113.

Fairbridge, R. W. 1960. The changing level of the sea. *Scientific American, 202* (5):70–79.

Farkas, T. 1955. Zur Brutbiologie und Ethologie des Steinrötels (*Monticola saxatilis*). *Die Vogelwelt, 76*:164–180.

Farner, D. A. 1945. The return of Robins to their birthplaces. *Bird-Banding, 16*:81–99.

Farner, D. S. 1955. The annual stimulus for migration: experimental and physiologic aspects. *in* Wolfson, A., *Recent Studies in Avian Biology*. University of Illinois Press, Urbana, Illinois.

Fisher, H. I. 1958. The "hatching muscle" in the chick. *Auk, 75*:391–399.

Fisher, J. 1951. *Watching Birds*. Penguin Books. Harmondsworth, Middlesex.

Fisher, J. 1952. *The Fulmar*. Collins, London.

Fisher, J., and R. A. Hinde. 1949. The opening of milk bottles by birds. *British Birds, 42*:347–357.

Fisher, J., and R. M. Lockley. 1954. *Sea-Birds*. Houghton Mifflin Company, Boston.

Fitch, H. S., F. Swenson, and D. F. Tillotson. 1946. Behavior and food habits of the Red-Tailed Hawk. *Condor, 48*:205–237.

Flower, S. S. 1938. Further notes on the duration of life in animals. IV. Birds. *Proceedings of the Zoological Society, London*, Series A, *108*:195–235.

Frank, F. 1941. Besondere Nistweise der Feldsperlings in Bessarabien. *Ornithologische Monatsberichte, 52*:156–157.

Frederikson, K. A. 1940. Über das Brüten der Lachmöwe, *Larus ridibundus* L., auf Felseninseln im Schärenhof und die Ursachen dazu. *Ornis Fennica, 17*:62–63.

Friedmann, H. 1929. *The Cowbirds*. Charles C. Thomas, Springfield, Illinois.

Friedmann, H. 1947. Geographic variations of the Black-bellied, Fulvous and White-faced Tree Ducks. *Condor, 49*:189–195.

Friedmann, H. 1955. The Honey-guides. *U.S. National Museum Bulletin 208*.

Friedmann, H., and M. Davis. 1938. "Left-handedness" in parrots. *Auk, 55*:478–480.

Frings, H., and J. Jumber. 1954. Preliminary studies on the use of specific sound to repel Starlings (*Sturnus vulgaris*) from objectionable roosts. *Science, 119*:318–319.

Frings, H., M. Frings, B. Cox, and L. Peissner. 1955. Recorded calls of Herring Gulls (*Larus argentatus*) as repellents and attractants. *Science, 121*: 340–341.

Frings, H., and M. Frings. 1957. Recorded calls of the Eastern Crow as attractants and repellents. *Journal of Wildlife Management, 21*:91.

Frisch, K. von. 1956. The "language" and the orientation of the bees. *Proceedings of the American Philosophical Society, 100*:515–519.

Frith, H. J. 1956. Temperature regulation in the nesting mounds of the Mallee-Fowl, *Leipoa ocellata* Gould. *Commonwealth Scientific and Industrial Research Organization, Wildlife Research, 1*: 79–95.

Frith, H. J. 1957. Clutch size in the Goldfinch. *Emu, 57*:287–288.

Frith, H. J. 1957. Experiments on the control of temperature in the mound of the Mallee-Fowl, *Leipoa ocellata* Gould (Megapodiidae). *Commonwealth Scientific and Industrial Research Organization, Wildlife Research, 2*:101–110.

Frith, H. J., and R. A. Tilt. 1959. Breeding of the Zebra Finch in the Murrumbridgee irrigation area, New South Wales. *Emu, 59*:289–295.

G

Gallet, E. 1950. *The Flamingos of the Camargue*. Oxford University Press, New York.

Gaultierotti, T., B. Schreiber, D. Mainardi, and D. Passerini. 1959. Orientation capacity and cerebellar potentials. *American Journal of Physiology, 197*:469–474.

Gause, G. F. 1934. Experimental studies on the struggle for existence in *Paramecium caudatum*, *Paramecium aurelia*, and *Stylonichia mytilus*. *Zoologischeskii Zhurnal, 12*.

George, J, C., and R. M. Naik. 1960. a. Some observations on the distribution of the blood capillaries in the pigeon breast muscle. *Auk, 77*:224–226.

George, J. C., and R. M. Naik. 1960. b. Intramuscular fat store in the pectoralis of birds. *Auk, 77*:216–217.

Gerstell, R. 1942. The place of winter feeding in practical wildlife management. *Research Bulletin No. 2*, Pennsylvania Game Commission, Harrisburg, Pennsylvania.

Gibb, J. 1947. Sun-bathing in birds. *British Birds, 40*: 172–174.

Gibb, J., and C. Gibb. 1951. Waxwings in the winter of 1949–50. *British Birds, 44*:158–163.

Gilfillan, M. C., and H. Bezdek. 1944. Winter foods of the Ruffed Grouse in Ohio. *Journal of Wildlife Management, 8*:208–210.

Gilliard, E. T. 1956. Bower ornamentation versus plumage characteristics in bower-birds. *Auk, 73:* 450–451.

Gilliard, E. T. 1958. *Living Birds of the World.* Doubleday, Garden City, N.Y.

Glover, F. A. 1956. Nesting and production of the Blue-winged Teal (*Anas discors* Linnaeus) in northwest Iowa. *Journal of Wildlife Management, 20:*28–46.

Goethe, F. 1941. Beobachtungen am Neusiedlersee und in dem Gebiet der Salzlachen. *Journal für Ornithologie, 89:*268–281.

Goethe, F. 1953. Soziale Hierarchie im Aufzuchtschwarm der Silbermöwen. *Zeitschrift für Tierpsychologie, 10:*44–50.

Goodall, J. D., R. A. Philippi, B. and A. W. Johnson. 1945. Nesting habits of the Peruvian Gray Gull. *Auk, 62:*450–451.

Goodpasture, K. A. 1955. Recovery of a Chickadee population from the 1951 ice storm. *Migrant, 26* (2):21–23.

Goodwin, D. 1956. Observations on the voice and some displays of certain pigeons. *Avicultural Magazine, 62:*17–33; 62–70.

Goodwin, D. 1956. *In* Hutson, H. P. W., *The Ornithologists' Guide.* Philosophical Library, New York.

Gould, E. 1957. Orientation in box turtles, *Terrapene c. carolina* (L.). *Biological Bulletin, 112:*336–348.

Gower, C. 1936. The cause of blue color as found in the Bluebird and the Blue Jay. *Auk, 53:*178–185.

Grassé, P. P. 1950. Organization des sociétés d'oiseaux. *Traité de Zoologie. Tome XV. Oiseaux.* Masson et Cie, Paris.

Graves, R. 1948. *The White Goddess.* Creative Age Press, New York.

Green, C. 1949. The Black-shouldered Kite in Masira (Oman). *Ibis, 91:*459–464.

Greenewalt, C. H. 1955. The flight of the Black-capped Chickadee and the White-breasted Nuthatch. *Auk, 72:*1–5.

Greenewalt, C. H. 1960. *Hummingbirds.* Doubleday, Garden City, New York.

Greenway, J. C. 1958. *Extinct and Vanishing Birds of the World.* American Committee for International Wild Life Protection, Special Publication No. 13, New York.

Griffin, D. R. 1943. Homing experiments with Herring Gulls and Common Terns. *Bird-Banding, 14:*7–23.

Griffin, D. R. 1953. Acoustic orientation in the Oil Bird, *Steatornis. Proceedings of the National Academy of Science, U.S.,* 39:884–893.

Griffin, D. R. 1955. Bird navigation. *In* Wolfson, A., *Recent Studies in Avian Biology.* University of Illinois Press, Urbana, Illinois.

Griffin, D. R., and R. J. Hock. 1949. Airplane observations of homing birds. *Ecology, 30:*176–198.

Grinnell, J., and T. I. Storer. 1924. *Animal Life in the Yosemite.* University of California Press, Berkeley.

Griscom, L. 1937. A monographic study of the Red Crossbill. *Proceedings of the Boston Society of Natural History, 41:*77–210.

Griscom, L. 1941. The recovery of birds from disaster. *Audubon Magazine, 43:*191–196.

Griscom, L. 1945. *Modern Bird Study.* Harvard University Press, Boston.

Groskin, H. 1950. Banding 4,469 Purple Finches at Ardmore, Pa. *Bird-Banding, 21:*93–99.

Gross, A. O. 1940. The migration of Kent Island Herring Gulls. *Bird-Banding, 11:*129–155.

Gross, A. O. 1947. Cyclic invasions of the Snowy Owl and the migration of 1945–1946. *Auk, 64:*584–601.

Gueniat, E. 1948. Beobachtungen an einem Massenschlafplatz von Bergfinken in der Ajoie im Winter 1946–47. *Der Ornithologische Beobachter, 45:*81–98.

Guhl, A. M. 1956. The social order of chickens. *Scientific American, 194* (2):42–46.

Gunn, W. W. H., and A. M. Crocker. 1951. Analysis of unusual bird migration in North America during the storm of April 4–7, 1947. *Auk, 68:*139–163.

H

Haartman, L. von. 1949. Der Trauerfliegenschnäpper. *Acta Zoologica Fennica.* Helsinki.

Haartman, L. von. 1953. Was reizt den Trauerfliegenschnäpper (*Muscicapa hypoleuca*) zu füttern? *Die Vogelwarte, 16:*157–164.

Haartman, L. von. 1954. Der Trauerfliegenschnäpper. III Die Nahrungsbiologie, *Acta Zoologica Fennica, 83:*1–96.

Haartman, L. von. 1956. Einfluss der Temperatur auf den Brutrhythmus. *Ornis Fennica, 33:*100–107.

Haftorn, S. 1933. Contribution to the food biology of tits . . . Part I. The Crested Tit (*Parus c. cristatus,* L.). *Det Kgl Norske Videnskabers Selskabs Skrifter,* 1953 (4):1–124.

Hailman, J. P. 1960. Hostile dancing and fall territory of a color-banded Mockingbird. *Condor, 62:*464–468.

Hall, T. S. 1951. *Source Book in Animal Biology.* McGraw-Hill Book Company, New York.

Hamilton, W. J. 1943. Nesting of the Eastern Bluebird. *Auk, 60:*91–94.

Hamilton, W. J., and M. C. Hammond. 1960. Oriented overland spring migration of pinioned Canada Geese. *Wilson Bulletin, 72:*385–391.

Hammond, M. C. 1948. Marsh Hawk kills Baldpate. *Auk, 65:*297–298.

Hann, H. W. 1937. Life history of the Oven-bird in southern Michigan. *Wilson Bulletin, 49:*145:237.

Hann, H. W. 1953. *The Biology of Birds.* Ulrich Book Store, Ann Arbor, Michigan.

Hanson, H. C., and R. H. Smith. 1950. Canada Geese of the Mississippi Flyway. *Bulletin of the Illinois Natural History Survey, 25:*67–210.

Hansen, L. 1952. Natuglens (*Strix a. aluco* L.) døgn-og årsrytme. *Dansk Ornithologisk Forenings Tidsskrift, 46:*158–172.

Harper, F. 1938. The Chuck-will's widow in the Okefenokee region. *The Oriole, 3:*9–13.

Harper, T. A., R. V. Boucher, and E. W. Callenbach. 1952. Influence of source and quantity of vitamin A ingested upon liver storage and survival time of Bob-white Quail. *Poultry Science, 31*:273–283.

Harris, R. D. 1944. The Chestnut-collared Longspur in Manitoba. *Wilson Bulletin, 56*:105–115.

Hartley, P. H. T. 1949. The biology of the Mourning Chat in winter quarters. *Ibis, 91*:393–413.

Hartley, P. H. T. 1950. An experimental analysis of interspecific recognition. In *Physiological Mechanisms in Animal Behaviour. Symposia of the Society for Experimental Biology. IV.* Academic Press, New York.

Haviland, M. 1926. *Forest, Steppe and Tundra.* Cambridge University Press.

Hawkins, A. S. 1940. Sex and age ratios in ducks. *Research News,* October, 1940. (mimeographed).

Hawksley, O. 1957. Ecology of a breeding population of Arctic Terns. *Bird-Banding, 28*:57–92.

Heilfurth, F. 1936. Beitrag zur Fortpflanzungsökologie der Hochgebirgsvögel. *Beiträge zur Fortpflanzungsbiologie der Vogel, 12*:98–105.

Heilmann, G. 1927. *The Origin of Birds.* D. Appleton and Company, New York.

Heinroth, O. 1910. Beiträge zur Biologie, namentlich Ethologie und Psychologie der Anatiden. *Verhandlung des V Internationalen Ornithologen-Kongresses:* 589–702. Berlin, Deutsche Ornithologische Gesellschaft, 1911.

Heinroth, O. 1922. Die Beziehungen zwischen Vogelgewicht, Eigewicht, Gelegegewicht und Brutdauer. *Journal für Ornithologie, 70*:172–285.

Heinroth, O. 1938. *Aus dem Leben der Vögel.* Julius Springer, Berlin.

Heinroth, O., and M. Heinroth, 1924–1933. *Die Vögel Mitteleuropas.* Berlin.

Heinroth, O., and K. Heinroth. 1958. *The Birds.* University of Michigan Press, Ann Arbor, Michigan.

Hensley, M. M., and J. B. Cope. 1951. Further data on removal and repopulation of the breeding birds in a spruce-fir forest community. *Auk, 68*:483–493.

Herman, C. M. 1938. Epidemiology of malaria in Eastern Redwings (*Agelaius p. phoeniceus*). *American Journal of Hygiene, 28*:232–241.

Herman, C. M. 1944. The blood protozoa of North American birds. *Bird-Banding, 15*:89–112.

Herman, C. M., and E. E. Wehr. 1954. The occurrence of gizzard worms in Canada Geese. *Journal of Wildlife Management, 18*:509–513.

Herrick, E. H., and J. O. Harris. 1957. Singing female Canaries. *Science, 125*:1299–1300.

Herrick, F. H. 1924. The daily life of the American Eagle: late phase. *Auk, 41*:517–541.

Herrick, F. H. 1935. *Wild Birds At Home.* D. Appleton-Century Company, New York.

Hess, E. H. 1956. Space perception in the chick. *Scientific American, 195* (1):71–80.

Hess, E. H. 1958. "Imprinting" in animals. *Scientific American, 198* (3):81–90.

Hess, E. H. 1959. Imprinting. *Science, 130*:133–141.

Hess, G. 1951. *The Bird: Its Life and Structure.* Greenberg, New York.

Hesse, R., W. C. Allee, and K. P. Schmidt. 1937. *Ecological Animal Geography.* John Wiley and Sons, New York.

Heydweiller, A. M. 1936. Sex, age, and individual variation of winter Tree Sparrows. *Bird-Banding, 7*: 61–68.

Hickey, J. J. 1942. Eastern population of the Duck Hawk. *Auk, 59*:176–204.

Hickey, J. J. 1943. *A Guide to Bird Watching.* Oxford University Press, New York.

Hickey, J. J. 1955. An elevated nest of a Barn Swallow. *Wilson Bulletin, 67*:135.

Hicks, L. E. 1934. A summary of Cowbird host species in Ohio. *Auk, 51*:385–386.

Hinde, R. A. 1952. *The Behaviour of the Great Tit (Parus major) and Some Other Related Species.* E. J. Brill, Leiden.

Hinde, R. A. 1954. Factors governing the changes in strength of a partially inborn response, as shown by the mobbing behaviour of the Chaffinch (*Fringilla coelebs*). I. *Proceedings of the Royal Society,* B. 142:306–331 (331–358).

Hinde, R. A. 1956. The biological significance of territories of birds. *Ibis, 98*:340–369.

Hindwood, K. A. 1955. Bird-wasp nesting associations. *Emu, 55*:263–274.

Hitchcock, H. B. 1955. Homing flights and orientation of pigeons. *Auk, 72*:355–373.

Hoffman, A. 1949. Über die Brutpflege des polyandrischen Wasserfasans *Hydrophasianus chirurgus* (Scop.). *Zoologische Jahrbücher.* 78:367–403.

Hoffman, K. 1954. Versuche zu der im Richtungsfinden der Vögel enthaltenen Zeitschätzung. *Zeitschrift für Tierpsychologie, 11*:453–475.

Hoglund, N., and K. Borg. 1955. Über die Grunde für die Frequenzvariation beim Auerwild. *Zeitschrift für Jagdwissenschaft, 1*:59–62.

Holm, E. R., and M. L. Scott. 1954. Studies on the nutrition of wild waterfowl. *New York Fish and Game Journal, 1*:171–187.

Holst, E. von, and U. von Saint Paul. 1962. Electrically controlled behavior. *Scientific American, 206* (3): 50–59.

Holzapfel, M. 1939. Analyse des Sperrens und Pickens in der Entwicklung des Stars. *Journal für Ornithologie, 87*:525–553.

Homberg, L. 1957. Fiskande Kråkor. *Fauna och flora, 5*:182–185.

Hoogerwerk, A. 1937. Uit het leven der witte ibissen *Threskiornis aethiopicus melanocephalus. Limosa, 10*:137–146.

Horton-Smith, C. 1938. *The Flight of Birds.* H. F. & G. Witherby, London.

Horvath, L. 1955. Red-footed Falcons in Ohat-Woods near Hortobagy. *Acta Zoologica Academiae Hungaricae, 1*:245–287.

Höst, P. 1942. Effect of light on moults and sequences of plumage in the Willow Ptarmigan. *Auk, 59*: 388–403.

Howard, H. 1952. The prehistoric avifauna of Smith Creek Cave, Nevada, with a description of a new gigantic raptor. *Bulletin of the Southern California Academy of Science, 51*:50–54.

Howard, H. 1955. Fossil birds with especial reference to the birds of Rancho La Brea. *Los Angeles County Museum Science Series No. 17.*

Howard, H. 1957. A gigantic "toothed" marine bird from the Miocene of California. *Santa Barbara Museum of Natural History, Bulletin No. 1.*

Howard, H. E. 1920. *Territory in Bird Life.* Murray, London.

Hüchtker, R., and J. Schwartzkopf. 1958. Soziale Verhaltensweisen bei hörenden and gehörlosen Dompfaffen (*Pyrrhula pyrrhula* L.). *Experientia, 14:*106.

Huggins, R. A. 1941. Egg temperature in wild birds under natural conditions. *Ecology, 22:*148–157.

Hustich, I. [Editor]. 1952. The recent climatic fluctuation in Finland and its consequences. *Fennia, 75:* 1–128.

Hutt, F. B. 1949. *Genetics of the Fowl.* McGraw-Hill Book Company, New York.

Huxley, J. S. 1939. A discussion on subspecies and varieties. *Proceedings of the Linnaean Society, London, 151:*105–106.

Huxley, J. S. 1942. *Evolution: The Modern Synthesis.* Harper and Brothers, New York.

Huxley, J. S. 1949. Wren feeding young on fish. *British Birds, 42:*185–186.

I

Irving, L. 1960. Birds of Anaktuvuk Pass, Kobuk, and Old Crow. A study in arctic adaptation. *U. S. National Museum, Bulletin 217.* Washington, D.C.

Isely, F. B. 1938. Survival value of acridian protective coloration. *Ecology, 19:*370–389.

Ising, G. 1946. Die physikalische Möglichkeit eines tierischen Orientierungssinnes auf Basis der Erdrotation. *Ark. Matematik, Astonomi, och Fysik, 32A, No. 18:*1–23.

J

Jahn, H. 1939. Zur Biologie des japanischen Paradiesfliegenschnäppers *Terpsiphone a. atrocaudata* (Eyton). *Journal für Ornithologie, 87:*216–223.

Jameson, W. 1960. Flight of the Albatross. *Natural History, 69* (4):62–69.

Jesperson, P. 1924. On the frequency of birds over the high Atlantic Ocean. *Nature, 114:*281–283.

Jesperson, P. 1929. On the frequency of birds over the high Atlantic Ocean. *Verhandlungen des VI Internationalen Ornithologen Kongresses. Kopenhagen, 1926.* Berlin, Feb. 1929.

Jollie, M. 1947. Plumage changes in the Golden Eagle. *Auk, 64:*549–576.

Johnson, R. A. 1941. Nesting behavior of the Atlantic Murre. *Auk, 58:*153–163.

Johnston, D. W. 1956. The annual reproductive cycle of the California Gull. *Condor, 58:*134–162.

Johnston, R. F. 1956a. Population structure in salt marsh Song Sparrows. Part I. *Condor, 58:*24–44.

Johnston, R. F. 1956b. Population structure in salt marsh Song Sparrows. Part II. *Condor, 58:*254–272.

Jordan, J. S. 1953a. Consumption of cereal grains by migratory waterfowl. *Journal of Wildlife Management, 17:*120–123.

Jordan, J. S. 1953b. Effects of starvation on wild Mallards. *Journal of Wildlife Management, 17:*304–311.

Juhn, M., G. H. Faulkner, and R. G. Gustavson. 1931. The correlation of rates of growth and hormone threshold in the feathers of fowls. *Journal of Experimental Zoology, 58:*69–111.

Jull, M. A. 1952. *Poultry Breeding.* John Wiley & Sons, New York.

Jungfer, W. 1954. Über Paartreue, Nistplatztreue und Alter der Austernfischer (*Hematopus o. ostralegus*) auf Mellum. *Die Vogelwarte, 17:*6–15.

K

Kalela, O. 1949. Changes in geographic ranges in the avifauna of northern and central Europe in relation to recent changes in climate. *Bird-Banding, 20:*77–103.

Kalmbach, E. R. 1938. A comparative study of nesting waterfowl on the Lower Souri Refuge, 1936–1937. *Transactions of the 3rd North American Wildlife Conference, Washington, D.C.:* 610–623.

Kalmbach, E. R. 1958. *In* Bent, A. C. Life Histories of North American Blackbirds, Orioles, Tanagers and their Allies. *U.S. National Museum Bulletin 211.* Washington, D.C.

Kalmus, H. 1956. Sun navigation of *Apis mellifica* L. in the southern hemisphere. *Journal of Experimental Biology, 33:*554–565.

Karplus, M. 1952. Bird activity in the continuous daylight of arctic summer. *Ecology, 33:*129–134.

Kearton, C. 1930. *The Island of Penguins.* Longmans, Green, New York.

Keast, J. A., and A. J. Marshall. 1954. The influence of drought and rainfall on reproduction in Australian desert birds. *Proceedings of the Zoological Society, London, 124:*493–499.

Kendeigh, S. C. 1940. Factors affecting length of incubation. *Auk, 57:*499–513.

Kendeigh, S. C. 1941. Territorial and mating behavior of the House Wren. *Illinois Biological Monographs, XVIII: No. 3:* 1–120. University of Illinois Press, Urbana, Illinois.

Kendeigh, S. C. 1945a. Nesting behavior of wood warblers. *Wilson Bulletin, 57:*145–164.

Kendeigh, S. C. 1945b. Resistance to hunger in birds. *Journal of Wildlife Management, 9:*217–226.

Kendeigh, S. C. 1952. Parental Care and its Evolution in Birds. *Illinois Biological Monographs, 22:*1–356.

Kendeigh, S. C. 1961. *Animal Ecology.* Prentice-Hall, Inc. Englewood Cliffs, N. J.

Kenyon, K. W. 1942. Hunting strategy of Pigeon Hawks. *Auk, 59:*443–444.

Kenyon, K. W., and D. W. Rice. 1958. Homing of Laysan Albatrosses. *Condor, 60:*3–6.

Kilham, L. 1958. Territorial behavior of wintering Red-headed Woodpeckers. *Wilson Bulletin, 70:* 347–358.

Kipp, F. A. 1958. Zur Geschichte des Vogelzuges auf der Grundlage der Flügelanpassungen. *Die Vogelwarte, 19:*233–242.

Kiriline, L. de. 1954. The voluble singer of the tree-tops. *Audubon Magazine, 56:*109–111.

Kirkman, F. B. 1937. *Bird Behaviour*. Nelson, London.

Kirkpatrick, C. M., and A. C. Leopold. 1952. The role of darkness in sexual activity of the quail. *Science, 116:*280–281.

Kleinschmidt, O. 1958. *Raubvögel und Eulen der Heimat*. Ziemsen Verlag, Wittenberg.

Klopfer, P. H. 1956. Goose-behavior by a White Leghorn chick. *Wilson Bulletin, 68:*68–69.

Klopfer, P. H. 1959. Imprinting. *Science, 130:*730.

Kluijver, H. N. 1935. Waarnemingen over de Levenswijze van den Spreeuw (*Sturnus v. vulgaris* L.) met Behulp van Geringde Individuen. *Ardea, 24:* 133–166.

Kluijver, H. N. 1951. The population ecology of the Great Tit, *Parus m. major* L. *Ardea, 39:*1–135.

Kluijver, H. N. 1955. Das Verhalten des Drosselrohr-sangers, *Acrocephalus arundinaceus* (L). *Ardea, 43(1/3):*1–50.

Kluijver, H. N., J. Ligtvoet, C. van den Ouwelant, and F. Zegwaard. 1940. De levenswijse van den Winterkoning, *Troglodytes tr. troglodytes* (L.). *Limosa, 13:*1–51.

Koch, H. J., and A. F. de Bont. 1944. Influence de la mue sur l'intensite de metabolisme chez le pinson, *Fringilla coelebs coelebs* L. *Annales Soc. Zool. Belg., 75:*81–86.

Koehler, O. 1951a. The ability of birds to "count." *Bulletin of Animal Behaviour, 9:*41–45.

Koehler, O. 1951b. Der Vogelsang als Vorstufe von Musik und Sprache. *Journal für Ornithologie, 93:* 3–20.

Kortlandt, A. 1942. Levensloop, samenstellung en structuur der Nederlandse aalscholverbevolking. *Ardea, 31:*175–280.

Kosin, I. L. 1942. Observations on effect of esterified androgen on sex eminence of the chick. *Endocrinology, 30:*767–772.

Koskimies, J. 1950. The life of the Swift, *Micropus apus* (L.), in relation to the weather. *Annales Academiae Scientiarum Fennicae, Series A, IV. Biologica, 12:*1–151.

Kramer, G. 1957. Experiments on bird orientation and their interpretation. *Ibis, 99:*196–227.

Kramer, G. 1961. Long distance orientation. *In* Marshall, A. J., *Biology and Comparative Physiology of Birds*. Academic Press, New York and London.

Kramer, G., J. G. Pratt, and U. von St. Paul. 1956. Directional differences in homing pigeons. *Science, 123:*329–330.

Küchler, W. 1935. Jahreszyklische Veränderung im histologischen Bau der Vogelschilddrüse. *Journal für Ornithologie, 83:*414–461.

Kuhk, R. 1960. Ein 31½ jähriger Grosser Brachvogel (*Numenius arquata*). *Die Vogelwarte, 20:*233.

L

Lack, D. 1937. The psychological factor in bird distribution. *British Birds, 31:*130–136.

Lack, D. 1939. The display of the Blackcock. *British Birds, 32:*290–303.

Lack, D. 1940a. Courtship feeding in birds. *Auk, 57:* 169–178.

Lack, D. 1940b. Qbservations on captive Robins. *British Birds, 33:*262–270.

Lack, D. 1943. *The Life of the Robin*. H. F. & G. Witherby, London.

Lack, D. 1945. The ecology of closely related species with special reference to Cormorant (*Phalacrocorax carbo*) and Shag (*Phalacrocorax aristotelis*). *Journal of Animal Ecology, 14:*12–16.

Lack, D. 1947. *Darwin's Finches*. Cambridge University Press, London.

Lack, D. 1948. The significance of clutch-size. III. *Ibis, 90:*25–45.

Lack, D, 1949. The significance of ecological isolation. *In* Jepson, G. L., E. Mayr, and G. G. Simpson, *Genetics, Paleontology, and Evolution*. Princeton University Press, Princeton, New Jersey.

Lack, D. 1954. *The Natural Regulation of Animal Numbers*. Oxford University Press, London.

Lack, D. 1955. British tits (*Parus* spp.) in nesting boxes. *Ardea, 43:*50–84.

Lack, D. 1958. The significance of the colour in Turdine eggs. *Ibis, 100:*145–166.

Lack, D. 1959. Watching migration by radar. *British Birds, 52:*258–267.

Lack, D. 1960a. The height of bird migration. *British Birds, 53:*5–10.

Lack, D. 1960b. The influence of weather on passerine migration. *Auk, 77:*171–209.

Lack, D. 1960c. Migration across the North Sea studied by radar. Part II. *Ibis, 102:*26–57.

Lack, D., and H. Arn. 1947. Die Bedeutung der Gelegegrösse beim Alpensegler. *Ornithologische Beobachter, 44:*188–210.

Lack, D., and E. Lack. 1952. The breeding behaviour of the Swift. *British Birds, 45:*186–215.

Lange, H. 1948. Sløruglens (*Tyto alba guttata* (Brehm)) Føde, belyst gennem Undersøgelser af Gylp. *Dansk Ornithologisk Forenings Tidsskrift, 42:*50–84.

Lanyon, W. E. 1958. The motivation of sunbathing in birds. *Wilson Bulletin, 70:*280.

Laskey, A. R. 1943. The nesting of Bluebirds banded as nestlings. *Bird-Banding, 14:*39–43.

Laskey, A. R. 1946. Snake depredations of bird nests. *Wilson Bulletin, 58:*217–218.

Laskey, A. R. 1948. Some nesting data on the Carolina Wren at Nashville, Tennessee. *Bird-Banding, 19:* 101–121.

Laskey, A. R. 1950. A courting Carolina Wren building over nestlings. *Bird-Banding, 21:*1–6.

Laven, H. 1938. Beiträge zur Brutbiologie des Halsbandregenpfeifers (*Charadrius hiaticula* L.). *Beiträge zur Fortpflanzungsbiologie der Vögel, 14:* 49–54.

Laven, H. 1940. Beiträge zur Biologie des Sandregen-pfeifers (*Charadrius hiaticula* L.). *Journal für Or-nithologie, 88:*184–287.

Lawrence, L. de K. 1948. Comparative study of the nesting behavior of Chestnut-sided and Nash-ville Warblers. *Auk, 65:*204–219.

Lay, D. W. 1938. How valuable are woodland clear-ings to birdlife? *Wilson Bulletin, 50:*254–256.

Leiber, A. 1907. Vergleichende Anatomie der Specht-zunge. *Zoologica,* Stuttgart, *20:*1–79.

Leopold, A. 1933. *Game Management.* Charles Scrib-ner's Sons. New York.

Leopold, A., and A. E. Eynon. 1961. Avian daybreak and evening song in relation to time and light in-tensity. *Condor, 63:*269–293.

Levine, S., and G. W. Lewis. 1959. Critical period for effects of infantile experience on maturation of stress response. *Science, 129:*42–43.

Lewis, F. T. 1944. The Passenger Pigeon as observed by the Rev. Cotton Mather. *Auk, 61:*587–592.

Lewis, H. F. 1941. Ring-billed Gulls of the Atlantic Coast. *Wilson Bulletin, 53:*22–30.

Lillie, F. R. 1940. Physiology of the development of the feather. *Physiological Zoology, 13:*143–175.

Lillie, F. R., and M. Juhn. 1938. Physiology of devel-opment of the feather. *Physiological Zoology, 11:*434–448.

Lincoln, F. C. 1928. The migration of young North American Herring Gulls. *Auk, 45:*49–59.

Lincoln, F. C. 1950. Migration of Birds. *Fish and Wildlife Service, Circular No. 16.* Washington, D.C.

Linsdale, J. M. 1938. Environmental response of ver-tebrates in the Great Basin. *American Midland Naturalist, 19:*1–206.

Lippens, L. 1939. Les oiseaux aquatiques du Kivu. *Le Gerfaut,* 28: Fasc. Spécial: 1–104.

Lockie, J. D. 1955. The breeding habits and food of Short-eared Owls after a vole plague. *Bird Study, 2:*53–69.

Loefer, J. B., and J. A. Patten. 1941. Starlings at a Blackbird roost. *Auk, 58:*584–586.

Lofts, B., and A. J. Marshall. 1960. The experimental regulation of Zugunruhe and the sexual cycle in the Brambling, *Fringilla montifringilla. Ibis, 102:*209–214.

Löhrl, H. 1951. Balz und Paarbildung beim Halsband-fliegenschnäpper. *Journal für Ornithologie, 93:*46–60.

Löhrl, H. 1957. *Der Kleiber.* Ziemsen Verlag, Witten-berg.

Lokietsch, P. 1957. Brut der Weiszen Bachsteltze auf fahrendem Lastkraftwagen. *Ornithologische Mit-teilungen, 9:*98.

Lorenz, K. Z. 1935. Der Kumpan in der Umwelt des Vogels. *Journal für Ornithologie, 83:*137–213; 289–413.

Lorenz, K. Z. 1937. The companion in the bird's world. *Auk, 54:*245–273.

Lorenz, K. Z. 1938. A contribution to the comparative sociology of colonial-nesting birds. *Proceedings of the 8th International Ornithological Congress, Oxford, July, 1934.* Oxford University Press, 1938.

Lorenz, K. Z. 1950. The comparative method of study-ing innate behavior patterns. In *Physiological Mechanisms in Animal Behaviour. Symposia for Experimental Biology. IV.* Academic Press, New York.

Lorenz, K. Z. 1952. *King Solomon's Ring.* Thomas Y. Crowell Company, New York.

Lovell, H. B. 1958. Baiting of fish by a Green Heron. *Wilson Bulletin, 70:*280–281.

Low, S. H. 1957. Banding with mist nets. *Bird-Band-ing, 28:*115–128.

Lowery, G. H., and R. J. Newman, 1955. Direct stud-ies of nocturnal bird migration. *In* Wolfson, A., *Recent Studies in Avian Biology.* University of Illinois Press, Urbana, Illinois.

Lydekker, R. 1901. *The New Natural History.* Merrill and Baker, New York.

M

Maclatchey, A. R. 1937. Contribution a l'etude des oiseaux du Gabon Meridional (Suite). *L'Oiseau et Revue Francais d'Ornithologie,* 7:60–80.

MacMullan, R. A., and L. L. Eberhardt. 1953. Toler-ance of incubating pheasant eggs to exposure. *Journal of Wildlife Management, 17:*322–330.

Magee, M. J. 1936. The wing molt in Purple Finches. *Bird-Banding, 7:*73–76.

Magee, M. J. 1940. Notes on the returns of the Eastern Purple Finch (*Carpodacus purpureus purpureus*), and their sex ratio. *Bird-Banding, 11:*110–111.

Makatsch, W. 1950. *Der Vogel und Sein Nest.* Akade-mische Verlagsgesellschaft, Leipzig.

Makatsch, W. 1952. *Der Vogel und Sein Ei.* Akade-mische Verlagsgesellschaft, Leipzig.

Mangold, E. 1929. Die Verdauung des Geflügels, im *Handbuch der Ernährung und des Stoffwechsels der landwirtschaftlichen Nutziere. Vol. II.* Julius Springer, Berlin.

Mangold, O. 1946. Die Nase der segelnden Vögel ein Organ des Strömungssinnes? *Die Naturwissen-schaften, 33:*19–23.

Marais, E. N. 1937. *The Soul of the White Ant.* Dodd, Mead & Company, New York.

Marks, H. L., P. B. Siegel, and C. Y. Kramer. 1960. Ef-fect of comb and wattle removal on the social or-ganization of mixed flocks of chickens. *Animal Behaviour, 8:*192–196.

Marler, P. 1955. Studies of fighting in Chaffinches. *British Journal of Animal Behaviour, 3:*137–146.

Marler, P. 1956. Behaviour of the Chaffinch, *Fringilla coelebs. Behaviour, Supplement V:*1–184. E. J. Brill, Leiden.

Marsh, C. O. 1880. *Odontornithes: a Monograph on the Extinct Toothed Birds of North America.* U.S. Government Printing Office, Washington, D.C.

Marshall, A. J. 1950. The function of vocal mimicry in birds. *Emu, 50:*5–16.

Marshall, A. J. 1954. *Bower-Birds.* Oxford University Press, London.

Marshall, A. J. 1960–1961. *Biology and Comparative Physiology of Birds.* 2 vols. Academic Press, New York and London.

Marshall, A. J., and D. L. Serventy. 1956a. The breeding cycle of the Short-tailed Shearwater *Puffinus tenuirostris* (Temminck) in relation to trans-equatorial migration and its environment. *Proceedings of the Zoological Society, London,* 127:489–510.

Marshall, A. J., and D. L. Serventy. 1956b. Moult adaptation in relation to long-distance migration in petrels. *Nature, 177:*943.

Marshall, H. 1947. Longevity of the American Herring Gull. *Auk, 64:*188–198.

Marshall, J. T. 1955. Hibernation in captive goatsuckers. *Condor, 57:*129–134.

Marshall, W. H. 1946. Cover preferences, seasonal movements, and food habits of Richardson's Grouse and Ruffed Grouse in southern Idaho. *Wilson Bulletin, 58:*42–52.

Mason, A. G. 1945. The display of the Corn-Crake. *British Birds, 38:*351–352.

Mason, E. A. 1944. Parasitism by Protocalliphora and management of cavity-nesting birds. *Journal of Wildlife Management,* 8:232–247.

Mathews, F. S. 1921. *Field Book of Wild Birds and Their Music.* G. P. Putnam's Sons, New York.

Mathiasson, A. 1957. Fågelsträcket vid Falsterbo. *Vår-Fågelvärld, 16:*90–104.

Matthews, G. V. T. 1954. Some aspects of incubation in the Manx Shearwater, *Procellaria puffinus,* with particular reference to chilling resistance in the embryo. *Ibis, 96:*432–440.

Matthews, L. H. 1939. Visual stimulation and ovulation in pigeons. *Proceedings of the Royal Society,* B., 226:423–456.

Mayaud, N. 1950. In Grassé, P., *Traité de Zoologie, Tome XV, Oiseau.* Masson et Cie., Paris.

Mayfield, H. 1952. Nesting-height preference of the Eastern Kingbird. *Wilson Bulletin, 64:*160.

Mayhew, W. W. 1955. Spring rainfall in relation to Mallard production in the Sacramento Valley, California. *Journal of Wildlife Management, 19:* 36–47.

Mayr, E. 1935. Bernard Altum and the territory theory. *Proceedings of the Linnaean Society of New York, 45–46:*15 pp.

Mayr, E. 1939. The sex ratio in wild birds. *American Naturalist, 73:*156–179.

Mayr, E. 1942. *Systematics and the Origin of Species.* Columbia University Press, New York.

Mayr, E. 1943. The zoogeographic position of the Hawaiian Islands. *Condor, 45:*45–48.

Mayr, E. 1945. Bird conservation problems in the Southwest Pacific. *Audubon Magazine, 47:*279–282.

Mayr, E. 1946a. History of North American bird fauna. *Wilson Bulletin, 58:*3–41.

Mayr, E. 1946b. The number of species of birds. *Auk, 63:*64–69.

Mayr, E. 1948. The bearing of the new systematics on genetical problems. The nature of species. In *Advances in Genetics, Vol. 2.* Academic Press, New York.

Mayr, E. 1949. Speciation and systematics. *In* Jepsen, G. L., E. Mayr, and G. G. Simpson, *Genetics, Paleontology and Evolution.* Princeton University Press, Princeton, New Jersey.

Mayr, E. 1950. Speciation in birds. *Proceedings of the Xth International Ornithological Congress, Uppsala, June 1950:* 91–131. Almqvist and Wiksells, Uppsala, 1951.

Mayr, E. 1954. Change of genetic environment and evolution. *In* Huxley, J., A. C. Hardy, and E. B. Ford, [Editors], *Evolution as a Process.* G. Allen and Unwin, London.

Mayr, E., E. G. Linsley, and R. L. Usinger. 1953. *Methods and Principles of Systematic Zoology.* McGraw-Hill Book Company, New York.

Mayr, E., and M. Mayr. 1954. The tail molt of small owls. *Auk, 71:*172–178.

Mazzeo, R. 1953. Homing of the Manx Shearwater. *Auk, 70:*200–201.

McAtee, W. L. 1940. An experiment in songbird management. *Auk, 57:*333–348.

McCabe, R. A., and H. F. Deutsch. 1952. The relationships of certain birds as indicated by their egg white proteins. *Auk, 69:*1–18.

McCabe, T. T. 1942. Types of shorebird flight. *Auk,* 59:110–111.

McClure, H. E. 1945. Reaction of the Mourning Dove to colored eggs. *Auk, 62:*270–272.

McIlhenny, E. A. 1937. Life history of the Boat-tailed Grackle in Louisiana. *Auk, 54:*274–295.

McIlhenny, E. A. 1939. Feeding habits of the Black Vulture. *Auk, 56:*472–474.

McIlhenny, E. A. 1940. Effect of excessive cold on birds in southern Louisiana. *Auk, 57:*408–410.

McKean, J. L. 1960. Movements of Cattle Egrets. *Emu, 60:*202.

McKernan, D. L., and V. B. Scheffer. 1942. Unusual numbers of dead birds on the Washington coast. *Condor, 44:*264–266.

McLean, I., and K. Williamson, 1960. Migrants at station "Juliett" in September 1959. *British Birds,* 53:215–219.

Meijknecht, J. T. V. 1941. Farbsehen und Helligkeitsunterscheidung beim Steinkauz (*Athene noctua vidalii* E. A. Brehm). *Ardea, 30:*129–174.

Meinertzhagen, R. 1954. *Birds of Arabia.* Oliver and Boyd, London.

Meise, W. 1954. Über Zucht, Eintritt der Geschlechtsreife, Zwischen- und Weiterzug der Wachtel (*C. coturnix*). *Die Vogelwarte, 17:*211–215.

Messmer, E., and I. Messmer. 1956. Die Entwicklung der Lautäusserungen und einiger Verhaltungsweisen der Amsel (*Turdus merula merula* L.) unter natürlichen Bedingungen und nach Einzelaufzucht in schalldichten Räumen. *Zeitschrift für Tierpsychologie,* 13:341–344.

Mewaldt, L. R., and R. G. Rose, 1960. Orientation of migratory restlessness in the White-crowned Sparrow. *Science, 131:*105–106.

Mickey, F. W. 1943. Breeding habits of McCown's Longspur. *Auk, 60:*181–209.

Mildenberg, H. 1940. Beobachtungen über Fitis-Weiden- und Waldlaubsänger im Rheinland. *Journal für Ornithologie,* 88:537–549.

Millay, E. St. V. 1922. *A Few Figs from Thistles.* Harper and Brothers, New York.

Miller, A. H. 1951. An analysis of the distribution of the birds of California. *University of California Publications in Zoology,* 50:531–644.

Miller, A. H. 1954. The occurrence and maintenance of the refractory period in crowned sparrows. *Condor*, 56:13–20.

Miller, R. C. 1958. Morning and evening song of Robins in different latitudes. *Condor*, 60:105–107.

Mitchell, K. D. G. 1955. Aircraft observations of birds in flight. *British Birds*, 48:59–70.

Moffit, J., and C. Cottam. 1941. The eel-grass blight and its effect on Brant. *U.S. Fish and Wildlife Service Leaflet* 204:1–26.

Moreau, R. E. 1936. Bird-insect nesting associations. *Ibis*, 6:460–471.

Moreau, R. E. 1940. Numerical data on African birds' behaviour at the nest. II. *Ibis*, 14th Series, 4:234–248.

Moreau, R. E. 1944. Clutch-size: a comparative study with special reference to African birds. *Ibis*, 86:286–348.

Moreau, R. E. 1948. Ecological isolation in a rich tropical avifauna. *Journal of Animal Ecology*, 17:113–126,

Moreau, R. E. 1952. Africa since the Mesozoic: with particular reference to certain biological problems. *Proceedings of the Zoological Society of London*, 121:869–913.

Moreau, R. E., and W. M. Moreau. 1938. The comparative breeding ecology of two species of Euplectes (Bishop Birds) in Usambara. *Journal of Animal Ecology*, 7:314–327.

Moreau, R. E., and W. M. Moreau. 1940. Incubation and fledging periods of African birds. *Auk*, 57:313–325.

Morgan, B. B., and E. F. Waller. 1941. Some parasites of the Eastern Crow. *Bird-Banding*, 12:16–22.

Morike, K. D. 1953. Der Leier-Überschlag der Monchgrasmucke. *Ornithologische Mitteilungen*, 5:90–95.

Mountfort, G. R. 1935. Manifestations visibles du developpement sexuel des oiseaux. *L'Oiseau et La Revue Francais d'Ornithologie*, 5:494–505.

Mountfort, G. 1957. *The Hawfinch*. Collins, London.

Mühl, K. 1954. Krähen und Elstern fressen Schafwolle. *Ornithologische Mitteilungen*, 6:236.

Mühlthalen, F. 1952. Beobachtungen am Bergfinken Schlafplatz bei Thun, 1950/51. *Der Ornithologische Beobachter*, 49:173–192.

Munro, J. A. 1938. The Northern Bald Eagle in British Columbia. *Wilson Bulletin*, 50:28–35.

Munro, D. A. 1954. Prairie Falcon "playing." *Auk*, 71:333–334.

Murphy, R. C. 1936. *Oceanic Birds of South America.* Macmillan, New York.

Musselman, T. E. 1941. Bluebird mortality in 1940. *Auk*, 58:409–410.

Musselman, T. E. 1946. Some interesting nest habits of the Eastern Bluebird (*Sialia sialis sialis*). *Bird-Banding*, 17:60–63.

N

Nero, R. W. 1951. Pattern and rate of cranial 'ossification' in the House Sparrow. *Wilson Bulletin*, 63:84–88.

Nero, R. W., and J. T. Emlen. 1951. An experimental study of territorial behavior in breeding Red-winged Blackbirds. *Condor*, 53:105–116.

Nestler, R. B. 1946. Mechanical value of grit for Bobwhite Quail. *Journal of Wildlife Management*, 10:137–142.

Nestler, R. B., *et al.* 1944. Winter protein requirements of Bob-white Quail. *Journal of Wildlife Management*, 8:218–222.

Nestler, R. B., and A. L. Nelson. 1945. Inbreeding among pen-reared Quail. *Auk*, 62:217–222.

Newton, A. 1896. *A Dictionary of Birds.* A. and C. Black, London.

Nice, M. M. 1937. Studies in the Life History of the Song Sparrow. I. A Population Study of the Song Sparrow. *Transactions of the Linnaean Society of New York*, 4:1–247.

Nice, M. M. 1938a. The biological significance of bird weights. *Bird-Banding*, 9:1–11.

Nice, M. M. 1938b. What determines the time of a Song Sparrow's awakening song? *IXe Congrès Ornithologique International, Rouen*:249–255.

Nice, M. M. 1939. The Social Kumpan and the Song Sparrow. *Auk*, 56:255–262.

Nice, M. M. 1941. The role of territory in bird life. *American Midland Naturalist*, 26:441–487.

Nice, M. M. 1943. Studies in the Life History of the Song Sparrow. II. *Transactions of the Linnaean Society of New York*, 6:1–328.

Nice, M. M. 1949. [Review]. *Bird-Banding*, 20:192.

Nice, M. M. 1953. The earliest mention of territory. *Condor*, 55:316–317.

Nice, M. M. 1954. Incubation periods throughout the ages. *Centaurus*, 3:311–359.

Nice, M. M. 1957. Nesting success in altricial birds. *Auk*, 74:305–321.

Nice, M. M. 1962. Development of Behavior in Precocial Birds. *Transactions of the Linnaean Society of New York*, 8.

Nickell, W. P. 1944. Studies of habitats, locations and structural materials of nests of the Robin. *Jack Pine Warbler*, 22:48–64.

Nicod, L. 1952. Augmentation des Hirondelles de cheminèe. *Nos Oiseaux*, 21:168–170.

Nicolai, J. 1956. Zur Biologie und Ethologie des Gimpels (*Pyrrhula pyrrhula* L.). *Zeitschrift für Tierpsychologie*, 13:93–132.

Nicolai, J. 1959. Familientradition in der Gesangsentwicklung des Gimpels (*Pyrrhula pyrrhula* L.). *Journal für Ornithologie*, 100:39–46.

Niethammer, G. 1937–1942. *Handbuch der Deutschen Vogelkunde.* Akademische Verlagsgesellschaft, Leipzig.

Noble, G. K. 1936. Courtship and sexual selection of the Flicker. *Auk*, 53:269–282.

Noble, G. K. 1939. The role of dominance in the social life of birds. *Auk*, 56:263–273.

Noble, G. K., M. Wurm, and A. Schmidt. 1938. Social behavior of the Black-crowned Night Heron. *Auk*, 55:7–40.

Nopsca, F. 1907. Ideas on the origin of flight. *Proceedings of the Zoological Society of London*, 1907: 223–236.

Norris, R. A., and F. S. Williamson. 1955. Variation in relative heart size of certain passerines with increase in altitude. *Wilson Bulletin*, 67:78–83.

Norris, R. T. 1947. The Cowbirds of Preston Frith. *Wilson Bulletin, 59:*83–103.

Novick, A. 1959. Acoustic orientation in the Cave Swiftlet. *Biological Bulletin, 117:*497–503.

O

Odum, E. P. 1941a. Variation in the heart rate of birds. *Ecological Monographs, 11:*299–326.

Odum, E. P. 1941b. Winter homing behavior of the Chickadee. *Bird-Banding, 12:*113–119.

Odum, E. P. 1943. Some physiological variations in the Black-capped Chickadee. *Wilson Bulletin, 55:* 178–191.

Odum, E. P. 1958. The fat deposition picture in the White-throated Sparrow in comparison with that in long-range migrants. *Bird-Banding, 29:*105–108.

Odum, E. P. 1959. *Fundamentals of Ecology.* W. B. Saunders Company, Philadelphia.

Odum, E. P., and J. D. Perkinson. 1951. Relation of lipid metabolism to migration in birds. *Physiological Zoology, 24:*216–230.

Oemichen, E. 1950. Le vol des oiseaux. *In* Grassé, P. P., *Traité de Zoologie, Tome XV, Oiseaux.* Masson et Cie., Paris.

Ogilvie, C. M. 1951. The building of a rookery. *British Birds, 44:*1–5.

Olsen, M. W. 1960. Performance record of a parthenogenetic Turkey male. *Science, 132:*1661.

O'Neill, E. J. 1947. Waterfowl grounded at the Muleshoe National Wildlife Refuge, Texas. *Auk, 64:* 457.

P

Pastore, N. 1954. Discrimination learning in the Canary. *Journal of Comparative and Physiological Psychology, 47:* 288–289; 389–390.

Payne, R. S. 1961. The acoustical localization of prey in the Barn Owl, (*Tyto alba*). *American Zoologist, 1:*379.

Paynter, R. A. 1955. Birds in the upper arctic. *Auk, 72:* 79–80.

Pearson, O. P. 1950. The metabolism of hummingbirds. *Condor, 52:* 145–152.

Pearson, O. P. 1953 a. The metabolism of hummingbirds. *Scientific American, 188* (1):69–72.

Pearson, O. P. 1953 b. Use of caves by hummingbirds and other species at high altitudes in Peru. *Condor, 55:*17–20.

Peet, W. M. 1959. Starlings affected by smog. *British Birds, 52:*238.

Peters, H. S. 1936. A list of external parasites from birds of the eastern part of the United States. *Bird-Banding, 7:*9–27.

Peters, J. L. 1931–1951. *Check-list of Birds of the World.* Harvard University Press, Cambridge, Massachusetts.

Petersen, A., and H. Young. 1950. A nesting study of the Bronzed Grackle. *Auk, 67:*466–476.

Petersen, E. 1953. Orienteringsforsøg med. Haettemåge (*Larus r. ridibundus* L.) og stormmåge (*Larus c. canus* L.) i vinterkvarteret. *Dansk Ornithologisk Forenings Tidsskrift 47:*153–178.

Peterson, R. T. 1941. *A Field Guide to the Western Birds.* Houghton Mifflin, Boston, Massachusetts.

Peterson, R. T. 1948. *Birds Over America.* Dodd, Mead, New York.

Petrides, G. A. 1944. Sex ratios in ducks. *Auk, 61:*564–571.

Pettingill, O. S. 1942. The birds of a Bull's Horn Acacia. *Wilson Bulletin, 54:*89–96.

Phillips, A. R. 1951. Complexities of migration: a review. *Wilson Bulletin, 63:*129–136.

Pincus, G., and T. F. Hopkins. 1958. The effects of various estrogens and steroid substances on sex differentiation in the fowl. *Endocrinology, 62:* 112–118.

Pitelka, F. A., P. Q. Tomich, and G. W. Treichel. 1955. Ecological relations of jaegers and owls as lemming predators near Barrow, Alaska. *Ecological Monographs, 25:*85–117.

Polyak, S. 1957. *The Vertebrate Visual System.* University of Chicago Press, Chicago.

Poole, E. L. 1938. Weights and wing areas in North American birds. *Auk, 55:* 511–517.

Portielje, A. F. J. 1921. Zur Ethologie bzw. Psychologie von *Botaurus stellaris. Ardea, 15:* 1–15.

Portmann, A. 1950. Le developpement postembryonnaire. *In* Grassé, P. *Traité de Zoologie, Tome XV. Oiseaux.* Masson et Cie, Paris.

Poulsen, H. 1951. Inheritance and learning in the song of the Chaffinch (*Fringilla coelebs* L.). *Behaviour, 3:*216–228.

Poulsen, H. 1953. A study of incubation responses and some other behaviour patterns in birds. *Vidensk. Medd. fra Dansk naturh. Foren., 115:*1–131.

Prevost, J. 1953. Formation des couples, ponte et incubation chez le Manchot Empereur. *Alauda, 21:* 141–156.

Prevost, J., and F. Bourlière. 1957. Vie sociale et thermoregulation chez le Manchot Empereur *Aptenodytes forsteri. Alauda, 25:* 167–173.

Price, J. B. 1936. The family relations of the Plain Titmouse. *Condor,* 38:23–28.

Prosser, C. L. *et al.* 1950. *Comparative Animal Physiology.* W. B. Saunders Company, Philadelphia.

Pumphrey, R. J. 1961. Sensory organs: Hearing. *In* Marshall, A. J., *Biology and Comparative Physiology of Birds.* Academic Press, N.Y.

Putzig, P. 1937. Von der Beziehung des Zugablaufs zum Inkretdrüsensystem. *Vogelzug,* 8:116–130.

Putzig, P. 1938. Der Frühwehzug des Kiebitzes (*Vanellus vanellus* L.) unter Berucksichtigung anderen Limicolen. *Journal für Ornithologie,* 86: 123–163.

Pycraft, W. P. 1910. *A History of Birds.* Methuen, London.

Pynnönen, A. 1939. Beiträge zur Kenntnis der Biologie finnischer Spechte. *Annales Zoologici Societatis Zoologicae-Botanicae-Fennicae Vanamo,* 7:1–166.

Pynnönen, A. 1950. Om Järpens Levnadsvanor. *Suonem Riista* [Helsinki], 5:7–27.

Q

Quaintance, C. W. 1938. Content, meaning and possible origin of male song in the Brown Towhee. *Condor*, 40:97–101.

Quiring, D. P. 1950. *Functional Anatomy of the Vertebrates*. McGraw-Hill Book Company, New York.

R

Räber, H. 1950. Das Verhalten gefangenen Waldohreulen (*Asio otus otus*) und Waldkäuze (*Strix aluco aluco*) sur Beute. *Behaviour*, 2:1–95.

Ramsay, A. O. 1953. Variations in the development of broodiness in fowl. *Behaviour*, 5:51–57.

Rand, A. L. 1936. The distribution and habits of Madagascar birds. *Bulletin of the American Museum of Natural History*, 72: 143–499.

Rand, A. L. 1943. Some irrelevant behavior in birds. *Auk*, 60:168–171.

Rankin, M. N., and D. H. Rankin, 1940. Additional notes on the roosting habits of the Tree Creeper. *British Birds*, 34: 56–60.

Raspet, A. 1950. Performance measurements of a soaring bird. *Aeronautical Engineering Review*, 9 (12): 1–4.

Rawles, M. E. 1960. The integumentary system. *In* Marshall, A. J., *Biology and Comparative Physiology of Birds*. Academic Press, New York.

Reinikainen, A. 1937. The irregular migrations of the Crossbill *Loxia c. curvirostra*, and their relation to the cone-crop of the conifers. *Ornis Fennica*, 14: 55–64.

Reinsch, H. 1953. Fahrinselbeobachtungen. *Ornithologische Mitteilungen*, 5:21–29.

Rensch, B. 1925 a. Experimentelle Untersuchungen über den Geschmackssinn der Vögel. *Journal für Ornithologie*, 73: 1–8.

Rensch, B. 1925 b. Verhalten von Singvögeln bei Änderung des Geleges. *Ornithologische Monatsberichte*, 33:169–173.

Rensch, B. 1931. Der Einfluss des Tropenklimas auf den Vogel. *Proceedings of the VIIth International Ornithological Congress, Amsterdam, 1930:* 197–205. Amsterdam, 1931.

Rensch, B. 1936. Studien über klimatische Parallelität der Merkmalsausprägung bei Vogeln und Saugern. *Archiv für Naturgeschichte*, N. F. 5:317–363.

Rensch, B. 1947. *Neuere Probleme der Abstammungslehre*. Ferdinand Enke Verlag, Stuttgart.

Rensch, B. 1959. *Evolution Above the Species Level*. Columbia University Press, New York.

Richdale, L. E. 1941. A brief summary of the history of the Yellow-eyed Penguin. *Emu*, 40:265–387.

Richdale, L. E. 1943. The Kuaka or Diving Petrel, *Pelecanoides urinatrix* (Gmelin). *Emu*, 43:24–48; 97–107.

Richdale, L. E. 1949. A study of a group of penguins of known age. *Otago Daily Times*, Dunedin, New Zealand.

Richdale, L. E. 1950. *Biological Monographs No. 4*. Dunedin, New Zealand.

Richdale, L. E. 1951. *Sexual Behavior in Penguins*. University of Kansas Press, Lawrence, Kansas.

Richdale, L. E. 1952. The post-egg period in albatrosses. *Biological Monographs, No. 4*. Dunedin, New Zealand.

Richdale, L. E. 1954. Breeding efficiency in Yellow-eyed Penguins. *Ibis*, 96:207–224.

Richter, R. 1939. Weitere Beobachtungen an einer gemischter Kolonie von *Larus fuscus graellsi* Brehm und *Larus argentatus* Pontopp. *Journal für Ornithologie*, 87:75–86.

Riddle, O. 1938. The changing organism. In *Cooperation in Research*. The Carnegie Institution of Washington. Publication No. 501:259–273.

Ridgway, R., and H. Friedmann. 1901–1950. *Birds of North and Middle America*. U.S. National Museum Bulletins, Washington, D.C.

Riley, G. M. 1937. Experimental studies on spermatogenesis in the House Sparrow, *Passer domesticus* (L.). *Anatomical Record*, 67:327.

Riley, G. M. 1940. Light versus activity as a regulator of the sexual cycle of the House Sparrow. *Wilson Bulletin*, 52:73–86.

Ringer, R. K., and K. Rood, 1959. Hemodynamic changes associated with aging in the Broad Breasted Bronze Turkey. *Poultry Science*, 38:395–397.

Ripley, S. D. 1947. *Trail of the Money Bird*. Longmans, Green, London.

Ripley, S. D. 1950 a. Birds from Nepal, 1947–1949. *Journal of Bombay Natural History Society*, 49: 355–417.

Ripley, S. D. 1950 b. Strange courtship of birds of paradise. *National Geographic Magazine*, 97: 247–278.

Ritter, W. E., and S. B. Benson. 1934. "Is the poor bird demented?" *Auk*, 51:169–179.

Rivière, B. B. 1940. House-martins rebuilding broken nest and feeding young. *British Birds*, 34:87–88.

Roberts, B. 1934. Notes on the birds of central and and south-east Iceland with special reference to food habits. *Ibis*, 4:252.

Roberts, B. 1940. The life cycle of Wilson's Petrel, *Oceanites oceanicus* (Kuhl). *Scientific Reports of the British Graham Land Expedition 1934–1937*, 1:141–194. London.

Roberts, N. L. 1942. Breeding activities of three common species. *Emu*, 41:185–194.

Roberts, N. L. 1955. A survey of the habit of nest-appropriation. *Emu*, 55: 110–126; 173–184.

Roberts, T. S. 1932. *The Birds of Minnesota*. University of Minnesota Press, Minneapolis.

Robinson, A. 1945. The application of 'Territory and the Breeding Cycle' to some Australian birds. *Emu*, 45:100–109.

Robinson, A. 1956. The annual reproductive cycle of the Magpie, *Gymnorhina dorsalis* Campbell, in southwestern Australia. *Emu*, 56:233–236.

Rochon-Duvigneaud, A. 1950. Les yeux et la vision. *In* Grassé, P. P., *Traité de Zoologie, Tome XV, Oiseaux*. Masson et Cie, Paris.

Rodbard, A. 1950. Weight and body temperature. *Science*, 111:465–466.

Rodbard, A. 1953. Warm-bloodedness. *Scientific Monthly*, 77:137–142.

Rollin, N. 1945. Song Thrush song. *British Birds, 38:* 262–270.

Rollin, N. 1958. Late season singing of the Yellowhammer. *British Birds*, 51:290–303.

Romanoff, A. L. 1934. Study of artificial incubation of game birds. *Bulletin of Cornell University Agricultural Station*, No. 616:1–39.

Romanoff, A. L., and A. J. Romanoff. 1949. *The Avian Egg.* John Wiley and Sons, New York.

Romer, A. S. 1955. *The Vertebrate Body.* W. B. Saunders, Philadelphia.

Rothschild, M., and T. Clay. 1952. *Fleas, Flukes, and Cuckoos.* Collins, London.

Rowan, W. 1921. Observations on the breeding habits of the Merlin. *British Birds*, 15:122–129.

Rowan, W. 1929. Experiments in bird migration. I. Manipulation of the reproductive cycle: Seasonal histological changes in the gonads. *Proceedings of the Boston Society of Natural History*, 39: 151–208.

Rowan, W. 1938. Light and seasonal reproduction in animals. *Biological Review*, 13:374–402.

Ruiter, C. J. S. 1941. Waarneminingen omtrent de levenswijze de Gekraagde Roodstaart, *Phoenicurus ph. phoenicurus* (L.). *Ardea, 41:*175–214.

Ruiter, I. de. 1952. Some experiments on the camouflage of stick caterpillars. *Behaviour*, 4:222–232.

Rüppell, W. 1944. Versuche über Heimfinden ziehender Nebelkrähen nach Verfrachtung. *Journal für Ornithologie*, 92:106–132.

Ryser, F. A., and P. R. Morrison. 1954. Cold resistance in the young Ring-necked Pheasant. *Auk*, 71:253–266.

S

Saalfeld, E. von. 1936. Untersuchungen über das Hackeln bei Tauben. *Zeitschrift für Vergleichende Physiologie*, 23:727–743.

Sadovnikova, M. P. 1923. A study of the behavior of birds in the maze. *Journal of Comparative Psychology*, 3:123–139.

Saint-Paul, U. von. 1954. Nachweis der Sonnenorientierung bei nächtlich ziehenden Vögeln. *Behaviour*, 6:1–7.

Salomonsen, F. 1938. Notes on the moults of the Rock Ptarmigan (*Lagopus mutus*). IXe *Congrès Ornithologique International, Rouen, 9–13 Mai, 1938:* 295–310. Secrétariat du Congrès, Rouen, 1938.

Salomonsen, F. 1947. Maagekoloniere paa Hirshomene. *Dansk Ornithologisk Forenings Tidsskrift,* 41:174–186.

Salomonsen, F. 1950. The immigration and breeding of the Fieldfare (*Turdus pilaris* L.) in Greenland. *Proceedings of the Xth International Ornithological Congress, Uppsala, June, 1950:* 515–526. Almqvist & Wiksells, Uppsala, 1951.

Sapin-Jaloustre, J. 1952. Découverte et description de la rookery de Manchot Empereur (*Aptenodytes forsteri*) de Pointe Géologie (Terra Adélie). *L'Oiseau, 22:*143–184.

Sapin-Jaloustre, J., and F. Bourlière. 1951. Incubation et developpement du poussin chez le Manchot Adelie, *Pygoscelis adeliae. Alauda, 19:*65–87.

Sauer, F. 1954. Die Entwicklung der Lautäusserungen vom Ei ab schalldicht gehaltener Dorngrasmücken (*Sylvia c. communis*, Latham) im Vergleich mit später isolierten und mit wildlebenden Artgenossen. *Zeitschrift für Tierpsychologie, 11:*10–93.

Sauer, F. 1957. Die Sternenorientierung nächtlich ziehender Grasmücken (*Sylvia atricapilla, borin, und curruca*). *Zeitschrift für Tierpsychologie, 14:* 29–70.

Saunders, A. A. 1947. The seasons of bird song: the beginning of song in spring. *Auk, 64:*97–107.

Saunders, A. A. 1948. The seasons of bird song: the cessation of song after the nesting season. *Auk, 65:*19–30.

Saunders, A. A. 1951. *A Guide to Bird Songs.* Doubleday, New York.

Saunders, A. A. 1959. Forty years of spring migration in southern Connecticut. *Wilson Bulletin, 71:* 208–219.

Savile, D. B. O. 1950. The flight mechanism of swifts and hummingbirds. *Auk, 67:*499–504.

Savile, D. B. O. 1957. Adaptive evolution in the avian wing. *Evolution, 11:*212–224.

Scheer, G. 1951. Über die zeitliche Differenz zwishen Erwachen und Gesangbeginn. *Die Vogelwarte, 16:*13–15.

Schifferli, A. 1949. Schwankungen des Schleiereulenbestandes *Tyto alba* (Scopoli). *Der Ornithologische Beobachter, 46:*61–75.

Schildmacher, H. 1929. Über den Wärmehaushalt kleiner Körnfresser. *Ornithologische Monatsberichte, 37:*102–106.

Schjelderup-Ebbe, T. 1923. Weiters Beiträge zur Social- und Individual-Psychologie des Haushühns. *Zeitschrift für Psychologie, 132:*289–303.

Schjelderup-Ebbe, T. 1935. Social behavior in birds. *In* Murchison, C., *A Handbook of Social Psychology.* Clark University Press, Worcester, Massachusetts.

Schmidt, W. J. 1952. Neuere Untersuchungen über Schillerfarben. *Journal für Ornithologie*, 93:130–135.

Schmidt-Koenig, K. 1960. The sun-azimuth compass: one factor in the orientation of homing pigeons. *Science*, 131:826–827.

Schmidt-Nielsen, K. 1959. Salt glands. *Scientific American*, 200 (1):109–116.

Schmidt-Nielsen, K. 1960. *Animal Physiology.* Prentice-Hall, Englewood Cliffs, New Jersey.

Scholander, S. I. 1955. Land birds over the western North Atlantic. *Auk*, 72:225–239.

Schorger, A. W. 1937. The great Wisconsin Passenger Pigeon nesting of 1871. *Proceedings of the Linnaean Society, New York*, No. 48:1–26.

Schorger, A. W. 1947. The deep diving of the Loon and the Old Squaw and its mechanism. *Wilson Bulletin*, 59:151–159.

Schorger, A. W. 1960. The crushing of *Carya* nuts in the gizzard of the Turkey. *Auk*, 77:337–340.

Schüz, E. 1936. The White Stork as a subject of research. *Bird-Banding*, 7:99–107.

Schüz, E. 1938. Über Biologie und Ökologie des Weiszen Storches (*Ciconia c. ciconia*). Proceedings of the Eighth International Ornithological Congress, Oxford, July, 1934: 577–591. Oxford University Press, 1938.

Schüz, E. 1943a. Brutbiologische Beobachtungen an Staren 1943 in der Vogelwarte Rossitten. *Journal für Ornithologie*, 91:388–405.

Schüz, E. 1943b. Über die Jungen aufzucht des Weiszen Storches (*C. ciconia*). *Zeitschrift für Morphologie und Oekologie der Tiere*, 40:181–237.

Schüz, E. 1944. Nest-Erwerb und Nest-Besitz beim Weiszen Storch. *Zeitschrift für Tierpsychologie*, 6:1–25.

Schüz, E. 1949a. Reifung, Ansiedlung und Bestandwechsel beim Weiszen Storch (*C. ciconia*). In *Ornithologie als Biologische Wissenschaft*. C. Winter, Heidelberg.

Schüz, E. 1949b. Die Spät-auflassung ostpreussischer Jungstörche in West-Deutschland durch die Vogelwarte Rossitten 1933. *Die Vogelwarte*, 2:63–78.

Schwartz, C. W., and E. R. Schwartz. 1951. An ecological reconnaissance of the pheasants of Hawaii. *Auk*, 68:281–314.

Schwartzkopff, J. 1949. Über den Zusammenhang von Gehör und Vibrationssinn bei Vögeln. *Experientia*, 5:159–161.

Schwartzkopff, J. 1955. On the hearing of birds. *Auk*, 72:340–347.

Scott, W. E. 1938. Old Squaws taken in gill nets. *Auk*, 55:668.

Serventy, D. L. 1938. Notes on Cormorants. *Emu, 38:* 357–371.

Serventy, D. L. 1957a. Duration of immaturity in the Short-tailed Shearwater, *Puffinus tenuirostris* (Temminck). *Wildlife Research*, 2:60:62. Commonwealth Scientific and Industrial Research Organization, Melbourne, Australia.

Serventy, D. L. 1957b. Recovery of a South Australian *Puffinus tenuirostris* in the Bering Sea. *South Austral. Ornith.*, 22 (4):56.

Serventy, D. L., and H. M. Whittell. 1950. *A Handbook of the Birds of Western Australia*. 2nd Edition. Paterson Press, Perth, W. Australia.

Sharp, W. M. 1957. Social and range dominance in gallinaceous birds. *Journal of Wildlife Management*, 21:242–244.

Shelford, V. E. 1945. The relation of Snowy Owl migration to the abundance of the Collared Lemming. *Auk*, 62:592–596.

Shelford, V. E., and L. Martin. 1946. Reactions of young birds to atmospheric humidity. *Journal of Wildlife Management*, 10:66–68.

Sherman, A. R. 1910. At the sign of the Northern Flicker. *Wilson Bulletin*, 22:135–166.

Sherwood, A. W. 1946. *Aerodynamics*. McGraw-Hill Book Company, New York.

Shoemaker, H. H. 1939. Social hierarchy in flocks of the Canary. *Auk*, 56:381–406.

Shreuers, T. 1941. Zur Brut- und Ernährungsbiologie des Neuentöters (*Lanius collurio*). *Journal für Ornithologie*, 89:182–203.

Shufeldt, R. W. 1909. Osteology of birds. *Bulletin of the New York State Museum*, No. 130:5–381.

Sick, H. 1939. Über die dialektbildung beim "Regenfur" des Buchfinken. *Journal für Ornithologie, 87:* 568–592.

Siivonen, L. 1939. Zur Ökologie und Verbreitung der Singdrossel (*Turdus ericetorum philomelos* Brehm). *Annales Zoologici Societatis Zoologicae-Botanicae-Fennicae Vanamo*, 7:1–289.

Simpson, G. G. 1940. Mammals and land bridges. *Journal of the Washington Academy of Science*, 30:137–163.

Simpson, G. G., C. S. Pittendrigh, and L. H. Tiffany. 1957. *Life—An Introduction to Biology*. Harcourt, Brace and Company. N. Y.

Skutch, A. F. 1931. The life history of Rieffer's Hummingbird, (*Amazilia tzacatl tzacatl*) in Panama and Honduras. *Auk,48*:481–500.

Skutch, A. F. 1940. Social and sleeping habits of Central American wrens. *Auk*, 57:293–312.

Skutch, A. F. 1942. Life history of the Mexican Trogon. *Auk*, 59:341–363.

Skutch, A. F. 1944a. The life-history of the Prongbilled Barbet. *Auk, 61*:61–88.

Skutch, A. F. 1944b. Life history of the Quetzal. *Condor, 46*:213–235.

Skutch, A. F. 1945. Incubation and nestling periods of Central American birds. *Auk*, 62:8–37.

Skutch, A. F. 1946a. Life history of the Costa Rican Tityra. *Auk*, 63:327–362.

Skutch, A. F. 1946b. The parental devotion of birds. *Scientific Monthly*, 62:364–374.

Skutch, A. F. 1949. Do tropical birds rear as many young as they can nourish? *Ibis*, 91:430–458.

Skutch, A. F. 1952. On the hour of laying and hatching of birds' eggs. *Ibis*, 94:49–61.

Skutch, A. F. 1954, 1960. *Life Histories of Central American Birds. Pacific Coast Avifauna*, Part I, No. 31; Part II, No. 34. Cooper Ornithological Society, Los Angeles 24, California.

Skutch, A. F. 1957. The incubation patterns of birds. *Ibis*, 99:69–93.

Skutch, A. F. 1959. Life history of the Groove-billed Ani. *Auk*, 76:281–317.

Sladen, W. J. L. 1953. The Adelie Penguin. *Nature*, 171:952–955.

Sladen, W. J. L., and N. A. Ostenso. 1960. Penguin tracks far inland in the Antarctic. *Auk*, 77:466–469.

Sladen, W. J. L., and W. L. N. Tickell. 1958. Antarctic bird-banding by the Falkland Islands Dependencies Survey, 1945–1957. *Bird-Banding*, 29:1–26.

Slud, P. 1957. The song and dance of the Long-tailed Manakin, *Chiroxiphia linearis. Auk*, 74:335–339.

Smith, A. G., and H. R. Webster. 1955. Effects of hail storms on waterfowl population in Alberta, Canada—1953. *Journal of Wildlife Management, 19:* 368–374.

Smith, K. D. 1955. The winter breeding season of land birds in eastern Eritrea. *Ibis*, 97:480–507.

Smith, S. 1942. Field observations on the breeding biology of the Yellow Wagtail. *British Birds, 35:* 186–189.

Snow, D. W. 1955. The abnormal breeding of birds in the winter 1953–1954. *British Birds,* 48:121–126.

Southern, J. 1952. Spotted Flycatchers feeding nestling Blackbirds. *British Birds,* 45:366.

Southern, W. E. 1959. Homing of Purple Martins. *Wilson Bulletin,* 71:254–261.

Sprot, G. D. 1937. Migratory behavior of some Glaucous-winged Gulls in the Strait of Georgia, British Columbia. *Condor,* 39:238–242.

Sprungman, O. I. 1941. Fish that eat ducks. *American Forests,* 47:507.

Sprunt, A. 1955. The spread of the Cattle Egret. *Smithsonian Report* for 1954:259–276.

Srb, A. M., and R. D. Owen. 1952. *General Genetics.* Freeman and Company, San Francisco.

Stager, K. E. 1941. A group of bat-eating duck hawks. *Condor,* 43:137–139.

Steinbacher, J. 1936. Zur Frage der Geschlechtsreife von Kleinvögeln. *Beiträge zur Fortpflanzungsbiologie der Vögel,* 12:139–144.

Steinbacher, J. 1951. *Vogelzug und Vogelzugforschung.* Kramer, Frankfurt A/M.

Steinfatt, O. 1938. Das Brutleben der Sumpfmeise und einige Vergleiche mit dem Brutleben der anderen einheimischen Meisen. *Beiträge Fortpflanzungsbiologie der Vögel,* 14:84–89; 137–144.

Stenger, J., and J. B. Falls. 1959. The utilized territory of the Ovenbird. *Wilson Bulletin,* 71:125–140.

Stewart, P. A. 1952. Dispersal, breeding behavior, and longevity of banded Barn Owls in North America. *Auk,* 69:227–245.

Stewart, R. E. 1956. Ecological study of Ruffed Grouse broods in Virginia. *Auk,* 73:33–41.

Stonehouse, B. 1956. The King Penguin of South Georgia. *Nature,* 178:1424–1426.

Storer, J. H. 1948. *The Flight of Birds.* Cranbrook Institute of Science, Bloomfield Hills, Michigan.

Storer, R. W. 1960. Adaptive radiation in birds. *In* Marshall, A. J., *Biology and Comparative Physiology of Birds.* Academic Press, New York.

Storer, T. I. 1943. *General Zoology.* McGraw-Hill Book Company, New York and London.

Streicher, E., D. B. Hackel, and W. Fleischmann. 1950. Effects of extreme cold on the fasting pigeon. *American Journal of Physiology,* 161:300.

Stresemann, E. 1927–1934. *In* Kükenthal, W., and T. Krumbach. *Handbuch der Zoologie. Sauropsida: Aves.* Berlin und Leipzig.

Stresemann, E. 1940. Zeitpunkt und Verlauf der Mauser bei einigen Entenarten. *Journal für Ornithologie,* 88:288–333.

Stresemann, E. 1947. Baron von Pernau, pioneer student of bird behavior. *Auk,* 64:35–52.

Stresemann, E. 1955. Die Wanderungen des Waldlaubsängers (*Phylloscopus sibilatrix*). *Journal für Ornithologie,* 96:153–167.

Sturkie, P. D. 1954. *Avian Physiology.* Comstock Publishing Associates, Ithaca, New York.

Sumner, F. B. 1934. Does "protective coloration" protect? Results of some experiments with fishes and birds. *Proceedings of the National Academy of Sciences,* 20:559–564.

Suomalainen, H. 1937. The effect of temperature on the sexual activity of non-migratory birds, stimulated by artificial lighting. *Ornis Fennica,* 14:108–112.

Sutter, E. 1951. Growth and differentiation of the brain in nidifugous and nidicolous birds. *Proceedings of the Xth International Ornithological Congress, Uppsala, June 1950,* 636–643. Almqvist and Wiksells, Uppsala, 1951.

Sutter, E. 1957. Radar als Hilfsmittel der Vogelzugforschung. *Ornithologische Beobachter,* 54:70–96.

Sutton, G. M. 1951. *Mexican Birds.* University of Oklahoma Press, Norman, Oklahoma.

Sutton, O. G. 1955. *The Science of Flight.* Penguin Books, Baltimore, Maryland.

Svärdson, G. 1949. Competition and habitat selection in birds. *Oikos,* 1:157–174.

Svärdson, G. 1957. The "invasion" type of bird migration. *British Birds,* 50:314–343.

Svärdson, G. 1958. Biotop och häckning hos skrattmåsen (*Larus ridibundus*). *Vår Fågelvärld,* 17:1–23.

Swanberg, P. O. 1951. Food storage, territory and song in the Thick-billed Nutcracker. *Proceedings of the Xth International Ornithological Congress, Uppsala, June 1950,* 545–554. Almqvist & Wiksells, Uppsala, 1951.

Swank, W. G. 1944. Germination of seeds after ingestion by Ringnecked Pheasants. *Journal of Wildlife Management,* 8:223–231.

Swarth, H. S. 1920. Revision of the avian genus *Passerella* with special reference to the distribution and migration of the races in California. *University of California Publications in Zoology,* 21:75–224.

T

Taber, R. D. 1949. Observations on the breeding behavior of the Ring-necked Pheasant. *Condor,* 51:153–175.

Tanabe, Y., K. Himeno, and H. Nosaki. 1957. Thyroid and ovarian function in relation to molting in the hen. *Endocrinology,* 61:661–666.

Tanner, J. T. 1941. Three years with the Ivory-billed Woodpecker, America's rarest bird. *Audubon Magazine,* 43:5–14.

Tanner, J. T. 1942. The Ivory-billed Woodpecker. *Research Report No. 1. of the National Audubon Society.* New York.

Thielke-Poltz, H., and G. Thielke. 1960. Akustisches Lernen verschieden alter schallisolierter Amseln (*Turdus merula* L.) und die Entwicklung erlernter Motive ohne und mit künstlichem Einfluss von Testosteron. *Zeitschrift für Tierpsychologie,* 17:211–244.

Thompson, D'Arcy W. 1942. *On Growth and Form.* Cambridge University Press.

Thomson, A. L. 1926. *Problems of Bird Migration.* Houghton Mifflin, Boston, Massachusetts.

Thomson, A. L. 1936. *Bird Migration.* H. F. and G. Witherby, London.

Thomson, J. A. 1923. *The Biology of Birds.* Macmillan, New York.

Thorndike, L. 1929. *A History of Magic and Experimental Science.* Macmillan, New York.

Thorpe, W. H. 1956a. The language of birds. *Scientific American, 195* (4):128–138.

Thorpe, W. H. 1956b. *Learning and Instinct in Animals.* Harvard University Press, Cambridge, Massachusetts.

Tiedemann, M. 1943. Ornithologische Beobachtungen aus dem Hornsund-Gebiet auf West Spitzbergen. *Journal für Ornithologie, 91:*239–267.

Tiemeier, O. W. 1941. Repaired bone injuries in birds. *Auk, 58:*350–359.

Time Magazine, June 23, 1958, p. 66.

Tinbergen, N. 1939a. On the analysis of social organization among vertebrates, with special reference to birds. *American Midland Naturalist, 21:*210–234.

Tinbergen, N. 1939b. The behavior of the Snow Bunting in spring. *Transactions of the Linnaean Society of New York,* V. 1–95.

Tinbergen, N. 1948. Social releasers and the experimental method required for their study. *Wilson Bulletin, 60:*6–51.

Tinbergen, N. 1951. *The Study of Instinct.* Clarendon Press, Oxford.

Tinbergen, N. 1953a. *The Herring Gull's World.* Collins, London.

Tinbergen, N. 1953b. *Social Behavior in Animals.* John Wiley and Sons, New York.

Tinbergen, N. 1957. Defense by color. *Scientific American, 194* (4):48–54.

Tinbergen, N., and D. J. Kuenen. 1939. Über die auslösenden und die richtunggebenden Reizsituationen der Sperrbewegung von jungen Drosseln. *Zeitschrift für Tierpsychologie, 3:*37–60.

Tinbergen, N., and A. C. Perdeck. 1951. On the stimulus situation releasing the begging response in the newly hatched Herring Gull chick (*Larus argentatus argentatus* Pont.). *Behaviour, 3:*1–39.

Törne, H. v. 1939. Allerlei aus der Brutperiode 1938 auf Schleimunde. *Beiträge zur Fortpflanzungsbiologie der Vögel, 15:*102–105.

Trautman, M. B. 1947. Courtship behavior of the Black Duck. *Wilson Bulletin, 59:*26–35.

Tschantz, B. 1959. Zur Brutbiologie der Trottellume (*Uria aalge aalge* Pont.). *Behaviour, 14:*1–100.

Tucker, B. W. 1943. Brood patches and the physiology of incubation. *British Birds, 37:*22–28.

Tucker, B. W. 1943. *In* Witherby, H. F., F. C. R. Jourdain, N. Ticehurst, and B. W. Tucker, *The Handbook of British Birds.* H. F. and G. Witherby, London.

Turček, F. J. 1952. An ecological analysis of the bird and mammalian population of a primeval forest on the Polona-mountain (Slovakia). *Bulletin international de l'Academie tcheque des Sciences, 53:* 1–25.

Twitty, V. C. 1959. Migration and speciation in newts. *Science, 130:*1735–1743.

Twomey, A. C. 1936. Climographic studies of certain introduced and migratory birds. *Ecology, 17:* 122–132.

U

Urner, C. A., and R. W. Storer. 1949. The distribution and abundance of shorebirds on the north and central New Jersey coast, 1928–1938. *Auk, 66:* 177–194.

V

Van Tyne, J. 1951. A Cardinal's, *Richmondena cardinalis,* choice of food for adult and for young, *Auk, 68:*110.

Van Tyne, J., and A. J. Berger. 1959. *Fundamentals of Ornithology.* John Wiley & Sons, New York.

Vleugel, V. A. 1951. A case of Herring Gulls learning by experience to feed after explosions by mines. *British Birds, 44:*180.

Vogt, W. 1938. Preliminary notes on the behavior and ecology of the Eastern Willet. *Proceedings of the Linnaean Society of New York,* No. 49, 1937:8–42.

Vogt, W. 1941. Food detection by vultures and condors. *Auk, 58:*571.

W

Wagner, H. O. 1941. Lange "Verlobungzeit" mexikanischer Tyranniden. *Ornithologische Monatsberichte, 49:*137–138.

Wagner, H. O. 1945. Notes on the life history of the Mexican Violet-ear. *Wilson Bulletin, 57:*165–187.

Wagner, H. O. 1946. Observaciones sober la Vida de *Calothorax lucifer. Anales del Instituto de Biologia, 16:*283–299. Mexico, D. F.

Wagner, H. O. 1954. Versuch einer Analyse der Kolibribalz. *Zeitschrift für Tierpsychologie, 11:*182–212.

Wagner, H. O. 1957. The molting periods of Mexican hummingbirds. *Auk, 74:*251–257.

Wagner, H. O. 1957. Variation in clutch size at different latitudes. *Auk, 74:*243–250.

Walkinshaw, L. H. 1939a. Additional information on the Prothonotary Warbler. *Jack-Pine Warbler, 17:* 64–71.

Walkinshaw, L. H. 1939b. Nesting of the Field Sparrow and survival of the young. *Bird-Banding, 10:* 107–114.

Walkinshaw, L. H. 1941. The Prothonotary Warbler, a comparison of nesting in Tennessee and Michigan. *Wilson Bulletin, 53:*3–21.

Walkinshaw, L. H. 1945a. Aortic rupture in Field Sparrow due to fright. *Auk, 62:*141.

Walkinshaw, L. H. 1945b. Field Sparrow, 39–54015. *Bird-Banding, 16:*1–14.

Wallace, A. R. 1876. *The Geographical Distribution of Animals.* Harper and Brothers, New York.

Wallace, A. R. 1889. *Travels on the Amazon and Rio Negro.* Ward, Lock, London.

Wallace, G. J. 1955. *An Introduction to Ornithology.* Macmillan, New York.

Walls, G. L. 1942. *The Vertebrate Eye and Its Adaptive Radiation.* Cranbrook Institute of Science. Bloomfield Hills, Michigan.

Watson, J. B. 1908. The behavior of Noddy and Sooty Terns. *Papers from the Tortugas Laboratory of the Carnegie Institution of Washington, 2:*187–255.

Weller, M. W. 1958. Observations on the incubation behavior of a Common Nighthawk. *Auk*, 75:48–59.

Welty, Joel Carl. 1934. Experiments in group behavior of fishes. *Physiological Zoology*, 7:85–128.

Wendland, V. 1958. Zum Problem des vorzeitigen Sterbens von jungen Greifvögeln und Eulen. *Die Vogelwarte*, 19:186–191.

Werth, I. 1947. The tendency of Blackbird and Song-Thrush to breed in their birthplaces. *British Birds*, 40:328–330.

Westerkov, K. 1956. Incubation temperatures of the pheasant, *Phasianus colchicus*. *Emu*, 56:405–420.

Wetmore, A. 1919. Lead poisoning in waterfowl. *U.S. Department of Agriculture Bulletin No. 793*.

Wetmore, A. 1931. *Warm-blooded Vertebrates. Smithsonian Scientific Series, Vol. 9*. Smithsonian Institution Series, New York.

Wetmore, A. 1936. The number of countour feathers in Passeriform and related birds. *Auk*, 53:159–169.

Wetmore, A. 1951. A revised classification for the birds of the world. *Smithsonian Miscellaneous Collections*, Vol. 117. No. 4.

Wetmore, A. 1952. Recent additions to our knowledge of prehistoric birds. *Proceedings of the Xth International Ornithological Congress, Uppsala, June 1950*, Almqvist and Wiksells, Uppsala, 1951.

Wetmore, A. 1955. Paleontology. *In* Wolfson, A. *Recent Studies in Avian Biology*. University of Illinois Press, Urbana, Illinois.

Wharton, W. P. 1931. Parasites on birds taken at Summerville, South Carolina. *Bird-Banding*, 2:34–35.

Whitaker, L. M. 1957. A resume of anting, with particular reference to a captive Orchard Oriole. *Wilson Bulletin*, 69:195–262.

Whitman, C. O. 1899. Animal behavior. *Biological Lectures of the Marine Biological Laboratory, Woods Hole, Massachusetts*, 1898:285–338.

Williams, G. G. 1950. Weather and spring migration. *Auk*, 67:52–65.

Williams, G. R. 1952. The California Quail in New Zealand. *Journal of Wildlife Management, 16*:460–483.

Williams, G. R. 1953. The dispersal from New Zealand and Australia of some introduced European passerines. *Ibis*, 95:676–692.

Williams, L. 1952. Breeding behavior of the Brewer Blackbird. *Condor*, 54:3–47.

Williamson, K. 1949. The distraction display of the Arctic Skua. *Ibis*, 91:307–313.

Williamson, K. 1959. The September drift movements of 1956 and 1958. *British Birds*, 52:334–377.

Willier, B. H. 1952. Cells, feathers and colors. *Bios, 22*:109–125.

Willier, B. H., and M. E. Rawles. 1940. The control of feather color pattern by melanophores grafted from one embryo to another of a different breed of fowl. *Physiological Zoology*, 13:177–199.

Wilson, J. E. 1959. The status of the Hungarian Partridge in New York. *Kingbird*, 9:54–57.

Wing, L. W. 1956. *Natural History of Birds*. The Ronald Press, New York.

Winterbottom, J. M. 1949. Mixed bird parties in the tropics with special reference to Northern Rhodesia. *Auk*, 66:258–263.

Winterbottom, J. M. 1950. Related species in mixed bird parties in Northern Rhodesia. *Ostrich, 21*:77–83.

Witherby, H. F., F. C. R. Jourdain, N. F. Ticehurst, and B. W. Tucker. 1943. *The Handbook of British Birds*. H. F. and G. Witherby, London.

Witschi, E. 1935. Seasonal sex characters in birds and their hormonal control. *Wilson Bulletin*, 47:177–188.

Wolfson, A. 1942. Regulation of spring migration in Juncos. *Condor*, 44:237–263.

Wolfson, A. 1945. The role of the pituitary, fat deposition and body weight in bird migration. *Condor*, 47:95–127.

Wolfson, A. 1954. Sperm storage at lower-than-body temperature outside the body cavity of some passerine birds. *Science*, 120:68–71.

Wolfson, A. 1955. *Recent Studies in Avian Biology*. University of Illinois Press, Urbana, Illinois.

Wood, C. A., and F. M. Fyfe. 1943. *The Art of Falconry*. Stanford University Press, Stanford, California.

Wood, S. F., and C. M. Herman. 1943. The occurrence of blood parasites in birds from southwestern United States. *Journal of Parasitology, 29*:187–196.

Woodbury, R. A., and W. F. Hamilton. 1937. Blood pressure studies in small animals. *American Journal of Physiology, 119*:663.

Woodcock, A. H. 1940. Observations on Herring Gull soaring. *Auk*, 57:219–224.

Woodcock, A. H. 1942. Soaring over the open sea. *Scientific Monthly, 55*:226–232.

Woolfenden, G. E. 1956. Comparative breeding behavior of *Ammospiza maritima*. *University of Kansas Publications, Museum of Natural History*, 10:45–75.

Wright, P. L., and M. H. Wright, 1944. The reproductive cycle of the male Red-winged Blackbird. *Condor*, 46:46–59.

Wynne-Edwards, V. C. 1930. On the waking time of the nightjar (*Caprimulgus e. europaeus*). *Journal of Experimental Biology*, 7:241–247.

Wynne-Edwards, V. C. 1939. Intermittent breeding of the Fulmar *Fulmaris glacialis* (L.). *Proceedings of the Zoological Society of London*, A. 109:127–132.

Wynne-Edwards, V. C. 1948. Yeagley's theory of bird navigation. *Ibis*, 90:606–611.

Y

Yamashina, M. 1939. A social breeding habit among Timaliine birds. *IXme Congrès Ornithologique International, Rouen; 9–13 Mai, 1938*:453–456. Secrétariat du Congrès, Rouen, 1938.

Yeagley, H. L. 1947. A preliminary study of a physical basis of bird navigation. *Journal of Applied Physics, 18*:1035–1063.

Yeagley, H. L. 1951. A preliminary study of a physical basis of bird navigation, Part II. *Journal of Applied Physics, 22*:746–760.

Yeatter, R. E. 1934. The Hungarian Partridge in the Great Lakes Region. *Bulletin No. 5*, University of Michigan School of Forestry and Conservation.

Yocum, C. F. 1943. The Hungarian Partridge (*Perdix perdix* Linn.) in the Palouse Region, Washington. *Ecological Monographs, 13:*167–201.

Young, H. 1951. Territorial behavior of the Eastern Robin. *Proceedings of the Linnaean Society of New York.* Nos. 58–62:1–37.

Young, H. 1955. Breeding behavior and nesting of the Eastern Robin. *American Midland Naturalist, 53:* 329–352.

Ytreberg, N. J. 1956. Contribution to the breeding biology of the Black-headed Gull (*Larus ridibundus*) in Norway. *Nytt Magasin for Zoologi, 4:*5–106.

Z

Zeuthen, E. 1942. The ventilation of the respiratory tract in birds. *Kgl. Danske Videnskabernes Selskab, Biologiske Meddelelser, 17:*1–51.

Zimmer, J. T. 1938. Notes on migrations of South American birds. *Auk, 55:*405–410.

Zimmer, J. T., and E. Mayr. 1943. New species of birds described from 1938 to 1941. *Auk, 60:*249–262.

Zuckerman, S. 1957. Hormones. *Scientific American, 196* (3): 76–87.

Index

525